Nigeria: Background to Nationalism

NIGERIA
Background to Nationalism

by James S. Coleman

University of California Press
Berkeley and Los Angeles
1960

The end-paper map has been reproduced
from the seventeenth-century original in the
Nigeria Liaison Office Library, Washington,
D.C., through the courtesy of the Nigeria
Liaison Officer.

University of California Press • Berkeley and Los Angeles
Cambridge University Press • London, England
© 1958 by The Regents of the University of California
Second Printing, 1960
Library of Congress Catalog Card No. 58-10286
Designed by Ward Ritchie
Printed in the United States of America

To MAR

In Memoriam

Preface

Any study of the recent political history of an emergent African state can, at this stage, be no more than exploratory. This is particularly true when one attempts, as I have done, to analyze the rise and growth of a phenomenon such as nationalism in a country the size of Nigeria. Data are too fragmentary and contradictory, passions are still too intense and perspectives too distorted to permit broad generalizations and firm conclusions. An exploratory study, therefore, invites, and ought to provoke, corrections in fact and in judgment; indeed, it is but an invitation to further research. This book claims to be no more than an introduction to selected aspects of the political history of modern Nigeria.

The data assembled in this book are the end product of countless interviews, extensive travel and observation, and the use of many centers of documentation in Nigeria, the United Kingdom, and the United States. In a brief note of acknowledgment, therefore, it is impossible to mention and to thank by name all individuals, both Nigerian and British, who have assisted me in one way or another during my field work. To British officials I am indebted for their courtesy and coöperation in allowing me complete freedom of movement and inquiry throughout my stay in Nigeria. Special thanks are due to the Right Honourable A. Creech Jones, Sir Hugh Foot, R. E. Brown, J. S. Dudding, D. A. Murphy, and D. A. Pott. To Professor W. Hamilton Whyte and D. N. Leich, former Director and Secretary, respectively, of the West African Institute of Social and Economic Research, I am particularly grateful for accommodation and research facilities, and many other forms of assistance willingly provided me throughout my tour. I am also appreciative of the coöperation and assistance received from Mrs. E. M. Chilver, Director, and the staff of the Institute of Commonwealth Studies, Oxford University, the Librarian and his staff at University College, Ibadan, and the Nigeria Liaison Officer, Washington, D.C. The Managing Director and other officials of the United Africa Company were also most helpful in providing data and other assistance.

Among the many Nigerians to whom I am indebted for assistance and hospitality, the following deserve special mention: the three regional premiers—Chief Obafemi Awolowo, Dr. Nnamdi Azikiwe, and Alhaji Ahmadu, Sardauna of Sokoto; J. O. Adigun, Alhaji Shehu Ahmadu (Madakin Kano), A. M. Akinloye, Chief S. L. Akintola, Abiodun Aloba, Chief Kolawole Balogun, Dr. Saburi Biobaku, Increase Coker, Isaac O. Delano, Dr. K. Onwuka Dike, Chief Anthony Enahoro, Ernest Ikoli, Eyo Ita, Mallam Aminu Kano, Dr. Eni Njoku, Dr. Chike Obi, Professor Ayo Ogunsheye, Adebola Onitiri, D. C. Osadebay, Mallam Maitama Sule, M. A. S. Sowole, M. A. Tokunboh, Dr. E. U. Udoma, and Chief F. R. A. Williams. I am particularly appreciative of the assistance and friendship of Samuel F. Ayo-Vaughn, Mallam Abba Gana, Dr. Abubakar Imam, Magnus Macaulay, and Ignatius C. Olisemeka.

To the United States Educational Commission in the United Kingdom I am indebted for a Fulbright travel grant which made it financially possible for me to visit the United Kingdom and to engage in field research in Nigeria during 1951–1952.

There are several friends and scholars who have read all or part of the manuscript in various stages and who have contributed many helpful comments and suggestions for which I am most grateful. The original manuscript was read in its entirety by Dr. T. Olawale Elias, Thomas Hodgkin, Elechukwu Njakar, and Professor Kenneth Robinson, Director of the Institute of Commonwealth Studies of the University of London. Portions of the manuscript were read by Professor William R. Bascom, Professor K. Onwuka Dike, Mallam Abba Gana, G. E. A. Lardner, P. C. Lloyd, and Professor Guy Pauker. The comments and criticisms of these individuals were invaluable in subsequent revisions. Needless to say, the final product is probably not as they would have written it, nor do they necessarily agree with all that I have said. All errors of fact and interpretation are my sole responsibility.

I am indebted to the University of London Press for permission to reproduce maps 2 and 12 from K. M. Buchanan and J. C. Pugh, *Land and People in Nigeria* (London: 1955), and to the Cambridge University Press for permission to reproduce maps 8 and 9 from F. D. Fage, *An Introduction to the History of West Africa* (Cambridge: 1955). I should also like to thank James Casper for his assistance in preparing and in putting into final form the other maps appearing in this volume, and Donald Crow for his help in preparing the statistical data used in the final chapter.

There are slight differences in ethnic boundaries between maps 6 and 13, pertaining to the Western Region, and between maps 7 and 14, pertaining to the Eastern Region, because maps 6 and 7 are based upon ethnographic maps and data, and maps 13 and 14 upon the boundaries of administrative divisions and provinces, which do not necessarily coincide.

As a result of special circumstances existing at the time of the final editing of the manuscript a very heavy burden was placed upon the editorial staff of the University of California Press. For her patience and coöperation I am particularly indebted to Mrs. Grace Stimson.

Finally, were it not for two individuals this study would not have been undertaken or completed. To an inspiring teacher and loyal friend, Dr. Rupert Emerson, Professor of Government at Harvard University, I owe special thanks—as does a whole generation of Harvard students—for wise counsel and constant encouragement. To my beloved wife, Margaret Tate Coleman, I owe my deepest debt of gratitude. The dedication of this book to her memory is but token acknowledgment of her share in the effort it has involved. It is really our book, for it would never have been written or published had it not been for her sacrifices and moral support, as well as the many hours she so enthusiastically gave to its preparation.

J. S. C.

Los Angeles, California

Contents

Contents

Illustrations

Maps

Illustrations

Introduction

One of the most significant developments in international relations during the past three decades has been the spread of the idea of national self-determination to the non-Western world, and particularly to those areas having a colonial status. Several new states have entered the mainstream of world politics, and more are approaching the threshold of independence. New areas of instability have been created and new situations of tension have developed. The "negative" power generated by the Arab-Asian-African bloc and displayed with increasing effectiveness within and without the United Nations has introduced radically new imponderables in international relations. Indeed, the full implications of the transformation in world power relationships which stems from the universalization of the national idea are only beginning to be realized.[1]

In many respects, this epoch-making development was neither anticipated nor desired. The reasons are not exclusively reactionary or ethnocentric. Admittedly, the global expansion of the principle of national self-determination threatened the strategic and economic interests of Western colonial powers. Also, important segments of Western leadership were committed to an ideology that rationalized Western tutelage in terms of certain unprovable superior-inferior assumptions. Yet once these obvious facts are acknowledged, it is important to note other less interest-bound reasons that also serve to explain the failure to predict, and the inclination to resist, this important change. These reasons were basically of two types, one relating to the applicability of the national principle to non-Western groups, and the other relating to the validity of the principle itself.

Introduction

In the judgment of some people, the principle of national self-determination was not applicable to the cultural realities of non-Western areas, and any effort to apply or realize that principle would lead to situations ethically more intolerable than Western colonial rule. The argument is a familiar one and has been succinctly expressed by Arnold Toynbee:

> During the last century and a half we have seen our Late Modern Western political institution of "national states" burst the bounds of its birthplace in Western Europe and blaze a trail of persecution, eviction and massacre as it has spread abroad into Eastern Europe, South-West Asia, and India—all of them regions where "national states" were not part and parcel of an indigenous social system but were an exotic institution which was deliberately imported from the West, not because it had been found by experimentation to be suitable to the local conditions of these non-Western worlds, but simply because the West's political power had given the West's political institutions an irrational yet irresistible prestige in non-Western eyes.[2]

Others went further and questioned the validity of the national principle itself. This current of thought was particularly strong during and near the end of World War II, a holocaust provoked by the excesses of German, Italian, and Japanese nationalism. The nation-state was viewed as an archaic institution peculiar to the ideology and technology of a particular period in human development which would inevitably give way to larger-scale patterns of human organization.[3] Moreover, nations were believed to be inherently undemocratic and aggressive.[4] In short, the preservation of the national state, as well as its universalization, was considered to be anachronistic and retrograde.

The peoples of tropical Africa, in particular, have been regarded as a part of humanity which might escape the scourge or the blessings of Western modes of human organization and Western patterns of political behavior. This perspective was in part the product of the belief that they were fundamentally different from the rest of mankind and that their destiny could and ought to be guided by the so-called advanced races. Indeed, of all major areas in the non-Western world, tropical Africa was believed the most unfit for the national principle. As Alfred Cobban put it: "National self-determination may in its normal political connotation be out of the question in Africa. . . ." [5] Again, in comparing tropical Africa with Asia, Margery Perham affirmed the very provocative and debatable proposition that

> The dealings between tropical Africa and the West must be different. Here in place of the large unities of Asia was the multi-cellular tissue of tribalism: instead of an ancient civilization, the largest area of primitive poverty enduring into the modern age. Until the very recent penetration by Europe the greater part of the continent was without the wheel, the plough or the transport-animal; almost without stone houses or clothes, except for skins; without writing and so without history.[6]

The general belief, expressed by an American historian, was that "the day is far distant when the peoples of Africa will be capable of organizing independent states." [7] As a consequence of this attitude, the outside world in general has been inclined to think of development and change in Africa in terms of refining techniques of colonial administration, or of strengthening and generalizing the principle of international accountability.

During the brief period 1945–1951 the outside world was shocked into a realization that Africans were determined to assert control over the pace and direction of their political development. In both the Gold Coast (now Ghana) and Nigeria the British government was compelled to make radical political concessions pointing toward the early creation of independent African states. These concessions were forced by nationalist movements inspired by the doctrine of national self-determination. Today the governments of these emergent states have passed or are passing into the hands of Africans. This wholly unexpected development has served as a dramatic notice to the world that for good or ill the peoples of tropical Africa are determined to inaugurate their own national era.

The present study is focused upon the social and historical background of the emergence of nationalism in Nigeria. Nigeria is far and away the largest of the dependent territories in what remains of the British Empire. It is also the most heavily populated of all political units in Africa and the twelfth most populous country in the world. It contains within its borders the three largest nationalities in Africa—each numbering more than five million. Moreover,

3

the groups that make up its population reflect the widest range of political organization of any territory on the continent. It is the only political entity in Africa where most of the main African language groups are found. In short, in terms of size and diversity, Nigeria has much to distinguish it from other areas.

These very features—Nigeria's immense size and its complex diversity—coupled with the fact that this study is necessarily exploratory, have dictated several sharp delimitations. Three criteria have been employed to establish boundaries to the subject matter. The first relates to the concept of "nationalism" here employed. A broad distinction has been made between the "primary resistance" of traditional African groups on the one hand, and, on the other, the movement to create new political nationalities (that is, Nigeria, Western Region, Eastern Region, Northern Region) as self-governing units in the modern world. For our present purposes "nationalism" refers to the latter. Such a distinction, however, does not suggest that in terms of the quest for freedom or of the resentment of alien rule there is really any fundamental difference between the two forms of expression. They are but two aspects, or phases, of the same phenomenon. Yet there is a time difference, and special focus on the second phase is useful not only analytically but also as a means of narrowing the period to be covered. A more detailed explanation of the concept of nationalism and other concepts employed in this study will be found in chapter 7 and in the Appendix.

Another means by which the study has been delimited is the selection of a terminal date. Here again our special concept of nationalism provides assistance. Just as 1900 marks the commencement of our time purview, since it was the date when "Nigeria" emerged as a political unit known to the world and to the peoples living within its boundaries, so 1952 is the terminal date, since it marks that point in time when the nationalist movement, divided though it was, became formally structured in political parties functioning within a political system fairly close to the threshold of independence. Again, this does not suggest that nationalism ended in 1952; on the contrary, since 1952 it has not only become more emphatic but has spread ever more widely and deeply. Political developments since 1952 are briefly examined in chapter 18; a more detailed description and analysis would require another,

4

somewhat different book. It is elementary that an essentially historical study must have a beginning and an ending. The emergence of formal political parties in 1952 would appear to be the most logical point at which to terminate a study of the background to nationalism in Nigeria. The conceptual distinction made in the Appendix between a "nationalist movement" and "political parties" explains this rationale in greater detail.

A third way in which the scope of the study has been reduced has been to exclude the rise and development of nationalism in the Cameroons under United Kingdom trusteeship. Because the northern section of the British Cameroons is effectively integrated into the Northern Region of Nigeria, and the Southern Cameroons constitutes a region in the Federation of Nigeria, this exclusion is in a sense arbitrary and unfortunate. In view, however, of the special international status of the Cameroons during the period of this study, as well as the rather different course nationalism has taken there, it is believed that the exclusion is justified. Here again, another study is clearly in order.

An author must not only seek focus; he must also ensure that his data and analysis are not misinterpreted. Three special points require emphasis. The first is that in generalizing about large categories of persons under such collectives as the "British administration," "officialdom," "missionaries," "nationalists," or "Ibo," there is the great danger of conveying the impression that the peoples thus categorized are monolithic, like-minded, and similarly motivated. Such an impression is a gross distortion, for in each category one can point to any number of exceptions. There have been "Colonel Blimps" and passionate Afrophiles among administrators, just as there have been irresponsibles and statesmen among nationalists. Generalization is a difficult art at any time, but particularly when dealing with group character.

The second point is that grievances—imaginary or real, frivolous or justifiable—constitute a major part of colonial nationalism. This means that any study focused specifically upon the phenomenon of nationalism inevitably tends to dwell upon situations, policies, and actions that produce grievances, at the expense of many other situations, policies, and actions that by any standard are laudatory. Thus, for example, the present study tends to point up unimaginative policies, errors in judgment, and the human frailties of offi-

5

cialdom, as well as the ethnocentrism of certain missionary activities, while understressing, perhaps, the vision and broad humanity of many officials and missionaries. This imbalance is further exaggerated by a rather striking time lag in the perspectives of many nationalists. British policies and attitudes in 1948 are often judged in terms of the policies and attitudes prevalent in an earlier period, and there seems to be a disinclination—understandable, perhaps —to recognize the many genuine and fundamental changes that have occurred. Moreover, as this is a study of the historical roots of nationalism, earlier policies receive close scrutiny, with the consequent danger that the reader may conclude that such policies have remained unchanged. Suffice it to say that a major thesis of this study is that nationalism—the quest for self-government—in Nigeria is as much a fulfillment as a failure of British policy.

Finally, to interpret the complex human motives and aspirations that form the content of nationalism in Africa today, one is obliged to be both tentative and humble. The concept of freedom has a special meaning for peoples living under alien rule, and it is a meaning not always comprehended or appreciated by non-Africans. It is no doubt an awareness of this fact which prompted Rita Hinden, in her survey of British imperial attitudes, to affirm that any study of colonial attitudes to imperialism, "if it is to ring true, can only come from someone who has himself experienced what it is to be a member of the 'subject race.' " [8] This is a view the author shares. Fortunately, two of Nigeria's leading nationalists have already expressed their attitudes in book form: the premier of the Western Region, Chief Obafemi Awolowo, in his admirable *Path to Nigerian Freedom*, and the premier of the Eastern Region, Dr. Nnamdi Azikiwe, in *Renascent Africa*.[9] The present study is but an exploratory effort to draw together the thoughts appearing in these and similar works, and to interpret them against the broad background of social change and Nigerian political development.

This case study of the rise of nationalism in Nigeria is based on certain fundamental assumptions. One is that the peoples of Nigeria are essentially not unlike other peoples. Another is that the most fruitful method of inquiry will be to look first for those underlying social changes that have precipitated nationalist movements in Europe and Asia. The discovery of uniformities and recurring patterns is not only of theoretical significance; it is also the fascinating aspect of the study of history. In his writings Lord Hailey has suggested that there is a fairly universal pattern in the appearance of nationalism. In fact, a theory of such a pattern has been advanced by Karl W. Deutsch.[10] The crux of his theory is that essentially the same forces and ideas that produced nationalism and nations in Europe have been and will be operative in the non-European world.

The material of this study is divided into four parts. Part I describes the relevant features of the physical, cultural, and historical setting. Part II is a critical analysis of the processes of social and political change, broadly subsumed under the rubric "Western impact," which have created situations predisposing the Nigerian peoples to nationalism. Part III contains a general historical survey of the rise and growth of nationalist sentiment and activity in Nigeria, and Part IV is a description and analysis of the development of the nationalist movement in the postwar period up to 1952, together with a brief survey of events since that date.

PART I
The Cultural and Historical Setting

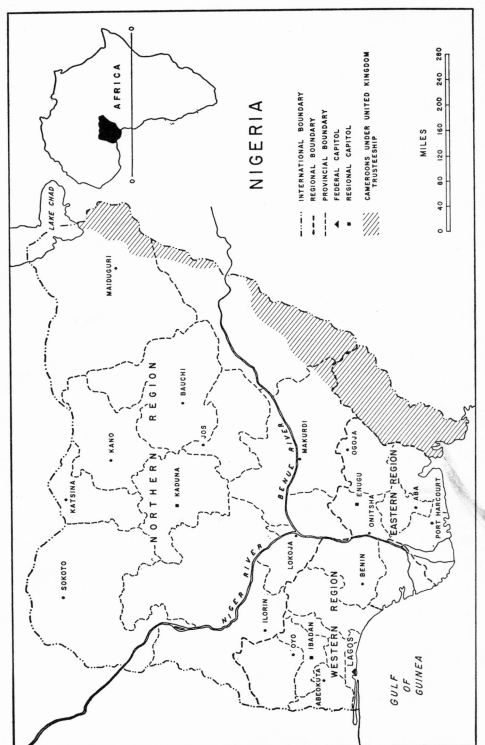

Map 1

CHAPTER 1

The Geography and Peoples of Nigeria

Nigeria lies at the extreme inner corner of the Gulf of Guinea in West Africa. It is a compact area of 373,000 square miles, extending from the Gulf of Guinea on the south to the Sahara Desert on the north, and bounded on the west and north by Dahomey and Niger territories of French West Africa, and on the east by Lake Chad and the Cameroons under United Kingdom trusteeship. Ranging from south to north, four physical regions can be distinguished. Along the coastline there is a dense belt of swamp and mangrove forest, varying from 10 to 60 miles in width, which is sparsely populated and little developed. Next is a fairly sharply defined belt of tropical rain forest and oil-palm bush from 50 to 100 miles wide, intersected by rivers and streams. This is followed by a 300-mile-wide belt of open woodland and grass savannah. Finally, the latter shades off into a vast undulating plateau with occasional hills, until at last the sandy tracts of the southern Sahara are reached. This gradation in vegetation and climate is the result of wide variations in rainfall produced by the seasonal inflow of humid air from the South Atlantic. The regional differences in soil fertility and food crops resulting from this natural differentiation have produced, in many instances, complementary economies.

The most prominent physical feature of Nigeria is the Niger River. It rises in the mountains northeast of Sierra Leone, traverses the whole of the French Sudan, enters Nigeria in the northwest, joins the Benue River at Lokoja, near the center of Nigeria, and then flows due south into the Gulf of Guinea. Despite its length and dispersion, Nigeria's river system has not been a great commercial waterway for trade with the outside world, nor has it contributed significantly to the growth of an internal exchange economy. Navigational obstacles such as seasonal variations in water levels and shifting sand bars at the mouth of the Niger have not only restricted its use to seagoing ships of very shallow draft, but also limited the development of river ports. Moreover, the heavily populated areas in the far north and in the west are at a considerable distance from these rivers. The river system therefore has not facilitated—indeed, in some respects it has positively hampered—economic intercourse among the major ethnic groups in Nigeria.

The physical location of Nigeria in the corner of the Gulf of Guinea has limited intercourse and encouraged isolation. Nigeria shares with the rest of the West Coast the dense and inhospitable belt of coastal swamp forest. As one report put it, "Nobody went along the West Coast of Africa unless he had very good immediate reason for his journey, and the further along the coast, the truer this became." [1] Nigeria is at the tail end, eastward from Portuguese Guinea, of this 1,500-mile stretch of West Coast swamp forest. North, toward the Sahara Desert, the absence of natural routes facilitating human intercourse is even more pronounced: "All roads out of West Africa, save one, lead either to the desert, or to the sea. To attempt to cross either was an undertaking indeed." [2] The one exception is the Niger-Nile traverse via Lake Chad, the historical route of mass travel from West Africa to the outside world. Until the modern development of roads, railroads, air travel, and ports and harbors, however, neither the land-borne impact from the Middle East nor the sea-borne impact from Europe was of any great significance in bringing Nigeria into the general stream of world events and forces.

In southern Nigeria two other factors combined to preserve this isolation as well as to condition the nature of agricultural development, land tenure, and social and political organization. The first was the physical density of the tropical swamp and rain forest; the second was the tsetse fly. The obvious resistance of the trees themselves prevented intercourse:

> You may reach a tropical forest on a broad front—you must pass through it by files. It is like a town a thousand miles long. The paths lead to perfectly definite spots, from one village to another. Every village is a road-block; the path comes to the village, breaks up to enter the houses, regathers itself, and leads out on the other side. [3]

The tsetse fly prevented the use of horses or oxen either for war or for draught. If imported by the inhabitants or if brought in by an invading army these animals did not survive. As a consequence, traffic in pre-British Nigeria was pedestrian and not vehicular. There were no wheels and there were no roads simply because the forest and the tsetse fly defied their use.

The absence of animals coupled with the challenge of the forest also contributed to the intensely local character of agriculture. Farming was an enterprise for family groups because communal effort was needed to clear the forest. Moreover, the localness of agricultural production and land tenure was extremely influential in determining the size of the traditional political organization. In the forest belt political units were small and dispersed, and, with exceptions noted later, were based on the extended family or the clan. By contrast, in northern Nigeria, where there is no forest and where cattle and horses can be used, the traditional units are larger. In any event, the small size of the traditional political unit—later perpetuated by the system of indirect rule—has been a contributing factor in the persistence of parochial attitudes and loyalties, which, combined with linguistic diversities, have been obstacles to economic and political integration in Nigeria. The smallness has also meant that, except for the Yoruba and the Bini, most Nigerians in the south lack experience in administering large-scale political organizations. This has affected both the leadership and the activities of nationalist movements, as well as other aspects of the nation-building process.

The importance of the causal connection between environment and size of sociopolitical organization can be exaggerated; but it is believed that in the past Western observers have ignored the relationship and have preferred to account for such peculiarities as the absence of the wheel, pedestrian transport, communal land tenure, and smallness in scale of agricultural production and political organization, in terms of a natural racial inferiority.

The great variety of cultures and of physical types produced by a protracted and extensive intermingling of immigrant stocks, together with wide differences in the scale and degree of political organization, has made it difficult to develop a scientific classificatory system for the peoples of Nigeria. For descriptive purposes ethnic distinctions have been drawn on the basis of language, aided to some extent by evidences of similarity in customs or other criteria. Ethnographical and anthropometrical surveys have been too limited in scope to provide a more accurate criterion of group demarcation. But language is frequently misleading; for example, the majority of those listed as Fulani speak the Hausa (not the Fulani) language as the mother tongue. It would be inaccurate to give ethnic and political attributes to all linguistic categories.

Although intermixture has made it impossible to correlate a physical type with a particular linguistic group, nevertheless, three of the many types within Nigeria can be broadly distinguished (see map 2). The overwhelmingly predominant type is

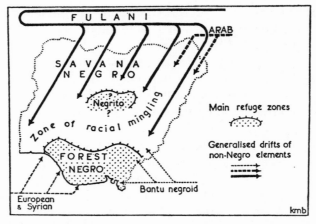

Map 2. Principal indigenous racial types (from K. M. Buchanan and J. C. Pugh, *Land and People in Nigeria*)

the "West Coast Negro." It is found in its most undiluted form in the southeastern forest belt, but it forms the basic substratum throughout most of Nigeria. The other two minor types are the Fulani (of Mediterranean extraction) and the Semitic Shuwa Arabs. The Fulani are widely dispersed throughout the Northern Region, and except for the nomadic herdsmen (called "Cow Fulani") who have retained the features of the true Fulani stock, this type has become assimilated to the predominant Negro type. The Shuwa Arabs in Nigeria are confined to the Lake Chad area of Bornu Province in the Northern Region. Between the pure Fulani or Shuwa Arab at the one extreme, and the pure Negro in the coastal forest region at the other, there are wide physiognomic variations (including traces of Mongoloid, Caucasoid, and Semitic features) which not only defy classification but disprove the common white belief that "all Africans look alike." In general, however, all but a relatively small number of Nigerians have essentially Negroid features, the most distinguishing of which are a dark skin and frizzled hair.[4]

TABLE 1

GEOGRAPHICAL DISTRIBUTION OF PRINCIPAL ETHNIC GROUPS OF NIGERIA
(Early 1950's)

Ethnic group and region of origin	Lagos Township	Western Region	Eastern Region	Northern Region	Total	Percentage of population of Nigeria
Western groups						
Yoruba	195,974	4,302,401	11,377	536,109 b	5,045,861	16.6
Edo	5,708	446,444	4,027	11,938	468,117	1.5
Others	5,051	486,902	a	a	491,953	
Total	206,733	5,235,747	15,404	548,047	6,005,931	
Eastern groups						
Ibo	31,887	342,335 c	4,916,736	166,910 d	5,457,868	17.9
Ibibio-Efik	4,505	5,265	809,387	12,759	831,916	2.7
Ijaw	3,925	79,079 e	258,962	a	341,966	1.1
Others	a	a	1,038,117	a	1,038,117	
Total	40,317	426,679	7,023,202	179,669	7,669,867	
Northern groups						
Hausa	3,847	41,374	10,288	5,488,446	5,543,955	18.2
Fulani	285	6,858	757	3,022,581	3,030,481	9.9
Kanuri	148	1,170	2,151	1,298,306	1,301,775	4.2
Nupe	444	6,980	2,811	348,979	359,214	1.1
Tiv	805	2,428	5,121 f	772,771	781,125	2.5
Others	202	4,110	a	5,051,380	5,055,692	
Total	5,731	62,920	21,128	15,982,463	16,072,242	
Other groups	14,626	356,680	151,228	101,874	624,408	
Grand total	267,407	6,082,026	7,210,962	16,812,053	30,372,448	

a Exact number not known; included in "Other groups."
b Of this number, about 480,000 constitute a border minority in the Northern Region.
c Of this number, about 285,000 constitute a border minority in the Western Region.
d Of this number, about 40,000 constitute a border minority in the Northern Region.
e Of this number, about 65,000 constitute a border minority in the Western Region.
f Of this number, about 4,500 constitute a border minority in the Eastern Region.
Sources: *Population Census of the Western Region of Nigeria, 1952* (Lagos: Government Statistician, 1953–1954); *Population Census of the Northern Region of Nigeria, 1952* (Lagos: Government Statistician, 1952–1953), pp. 26–29; *Population Census of the Eastern Region of Nigeria, 1953*, Bulletin no. 1 (Lagos: Government Statistician, 1954), pp. 18–19.

Within the boundaries of Nigeria there are approximately 248 distinct languages. Scientific linguists have not agreed upon any single classificatory scheme for African languages, but it is generally recognized that Nigeria is one of the principal "linguistic crossroads" of Africa.[5] Map 3 illustrates the number and distribution of the major linguistic aggregations represented in Nigeria.

Nigerian linguistic groups range in size from tiny units consisting of less than 700 people to groups numbering well above 5,000,000.[6] The size of the largest of these groups is shown in

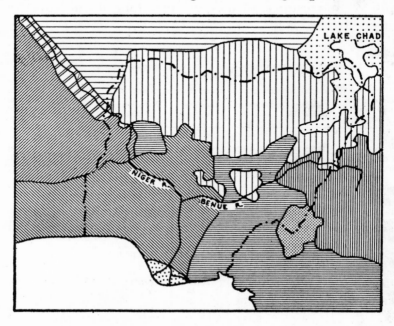

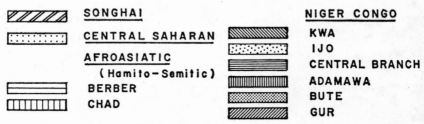

	SONGHAI		NIGER CONGO
	CENTRAL SAHARAN		KWA
	AFROASIATIC		IJO
	(Hamito-Semitic)		CENTRAL BRANCH
	BERBER		ADAMAWA
	CHAD		BUTE
			GUR

Map 3. Major language families represented in Nigeria (adapted from Joseph H. Greenberg, *Studies in African Linguistic Classification*)

table 1. It will be noted that certain of the larger groups are transregional (see map 4). Somewhat less than 500,000 Yorubas, for example, are resident in Ilorin and Kabba provinces in the Northern Region; the Ijaws are divided in the Niger Delta between the Eastern and Western regions, and more than 300,000

Nationalist arenas—The city

A NORTHERN CITY. (*Photograph, courtesy of British Information Services.*)

A SOUTHERN CITY. (*Photograph, courtesy of British Information Services.*)

Nationalist arenas—The village

A NORTHERN VILLAGE. (*Photograph, courtesy of British Information Services.*)

A SOUTHERN VILLAGE. (*Photograph, courtesy of British Information Services.*)

Other nationalist arenas

THE LEGISLATIVE ASSEMBLY. (*Photograph, courtesy of British Information Services.*)

THE MASS MEETING. (*Photograph, courtesy of British Information Services.*)

THE MARKET PLACE. (*Photograph, courtesy of British Information Services.*)

Nationalist media

THE PUBLIC PLATFORM. (*Photograph, courtesy of* West Africa.)

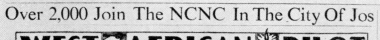

THE PRESS

Some traditional leaders in the north

EMIR OF KANO. (*Photograph, courtesy of British Information Services.*)

EMIR OF GWANDU. (*Photograph, courtesy of British Information Services.*)

EMIRATE OFFICIALS. (*Photograph, courtesy of British Information Services.*)

Some traditional leaders in the south

OGIRRUA OF IRRUA (left) AND OBI OF IDUMJE OGBOKO. (*Photograph, courtesy of British Information Services.*)

ALAKE OF ABEOKUTA (left) AND OBA OF BENIN. (*Photograph, courtesy of British Information Services.*)

The regional premiers

CHIEF OBAFEMI AWOLOWO, PREMIER, WESTERN REGION. (*Photograph, courtesy of Nigerian Federal Information Service.*)

DR. NNAMDI AZIKIWE, PREMIER, EASTERN REGION. (*Photograph, courtesy of Nigerian Federal Information Service.*)

ALHAJI AHMADU, SARDAUNA OF SOKOTO, PREMIER, NORTHERN REGION. (*Photograph, courtesy of Nigerian Federal Information Service.*)

The federal leaders

SIR JAMES WILSON ROBERTSON,
GOVERNOR-GENERAL

ALHAJI ABUBAKAR TAFAWA BALEWA,
PRIME MINISTER

THE COUNCIL OF MINISTERS

Ibos live on the west bank of the Niger in the Western Region and in the southern parts of Benue Province in the Northern Region. This division of ethnic groups by regional (political) boundaries helps to explain the later emergence of Irredentist and separatist movements among the groups affected.

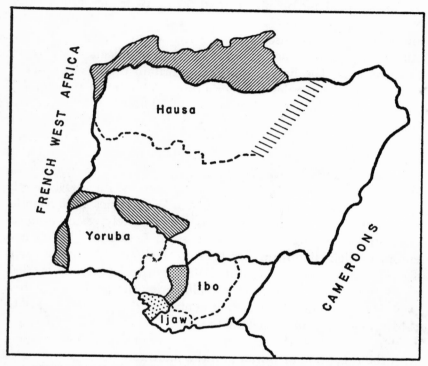

	YORUBA MINORITY AREA OF NORTHERN REGION AND FRENCH DAHOMEY
	IJAW MINORITY AREA OF WESTERN REGION
	IBO MINORITY AREA OF WESTERN REGION
	HAUSA—SPEAKING AREA OF FRENCH NIGER
	SHATTER BELT: HAUSA AND OTHER CHAD GROUPS

Map 4. Ethnic minorities created by regional and international boundaries (adapted in part from K. M. Buchanan and J. C. Pugh, *Land and People in Nigeria*)

It will also be noted that some groups are divided by the international boundaries separating Nigeria from its western and northern neighbors in French West Africa. Thus, sizable areas of southeastern Dahomey, including the port town of Porto Novo, are inhabited by Yoruba-speaking peoples. Also, areas inhabited by Hausa-speaking peoples extend 50 to 100 miles into French Niger territory in the Northern Region. The Kanuri, and several minor groups, have also been affected. Until the present, these ethnic divisions have not acquired political significance for at least three reasons. The first is that, since Britain established control over most of the peoples of Nigeria through the treaty process, full states such as the Egba Kingdom, the Ilorin Emirate, and the Sokoto Sultanate were brought under British jurisdiction intact. Secondly, the sharp contrast between French and British colonial policies has resulted in the subjection of segments of the divided groups to very different cultural influences. Finally, there has been extensive freedom of movement across frontiers. Each year nearly a quarter-million Africans from French West Africa visit Nigeria. If it develops at all, Irredentism will most likely result from an effort of the Yoruba of Nigeria's Western Region to liberate and embrace their linguistic brothers in Dahomey. The divisions among ethnic groups along the eastern border of Nigeria are less clear-cut, and, because of the smallness of the tribes concerned as well as the high degree of fragmentation, the problem of political Irredentism is not expected to arise.

Before the British occupation the present Northern Region, with the exception of Bornu and the more remote pagan areas of the Jos plateau, was broadly speaking coterminous with the Fulani Empire; the present Western Region, with the exception of a few small Delta groups and Ibo and Ijaw minorities, was organized into sizable Yoruba and Edo kingdoms; and the present Eastern Region consisted of small semiautonomous communities of Ibo- and Ibibio-speaking peoples and other more politically fragmented tribes. The peoples of Nigeria, therefore, can be most conveniently described by region.

THE PEOPLES OF THE NORTHERN REGION

The Northern Region (see map 5) includes more than 75 per cent of the total land area of Nigeria, and claims nearly 60 per cent of

18

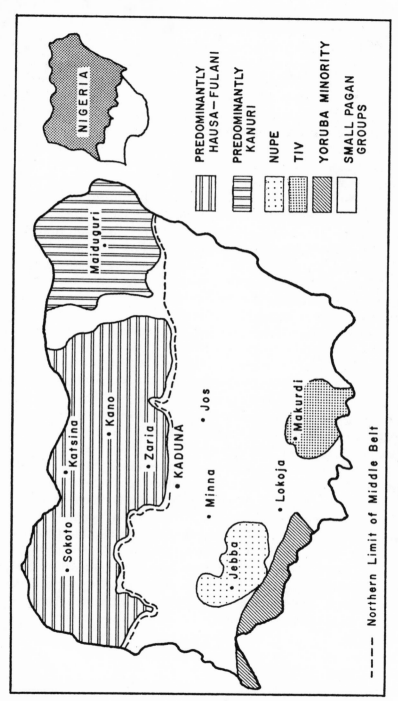

Map 5. Principal ethnic groups in Northern Region

PREDOMINANTLY
HAUSA—FULANI

PREDOMINANTLY
KANURI

NUPE

TIV

YORUBA MINORITY

SMALL PAGAN
GROUPS

NIGERIA

Maiduguri

Sokoto

Katsina

Kano

Zaria

KADUNA

Jos

Minna

Makurdi

Lokoja

Jebba

- - - - Northern Limit of Middle Belt

its peoples, including 5 of the 10 largest linguistic groups (Hausa, Fulani, Kanuri, Tiv, and Nupe), and all but 14 of the 239 small groups. Broadly speaking, at the time of the British occupation in 1900 the peoples of this area were divided politically into three main groups: (1) in the northeast, the Kanuri-speaking peoples of Bornu and Lake Chad area were the subjects of the *Shehu* of Bornu; (2) in the west the Fulani- and Hausa-speaking peoples were organized into a large number of semi-independent emirates, governed by a Fulani aristocracy, which recognized the religious leadership of the Sultan of Sokoto (Sarkin Musulmi); and (3) in the Middle Belt, on the Jos plateau, and interspersed elsewhere throughout the lower half of the region, were the Cow Fulani, the Tiv, the Birom, the Gwari, and more than 200 other small linguistic groups—so-called "pagan tribes"—either leading a precarious autonomous existence or constituting the bulk of the population of the Fulani emirates. Within these broad groupings, the peoples were at various stages of political development ranging from unconsolidated village groups to the centralized sultanates of Sokoto and Bornu.

During the several centuries before the British intrusion into the Northern Region, intertribal wars, migrations, and the internal slave trade tended thoroughly to mix up its peoples. These factors, together with the almost total lack of accurate ethnographic data, make it impossible to determine to what extent the linguistic groups of that area have had a tribal or national self-consciousness, or a political focus above the level of the extended family or village group. The fact that since the British occupation administrative divisions, with a few exceptions, have not been coterminous with linguistic groups has added to the confusion, particularly in the Middle Belt. There is also evidence of considerable internal assimilation. For example, elements of the Gwari-speaking peoples living in the Zaria Emirate have become markedly differentiated from the original Gwari stock. Similarly, Nupe-speaking peoples resident in Yorubaland have tended to become Yorubaized. With significant exceptions, to be noted subsequently, there has been a tendency for the smaller and more fragmented groups to lose their identity and gravitate toward the predominating groups, particularly the Hausa.

The Fulani-speaking peoples are spread throughout North and

West Africa, from the upper Nile to the Senegal, and are found either as unassuming nomadic herdsmen or as a settled alien ruling group. Their origin is obscure, and has given rise to many conflicting theories.[7] During the past century and a half they have been the dominant political power in the Northern Region. Their empire, centering around Sokoto, was established as a consequence of the successful jihad which started in 1802 under the leadership of a Fulani sheik, one Othman dan Fodio. Their conquest was carried out in two phases and by two methods: a gradual infiltration of the Hausa kingdoms over a period of centuries, and then, military conquest. The Fulani imperial superstructure was loosely organized and highly decentralized, and toward the latter part of the nineteenth century the emirates became increasingly independent. In certain respects the Fulani overlords, like the Manchu dynasty of China, tended to become culturally assimilated to their subjects. As a result of wide-scale intermarriage these "settled" Fulani have lost most of the distinguishing physical characteristics of their race, and the majority of them speak only Hausa as their mother tongue. Although they have become Hausa-ized, most of them continue to claim descent (usually only in the male line) from the true Fulani stock. Aside from this manifestation of national consciousness, possibly based on the urge to identify themselves with the ruling community, there is little evidence of a separate group consciousness, except, of course, among the undiluted Cow Fulani. The wide geographical dispersion of the Fulani throughout all parts of the Northern Region of Nigeria (concentrated mainly in Adamawa, Bauchi, Kano, Sokoto, and Zaria provinces) and elsewhere in West Africa, has also been an inhibiting factor.

More than 40 per cent of the population of the Northern Region speak Hausa as their mother tongue. The Hausa are basically only a linguistic group which includes a wide variety of cultures and physical types. Although concentrated mainly in Kano, Sokoto, Katsina, and Zaria provinces, they are found in sizable numbers in all areas of the north. There are more than 50,000 in the southern regions, and in Lagos alone they number more than 4,000. Hausa traders are located in all urban communities throughout West Africa. The Hausa, and the groups they have assimilated over the centuries, are identified principally by the Hausa language, which has become a lingua franca of the western Sudan; the Muslim faith; the Hausa gowns and skullcap; and skill in trading. The Hausa possess an intense cultural consciousness, and no matter where they travel abroad, or how long they remain, they retain a profound pride in being Hausa. They have displayed little desire to emulate or imitate the white man.

The Hausa have exercised a powerful cultural attraction on the smaller tribes of the Middle Belt as well as on some southern nationalists, particularly those from the Eastern Region. For this there are several reasons. The first is that many features of Hausa culture give it dignity, status, and prestige: a comparatively rich historical tradition; a distinctive architecture; the pomp and splendor of its ruling class; its easily learned and useful language; and the Islamic faith. The second, following from the first, is that the culture provides an alternative to the white European culture which the Hausa have been taught to emulate. As an Islamic culture, its links are with the East, via the Maghreb, Tripolitania, and Egypt. Of all Nigerian cultures, the Hausa culture is connected most intimately with the medieval kingdoms and empires of the western Sudan. Culturally conscious Nigerians, both Hausa and non-Hausa from the south, seek to identify themselves with this tradition. In their view it provides positive proof that the white man is mistaken when he states that Nigerians have no culture, no history, and no experience in large-scale political organization. This tendency toward identification is manifest even among educated Nigerians from the south who do not take on the externals of Hausa culture.

The original Hausa moved into what is now the Northern Region of Nigeria long before the spread of Islam to that area in the thirteenth century. Under Islamic influences they developed a fiscal system and a trained judiciary administering the Maliki code of Mohammedan law. During succeeding centuries they suffered from internecine wars, invasions from the Empire of Songhai, as well as from the Jukun pagans of the Benue valley. By the middle of the eighteenth century one of the states (Gobir), ruled by pagans, became dominant throughout Hausaland. The resultant decline of Islam was one of the factors that precipitated the Fulani jihad in 1802.[8]

The Kanuri-speaking people are mainly localized in the Chad

Basin. The original Kanuri (a collective term applying to allied peoples who came from Kanem) invaded that area in successive waves during the thirteenth and fourteenth centuries. Before their intrusion the area was peopled by a variety of fragmented groups, which eventually succumbed to the dominant Kanuri culture. The Kingdom of Bornu was established and the Kanuri peoples and their satellites of this area were brought together and developed a high level of unity as early as the fourteenth century. This unity was further strengthened during the nineteenth century under the leadership of Muhammed el Kanemi, who repulsed the Fulani invasion into Bornu. The Kanuri peoples have been Muslims for centuries; they are characterized by considerable physical homogeneity; and they have a political focus in the ancient Kingdom of Bornu.[9]

The Nupe, the fourth and smallest of the predominantly Moslem groups in the Northern Region, are partially localized in the Niger River valley above its confluence with the Benue. Prior to the Fulani jihad, a Nupe kingdom had existed since the fifteenth century. The Fulani conquerors—a small minority—were absorbed completely by the Nupe culture; moreover, even after the Nupe were divided among several separate states by the Fulani, and later by the British administration, they retained their sense of unity. A common historical tradition, the unifying symbol of *etsu* Nupe (king of the Nupe), and a common culture and language have perpetuated a feeling of Nupe consciousness. The Nupe have gravitated toward the Hausa in certain respects, but have still retained their individuality. As a result of their early contact with the Royal Niger Company and European trading stations, their geographical location astride the main internal trade routes between the far north and the coast, and a limited amount of Christian evangelism and Western education, they have undergone a higher degree of Western acculturation than any other Moslem group in the north.[10]

The Tiv (Munshi) tribe is a distinct group highly concentrated in one compact area south of the Benue River. Although the tribe has never had a central government, the conspicuous uniformity of their language and physique, their common customs, and their belief in a common origin have combined to produce an intense feeling of individuality and "Tiv-ness." They were not conquered by the Fulani, and they were one of the last groups to be pacified by the British. They are relatively unacculturated in regard to either Hausa-Islamic culture or European-Christian culture. Their political unity has been consciously fostered by the British administration, and in 1947 a central all-Tiv council and chief were appointed. Because of pre-British intertribal wars with the Hausa, and because of considerable recent Ibo migration northward, the Tiv tend to be hostile to these two larger groups.[11]

The foregoing groups (Fulani, Hausa, Kanuri, Nupe, and Tiv) constitute the "Big Five" of the Northern Region, and together make up approximately 65 per cent of its population. The first four share a common Islamic culture, and, despite such differences as the strong group feeling of the Kanuri and the Nupe, their cultural unity marks them off sharply not only from the non-Moslem Tiv, but also from the other peoples of Nigeria.

The remaining 35 per cent of the population of the Northern Region is made up of the so-called pagan tribes. Prior to the imposition of the Fulani-British superstructure, some of these were organized into unconsolidated village groups (for example, Nunji and Warji), and some into loose confederacies for war purposes (for example, Angas and Warjawa); others (for example, Igbirra, Bede, Bachama, and Igala) had achieved a certain measure of tribal unity. In the century and a half since the Fulani jihad, there have been two somewhat contradictory developments: the tendency of the leaders and more educated members of these small groups to become assimilated to the dominant Fulani-Hausa culture; and the British effort to render these groups administratively and politically less subordinate to the Fulani-Hausa aristocracy by encouraging pantribal federations which, in turn, have been made independent native authorities. These peoples have thus been caught between the expanding influence of Hausa culture and a countervailing British effort to stimulate their own group consciousness. Intermingled with these two influences has been the energetic evangelization of these peoples by Christian missionaries. Under the impact of many conflicting external influences, these Middle Belt groups are being stirred to consciousness; the rate and direction of their cultural and political development are among the most important but unpredictable aspects of future Nigerian politics.

The Yoruba peoples (see map 6) might rightly claim to be the largest cultural aggregation in West Africa with a history of political unity and a common historical tradition. Yoruba myths trace their origin to Ile Ife, a town in the center of Yorubaland where the grave of Oranyan, the mythical second King of the Yoruba, is still shown. Other theories regarding their origin point to Mecca and upper Egypt as their point of departure and the second millennium B.C. as the period of their migration to Ile Ife.

During most of the eighteenth century the Yoruba—except for the Ijebu subtribe—were united into one kingdom ruled from Old Oyo. By 1780, however, they were split into four states (Oyo, Egba, Ketu, and Jebu), and by 1850, as a result of the Fulani conquest of Ilorin, four new states emerged (Ibadan, Ilesha, Ife, and the Ekiti Parapo). By the turn of the century, when British authority was asserted over Yorubaland, additional fragmentation had occurred. Since then the disintegrative process has continued. In some instances it has been encouraged or at least tolerated by the British, pursuant to a policy of favoring "local autonomy": for example, the Ekiti Federation was split administratively into sixteen separate units; Ibadan severed itself completely from Oyo, and in turn the seven outlying districts of Ibadan (Oshun Federation) seceded; Ijebu-Remo was separated from Ijebu-Ode; and the Egbado subtribe has maintained only a very tenuous attachment to the Egba.[12]

Despite political fragmentation and regional dialectical differences (Ekiti and Ijebu dialects differ substantially from those of Oyo and Egba), regional variations in religious and ceremonial forms, and tensions produced by former slave or trade wars and struggles for independence or by current land and chieftaincy disputes, a comparatively strong Yoruba-consciousness has persisted. The belief in a common origin, a fairly recent all-tribal political unity, widespread intermarriage within the tribe, and the possession of Pan-Yoruba *orisha's* (tribal deities), have been integrative influences.

Additional distinguishing features of the Yoruba are of significance. One is the comparatively large-scale political organization which existed before the British intrusion. The *Alafin* of Oyo and

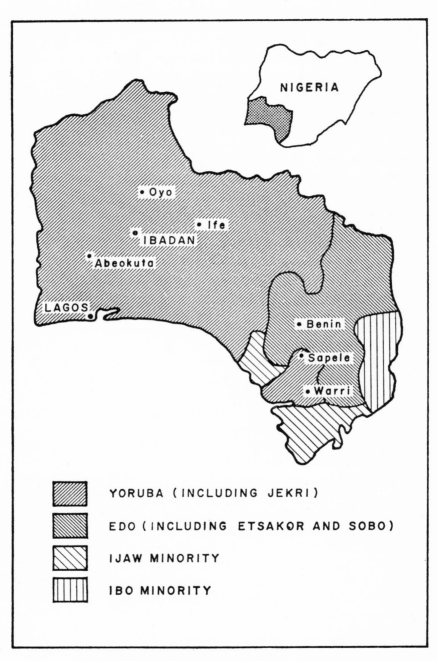

Map 6. Principal ethnic groups in Western Region

his council ruled over a kingdom which surpassed in size any of the northern emirates with the exception of Kano and Sokoto. The Egba Kingdom (ruled by the *Alake* of Abeokuta), the Ekiti Federation, and the Kingdom of Ijebu-Ode had populations exceeding 200,000. A second feature, already noted, was the substantial degree of urbanization which prevailed in pre-European times. Finally, apart from the Efik of Old Calabar and a few sections of the Ijaw on the Niger Delta, the Yoruba peoples have been subjected to more intensive westernization than any other group in Nigeria. Christian missionaries entered Yorubaland in 1841; and Lagos, a predominantly Yoruba city, was annexed to the British Crown in 1861. Since Lagos is the principal port of Nigeria, a large percentage of Nigeria's exports and imports have traversed Yorubaland. All these factors have combined to differentiate the Yoruba markedly from other groups in Nigeria.

The Edo, centered in the old Kingdom of Benin, are the other principal group of the Western Region. Yoruba traditions describe the Edo-speaking peoples (as well as the smaller Jekri tribe) as merely an offshoot of the Yoruba. The early rulers of the kingdom were Yoruba, and there are certain Edo institutions markedly similar to those of the Yoruba. On the other hand, the Edo and Yoruba languages are mutually unintelligible, and few if any Edo politicians would support the claim that the Edo people are part of the Yoruba nationality.

When the Portuguese visited Benin City at the end of the fifteenth century, they found a powerful kingdom. At that time the Kingdom of Benin was the most centralized state on the Guinea Coast. It once included Lagos, as well as the peoples belonging to smaller Edo-speaking subtribes (Kukuruku, Ishan, and Sobo), and to the Ika subtribe of the Ibo. The power of the kingdom gradually contracted and at the time of the British intrusion (1897), the authority of the *Oba* (king) of Benin was limited mainly to the two subtribes of Bini and Esa. The latter constitute only about 20 per cent of the total Edo-speaking population. The outlying Edo subtribes to the north (Ishan and Kukuruku) and to the south (Sobo), although acknowledging a former subservience to the Oba of Benin, are politically fragmented and have acquired local autonomy under the British administration. This fact, together with a separate subtribal consciousness in each of

27

the outlying groups and their wide dialectical differences, has inhibited the growth of an all-Edo national unity.[13]

As noted above, the old Kingdom of Benin included the Ika subtribe of the Ibo, numbering about 250,000, which inhabited a compact area between Edo territory and the western bank of the Niger River. The *obi* (an Ibo term—of likely Yoruba origin—for king or chief) was appointed by the Oba of Benin, and the Ika acknowledged allegiance to him. The decline of the Kingdom of Benin and the establishment of the British administration caused these Ibo-speaking peoples to develop traditions of local autonomy and independence from Benin. The fairly recent growth of a Pan-Ibo national consciousness has further weakened what remained of their traditional attachment to Benin.[14]

The Ijaw tribe, divided almost evenly between the Western and the Eastern regions, is perhaps the most ancient in West Africa. Its language has little affinity with any other in Nigeria. Except for a small enclave of Jekri, the Ijaw are the principal inhabitants of the Delta region of the Niger. So situated, they were among the first to feel the impact of westernization through their contact with the European trader and later the missionary. Their political fragmentation, caused in part by the dense swamp forest and the hundreds of small creeks in the Delta, has been perpetuated by their administrative division, first between provinces, and latterly between regions.[15]

THE PEOPLES OF THE EASTERN REGION

A large part of the Eastern Region is covered by a dense forest. This accounts in part for the fact that the peoples inhabiting that area (see map 7) have had a more decentralized political structure than any other major group. Another contributory factor may have been the absence of invasions or mass migrations which would have induced or compelled them to form large states administered by a centralized authoritative leadership. Finally, the alleged "individualistic" temperament of the peoples of this area —and there is strong evidence of a cultural emphasis upon individual achievement affecting rank status—tended to prevent the emergence of large-scale centralized organizations. In any event, the basic social unit among the Ibo and Ibibio has been a single extended family or a kindred composed of several such families,

28

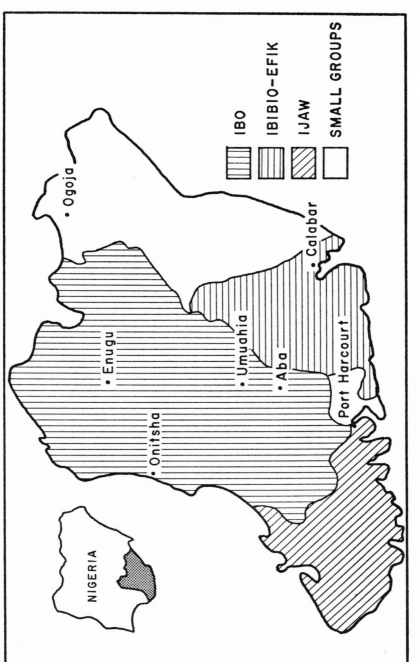

Map 7. Principal ethnic groups in Eastern Region

and the largest political unit has normally been the village group. Although the Ibo nationality is the second largest in Nigeria, it is divided into 30 subtribes, 69 clans, and some 500 fairly autonomous villages or village groups.[16]

Even though the village group has normally been the highest level of recognized common authority, there have been times when consciousness of a wider unity existed, or could be awakened. In some areas of Iboland there is a tradition of hereditary kingship, and the kingdom is usually larger than the village group. Also, many clans are not necessarily localized, but cut across large sections of Iboland. The members of most clans are vaguely aware of belonging to a group higher than the extended family or village. The Ngwa clan (more than 100,000) is a case in point. Most Ngwas are united by a belief in a common ancestry. According to clan legends, the original Ngwa crossed the Imo River and settled at a place called Ekelafor, which became thereafter the annual place of meeting for all senior *onye-mue-ala*'s representing the 15 village groups and 215 villages into which the clan was fragmented. Although physical conditions, and early British encouragement of decentralization, prevented the political expression of a higher corporate unity, there did exist an Ngwa consciousness. In the late 1930's, the British administration, with the help of educated Ngwas, established the All-Ngwa Clan Council as a central organ of government. Today, Ngwa consciousness is quite strong.

Ibo women have developed organizations based upon both their natal and marital villages, and these societies have transcended village groups and even clan boundaries. This was effectively demonstrated in the Aba Riots of 1929, and in the more recent women's riots in 1947–1948. Also, Iboland abounds in titled male societies, membership in which is based in many instances upon the possession of wealth, and this system of titles tends to cut across and frequently to eclipse the family and village organization. Moreover, one Ibo group, the Aro, maintained an all-tribal oracle at Arochuku, and, by one account, as early as the fifteenth century inaugurated a trading system that covered most of Iboland.[17] Finally, intratribal disputes between villages or village groups have traditionally been settled by councils representing the wider groups to which the disputants belong. Despite the *ad hoc* nature of such councils, they provide evidence that higher levels of authority can emerge spontaneously when needed. Thus, as Dr. K. Onwuka Dike has pointed out in his recent study: "Beneath the apparent fragmentation of authority lay deep fundamental unities not only in the religious and cultural spheres, but also . . . in matters of politics and economics."[18] These unities provided the basis for the later emergence of a Pan-Ibo consciousness which profoundly affected the Nigerian nationalist movement.

As previously indicated, there are many similarities in the social structure of the Ibo and the Ibibio peoples. The latter constitute the second and only other large group in the Eastern Region. But such resemblances, and the fact that the two groups are contiguous, do not mean that they have strong cultural or linguistic affinities. The Ibo and Ibibio languages belong to different branches of the large Niger-Congo linguistic family.[19] Moreover, there are many bases, mainly historical, for Ibo-Ibibio hostility and tension. The early maraudings of the Arochuku Ibo in Ibibioland, and the frequent clashes between neighboring clans of the two groups, even in recent times, have sharpened the basic cultural-linguistic differentiation.

Just as there is a historical cleavage between the Onitsha Ibo and the main body of Ibo (referred to commonly as the "non-Onitsha Ibo"),[20] so is there a marked differentiation between the Ibibio and the Efik. The latter inhabit Calabar and its environs. They have been in long and continuous contact with external cultural influences. Because of this and other factors, the Efik have tended to regard themselves as very different from the Ibibio. They claim an independent origin, and strongly resent any identification with the Ibibio, although both speak basically the same language.[21]

Apart from the Ibo, the Ibibio-Efik, and the Ijaw, the other peoples of the Eastern Region are divided among nine small groups, speaking different languages. The majority of them inhabit Ogoja Province, which was the last area to be brought under British control, and consequently the last to be favored with communications and social services; hence they are the least developed of all groups in the region. Until recently they have been politically inarticulate, and, unlike the smaller groups in the north, show

31

no definite signs of cultural orientation toward any of the major groups in the Eastern Region.

The foregoing survey of the major groupings of Nigeria has made reference mainly to the scale of political organization achieved by each. The diversities are greater than in any other territory in Africa. The groups vary from the highly organized Fulani-Hausa emirates in the north, and the sizable kingdoms of the Yoruba and the Edo in the west, to small autonomous or semi-autonomous groups in the Middle Belt and the Eastern Region. These qualitative differences in scale of political organization, however, do not hide a fairly basic uniformity in social structure. Throughout Nigeria the fundamental kinship unit is the lineage (Ibo-*umunna*, Hausa-*dangi*, Yoruba-*idile*), a portion of clan living together in a given locality.[22] Heretofore it has commanded the strongest loyalty because it is the primary social and economic unit. There has unfortunately been a tendency in the past for observers to evaluate group differences according to European preconceptions; that is, those groups that had transcended the clan in scale of political organization were considered more advanced, civilized, and superior, and those that had not were classified as backward, primitive, and inferior. The present writer finds this classical Lugardian method of differentiating the peoples of Nigeria unacceptable. The difference in scale of political organization is a useful classificatory tool for descriptive analysis; at the same time it is essential to keep in mind that a fairly common African pattern of social organization underlies the varying political superstructures.

Kinship government, at the lineage level and below, is basically the same throughout Nigeria. It is at the higher levels of the traditional political structures that wide variations are to be noted. At the time of the British occupation, the Fulani-Hausa and Kanuri states in the Northern Region were dominated by rulers who were theoretically absolute. They ruled with the advice of councilors who were either fief-holders or their official appointees. Below them and their advisory councils (inner councils) were district heads and village heads appointed by them and accountable to them through a rigorous hierarchical organization. The whole superstructure was alien to the peoples, except for the village head, who, although an appointee of the Fulani emir, was in practice usually selected by the people according to traditional methods. The district heads either were members of the emir's own or of other important Fulani families, or were, in states having large pagan tribes, the traditional chiefs of the subject peoples. Among the Yoruba, the chiefs (obas) of the subtribes were either hereditary or were elected from among a limited number of royal families who ruled in turn. The whole Yoruba system was marked by checks and counterchecks, and the superstructure was essentially that of a constitutional monarchy. Finally, among the Ibo and the Ibibio, with several exceptions, "authority is dispersed among groups rather than centralized in any one individual or body." Traditional societies and age-grade organizations played an important role in the indigenous governmental process. In general, government was the business of the whole community, and according to most Ibos it was essentially democratic.

NON-NIGERIAN ELEMENTS IN THE POPULATION

Of all territories in tropical Africa, Nigeria is unique in that alien or foreign elements make up only a small proportion of its total population. In Nigeria these elements fall into three distinct categories: Europeans, Levantines and Indians, and "native foreigners." The growth in the size of these groups is shown in table 2.

TABLE 2

NON-NIGERIAN ELEMENTS IN THE NIGERIAN POPULATION

Year	Non-African elements			Total non-Africans	Non-Nigerian Africans
	British officials	Other Europeans	Levantines and Indians		
1911	1,000	1,200	100	2,300	b
1921	2,039	1,829	188	4,056	19,300
1931	2,695	4,582	498	7,775	27,207
1938	2,001	6,188	1,034	8,223	b
1952–53	a	a	a	15,354	39,680

a Separate figures not available; included in "Total non-Africans."
b Not known.

Sources: P. Amaury Talbot, *The Peoples of Southern Nigeria* (London: 1926), Vol. IV; C. K. Meek, *The Northern Tribes of Nigeria* (London: 1925), Vol. II; *Census of Nigeria, 1931* (Lagos: Government Printer, 1932); *Population Census of the Western Region of Nigeria, 1952* (Lagos: Government Statistician, 1953–1954); *Population Census of the Eastern Region of Nigeria, 1953* (Lagos: Government Statistician, 1953–1954); *Population Census of the Northern Region of Nigeria, 1952* (Lagos: Government Statistician, 1952–1953).

33

Only brief mention of these non-Nigerian elements need be made here, since they will be discussed in greater detail at appropriate points throughout the study.

Nigeria has the smallest proportion of Europeans to Africans on the continent of Africa. The smallness of the resident European population has had a decisive influence upon the rise and course of nationalism, particularly since few, if any, Europeans have considered themselves permanent residents of Nigeria. Most of them are missionaries, employees of European firms, or civil servants. While the number of European businessmen has increased steadily since 1921, the number of government officials remained fairly constant until the beginning of World War II. After the war the number of officials increased as a result of the expansion of education and of activities connected with economic development. However, with the approach of self-government, and the greatly accelerated program of "Africanization," the number of Europeans in the official category is bound to decrease very rapidly.

The Levantines (Greeks, Syrians, Lebanese) and the Indians have helped to fill the gap between large European firms and petty African traders. After 1921 they arrived in increasing numbers, and the influx was not arrested until immigration restrictions were imposed in 1947. The overwhelming majority of Levantines and Indians have been engaged in retail trade. Lacking color consciousness, willing to live in the African quarters of urban centers, and content with small-margin profits, they have not created the psychological barrier that has separated Europeans and Africans elsewhere in Africa. They have scrupulously avoided politics, although a few of their more farsighted leaders began to court the nationalists at an early date. With certain exceptions there is little evidence that Levantines and Indians consider Nigeria their permanent home.

A "native foreigner" is defined by law as "any person (not being a Native of Nigeria) whose parents were members of a tribe or tribes indigenous to some part of Africa and the descendants of such persons, and includes any person, one of whose parents was a member of such a tribe." [23] For the purposes of this study, these non-Nigerian Africans can be put into two categories: those who are educated and those who are not. Educated native foreigners include, *inter alia*, West Indians, Ghanians, Sierra Leonians, and

Dahomeans who flocked to Nigeria in the early years of British penetration and took up positions as clerks and artisans in the government and in business firms. Although they spend their working life in Nigeria, the majority intend to retire to their homelands. Many of them became prominent in early organizational activity of a nationalist flavor, as will be noted later. The uneducated native foreigners are the semipermanent or seasonal laborers who visit Nigeria from neighboring French territories to work as farm helpers or as laborers in the tin mines. Politically they are an unknown quantity.

CHAPTER 2

The Historical Background

British administration in Nigeria did not formally commence until 1861, the year that Lagos was ceded to the Crown. For many centuries before then, however, northern Nigeria had been subjected to external influences from the large medieval kingdoms of the western Sudan (Ghana, Melle, and Songhai), from the Maghreb and Tripolitania, and from Egypt via Lake Chad and the Nile-Niger traverse previously mentioned. The important immigrations of northern Nigerian groups (Fulani, Hausa, Kanuri) were directly connected with disturbances resulting from the spread of Islam in Egypt and North Africa in and after the seventh century. The empires of Melle and Songhai were Islamic, the rulers having been converted to Islam in the middle of the eleventh century. In 1493 a Negro (Mohammed Askia) seized the throne of the Empire of Songhai, and during the succeeding two centuries most of the Hausa states were brought within that empire. In the meantime, Katsina and Kano had become famous as centers of Islam, and Kano emerged as a great commercial entrepôt. Historically and culturally, the Muslim areas of northern Nigeria belong to the western Sudan (see map 8).[1]

Until the arrival of the British, northern Nigeria was economically oriented toward Tripoli and Egypt (see map 9). Kano was famous throughout and beyond the Sudan for the weaving and embroidery of cloths, the tanning of skins, and ornamental leatherwork. The latter product, known as "Morocco leather," was exported across the Sahara to North African ports; the caravans brought back to Kano European trade goods, mostly cloth, metal

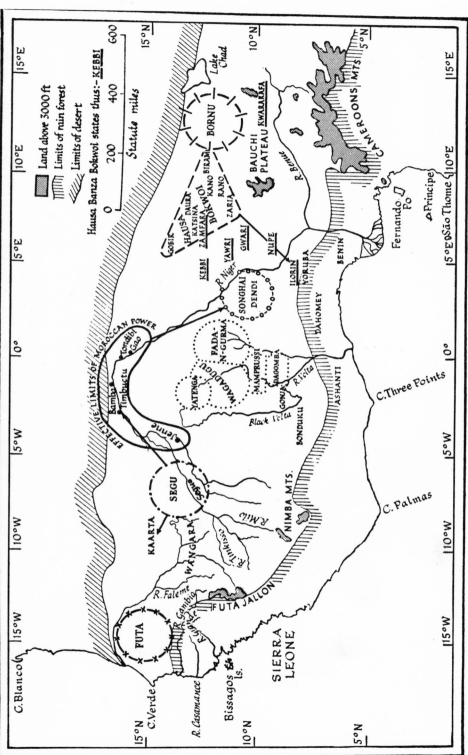

Map 8. The states of the western Sudan in the seventeenth century (from J. D. Fage, *An Introduction to the History of West Africa*)

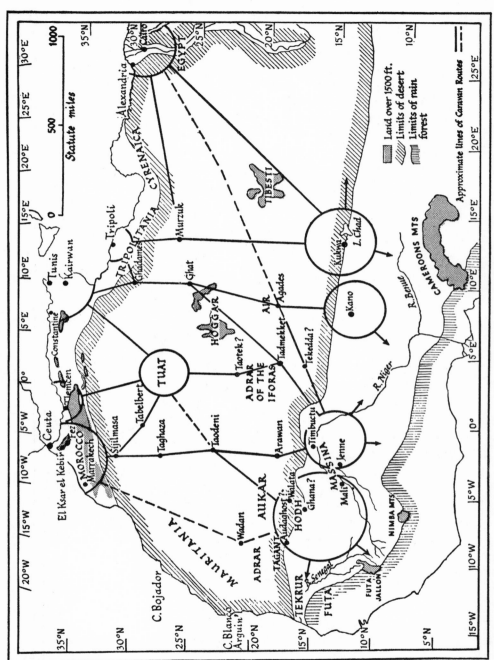

Map 9. Relations between North and West Africa. (from J. D. Fage, *An Introduction to the History of West Africa*)

articles, and glass. The outstanding economic development in northern Nigeria since the British occupation has been the virtual cessation of this historic trans-Saharan trade, and the diversion of export products to the Guinea Coast as a result of the imposition of an artificial frontier above Kano and the development of a modern transportation system within Nigeria.

Islam was firmly established in northern Nigeria by the end of the fifteenth century, and its effects were profound. Although Islam, like Catholicism, is not necessarily conservative, the political elite which emerged in northern Nigeria used certain interpretations of Islam to impose centralized government and a rigid class hierarchy and to inculcate habits and attitudes of political deference and subordination. The Hausa language absorbed hundreds of words of Arabic origin and was adapted to Arabic script. Islam provided a transtribal bond which has been one of the most powerful integrative factors in northern Nigeria. It also provides a link with the modern Middle East, as evidenced by the thousands of pilgrims who travel from northern Nigeria to Mecca each year, and by the growing contacts with the Sudan, Egypt, and other Muslim countries.[2]

These early influences from the Maghreb and North Africa were not restricted exclusively to the north. In a diluted form they filtered down into the more physically accessible parts of Yorubaland. Today there are as many Yoruba Muslims as Christians, although Yorubaland has been subjected to intensive Christian evangelization for more than a century. Some authorities believe that certain Yoruba and Edo cultural traits can be traced with certainty to Egypt: the divinity of kings, ceremonies of reinvestiture and rejuvenation, and beliefs similar to the Egyptian ka.[3] The spread of Islam was halted, however, wherever the rain forest became dense and inhospitable. Environmental factors, among others, prevented the southeastern part of Nigeria from feeling its impact.

During the fifteenth century, when Islam was consolidating its hold over northern Nigeria, the impact of the export slave trade, commenced by Portugal, was being felt in the south. By 1455 more than 700 slaves were being shipped annually to Portugal from the West Coast of Africa; and under the inspiration and guidance of Henry the Navigator the whole of the Guinea Coast was known by 1500. Portuguese traders and missionaries briefly visited Benin City in the 1480's, and from the latter part of the fifteenth century until the beginning of the nineteenth century they exercised an appreciable influence in the Itsekiri Kingdom of Warri.[4]

During the three centuries following 1500 most of the leading European nations participated in the slave trade, which became lucrative after the discovery of America and the establishment of Spanish colonies in the West Indies had created a heavy demand for slaves. In 1712 the British secured a virtual monopoly over slave dealing on the West Coast. A century later, in 1807, Great Britain declared the slave trade illegal. British abolition produced no revolutionary change, however, because foreign slave dealers, mainly Portuguese, rushed in to fill the vacuum. In fact, the trade actually increased, and was not finally ended until the mid-1840's.[5]

European slave dealers had no strong incentive to explore the Nigerian hinterland, and few of them left their vessels. Procurement of the slaves was left to African enterprise. Chiefs and African slave traders readily undertook the role of middlemen and brought the slaves to shipside in exchange for European trinkets. Thus they acquired a vested interest in the slave traffic and were as much aggrieved by its cessation and their consequent displacement as were the white slave dealers. The first Nigerian middle class was liquidated by the abolition of the external slave trade.[6]

Nigeria was known as the "Slave Coast" until the middle of the nineteenth century. Its peoples felt the brunt of four centuries of European-African contact resulting from the traffic in slaves. Africanisms traceable to Yoruba culture have been found in Negro communities in Brazil, the West Indies, and elsewhere in the New World.[7] Many of the creoles of Freetown, Sierra Leone, are descendants of early Yoruba freed slaves. The total effect of the slave trade upon Nigerian society, institutions, and peoples will perhaps never be known. Certain general effects are obvious. The trade was one of the main causes of the devastating internecine strife that prevailed in southern Nigeria during the centuries preceding abolition. Not only were tribal institutions disorganized, but the energies and talents of the people were consumed either by raiding or being raided in order to meet the great demands for slaves. Hundreds of thousands of the most virile members of their race were physically withdrawn from African society over a period of 400 years. The same period saw Europe emerge from medieval stagnation and pass through her agricultural, industrial, and intellectual revolutions.

The slave trade not only profoundly affected institutions, but it left a psychological legacy of suspicion, servility, or hostility which has been one of the most serious obstacles in Eurafrican relations. Many educated Africans privately believe that the slave trade is the main explanation for their so-called primitiveness. They bitterly resent the stigma of inferiority implicit in the fact that their race was once a race of slaves. They feel that they were victims of history, held back while other peoples were advancing.

BRITISH ACQUISITION OF NIGERIA

After the British government had declared the slave trade illegal in 1807, European traders were compelled to turn to legitimate trade in such commodities as palm oil and ivory. The adjustment was made quickly, however, and as early as 1826 twelve British merchant ships were reported to be in the Bonny River at one time. The discovery in 1830 that the Niger entered the Bight of Biafra served as an invitation for traders to penetrate the hinterland. During the succeeding seventy years the trade in Nigerian products grew very rapidly and was conducted first by private European traders and companies, and later (1886–1900) by the chartered Royal Niger Company, formed under the leadership of Sir George Goldie as a result of his amalgamation of all rival companies.[8] The Berlin Conference of 1885 acknowledged British claims to the Niger Basin, and Britain gave the Royal Niger Company power "to administer, make treaties, levy customs and trade in all territories in the basin of the Niger and its affluents."[9] Armed with this mandate the company in the next fifteen years established a firm monopoly over all trade in the Niger Basin. In 1900 the British government took over from the Royal Niger Company, and Sir Frederick Lugard, as high commissioner, proclaimed the Protectorate of Northern Nigeria.

In the meantime, British trading interests along the coast had secured sufficient political support from a reluctant home government to have a British consul appointed in 1849. Stationed on the Spanish island of Fernando Po, the consul was charged with

41

supervising trading activities in the Bights of Benin and Biafra. In 1872 certain judicial and administrative powers were conferred upon him, including the levying of fines and the taking of punitive measures against Africans who resisted "peaceful" commerce. In 1885 Britain, when given a clear hand at the Berlin Conference, formally declared the Niger Delta area, over which the consul had been exercising limited powers, the Oil Rivers Protectorate. During the next seven years an armed constabulary was raised, armed launches were secured, and consuls and vice-consuls were appointed to the various rivers over which they were given control by the commissioner and consul general resident at Old Calabar. Finally, in 1893, Britain extended the protectorate over the hinterland and renamed it the Niger Coast Protectorate.

More than three decades earlier, in 1861, the British government had annexed the settlement of Lagos as a colony, ostensibly for the purpose of stopping the slave trade. For twenty years this famous slave mart was successively under the jurisdiction of the governor of the West African Settlements, resident in Sierra Leone (1866–1874), and the governor of the Gold Coast Colony (1874–1886). Lagos was finally severed from the Gold Coast (now Ghana) in the same year that the Royal Niger Company was given its charter and the Oil Rivers Protectorate was established. In 1900 the Niger Coast Protectorate became the Protectorate of Southern Nigeria, and six years later it was amalgamated with Lagos under the title of Colony and Protectorate of Southern Nigeria. Finally, in 1914, the two protectorates (northern and southern) were amalgamated to form the Colony and Protectorate of Nigeria.

The foregoing is a necessarily brief history of how three separate, independent, and uncoördinated forces, centered respectively at Lagos (under a colonial governor), Old Calabar (under a Foreign Office consul), and Lokoja (under a chartered trading company), spread out from their bases and ultimately acquired control over an immense block of tropical Africa endowed with the name of Nigeria. These historical developments are illustrated by map 10. The fact that such acquisition was piecemeal and occurred in successive stages accounts in part for the extreme unevenness in the degree of social change and modernization among the various groups and areas of Nigeria. This unevenness has added internal stress to already existing tensions.

THE EMERGENCE OF MODERN NIGERIA

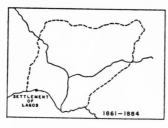

PORT AND ISLAND OF LAGOS CEDED
TO GREAT BRITAIN IN 1861

------ NIGERIAN BOUNDARY (1900)

||||||| COLONY AND PROTECTORATE
OF LAGOS

OIL RIVERS PROTECTORATE
(1887)

NIGER COAST PROTECTORATE
(1893)

////// BRITISH SPHERE OF INFLUENCE
(1894)

------ NIGERIAN BOUNDARY (1900)

||||||| LAGOS AND COLONY

PROTECTORATE OF SOUTHERN
NIGERIA

////// PROTECTORATE OF NORTHERN
NIGERIA

COLONY AND PROTECTORATE
OF SOUTHERN NIGERIA

////// PROTECTORATE OF NORTHERN
NIGERIA

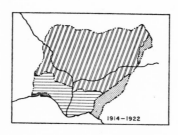

COLONY AND PROTECTORATE OF NIGERIA
(1914)

||||||| COLONY

PROTECTORATE:

////// NORTHERN PROVINCES

SOUTHERN PROVINCES

CAMEROONS MANDATE (1922)

Map 10

Until the turn of the nineteenth century the areas embraced in whole or in part by the then geographical expression now named "Nigeria" were referred to by a variety of names. The immediate predecessors have been noted: the Colony of Lagos, the Niger Coast Protectorate, and the "territories in the basin of the Niger and its affluents" administered by the Royal Niger Company. Other earlier names, reflecting the caprice of the cartographer or traveler, included "Soudan or Nigritia," "Houssa" states, Central Sudan, Guinea Coast, Slave Coast, Niger Empire, and Niger Sudan. The first official recognition of the name "Nigeria" appeared in the debate in the House of Commons on the Royal Niger Company Bill in July, 1899. Several persons have tried, however, to discover who coined the name. According to A. H. M. Kirk-Greene it was the London *Times*. In the January 8, 1897, issue the *Times* suggested that,

> . . . as the title "Royal Niger Company's Territories" is not only inconvenient to use but to some extent is also misleading, it may be permissible to coin a shorter title for the agglomeration of pagan and Mohammedan states which have been brought, by the exertions of the Royal Niger Company, within the confines of a British Protectorate, and thus need for the first time in their history to be described as an entity by some general name. To speak of them as the Central Sudan, which is the title accorded by some geographers and travellers, has the disadvantage of ignoring political frontier lines. . . . The name "Nigeria," applying to no other portion of Africa, may, without offence to any neighbours, be accepted as co-extensive with the territories over which the Royal Niger Company has extended British influence, and may serve to differentiate them equally from the British colonies of Lagos and the Niger Protectorate on the coast, and from the French territory of the Upper Niger.[10]

Thus in the historical development of the country of Nigeria the north was in a sense tacked on to the south, but the name "Nigeria" was first given to the north.

BRITISH POLICY IN NIGERIA

The general outlines of British policy in Nigeria since 1900 require but brief mention. Specific features relating directly to the rise of nationalism will be discussed in following chapters. At the outset a distinction must be drawn between the British superstructure and the system of native administration. The former included the governor, lieutenant governors, the colonial bureaucracy, the field staff of residents and district officers, and the army and police. Beneath this central governing apparatus which initiated all policies and promulgated all laws were more than 200 separate units of local government (native administrations) of varying sizes and types, possessing delegated powers and subject to central supervision in the exercise of those powers. The superstructure was, with a few exceptions, all British; the mass base was all African.

The artificiality of Nigeria's boundaries and the sharp cultural differences among its peoples point up the fact that Nigeria is a British creation and the concept of a Nigerian nation is the result of the British presence. There are many nations in the world, of course, which began as "geographical expressions" inhabited by peoples of widely different cultural backgrounds, and yet subsequently achieved nationhood under a unified administration imposed either by a dominant group within or by an alien invader from without. There are two principal ways in which an alien invader can facilitate the growth of a feeling of identity: (1) the creation of internal peace and the maintenance of law and order, and (2) the imposition of a common government which all recognize and to which all give obedience, allegiance, and loyalty. Undeniably, the greatest contribution the British have made to Nigerian unity is the pacification of the country, the establishment of central police forces, and the maintenance of a minimum standard of justice. As Margery Perham has written:

> European rule was imposed like a great steel grid over the amorphous cellular tissue of tribal Africa and the hundreds of independent and often hostile communities were held within its interstices in peace. This peace has allowed—and this has been one of the greatest hopes and justifications of colonial rule—full and free movement for the first time over wide areas not only for commerce but also for ideas and for men who could never know each other before.[11]

The present unity of Nigeria, as well as its disunity, is in part a reflection of the form and character of the common government

45

—the British superstructure—and the changes it has undergone since 1900. In that year the area now known as Nigeria was divided into three separate colonial territories (the Colony of Lagos and the protectorates of Southern and Northern Nigeria), each independently administered by three different administrators directly responsible to the United Kingdom. In 1904 the two southern administrations were brought under the same governor (Sir Walter Egerton), and two years later the Colony and Protectorate of Southern Nigeria, under a united colonial bureaucracy, came into being. For the next six years Northern and Southern Nigeria were administered as separate colonial territories, even to the extent of having frontier controls. In 1914 the colony and the two protectorates were amalgamated and ostensibly became a single political unit called the Colony and Protectorate of Nigeria, with the capital at Lagos. The only bond of political unity, however, was the person of Sir Frederick Lugard, the new governor-general.

Despite this final amalgamation of 1914, the administrative individuality of the former separate territories was maintained. The Colony of Lagos preserved its unique legal status. Like other early West African trading stations, Lagos and its environs had been annexed and made a colony. The peoples became British subjects owing allegiance to the British sovereign, and British law was imposed on African law. The colony's separate status continued until the inauguration of the Constitution of 1951. Moreover, the amalgamated protectorate of 1914 was divided into two groups of provinces (northern and southern) which corresponded identically with the formerly separate protectorates. Each of these two groups of provinces was administered by a separate lieutenant governor, reporting directly to the governor, and by a distinct colonial bureaucracy.

Although the broad principles of the native administration system were slowly extended from the north to the south, the different policies and conceptions of colonial administration which had evolved in each of the two protectorates during the fourteen years of their separate existence continued to dominate official thought and action. Also, different policies regarding native land prevailed in the two areas. The only occasions on which the higher officials of the two separate bureaucracies could meet was at the annual session of the Legislative Council in Lagos. The northern bureaucracy, reflecting somewhat the conservatism of Moslem culture, continually agitated for distinct and separate development of the north, even to the point of suggesting that it be cut off from the south. A frequently heard quip was that if all the Africans were to leave Nigeria the northern and southern administrations would go to war. The officials of the two bureaucracies spoke different official languages. In the north it was Hausa; in the south—because of the complex polytonic languages—it was English. Thus there was a distinct and independent administrative development as between the north and the south which has continued until the present day. The fact that the Northern and Southern protectorates were never effectively united has tended to perpetuate the sharp cultural differences between the peoples of the north and of the south.

In the meantime, a process of administrative integration and disintegration had occurred within the southern provinces. When the Southern Protectorate was created in 1900, it was administratively organized into three groups of provinces, each headed by a resident who reported to a lieutenant governor. These were subsequently amalgamated into one united administration with a free-circulating bureaucracy and with headquarters first in Lagos and subsequently in Enugu. Throughout this period of southern unity, administrative policies were essentially uniform, with adaptations for obvious sectional or tribal peculiarities. In 1939 the awkwardness of Enugu as a headquarters, together with other factors, brought about a division of the south into two groups of provinces (western and eastern), with the Niger River as the boundary.

Thus, at the outbreak of World War II, Nigeria was divided into four artificial administrative units: the colony, the Western Provinces, the Northern Provinces, and the Eastern Provinces. During the war the shortage of administrative personnel, plus the growing congestion in Lagos, forced substantial delegation of powers and functions from Lagos to the headquarters of the three groups of provinces. By the end of the war the degree of administrative devolution had been of such magnitude as to endow the three main areas with an individuality. This was strengthened and formalized by the Richards Constitution of 1946, which gave each unit fairly broad powers. The Constitution of 1951 changed

47

their designation to "region," and they formally became constituent units in a quasi-federal system. The colony was obliterated
in the same year by its amalgamation with the Western Region.
The revised Constitution of 1954 gave the regions greater autonomy in the Federation of Nigeria, and made Lagos the federal
capital. Thus, accidents of historical acquisition together with the
changing imperatives of administrative convenience were among
the determinants of the present division of Nigeria into three regions (see map 11). They were also factors in the "regionalization" of nationalism discussed in chapter 15.

A second feature of the territorial organization of the superstructure was the hierarchical subdivision of the country into
provinces and of these, in turn, into districts or divisions, under
the control of British residents and district officers respectively.
The boundaries of these subdivisions were based, insofar as possible, upon the territorial boundaries of the indigenous political
units. The complexity of the tribal mosaic frequently prevented
full application of the principle, and where there was a conflict it
was administrative convenience that determined what peoples
would be included in a district.[12] After the superstructure was
established there were several adjustments, but provincial and
district boundaries usually remained fairly constant. As a result
some of the provinces and districts have become the focus of a
new loyalty and thus have progressed from the status of an artificial administrative unit to that of a political unit possessed of its
own individuality. The majority of Nigerians, when queried about
their homeland, will usually identify themselves with the name of
their division or of the province in which it is located. It is not
unlike the identification of an American with his home state.

An indispensable part of the British superstructure was the
African staff made up of clerks, technicians, and subalterns who
performed the perfunctory and routine tasks of administration.
Recruited from all tribes—but mainly from those of southern
Nigeria which had early advantages in education—the members
of this group were liable to service in all parts of Nigeria. Moreover, because it feared corruption, undue influence, and the like,
the government tended to assign members of the African staff to
areas different from those of their birth. This corps of educated
Nigerians, most of whom had served in various parts of Nigeria,

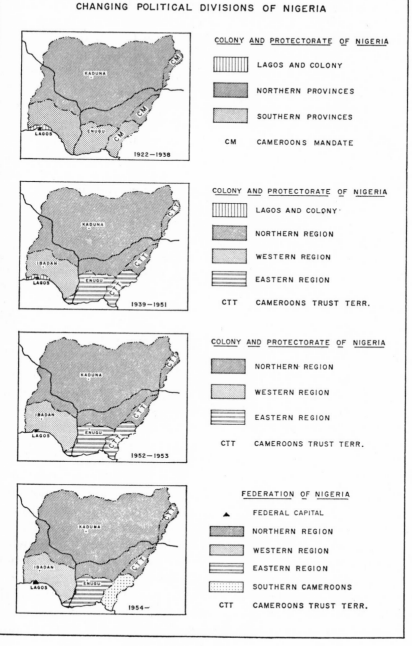

CHANGING POLITICAL DIVISIONS OF NIGERIA

COLONY AND PROTECTORATE OF NIGERIA

LAGOS AND COLONY

NORTHERN PROVINCES

SOUTHERN PROVINCES

CM   CAMEROONS MANDATE

1922—1938

COLONY AND PROTECTORATE OF NIGERIA

LAGOS AND COLONY·

NORTHERN REGION

WESTERN REGION

EASTERN REGION

CTT   CAMEROONS TRUST TERR.

1939—1951

COLONY AND PROTECTORATE OF NIGERIA

NORTHERN· REGION

WESTERN REGION

EASTERN REGION

CTT   CAMEROONS TRUST TERR.

1952—1953

FEDERATION OF NIGERIA

▲   FEDERAL CAPITAL

NORTHERN REGION

WESTERN REGION

EASTERN REGION

SOUTHERN CAMEROONS

CTT   CAMEROONS TRUST TERR.

1954—

Map 11

developed a Nigeria-wide outlook. Thus they came to sense the unity and sameness of the British administrative apparatus. It is therefore not surprising to find that they and their counterparts in European trading firms later made up the majority of active members in the centrally-minded nationalist movement and were the most articulate crusaders for Nigerian unity. It is estimated that by 1945 they numbered about 50,000. Their creation has been the most important contribution of the British superstructure to the concept of Nigerian unity and to nationalism.

The Legislative Council was another institution that could have served as a unifying political focus. Established in Lagos immediately after annexation (1861) in accordance with British policy for crown colonies, it advised the governor in the framing of legislation for the colony only. In 1923, the council was reorganized to provide for four elected African members (the first in British tropical Africa), and its purview was extended to include all southern Nigeria. This body endured until 1947 when it was replaced by the more representative all-Nigerian council established under the Richards Constitution. In 1913 a Nigeria-wide advisory body, known as the Nigerian Council, was established by Lord Lugard. It was abandoned in 1922 mainly because the six appointed chiefs rarely attended and its proceedings evoked little interest.

It should be noted that until 1947 (except for the abortive Nigerian Council) the people of the Northern Provinces did not participate in the Legislative Council. This not only accentuated the separate development of that region, but meant that during the most crucial twenty-five-year period of Nigeria's development (1922–1947) there was no central representative institution which could have become an instrument for inculcating a sense of Nigerian unity. In short, before 1947 there was little opportunity for a Nigerian to feel that he was under a common government which commanded his obedience, allegiance, and loyalty. The situation was further aggravated by the educational system which aimed at cultivating a "love of tribe," as well as by the system of native administration, to which we now turn.

Beneath the upper level of institutions which constituted the central, coördinating, and directing part of the machinery of government was a vast aggregation of indigenous political units termed native administrations. The crown colony form of government was manifestly inappropriate for the administration of the vast hinterland regions of the protectorate. Hence, when Lord Lugard established British authority in northern Nigeria, this fact, coupled with the lack of funds and staff and the existence of strong, well-organized indigenous states (emirates) in that area, convinced him that the emirates should be preserved and used as instruments of colonial rule. In the decade that followed he rationalized a system of local administration popularly known as indirect rule. Its essential features were the preservation of traditional political institutions and their adaptation, under the tutelage and direction of the British administration, to the requirements of modern units of local government. One result of the amalgamation of 1914 was the extension and adaptation of this system to the Southern Provinces.[13]

In the Muslim areas of the Northern Provinces the system of indirect rule functioned extremely well. One reason was that the British had merely taken over and consolidated the slowly disintegrating Fulani Empire which had been established a century before. Another was the existence of highly centralized, hierarchically organized authoritarian states. Furthermore, the emirates had developed well-defined procedures for tax assessment and revenue collection which antedated the British occupation; in the rest of Nigeria the idea of systematic direct taxation was unknown. These three elements—all present in the north but largely absent in the south—explain the great difficulty encountered by the British in extending indirect rule to the southern areas.

Only a qualified success was attained in the Western Region (Yorubaland and Edoland). Although fairly strong traditional authorities were in power in that area, the kings (obas) were ultimately accountable to, if not the mouthpieces for, councils of hereditary titleholders and representatives of societies. The idea of direct taxation was only slowly and reluctantly accepted. Moreover, the intertribal wars which preceded an uncertain, delayed, and protracted British occupation of this area had made the situation very delicate and unsettled.

In what is now the Eastern Region, even greater difficulty was encountered. British efforts were consumed in a ceaseless quest for the elusive traditional authorities. By the time they were discovered, full application of indirect rule would have meant undoing much that had already been done. Finally, in 1950, the whole effort was abandoned and the British authorities, in cooperation with African leaders, undertook to establish a modified form of English local government throughout the Eastern Region.[14]

Several aspects of the development of native administration are relevant to this study. The first centers around the fairly consistent and firm support given by the British administration to the integration of tribal groups which either had failed to achieve unity, or had lost it during intertribal wars. The smaller pagan groups within or on the periphery of the large northern emirates were given substantial autonomy and, wherever possible, were removed from the Fulani overlordship. Other groups, such as the Birom and the Tiv, whose scale of political organization had risen no higher than the extended family or lineage, were progressively federated at successively higher levels, and finally all-tribal chiefs were appointed as an integrative symbol, largely in response to popular demand.[15] In Iboland and Ibibioland the British made every effort to induce fragmented elements of clans to federate and establish clan, district, or divisional councils. It is here that the artificial administrative units acquired political significance.

At a higher level, chiefs of the larger tribal groups (Hausa and Yoruba) were, from the early 1930's on, brought together in annual durbars or conferences in order to break down parochialism and develop a wider regional approach to their problems. Although these early efforts were usually unsuccessful in terms of immediate practical results, they did provide a background for the postwar regional "houses of chiefs," [16] and for the emergence of a regional consciousness among the participants. On the other hand, in contradistinction to these integrative efforts, the British authorities had great difficulty in resisting the fragmentation of larger units, either to placate a disgruntled minority or to satisfy the *amour-propre* of a misplaced group. Nearly every group, irrespective of size, agitated for its own local council. The fluctuating process of building up and tearing down has, in any event, always been within the confines of one tribe. In the balance, the overwhelming emphasis has been upon greater tribal integration.

Whatever else might be said of the application of indirect rule in Nigeria—and a very strong case can be made for it—there can be little doubt that it has complicated the task of welding diverse elements into a Nigerian nation. The contrast with neighboring French territories is quite striking. British policy undoubtedly encouraged or reinforced a natural parochialism, which has been difficult to eradicate in the higher councils at regional and central levels. It is probably true that the real public life of the people has been centered about their traditional communities, and much can be said for the British emphasis upon local government as a training ground for greater political responsibilities. Indeed, given the prewar assumptions regarding the pace of Nigerian political development, it is difficult to see what other theory or system could have been devised. Latter-day nationalists, however, regard such a policy as a deliberate effort to divert attention from the issue of who is to control the superstructure.

Two other features of the native administration system should be noted here. The first is that until the mid-1930's (and late 1940's in the Northern Provinces) the educated elements did not participate in the system to any meaningful extent. This aspect, and its consequences for the growth of nationalism, will be discussed in greater detail in a later chapter. The second point is that, although the theory of indirect rule took into account the interrelatedness of the different aspects of African social systems (that is, that political and economic institutions, kinship organizations, and the ritual life are all interdependent and intimately related), the practice did not. The theory envisaged not only the support of traditional authorities, but also the preservation of indigenous systems of land tenure, the encouragement of "peasant production," and after 1925 a tribal and rural emphasis in school curricula. In practice, however, there was a failure to appreciate the disintegrative effect of peasant cultivation of cash crops. While the government was conscientiously endeavoring to preserve the political institutions of traditional society and the patterns of land tenure, new and largely unregulated economic forces were weakening or altering traditional economic institutions, and missionary activities and Western education were undermining the ritual life. The theory of indirect rule presupposed a substantial degree of totalitarianism (that is, complete control by government over all forces of change), but neither British ideals nor British economic interests and policy would have permitted such an arrangement.

Nigerian political history until the late 1940's is primarily a record of interactions among the British superstructure, the native authorities, and a third element largely excluded from both—the educated class. The relations between the first two were never in fact what the votaries of indirect rule had hoped they would be. Until the postwar period, when a substantial devolution of political and fiscal authority occurred, the native administrations were in effect but local extensions of the British superstructure. Although the British paid no little attention to matters of form and ceremony, everybody knew where real power was vested. No group was more aware of this than the traditional authorities themselves. Emirs, obas, and elders realized that their positions and perquisites depended as much upon the good will of district officers, residents, and chief commissioners as upon the consent of their peoples.

This broad generalization must be qualified in several respects. Most important, the stringency of supervision was not necessarily the result of a hunger for power, but rather of a passion to achieve and maintain certain minimum standards of justice and administrative efficiency. Once this fact is noted, however, the minuteness of British control and the ease with which traditional authorities could be removed and installed at the will of British officials can be documented sufficiently to support the generalization. At least there was enough truth in it to warrant an almost unanimous conviction among educated elements that chiefs were the unwitting or reluctant tools of the government, and not the representatives of the people, in either the African or the European sense. It is this aspect of the relationship which is directly relevant to this study.

If British administrative and political policies tolerated or encouraged tribal and regional separateness, the government's economic and fiscal policies were powerful counterweights in the direction of unity. In order to further British economic interests in Nigeria it was necessary to establish political control, and then to construct communications, institute a common currency, and encourage African production of tropical export crops, and finally to stimulate a desire for European manufactured goods. When Joseph Chamberlain became Colonial Secretary in 1895 a broad attack was made along all four fronts. Under his guidance, the first objective was achieved by 1900; the second, the development of communications, was begun in 1896 and went on *pari passu* with pacification. Communications were vital for effective occupation and administration. These were the primary hurdles; the others were tackled later.

Before 1900 it was said that "Europeans travel in two ways, either by sea in a canoe, or by land in a hammock." [17] Between 1879 and 1892 private enterprise had sought to open up the hinterland by constructing a railroad, but the government opposed the project. One of the supporters of this early effort expressed the enthusiasm of the day:

> Think of the benefit that it would be to England in increasing markets for manufactured goods and receiving additional produce in return; . . . it would civilize the savage and prepare him for the missionary.[18]

The Lagos-Ibadan line (120 miles) was completed by 1900; Kano (704 miles from Lagos) was reached in 1911; and during the next fifteen years an additional 600 miles of line were laid connecting Kano with Port Harcourt, the eastern terminus. By 1936 a railway network of 2,178 miles of track covered Nigeria. In the meantime, harbor development had been energetically pursued at Lagos and Port Harcourt. The former became the exclusive gateway to western and northern Nigeria and completely eclipsed the river Niger as an artery of transport and communication. When the Udi coal fields were discovered in 1912, Port Harcourt was constructed to serve that industry as well as to empty the Benue Basin of its products.

During the first two decades of British occupation very few road were built. In 1900 roads were nonexistent; by 1906 only 30 miles of roads had been constructed; and as late as 1914 it was reported that "away from the railway line head porterage is the rule, and it is not likely that the carrier . . . will ever be displaced." [19] Europeans traveled by bicycles, horses, or hammock. After World War I, however, it was discovered that the light Ford car could travel on the rough African bush paths. As a consequence, Nigeria began to be flooded with Fords; by 1923 there were more than 600 in Lagos alone. The Ford car was the impetus needed for road construction; by 1926 more than 6,000 miles had been built. In the next decade the mileage trebled, and by 1950 there were more than 28,000 miles of roads.[20] The real significance of this development is that the roads were purposely constructed as feeders to the railroad lines, so as to open up fresh districts to commerce: ". . . motors are doing a great excellence in extending the culture of cocoa by affording economic transport to regions otherwise outside the profitable ambit." [21] The growth of an intraterritorial telegraphic, and later a telephonic, system was equally remarkable in its rapidity and extensiveness. By 1922 more than 40 per cent of the revenue of the country was being devoted to the construction and maintenance of communications facilities.[22] Even as late as 1939, expenditures for such facilities took up nearly one-quarter of the annual estimates. This passion for communications is vividly portrayed by the road-conscious district officer in Joyce Cary's novel *Mister Johnson.*

The consequences of this rapid development of communications where none had existed before were profound. The export trade in tin, cotton, and groundnuts has been in large measure the direct result of building the railroad. Before a line was constructed to the plateau, tin ore was carried by head porterage by more than 23,000 Africans for a distance of 200 miles.[23] When the railroad reached Kano in 1911 the exports of groundnuts jumped from 1,179 to 19,288 tons in one year.[24] The railroads and roads not only provided the indispensable means for developing the export trade of bulky and heavy items, such as groundnuts and tin, but they facilitated to some extent a diversification which relieved Nigeria of a dangerous monocultural position. In 1900 palm products made up 82 per cent of Nigeria's total exports; by 1937 this item had been reduced to 31 per cent.

A second factor tending to stimulate the production of export crops and the importation of European manufactured goods, as well as to bring order and rationality to economic activity and the task of government, was the introduction of an easily portable, universally accepted medium of exchange. Barter had been the indigenous means of conducting trade, but as a result of the growth of legitimate European-African trade during the nineteenth century, barter had gradually been replaced by commodity currencies. The latter consisted of cases or bottles of gin, slaves, brass pans, and, later, more standard articles such as cowrie shells, copper wires, and small alloy horseshoes called "manillas." As late as 1919, however, Lord Lugard reported that "trading by barter is still carried on in some parts of Nigeria in spite of all efforts of the Government to put a stop to it." [25] In the southeastern areas of Nigeria manillas were not completely abandoned until 1950, when redemption was made compulsory.[26]

Another development that encouraged the use of a standard currency and assured the government of necessary revenue was the introduction and generalization of a system of direct taxation. Except in the Muslim emirates in the north, where an indigenous system of taxation had evolved, it was contrary to custom in most Nigerian societies to pay fixed recurrent taxes, although an equivalent prevailed in the form of tribute paid to chiefs for services rendered. Mainly because of this fact, the British authorities studiously avoided the imposition of taxes in pre-Lugardian days. West Coast operations were financed either by imperial subsidies or through local customs duties. The reason for this caution was explained by the governor of Lagos in 1864:

> . . . all semblance of direct taxation or any system which would press immediately upon the natives has been deliberately eschewed as injudicious in the present unsettled state of the Settlement, and as liable to cause friction in the transition to English rule.[27]

After 1900, Lugard preserved and rationalized the established system in the north, and in 1916 attempted to extend it to the south. Despite some initial resistance, particularly in Egba country, it was generally accepted in Yorubaland, and by the end of 1924 direct taxation was in force throughout the whole of the Western Provinces. Efforts to extend the system to the Eastern Provinces contributed to the famous Aba Riots of 1929; but taxation was finally accepted in that area in the 1930's, although with a somewhat modified basis of assessment. The relevance of this progressive imposition of direct taxation to the increase in currency circulation is that tax payments could legally be made only in the new currency. As a result, every household was eventually required either to turn to wage labor or to produce cash crops. Thus, despite its delayed and uneven application, systematic taxation was one of the most effective government measures in the development of a money economy.

Long before the effects of systematic taxation were being felt, however, the government had given Nigerians every encouragement to produce crops for export. Before World War I, isolated but significant efforts had already been made. In 1887, the Lagos Botanic Station was established to explore the possibility of introducing cocoa culture in the Western Region. In 1902 the British Cotton-Growing Association was formed to encourage the production of cotton—mainly in the Sudan and Nigeria—for Lancashire. A prominent feature of Chamberlain's program for economic development in the colonies was to study tropical agriculture; hence early reports made frequent reference to the shipment of bits of soil or vegetation to the imperial institutes in England for analysis.

It was during the interwar period, however, that the greatest strides were made in accelerating export production. The task of stimulating production was turned over to three of the technical departments of the government (Agriculture, Forestry, and Veterinary), and, despite the substantial retrenchment of staff in the early 1930's, the technical personnel of these departments trebled. The program included not only the further development of existing exports (palm oil, cocoa, groundnuts, cotton, and rubber), but the fostering of new products (ginger, rice, and gum arabic). In general, administrative and technical services as well as commercial interests concentrated mainly on production for external markets, to the neglect of subsistence and internal exchange economies.

Another facet of British economic policy in Nigeria relevant to this study was official recognition and support of the indigenous form of landownership. Land, in most African societies, is owned by the community; allocation and use in the form of a usufruct is controlled by the traditional authorities (emir, chief, elders) who act as trustees for that community. But normally a family, once given its share, is free to use the land as it wishes, except that it cannot sell the land or otherwise alienate it from the community. The community in Nigeria varies in size according to the scale of socioeconomic organization of the group. Normally, the trustee of the land is equivalent to the native authority; hence the official preservation of traditional forms of landownership was, in effect, the economic corollary to the political policy of indirect rule.[28]

This land policy has had several important consequences. The first and most obvious is that it prevented the growth of a white-settler community. As already noted, of all territories in Africa, Nigeria has had the lowest proportion of Europeans to Africans. Secondly, it has been a deterrent to the investment of private capital in the development of the Nigerian economy. Apart from the Royal Niger Company (and subsequently the United Africa Company), foreign enterprise has done less toward the development (as distinguished from trading operations) of British West Africa than of any other area in the British Empire.[29] In 1911 and again in 1920 the governor of Nigeria emphatically rejected efforts by foreign interests to establish plantations. With the exception of a small palm-oil plantation in Calabar and a rubber plantation in Benin Province, there are no agricultural units owned or controlled by European enterprise. Although this has on the one hand protected the Nigerian peasant producer and prevented interracial conflicts over landownership, it has, on the other hand, placed Nigeria in a very poor competitive position vis-à-vis the plantation economies of the Belgian Congo and southeast Asia.

The official policy of preserving traditional forms of land tenure has had more specific results. First, it has inhibited freedom of migration and residence of Nigerian peoples. Iboland is extremely overpopulated, but Ibos have been unable to migrate to other areas because the native authorities in those areas have refused them entree. In the exercise of this group right of group exclusion, the native authorities have been strongly supported by the government (for example, Benin, Idoma, Tiv, and Igala native authorities versus Ibo settlers). A similar situation has existed within the same tribe (for example, Ibadan native authority versus Ijebu settlers). As a result, intertribal and intratribal tensions have been aggravated. Secondly, the government has pursued two separate and distinct protective policies regarding landownership as between the north and the south. In the former area its powers are theoretically more absolute; but the important point is that in practice the administration in the north has prohibited any non-Nigerian, as well as any Nigerian (whether a native of the north or of the south) from acquiring freehold title, whereas in the south individual tenure has developed extensively in urban and periurban areas without government opposition. This policy of differentiation in the administration of its trusteeship over land has not only strengthened the separateness of the north, but created grievances among many southerners having economic interests or aspirations in the north. Nationalist criticism of land policy has usually been made by southerners and has been focused upon what they considered discriminatory treatment.[30] On the other hand, many northern nationalists are grateful for this policy.

Apart from establishing this specific policy regarding indigenous land tenure, the provision of essential public works and utilities, and the development of the Enugu coal fields, the government, as Margery Perham put it, played the role of an "inattentive umpire while private traders . . . on the one side, and native producer-consumer-labourers on the other, played out their economic game." [31] Until World War II the great European trading firms, which largely controlled Nigeria's export-import trade, were not subjected to any regulation. The consequences of this prewar laissez-faire policy will be discussed in greater detail in chapter 3. Suffice it to state here that postwar nationalists, when contemplating the gap between their aspirations regarding Nigeria's economic potentialities on the one hand, and the prewar laissez-faire policy on the other, tended to blame the government not only for the underdevelopment of the Nigerian economy but also for the disproportionate economic power that had gravitated into the hands of European firms. The contradiction between the statism necessary to fulfill their aspirations and the bourgeois interests of many of their leaders has not yet been resolved.

PART II

*The Western Impact and the
Roots of Nationalism*

CHAPTER 3

Western Economic Forces

Since the establishment of British administration in Nigeria, Western economic forces have profoundly changed both the structure of traditional Nigerian societies and the perspectives of Nigerian peoples. The tempo and character of the changes created situations and attitudes that have predisposed many Nigerians to racial consciousness and nationalist activity. The operation of these new economic forces, however, was governed to an important degree by the British policies discussed in the preceding chapter: establishment of internal peace and security; development of a communications network and transportation grid; imposition of systematic and universal taxation; compulsory use of a standard coin currency; and encouragement of the production of export crops. A sixth factor—extraterritorial enterprise—and the special grievances engendered by its operations will be analyzed later in this chapter. Two other indirect influences—Christian missionary activity and Western education—are given detailed treatment in subsequent chapters.

At the outset three special features of Nigerian economic development must be emphasized. One is that Western economic forces and ideas have not been imposed upon unwilling and protesting peoples. There were instances at first of a strong and instinctive resistance to new ideas and techniques, but once they were found useful the ordinary African accepted them with alacrity. The utility, attractiveness, and prestige-giving qualities of imported European goods served as a powerful stimulus. When illiterate African laborers, who had been press-ganged into building the railroads, found themselves paid in a new medium which would buy these highly prized goods, they were converted. The classic example of African ingenuity, enterprise, and adaptability is the development of the Ghana (Gold Coast) cocoa industry.[1] The same has been true, to a lesser extent, of the growth of that industry in western Nigeria. Indeed, one reason for the rapidity of change and the intensity of the social and economic ferment in Nigeria is that the government's conscious encouragement of Western economic forces was balanced by the eagerness and receptivity of the African.

A second consideration related to, and somewhat qualifying, the foregoing concerns the differential tribal response to the new economic forces. In the past there has been a tendency to regard all African societies indiscriminately as highly communalistic and familistic collectivities whose response to the same stimuli would be uniform, and in which individual ownership of property and the acquisition of status and political power through wealth are unknown.[2] This distorted picture may be partly the result of a sentimental urge to idylize simple communal societies and to deprecate the individualism and materialism of modern industrial society. But tribal response to the impact of modern economic forces has been highly varied in Nigeria, not only because of geographical, topographical, and historical differences, or of variations in the distribution of resources (for example, some areas are suitable for growing cocoa and others are not), but also because of cultural differences in the capacity and predisposition of different groups and subgroups to adapt to the new forces.

These cultural differences have been determined in part by the traditional social structure and the degree of upward mobility within that structure, the attitudes toward property and toward wealth individually acquired, and the relationship between wealth and political power. In traditional Ibo society, for example, there was much upward mobility and a fairly close correlation between the individual acquisition of wealth and the exercise of legitimate political power. In Hausa society a very different cultural pattern prevailed.[3] Again, one finds further cultural variations, such as Yoruba youths refusing to turn to wage labor if it involved being a servant, Hausa traders finding clerkship unattractive, and the Niger Delta peoples holding on to their manillas until 1950. These tribal variations are significant because they have partly determined the tribal composition of the commercialized and economi-

64

cally involved elements. Tribal disparities among the latter have been, in turn, partly responsible for tensions within the nationalist movement.

The third important feature is that several groups in Nigeria had had centuries of contact with Western economic forces prior to the formal establishment of British administration in 1900. For at least three centuries the coastal groups were deeply involved in a semicommercialized economy, first through the slave trade, and later, during the latter part of the nineteenth century, through legitimate trade in palm oil and other products. The magnitude of African trading activities in the Niger Delta region during the nineteenth century is described in great detail in Dr. K. Onwuka Dike's recently published pioneering study.[4] In the far north, sizable commercial communities had grown up around such centers as Kano City, which had been linked with Mediterranean cities via caravan trade since the Middle Ages. The cash nexus and economic individualism, therefore, are not a product solely of recent British political control. Nevertheless, that control provided a framework and an arena in which the new economic forces were allowed greater scope and their consequences were more sharply delineated.

In particular, the establishment of internal security, the development of communications and roads, and the imposition of a common currency permitted far greater mobility and social communication than had previously been possible. This in turn facilitated the growth of an internal exchange economy, transcending ethnic and political boundaries, which has greatly increased in scope and importance during the past several decades.[5] Within the Northern Region alone at least fourteen basic commodities are produced in one area for consumption in other areas. Between the Northern Region and the southern regions a very active trade has developed; the north ships dried fish, skins, leatherwork, cloth, and cattle to the south and receives kola, citrus, and other foodstuffs in return. The Middle Belt in the Northern Region is a food-surplus area supplying yams to food-deficit areas such as the plateau mining areas in the north and the cocoa-growing areas in the Western Region. Coal from the Enugu mines in the Eastern Region supplies the whole country. In addition, there has grown up in almost every area where urbanization has occurred, or where there is a heavy

65

dependence on an export economy, a rather extensive exchange of goods between urban centers and rural areas.

All these new patterns of economic intercourse have contributed to the growth of integration and of interdependence, as well as to the emergence of economic—and latterly political—groups tending to support a territory-wide political system. Other factors, however, have operated to minimize such developments. For example, area differentials in modern economic development also stimulated separatist tendencies of even greater political significance. Certainly regional disparities in the value of export products and in per capita income, as indicated in table 3, suggest

TABLE 3

Regional Differences in Agricultural Export Production and
Per Capita Income in Nigeria

Item	Western Region	Eastern Region	Northern Region
Agricultural export production [a]			
Value in million pounds sterling	11.4	7.3	9.75
Value per capita in pounds sterling	2.8	1.4	0.72
Value per square mile in pounds sterling	249.0	159.0	34.0
Per capita income			
Value in pounds sterling [b]	34.0	21.0	17.0

[a] From K. M. Buchanan and J. C. Pugh, *Land and People in Nigeria* (London: 1955), p. 128. Figures are as of 1948.

[b] From *The Economic Development of Nigeria*, International Bank for Reconstruction and Development (Baltimore: 1955), table 7, p. 616. Figures relate to per capita estimates of gross national income for 1952–53. Figure for the Eastern Region includes the Southern Cameroons.

an explanation for differing attitudes toward regional versus Pan-Nigerian nationalism. Thus economic development can be both integrative and disintegrative. Certainly both tendencies have been operative in Nigeria.

THE GROWTH OF A MONEY ECONOMY

Systematic taxation, a common portable currency, the desire for European goods, the opportunity to pursue the profit motive, support or tolerance from the government—all these have been significant elements in the historic shift from an almost wholly subsistence economy to a predominantly money economy. By about 1948 roughly 43 per cent of the adult male population of Nigeria was actively concerned in the cash nexus. Table 4, which shows the growth in the volume of selected exports, indicates that this shift to a commercialized economy has occurred mainly within the last fifty years.

TABLE 4

GROWTH OF NIGERIAN EXPORT TRADE
(Selected commodities in thousands of tons)

Period	Selected exports				Value of total exports in millions of pounds
	Palm products	Groundnuts	Cocoa	Cotton	
1861	40	0	0	0	ª
1899–1901	66	12	ª	ª	ª
1919–1921	272	45	20	4	ª
1934	402	245	78	6	8.9
1939	426	147	114	4.4	10.5
1944	439	156	70	4.3	17.2
1949	546	378	103.6	10	81.1
1951	497	141	121.5	15.4	120.1
1953	604	327	104.7	17.7	125.3

ª Figures unknown.
Sources: Margery Perham, ed., *Mining, Commerce, and Finance in Nigeria* (London: 1945), p. 9; P. T. Bauer, *West African Trade* (Cambridge: 1954), p. 195; *The Economic Development of Nigeria*, International Bank for Reconstruction and Development (Baltimore: 1955), pp. 18–19.

By the 1940's only a few Nigerian communities remained in complete isolation and preserved a subsistence economy. Daryll Forde pointed out in 1946 that even a remote Ibo, Yoruba, or Hausa village, "while clearly exhibiting the predominance of the subsistence element will also include in its economic system internal and external exchange elements to a substantial degree." [6] Moreover, Nigeria has four primary export crops, which safeguard the country as a whole, though not its regions taken separately, from the dangers of a monocultural economy.[7] These factors explain in part why there was comparatively little suffering or nationalist protest when the value of Nigerian exports dropped 50 per cent immediately after World War I and again in the early 1930's. By the late 1930's, however, the external exchange element had become dominant, particularly in cocoa and groundnut areas.

Several important social, and ultimately political, consequences of the transformation from a subsistence to a money economy are significant in the development of nationalism. The first is that the shift has loosened or extinguished the coöperative ties binding the individual to his clan or lineage members. Lineage bonds have been corroded by the strong attractions of the individual profit motive and by extralineage opportunities. Old standards of values have been upset, new opportunities created, and new methods of accumulating wealth evolved. Moreover, there has been a positive movement in the direction of individualizing landholdings, especially in the cocoa areas of the Western Region and in the urban and semiurban areas of southern Nigeria.[8] It should, however, be emphasized that in Nigeria this has been no more than a tendency increasingly manifest in the past three decades; in rural and agricultural areas the traditional system still exerts a strong resistance to these disintegrating influences. Even in Lagos, where British ideas regarding property ownership have been operative for nearly a century, Dr. T. O. Elias reports that the "institution of family ownership is still a very live force."[9] Nigeria therefore stands out in rather sharp contrast to Ghana (the Gold Coast), where many owners of cocoa farms are *individual* absentee landlords belonging to the educated classes living in the coastal towns. This striking difference between the two territories is mainly the result of the early policy of the Nigerian government in preserving the indigenous system of land tenure.[10]

Another consequence of the shift to a money economy has been the drift toward wage employment. By 1938 the number of persons more or less permanently employed for wages was approximately 150,000.[11] Ten years later the number had increased to about 260,000, and by 1951 it was slightly more than 300,000. Since Nigeria's total population is more than 30 million, this is a remarkably small full-time labor force. Indeed, as the data in table 5 indicate, the degree of commercialization of labor in Nigeria was much smaller than in several other African territories. In 1948 the number employed for wages constituted only about 4 per cent of the total adult male population of Nigeria. Moreover, in the same year wages and salaries made up only 10 per cent of the total money income of the country; the remaining 90 per cent went to agricultural producers in the commercialized sector of the economy. As table 5 further shows, a similar ratio of distribution of income also applied to the Gold Coast. Thus the two countries in tropical Africa where nationalism is most advanced have had the smallest proportionate number engaged in wage labor.

TABLE 5

COMMERCIALIZATION OF LAND AND LABOR IN SELECTED AFRICAN TERRITORIES

Country or territory	Adult male population				Total number in wage labor force	Percentage distribution of total money income	
	Agricultural production		Percentage in wage employment	Percentage involved in money economy (cols. 2 and 3)		Wages and salaries	Agricultural producers
	Percentage in subsistence production	Percentage in commercialized production					
	(1)	(2)	(3)	(4)	(5)	(6)	(7)
Nigeria	57	39	4	43	257,500	10	90
Gold Coast (Ghana)	21	64	15	79	184,300	8	92
Uganda	59	29	12	41	171,200	22	78
Kenya	70	5	25	30	420,800	74	26
Southern Rhodesia	51	9	40	49	458,000	87	13
Belgian Congo	41	29	30	59	962,000	58	42

Source: *Enlargement of the Exchange Economy in Tropical Africa, 1954,* UN Document E/2557/ST/ECA/23, pp. 15, 17, 19, 24. Dates for data are various but all within period 1947–1950.

Although the foregoing suggests a low correlation between the degree of commercialization of labor and the existence of nationalism, it does not necessarily mean that the elements drawn into permanant wage employment have been unimportant in nationalist development. Indeed, the main weight of active nationalist support came from the 100,000-odd clerks, artisans, and skilled

TABLE 6

NUMBER OF PERSONS EMPLOYED IN PRINCIPAL INDUSTRIES
AND SERVICES IN NIGERIA, 1951

Industry or service	*Supervisors, foremen, etc.*	*Clerical*	*Craftsmen and artisans*	*Skilled labor*	*Laborers, apprentices, women*	*Total*
Government, central	271	2,195	1,343	1,678	3,134	8,621
Government, local	1,882	6,887	2,642	8,671	34,239	54,327
Transport services	1,690	3,554	5,916	8,996	14,415	34,571
Trade (firms)	372	5,681	737	1,383	9,844	18,017
Communications	283	1,418	720	261	1,095	3,777
Banking and insurance	75	927	14	58	397	1,471
Public utilities	79	294	749	1,061	1,699	3,882
Construction and repair industry	560	708	11,825	7,021	23,227	43,341
Manufacturing (secondary)	445	916	1,888	1,661	6,824	11,734
Mining and extraction	519	1,062	1,600	7,701	50,848	61,730
Forestry and logging	239	741	1,083	1,424	11,072	14,559
Agricultural and live-stock production	2,099	1,195	2,107	6,237	28,038	39,676
Other	180	944	1,249	1,015	14,327	17,715
Total	8,964 ᵃ	26,552	31,873	47,170	199,159	303,421

ᵃ The majority of these persons are Europeans.

Source: *Annual Report,* Department of Labor, 1951–52 (Lagos: Government Printer, 1953), pp. 37–39. The report includes only those persons working in establishments employing ten or more persons, and does not include teachers.

laborers employed in the industries indicated in table 6 (particularly government, transport, trade, and mining). It is not the number of wage laborers or of salaried workers, but their strategic position in the structure of the economy and the administration which has made this support possible.

Apart from taxation and the desire for European goods, the principal stimulant to wage employment was that monetary wealth gradually became the key to status and the criterion of success in the emerging social structure. In most areas the bride price increasingly had to be paid in the new currency rather than in labor, cowries, or goods as before; hence wage employment became an essential precondition for the acquisition of a wife. Once currency was generally accepted as the standard of measurement for and the means of acquiring all good things, the shift to wage employment was inevitable.

Since the production of palm oil, groundnuts, and rubber, and the ownership of a cocoa farm are normally based upon family enterprise, they have not necessarily removed the producer from his traditional environment. This is highly significant, for in many areas of Nigeria the lineage has been adapted to commercialized production. Services for an employer or as a professional person, however, are necessarily individual in performance and remuneration. Furthermore, wage employment has usually been a phenomenon of urban centers. As a consequence, the drift toward such employment has profoundly affected both wage earners and the communities they left behind. The equilibrium of the rural village community was weakened, age-grade societies began to lose their customary powers and functions, and traditional crafts were abandoned. This process of community disintegration was accelerated by seasonal or migrant laborers, who, when they returned to their villages, brought back new ideas, tastes, and habits. Full-time salaried employees in urban centers were subjected to strong individualizing influences. Physical isolation from the traditional milieu and the receipt of a personal money income created profound tensions in many of them. The struggle between the strong urge to cut himself adrift from his family and live his own life, on the one hand, and the wish to sacrifice his own comfort and happiness to fulfill deeply engrained family and communal obligations on the other, has been a painful dilemma every wage-earning Nigerian has had to face.[12] Comparatively few succumbed to the temptation of complete severance. The majority sought a delicate compromise, making a gesture toward satisfying the demands of the lineage at home while trying at the same time to pursue their own insatiable quest for a higher living standard in the emergent urban society. As wages and salaries were not large enough to meet African family obligations, the wage-earning Nigerian inevitably faced an agonizing debt, which induced bit-

71

terness over his meager wages and the high cost of living.[13] This led to materialism, venality, and an almost pathological obsession regarding money.[14]

THE DEVELOPMENT OF URBAN CENTERS

With political stability and internal security assured by the British presence, the new economic forces gave rise to new urban centers and accelerated the growth of most traditional centers. Since the major employing agencies (government and commercial firms) had their headquarters in cities, the majority of Nigerians drawn into salaried and wage employment became urban dwellers. As entrepôts in the expanding market economy, cities became the centers of activity for the new urban class of traders and merchants. Most of the secondary schools were located in or near the larger cities (for example, Lagos, Ibadan, Onitsha, Calabar, and Zaria), which meant that each upcoming generation of schoolboys in training for clerkdom were inured to and seduced by city life long before they secured their first jobs. The cities became not only melting pots, but the breeding and training grounds, as well as the arenas, of Nigerian nationalism.

A direct consequence of urban life has been the intensification of the division of labor. As urban Nigerians became increasingly dependent upon their occupational specialties or salaried jobs, they lost the economic and psychological security of the lineage and the self-sufficient rural community. Their physical removal from customary sanctions, traditional authorities, and parental surveillance alone gave them a sense of personal freedom—and anxiety—not previously experienced. Furthermore, the impersonality, heterogeneity, and competitiveness of urban life accentuated their personal insecurity as well as their individualism. The latter became more pronounced as a result of the quest not only for survival but also for status and prestige within the urban social structure. Stratification within that structure depended on education and wealth, and both were the products of individual enterprise. These two sets of factors—the insecurity and individualism caused by physical detachment from the village-based lineage as well as by the characteristics of city life, and the compulsive urge to win security and status within the new urban society—were critical ingredients in the development of new and assertive leadership and in the creation of variable and easily manipulated mass followings.

The city was also a center for intensive acculturation.[15] There Nigerians not only came into daily and intimate contact with Europeans and with educated and sophisticated Africans, but also saw varieties of European-made gadgets and goods on conspicuous display. Motion pictures and the latest newspapers and magazines were available. It was in the city that new tastes and wants were created, new values adopted, and emulative urges asserted. The acculturating influence of the city was in turn carried to rural homelands through kinship associations and tribal unions, or by the vivid oral reports of returning migrants. Urban dwellers became acutely aware of the wide gap between the higher standards of living and the greater amenities of the city—especially in the European quarters—and the poverty of their rural villages. They therefore consciously endeavored to take the enlightenment, modernity, and "civilization" of the urban centers to the villages. Tribal unions were the main agents in this process of early diffusion, just as they were later in spreading to the rural areas the political consciousness and nationalist ideas born in the urban centers.

These general consequences of urbanization must, however, be somewhat qualified. The developments noted were, at best, only broad tendencies,[16] with wide variations in their occurrence. Such variations are partly explained by the differing patterns of urban development in Nigeria. As indicated in table 7, there has been a substantial increase in the urban population during the past forty years. Yet the most revealing fact is that until the last census, in 1952, all but one (Kano) of the ten Nigerian cities with a population of more than 40,000 were located in Yorubaland in the west and north. Moreover, the existence of urban centers in Yorubaland has not been the direct result of Western acculturation; rather, it is a traditional Yoruba pattern antedating British control.[17] These Yoruba cities were heterogeneous in terms not only of craft specialization but also of social-class and reference-group identifications. A Yoruba city in pre-British Nigeria was a large-scale aggregation of lineages—the primary groups—bound together by a common government and constituting a single political community.

73

TABLE 7

POPULATION OF PRINCIPAL URBAN CENTERS IN NIGERIA

Western Region	1911	1921	1931	1953
Traditional centers				
Ibadan	175,000	238,094	387,133	459,196
Lagos	73,766	99,690	126,108	267,407
Ogbomosho	80,000	84,860	86,744	139,535
Oshogbo	59,821	51,418	49,599	122,728
Ife	36,231	22,184	24,170	110,790
Iwo	60,000	53,588	57,191	100,006
Abeokuta	51,255	28,941	45,763	84,451
Oyo	45,438	40,356	48,733	72,133
Ilesha	ᵃ	ᵃ	ᵃ	72,029
Benin City	ᵃ	ᵃ	ᵃ	53,753
Iseyin	33,362	28,601	36,805	49,690
Ede	26,577	48,360	52,392	44,808
New Centers				
Sapele	2,107	2,151	4,143	33,638

Eastern Region	1911	1921	1931	1953
New Centers				
Onitsha	ᵃ	10,319	18,084	76,921
Enugu	ᵃ	3,170	12,959	62,764
Port Harcourt	ᵃ	7,185	15,201	71,634
Aba	ᵃ	2,327	12,958	57,787
Calabar	ᵃ	15,438	16,958	46,705

Northern Region	1911	1921	1931	1952
Traditional centers				
Kano	ᵃ	49,938	97,031	130,173
Yerwa (Maiduguri)	ᵃ	16,274	24,359	54,646
Zaria	ᵃ	25,000	28,000	53,974
Katsina	ᵃ	17,489	22,349	52,672
Sokoto	ᵃ	19,335	20,084	47,643
Ilorin	36,342	38,668	47,412	40,994
New centers				
Gusau	ᵃ	10,412	14,878	40,202
Kaduna	ᵃ	5,428	10,628	38,794
Jos	ᵃ	2,000	2,467	38,527
Minna	ᵃ	2,000	5,143	12,810

ᵃ Exact number not known.

Sources: P. Amaury Talbot, *The Peoples of Southern Nigeria* (London: 1926), Vol. IV; C. K. Meek, *The Northern Tribes of Nigeria* (London: 1925), Vol. II; *Census of Nigeria, 1931* (Lagos: Government Printer, 1932); *Population Census of the Western Region of Nigeria, 1952* (Lagos: Government Statistician, 1953–1954); *Population Census of the Eastern Region of Nigeria, 1953* (Lagos: Government Statistician, 1953–1954); *Population Census of the Northern Region of Nigeria, 1952* (Lagos: Government Statistician, 1952–1953).

In its early urban development Yorubaland was unique among the societies of pre-British Nigeria. Benin City, the capital of the ancient Kingdom of Benin, was an urban aggregation only in a qualified sense. Elsewhere, in the Eastern Region and throughout most of the Middle Belt of the Northern Region, there were no cities at the time of the British intrusion. Most closely approximating the Yoruba pattern were the capitals of the Fulani emirates (Sokoto, Zaria, Katsina, and Kano) and of the Kingdom of Bornu (Yerwa). The walled city of Kano, of course, was a famous medieval entrepôt and metropolis.

The tribal variations in urban development prior to the Western impact are significant in an evaluation of the economic, social, and political consequences of that impact. The data in table 8 reveal that the Yoruba are the most highly urbanized people in Nigeria; yet during the period 1921–1952 they had the lowest rate of urban growth, and the populations of their cities were the least heterogeneous in all Nigeria. The Yoruba cities other than Lagos have, therefore, been least affected by the urbanization resulting from the Western intrusion.

This does not mean that the urbanized Yorubas have been unaffected. Indeed, as will be seen, Western education, missionary activity, and a variety of other forces and influences have operated to weaken, and often to extinguish, the behavioral patterns, values, and controls of traditional Yoruba culture. It does suggest, however, that the disintegrating and unsettling consequences of modern urbanization have been minimized in Yorubaland as a result of the preëxistence of structured urban communities based upon lineages. Yoruba city dwellers could absorb the characteristic aspects of urbanization without being physically uprooted. In short, the new economic forces resulted in the commercialization and adaptation of a relatively homogeneous and structured community, with minimal changes in social stratification, political authority, and place of domicile.[18]

The pattern of urban development in the Eastern Region, and particularly among the Ibo peoples, sharply contrasts with the Yoruba pattern. There were no preëxistent cities. As late as 1931 there were no cities with a population of more than 20,000 throughout that vast and heavily populated area. By 1952, however, there were four cities, each with a population of more than 50,000,

TABLE 8

REGIONAL VARIATIONS IN DEGREE, RATE, AND CHARACTER OF URBANIZATION
IN NIGERIA

Region	Percentage of total popula- tion urbanized [a]	Percentage increase in popula- tion of main urban centers, 1921–1952	Per- centage of ur- ban population nonindigenous
Lagos district	52.9	168	26.7
Western Region	26.0	[g]	[g]
Yoruba areas	30.3	112 [b]	3.8 [b]
Non-Yoruba areas	2.2	[g]	18.7 [c]
Eastern Region	8.0	688 [d]	25.7 [d]
Northern Region	3.5	[g]	[g]
Traditional centers	[g]	128 [e]	23.5 [e]
New urban centers	[g]	522 [f]	[g]

[a] Percentage of population living in centers of 20,000 or more at time of 1952–1953 census.

[b] Calculated on basis of population increases in, and the population composi- tion of, the ten Yoruba cities having a population of more than 40,000 in the 1952– 1953 census.

[c] Benin City in Edoland, the only non-Yoruba city in the Western Region with a population of more than 40,000 in the 1952 census.

[d] Calculated on the basis of population increases in, and the population com- position of, the five cities of the Eastern Region having a population of more than 40,000 in the 1952–1953 census.

[e] Calculated on the basis of population increases in, and the population com- position of, the six cities of the Northern Region having a population of more than 40,000 in the 1952 census.

[f] Gusau, Kaduna, Jos, and Minna.

[g] Figures not known.

Sources: P. Amaury Talbot, *The Peoples of Southern Nigeria* (London: 1926), Vol. IV; C. K. Meek, *The Northern Tribes of Nigeria* (London: 1925), Vol. II; *Census of Nigeria, 1931* (Lagos: Government Printer, 1932); *Population Census of the Western Region of Nigeria, 1952* (Lagos: Government Statistician, 1953– 1954); *Population Census of the Eastern Region of Nigeria, 1953* (Lagos: Govern- ment Statistician, 1953–1954); *Population Census of the Northern Region of Ni- geria, 1952* (Lagos: Government Statistician, 1952–1953).

of which 85 per cent was Ibo. The rate of growth of these eastern urban centers during the three decades from 1921 to 1952 (688 per cent) was far higher than elsewhere in Nigeria. Yet this rapid and intensive urbanization of the Ibo peoples since the British occupation is a phenomenon not only of the Eastern Region, their homeland. Ibos also constitute more than one-third of the non- indigenous population of the urban centers in the Northern and Western regions. As the figures in table 9 reveal, the proportion is much higher for several non-Ibo cities. These figures are important not only as evidence of the intensive, rapid, and widespread urbanization of the Ibo peoples, but also as a partial insight into their vanguard role in the nationalist movement.

TABLE 9

DEGREE OF IBO URBANIZATION OUTSIDE IBOLAND
(Early 1950's)

City	Indigenous group	Percentage of Ibos in nonindigenous population
Lagos	Yoruba	44.6
Benin City	Edo	53.5
Sapele	Urhobo	46.0
Calabar	Efik	50.7
Kano	Hausa	38.0
Zaria	Hausa	39.0
Kaduna	Mixed	40.7

Sources: *Population Census of the Western Region of Nigeria, 1952* (Lagos: Government Statistician, 1953–1954); *Population Census of the Eastern Region of Nigeria, 1953* (Lagos: Government Statistician, 1953–1954); *Population Census of the Northern Region of Nigeria, 1952* (Lagos: Government Statistician, 1952–1953).

It is necessary to distinguish sharply between "traditional" and "new" cities, as has been done in table 7. The former category includes centers, such as those of the Yoruba, which were in existence when British control was established. The "new" cities are the urban aggregations that have subsequently emerged. None of the cities—traditional or new—are industrial cities; rather they are subcategories of the "preindustrial" type.[19] With the qualified exception of Lagos and Sapele, and a growing number of other cities where secondary industries have been established since 1945, Nigerian cities are mining-commercial-administrative centers and not manufacturing cities as known in the West. Some anthropologists prefer "commercial center" to "urban center." Moreover, whereas all new cities are of the commercial-administrative type, traditional cities vary in the extent to which they have been affected by modern urban developments.[20] In general, the unsettling and disorganizing effects of urbanization have been most in evidence in the cosmopolitan new cities and in those traditional cities that became principal centers of trade, administration, or transportation, and, *pari passu*, more ethnically heterogeneous in character. Yet even in the new cities compensating mechanisms and developments have cushioned the corrosive impact of urban life. Kinship associations and tribal unions sprang into being and helped to maintain lineage attachments and a sense of belonging and relatedness. Even the most artificial of the new cities were not agglomerations of detribalized and disorganized individuals—"a glob of humanity"—but aggregations of tribal unions.[21] Only the "Boma Boys" * were insecure, and they always managed to get by. With the passage of time new primary-group identifications were established and the new cities began to acquire a structure and civic leadership, frequently in the form of multitribal community leagues which endeavored to foster civic consciousness.

In traditional cities, the British policy of indirect rule and non-alienation of land has limited and restrained the extreme disorganizing effects of urbanization. Except for Lagos, where the traditional House of Docemo was frequently ignored or treated in rather cavalier fashion, British officials recognized and supported the authorities in the traditional cities of Yorubaland, Benin, and the Hausa-Fulani emirates. Urbanization in these centers, in terms of an increase in population since the British occupation, has occurred in two clearly definable sectors: (*a*) the traditional sector (which in Hausaland was usually demarcated by a city wall) where increases resulted from biological growth or from the influx of rural peoples of the same lineage, clan, or tribe as the indigenous urban dwellers; and (*b*) the "stranger" sector, tribally heterogeneous and situated on the periphery of the traditional city. As traditional city authorities controlled land rights and the political system, "strangers" were compelled to settle on the outskirts of the city in specifically demarcated zones and were excluded from political life.

This two-sector pattern of urban development in traditional cities has significantly minimized the unsettling consequences of urbanization in the indigenous sector. The tribal homogeneity of indigenous peoples was to a large extent preserved. It was in the

---

* A "Boma Boy" is an unemployed ruffian or petty thief. Collectively, "Boma Boys" are not unlike American street-corner gangs.

stranger sector on the periphery of the traditional city that one found heterogeneity, a weakening of lineage ties, and evidence of the instability, insecurity, and atomism frequently attributed to modern urban life.* But even here lineage attachment and responsibility were partly preserved through tribal unions. This compartmentalization of urban life in western and northern cities has, however, inhibited political integration and the development of a cosmopolitan or "nationalist" outlook. The stranger sectors have been the centers of nationalist activity, partly because of the higher education and tribal composition of the population and the greater impact of a cosmopolitan urban life, but also because of grievances and frustrations felt by the strangers at being treated as outcasts and subjects of the traditional city heads, who, of course, were supported by British authority.[22]

These different patterns of urbanization in Nigeria are relevant to a study of the roots of nationalism in that we can give but qualified acceptance to the proposition that urbanization leads to social disintegration and a greater susceptibility to nationalism and political activity. We have seen that the consequences of urbanization are highly relative. Once these qualifications and reservations are made, however, there can be no doubt that urbanization, when accompanied by increased mobility, physical detachment from traditional authority and lineage bonds, social restratification, and a tribally heterogeneous milieu, has rendered the peoples concerned more vulnerable to nationalist appeals than others not so situated. In its early stages nationalism in Nigeria was a wholly urban phenomenon, but it was not a phenomenon of *all* urban centers.

ECONOMIC GRIEVANCES AND NATIONALISM

Increased mobility, urbanization, the drift from a subsistence to an internal or external exchange economy, the diversification of labor and the specialization of crops, and the trend toward wage employment have been the prominent features of the social and economic ferment in Nigeria since the Western intrusion. These revolutionary changes profoundly affected traditional loyalties, patterns of behavior, and social obligations. They also created new

---

* In Hausaland the stranger settlement is called a *sabon gari;* in Yorubaland it has a variety of local names, all indicating its "foreign" character.

79

tensions, and an embittering economic insecurity, as well as individualistic and materialistic attitudes and values. Their impact was cushioned, and the rate and degree of disintegration were held in check, by the tenacity of the kinship bond. At most, however, this ferment provided only the predisposing conditions or background for the rise of political consciousness and of nationalist sentiment. In the economic realm we must look more specifically at the grievances generated by the policies and practices of those who controlled economic power, the government and European traders and commercial firms.

Until World War II the Nigerian government did not systematically control the marketing of export crops, though it did much to promote and facilitate their production; nor was it interested, apart from regulating the liquor and arms traffic and collecting customs duties, in the importation and sale of European manufactured goods. The government's main policy, indeed its *raison d'être*, was to maximize such exports and imports. It left everything else to free enterprise which, because of superior economic power, was overwhelmingly European. The most direct statement made by a Nigerian governor on this subject was that of Sir Arthur Richards (now Lord Milverton) in 1945: "It is the policy of this Government to work with Africans and with 'big business' in a tripartite partnership for the good of the people. . . . within the framework of Government regulation private enterprise has a great contribution to make to the future welfare of Nigeria. . . ." [23]

In large measure, African resentments and grievances stemmed from the concentration of economic power in the hands of expatriate firms, particularly the major firm, the United Africa Company (UAC).[24] Since 1930 the UAC has exercised a prominent and at times a dominant role in the Nigerian economy. By the late 1930's it controlled more than 40 per cent of Nigeria's import-export trade, and as late as 1949 it handled 34 per cent of commercial merchandise imports into Nigeria and purchased, on behalf of Nigerian marketing boards, 43 per cent of all Nigerian nonmineral exports.[25] Moreover, the UAC, with five other old, established European firms, organized the Association of West African Merchants (AWAM) through which they occasionally made import agreements and allocated export quotas. In 1949 the six firms in the AWAM handled about 66 per cent of Nigeria's imports and nearly 70 per cent of her exports.[26] Moreover, until recently most of these firms engaged in extensive retail and semiwholesale trade at widely dispersed upcountry stations. In addition to the predominant role of AWAM firms, there also existed a very heavy concentration in the European ownership and control of banking and shipping facilities.[27] This near-totality of economic power exercised by a small group of European firms, together with apparent governmental support or toleration of that power, gave rise to a popular image of alien collusion and exploitation.

This image of a close association between alien political control and an alien economic oligopoly was not without substance. Although the Nigerian government steadfastly opposed, with few exceptions, European acquisition of land and the establishment of European plantations, it dealt mostly with a few large firms in the allocation of trading licenses, the administration of trade controls, and the formulation of tax policies. This does not necessarily mean that ideological or national affinities linked government and management, although the possibility cannot be excluded. Nor does it necessarily suggest a conscious official opposition to African enterprise. Had there been large established African firms, they would in all likelihood have been given the same opportunities as European firms. It is not unreasonable to assume that the government's willingness to deal with expatriate firms represented primarily a bureaucratic predilection based on a preference for well-established contacts and on the imperative of administrative convenience.[28]

The popular belief in a government-oligopoly conspiracy, however, was greatly strengthened by the wartime controls imposed on export trade. For various reasons, such as the effective Allied prosecution of the war and the protection of African primary producers, the British government in November, 1939, established an official monopoly over the purchase, export, and marketing of all West African agricultural products. The export-control system was operated by the West African Produce Control Board, a statutory corporation. Again, for reasons of administrative efficiency and simplicity, the board designated the large established expatriate firms as its buying agents. Each firm's share of trade was determined on a quota basis according to past performance, which meant, of course, that new firms (European or African) could not participate. Thus the government in effect froze, legitimized, and perpetuated for the duration of the war the prewar alien oligopoly in Nigeria's export trade.[29]

Two groups were especially affected by and resentful of the power and competitive advantages of the expatriate firms: (1) the emergent entrepreneurial class, and (2) consumers who had developed tastes for imported goods. Two rather different views have been expressed concerning the first group, the budding Nigerian middle class. One view suggests that since the end of the nineteenth century European enterprise has consciously and systematically—and, by implication, malevolently—endeavored to prevent the emergence of a strong African business community.[30] The other view, expressed most recently in P. T. Bauer's much debated study, is that the large expatriate firms were obliged to assume a dominant position and to acquire vested interests simply because a strong local capitalist class did not develop.[31] Actually, there is evidence to support both positions, depending upon the period and the area of economic activity. There is not enough evidence, however, to support a definitive historical judgment. An objective economic history of Nigeria has yet to be written. The politically relevant facts, of course, are that certain aspiring entrepreneurial groups in Nigeria felt themselves denied opportunities they regarded as theirs, and the responsibility for such denial was projected first upon the alien oligopoly and later upon the British administration, and that the entrepreneurial groups were strong and active in their support—both verbal and financial —of the nationalist movement.

During the century of trading activity before World War II, several Nigerian business groups were displaced, or suffered frustration in their entrepreneurial pursuits, as a result of the operations of expatriate firms; or they disappeared for other reasons. One group comprised those African middlemen in the Niger Delta area who during the first half of the nineteenth century had become the recognized intermediaries between European traders on the coast and the peoples of the hinterland. They bought the products of the interior (largely palm oil and kernels) and sold them at their own price on the coast. In return they received European trade goods which they later sold in the interior. In the main, this emergent capitalist class was made up of coastal chiefs or enterprising commoners from the maritime or riverain tribes. During the last few decades of the nineteenth century, however, this group was effectively eliminated by European trading firms. Subtle measures—the exaction of heavy trade licenses or the enforcement of stringent regulations regarding the marketing of African produce—were frequently the techniques used, when these failed more positive steps were taken, including punitive expeditions against resisting groups and the deportation of their leaders, among whom King Ja Ja was perhaps the most famous.[32]

Another group included those middlemen (mainly chiefs, but also commoners) who acted as the vanguard of the European commercial houses in penetrating the remoter areas. In the two decades preceding World War I many of the more enterprising members of this group amassed sizable fortunes and became substantial traders and exporters on their own account. Two developments, however, tended to weaken and eliminate this group. One was the progressive extension of the operations of European firms into the bush, including the establishment of retail outlets through which they traded directly with African producer-consumers. This was possible largely because of (1) their overwhelming financial power and consequent competitive advantage, (2) the climate of security created by the British presence, and (3) the development and expansion of communications and transportation facilities in the interior. The second development, which virtually liquidated those African traders who survived the superior competitive power of the firms, was the sudden depression of 1920–1921, in which most African entrepreneurs were caught with large inventories and exhausted credit. The result was that their businesses passed to the European firms.[33]

The extension of the trading operations of large firms into the interior did not eliminate all middlemen; it mainly affected those who distributed and retailed imported goods. Trade is a two-way operation, however, and it has been estimated that during the interwar period the number of middlemen engaged in the marketing of major Nigerian exports (primary products such as cocoa and palm oil and kernels) was about 100,000.[34] These middlemen formed a crucial part of the marketing machinery. With advances of cash from the firms, they purchased produce from the farmers and in turn were credited by the firms. Their excess profits, which it is generally agreed were large, depended upon their skill in taking advantage of price changes as well as upon the illiteracy of the primary producer. Many of them also became moneylenders and retailers on their own account. Here again statutory marketing arrangements tended to thwart the activities of this increasingly affluent group. Under these arrangements the firms became licensed buying agents and the middlemen became accredited to the firms, and prices and profits for both groups were largely predetermined by the marketing boards. This system, in effect since 1939, has drastically limited the opportunities, once possessed by the middlemen, to amass capital—often, admittedly, in an exploitative manner—and use it in other entrepreneurial activities.[35]

Although these wartime marketing controls could be justified on most economic counts, the regulations were remarkably insensitive to the aspirations and claims of another African entrepreneurial element, the tiny group of small-scale African exporters. Their total share in the wartime export trade was less than 1 per cent, and, as previously noted, the criterion of past performance made it impossible for them to expand their participation. With few structural changes the system became a permanent feature of postwar Nigerian government. Although attacked by nationalist leaders during the war, the system increasingly won their support. This support was attracted only because Nigerian leaders were able to acquire control over the boards, the system of quotas based on past performance was abolished, and Nigerian exporters were given special encouragement and support.[36] Prior to these changes, the system was understandably a nationalist target.[37]

In the historic displacement or curtailment of successive entrepreneurial groups in Nigeria, the decisive determinant, apart from such political factors as the support given the Royal Niger Company by the imperial government and the discriminatory quota system governing wartime exports, has been the overwhelming economic power of the expatriate firms. At the outset we will assume that this concentration of power is not the result of the malevolence and rapaciousness of the firms. "Evil men" explanations of human affairs are unconvincing, whether they derive from

Marxian premises, a sense of racial persecution, or mere nationalist oratory. We will further assume that the expatriate firms, like any business enterprise, European or African, desired to maximize profits and minimize losses. Once these assumptions are made, it is necessary to look for other explanations. Two are regarded as significant. One is that the popular restraints normally felt by the business community in other societies were not directly or fully operative in Nigeria. The obvious conclusion is that Nigeria needed its own government to make these restraints effectual. The other explanation is that certain features of the Nigerian situation have, as P. T. Bauer suggests, favored firms with large capital resources.[38] The capital requirements for mere entry into the race and for survival have been comparatively larger in Nigeria than elsewhere. In the eyes of most Nigerian businessmen, the equally obvious conclusion is that Africans should have access to adequate capital, and that this would be possible only when they had their own government.

Given these two factors—the successive displacement of emergent Nigerian capitalists in potentially profitable enterprises, and the extremely high capital requirements peculiar to Nigeria— it is understandable that the issue of bank credit and the allegedly discriminatory practices of European banks were sources of grievance and a stimulus to nationalist sentiment. There can be little doubt that credit, though readily available to Europeans and to the ubiquitous Levantines, was extremely difficult for most Africans to obtain from European banks. In the view of many Africans, such differential treatment was positive evidence that the banks were pursuing a policy of conscious discrimination.

Although racial prejudice may well have been operative in certain instances, other factors helped to account for the extreme conservatism of European banks. One is that two British banks (Barclay's and the Bank of British West Africa) exercised a virtual monopoly in Nigeria. Since their favored position assured them of an adequate return from routine operations, these banks could avoid lending activities that seemed to involve undue risk. Because many affluent Africans hesitated to disclose their financial status, or because the security they offered contained elements of uncertainty, or because a wide social gap sometimes separated bank managers and African business leaders, most loans to Africans

were believed to contain a large element of risk.[39] These explanations, however, do not alter the fact that banking conservatism
was interpreted by Nigerians not only as another manifestation of
racial prejudice, but also as part of the total complex of European
domination aimed at keeping the African down.

The foregoing circumstances stimulated Nigerians to organize
their own bank, and 1933 the National Bank of Nigeria was
founded. Immediately after World War II several others appeared.[40] The owners of these banks particularly resented British
designation of a European bank as the official bank for the government of Nigeria. As the annual report of a Nigerian bank put
it: "It would have been a great help to Nigerian Enterprise if the
Nigerian Government . . . [had extended] . . . her patronage to
at least some of the African-owned Banks in Nigeria." [41] It is not
without significance that at least two of these African banks gave
financial support to the nationalist movement, and that, not long
after the accession to power of all-Nigerian governments in the
Eastern and Western regions, African banks were awarded a substantial share of government business. In the Eastern Region this
led to the bank crisis of 1956 discussed in chapter 18.[42]

Another category of Nigerian entrepreneurs affected by the
operations of expatriate firms included the hundreds of thousands
of petty women traders in urban centers. These women purchased
goods from European firms and sold them in local African markets
on a "penny-penny" basis. During the postwar period the market-
women were particularly aggrieved over a practice of the firms
known as "conditional sales." [43] Their strong opposition was significant in certain of the postwar protest movements in urban centers. They repeatedly demonstrated a remarkable capacity for
organization and unity of action, and an unusual degree of political sophistication. The Lagos market-women, for example, were
the main mass base of Nigeria's oldest political organization, the
Nigerian National Democratic party. In short, the market-women
were constituents whom any urban politician or nationalist leader
would ignore at his peril.

The activities of the expatriate firms were also strongly resented
by the producers of export commodities and consumers of imported goods. The firms, as the principal purchasers of export

products and the principal importers of European goods, were blamed both for low prices paid the producers and for high prices charged the consumers. Although statutory marketing arrangements relieved the firms of any responsibility for the former from 1939 on, perspectives are slow to change. Nigerian producers were unable to forget that the firms were largely responsible for prices in the prewar period, even though it was Nigerian middlemen who actually bought their produce and frequently made the highest profit. The big firms were commonly regarded in the earlier period as an exploitative oligopoly. This belief led to the cocoa holdups of 1932 and 1937 in the Gold Coast, and occasioned no little bitterness and agitation in the cocoa-growing areas of Nigeria. The AWAM, like the "big trusts" in other countries, became the symbol of exploitation and oppression.

Although the expatriate firms were ultimately relieved of responsibility for prices and profits connected with export products, they remained the primary target of grievances over the prices of imported goods. Here the AWAM meant import monopolies, price fixing, and extortionist profits. Popular resentment was particularly acute in both Nigeria and the Gold Coast in the immediate postwar period when pent-up wants and expectations were at peak levels, but consumers' goods were in extremely short supply. This situation led to a boycott in the Gold Coast and serious unrest in Nigeria.[44] It intensified hostility not only toward the expatriate firms but also toward the government, which by its silence and inaction was presumed to be supporting the firms, or at least allowing them complete freedom of action.

Before the war the only other major economic activity in Nigeria was the mining of tin, gold, columbite, and silver-lead. In 1899, when its charter was revoked, the Royal Niger Company ceded the government "all its land and mining rights of whatever sort" in northern Nigeria, and agreed to accept a flat payment of £150,000 and half the proceeds of a royalty for a period of ninety-nine years.[45] This protective measure, taken by the government to acquire all mining rights before any development had occurred, saved Nigeria the fate of other African territories where exclusive mining rights were granted to private enterprise. Since 1900 mining in Nigeria has been controlled by minerals ordinances, and

European miners or mining companies have been obliged to obtain prospecting licenses and mining leases from the government, as well as to meet certain other conditions.

The history of European mining enterprise is much the same as the history of the commercial firms. There was the same insensitivity to the aspirations of the Nigerians. Before the European intrusion, Africans had mined tin, galena, salt, and other surface minerals, although on a comparatively small scale. Once Europeans began to exploit Nigerian mineral deposits, Africans had little opportunity to enter mining enterprise except as unskilled labor. Until 1927, legislation specifically discriminated against Nigerians by requiring that the agent in charge of a mining lease be a European. Even after that provision was removed, Africans were effectively disqualified because they lacked the capital necessary to secure leases. Theoretically, of course, the new licensing procedure was in no way discriminatory; it was intended to secure the most efficient operation of the mines. Under the circumstances, however, it had the effect of excluding Africans. The situation was further aggravated because neither the mining firms nor the government made any effort to train Nigerians for responsible posts or technical positions in the mining industry.

In analyzing economic grievances against expatriate enterprise and their relationship to the rise of nationalism in Nigeria, we must distinguish two levels: (1) the level of immediate personal grievances of individuals affected, and (2) the "national" level at which the grievances are cast in collective terms. Individual grievances may find an outlet in uprisings, local boycotts, strikes, and protest movements, or even in individual reprisals. Or elements with common grievances may become pressure groups. It is usually the aim and function of the nationalist leader, however, to aggregate and articulate individual and group grievances into something more than simply a catalog of complaints, so that they relate to a larger "national" whole which has its own grievance against another whole. Thus, even though the grievances of aspiring exporters might be assuaged by a change in the policy of the government or of the firms, such ameliorative action would not assuage the grievance of the nation. The grievance of the nation subsumes all individual grievances. Thus there arises the notion of a reciprocity of dependence—the national grievance is dependent on individual grievances, but the latter can be completely eliminated only by national liberation.

In performing this aggregating and symbolizing function, nationalists endeavored to identify and draw attention to "national" economic grievances resulting from the domination of the Nigerian economy by expatriate enterprise and from the neglect of Nigeria's potentiality. Among such grievances were the following: the annual profits and royalties of alien firms exceeded annual expenditures on education; the salaries of the 3,000-odd European employees exceeded the wages paid the 100,000-odd Africans employed by the firms; the bulk of European salaries and firm profits were not reinvested or spent in Nigeria for industrialization, but were transferred to the United Kingdom; the mining royalties paid to one firm over a ten-year period equaled nearly one-sixth of the total Nigerian budget. It is quite likely that many of those holding individual grievances were insensitive or indifferent to this larger concept of exploitation. In emphasizing the exploitation of "Nigeria" rather than of individual Nigerian groups, however, the nationalist leaders sought by one sweep to involve thirty million people in the individual grievances of a few hundred thousand. This is a measure of the power of identification with the national symbol.

Nationalism is not merely the sum of accumulated grievances; it is equally an awareness of greater possibilities and opportunities. Here the large expatriate firms have also had an impact by providing entrepreneurial capital and career training and preparation, and, more generally, by sparking economic growth. Although it is true that certain emergent capitalist groups were displaced or eliminated by the superior economic power of the firms, it is also true that the firms have been the major source of initial credit for the present generation of Nigerian traders, who, of course, constitute the bulk of what might be called the middle class. Virtually the whole pattern of trade (including both the retailing of imports and the purchase of exports) has been based upon capital advances or credits made by expatriate firms to Nigerian middlemen and market-women. A substantial number of Nigerians have subsequently moved out on their own to become independent traders, operating on an ever-increasing scale. This development has been greatly accelerated since the war by the conscious back-to-the-ports movement of the larger firms, which has caused retail trade to pass increasingly into the hands of Nigerians, many of them former firm employees.[46]

Employment in the firms has been one of the main channels of advancement for a large number of the present Nigerian economic and political elite. Of the eighty members of the first Western House of Assembly (1951–1956), eighteen, or 22 per cent, commenced their careers as clerks in the firms. Of these eighteen, one became an organizational leader, two became lawyers, eight achieved managerial status in their respective firms, and ten went into business on their own. The latter no doubt took with them not only savings with which to launch their businesses, but also *expertise* acquired by their experience in the firms. Moreover, the Africanization of the managerial staff of the firms has kept pace with that of government, at least in nontechnical positions. By 1952, for example, 99 of the 365 positions in the management of the United Africa Company operations in Nigeria were held by Nigerians.[47]

In addition to these direct accomplishments, expatriate enterprise has made a broader contribution by generating general economic growth. Nigeria was part of what Sir Keith Hancock has described as the "traders' frontier," in which the concept of "exploitation" must be treated with great reserve.[48] More recently, P. T. Bauer has emphasized the fallaciousness of the notion that the wealth of the expatriate traders in West Africa had been "taken or extracted" from the Africans, because trade is in itself productive and creative.[49] Although expatriate firms often ruthlessly manipulated the market by aggressive buying and selling or by market-sharing agreements and other restrictive practices, their operations accelerated the commercialization of the Nigerian economy, increased the number of Nigerians participating in the economic life of the new society, and in other respects fostered economic growth and development. All these services helped to lay the groundwork and provide a wider mass base for the postwar nationalist movement.

CHAPTER 4
Christianity and European Missionaries

Through their extensive evangelical activity and long monopoly in the field of education, Christian missionaries played a critical role in the rise of nationalism in Nigeria. Unlike traders, they did not limit their endeavors to port towns, rail or river lines, or commercial centers; rather, they undertook to penetrate the most remote areas in the interior with the determination to remain there until Christianity was firmly established. Unlike government administrators, they did not seek to preserve traditional society, but rather to transform it. Without the missionary enterprise both the timing and nature of the awakening of racial and national consciousness would probably have been very different.

Tropical Africa was of special interest to Christian missionaries.[1] The heathen was the missionary target, and of all peoples in the non-European world the African was believed to be the most heathen. In early missionary literature Africa was characterized " 'as one universal den of desolation, misery, and crime;' and certainly, of all the divisions of the globe it has always had an unfortunate preeminence in degradation, wretchedness and woe."[2] The reports of many early traders, explorers, and pioneer missionaries contained vivid and frequently exaggerated accounts of primitive savagery and barbarism. In 1873 a returned missionary said: "The Chinaman meets you with the stolid morality of his Confucianism; the Hindoo with astute logic for his Pantheism. . . . When I carry my torch into the caves of Africa, I meet only filthy birds of darkness. . . ."[3] Thus, whereas the non-Christian East was portrayed as having traditions of ancient civilizations, Africa was believed to have nothing but "moral darkness." This early missionary perspective of Africa was but a reflection of the general, and persistent, belief that the peoples of tropical Africa were fundamentally different from the rest of mankind.

There was a tendency not only to believe that Africans were in far greater need of Christian salvation than other peoples, but also that, compared with other areas of the non-Christian world, Africa offered far greater opportunities for Christian evangelical activity. The exceptional stubbornness of Islam and the strong resistance of Hinduism in India, of Confucianism in China, and of Buddhism in Burma, Ceylon, and Japan, made pagan Africa appear especially inviting as a mission field. And missionary

TABLE 10

COMPARATIVE INCREASE IN PROTESTANT COMMUNICANTS IN
MAJOR AREAS OF THE NON-WESTERN WORLD

Date	Asia and Middle East (1,000,000,000) [a]	Latin America (120,000,000) [a]	Africa (135,000,000) [a]
1903	622,460	132,388	342,857
1911	875,322	369,077	566,608
1925	1,533,057	368,228	1,015,683
1938	2,206,822	695,363	2,163,301

[a] Approximate population.

Source: Joseph I. Parker, ed., *Interpretative Statistical Survey of the World Mission of the Christian Church* (New York: International Missionary Council, 1938).

expectations regarding tropical Africa were in a large measure fulfilled. Whereas by 1938 only 1.7 per cent of the population of India (1.3 per cent of the population of all Asia) had accepted Christianity, more than 7 per cent of the peoples of tropical Africa were Christian adherents.[4] This comparatively wider acceptance of Christianity by Africans is further illuminated by the increase in the number of Protestant communicants in major areas, as indicated by the statistics in table 10.

Certain special factors in West Africa stimulated a missionary interest. As the "white man's grave" the area presented an opportunity for personal risk and sacrifice as well as for heroic martyrdom. Also, interest in the West Coast had been quickened by the slave trade, religious enthusiasm had been generated in the movement for its abolition, and Christian consciences had been stung by the white man's association in that traffic. At least these considerations figured largely in the missionaries' own rationale of their motivation and purpose. Indeed, a historian of the Church Missionary Society, the largest Protestant missionary movement in Nigeria, reported that the founders of the society, "commiserating the condition of the people, and more particularly of the Negro race, on account of the cruel wrongs which the slave-trade had inflicted upon them, selected Africa as their first field of missionary enterprise." [5] During the period of the slave trade, Nigeria was known as the "Slave Coast." It is not without significance that among the first agents of Protestant Christianity in Nigeria were freed slaves who returned to Nigeria from Sierra Leone.

Another consideration that sharpened missionary interest in Nigeria was apprehension regarding the spread of Islam. At both the Edinburgh and Lucknow World Missionary Conferences, held early in the present century, it was stressed that the "whole strategy of Christian missions in Africa should be viewed in relation to Islam. . . ." [6] In particular, the Lucknow conference resolved:

> We are strongly of opinion that concerted action among missionary boards and organizations is necessary, in order thoroughly to coordinate the forces now at work in Africa, and to regulate their distribution in such a manner as to provide a strong chain of mission stations across Africa, the strongest link of which shall be at those points where Moslem advance is most active. [7]

Northern Nigeria was one of the most thoroughly Islamized areas in tropical Africa, and Islam was also making significant advances among the peoples of central and southwestern Nigeria. Indeed, one missionary strategist proposed that southern Nigeria be regarded as a core area from which to make the first main line of Christian advance up the Niger and Benue looking toward the Nile via Lake Chad. [8]

Although Roman Catholic missionaries arrived in Benin as early as 1516, and remained until 1688, their efforts failed to make any significant or lasting impression. [9] Nearly two centuries elapsed before Nigeria became a target for renewed missionary activity, although Protestant evangelists were established in the Gold

Coast as early as 1752. In the mid-1840's, the Wesleyan Methodist Missionary Society and the Church Mission Society began work in Badagry and Abeokuta in southwestern Nigeria. During the next half-century these early pioneers were followed by six more missionary societies, and by the end of World War I fifteen European and American evangelical groups were operating in the southern provinces and the Middle Belt of Nigeria. More than 600 European missionaries, assisted by nearly 5,000 Nigerians, had established close to 3,000 churches, and Christendom claimed more than 800,000 communicants.[10]

The aspects of this missionary enterprise which have special relevance here are its timing and geographical incidence. These are illuminated by the figures on the differential development of Christianity in Nigeria set forth in table 11. The significant points revealed by these data are (1) the recency of the encounter between Christianity and many of the groups being proselytized; (2) the delayed impact upon the Ibo and Ibibio peoples, and the comparatively higher proportion of converts to Christianity among these groups in a very short period of time; (3) the earlier and more intensive Christian influence upon the Yoruba and Efik peoples (centering around Abeokuta, Lagos, and Calabar); and (4) the slight effect of missionary enterprise upon the peoples of the Northern Region before 1931, but the rather substantial increase in Christian adherents in the Middle Belt during the past two decades.[11] These temporal and areal variations in the impact of Christianity assume considerable importance— especially since schools accompanied missionary stations—in explaining the ethnic composition of early nationalist leadership and the subsequent appearance of ethnic and regional tensions within the nationalist movement.

Such differences are only partly explained by geographical accessibility and historical accidents. Two other factors were important determinants. One was the official policy, adopted mainly for political reasons by Lord Lugard, of excluding Christian missionaries from the predominantly Muslim areas of the Northern Region. The other variable was the cultural factor. On the one hand there was a cultural resistance to Christian activity by groups already Islamized or by those characterized by rigid stratification and bureaucratic organization in which influential

TABLE 11

Differential Impact of Christianity in Nigeria

Region and ethnic group	Number of mission stations by principal ethnic group			Number of Christian adherents by region				Christian adherents as percentage of total regional population 1952–1953
	1875	1900	1925	1880–1885	1900–1910	1920	1952–1953	
Western Region								
Yoruba	12	24	47 }	6,500	17,700	260,500	ª	ª
Edo	ª	3	15					
Eastern Region								
Ibo	2	7	28 }	few	18,500	514,395	3,915,500	50
Ibibio-Efik	4	12	24					
Northern Region								
Muslim North groups	0	0	5 }	few	few	19,200	558,000 ᵇ	3.3 ᵇ
Middle Belt groups	2	2	57					

ª Number not known.

ᵇ Of the Christians in the Northern Region, 73 per cent live in the Middle Belt provinces.

Sources: P. Amaury Talbot, *The Peoples of Southern Nigeria* (London: 1926), IV, 110 ff.; J. Lowry Maxwell, *Nigeria, the Land, the People and Christian Progress* (London: 1931), pp. 105 ff.; *Population Census of the Northern Region of Nigeria*, 1952 (Lagos: Government Statistician, 1952), pp. 11, 32–33; *Population Census of the Eastern Region of Nigeria*, 1953, Bulletin no. 1 (Lagos: Government Statistician, 1954), pp. 4–5.

elements were apprehensive about the unsettling effects of Christian activity (for example, the northern emirates and certain areas of Yorubaland). On the other hand, certain groups displayed a marked receptivity to missionary penetration, particularly the Ibo and Ibibio peoples, as well as those in the Middle Belt of the Northern Region. Considerations other than the absence of Islam and hostile traditionalist elements were clearly involved. It is difficult to explain the amazingly rapid and mass adoption of Christianity by the Ibo peoples without reference to the heavy pressure of population upon the land, the emphasis upon achieved —as distinguished from ascribed—status, the passion for Western education in order to "catch up," and the consequent tendency to look upon Christianity in essentially instrumental terms. In short, the impact of Christian missionary endeavor has been determined as much by the cultural predispositions and situations of the several respondent groups as by the efforts and activities of the missionaries. The former variables provide significant clues to an understanding of the influence of Christianity upon the rise of nationalism, as well as of the attitudes of nationalists toward the Christian endeavor.

Propositions regarding causal relationships between Christian missionary activity and the rise of nationalism can be advanced only with the greatest tentativeness and caution, and then only at the highest level of generalization. Certainly they cannot be quantitatively stated.[12] For example, there are some remarkable parallels in the nationalist predispositions of the Kanuri, the least Christianized elements in Nigeria, and the Ibo, who are among the most Christianized groups.[13] Again, Old Calabar, with its century-old contact with missionary forces and an overwhelmingly Christian population, became a haven for pro-British respectability, and its indigenous inhabitants, like the Creoles of Freetown, Sierra Leone, were stimulated to nationalist activity rather late in the day. Perhaps the most that can be said is that the missionary impact has been profound though not determinative, unintentional and indirect in some ways, and purposive but contradictory in others. Apart from its educational aspect, to be discussed later, the missionary enterprise may be analyzed under three different headings: (1) its initiation and acceleration of social change and of the disorganization of traditional African societies; (2) its provision of a basis for societal reintegration on a new and larger scale; and (3) its stimulation of racial and political consciousness.

THE IMPACT OF CHRISTIANITY UPON TRADITIONAL AFRICAN SOCIETIES

The early missionaries were inclined to feel that the African was in the grip of a cruel and irrational system from which he ought to be liberated. Their early experiences and observations in Africa confirmed their belief that in the African scheme of things human life itself meant very little. In their eyes ritual murder, human sacrifice, and cannibalism were sufficient to condemn the whole system, even after British police power had suppressed these more repugnant practices. The missionaries were inclined to go beyond the mere limits of "natural justice" which the British imposed upon African chiefs in their treaties of protection; they included among the preconditions for entry into the Christian fold the abandonment of such customs as initiation ceremonies (a crucial phase in the African system of education), dancing (a vital part of the aesthetic and recreational life of the African), marriage payment (a bond linking the families of the bride and the groom), polygyny (at the core of the entire African family system), secret societies (very often key institutions in the traditional political system), and ancestor worship (the symbol of community which linked the individual to a larger whole through time), not to mention so-called witch doctoring, seminudity, African names, and traditional funeral ceremonies. Renunciation of the old order of things was a prerequisite to acceptance of the new. A spokesman for the International Missionary Council affirmed this purpose in very clear language:

> The missionary is a revolutionary and he has to be so, for to preach and plant Christianity means to make a frontal attack on the beliefs, the customs, the apprehensions of life and the world, and by implication (because tribal religions are primarily social realities) on the social structures and bases of primitive society. The missionary enterprise need not be ashamed of this, because colonial administrations, planters, merchants, western penetration, etc., perform a much more severe and destructive attack.[14]

97

This rationalization was based squarely upon a persistent major assumption, stated by the same author, that "the primitive religions are all destined to perish and disappear." [15]

Coupled with this negative purpose of extinction was the positive desire to help, to lead Africans to the good life. One strand was an ameliorative humanitarianism. In the words of David Livingstone: "I resolved to devote my life to the alleviation of human misery." [16] The other strand was aimed at ultimate African liberation, in the spiritual sense, via the Kingdom of God. As one ardent missionary put it:

> The Christian Church is concerned with a greater problem, that of the annexation of the tribes and peoples for the kingdom of God and the proclamation among them of that reign of righteousness and peace which will alone work the true redemption of Africa, the liberation and development of her peoples to take their rightful place in the life of the world.[17]

This vigorous and benevolent concept of tutelage was but a manifestation of an idea dominant in Europe at the time—the idea of progress, European cultural superiority, and ethnocentric nationalism. Christianity, progress, European culture, and moral excellence were all regarded as aspects of a monolithic whole, the concept of Christian civilization.[18] Not only was European religion presumed to be higher than African religion, but European values and institutions were considered superior to those of the African. Unable to transcend the assumptions of their day, the early missionaries were enthusiastic and dedicated agents of thoroughgoing Europeanization.[19] But even had missionaries not identified Christianity and European culture, the African would still have considered them indivisible. His conception of religion was not unlike that of the medieval European who regarded Christianity and civilization as coterminous.[20] In short, the missionary, guided by ethnocentric preconceptions, and the African, responding with a communal conception of religion, became unwitting partners as donor and recipient in the process of westernization.

The early missionary objective of total religio-cultural conversion was the product of evangelical theology and the prevailing assumptions of the nineteenth century. By World War I the attitude of several thoughtful missionary leaders appeared to be changing. The idea of a new approach was partly due to a growing concern, even alarm, over the disintegrating consequences of past missionary activity. Instances of the secession of African Christian groups from the Church were becoming more common, and loyal African evangelists were reporting that such desertions were due to the stiff and unbending opposition of missionaries to customs that Africans did not regard as evil.[21] The new attitude was in part attributable to increased knowledge of African cultures and the growth of a new interest in and sympathy toward the meaningful and useful aspects of those cultures. It is summed up best in the words of Donald Fraser: "I fear the evangel which denationalizes."[22]

In 1926 a special conference at Le Zoute, Belgium, was attended by leading representatives of colonial administrations and of Protestant missionary societies working in Africa, and by African Christian leaders. The conference gave official expression to a new approach: "There is less of pity and more of respect for the Africans and for their past. . . . The western concepts of nationality, of language and somewhat even of religion are being replaced by the meekness, the love, that inherits all."[23] This changed position was linked to new attitudes of governments toward dependent peoples, to the awakening of political consciousness in Asia and Africa, and to a rapidly developing world consciousness of the African continent, which were all part of the general ferment following World War I. The Laymen's Foreign Missions Inquiry in 1930–1932, with special reference to the rise of nationalism in the non-European world, concluded:

"The connection of Christianity with Western life, formerly a matter of prestige, now has its disadvantages. For the sake of securing for Christianity a fair hearing it is necessary to separate it, as far as possible, from our history and our promoting agencies and to present it in its universal capacity."[24]

Thus the identification of Christianity with European culture was not only considered ethnocentric, but it was also an obstacle to Christian victory.

To implement this new outlook missionaries were urged to draw upon the insights of anthropologists.[25] The idea of destruction remained, but it was to be less provocative and more discriminating. As Kraemer put it: "Repression and ignoring is driving to the background, not destroying. To put something in its place is the best way of destroying."[26] Missionaries were counseled not to oppose an institution or a custom that provided for a natural and vital need unless they had found a meaningful substitute. Indeed, by the early 1940's missionary leaders had begun to stress a sympathetic and eclectic approach toward traditional African culture and religion.[27]

Despite the soul-searching and self-criticism that prevailed among many Protestant missionary leaders, there is little evidence to suggest that the new approach had any immediate or profound effect upon the attitudes and activities of the ordinary missionary in the field. There were changes in field personnel and particularly in educational policy, but the dramatic reorientation required by the new approach was not easy to accomplish, particularly among persons face to face with concrete field situations tending to confirm traditional ethnocentric modes of thought. In any event, it is doubtful if the assumptions underlying the new strategy would have permitted its application in areas where social change was far advanced. There is also little to suggest that nationalists, agitated over the self-conscious cultural arrogance of many of the early missionaries, would be sensitive to or impressed by a new set of attitudes. Indeed, even if the latter were genuine and found positive expression in missionary activity, the older missionary prejudices and perspectives had an instrumental value to the nationalists in their efforts to amass grievances and to create and propagate the image of an unregenerate imperialism.

The main consequences of the early negative approach of missionaries were the undermining of parental authority, the weakening of traditional sanctions, the general alienation of Christian elements from the balance of the community, and the inculcation of disrespect for traditional African cultures. Of course, the individualism implicit in the Christian faith and explicit in the missionary technique also tended to have a disintegrating effect not only upon African societies, as ongoing social systems, but also upon the personality structure of many of the individuals who came within the orbit of Christian missionary activity. In most traditional African societies the group (family and lineage) is supreme over the individual, and religion is an intensely communal and legalistic affair saturating all aspects of the culture. Once the genuine African convert had embraced Christianity, the difficulties of individual adjustment to a sociopolitical structure incapable of realizing Christian ideals became insuperable. As the aim of most Protestant missionaries was not to Christianize a people en masse, but "to gather together a flock of converted individuals," successful evangelization created cleavages within the African community by ideologically and institutionally alienating converts from their communal life.[28] It also gave ever-increasing numbers of African adherents powerful weapons— the Christian doctrine of human equality and the old religious ideal of the brotherhood of man—with which to challenge the ethical basis of colonial rule as well as the more rankling pretensions of white superiority.

By their mere physical presence in Nigeria missionaries were important agents in the acculturation process. Few of them "went native" in their living habits. Scattered throughout the country in isolated stations, they endeavored to approximate European living standards, notwithstanding the obstacles of climate, lack of materials, and absence of basic services. Normally missionary societies at home were generous in providing funds to render existence tolerable. As a rule, until World War II, missionaries were the only Europeans who brought their families to Nigeria. As a white man the missionary was an object of great curiosity and emulation. Large numbers of Africans untouched by his evangelical and educational activity were nonetheless acutely aware of his presence, his gadgets, and his mode of life. This awareness awakened new aspirations and fostered such tendencies as imitation, emulation, and Europeanization, which have been significant in the total acculturation process. The emulative effect was reflected in the report of a missionary in the 1880's that "it was fast becoming the fashion in Yorubaland to call oneself a Christian." [29]

CHRISTIANITY AND REINTEGRATION

Missionary enterprise was not merely unsettling in its effect upon Nigerians, but in several respects it provided the instruments for reintegration. One of its most important contributions was as an unwitting stimulus to African cultural, and later, political nationalism through the use of the vernacular in religious and educational work and the development of the vernacular press. Missionary societies were the first to undertake seriously the systematic study of African languages. They financed and sponsored not only the development of a system of orthography but also the translation of the Bible and of Christian and educational literature into the vernacular. They played a role similar to that of the Catholic clerics in medieval society who, as Baron has observed, were also the main "promoters of national literature and recorders of national history." [30]

As early as 1851 the Church Missionary Society sent Bishop Samuel Crowther (a Yoruba ex-slave) to England where he compiled a Yoruba grammar and a Yoruba-English dictionary, and translated many books of the Bible into Yoruba.[31] In the 1860's, the Reverend J. C. Taylor (son of Ibo ex-slaves) was sent to England by the same society to translate portions of the Bible into Ibo, and in 1913 a Union Ibo Bible was published.[32] By 1925 the complete Bible had been translated into Ibo, Hausa, and Efik, and varying portions of the Scriptures into forty-five other Nigerian languages.[33] In twenty-one of these languages (including Hausa, Ibo, Yoruba, Efik, Nupe, and Fulani) there was a growing body of secular literature, including not only school books and language texts (grammars, phrase books, vocabularies), but also stories, legends, and proverbs taken from the histories of the cultures concerned and written by Nigerian authors.[34]

At the 1926 Le Zoute conference, representatives of all Protestant missions in Africa agreed that "Africa will best be evangelized by her own children." [35] Actually, in varying degrees of timing and techniques of control, Protestant missions in Nigeria from the beginning had endeavored to elevate Africans to the clergy and to establish and encourage the "indigenous Church." [36] In 1850 there was only 1 Nigerian clergyman (Bishop Samuel Crowther), but by 1900 there were 23, and twenty years later the number had increased to 169. As indicated by table 12, the Nigerian clergymen of the Church Missionary Society alone numbered 226 in 1953. By 1920, all Protestant evangelical activity in the Northern Provinces was carried on by African clergymen without assistance from European missionaries; in the same year southern Nigeria claimed 14 indigenous Christian churches with 175,000 adherents and more than 1,000 church buildings scattered throughout ten of the twelve provinces.[37] The official his-

TABLE 12

GROWTH OF THE CHURCH MISSIONARY SOCIETY IN NIGERIA

	Western Region				Eastern Region			
	Clergy		Mem- bers	Adherents	Clergy		Mem- bers	Adherents
Year	Euro- pean	Afri- can			Euro- pean	Afri- can		
1849	5	1	122	ᵃ	0	0	0	0
1859	6	5	916	ᵃ	0	0	0	0
1879	6	10	1,612	4,075	3	3	ᵃ	ᵃ
1894	10	20	2,341	6,690	8	3	381	1,496
1938	13	89	26,514	147,148	18	44	24,281	79,116
1953	12	149	ᵃ	(403,882) ᵇ	15	77	ᵃ	(403,882) ᵇ

ᵃ Number unknown.
ᵇ This figure represents the total for both regions; breakdown not available.
Sources: *The Church Missionary Atlas* (London: Church Missionary Society, 1896), pp. 35–44; *Annual Report of the Church Missionary Society* (London: Church Missionary Society, 1953), pp. 33–40; *World Christian Handbook* (London: World Dominion Press, 1952), pp. 193–194; Joseph I. Parker, ed., *Interpretative Statistical Survey of the World Mission of the Christian Church* (New York: International Missionary Council, 1938), pp. 18–21; J. Lowry Maxwell, *Nigeria, the Land, the People and Christian Progress* (London: 1931); P. Amaury Talbot, *The Peoples of Southern Nigeria* (London: 1926), IV, 119 ff.

torian of the Church Missionary Society recorded the principal reasons for supporting this Africanization of religion: ". . . as it was the inadequate supply of men that led the Society to employ more Natives, so it was the inadequate supply of funds that led it to make resolute efforts to throw the Native Churches on their own resources." [38]

The first major effort to Nigerianize the clergy and promote self-governing church bodies was made by the Church Missionary Society. Bishop Samuel Crowther was placed in charge of the Niger Mission. Toward the end of his episcopate the society criticized him for laxity in supervision and for "heathenish practices" among his subordinates, and concluded that its first experiment was a "lamentable failure." A purging committee under a new European bishop undertook to reorganize the mission, which provoked a secessionist movement in the Delta area and a repudiation of European authority. The net result of the episode was that the mission authorities backtracked in their policy of Africanizing the senior positions in the clergy, and renewed their insistence upon rigorous moral standards.[39] Both measures provided the grounds for future disaffection and grievance, ultimately resulting in the formation of nativistic and anti-white syncretistic movements.

The policy of Africanizing the priesthood and encouraging the indigenous Church—dictated as much by practical as by idealistic motives—had important consequences. It gave the educated Nigerian at least one avenue to a professional career approximating "senior service" or "white man" rank, and thereby an opportunity to achieve some measure of dignity, social status, and leadership.[40] It also provided members of this new elite with a platform enabling them to protest against any desertion by the missionary societies of their stated aims. Moreover, Nigerians could claim, as some of them later did, that Africanization in one sphere of European-controlled enterprise (the Church) should by ethical right be extended to other spheres (government and business). On the organizational side, the indigenous Church provided a new focus of loyalty and interest apart from the tribe. It brought Nigerians together for a common cause, trained them for common action, and created an organized following for Nigerian leaders.[41]

Christianity was an integrative force in that it provided a transtribal bond uniting individuals of different and formerly hostile traditional communities. The two largest Christian missions in Nigeria (the Church Missionary Society and the Roman Catholic Mission) distributed their evangelizing efforts among virtually all the provinces and groups of southern Nigeria. Annual church conferences attended by African clergymen and lay agents of diverse cultural backgrounds helped to break down parochialism and awaken a wider view and a consciousness of racial identity. Moreover, in the rapidly growing multitribal urban communities Christian churches provided a link among converts of different tribes and a new basis of loyalty in which ethnic origin became less relevant. As the missions had a monopoly over education, the Christians in urban communities included most of the educated elements, who were later to become the leaders in protest movements and in the awakening of a political and transtribal national consciousness.

CHRISTIAN MISSIONS AND NATIONALIST GRIEVANCES

To the extent that conversion produced in the African a genuine loyalty and devotion to the Christian ethic and the Christian Church, the missionaries contributed to political moderation and to a concentration of interests upon otherworldly matters.[42] It was among the apostates, the near-converts, and the many Africans exposed but unconverted to Christianity, especially through the educational system, that disillusionment was bitter and politically consequential. And the significant fact about the latter category was not that the number of Christian souls was reduced, but that the disaffected Africans had been detached from their traditional culture and, lacking Christianity as a focus for their interests and loyalty, were adrift and ripe for an integrating ideology. Thus it is the failure rather than the achievement of missionary endeavor that has special relevance.

Most of the Africans who came under the influence of missionaries were already acutely conscious of the superiority of European technology. Because they were technologically superior, Europeans came to Africa convinced of white supremacy in all things, and in the early phase many Africans accepted the same idea. The missionaries in Africa fostered this belief to the point that E. D. Morel, one of their most pungent critics, accused them of being, unwittingly, the strongest allies of the "damned nigger" school: "It is from them in the main that has grown up the conviction . . . that nothing in the structure of African social life is worth preserving; that everything, indeed, is bad and corrupt, and must be pulled down—tribal systems, communal tenure, and marriage laws."[43]

Africans were ultimately bound to protest or revolt against several aspects of the early missionary approach. In the first place, the attitude of many missionaries toward African customs and institutions tended to perpetuate—long after more thoughtful and knowledgeable observers had abandoned them—such ethno-centric preconceptions as that the Africans had no history, no culture, and little virtue. One has only to observe recent Holly-wood motion pictures with an African theme to grasp the tenacity of distorted, pejorative, and condescending viewpoints. The real importance of these self-perpetuating myths is not what the out-side world continued to believe, but what the denial of a history or a culture did to the pride of the thoughtful African. The pas-sionate quest for a history and the glorification of African culture later undertaken by race-conscious nationalists were a direct re-sponse to what they felt had been a deliberate deception on the part of a missionary-government conspiracy—a subtle imperial technique to make Africans meek, passive, ashamed, and, above all, respectful. This reaction indiscriminately affected Christian-ity, the doctrine of white superiority, and ultimately colonial rule.

Some missionaries permitted their preconceptions regarding the inferiority of African culture to influence their personal deal-ings with individual Africans. As early as 1876, Blyden referred to this tendency:

> Coming to the coast under such teaching [the idea of African inferiority] they are induced to adopt a method of dealing with the natives, and to maintain a demeanour which, in spite of their educational and other services, inspire the people among whom they labour with feelings of impatience, if not of dislike.[44]

Condescension and arrogance, coupled with a paternalism that, however well meant, implied inferiority, added fuel to the fire of resentment and protest being kindled in the souls of Africans.

Nigerians ultimately protested against not only the missionary view of their inferiority, based on their alleged lack of history and culture, but also against the pretensions of white virtuousness. As Blyden put it:

> . . . from the time of the discovery of the Negro country by the Portuguese to the present, Europe has sent to the coast as traders some of its vilest characters. . . . The intelligent natives of the interior with whom we have conversed in our travels between Sierra Leone and the head-waters of the Niger, look, with hardly an exception, upon the religion and books of the white man as

intended not to teach men the way to heaven, but how to become rich and great in this world.[45]

The Nigerian had been taught that the European race was superior because it was Christian; hence he was acutely conscious and critical of any un-Christian behavior by a white man. Isolated deviants could be overlooked, but when many members of the white community in Nigeria appeared indifferent to the precepts of Christianity, the Nigerian was not only disenchanted but annoyed at being duped by humbuggery and a holier-than-thou attitude. As one nationalist newspaper editorialized: ". . . Europeans came to Africa with Christ and the gospel. It appears that on their way back they left both there. The gospel must be taken back to Europe. Europe must be re-educated, . . . re-civilized. Europe needs African evangelists." [46] The Nigerian's disaffection was given additional support by Nigerian students returning from Europe or America with reports on the character and behavior of the ordinary white man. His disillusionment tended to make him cynical and critical of all white pretensions, and thereby contributed to the rapid collapse of the doctrine of white superiority. Moreover, as Blyden suggested, it encouraged a materialistic attitude and a belief that the real secret of European strength and success was not the Bible, but exploitative skill. This shift in attitude had political overtones; emulation of the white man's religion would lead to moderation, humility, and passivity, whereas emulation of the European's exploitative skill would inevitably challenge the white man's privileged position.

The Nigerian reacted not only against the attitudes of missionaries, but also against their aim of total Europeanization, especially when the abandonment of many meaningful customs and institutions was made a precondition for entry into the Kingdom of God. The most tenacious and contentious of these customs was polygyny, over which a bitter battle was waged from the beginning of missionary activity. Most articulate Africans, anthropologists, administrators, and liberal clergymen were highly critical of the obdurate position of the missionary societies, but without avail.[47] The uncompromising attitude of Christian missionaries regarding polygyny and other African customs was one reason for the wide appeal and success of Islam in southern Nigeria. On the organizational side it was the precipitating factor in the secession and formation of syncretistic African churches, and in the awakening of a cultural and racial consciousness. A leading Nigerian Christian stated:

> . . . Christ and Western Civilization came together; no one could distinguish one from the other. Collar and ties, or the Bible. The early native Christians were known by their western dresses. Now it is dawning upon the African of today that he can have one without the other. This is the tremendous significance of this stage of our progress. . . . What is demanded today is Christianity without the system that has been built around it in the West.[48]

The same sentiment had been expressed by leading African Christians, as well as by such European sympathizers as E. D. Morel and Mary Kingsley, from the latter part of the nineteenth century on. And, as previously noted, it emerged as a prominent theme in the replanning of missionary strategy during the interwar years.

A final object of Nigerian protest was the link that existed or, just as important, was believed by the Nigerian to exist between Christian missions and the imperial and colonial governments. To the unsophisticated the tie was axiomatic, since both the missionary and the administrator were white men. Missionaries were the victims of several early manifestations of an instinctively hostile resentment against the white man's intrusion. In many areas the missionary was in fact supported by government military power. The Western-educated Nigerian, however, suspected a more insidious motive. As a noted Christian nationalist put it:

> The word "Christ" has always been identified here with the British Empire . . . [and] the general feelings are that the Missionaries have been the front troops of the Government to soften the hearts of the people and while people look at the Cross white men gather the riches of the land.[49]

The suspicion of a missionary-government conspiracy was quite common, even though three of the largest missions in Nigeria were non-British (the American Baptist Mission, the Catholic Mission, and the Canadian Sudan Interior Mission), and many white Christian leaders in the United Kingdom and elsewhere had supported nationalist sentiment and activity, both directly and indirectly.

Aside from the obvious identity of color, culture, and living standards, other factors helped to foster such a suspicion. Was not the monarch of England head of the Anglican Communion? Moreover, a key clause in most of the original protectorate treaties between the traditional authorities of southern Nigeria and the representatives of the British Crown was: "All white Ministers of the Christian Religion shall be permitted to exercise their calling within the territories of the aforesaid King and Chiefs, who hereby guarantee to them full protection." [50] Beginning in the early 1930's, mission schools came increasingly under the control of the Nigerian government, and as a result the inadequacies and failures of the educational system—the most deeply felt of all nationalist grievances—were blamed upon the missions and the government as partners in repression.[51]

To the Nigerian nationalist, however, the most persuasive factor was the silence of missionaries on such subjects as discrimination, inequality, exploitation, denial of opportunity, and all the other features characteristic of alien rule. Nigerians considered these evils patently un-Christian and contrary to missionary teachings. They were not convinced by the argument that open opposition to or criticism of the government by missionaries might have meant the curtailment of mission activities and possibly the expulsion of missionaries from Nigeria. Missionaries were obliged to accept the stigma of being allies of imperialism because they could not be open critics; they depended upon colonial governments for leases of land and for financial subsidies for their educational activities. The suspicion of collusion was strengthened when, in the early postwar period, certain missionaries openly condemned "Zikist nationalism" in their sermons; this approach facilitated the nationalist effort to spread the notion that missionaries were opposed to African freedom.

From the standpoint of racial and political awakening, the African view of missionary-government relations was significant because it strengthened the Nigerian's conviction that all white men were allied in some way against Africans, and that even if he became a Christian his worldly status of economic and political subordination would not be improved. The Nigerian's viewpoint reinforced his feeling of identity with other Nigerians, and made the struggle for equality and emancipation appear to be one of all black against all white, rather than of Christians of all races against non-Christians. He became increasingly cynical and suspicious of the motives behind white endeavors, even those of a charitable and humanitarian nature. In short, irrespective of its basis and justification, the Nigerian attitude was of crucial psychological significance in predisposing many Christianized natives toward racial and nationalist sentiment and activity.

The absence of open criticism of the government did not necessarily indicate missionary silence or indifference. In large measure it simply reflected the widely held concept of the proper role of the missionary vis-à-vis political matters, most characteristically expressed by J. Merle Davis in his *Modern Industry and the African:*

> The missionary, through his intimate contact with the people, is in a favourable position for observing the effect of Government measures on Native life, and may often with advantage call the attention of the Administrator to possible undesirable effects of such measures as well as to breaches of the law and the miscarriage of justice. Before taking any such action, however, the missionary should be sure of the accuracy of his facts, should be fully informed of the laws relating to the matter in question, and should endeavour to understand the difficulty which confronts the official in administering them. The missionary should never appeal to outside public opinion for the righting of what he considers to be a public wrong until he has first brought the matter privately to the attention of the responsible authorities and exhausted every means of inducing them to set matters right.[52]

Thus missionaries, though admonished not to criticize government openly and certainly not to challenge the imperial connection, did have the right and the duty to advise the government regarding injustices and undesirable policies. Indeed, a substantial body of evidence suggests that, within a rather narrow framework, missionaries in Nigeria were vigorous critics on behalf of the African, both behind the scenes and on government advisory committees. But as a rule their mild prodding fell far short of the uncompromising frontal assault upon government and imperialism which nationalists demanded of their supporters.

In at least two respects Christian agencies have been positive and open in their encouragement and sponsorship of nationalism. First, certain missionaries and Christian leaders and groups in the United Kingdom and in the United States had a strong pro-African orientation. Leading figures like the late Reverend J. H. Harris, the Reverend Reginald Sorenson (long-time patron of the West African Students' Union), and the Reverend Michael Scott are examples. Christian groups in both countries have been very active in encouraging and sponsoring African students, and in arranging discussion groups and forums in which the students could voice their political aspirations. In many instances such groups, or prominent individuals in them, have openly espoused the demands of the Africans for whom they were hosts. Indeed, the host function of Christian groups and individual Christian spokesmen in the two countries has been a significant element in the development of Nigerian nationalism. More conservative or more cautious Christians might have considered such activity as premature or improper, or even "left-wing"; nevertheless, it is a strand in the Christian-missionary influence which has been underestimated, particularly by the nationalists themselves.[53]

Second, certain more formal actions of Christian agencies supported what might broadly be interpreted as the African cause. Examples are resolutions adopted annually by the Foreign Missions Conference of North America, pronouncements from the Vatican and by the Archbishop of Canterbury, and occasional statements of the Conference of Missionary Societies in Great Britain and Ireland and of the British Council of Churches. In 1945 the latter two agencies were particularly strong in their criticism of discrimination and denial of opportunities. They agreed in a public declaration that "the Conference of Missionary Societies . . . is deeply thankful for the repeated affirmation of responsible statesmen of the United Nations that there must be full freedom of opportunity for all the peoples of the world, without discrimination on racial grounds."[54] Such formal pronouncements were occasionally the product of pressures from missionaries in the field. Although they did not challenge alien rule directly, they served to legitimize nationalist ideals at the highest level.

In general, the public position of Christian agencies on political matters has been determined by their appraisal of the political situation and of the strength and direction of political forces. They readily accommodated themselves to the changed political situation once nationalism had "caught on" and was clearly the "wave of the future." This could be interpreted by nationalists as simple opportunism; but it could also be interpreted as a response to changes in the manifest desires and capacities of the Nigerian peoples. In any event, in 1951, when nationalists acquired substantial control over the government, the Archbishop of Canterbury personally inaugurated the Ecclesiastical Province of West Africa, successor to the missionary dioceses of the colonial period, and thereby placed Nigeria and the other territories of British West Africa on the same level, within the Anglican Communion, as the white dominions and the new states of India, Burma, and Ceylon. In the same year Father Slattery, the energetic editor of the *Nigerian Catholic Herald,* established a policy of supporting, in editorials and news articles, the broad objectives of the nationalist movement. These dramatic changes suggest that Christian agencies, though not in the vanguard of the movement, have not been obstructive or obdurate in accepting nationalism and the political leadership produced by it.

Despite nationalist grievances regarding certain features of missionary enterprise, there is evidence to suggest that in the long run the total missionary contribution to Nigeria will be placed in its proper perspective by the nationalists themselves. As the Honorable Dennis Osadebay, founder of the Ibo State Union and a leader of the National Council of Nigeria and the Cameroons, has written:

> . . . the missionary has made the African soil fertile for the growth of imperialism . . . [but] he has equally helped to lay the foundations for the present spirit of nationalism. . . . When African historians come to write their own account of the adventure of Africa with imperialism, they will write of the missionaries as the greatest friends the African had.[55]

CHAPTER 5

Western Education

One of the most revolutionary influences operative in Nigeria since the beginning of the European intrusion has been Western education.[1] Although this influence was felt directly by only a small minority of the population before 1951, its broad scope, systematic nature, and continuity during the crucial formative years made it far more effective and penetrating than the more superficial economic and social aspects of culture contact.

From the very beginning education was a virtual monopoly of the Christian missionary societies:

> To all intents and purposes the school is the Church. Right away in the bush or in the forest the two are one, and the village teacher is also the village evangelist. An appreciation of this fact is cardinal in all considerations of African education.[2]

Until 1898 all education was under the direct control of missionaries. As late as 1942 they controlled 99 per cent of the schools, and more than 97 per cent of the students in Nigeria were enrolled in mission schools. By 1945 there were comparatively few literate Nigerians who had not received all or part of their education in mission schools.[3]

THE SOCIAL AND POLITICAL CONSEQUENCES
OF WESTERN EDUCATION

From the standpoint of acculturation, the real significance of the missionary monopoly over education lay in the evangelical approach of mission schools. The mission school was an instrument, a very powerful instrument, for the rapid Christianization (and hence Europeanization) of the youth of Nigeria. It was an institution in which the full pressure of accultural influence was applied. The schools taught young Nigerians to aspire to the virtues of white Christian civilization. They consciously encouraged the emulation of European culture, and unwittingly fostered disdainful feelings toward the "heathen" brothers of their students. Consistent with their preconceptions regarding African culture, the missionaries tended to ignore "African" forms of education because they considered them either evil or nonexistent. The African was treated as a *tabula rasa* upon which could be written a completely new civilization.[4]

The content of Western education, which was, of course, largely but not wholly determined by the missionary motive, was equally significant. The extensive use of the English language in school curricula, made necessary by Nigeria's linguistic diversity, was a decisive contribution to acculturation. From the very beginning missionaries found the vernacular languages useful vehicles for the propagation of the gospel. Despite the missionaries' commendable efforts to develop orthographies and systems of writing, however, these languages had serious limitations as media for formal, and particularly for higher, instruction.[5] As a consequence, they were used only in the first stages of elementary education. All instruction at higher levels was in English. The Nigerian who acquired a knowledge of English had access to a vast new world of literature and of ideas, and his contact with it awakened new aspirations, quickened the urge toward emulation, and provided the notions and the medium for the expression of grievances. Moreover, the English language (and its corrupted form, pidgin English) served as a lingua franca for communication among the educated elements of all tribes, a bond of decisive importance in the development of a Pan-Nigerian, or even a regional, nationalist movement.

With a few notable exceptions, education in Nigeria was based on learning to read, write, and calculate in the English language. Later additions to the curriculum were British Empire history and European geography, plus a few practical subjects such as gardening, sanitation, and personal hygiene. As African history was considered either nonexistent or unimportant, the great men who were studied in the schools were the kings of England and the early white empire builders who came to Nigeria with a new and superior civilization. The great events and historical developments that were taught were European and colonial wars of pacification, the evolution of the British constitution, and the growth of the British Empire. In literature, Shakespeare and the Bible held the stage. Even today, it is not uncommon to find a semieducated Nigerian working as a steward who can name the principal English cities, quote the Bible, and recite Hamlet, but who has little knowledge of the geography, the proverbs and folk tales, or the prominent leaders and outstanding events in the history of his own country.[6]

The result of this concentrated and institutionalized indoctrination was the creation of a new class. Conversion to Christianity, knowledge of and preference for English, imitation of European behavior, and postschool employment in an urban milieu all helped to isolate the educated African from his traditional environment. Moreover, there was an inherent contradiction between the role expected of the young Nigerian in accordance with tradition and custom, and the role expected of him as a result of his Western education. Westermann has emphasized that indigenous education focused attention on the group and not on the individual. "The child is not regarded as a developing personality, but as a member of the group . . . 'birth fixes for life the social status of each individual.'"[7] The European educational ideal placed primary stress upon the individual as an autonomous personality. The resulting incompatibility between African tribal life and Western education made reintegration into the tribal community very difficult.

Western education did not merely facilitate the emergence of a separate class; it endowed the individuals in that class with the knowledge and skills, the ambitions and aspirations, that enabled them to challenge the Nigerian colonial government and ultimately to wrest control over the central political power from it. By the latter achievement the Western-educated elements placed themselves above the traditional African authorities in the new Nigerian political system. Thus, within the short span of two generations, Western education made possible a nearly complete reversal in the status of Nigerian political leaders. The rapidity of upward mobility in this revolutionary transformation is possibly unparalleled in history.

This status reversal is particularly striking in that a substantial number of Western-educated Nigerians were drawn from the lower strata (frequently the slave class) of traditional society. Indeed, many of Nigeria's most prominent political leaders are but one generation removed from the most humble status. Western education was therefore an instrument by which many from the lowest strata in traditional societies were catapulted into the highest strata in the modern territorial system. The causal link between Western education and rapid restratification is thus apparent.

One of the most burning issues in the development of Nigerian nationalism was the qualitative and quantitative inadequacy of Western education. As to content, the schools equipped the African with little more than an elementary knowledge of the English language for an economic future in which a senior clerkship was the upper limit of his permissible advancement. In terms of need and desire, there were hundreds of candidates for every school vacancy.[8] Nigerian resentment over British educational policy was one of the principal stimulants for later organizational activity, according to one nationalist:

> Leaders of thought began first to agitate for a change in educational policy, but unfortunately the Government paid little heed. Consequently, to achieve their ends these political leaders turned their attention to an intellectual fight for political emancipation which would enable the country to rectify the mistakes made in education by the British Government in Nigeria.[9]

But Nigerians were not alone in their dissatisfaction over the educational system. The "detribalizing" and grievance-producing effects of educational policy were discussed and criticized by Europeans in and out of Nigeria for nearly a century. It is remarkable that such criticism had so little impact upon government and missionary educational activity in Nigeria. Most of the criticism centered on the literary and academic shortcomings of the curriculum. Critics advocated a shift from the Anglicizing literary training, which merely produced a disaffected clerk class, to a more practical education which would teach the vernacular, agriculture, tribal loyalty, handicrafts, religion, and domestic and industrial skills. At the core of the new concept of education was the belief that the African should be educated "along his own lines." This, of course, was meant to be the educational aspect of the policy of indirect rule. Motives varied among the critics. Some of them feared the growth of a minority of potential agitators who would stir up political consciousness just as their Anglicized counterparts had done in India; [10] others—Afrophiles, anthropologists, and professional educators—were troubled less about the ultimate political consequences of a literary education than about its effect upon the psychological and social well-being of the African. [11]

As early as 1847, the Privy Council's Committee on Education recommended the establishment of industrial day schools and model farm schools for the purpose of "securing better conditions of life and the development of the African as a peasant on the land." [12] This first statement on African education proved to be nothing more than a pious aspiration, for no steps were taken to formulate an imperial policy until 1925. In that year the Advisory Committee on Native Education, established in 1923, published a comprehensive statement of imperial policy. It emphasized the need for greater government activity in education, closer co-operation with missionary societies, expanded technical and vocational training, maximum use of the vernacular, and acceptance and utilization of useful and healthy elements in the traditional culture. The aim of education was "to raise the standard alike of character and efficiency of the bulk of the people." [13]

In 1935 the committee published a detailed statement of policy regarding the education of the African rural masses, which expanded the ideas stated in the 1925 memorandum. It advocated a clear recognition of the intimate connection between educational and economic policy, and stressed the need for education in rural communities, because "the basis of African life is, and is likely to remain, agricultural." [14] Another feature of the post-1925 policy of the Colonial Office was the endeavor to link education with the system of indirect rule: ". . . education should strengthen the feeling of responsibility to the tribal community." Religion was emphasized in the statement that "the greatest importance must . . . be attached to religious teaching and moral instruction," which should be accorded "equal standing with secular subjects." [15]

It was in Protestant missionary circles, however, that self-criticism was most pronounced. The 1920's were a period of ferment in European attitudes regarding the evangelization and education of the African. After much soul-searching, missionary leaders recommended changes in the school curricula. In 1920 a commission sponsored by the Phelps-Stokes Fund and the Foreign Mission Societies of North America visited Nigeria and strongly urged the development of teaching in simple industries and agriculture.[16] In 1923 the Conference of Missionary Societies of Great Britain and Ireland successfully memorialized the Colonial Office to establish the Advisory Committee on Native Education. Prominent missionary leaders were the original sponsors of the International Institute of African Languages and Cultures, established in 1926. In the same year the International Le Zoute Conference of Protestant Missionary Societies recommended that "the curriculum of all types of schools should be drawn up with complete awareness of the life of the community. . . . Agriculture and industry should be taught in the classroom as well as practised in the field and workshop." [17]

Government officials in Nigeria also frequently expressed dissatisfaction with the educational system. In 1900 the Lagos Board of Education resolved, on the recommendation of Governor Sir William MacGregor, that

> It is not possible for our schools to produce really good results unless we are less apathetic about education and unless we . . . provide a comprehensive scheme of public instruction, which shall not only supply the wants of a clerkly class, but shall also prepare youth for husbandry and handicrafts.[18]

In a remarkable address in 1920, Sir Hugh Clifford admonished the Nigerian Council that "the curricula in use in the government and in the assisted schools . . . require to be very considerably revised." [19] In 1926 the director of education stated that the recommendation of the Lagos Board in 1900 was still applicable. In the same year the Board of Education expressed the belief that "not only should it be possible to devise a system of education which will fit students for life in the farm but the pressing need of artisans calls for the organization of classes for apprentices in workshops." [20] As late as 1942, Governor Bourdillon confessed:

> There is no doubt that the type of education provided in the past, especially in the elementary and primary schools, has been too academic. . . . The first consideration is to provide elementary education in the villages with a strong rural bias.[21]

Despite protracted criticism and repeated resolutions of new purpose, however, only a beginning was made before World War II in substituting a rural and vocational emphasis for the academic and literary bias in Nigerian school curricula.[22]

EDUCATION AND NATIONALIST GRIEVANCES

Most Western-educated Nigerians were critical of school curricula, but they were not united in their views as to what the purpose of education ought to be. The division was along much the same lines as the well-known differences between the views of two American Negro leaders: Booker T. Washington, who advocated the agricultural and vocational training of the masses, and Dr. W. E. B. Du Bois, who believed that education should first of all deal with the "talented tenth." [23] The minority of educated Nigerian critics inclined toward the Booker T. Washington school of thought. They resented the de-Africanizing tendencies of an exclusively Christian-European curriculum; and they lamented the lack of agricultural and handicraft training which had produced the cult of the detribalized clerk. In a sense they represented the instinctive cultural reaction of Africans to the disorganizing implications of European education, and to that extent even their protest was symbolic of a cultural awakening. They might also be categorized as the "accommodationists" among the westernized minority.

While sharing some of the views of this minority, especially its resentment over the deprecation of African culture, the majority of educated Nigerians were inclined toward Du Bois's "talented tenth" or elitist view. They also were dissatisfied with the quality of Nigerian education, but for reasons quite different from those of European critics. Their reasons are best summed up in their oft-repeated query: "Are we always to be 'hewers of wood and draw-

119

ers of water?' " [24] They were not impressed with the arguments of European Afrophiles or Christian educationalists, or even of their American Negro brethren, for an increasing rural, tribalistic, vocational, vernacular, and moral bias in Nigerian educational curricula. They felt that agricultural training would merely perpetuate the status of "hewers of wood and drawers of water" against which they were revolting. Education for citizenship in and responsibility toward the old tribal community seemed unreal, if not diversionary from a broader racial or national sentiment. Vocational training in such skills as carpentry, tailoring, and African handicrafts was not their concept of technical education, because it too would perpetuate an employment system wherein the African worker was subject to the European master. Use of the vernacular in education, gratifying though it might be to the cultural consciousness of Africans, smacked too much of a conscious effort to deprive them of an instrument of emancipation from a subordinate status. Finally, the monotonous repetition by missionaries and officials of the need for more and more "moral," "character," and "spiritual" training was to these critics a condescending holier-than-thou attitude which stung their pride and reinforced their growing conviction that the government and the missionaries were joined in an unholy alliance aimed at educational repression.

One of the major grievances of most educated Nigerians was not that Western education was literary in character, but that there was not enough of it. They wanted neither a glorified system of African education, nor European-sponsored schemes for educating them along their own lines. As long as their political and social status was one of inferiority they believed that education "along their own lines" would only reinforce that inferiority.

The school-leaving certificate, and consequently examination standards and the curriculum, of Nigerian secondary schools had been modeled after those of English grammar schools. When the government began to take a more active interest in education in the 1930's, and suggested that the curriculum be based on an African rather than an English standard, educated Nigerians protested strongly. They had three reasons for opposing the recommended alteration. The first and most obvious reason was that they did not like the rural, tribal, vocational, vernacular, and moral instruction that the government intended to substitute. Secondly, parity of examination standards had become highly symbolical. As a group these Nigerians aspired to European standards, and the English school certificate represented at least one area where nominal equality had been achieved. Finally, the possession of the certificate was a prerequisite not only for employment in Nigeria, but also for entry into universities abroad. Changing the curriculum and abolishing the certificate implied retrogression and greater frustration. Only complete and unadulterated Western education would satisfy their material and psychological aspirations.

The transcendent grievance of educated Nigerians, however, centered about their unsatisfied quest for higher education. They wanted an educational system that would train them to assume positions in the professions, in the technical and administrative branches of the civil service, and in commercial, industrial, and agricultural enterprise on the basis of absolute equality with the white man.

Before 1945 most educated Africans would probably have agreed with the British argument that the establishment of self-government in Nigeria depended upon the quality and number of Nigerians professionally equipped to assume positions of responsible leadership. But when British officialdom, in both London and Lagos, seemed unwilling or unable to reform the educational system or create educational opportunities for Africans, educated Nigerians became more and more convinced that the government was deliberately trying to keep them from qualifying for such positions. Indeed, one of the important motivations for the rise and growth of Nigerian nationalism was frustration among the educated classes, for the British government, while repeatedly affirming its policy of elevating qualified Nigerians to responsible "European" positions, at the same time did not, according to the African view, provide the necessary opportunities.

The memorandum on education policy (1925) had stated that the aims of education "must include the raising up of capable, trustworthy, public-spirited leaders of the people, belonging to their own race." [25] In 1936 the Advisory Committee on Native Education presented its views on higher education in Africa. Warning of the undesirability of increasing the number of Afri-

121

cans studying overseas in Europe and America, it urged the elevation of institutions in Africa to the university level. It admitted that such a program would be costly, but argued that "the development of education and the demand for it necessitate the facing of the situation if years of strain and the alienation of enlightened native opinion are to be avoided." [26] A more persuasive argument, stemming from self-interest, was that educational development in Africa would save the government money, since it would permit the replacement of costly European officers in the civil service by African officers. The committee further suggested that courses in medicine, engineering, agriculture, veterinary work, commerce, and applied sciences be given priority, although it did not oppose the granting of a liberal arts degree. Six years later, in 1942, the Secretary of State for the Colonies appointed a commission to make recommendations for future university development in British West Africa. The commission's report, presented to Parliament in June, 1945, became the basis for significant postwar developments in higher education in Nigeria.

Officialdom in Nigeria, however, was indifferent if not opposed to higher education for Nigerians. When the late Dr. Edward Blyden visited Nigeria in 1896 he memorialized the governor to assist in the establishment of a training college and industrial institute in Lagos. The governor, agreeing that it was highly undesirable for African youth to be educated in Europe, pointed out that

> . . . the young African educated in Europe imbibes ideas which, instead of assisting him in after life, tend rather to make him dissatisfied with his surroundings when he returns to his country and really unfit him for the part he is destined to take in his natural sphere.[27]

Blyden's project was never realized, mainly because of lack of financial support by both the government and African leaders. Thirty years later, in 1926, the Union of Students of African Descent, and African students at universities in the United Kingdom, petitioned the Secretary of State for the Colonies to award two annual government scholarships (one for study in the United Kingdom, the other for study in Africa) to eligible Africans in each colony.[28] Officialdom in Lagos, though unattracted by the idea of government scholarships for study at British universities, looked more favorably upon scholarships at Fourah Bay and Achimota colleges in Sierra Leone and Ghana (then the Gold Coast). In the meantime, however, plans for higher education in Nigeria were crystallizing.

Higher education in Nigeria really began with the opening of a medical school in 1930. Four years later the government formally opened Yaba Higher College. Unlike Fourah Bay College in Sierra Leone, neither of these institutions was affiliated with an English university; hence their examination standards and diplomas were Nigerian, not European. Although this governmental attempt to provide advanced educational opportunities for Nigerians was considered "commendably bold . . . in the prevailing circumstances of finance and the standard of secondary school education," [29] it did very little to assuage the grievances of the rapidly increasing educated class. In the first place, educated Nigerians resented the inferiority implicit in the fact that only a Nigerian diploma was obtainable. This meant that university-educated persons, in Nigeria and elsewhere, would look down upon graduates of these schools as a semieducated lesser breed. Second, admission to the two Nigerian institutions was restricted in two respects. The number of openings was limited to contemplated vacancies in government technical departments. Only 18 students were admitted in 1934, and in the following ten-year period the highest entry figure for one year was 36, whereas about 150 candidates applied for admission each year. Moreover, most candidates were selected from among the graduates of only a few—mainly government schools—of the thirty-four secondary schools in Nigeria. Third, those who were admitted had little or no freedom to choose their professions; they were usually assigned to courses according to government needs rather than according to their own preferences and aptitudes. Fourth, there was little visible evidence before World War II that completion of the courses would give graduates the status they felt higher education should bestow. Of the first 181 graduates only 38 became assistant medical, agricultural, and forestry officers; 19 were appointed as engineers and 6 as surveyors in the Public Works and Survey departments; the rest were ab-

sorbed into educational services, or into technical and administrative services as subordinate technicians and clerks.[30] Finally,
the training was predominantly vocational. No Nigerian at Yaba
was instructed in subjects like public administration and economics, which would qualify him to enter the administrative
service. In short, even though the opening of these two schools
was a step in the right direction, it was not a full and complete
step, and it did not impress educated Nigerians as an adequate
government effort.

During the late 1930's, dissatisfaction with Yaba increased and
agitation for overseas education became more intense. Finally, in
1937, the Nigerian government, reversing its long-standing opposition to education abroad, inaugurated a program of granting
scholarships for study in the United Kingdom. By 1945 a total
of 69 awards had been made, but only 7 of the recipients had
returned to Nigeria. Furthermore, the scholarships did not cover
the fields of study in which Nigerians were most interested. Of
the 193 Nigerian students in the United Kingdom in 1945—44
of them were government scholars—nearly two-thirds were pursuing programs of study for which few awards had been made: [31]

Subject	Private students	Government scholars
Law	55	2
Medicine	51	0
Engineering	12	3

Thus, even the pre-1945 scholarship program of the government
did not appreciably relieve the grievances of educated Nigerians.
They not only considered it grossly inadequate, but also felt that
it was so administered as to prevent Nigerians from entering
really responsible positions in the professions and the administration.

Although it is true that most educated Nigerians leaned toward
the Du Bois "talented tenth" concept of education and were dissatisfied with the quality and quantity of education available
to them as a group, yet they were acutely aware of the strong
desire of the unsophisticated masses for education. The latter
believed that Western education, and especially a knowledge
of the English language, would equip them with the techniques
and skills essential for the improvement of personal status in

the emergent economic and social structure. The higher living standards of their educated brothers offered positive proof of this. In this personal sense it was not the desire for education qua education, but rather the aspiration for knowledge essential for obtaining a salaried job. Africans also had a strong conviction that the real secret of the white man's strength and superiority was not his religion, but his education. Thus, in the new scale of values, education was not simply a desirable thing in itself, like medical services or good roads, but the absolute precondition for political, economic, and social emancipation of the race. As a Nigerian editor wrote: "Through education Japan has become the Britain of the East . . . and it is through education that we Africans can hope to make sure our ultimate Redemption." [32]

Educated Nigerians who aspired to leadership recognized, as the British government in Nigeria apparently did not, how the aspiration for education had become a powerful political force. Hence the educated elite in Nigeria, as in India, took the lead in insisting upon dramatic progress in mass education. The idea of compulsory, universal free education was a familiar theme in campaign oratory, in debates by Nigerian members in the Legislative Council, and in the Nigerian press. The apparent indifference of the government made it vulnerable to the charge that it was pursuing a deliberate policy of keeping the African down. It was the articulation of this grievance, fancied or real, which helped to link the educated Nigerian to his unsophisticated but emulative brethren. [33]

Despite the commendably far-sighted policy pronouncements of the Colonial Office Advisory Committee in the period 1925–1935, and its own statement of aims in 1930, the Nigerian government consistently treated education as a low-priority item in its annual estimates, as shown in table 13. It will be noted that between 1929 and 1939 there was no increase in the percentage of Nigerian revenue allocated to education. In 1938 the government-appointed Board of Education for the Colony and Southern Provinces pointed out that "this country is in the invidious position of providing fewer opportunities in regard to elementary education than any other British possession in Africa." [34] It emphasized that the development of a more practical curriculum, which would add facilities for technical and agricultural education, could not be undertaken without additional expenditure, and recommended that the government endeavor to raise additional revenue "to meet a desperate situation." [35]

TABLE 13

EXPENDITURE FOR EDUCATION IN NIGERIA
(SELECTED YEARS, 1877–1952)

Year	Expenditure for education	Total expenditure	Percentage of total expenditure
1877–1882	£ 200	*	*
1896	2,000	*	*
1918	45,747	£ 3,459,774	1.0
1923	100,063	6,509,244	1.5
1925	116,301	6,136,487	1.8
1929	263,457	6,045,621	4.3
1933	237,732	6,898,816	3.3
1936	231,983	6,585,458	3.5
1939	282,820	6,576,835	4.3
1951–1952	8,324,000	49,131,000	16.9

* Exact figures not known.
Sources: *Annual Report,* Department of Education, 1926 (Lagos: Government Printer, 1927), p. 4; *Nigeria Handbook, 1926* (Lagos: Government Printer, 1927); *Nigeria Handbook, 1936* (Lagos: Government Printer, 1937), p. 164; *The Economic Development of Nigeria,* International Bank for Reconstruction and Development (Baltimore: 1955), pp. 626–633.

Despite this urgent advice, Nigerian official thought regarding educational development remained distinctly conservative. At the outbreak of World War II only 12 per cent of the Nigerian children of school age (350,000 out of 3,000,000) were receiving instruction.[36] In a wartime despatch Governor Bourdillon proposed to the Secretary of State for the Colonies a postwar expansion scheme to provide for the education of an additional 176,000 over a ten-year period, although the population increase in Nigeria during that same period would be 4 per cent. This would have meant that in ten years after the end of the war the number of Nigerian children in school would be raised only by approximately 6 per cent. The governor apologized for the modesty of his proposal, and gave the following reason:

. . . a low percentage of expenditure on social services is inevitable in a poor country like Nigeria, in which essential expenditure on administration and security, and on the service of the public debt, must absorb an unduly large percentage of the available revenue.[37]

In commenting on this proposal the Advisory Committee on Education in the Colonies stated: ". . . the scheme outlined in the despatch hardly touches the fringe of the educational problem. It follows that the present trend of events demands a more radical treatment on a far wider front." [38]

The government's prewar neglect of education created several other grievances which eventually became significant in the growth of racial and nationalist sentiment. A highly influential, and numerically by far the most important, element of the educated classes—the mission teachers—were painfully and directly affected. During the depression these teachers, who by 1939 numbered more than 10,000, were obliged to accept a 15 per cent salary reduction. Again, in 1936 the government reassessed its allocation of revenue to mission schools and made a "short payment" of 14.5 per cent in the grants-in-aid for the period 1936–1938. The teachers in one mission school were so aggrieved that they went out on strike, an unprecedented step in Nigeria. During the late 1930's and early 1940's additional threatened or actual salary cuts caused a steady flow of these trained, experienced mission teachers into other occupations. The resulting personal inconvenience and disorganization created deep bitterness toward both the missionary societies and the Nigerian government. It is therefore not surprising to find that some of the most active nationalists were former teachers of the prewar period.

Another important group critical of the government's educational policy consisted of individuals and groups who on their own initiative had established private schools, and either were forced to close or were refused grants-in-aid because their standards were below those prescribed by educational ordinances. They alleged that government standards were stifling educational development, and that the disinclination to support their schools was a contradiction of the officially stated policy of encouraging self-help. This resentment was intensified later when the plans of tribal unions and native administrations to open their own secondary schools or to award scholarships for study at universities abroad did not receive government encouragement. Although such resentment is understandable, nevertheless there is no lack of evidence that the government encouraged private self-help educational projects when the sponsors were willing to meet established standards. Only a few sponsors could meet the standards, however, and the general feeling was that the stringency of government control and supervision over such projects implied a policy of educational limitation.[39]

A third group disaffected by the prewar educational system consisted of unemployed "Standard VI Boys" unable to find jobs in urban centers. Before the number of secondary schools was increased in 1930, possession of the primary school certificate (Standard VI) was the main prerequisite for a clerkship in one of the business firms or with the government. After a higher level of education was made available in the early 1930's, these two employing agencies raised their standards and ultimately made the Cambridge Certificate (secondary school diploma) the minimum qualification for a clerk's job. Thus primary education automatically lost its instrumental value, except for those who were financially able to continue their studies. During the decade preceding 1942, more than 300,000 students entered the primary schools of Nigeria, yet even in that year the secondary schools could absorb less than 2,000.[40]

Despite this revolutionary development in the supply-demand situation, the literary emphasis in the primary schools persisted, and the boys leaving them continued to gravitate to urban centers where the prospect of employment was small. They had gone to school with the aspiration to become clerks; their parents, mainly out of self-interest, had made sacrifices so that they could achieve that status; and the primary schools had given them the type of education which theretofore had been appropriate for a clerkship. Yet they found themselves in increasing numbers either unemployed or working as laborers in the townships, obliged to live off their more affluent "brothers." Some of them reluctantly returned to their villages and worked as farm hands—a distasteful if not an ignoble fate. These economically insecure and unintegrated "Standard VI Boys" formed the bulk of that group contemptuously referred to by European observers as "semieducated Africans." It was the members of this group who, for self-evident reasons, were increasingly attracted to nationalist ideas and antiwhite sentiment, and who ultimately provided the mass base for the postwar nationalist movement.

The fact that education was not free, as it was in French and Belgian colonies, was an additional source of grievance. Tuition and board in secondary schools in the Southern Provinces averaged about £15 per year, and in primary schools about £12.[41] This meant that educational opportunities were limited either to those fortunate enough to get scholarships, to children of wealthy parents, or, in most instances, to youths whose families made heavy sacrifices. The absence of free education, at least at the primary level, aroused protest not only from those who aspired to education but could ill afford it, but also from the majority of educated clerks and artisans who had to draw upon their meager salaries for school fees for their own children and, because of family obligations, for younger "brothers" as well.

Several factors were responsible for the disinclination of the Nigerian government to adapt the content of education to the country's changing needs, and to introduce reforms that would meet the aspirations of articulate Nigerians. In the first place, the fact that Britain's primary interest in Nigeria was economic dictated its own imperatives: territorial self-sufficiency, balanced budgets, and stringent economy. The undeveloped and precarious character of the Nigerian economy meant that there was insufficient revenue for costly programs of vocational training and educational expansion. Moreover, economy in government expenditures required maximum employment of Nigerians as clerks in order to obviate the need for importing higher-salaried Europeans.

Second, from a political standpoint, the stated aims of British rule in Nigeria, as they were understood and applied, were the maintenance of law and order and the gradual development of native administration. Hence educated Nigerians were needed only as clerks and artisans in civil service and commercial firms, and as educated subordinates in the police force and the army. A small beginning was made in training Nigerians for higher positions in technical services, and there was a fitful interest in a project to educate native administration officials and chiefs' sons, but in the south, at least, the results after fifty years of British rule were inconsequential. Political considerations were not deemed urgent enough to compel the Nigerian government to give education a higher priority. A British educator summed it up as follows:

> . . . the conception of the aim of education was, that it should make useful citizens, and when we say useful citizens we mean literally citizens who would be of use to us. The conception was one of exploitation and development for the benefit of the people of Great Britain—it was to this purpose that such education as was given was directed.[42]

Third, even if the Nigerian government had possessed sufficient revenue for educational expansion and reform, it is doubtful that there would have been a significant difference in the record. A literary curriculum not only provided government officials with useful English-speaking clerks and assistants, but it accorded with British preconceptions regarding education. Nigerian officialdom was itself the product of the English literary tradition, and believed that it offered the best type of education. In state-sponsored technical and vocational education, England had lagged far behind other Western industrial countries. In short, the traditional British philosophy of education conditioned the attitudes and reinforced the conservatism of colonial officialdom.

The imperial government itself took few positive steps to implement the policies formulated by the Advisory Committee on Native Education and announced by the Colonial Office. Before 1940 there were no imperial grants for education; rather, the first duty of a colonial government was to live within its means. Moreover, the Colonial Office approved the Nigerian budget each year, and there is no evidence that it endeavored at any time before 1940 to raise the priority given to education. The Colonial Office would have violated the time-honored principle of devolution of responsibility and authority had it prescribed in detail either the size or disposition of educational funds. Indeed, the two pronouncements of imperial policy, in 1925 and again in 1935, stipulated that recommended changes in educational policy would be made "as resources permit . . . ," and that "educational programmes must be largely, though not wholly, limited by the capacity of the people to bear the cost." [43]

Another explanation for prewar governmental inactivity was the eagerness of missionary societies to establish schools, with a simple curriculum of the four R's (religion, reading, writing, and arithmetic), to train African evangelists, teachers, and clerks. Missionary assumption of the educational burden was welcomed and encouraged, and later financially subsidized by the government. Not only did such an arrangement facilitate economy in government expenditures, but missionary education, like Nigerian officialdom, placed special emphasis upon moral and character training. This marriage of convenience and mutual benefit between government and missionary societies increased the former's indifference toward education as a function of government, and rendered the latter more and more suspect of colluding with the government and, in the eyes of Nigerian nationalists, with imperialism itself. The main interest of the missionary was the evangelization of the African, and a literary education was deemed adequate for the purpose. Moreover, such training was the least expensive, since equipment for technical and agricultural training was costly in men and in money. As the government was financially unable or unwilling to go beyond small subsidies, and as the missionaries, increasingly pinched for funds, desired to spread their resources as widely and consequently as thinly as possible, they lacked a strong motive for changing the content of education.

In vocational and technical training, government inactivity resulted largely from the absence of strong pressure for a policy of economic development and industrialization to provide employment opportunities for Nigerians who had completed such training. Prewar government reports consistently stressed the fact that existing departmental schemes for training artisans more than met the demand.

A final explanation was the insensitivity, if not the antipathy, of responsible Nigerian officials to the growing demands of nationalists for educational reform. Yet these officials received little aid or encouragement from the educated African members of the Legislative Council during the period 1923–1946. The persistent demands of this group for more and better education did not square with their even more emphatic insistence upon lower taxes and greater economy in government expenditures. Nigerian officialdom had little assurance that these members would have supported a significant increase in taxation to pay for improved education, although they would admittedly have been the first to insist that revenue saved by cutting European allowances should go to education.

Moreover, there was at the time little evidence of a strong and articulate demand from the great mass of Africans for a change in the clerk-producing system.[44] Clerical work was recognized as the proper field of employment.[45] The clerk had achieved an exalted position in the new urban social structure. He was literally and figuratively closest to the European; he was able to approximate the European's manner of living, speech, dress, and behavior; he was the most highly paid in the new medium of exchange; and he was the most educated. In short, the clerk had become a superman: the keeper of the keys, the symbol of power, the object of emulation.

Even if the Nigerian government had possessed the will and the means to institute the thoroughgoing educational reforms proposed by the Advisory Committee in 1925 and 1935, it is doubtful that such reforms would have arrested the tempo or shifted the direction of social change and political awakening. A literary education, with special emphasis upon the English language, had already acquired prestige and become a symbol in the eyes of most Nigerians. Moreover, the assumption underlying the proposed reforms was that social change could be decisively controlled by educating the African "along his own lines." It was a questionable assumption, founded upon the image of an idyllic and unchanging native village as the quintessence of African culture. The point was aptly expressed by a British educator, who in 1929 affirmed that

> For good or ill the African is now in the stream of the world's life. It is quite impossible for him to develop apart from the white man, even if he would. New desires have been awakened; . . . it can hardly be that a huge section of the human race should forever find their self-expression in agriculture and rural industries for no other reason than that these were their occupations when the white man came.[46]

THE DIFFERENTIAL IMPACT OF WESTERN EDUCATION

Differences in the timing and intensity of the impact of Western education on different tribes and regions have had an important bearing on the evolution of nationalism in Nigeria. The most striking difference, of course, is that between the Northern Region and the two southern regions (Eastern and Western), which were known as the Southern Provinces until 1939. As the data in table 14 indicate, the Northern Region has lagged behind the southern regions in the development of Western educational facilities. The gap is particularly noticeable and significant at the level of secondary education. Although the Northern Region possesses 54 per cent of the population of Nigeria, by 1947 only 251 northern students were attending secondary schools; this figure represented 2.5 per cent of the total secondary school enrollment in Nigeria.

The north-south disparity is further illuminated by the literacy statistics in table 15. In 1952, of the total population over seven years of age, 8.5 per cent were literate in roman script in all Nigeria, 16 per cent in the Eastern Region, 18 per cent in the Western Region, and 2 per cent in the Northern Region. Yet even within the Northern Region there were (and still are) significant differences. In the predominantly pagan provinces of the Middle Belt, 3.3 per cent were literate, whereas only 1.4 per cent were literate in the northern, predominantly Muslim, provinces.[47]

These areal differentials can be explained in part by geography and the historical sequence of impact; proximity to the coast meant earlier and more protracted contact with missionaries, the carriers of Western education. Perhaps the most important factor, however, was the hostility of the traditional Muslim rulers of northern Nigeria to Christian evangelization and Western education, and the British policy of sustaining them in their opposition. When the late Lord Lugard became high commissioner of the Protectorate of Northern Nigeria on January 1, 1900, he agreed to maintain, on behalf of Queen Victoria, all pledges and undertakings which had been assumed by the Royal Niger Company, including its policy of not supporting Christian missions in the Muslim North.[48]

There were, however, two important exceptions to the policy of missionary exclusion. First, the policy was generally applicable only to the predominantly Muslim emirates (Bauchi, Bornu, Kano, Katsina, Sokoto, and Zaria), peopled mainly by the Hausa, the

TABLE 14

DIFFERENTIAL DEVELOPMENT OF WESTERN EDUCATION IN SOUTHERN AND NORTHERN NIGERIA

| Year | Southern Nigeria (Eastern and Western regions) | | | | Northern Nigeria | | | |
| | Schools | | Pupils in attendance | | Schools | | Pupils in attendance | |
	Primary	Secondary	Primary	Secondary	Primary	Secondary	Primary	Secondary
1906	126	1	11,872	20	1	0	a	0
1912	150	10	35,716	67	34	0	954	0
1926	3,828	18	138,249	518	125	0	5,210	0
1937	3,533	26	218,610	4,285	539	1	20,269	65
1947	4,984	43	538,391	9,657	1,110	3	70,962	251
1957	13,473 b	176	2,343,317 b	28,208	2,080	18	185,484 c	3,643

a Number unknown.

b Figures include 30,602 pupils attending 94 secondary modern schools where post-primary instruction is given for three additional years for pupils who either are academically not up to the standards of full secondary schools or who cannot afford the higher fees.

c Figure for 1956.

Sources: *Annual Report*, Colony of Southern Nigeria, 1906, pp. 199 ff.; *Annual Reports*, Northern Nigeria, 1900–1911; *African Education* (Oxford: Nuffield Foundation, 1953), pp. 47–48; letters to the author from the Ministry of Education in each of the three regions of Nigeria, February–March, 1958.

TABLE 15

REGIONAL VARIATIONS IN LITERACY IN NIGERIA, 1952

Regions and provinces	Literacy in Roman script						Literacy in Arabic script	
	Standard II–IV or higher [a]		Others literate in roman script		Total			
	Num-ber	Per cent [b]	Num-ber	Per cent [b]	Num-ber	Per cent [b]	Num-ber	Per cent [b]
Eastern Region								
Onitsha	114,246	8.8	65,261	5.1	179,507	13		
Owerri	202,267	14.0	91,257	6.3	293,524	20		
Rivers	28,054	5.2	69,855	12.9	97,909	16	•	•
Calabar	136,164	12.7	87,203	8.1	223,367	21		
Ogoja	23,609	3.0	16,350	2.0	39,959	5		
Total	504,340	10.2	329,926	5.4	834,266	16		
Western Region (Yoruba areas)								
Ondo	57,854	8.7	69,311	10.2	127,165	19		
Ijebu	27,562	10.6	18,719	7.4	46,281	17		
Oyo	50,094	9.2	37,509	6.9	87,603	16		
Ibadan	105,329	9.7	79,286	7.3	184,615	16		
Abeokuta	31,197	6.8	20,278	4.4	51,475	11	•	•
(Other areas)								
Benin	58,912	9.3	22,675	3.6	81,587	13		
Delta	43,895	13.5	13,853	4.3	57,748	13		
Colony (Lagos)	44,008	21.4	89,451	43.2	133,459	64		
Total	418,851	10.7	351,082	6.6	769,933	18		
Northern Region (Middle Zone)								
Adamawa	5,769	.7	12,979	1.6	18,748	2.2	38,799	4.7
Benue	9,332	.9	10,511	1.0	19,843	1.8	11,094	1.0
Ilorin	11,197	2.9	9,232	2.4	20,429	5.3	9,108	2.4
Kabba	9,280	1.9	13,488	2.8	22,768	4.7	8,361	1.7
Niger	5,190	1.0	9,584	1.8	14,774	2.8	21,092	4.0
Plateau	15,258	2.4	17,909	2.8	33,167	5.2	13,879	2.2
(Subtotal)	(56,026)	(1.4)	(73,703)	(1.8)	(129,729)	(3.3)	(102,333)	(2.6)
(Northern Zone)								
Bauchi	8,246	.8	10,046	1.0	18,292	1.7	79,454	7.6
Bornu	4,961	.4	5,457	.5	10,418	.9	24,357	2.1
Kano	13,066	.5	10,339	.4	23,405	.9	201,044	8.1
Katsina	5,787	.5	11,228	1.0	17,015	1.6	51,996	4.8
Sokota	8,839	.5	10,858	.6	19,697	1.0	135,502	7.1
Zaria	17,306	3.0	14,845	2.6	32,151	5.6	61,573	10.8
(Subtotal)	(58,205)	(.7)	(62,773)	(.7)	(120,978)	(1.4)	(553,926)	(6.9)
Total	114,231	.9	136,476	1.1	250,707	2.0	656,259	5.4
All Nigeria	1,037,422	4.7	817,484	3.7	1,854,906	8.5	656,259 [d]	5.4

[a] Standard II (Eastern and Western regions) and Standard IV (Northern Region).
[b] Percentage of total population 7 years old or older in the area concerned.
[c] Data unknown for Eastern and Western regions, but number believed to be small.
[d] This number includes some who were also literate in roman script.
Sources: *Population Census of the Western Region of Nigeria, 1952* (Lagos: Government Statistician, 1953–1954); *Population Census of the Northern Region of Nigeria, 1952* (Lagos: Government Statistician, 1952–1953); *Population Census of the Eastern Region of Nigeria, 1953*, Bulletin no. 1 (Lagos: Government Statistician, 1954).

Fulani, and the Kanuri. Missionaries were encouraged to work in the pagan Middle Belt. In 1903 Lugard stated: "I have . . . held out every encouragement to establish missions in pagan centres, which appear to me to need the influence of civilization and religion at least as much as the Mohammedans." [49] The second exception was the gradual relaxation of official hostility, and the granting of authority for missionary societies to open stations and schools in Muslim emirates if invited by the emirs. It was under this tolerance that the Church Missionary Society opened a school in the Nupe country in 1903 at the invitation of the Emir of Bida, and the famous Walter Miller, a CMS missionary, later opened his school in Zaria in 1905 at the request of the Emir of Zaria.[50] These two exceptions were important in the awakening of racial consciousness and nationalism in the Northern Provinces, because a few of the early leaders of organized nationalist activity in the north were northerners who had received their early education in these and other mission schools.[51]

There were several reasons for the Lugardian policy of closing the far north to missionary societies. The most frequent official excuse has been Lugard's promise to the emirs after the conquest that the British administration would not interfere with their religion. He did not promise, however, to forbid Christian evangelization, nor did he make any legal commitment regarding noninterference; the day after he made his promise Lugard announced that by their hostile action the emirs themselves had abrogated all existing promises, agreements, pledges, and treaties: "The old treaties are dead; you have killed them." Thereafter, Lugard claimed, the right to rule over the country belonged absolutely and unconditionally to the British authorities. Actually, the policy of missionary exclusion was based on Lugard's conviction that missionary evangelization would contribute to political unrest because the emirs were violently opposed to Christianity: ". . . without the support of Government, these missions would not be tolerated. In effect, therefore, the mission obtains its footing on the support of British bayonets. . . ." [52]

Christianity and mission schools were not excluded simply because their presence would indirectly violate a promise or would offend the religious sensibilities of the Muslim population. Another reason was Lugard's belief that Christian ideas and Western education would militate against the successful development of his system of indirect rule.

> . . . the preaching of equality of Europeans and natives, however true from a doctrinal point of view, is apt to be misapplied by people in a low stage of development, and interpreted as an abolition of class distinction.[53]

> . . . the premature teaching of English . . . inevitably leads to utter disrespect for British and native ideals alike, and to a denationalized and disorganized population.[54]

In this connection it should be noted that, by the time British rule was established in northern Nigeria, some areas of southern Nigeria had been under the influence of Christianity and Western education for nearly fifty years, and the products of these two accultural media were generally lamented by European officialdom.[55] The Muslim areas of northern Nigeria, therefore, provided the British administration with a unique opportunity for controlling the rate and direction of acculturation.

The evolution of official policy regarding education in northern Nigeria can be divided into three distinct periods. The first, 1900–1909, was characterized by almost total inactivity, owing in part to Lugard's attitude toward education, and in part to the lack of funds. A familiar theme in Lugard's annual reports was the statement that "as in former years, the resources have not permitted any general scheme of education." [56] By the end of the period, however, Lugard had announced his over-all educational scheme, which included four types of schools: (1) schools to train the *mallamai* * as clerks to replace southerners, and as teachers in primary schools; (2) schools to instruct the sons of chiefs; (3) schools to teach the masses primary education in the vernacular; and (4) cantonment schools to educate the children of southern clerks, who as Christians should be isolated from northerners.[57] This school system was to be a superstructure built upon the 20,000 or more Koranic schools already in existence.

During the second period, 1910–1929, a carefully controlled

---

* *Mallamai* (Hausa) originally referred to the "learned" Koranic teachers; however, it now refers to the educated class generally, and *mallam* has become a title of courtesy (equivalent to English "mister") prefixed to the name of a man from the Muslim areas of the north.

government-sponsored educational system was established in the north. The model was not that of southern Nigeria, but that of the (Anglo-Egyptian) Sudan. An Education Department was organized, and the following types of schools were opened: elementary schools emphasizing health, native arts, gardening, and character training, taught by northern mallamai in the vernacular; primary schools for the mallamai, which employed the English language at the upper levels; arts and crafts schools for training in indigenous handicrafts and for instruction in carpentry, metal- and leatherwork, and motor repair; and the Katsina Teacher Training College, opened in 1921. The British authorities made scrupulous efforts to insure that the schools would not disrupt the existing social system. Since the schools were constructed and maintained by the native authorities, the emirs had a proprietary interest in them and undertook to fill them with students. Religion and Arabic were prominent subjects in the curriculum. In all matters of dress, behavior, and traditional forms of salutation, including prostration, the students were required to conform to local customs. In short, every effort was made to adapt the educational system to the environment and thereby avoid a repetition of the southern pattern.

In 1930 the education departments of the Northern and Southern Provinces were merged into a central department. The only significant developments in the following decade were the elevation of the Katsina Teacher Training College to the status of a full secondary school, and its transfer to Kaduna; the increasing coöperation of government technical departments in the training of artisans and agricultural inspectors, and the gradual awakening of the northern people to the desirability of education. The government abandoned an original plan to develop Katsina College into a university college along the lines of Yaba Higher College in the south. This meant that northerners were obliged to go south for training as medical technicians, pharmacists, and engineering assistants. In general, educational expansion was limited in scope and followed the direction taken in the earlier period.

Before the end of World War II there was little open criticism of education by Nigerians in the north. At the policy level, the initiative for and sponsorship of increased education seemed to come consistently from the British administration and not from the emirs and their councilors, at least according to official reports. One reason for the absence of protest was that in the authoritarian milieu of the north criticism from any person below the emirs would have been considered seditious and would instantly have been stifled by the emirs, or by the British on their behalf. Another and more important reason was that the demand in the north for educated northerners far exceeded the supply, and a frustrated educated proletariat like that in the south was never created. Again, the "dead hand" of Islam (as institutionalized in the north), unmolested by the disorganizing influence of individualistic Christian ideals and of an English-oriented literary educational system, and strengthened by an ultraconservative political superstructure, had not allowed the idea of progress to become an operative ideal in the north. It is probably true that most northerners were content with their Koranic schools and Islamic culture. The object of emulation seemed not to be the European administrator or the southern clerk, but the mallam who was fluent in Arabic and learned in Koranic law.

The outward appearance of contentment tended to strengthen the Lugardian ideal of a perfectly controlled educational program. Official attitudes remained conservative, as illustrated by a policy statement prepared in 1928 by the education officer for Kano Province:

[Students] . . . should as a rule follow in the occupation for which they were destined. The standard should be low so that the boys will not be alienated from their friends and parents by too great a sense of superiority. After a generation or more, the standard might be raised.[58]

According to this plan, Kano Province, with a population of more than 3 million, would have had 180 boys in primary school and 900 in elementary school by 1938. Yet beneath the surface there were signs of an awakening desire on the part of northern youth for wider educational opportunities. Nevertheless, by 1937 only one northerner had gained entry into Yaba Higher College, and as late as 1951 the 16 million people of the north could point to only one of their number who had obtained a full university degree—and he was a Zaria Fulani convert to Christianity educated in England by Walter Miller.

Western Education

This striking contrast in the missionary and educational impact upon northern and southern Nigeria is of crucial significance in understanding the nationalist awakening in Nigeria. In the first place, the absence of an English-speaking educated class in northern Nigeria in the early period necessitated the importation of thousands of southerners into the north as clerks and artisans. In 1920 Sir Hugh Clifford lamented:

> . . . after two decades of British occupation, the northern provinces have not yet produced a single Native of these provinces who is sufficiently educated to enable him to fill the most minor clerical post in the office of any government department.[59]

These small groups of educated southerners, concentrated in the sabon garis of northern townships, became centers of intensive secondary acculturation and the foci of the northern awakening. Second, when nationalist activity began to gather momentum in the south after 1943, northern leaders and educated elements were stung into the realization that in a self-governing Nigeria the north, because of its educational backwardness, would be dominated by educated southern nationalists. This fear, allegedly encouraged by the northern administration, stimulated educated northerners into a frenzy of organizational activity and, more significantly, awakened a strong cultural nationalism directed not only against the educated southerner, but also against the British administration. In the long run events demonstrated the futility of attempting to direct the forces of acculturation, especially when circumstances permitted effective control over only one of the accultural influences (that is, formal education) which were operative in the north.

CHAPTER 6
The Westernized Elite

The leaders and most of the active supporters of the Nigerian nationalist movement came from the ranks of those who had been most strongly affected by Western influences, and in particular from the Western-educated, English-speaking minority. By the early 1950's, when nationalism was well advanced, this group at most constituted no more than upwards of 6 per cent of the total population of Nigeria. On the basis of census data, where they exist, and of certain rough estimates, the numbers at different educational levels within this group are shown for two different periods in table 16.

TABLE 16

ESTIMATES OF WESTERN-EDUCATED AFRICANS IN NIGERIA, 1920's AND 1950's

Category	Early 1920's	Early 1950's	
	Number	Number	Percentage of total population
University education			
Completed	30	1,000 ⎱	.014
In progress	20	3,400 ⎰	
Post-primary education			
Completed	200	31,000 ⎱	.2
In progress	838 [a]	31,500 ⎰	
Primary education			
In progress	143,459 [a]	1,100,000	3.6

[a] Exact figures for 1926.

Sources: Figures calculated from P. Amaury Talbot, *The Peoples of Southern Nigeria* (London: 1926); *Annual Report,* Department of Education, 1953 (Lagos: Government Printer, 1954); *Population Census of the Western Region of Nigeria, 1952* (Lagos: Government Statistician, 1953–1954); *Population Census of the Eastern Region of Nigeria, 1953* (Lagos: Government Statistician, 1953–1954); *Population Census of the Northern Region of Nigeria, 1952* (Lagos: Government Statistician, 1952–1953); *African Education,* Nuffield Foundation (Oxford: 1953), pp. 47–48.

Westernized Elite

The articulate nationalist elements within the educated category came from a much smaller subgroup consisting mainly of barristers, physicians, teachers, clerks, and skilled laborers and artisans. The size, occupational components, and tribal origins (where known) of this smaller group are roughly shown for two different periods in table 17. This subgroup also included jour-

TABLE 17

Estimated Number of Nigerians in Key Occupational Groups in
Early 1920's and Early 1950's

Occupation	Early 1920's		Early 1950's	
Barristers	15	{ 12 Yorubas 3 Native foreigners	150 [a]	
Physicians	12	{ 8 Yorubas 4 Native foreigners	160	{ 76 Yorubas 49 Ibos 1 Hausa-Fulani 34 others
Teachers and clerks	21,000		70,000	
Artisans and skilled laborers	8,000		80,000	

[a] Ethnic breakdown not available.

Sources: Figures calculated from P. Amaury Talbot, *The Peoples of Southern Nigeria* (London: 1926), Vol. IV; C. K. Meek, *The Northern Tribes of Nigeria* (London: 1925); *Nigeria Gazette*, vol. 40, no. 10 (Jan. 26, 1953), 170–176; *Annual Report*, Department of Labour, 1951–1952 (Lagos: Government Printer, 1953), pp. 37–39.

nalists, organizational leaders, and a sizable number of traders and businessmen. These active core elements, however, would constitute at most a little more than .5 per cent of the total population of the country. And even in the subgroup, as Premier Obafemi Awolowo pointed out in 1947, "only a very small percentage are politically conscious." [1]

There have been substantial differences in tribal representation in these critical groups. Table 17, which shows these differences for barristers and physicians, clearly indicates the early and sustained lead of the Yoruba, the rapid advances made by the Ibo, and the wide gap separating the Hausa-Fulani from other groups.[2] Although recent data are not available, the figures in table 18, drawn from the 1921 census, further illuminate the substantial Yoruba lead in education and in several key occupational categories. In 1921 educated Yorubas and "native foreigners" held an

overwhelming majority (78 per cent) of the positions that required knowledge of the English language, and yet they constituted only 47 per cent of the educated group and less than 16
per cent of the population of townships. The Ibibio were the
most underemployed group in terms of education. Neither the
Ibibio nor the Ibo were represented in the professional ranks, al-

TABLE 18

TRIBAL REPRESENTATION IN SELECTED OCCUPATIONS IN THE TOWNSHIPS
OF SOUTHERN NIGERIA (EASTERN AND WESTERN REGIONS), 1921

Tribe	Per cent of total educated	Occupational categories			
		Profes-sional	Teachers and clerks	Artisans	Total
Yoruba	40.3	47	4,882	5,769	10,698
Native foreigners	7.3	26	1,732	978	2,736
Ibo	11.0	*	1,132	642	1,774
Ibibio	25.0	*	509	179	688
Edo	3.0	*	226	172	398
Other	13.4	*	406	347	753

* None or unknown.
Sources: Figures calculated from P. Amaury Talbot, *The Peoples of Southern
Nigeria* (London: 1926), IV, 160–171. The listings are made and the percentages
computed on the basis of data contained in references cited, coupled with other
population data.

though they made up 19 per cent of the population of townships
and 36 per cent of those who had received Western education.
These early differentials provide a partial clue to the later manifestation of Ibibio and Ibo tribal consciousness, and to a Yoruba
reaction that had a significant effect on the evolution of the
nationalist movement. During the three decades following 1921,
the Ibibio and Ibo fought desperately to overcome their early
handicap, and in the postwar period the same urge animated the
Hausa-Fulani in the north. Uneven acculturation, resulting in
part from the uneven tribal acquisition of Western education and
the uneven spread of "status" employment, produced competitive tensions within the educated categories which were powerful
stimulants to tribal as well as to territorial nationalism.

In addition to disparities in tribal representation, there has
also been unevenness in the geographical distribution of the edu-

cated elements. In 1921 approximately 40 per cent of those classified as "educated" in southern Nigeria were living in thirteen
townships, which collectively could claim less than 2 per cent of
the total population. In 1953, a similarly heavy percentage of the
educated lived in urban centers. Thus, 34 per cent of those who
had acquired a Standard II education in Onitsha Province lived
in Onitsha Town and Enugu; 60 per cent in Rivers Province lived
in Port Harcourt; 61 per cent in Ibadan Province lived in Ibadan;
and 89 per cent of those who had completed an Elementary IV
education or higher in Kano Province resided in Kano City.[3]

The reasons for the heavy concentration of westernized elements in urban centers have already been examined. Like most
educated groups, Western-educated Nigerians preferred the ex-
citement, the modernity, and the higher living standards of the
cities. They found bush farming unattractive and unremunerative.
They had sought and obtained an education to secure salaried
employment, which was largely an urban phenomenon. There
were several specific reasons for the large percentage of educated
elements in the three cities of Lagos, Calabar, and Port Harcourt.
First, these cities, as port towns, were the chief commercial
centers. Second, Lagos and Calabar had had a longer contact
with the West and possessed a disproportionate share of educational facilities; Lagos alone had 20 per cent of Nigeria's schools.
Third, Lagos was not only the political capital, but the headquarters of most European commercial enterprise; in 1921, 43
per cent of the Europeans in Nigeria lived in Lagos. Thirty years
later 60 per cent of the Europeans of the southern regions lived in
Lagos.

The concentration of educated Nigerians in a few port towns,
particularly in Lagos, fostered the European notion that a basic
urban-rural, and consequently an educated-illiterate, cleavage
existed; this in turn strengthened the belief that educated Africans were manifestly unrepresentative of the Nigerian masses.
This estimate of the situation continued to dominate European,
and particularly official, attitudes long after the early 1920's. Yet
even at that time, despite the tendency toward urbanization,
nearly 60 per cent of those listed as "educated" were living outside the townships. In 1921, in Calabar Province alone, more than
85 per cent lived in rural areas, and by 1953 the proportion had

increased to 92 per cent. During the interwar period urbanization did not keep pace with the growing number of "Standard VI Boys." Indeed, after the depression of the early 1930's there was severe retrenchment in both government and commercial enterprise, and job openings in urban centers were drastically reduced. Although it is true that thousands of the "Standard VI Boys" continued to flock to Lagos and other cities, nevertheless other thousands returned to their villages.

EUROPEAN ATTITUDES TOWARD THE EDUCATED ELITE

The special grievances of the westernized elements were crucial factors in the awakening of racial and political consciousness. Much of their resentment, of course, was the inevitable outcome of the disorganization following rapid social change. Their desire to emulate Europeans tended to separate them from their traditional milieu. Had they been accepted completely and unconditionally as dark-skinned Englishmen—as, in fact, certain members of the first generation were accepted—and had they been permitted to achieve a social and economic status that was both psychologically meaningful and materially satisfying, the course and the pace of Nigerian nationalism would most likely have been quite different. This did not happen, however, mainly because of the attitudes of many of the European residents and the policies of the British administration in Nigeria. In the trenchant words of Sir John Rodger: "We are busy manufacturing black and brown Englishmen—turning them out by the score, and cursing the finished article when the operation is complete. . . . [We] create an alien and then leave him to work out his own salvation." [4]

With many notable exceptions, the characteristic attitude of resident Europeans toward the educated African was one of contempt, amusement, condescension, or veiled hostility, depending upon the individual relationship. From the turn of the century until the late 1940's, many visitors to Nigeria, and to other parts of British West Africa, commented on the tension and animosity between Europeans and educated Africans. An observer in 1912 noted that "the relations between the Anglo-Saxon and the Anglicized African in West Africa are delicate and difficult." [5] In 1925 another observer said: ". . . one frequently hears people of all kinds remark how superior the untutored primitive villager

145

is to the African who has come into contact with Europeans." [6]
Charles Roden Buxton made a similar observation in 1935: "Few
white people have a good word to say for the educated African.
. . . [His] failings and absurdities are one of the stock subjects of
conversation among White people in West Africa." [7]

Apart from color prejudice, certain aspects of the Nigerian
situation helped to create the disparaging attitude of Europeans
toward the educated African. In the first place, some educated
Africans, particularly in the pre–World War II period, appeared
comical, and perhaps ridiculous, in their awkward attempts to
imitate the mannerisms in dress, speech, and behavior of the
"English gentleman." Because they made the latter their proto-
type, rather than the common English clerk, farmer, or laborer,
their endeavors were all the more ludicrous. Their efforts were not
unlike those of certain upper-class Negroes in America who, as
Myrdal has pointed out, try to imitate the "highest" standards of
white people, and go to extremes of conspicuous consumption
in their quest for status and acceptance. [8] There were also similarities in the misuse or overuse of long words, in the use of
pompous oratory, and in the ostentatious display of educational
attainments.

There are, of course, obvious explanations for the exaggerated
imitative tendencies of the educated Nigerian. He had been taught
in school to imitate the "English gentleman"; most of the advertisements he saw in newspapers and magazines, particularly
in the early days, were addressed to such a type; and, except for
traders and missionaries, most Europeans in Nigeria were colonial
officials who until recently were of the aristocracy or *haute
bourgeoisie*, and tried to perpetuate in Africa the mode of living
of the English upper classes. [9] In a sense, therefore, European attitudes were the product of class snobbery. As A. Victor Murray
has pointed out in a stimulating analogy between the medieval
Englishman and the modern African: "Nothing would have been
more unlikely to the mind of the mediaeval baron or abbot than
the evolution of the boorish peasant into the modern English
citizen." [10]

European resentment of the educated African stemmed in part
also from the universal urge to ridicule the imitator. Of course,
in the early period of colonialism, missionary effort, the educa-

tional system, and other Western forces and institutions were explicitly aimed at transforming the African into the European image. And any human relationship cast in the model-imitator mold tends toward a superior-inferior stratification of attitudes. It is psychologically difficult for a model to regard an imitator as his equal; he is hypercritical of, rather than flattered by, awkward efforts at imitation. It was no doubt the confession of inferiority implicit in extravagant imitation that led many postwar nationalists to lampoon the earlier generation of educated Africans, frequently with the epithet of "hat-in-hand Uncle Tomism." [11]

One can in fact draw a rather sharp distinction between the first generation of educated Nigerians, who revealed a strong urge to imitate, and the generation that came of age in the late 1930's and early 1940's. This difference in perspectives and behavioral patterns is of crucial significance. Generalizations about the perspectives and predispositions of one generation are likely to be invalid for its successor. In Nigeria there is fairly strong evidence that the attitudes of the second generation were partly determined by a reaction against the attitudes of the earlier generation. Indeed, one of the main themes in Premier Nnamdi Azikiwe's *Renascent Africa* was an appeal to the upcoming generation for "mental emancipation" from the attitudes of the older generation.[12] All this, of course, was closely linked with the development of cultural nationalism in the second generation of educated Nigerians.

Many resident Europeans also felt that the educated African was congenitally dishonest or unscrupulous, or had otherwise failed to achieve the minimum standards of character prescribed by the model of an acceptable European. This sentiment was reflected in the great emphasis placed upon moral and character training in the schools by European educators and officials. It also appeared in the disinclination of the European banks to grant credit to Nigerians, and in the unwillingness of commercial firms to elevate Nigerians to positions of responsibility, especially those involving financial matters. The feeling was not unlike that observed by Myrdal: ". . . whites *believe* the Negro to be innately addicted to crime." [13]

European beliefs and feelings about African financial dishonesty were not, of course, without foundation. The incidence of theft, corruption, and dishonesty on the part of Africans in contact with Europeans was high, but not necessarily higher than in similarly placed groups in other societies. Insofar as it was abnormal, however, there are several explanations. Some of these have been suggested by Mars:

> In a primitive community most goods become private property only through appropriation, and the respect for private property is accordingly exceedingly weak. The moral objection to stealing is largely confined to stealing from members of the extended family, village or tribe. The moral obligation to support the extended family is held to condone theft from others. Africans have still little compunction about embezzling white men's money, partly because they are resentful on account of the wrongs which they imagine they have suffered at their hands. Their extreme poverty makes practically all Africans pre-disposed to admire all methods, fair or foul, of getting rich quick . . . imprisonment is no stigma. . . . Nor must it be forgotten that as far as the financial unreliability of African employees of companies is concerned this was often a case of "like master like man" in days gone by. African employees were apt pupils of financially unscrupulous superiors.[14]

Moreover, punishment for crimes in tribal societies was severe; British justice and penal treatment were mild by contrast. There was a wide gap between the incomes of Africans and their unsatisfied material aspirations, which were intensified by daily contact with affluent white men, and by heavy doses of commercial advertisements. And, in general, the disorganization produced by the Western impact weakened moral standards and diminished the power of both traditional and European sanctions.

Other factors caused Europeans to consider the educated African deficient in character. They believed that an African who obtained a position of power over other Africans would exploit them mercilessly for his own ends. This charge was usually documented by references to the arrogance and exploitative practices of the Afro-American ruling minority in Liberia; or to the fact that employees of African firms were paid less and treated worse than employees of European firms; or to Lagos barristers who charged unconscionable legal fees and deliberately provoked costly litigation in which the illiterate bush farmer was the financial victim; or to the pomposity, venality, and nepotism, and the ruthless exaction of bribes from illiterate members of the public, on the part of African clerks, male nurses, customs employees, and police. This petty oppression by many educated Africans confirmed and strengthened European prejudice. The nature of this prejudice is reflected in the following comment of one European:

> It will certainly be several generations before the West African native, however carefully trained he may be, will have gained that force of character which the Englishman now inherits as a sort of birthright, and which will fit him to be placed in an independent position of authority, whether in the service of the church or the state.[15]

Although prejudice might account for the condescension or contempt of Europeans toward educated Africans, it did not explain their veiled or frequently open hostility. Friction was most acute at the personal level. Many Europeans felt that educated Africans were insulting, assertive, and "uppity"; that they refused to reciprocate social overtures and created imaginary disabilities, slights, and rebuffs; and that they maintained a "chip-on-the-shoulder" attitude in their personal relationships. The situation was similar to that described by Myrdal: "The trait which the whites perhaps associate most with Negroes is a tendency to be aggressive." [16]

Tensions of this character, of course, are well-known phenomena in interracial situations. The Nigerian problem, however, has distinctive features. In the first place, until recently the vast majority of educated Nigerians were political and social outsiders in their own country. Second, the educated Nigerian suffered more than anyone else from the discriminatory behavior of the white community, not only because he aspired most intensely to the status of equality, but also because he was the thankless intermediary between European officials and the Nigerian public. Most educated Nigerians either served directly under or were only one stage removed from daily contact with the white man, and the relationship was on a master-servant basis. The Nigerian's aggressiveness was either a defense mechanism hiding a

deeply ingrained inferiority complex, or a natural human retaliation to the insults, imaginary or real, which he received from his
European superior. John H. Harris pointed out in 1912 that

> . . . [although] no traveller in West Africa would claim that
> the natives, particularly the educated ones, are invariably cour-
> teous to White officialism, . . . [nevertheless,] if comparisons
> in discourtesy are to be made, none would assuredly hesitate
> as to where the chief blame rests.[17]

The antagonism of the white community, and especially of
officialdom, toward educated Nigerians became more pronounced
when it was realized not only that they were the source of political agitation, but also that they aspired to greater participation
in the government with the ultimate aim of displacing the white
administration. It was the educated Nigerians who organized
mass meetings in Lagos, provoked disturbances in the provinces,
published vituperative articles in the local press, and made life
miserable and insecure for British administrators. There was nothing a district officer, a resident, or a governor dreaded more than
political disturbances and unrest during his tour of duty. He
would have to face the inevitable parliamentary question, or a
visiting commission of inquiry, not to mention added work and an
unfavorable efficiency report. In a colonial milieu political tranquillity was the norm, and an administrator's failure to achieve
that norm was presumed to be a reflection upon his ability. The
educated African was the bête noire of the European administrator. In 1936 one district officer bluntly stated his apprehensions:

> Not only is the literate class a tiny fraction of the Nigerian popu-
> lation, and unrepresentative of the interests of the Nigerian
> population as a whole, but their bluff can be called easily now.
> But give a continuation of the policy . . . that now exists and
> insist on the same attention to their demands and cries for another
> decade or two and the Government will find that it has, like
> Frankenstein, raised up a monster which will consume it.[18]

On occasion the governor of Nigeria attempted to reduce the
tension between Europeans and educated Nigerians. An example
of such efforts at the highest level is the following statement made
by Sir Hugh Clifford, one of Nigeria's most colorful governors,
before the Nigerian Council in 1920:

Turning . . . to the more highly educated sections of the African communities of Nigeria, I maintain that every European in this country has toward them very special obligations and responsibilities which should inspire him with a deep sympathy for them and with an eager desire to aid and to befriend them. It is our civilization which, for educated Africans, has replaced, more or less completely, that which their forebears had developed for themselves. . . . The ideas which they have imbibed, the aspirations which they cherish, the hopes which they entertain, the desires by which they are animated are, in the main, ideas, aspirations, hopes and desires which originated with us, and which we, as a nation, have kindled in them. These, I suggest, are facts which should make a special appeal to the sympathy of every European who has dealings with educated Africans in Nigeria; which should inspire in him a meticulous courtesy in all his dealings with them; which should arm him with a more than ordinary measure of consideration, of patience, and of leniency in his converse with, and in his judgment of, them.[19]

The practical effect of such advice is, of course, uncertain. In later days nationalists could easily have interpreted it as an infuriating example of paternalism, however well intended.

It was in the social sphere, however, that European attitudes and prejudices toward educated Africans were most embittering. The vast majority of Nigerians—the illiterate and unsophisticated—were little disturbed by white pretensions to superiority, but educated Africans were genuinely resentful. In the early days, when Nigeria was indeed a "white man's grave," separate European and African residential areas and hospitals might have been justified on grounds of sanitation and public health. Yet long after modern prophylaxis had rendered Nigeria suitable for white habitation, the distinction was rigidly maintained. Separateness was not only openly asserted and therefore officially supported in the civil service, residential areas, and hospitals, but it existed in most places where interracial contact occurred, including motion picture theaters, social clubs, and recreational facilities.

And yet it was not the separateness, but rather the qualitative differences in the facilities provided for the two races, which aroused the greatest hostility. The extreme contrast between the well-paved roads, the street lighting, and the palatial homes in the European quarter on Lagos Island (Ikoyi), and the chaotic

151

squalor of the native quarter, was a constant reminder to educated Nigerians living in Lagos and other urban areas of the wide gap between their style of living and the "white" standard to which they aspired. Moreover, the refinements and comforts of European facilities were supported by taxes paid by Nigerians. In shops, post offices, banks, and railway stations, Europeans were customarily served ahead of Africans. The color bar did not distinguish between the educated and the illiterate, or between the bushman and the aspiring "black Englishman."

Color discrimination, as it was practiced in Nigeria, was the product not only of preconceptions regarding African inferiority, reinforced by a magnification of the faults of educated Africans, but also of the firm conviction that peaceful colonial administration and the perpetuation of imperial rule were directly dependent upon the doctrine of white superiority. This attitude is most poignantly brought out in Joyce Cary's novel *The African Witch.* Even those Europeans in Nigeria who were not color-conscious— and there were many, and at high levels—were effectively prevented from reducing social tensions and establishing rapport between European groups and educated Africans. The ban against familiarity, the rigid maintenance of separate African and European standards and facilities, and the painful, albeit subtle, penalties inflicted upon Europeans or educated Africans who violated the color bar were all part of a determined effort to preserve the doctrine of white superiority, not necessarily for its own sake, but for political tranquillity. Nor was this simply an unwritten code, as evidenced by the following wartime instructions given to white troops stationed in West Africa:

> In all contact with the natives, let your first thought be the preservation of your own dignity. The natives are accustomed to dealing with very few white people and those they meet hold positions of authority. The British are looked up to, put on a very high level. Don't bring that level down by undue familiarity.[20]

OFFICIAL POLICY TOWARD THE EDUCATED ELITE

From the beginning of formal British administration in Nigeria the government faced a serious dilemma in connection with the status and role of the educated elements. On the one hand, educated Nigerians were absolutely indispensable not only for the government of the country, but also for its development, as intermediaries between the tiny group of European officials and the vast mass base.[21] On the other hand, under British prewar policies, particularly indirect rule, there were few roles beyond clerkdom which educated Nigerians could be permitted to perform. Of course, the size of Nigeria and the small number of British officials made indirect rule itself a requisite of imperial control. In order to govern Nigeria the British needed both the educated elite and indirect rule, yet each pointed toward a very different political formula. One of the important strands in the political history of British administration in Nigeria has been the effort to resolve this internal contradiction.

Central Government

Before World War II the educated elements, with few exceptions, were excluded not only from the central government but also from the native administration of local government.[22] At the central level only four Africans were elected as members of the Legislative Council between 1923 and 1946.[23] Three were elected from the township of Lagos and one from Calabar, by an electorate composed of the wealthier members of the communities. In addition, the governor appointed seven Africans to the council during the period 1923–1938, and ten during the period 1938–1946, to represent the interior of the Southern Provinces. Before 1946 there was no African representation from the Northern Region.[24] All the elected and appointed African members came from the educated class (five clergymen, six lawyers, one journalist, one wealthy trader, and one district chief from the Cameroons). Yet only two of them, both elected from Lagos, would have been considered nationalist-minded at the time they served, and they were all repudiated by postwar nationalists.

Two educated Africans (Sir Adeyemo Alakija and Justice S. B. Rhodes) were appointed to the governor's Executive Council in 1943, but both were considered by the nationalists to be "safe" government men. Before 1943 no African had participated directly in policy formulation at the central executive level. Furthermore, with few exceptions, Africans were excluded from the various functional councils and boards appointed by the government to advise on specific problems. For example, membership on the Town Planning Committee appointed by the governor in 1926 to plan layouts for urban communities in Nigeria was limited to Europeans. As late as 1938 provincial committees were created to advise on pay rates for employees, but it was not until 1941 that an African was named to one of these committees. The two exceptions to this prewar policy of exclusion were (1) the African representative of the Nigerian Union of Teachers appointed to the Educational Advisory Board in 1933; and (2) the African representative of the African Motor Vehicle Owners' Union designated as a member of the Transport Advisory Board in 1937. There is, however, little evidence that before World War II the government considered the Africanization of these advisory bodies politically expedient, notwithstanding African criticisms in the Nigerian press and elsewhere.

It was their exclusion from the administrative, judicial, and technical branches of the senior (European) civil service, however, which the educated elements felt most keenly. Despite the comparatively large number of Nigerian barristers, the Nigerian judiciary remained predominantly European until the 1940's. By 1939, there were only twenty-three educated Africans in the senior service. But educated Nigerians were unimpressed by these appointments. One reason was that most of the appointees were either repatriated "Brazilians" * or native foreigners, and not "sons of the soil." The three most senior Africans in the senior service belonged to the alien categories, as did most of the early appointees to the judiciary. The two members of the Executive Council, Rhodes and Alakija, were Sierra Leonian and Brazilian respectively. Second, it was believed that even those few Africans who were elevated to senior-service rank did not enjoy equality with Europeans in the perquisites and conditions of service. One senior African, for example, had a European subordinate who received a higher salary than he did. Finally, educated Nigerians believed that Africans appointed to office were selected because

---

* "Brazilians" were persons of African descent whose ancestors were taken to Brazil by the Portuguese as slaves. After slavery was abolished in Brazil several of these families, mainly Yoruba, returned to Nigeria and settled in Lagos. Many of the early leaders in Lagos society, like the Alakijas, were "Brazilians."

they had ingratiated themselves with Europeans and not because they were more competent than others.[25]

Salary scales in the African clerical service ranged from £36 to £400 a year. The highest salary accrued only to the oldest and most senior African chief clerks, about twenty-five in number. Most Africans in the civil service received an annual salary of £100 or less. By contrast, a European official fresh from his university in England started at £450 a year, and within seventeen years his salary could increase to more than £1,000. The gap between the two services was further widened by the more favorable conditions of service and the higher perquisites in the senior service.

The feeling of denial regarding elevation to the (European) senior service might have been assuaged had a more fluid situation existed within the African civil service. But even in that service only 3 per cent of the positions (185 out of 5,841) had been classified as senior (that is, with a salary above £100 a year) by 1936.[26] This meant that the great bulk of government employees were competing for a few highly prized positions with a very slow turnover. The African's frustration was further aggravated because most of the senior posts in the African service were held by native foreigners. Since the government service provided the pattern for other employing agencies in Nigeria, this situation was general throughout the country.

It is also possible that the grievances of African civil servants would have been lessened had they been eligible for promotion from the ranks. As it was, the sharp differentiation between the European and African sectors of the civil service created or exacerbated tensions which developed along racial rather than purely economic lines. The few Africans who were appointed to the senior service had no bonds or feeling of identity with the thousands of Africans in the junior service, either because they were native foreigners, or because the gap between the two services was so wide that the great mass of Nigerian clerks did not feel that one of their own kind had been promoted.

In a large measure, however, the rigid stratification in the civil service simply represented the transfer to Nigeria of the bureaucratic organization characteristic of the British civil serv-

ice, in which there was, until recently, a marked distinction between the administrative class and the clerical services. In Great
Britain, of course, the distinction largely followed class lines,
whereas in Nigeria it automatically followed racial lines. In any
event, although the Nigerian pattern was not necessarily devised
to preserve white supremacy or to discriminate against Africans,
it nevertheless had that effect which, from a political standpoint,
is just as significant.

The virtual exclusion of educated Nigerians from meaningful
roles in the central government was an explicit policy of the
British administration. It was based upon the following oft-
quoted principle, enunciated by Lord Lugard in 1920:

> It is a cardinal principle of British Colonial policy that the inter-
> ests of a large native population shall not be subject to the will
> . . . of a small minority of educated and Europeanized natives
> who have nothing in common with them, and whose interests
> are often opposed to theirs. . . .[27]

The same principle was stated even more forthrightly by Sir
Hugh Clifford in his famous 1920 address before the Nigerian
Council. His remarks were largely provoked by the demands of
the National Congress of British West Africa:

> "There has during the last few months been a great deal of
> loose and gaseous talk . . . which has for the most part ema-
> nated from a self-selected and a self-appointed congregation of
> educated African gentlemen who collectively style themselves the
> 'West African National Conference.' . . . It can only be de-
> scribed as farcical to suppose that . . . continental Nigeria can
> be represented by a handful of gentlemen drawn from a half-
> dozen Coast tribes—men born and bred in British administered
> towns situated on the sea-shore, who in the safety of British
> protection have peacefully pursued their studies under British
> teachers. . . ."[28]

The denial of the political claims of educated Nigerians was
based not only on the smallness of their number, but also on the
belief that the educated minority lacked cultural identity with the
masses. During Lugard's governorship, and indeed until the early
1930's, there was evidence to support such a belief. In 1921 approximately 18 per cent of the English-speaking Africans in

Nigeria were native foreigners (that is, educated Africans mainly from the Gold Coast and Sierra Leone). In the townships of the Northern Provinces, with which Lugard was more intimately acquainted, the proportion was nearly 40 per cent. As late as 1936, this alien group still tended to dominate the upper ranks of the African civil service and the clerkship hierarchy in commercial firms. It is more likely than not that most of the educated Africans whom Lord Lugard and other high-ranking European officials encountered in the early 1920's were not Nigerians at all, but native foreigners.[29] Indeed, Sir William Geary reports that in the early period the terms "native foreigner" and "educated native" were virtually synonymous.[30]

If Lugard was referring to this group when he spoke about educated Africans, he was quite right—they had no identity with the indigenous Nigerian masses. Moreover, the Nigerians themselves, unlike Europeans who did not differentiate among Africans, knew that the native foreigners were not sons of the soil even though they were dark-skinned. Few of them spoke or were able to speak in the Nigerian vernacular. Most of them, coming from the Creole community in Freetown, Sierra Leone, or from the coastal areas of Ghana (then the Gold Coast), had been under British influence since birth; they were the real "black Englishmen" who dressed only in European clothes. Nearly 83 per cent of them were Christian, and had been born into that faith. The majority of them had no intention of settling in Nigeria, but were saving their money for eventual retirement in their home territories. As late as 1936, outward remittances by native foreigners totaled £545,875 a year, which exceeded Nigeria's average prewar annual expenditure on education.[31] In the decade 1921–1931, however, the number of native foreigners declined, and by the end of World War II native-born Nigerians constituted all but a tiny fragment of the educated elements.[32]

It is, of course, an open question whether educated Nigerians accurately represented the views of the inarticulate masses, or whether the interests of the two groups diverged. In any event, the principal basis for the charge that they were unrepresentative was that they had become "detribalized." This was a frequently expressed, and much resented, European stereotype of the educated Nigerian. The concept of "detribalization," useful though it may be in referring to social change as a general process, frequently conveys a false picture when applied to groups or individuals. As stated elsewhere, "the concept tends to evoke the distorted image of polar extremes—of 'tribalized' witch doctors and secret societies on the one hand and of 'detribalized' barristers and their 'national congresses' on the other, with very little connection between the two." [33] Most educated Nigerians either sought to recapture, or had never lost, a significant measure of identity with their lineage and with African culture.

There were many ways in which educated Nigerians manifested the tenacity of the lineage and tribal attachment. The wealthier professional classes made efforts to procure chieftaincy titles or councilorships in their native villages. They also coöperated with teachers, clerks, and artisans to organize and maintain lineage or tribal unions in urban communities. These unions were an organizational expression of the persistent feeling among educated groups of loyalty and obligation to the kinship group and to the town or village where the lineage was localized. Their widespread existence, their strength, and the devotion and interest of their members, including most of the educated Africans, provide positive evidence that Europeans have grossly exaggerated the detribalization of the educated class. On the other hand, some educated Nigerians, especially those who glorify African culture, have endeavored to minimize the extent of their own acculturation by denying that their European values, loyalties, behavior patterns, and aspirations were in any sense un-African or were blindly copied from Europeans. Race-conscious Africans have resented terms like "detribalization" and "Europeanization" as implying that Africans abandoned their own culture because it was inferior and embraced European culture *in toto* because it was superior.

Another official argument for limiting the participation of educated Africans in government was that they were not qualified to hold political power or responsibility. Lord Lugard claimed that "the educated native, generally speaking, [has not] shown himself to be possessed of ability to rule either his own community or backward peoples of his own race, even under favourable conditions." [34] Apart from his personal prejudices, Lord Lugard was influenced in his views by the exploitative and oligarchical character of Negro self-government in Haiti and Liberia. It is therefore significant that Premier Nnamdi Azikiwe entitled his first major work *Liberia in World Politics*, and sought in it to vindicate the Liberian experience. In any event, to the generation of educated Nigerians who came of age in the late 1930's and early 1940's, disqualification by analogy was as empty as an argument that Europeans were incapable of self-government because of the Nazi and Fascist dictatorships.

A persistent theme in official responses to the demands of educated Nigerians for the Nigerianization of the senior service was that the high standards of the service could not be compromised, and that few educated Africans could meet them.[35] In the abstract, of course, the maintenance of high standards is laudable, but to the educated Nigerian the argument smacked of sophistry. Government clerks who worked daily and intimately under European administrators resented it most. As they gained experience in routine administrative tasks, they realized that they were frequently doing much of the work and assuming a measure of the responsibility, while their white superiors had the power, the perquisites, and the status. They felt that the inequality was personal as well as racial, an attitude that is often thought to accord with a "subaltern mentality." In any event, African clerks were acutely aware of the striking contrast between their own salaries and conditions of service and those of the Europeans under whom they worked, and were convinced that they could readily replace the Europeans without reducing efficiency or lowering standards. In fact, some such replacements could undoubtedly have been made, commencing with routine jobs and extending upward to higher positions of responsibility and authority.[36]

But educated Africans were not totally excluded from government at the central level. Although Lord Lugard refused to give them power over the African masses, nevertheless he permitted them a limited outlet for their energies. In his view self-government for Europeanized Africans should be "along the same path as that of Europeans—increased participation in municipal affairs until they prove themselves fitted for the larger responsibilities of Government of their *own* communities. . . ."[37]

In 1936 Margery Perham, a careful student of Nigerian affairs and a close friend and biographer of the late Lord Lugard, examined the problem of the educated groups vis-à-vis the central government. Her recommendations, which to some extent reflected and influenced thought in official circles, emphasized the need to divert the educated elements from their preoccupation with the central structure of government. They should be given new opportunities in positions of trust in that structure, but they should *not* be permitted to enter the administrative (senior) service because it "should be regarded as the temporary [British] scaffolding round the growing structure of native self-government. . . . To build them [Africans] into the scaffolding would be to create a vested interest which would make its demolition at the appropriate time very difficult." [38] Since Miss Perham deemed the central Legislative Council unsuitable as the future focus for Nigerian political development, she recommended that

> In so far as the political ambitions of the educated are centred upon the Legislative Council, they should be met not by giving them an extension of power over the more backward masses, but by increasing their responsibilities, and therefore their sense of political realities, in the Colony, and in urban and other advanced areas.[39]

This is clearly a reaffirmation of the basic principles laid down by Lord Lugard nearly fifteen years earlier. It would not be incorrect to say that it represented the official prewar policy regarding the role of the educated elements vis-à-vis the central government.

Yet there was another strand in official policy which resulted in a fatal dualism. This strand comprised institutional arrangements and explicit official statements pointing toward ultimate self-government for a united Nigeria. A few educated Nigerians had actually been admitted to the central administrative service. They had also been appointed to serve as unofficial members of the Legislative Council, whose purview included not only the colony, but also the Southern Provinces and, for certain financial purposes, the Northern Provinces of Nigeria. Indeed some educated Africans had been members of the Legislative Council since the beginning of the century, and new members had been appointed during the 1930's.

These actual developments were buttressed by explicit official statements which clearly gave educated Nigerians the notion that all Nigeria would ultimately be governed by a central administration controlled by Africans. When discussing the reconstitution of the Nigerian Council in 1921, Sir Hugh Clifford stated that the new body should be "a *serious* factor in the Government of the Colony *and Protectorate*" and as "truly and practically representative of *all* Nigerian interests" as possible. He also expressed the hope that it would ultimately be "the Supreme Council of State—the 'Parliament' of Nigeria." [40] In her own recommendations Miss Perham assumed that "it will be towards some form of representative parliamentary government that a united Nigeria will one day aspire." [41] In both instances, however, the ultimate goal was considered to be in the distant future, and could be realized, as Sir Hugh had in fact stated, only "when the Native Chiefs become properly and efficiently organised throughout the country." [42] Yet this qualification did not dim the brightness of the future envisioned by educated Africans; it merely meant that they would have to mark time. This they were not content to do.

In retrospect, the tempo and course of Nigerian nationalism might have been different had the British authorities avoided the dualism of excluding educated Africans on grounds of principle, but at the same time giving them the vision of ultimate control. The policy of dualism created frustration and bitterness which a more consistent policy, pursued steadfastly from the commencement of British rule, might have prevented.

Local Government

As noted previously, prewar British policy stressed the modification and adaption of the native administration system. As Lord Lugard had stated, self-government for the African masses, as distinguished from the educated elements, was to be achieved by the "education of their own rulers, and the gradual extension of their powers, [rather] than by the introduction of an alien system of rule by British-educated and politically-minded progressives." [43] In his view, the traditional authorities were not only convenient and economical instruments for an imperial power, but they were the only authorities who, once reformed and educated, could conceivably claim to represent the people. The necessary reform and education were to be accomplished by training district officers and chiefs' sons, not by grafting Western-educated elements onto the traditional structure. The desire to minimize the contact between educated Africans and the illiterate masses was implicit in Lugard's plan for a government educational system in the Northern Provinces, which included (1) cantonment schools for educated southerners, to confine them to urban communities and isolate them from the native administration system; (2) the training of northern mallamai to replace Western-educated clerks; and (3) the education of chiefs' sons, which had been the main motivation for opening Nassarawa School in Kano and King's College in Lagos in 1909.

The Lugardian policy of excluding educated elements from the native authority system and of preventing their contact with the masses was not peculiar to the north, although it was more thoroughgoing and endured much longer there than elsewhere. It was characteristic of the official attitude throughout Nigeria until the early 1930's, when signs of change began to appear. In 1933 the governor of Nigeria noted that

> "It was almost a tendency not so many years ago to discourage too close an association between the educated African and the unsophisticated members of the community. One of the main reasons why educated Africans sought refuge in the towns was the intolerance shown to the class by Administrative Officers and other Europeans." [44]

In effect, therefore, government policy not only presumed that educated Africans were unrepresentative, but it operated to keep them that way.

Guided by the Lugardian principle of separating educated Nigerians from the masses, the British administration delayed coming to grips with the problems of where the educated classes would fit into the total picture, and of who would control the superstructure holding the native authorities together in a modern political unit. Educated Nigerians became convinced that they were destined to serve forever as clerks and subalterns, and that the superstructure was, as Lugard perhaps assumed, a perpetual British preserve. A correspondent of the London *Times* recognized the basic dilemma as early as 1912:

> [Educated Africans] . . . have, naturally, developed ambitions which, however legitimate, are unrealizable unless we are prepared to share supreme administrative controlling power with them; to reverse, therefore, our policy, and to place the Anglicanized African on an equality with ourselves in the work of government over the heads of the native rulers.[45]

In the early 1930's, however, official thought regarding the relationship between educated groups and the native authority system, particularly in the Southern Provinces, began to change. Several factors were responsible. The most obvious was the great increase in the number of educated Nigerians. It was no longer a problem of a few thousand concentrated in Lagos and other urban centers, but of hundreds of thousands scattered all over southern Nigeria. In the decade after World War I the number of secondary schools had jumped from two to twenty-six. The second factor was the sudden burst of organizational activity among educated groups in the early 1930's, which reflected their strong desire to participate in the affairs of their home villages or districts. Organized into lineage and tribal unions, educated sons abroad asserted a claim to have their voices heard in native authority councils. In general, their demands were moderate and showed a sense of responsibility. The British change in policy was in part a response to this challenge. In the late 1930's and early 1940's, the government gave increasing encouragement to the activities of these unions. At the same time it insisted that the educated influence must be persuasive rather than dictatorial, and that it must be channeled through and have the consent of the traditional authorities. In short, although Lugard's idea of keeping all political development in Nigeria within the framework of the traditional system was retained, his policy of educating and reforming that system from within, which had meant the exclusion of the educated elements, was abandoned.

Policy changes were further stimulated by warnings from observers and students of the African scene, who felt that meaningful roles must be provided for the previously excluded and unwanted group of educated Nigerians. In 1935 Charles Roden Buxton warned that "we neglect the *intelligentsia* at our peril," and added:

> The educated Indian—the Babu—was regarded with precisely the same mixture of contempt and jocularity as the educated African is today. Yet, what has happened? In less than a half a century those Babus, whom we thought we could ignore, . . . had become the statesmen of India. . . . They were still a tiny minority, but they had become the people without whose consent and cooperation we could no longer carry on the government of India at all. I venture to prophesy, confidently, that it will be the same in Africa. . . .[46]

In similar vein, Lucy P. Mair, one of Britain's leading Africanists, pointed out in 1936 that demands for change had always come from minorities with specific grounds for discontent and that the African educated class would ultimately triumph.[47]

Perhaps the most direct examination of the problem in its Nigerian setting was undertaken by Margery Perham in 1936. Acknowledging that the emergence of the educated Nigerian was absolutely necessary for Britain's colonial mission, she urged that it be accomplished by (1) employing more Nigerians in "positions of trust" (but not in the administrative service), and (2) "doing everything possible to find or create opportunities for them within the Native Administrations."[48] Obviously referring to Nnamdi Azikiwe, she raised this question: "But what scope . . . can the rudimentary Ibo groups offer to one of the tribe who has spent ten years at American universities accumulating academic qualifications?"[49] The question was answered by Azikiwe himself; ten years later he was the leader of a Nigeria-wide nationalist movement, and twenty years later the premier of Eastern Nigeria.

As subsequent events proved, this late prewar effort to channel the energies of educated Nigerians into the traditional structure did not satisfy their aspirations. It is difficult to make broad generalizations because of wide tribal variations in the composition of native authorities, the uneven tribal and geographical distribution of educated Nigerians, and the division of the group into sharply defined conservative, moderate, and radical elements.

The attitudes of educated Nigerians in prewar Lagos, the most sophisticated and enlightened urban center, provide a few clues. The older and more conservative progovernment members of the Lagos intelligentsia gave unquestioning support to the system of native administration in the provinces, but strongly objected to extending the system to Lagos or the colony area. Were they not "British subjects"? Lagos barristers, who comprised about half of the total African representation in the pre-1946 Legislative Council, opposed one aspect of the system of indirect rule on personal and professional grounds. They protested their exclusion as counsel from the native court system.[50] As more barristers arrived from the London Inns of Court, the protest became louder. The thousands of educated clerks, artisans, and subalterns in Lagos expressed their dissatisfaction over the exclusion policy through their lineage and tribal unions. Whether moderates who sought partial representation, or radicals who pressed for total control, they all wanted the old and illiterate members of the native authority councils replaced by the young and educated— namely, themselves.

By the time of World War II the grievances of educated Nigerians had increased and the radical tendency had become dominant. There were two principal reasons for this development. First, the British administration was either disinclined or unable, because of the war and the strong resistance of traditionalists, fully to integrate the educated elements into the traditional structure. The scattered efforts that were made affected so limited a number of educated Nigerians that few sensed any change in policy. The second reason was increasing acceptance of the notion that the system of indirect rule was "not only a form of government specially invented for backward peoples, but one designed to perpetuate their backwardness by preserving their isolation and tribal divisions." [51]

The antipathy of the educated elements toward the system of indirect rule had become more pronounced by the late 1930's. The Youth Charter of the Nigerian Youth Movement, published in 1938, contained the following statement:

We are opposed to the term "Indirect Rule" literally as well as in principle. Honest trusteeship implies direct British Rule with a view to ultimate self-government. We shall therefore strive for the complete abolition of the indirect rule system. Native Administration should be a form of local government, and it is for that reason that we will encourage and support it.[52]

Although several of the leaders of the movement were Lagos barristers—including the general secretary, just back from the London School of Economics—the adherence of the majority of educated Nigerians to such an attitude requires further explanation. The expression "indirect rule" had taken on imperialistic connotations because educated Nigerians believed that district officers, residents, and governors sometimes insulted chiefs and elders or emasculated their powers by vetoing their actions, dictating taxes, arbitrarily establishing local rules, appointing and deposing titled chiefs, and interfering with local customs; in short, the British administration, in their view, imposed a petty autocracy under the pretense of training Nigerians for self-government.

There was a second reason for the opposition to indirect rule. Because emirs and chiefs held office at the pleasure of the resident or the governor, they seemed to be merely puppets—"imperialist stooges" in nationalist jargon—of the colonial government, and hence could not be independent representatives of the people, least of all of the educated groups. It was the subservience of most traditional authorities to the white man, whether fancied or real, which provoked the more race-conscious educated Nigerians into uncompromising hostility to the whole system of indirect rule. The fact that British plans for constitutional reform did not deviate from the basic Lugardian purpose of channeling Nigerian energies and power through the native authority system, served only to strengthen the suspicion that the traditional authorities were agents of imperialism. This aggravated the growing antagonism between the educated elements and the chiefs, which in turn increased the latter's subservience to the British and the former's demands for control at the center. Members of the intelligentsia became convinced that the only sure way of making their influence felt was to wrest control of the superstructure from the British.

PART III

The Rise of the Nigerian Nationalist Movement

CHAPTER 7

Early Resistance and Protest Movements

Since the first encounter between Europeans and the peoples inhabiting Nigeria there have been a variety of manifestations of
what might broadly be called nationalism, if by the latter one
means sentiment or activity opposed to alien control. In this sense,
nationalism would include not only the recent and contemporary
movement among Nigerians to create a self-governing Nigeria,
but also the early militant resistance of the Delta rulers, such as
the famous King Ja Ja, to European penetration of the interior;
the defiance of King Kosoko of Lagos and of the Sultan of
Sokoto; and the Aba women's riots in eastern Nigeria in the late
1920's. In this broader sense, a history of nationalism in Nigeria
would necessarily encompass Euro-Nigerian relations during the
past four centuries.

Although all these various forms of resistance and assertion
might thus legitimately come under the rubric of "nationalism,"
it is useful for analytical purposes, and imperative in terms of
manageability and focus, to make the following distinctions:

1) Traditional nationalism includes movements of resistance
to the initial British penetration and occupation, early revolts
provoked by the imposition or operation of alien political or
economic coercions, and nativistic or messianic movements
which provided psychological or emotional outlets for the tensions and frustrations produced by rapid cultural change. All
these were probably as intensely nationalistic and anti-European
as subsequent movements, but for purposes of exposition and
analysis it is useful to distinguish them from later manifestations.

2) Modern nationalism includes sentiments, activities, and
organizational developments aimed explicitly at the self-govern-

169

ment and independence of Nigeria as a nation-state existing on a basis of equality in an international state system. Its distinguishing features are (*a*) the explicit goal of Nigerian self-government; (*b*) the concept of Nigerian unity; (*c*) the predominance of westernized elements in leadership groups; (*d*) the development of permanent political associations to pursue nationalist objectives; and (*e*) the predominance of modern political values and ideals. This study is primarily concerned with the latter range of phenomena, which might loosely be called twentieth-century Nigerian nationalism. The earlier manifestations of nationalism, however, are not without relevance for an understanding of later developments.

EARLY RESISTANCE MOVEMENTS

Throughout the four centuries preceding the imposition of formal British control, African chiefs in the Niger Delta area effectively prevented intrusions of the white man. In his recently published study, Dr. K. Onwuka Dike has emphasized that such opposition, and not disease, was the primary force tending to exclude the white man from the hinterland.[1] The opposition compelled European traders to recognize the sovereignty of African states, and remained effective so long "as Africans had the equipment, the means, and the numbers to maintain their independence."[2] But there were two developments that weakened or overcame this barrier to penetration. One was the decline in the power of the semimilitary coastal kingdoms which resulted from revolutionary economic changes, as well as from other internal developments. The other was the decision of the British government in 1885 to support a more determined and systematic penetration of the interior which was to culminate, fifteen years later, in the establishment of a formal protectorate supported and controlled by British power.

Once Britain had made this decision, the occupation and pacification of Nigeria were carried out with comparatively little difficulty and with relatively little expense in arms, money, and men. In general, the acquisition was accomplished by force, or by the threat of force. The British obtained the cession of Lagos by duress, after launching an armed attack during which most of the town was destroyed by fire.[3] In the Western Region, the

Ijebu and the Bini were both the victims of military conquest, the latter after putting up substantial resistance. In the Delta area, the Royal Niger Company met sporadic opposition to the establishment of its authority from the riverain tribes, whose bitter resentment over the white intrusion was well demonstrated in the Akassa Massacre. In the Eastern Region, between 1900 and 1920, several expeditionary forces (Aro, Northern Hinterland, Niger–Cross River, North Ibibio) were necessary to establish British control, and as late as 1918 constant patrolling was still the order of the day. In the north, the Nupe and the Ilorin, with armies of 30,000 and 8,000, respectively, resisted the forces of the Royal Niger Company. After the company's charter was revoked, and during the transition to formal British rule, the Nupe and the Kontagora revolted against British authority. The Yola, Kano, Sokoto, and Hadeija emirates were all conquered in 1903 by Lugard's forces, after offering initial resistance.[4] The vast areas of the Middle Belt were not completely pacified until the end of World War I. Even after pacification, however, there were frequent revolts in this area, which Sir Alan Burns has suggested were prompted "less by a zeal for independence than by a desire to continue the habits of murder, robbery, and cannibalism, which had become the second nature of these primitive people."[5]

To what extent was their conquest by superior forces, after they had offered maximum resistance, a factor in sparking a nationalist reaction among Nigerian peoples? It is suggestive that the Ijebu, the Bini, the Nupe, and several of the Ibo groups, who resisted the British most strenuously, have had a disproportionately heavy representation in the nationalist movement; yet there are other factors that could serve as an explanation. Part of the prejudice of many nationalists against indirect rule stemmed from the replacement of chiefs who resisted the alien intrusion by chiefs who were "good boys" and who willingly signed protectorate treaties. Certainly the protracted agitation of educated elements in Lagos was partly stimulated by their resentment over the duress employed by the British in acquiring the colony, and over the lowered status of the House of Docemo.

There seems to have been nothing in the conquest of Nigeria to compare to the famous Ashanti wars of Ghana. Moreover, the thoroughgoing application of indirect rule in Nigeria helped to alleviate the initial sting of subjugation. At most it can be said that the ease of British conquest and rule was a factor in creating an exaggerated belief in white superiority and black inferiority among the first generation after occupation, and that the reaction of educated Nigerians to white lordship and black depreciation ultimately had nationalistic implications. Being made acutely aware of one's own weakness by superior force can be a powerful stimulus to subsequent self-assertion and retaliation. Nationalists could later appeal to resentment based upon the indignities and injustices, the shame and wounded pride of subjugation, and could use it as a focus for mobilizing resistance to foreign rule.[6]

Except for descriptive purposes no sharp line can be drawn between the initial resistance to the establishment of British authority and later protest or revolt against specific administrative actions which Africans deemed offensive. In both instances, the response was an impulsive negative retort to an alien disruptive force. Yet there is clearly a difference of degree in native consciousness of alien control between compelling a chief under military threat to rule his people with the guidance of a British administrative officer, and directing the same chief to impose unaccustomed taxes upon his people. Moreover, there is an important time differential: the bewilderment and resentment over and the resistance to initial intrusion ended with pacification, whereas the sporadic revolts against specific administrative actions occurred after final submission and temporary accommodation to superior force. Nationalist leaders could capitalize on the latter by channeling grievances into the nationalist movement; the former, except as a rankling memory to be kept alive, had less utility.

Precipitated and fed by specific grievances, postpacification revolts were territorially uncoördinated, and haphazard in their occurrence. Subject to local leadership which before 1938 normally had no affiliation with or direction from strategists outside, they were usually short-lived, collapsing at the show of force, the release of emotional tension, or the removal of the grievances. Among the many instances of localized protest, only three warrant special mention: the Akassa Massacre of 1895, the Egba Uprising of 1918, and the Aba Riots of 1929. In the Akassa affair, the Brass middlemen, partly displaced by the expansion of the Royal Niger Company into the hinterland, organized a force of 1,500 men which attacked and destroyed the company's property at Akassa. This was followed by a punitive expedition, although the Brassmen assured the British consul of their loyalty to Queen Victoria, pointing out that they "did not kill the Queen's men." [7] Despite violence on both sides, the uprising had little political significance at the time. Later on, however, it became an item in the historical stock of nationalist grievances.

The Egba Uprising (or "Adubi War") of 1918 was a minor revolt in which one European and one chief were deliberately killed. The Egba Kingdom in Yorubaland had retained a substantial measure of autonomy until 1914, when the "independence" treaty governing its relations with the British government was terminated and indirect rule inaugurated. Accumulated grievances over administrative innovations of the British authority, especially the imposition of direct taxation in 1918, led the people to rebel. The revolt was quickly crushed, and the ensuing inquiry revealed that educated Egbas resident in Lagos had aided and abetted the uprising, partly because of resentment over the termination of Egba independence, and partly because of their own grievances over the Lagos water rate.[8] This was the first instance of a pattern that later became significant—the provocation of local disturbances in the interior by educated elements abroad,* who then used the uprisings to further the nationalist struggle. Such disturbances were invariably based on local grievances, but were frequently precipitated by educated "sons abroad." The ability of the intelligentsia to engineer interior disturbances by remote control was a source of strength which the administration did not fully appreciate; but the localization of such disorders and their flash-in-the-pan character were evidences of the weakness of the same group. These characteristics go far to explain the violent fluctuations in the intensity of local uprisings, which nationalist leaders later claimed were manifestations of nationalist activity, and which they wanted to harness to the nationalist movement.

---

* As used here, and as used by many Nigerians, the word "abroad" means away from one's home village (usually in an urban center), not necessarily overseas or in a foreign country.

The third major pre–World War II disturbance, which has figured large in the annals of an otherwise uneventful political history, was the Aba Riots of 1929. The rumor that women were to be taxed, and dissatisfaction over the abuses of native court members and warrant chiefs, precipitated a women's movement that spread like wildfire through two of the most densely populated provinces of the Eastern Region at the end of 1929. Chiefs and Europeans were attacked indiscriminately and there was widespread destruction of property and goods, belonging mainly to trading firms. The riot was not quelled until the police, in an overwhelming show of force, killed fifty women and injured an equal number. An unusual feature was that the women, all illiterate, not only initiated but also were the only participants in the uprising. The whole affair was entirely spontaneous and received no support from either the men or the literate elements of the provinces. It revealed an amazing capacity for organization and united action which transcended clan and tribal boundaries. Two commissions of inquiry were appointed. The first was purely official and submitted a report tending to exonerate the officials involved; the second, including two prominent Nigerian barristers, was highly critical of the administrative ineptness that had precipitated the uprising. The Secretary of State for the Colonies accepted the second report, but refrained from criticism except to note that the fundamental cause of the disturbance was faulty intelligence: ". . . the Government had insufficient knowledge of the indigenous institutions and life of the people." [9]

In addition to the foregoing protest movements, which sought amelioration of specific local grievances, mostly of an economic nature, others apparently unconnected with any clearly defined resentment have flared up. Usually religious in character, they fall into the category of protest phenomena described by Linton as "magical nativism," in which the participants try to re-create aspects of the traditional situation which appear desirable in retrospect.[10] In 1925, a nativistic religious movement in Iboland was allegedly a response to a miraculous message from *Chi-ukwa* (God). Bands of dancing women marched up and down the country denouncing such innovations as British currency and native courts and demanding a return to the customs of olden times.[11] It should be noted that the locale of the 1925 nativistic revival was the same as that of the Aba Riots which occurred four years later. Both movements not only were feminist, but had marked reactionary overtones. Just as the women of 1925 agitated for a return to customary currency and village councils, so the women of 1929 demanded that "all the white men should go to their country so that the land in this area might remain as it was many years ago before the advent of the white man." [12]

During the interval between the initial shock of alien control and 1950, minor nativistic religious movements arose throughout southern Nigeria. They reflected accumulated tensions within the social fabric of the community—tensions created by the shock of rapid culture change and urgently demanding release or dissipation.[13]

In the Moslem areas of northern Nigeria, a related type of protest occurred during the decade immediately following initial pacification. Several minor uprisings, which were led by local Mahdis, did not present any serious challenge to the political order (Fulani or British). But in order to crush an outbreak of Mahdism at Satiru in Sokoto Province in 1905, the British had to rush troops from Lagos and from the Tiv country where pacification was still in progress.[14] Since World War I there have been no known incidents of this nature, which is attributable at least in part to the British policy of not offending Moslem sensibilities. These early outbreaks, together with the fact that the Fulani jihad was part of the famous Wahabi movement, were evidence of the ever-present potentiality of religious revolt.

RELIGIOUS SECESSIONIST MOVEMENTS

Another form of protest which appeared quite early, and represents the religious strand in Nigerian nationalism, concerns the religious groups that seceded from the white-dominated Christian churches in Nigeria.[15] The first of these was the United Native African Church, which in 1891 seceded from the Anglican Church. The resolution of secession, dated August 14, 1891, reveals the dominant motive for the action:

That this meeting in humble dependence upon Almighty God is of opinion that Africa is to be evangelized, and that the foreign agencies at work at the present moment, taking into considera-

175

tion climatic, and other influences, cannot grasp the situation.
. . . Resolved that a purely Native African Church be founded,
for the evangelization and amelioration of our race, to be governed by African.[16]

The secession of the United Native African Church was partly
influenced by Dr. Edward Blyden, a famous African spokesman
from Liberia. In 1887 he published a book in which he bitterly
criticized the established Christian churches for their condescension toward African culture, and particularly for their intolerance of such African customs as polygyny. Late in 1890 he
visited Lagos and urged prominent African Christians to establish a native church on the pattern of Negro churches in the
United States. The editor of the leading nationalist paper in
Lagos wrote:

> It is Dr. Blyden who has set the African thinking and caused
> him to see and understand that no people or nation has said
> the last word for the world and that it is safer and better for
> the world that each race should retain and develop upon its own
> natural racial lines. . . .[17]

Ten years later, in 1901, another large group seceded from the
Anglican faith and formed The African Church (Inc.). This
secession removed so large a group that for several years it
seriously affected the membership and financial position of
European churches in Lagos.[18] In 1917 a third group seceded,
this time from the Methodist Church, and a few years later another group declared its independence from the Baptist Church.
During the interwar period several more groups seceded or, like
the Order of the Seraphim and Cherubim, were organized independently.[19] With certain exceptions, these separatist sects remained essentially Christian, and many retained the prayer books
and most of the ceremonial forms of the parent European
churches. The majority tended toward Biblical literalism: ". . .
our safest course is to study the religion mainly from the Bible
and from the life of its divine author Christ for ourselves and
have Him before us as our model." [20]

Some of these sects had received encouragement from American Negro sects. Blyden's attitude was undoubtedly a reflection
of such influence. Moreover, after the United Native African

Church had been firmly established, American Negro clergymen visited Nigeria in 1899 and ordained the ministers of the new Church. Many of the minor sects that came into being after the turn of the century, either by secession from a European church or as a spontaneously organized group, were the direct product of the encouragement of small American sects (white and Negro) which provided literature, hymn books, and leaflets.

These separatist movements were remarkably early manifestations of protest against white domination and the status of inferiority. Their greatest weakness, aggravated by the influence of American Negro sects, was the strong tendency toward endless schism. Small differences of opinion or petty personal rivalries would frequently cause the leader of one faction to break off and establish his own little sect. Repeated efforts to form a federation, an "African Communion," failed to achieve lasting results. Many of the African churches looked to the British government, with its policy of toleration, for support in their efforts to evangelize the interior. Some of the groups formed later, however, were openly antiwhite and anti-imperialist. A movement that occurred in 1914 in the Delta region under the leadership of a Nigerian who called himself the Second Elijah was essentially puritanical and Christian in character, but the leader became progressively anti-European and was finally convicted of sedition by the British authorities. Another movement, called "Orunlaism" by its prophet, was even more emphatic: "Scrap the imported religions. . . . [There can be no] political emancipation without spiritual emancipation. . . . Paint God as an African, . . . the angels as Africans, . . . the Devil by all means in any colour than an African, . . . and thou shalt be saved." [21] Two religious groups of anti-imperialist cast, God's Kingdom Society and the National Church, were adjuncts of the nationalist movement in the 1940's, and will be discussed later.

The pre–World War I secessionist groups were not devoid of political importance. Unlike the more tradition-oriented nativistic movements, they were led by educated Africans who had been under Christian and European influence in Lagos since 1852. Their assertions of independence support the view that the reactions of a subordinate culture to a dominant culture fall into a pattern, and that in the most acculturated groups the reaction is usually a phenomenon of the second generation. Some of the leaders of these groups were active in early Lagos protest movements which had a definite political character. Patriarch J. G. Campbell, organizer of the West African Episcopal Church, for example, was a prominent figure in pre–World War I Lagos politics and assumed the leadership in the National Congress of British West Africa immediately after the war. These groups were African associations which gave race-conscious leaders an outlet for their energies, a platform for their ideas, and an organized following. Despite their small number, the groups brought Africans together in a common cause and provided a milieu in which they could feel that they were masters of their own destiny. None of the groups caused the British administration serious apprehension, but they were symptomatic of an undercurrent of frustration and grievance which ultimately found an outlet in political nationalism.

EARLY PROTEST MOVEMENTS IN LAGOS

On several occasions in the two decades preceding World War I, residents of Lagos vigorously protested actions of the British government in Nigeria. Five of the protests will be examined.[22] The measures that were resented were largely necessary to the government's program of establishing formal British rule over Nigeria at the turn of the century. These early protests were in the nature of "primary resistance" to the British presence, in that they were particular responses to particular imperial measures deemed oppressive or onerous, rather than fundamental challenges to imperial rule or positive affirmations of the objective of Nigerian self-government. But the rancor produced by the official measures, and the political awakening that accompanied demonstrations of popular resentment, helped not only to foment distrust of British intentions, but also to lay the groundwork for a more programmatic form of nationalism.

The first incident occurred in 1895 when the governor proposed a house and land tax on the inhabitants of Lagos. In response, about 5,000 Lagos citizens went to Government House to demonstrate their strong opposition, and as a result the tax measure was never enforced.[23] The second wave of protest, occurring late in 1907 and early in 1908, was provoked by government expropriation of property on Lagos Island under the Land Acquisition Ordinance in order to provide sites for official residences. The resulting popular discontent was expressed in a petition sent to the Secretary of State for the Colonies. According to one report,

> The natives are openly talking of stopping trade in order to make the Governor feel how much they resent it. Several mass meetings have been held in Lagos, and the crowd went so far as to throw stones at the houses along the front, and in one case pulled a European merchant off his bicycle; . . . it is not only the Government officers who are involved, but every White Man in the colony. . . . The natives begin to see that it is they who are finding money to build all these fine palaces; . . . the people look at their own poor little huts alongside the palatial buildings of the European and wonder how long and how far this thing is to go. . . . They see these Government officers coming out for twelve months at a time, and then go away for six months on full pay; they see a pension list annually being added to; they see jinrickshas and servants, horses and stable boys, addition to the salaries of these officials. . . . The extravagance of the Government is becoming more than the people can stand. It is particularly visible in the luxuries of official Lagos life.[24]

In January, 1908, a third government measure aroused an even stronger outburst of popular resentment, which found expression on several occasions in the following eight years. The government levied a water rate on the local population in order to pay loan and maintenance expenditures arising from the development of a potable water supply for Lagos.[25] There were several bases for the strong opposition to the water rate. One was the belief that it was discriminatory; as one educated Lagosian put it,

> The motive of this measure is not, primarily, to benefit the people, but the Europeans; . . . the electric light scheme was inaugurated under similar pretenses. . . . Indirect taxation was imposed for this purpose by raising the ad valorem duty from five to ten per cent. . . . This increased taxation falls, of course, upon the native community, and that community has had the satisfaction of seeing electric light imported and installed in the houses of European officials. . . . Native quarters are, as a rule, as dark as Erebus; . . . so it will be with the water scheme. . . .

179

The Europeans will benefit from it, and some excuse will be invented to deprive the natives of it.[26]

It was also argued that the new scheme was unnecessary. As the Lagosians themselves did not lack water, it followed in their view that the water supply was intended only for the European community.[27] The administration took the position that "the Government is the father and the people the children. The father has seen that the water his children are drinking is not good." [28] The people also resented the imposition of the water rate because the Secretary of State for the Colonies had made his approval conditional upon (1) "full and open discussion," and (2) the absence of "formidable opposition." When the governor pointed out that the measure had received the unanimous assent of the unofficial members of the Legislative Council, the response of protesting Lagosians, heard frequently in the next thirty years, was that the unofficial members "are merely the Government nominees. . . . They do not represent the people in any sense." [29] Thus at the core of the protest were two powerful grievances: racial discrimination and taxation without representation.[30]

Although the Lagos people, after a brief riot in Tinubu Square, finally bowed to the collection of the rate, the protest movement had generated much bitterness. In a letter to the editor of the *African Mail* one Lagosian said: "What we daily feel, and every action of the present Administration justifies and deepens, is that we are exploited for the benefit of those who come among us. . . . The distrust that is consequent on such feeling is spreading more and more widely and nothing is done to stem or counteract it." [31] Also, for the first time, educated Lagosians organized a formal association as a vehicle for popular protest. In 1908 two leading African doctors of Lagos organized the People's Union for the purpose of defending native rights in general, and of opposing expropriation, changes in land tenure, and the water rate in particular. The failure to prevent the levying of the water rate, plus disagreements among the leaders, and the changes produced by World War I, caused the union to become moribund after 1916. It was, however, reorganized in 1923.

Another government action that precipitated no little protest and organizational activity was the Colonial Office appointment of the West African Lands Commission in 1912 for the purpose of determining the feasibility of applying the northern Nigeria system of land tenure to southern Nigeria. Since under that system all rights over land were "under the control and subject to the disposition of the Governor," leaders of opinion in Lagos regarded the proposal as an imperial move to deprive Africans in southern Nigeria of the right to own land. A mass meeting was organized in Lagos and deputations were dispatched to the Yoruba hinterland to awaken the chiefs and people to this alleged threat. In the meantime, in response to encouragement from the Reverend J. H. Harris, the famous Afrophile, the Lagos auxiliary of the Anti-Slavery and Aborigines Protection Society was founded to express Nigerian attitudes on land tenure.[32] A Nigerian delegation, composed of both educated Lagosians and chiefs from such interior centers as Abeokuta, Ibadan, Ijebu-Ode, Ilesha, and Ife, was dispatched to London in 1913. Several factors, including the growth of factionalism and the characteristic difficulty with funds, tended to bring the delegation into disrepute. In any event, although the whole episode was based upon the fear, rather than the actuality, of some new imperial coercion or deprivation, it resulted in the political mobilization of new elements of the population and brought together for the first time educated Lagosians and chiefs from the interior.[33]

The government responded to the outburst of political agitation and press criticism in 1908 by passing the Seditious Offenses Ordinance in 1909. Articulate Lagosians regarded the act as an intolerable and un-British stifling of criticism. In moving the rejection of the bill in the Legislative Council, the Honorable Sapara Williams pointed out that the "freedom of the Press is the great Palladium of British liberty. . . . Sedition is a thing incompatible with the character of the Yoruba people, and has no place in their constitution. . . . Hyper-sensitive officials may come tomorrow who will see sedition in every criticism, and crime in every mass meeting." [34] The editor of the *Lagos Weekly Record* charged that,

> . . . subjected to methods and measures of government so distinctly unconstitutional and arbitrary, the people dare not by any act, word, deed or sign signify their displeasure or dissatisfaction with the regime of government without entailing the risk of the penalty of the law for sedition.[35]

Notwithstanding a strong demonstration of protest, including one mass meeting of about 6,000, the bill became law; indeed the above-cited editor was one of the first to be prosecuted under it.

In general, membership in the early political associations in Lagos was limited to a few leaders who sought to defend what they considered the natural rights of Africans, and their acquired rights as British subjects, against the policies of a colonial government in the first phase of expansion and development. Such associations were primarily instruments for achieving a united front in protesting against particular grievances, and little effort was made to build them into permanent associations. Once the grievance was disposed of, the organizations either became moribund or split into hostile factions. Indeed, in 1921, Sir Hugh Clifford complained of the absence of any group from which he could obtain African views.[36] Two years later the editor of the *Nigerian Advocate* lamented that the "fault in us in Nigeria is that we cannot exercise tolerance with one another, and we quarrel over things that do not count." [37] In retrospect, it could be argued that one of the reasons for such weaknesses among Nigerians was the absence of meaningful political roles for them to play, or of an arena of legitimate political activity. They lacked a strong sense of purpose upon which associational development might be built. In this respect, the Constitution of 1923 opened a new phase in Nigerian political development.

CHAPTER 8

The Beginnings of Nationalist Thought and Activity

Two native foreigners were among the early founders of modern Nigerian nationalism. They were contemporaries, and both had close links with Liberia. One, the late Edward Wilmot Blyden, spent very little of his life in Nigeria, but the impact of his writings and speeches was of such scope that the late Casely Hayford of the Gold Coast (now Ghana) bestowed upon him the fatherhood of African nationalism. Blyden, who was born on the island of St. Thomas, Virgin Islands, called himself a "pure Negro," and his obituary identified him with the Ibo (Eboe) tribe.[1] Many elements in his thought linked him closely to American Negro intellectuals of his period.[2] The other man so important to Nigerian nationalism was the late John Payne Jackson, a Liberian. He was a close confidant of Blyden's, and for twenty-eight years (1890–1918) lived and wrote in Lagos. The early writings of Blyden and Jackson reveal the main themes of latter-day nationalist ideology. Blyden emphasized cultural nationalism, Jackson the more political aspects of nationalism.

The dominant note in Blyden's thought was that Africans should not indiscriminately emulate other races, but should seek the regeneration of their continent by bringing forth and demonstrating its unique contribution to humanity. His writings span a period of more than forty years, beginning with his first published work, *Liberia's Offering*, in 1862 and ending with *West Africa before Europe* in 1905. Casely Hayford wrote the introduction to the latter.[3] It is not without significance that for nearly forty years a large portrait of Dr. Blyden has hung on the wall of Glover Memorial Hall, the principal arena of Nigerian nationalism and the birthplace of the National Council of Nigeria and the Cameroons (NCNC).

From 1891 to the early 1930's the *Lagos Weekly Record,* owned and edited by John Payne Jackson (and after his death in 1918 by his son Thomas Horatius Jackson), was a determined agent in the propagation of racial consciousness. In commenting on this early period, Ernest Ikoli, the dean of Nigerian journalists, stated that a "newspaper's popularity was often measured by the intensity of its assault on the only target [that is, the government] that was available." [4] By this standard, Jackson's *Record* was far and away the most popular of all papers. His pungent criticism, expressed in lengthy editorials, always hung on the edge of sedition:

> One cannot refrain from speculating upon the bankruptcy of the New Imperialism and the apparent decay of British Imperial genius, so long as Great Britain continues to transcend the limits of political righteousness; to harbour the colour prejudice (the logical outcome of the Americanisation of England . . .) . . . ; to legislate away the rights of her coloured subjects (as witness the South African Union Act); and to remain indifferent to the wishes of her subject dependencies. [5]

> There can be no question that if the Nigerian system is not scrapped within the next five years, the unfortunate experiences of the Indian agitation will be witnessed in West Africa. . . . [6]

> . . . every constitutional effort directed against the nullification of the Nigerian System is a consecrated duty, a moral duty and a national duty. . . . Resistance to oppression is not only justifiable but necessary. . . . [7]

> . . . British politicians and administrators have been shouting us almost deaf with such catch phrases as trusteeship for the subject races, but there does not seem to be any definite programme as to how we are to be educated to take over the trusteeship. Not that we take these political utterances very seriously, but we know from the ordinary processes and laws of evolution that some day we should be obliged to take upon our own shoulders the black man's burden, and the sooner our good masters give us the opportunity of cultivating the necessary qualities for the task the better. [8]

Jackson ceaselessly urged Africans to unite and be aware of their common nationality:

> West Africans have discovered today what the Indians . . . discovered 35 years ago, that, placed as they were under the controlling influence of a foreign power, it was essential to their well-being that they should make a common cause and develop a national unity. . . . We hope the day will soon come when . . . Hausas, Yorubas, and Ibos will make a common stand and work hand in hand for their common fatherland.[9]

> Liberty was never conferred upon any nation; . . . it has to be won and even at that it has its price. . . . It is only through sacrifice or martyrdom on the altar of patriotism that success can be finally achieved.[10]

For forty years the *Record* campaigned in defense of West Africans and Africans against alien white rule. As A. B. Laotan concluded:

> The *Record* was so powerful that at one time, on account of its uncompromising attitude in the national interest, all foreign advertisements were withdrawn, but it stood its ground unflinchingly. . . . [It] was by far and away the best paper in West Africa. . . .[11]

Until 1914 the government, aside from its power to invoke charges of sedition, was unprotected against the onslaughts of Jackson's paper. In that year Sir Kitoyi Ajasa launched the *Nigerian Pioneer*, which took a conservative, progovernment line. Since Sir Kitoyi and Governor Lugard were close friends, and Lugard was extremely sensitive to and irritated by Jackson's journalism, it was believed that the *Pioneer* was in effect a government paper. Sir Kitoyi represented the older generation of "black Englishmen" for whom Lugard and other officials felt a strong affinity.[12] Jackson exemplified the other extreme, the race-conscious and uncompromising nationalist. Whereas Jackson gave strong support to all pre–World War I protest movements, Ajasa defended the government on most issues and opposed leaders and movements that earned government displeasure. Thus each man represented a distinct type within the educated African group. It was, of course, the Jackson point of view that ultimately won out.

There were other pre–World War I newspapers edited and published by Lagosians.[13] In 1903 the *Lagos Standard* appeared, in 1908 the *Nigerian Chronicle,* and in 1914 the *Nigerian Times.* The early growth of the Nigerian press led the government to pass an ordinance in 1903 requiring the registration of all newspapers, and another in 1917 requiring the bonding of all editors. The avenue for African expression was further widened in 1910 by the establishment in Lagos of the Tika-Tore printing works, the first in a country-wide network of small presses printing polemical literature, which grew up during the following forty years. African-owned newspapers and presses were the media through which the nationalistic ideas of educated Africans found an outlet; they were partly responsible for the ever-growing number of Nigerians predisposed to a nationalist ideology. There can be little doubt that nationalist newspapers and pamphlets have been among the main influences in the awakening of racial and political consciousness.[14]

Long before Nigeria's Jacksonian era, however, the idea of African self-government found expression. In a frequently cited work published in London in 1868, James A. B. Horton advocated self-government for the peoples of British West Africa.[15] Again in 1881, when Lagos was a settlement under the governor of the Gold Coast Colony, a local newspaper editorialized:

> . . . we are not clamouring for immediate independence . . . but it should always be borne in mind that the present order of things will not last forever. A time will come when the British Colonies on the West Coast will be left to regulate their own internal and external affairs.[16]

In her excellent bibliography of Nigerian nationalist literature, Ruth Perry has drawn attention to the small but growing number of publications, written by educated Africans, which began to appear during the latter part of the nineteenth century and the early part of the twentieth.[17] One of the first was John Augustus Payne's *Lagos and West African Almanack* (1874), which was followed by his *Table of Principal Events in Yoruba History* (1893). The latter was the first of many tribal histories written by educated Africans during the succeeding sixty years. The earliest and perhaps the best known of these was Samuel Johnson's history of the Yoruba, written in 1897 but not published until 1921.[18] These tribal histories were a crucial strand in the development of both African and tribal cultural nationalism, a phenomenon examined in greater detail in chapter 15.

Before World War I, a few Nigerians either participated in or were influenced by certain developments abroad. In 1895, for example, Orishetukeh Faduma, a Yoruba, read a paper entitled "The Religious Beliefs of the Yoruba People" at the Congress on Africa held at Atlanta, Georgia, on the theme "Africa and the American Negro."[19] In 1911 W. E. B. Du Bois, Edward Blyden, and Mojola Agbebi, African pastor of the Niger Delta Mission, attended the First Universal Races Congress in London; Agbebi read a paper entitled "The West African Problem," which was published in the proceedings.[20] In the same year Booker T. Washington convened the International Conference on the Negro which was attended by representatives from many countries, including Casely Hayford, who contributed a paper entitled "The Progress of the Gold Coast Native."[21] Such external contacts helped to increase the awareness of the main currents of thought in the outside world among a small but growing number of West African intellectuals.

WORLD WAR I AND THE NATIONAL CONGRESS

In surveying the impact of World War I upon Africa, Sir Harry Johnston observed that most of the territories in British tropical Africa "and—notably—Nigeria, have shown themselves thoroughly loyal portions of the British Empire. . . . "[22] Of course, Nigeria was not deeply involved in the war. A few thousand Nigerian soldiers saw service in the Cameroons and in East Africa. There was a temporary drop in shipping, but Britain's need for vegetable oils soon restored trade to normal. Some educated Africans appeared to be apathetic toward, if not hopeful of, a German victory. German trading firms had always been more lenient with their credit facilities than British firms.[23] Actually, however, the volume of Nigerian import-export trade increased fourfold during the war, which thus became a period of comparative prosperity.

Despite Nigeria's relative noninvolvement in the war, important external developments had a significant impact upon the thoughts, aspirations, and activities of literate and articulate Nigerians. The statements of President Wilson and Prime Minister Lloyd George regarding self-determination strongly affected a few leaders, despite General Smuts's assertion that Africa was inhabited by barbarians who could not possibly govern themselves. Special weight was given to Lloyd George's statement in 1918 that the principle of self-determination was as applicable to colonies as to occupied European territories. Even though subsequent qualifications made it clear that his statement did not refer to African territories, it had aroused the aspirations of some Nigerians, who were stimulated to ask "Why?" and "If not now, when?"

In the latter part of the war and the immediate postwar period, two developments among Negro groups outside Nigeria further stimulated the growth of nationalist sentiment. One was the convening of the first Pan-African Congress in Paris in 1918–1919 by W. E. B. Du Bois and Blaise Diagne, African deputy from Senegal. Du Bois reports that he went to Paris "with the idea of calling a Pan-African Congress, and to try to impress upon the members of the Peace Conference . . . the importance of Africa in the future world." [24] Neither Du Bois nor Diagne argued for the immediate inauguration of self-determination; indeed, Du Bois specifically stated that the principle could not be applied to "uncivilized peoples." [25] Twelve of the fifty-seven delegates attending the congress were from Africa. In its resolution to the Allied powers the congress demanded:

> . . . the natives of Africa must have the right to participate in the government as fast as their development permits, in conformity with the principle that the government exists for the natives, and not the natives for the government. They shall at once be allowed to participate in local and tribal government, according to ancient usage, and this participation shall gradually extend, as education and experience proceed, to the higher offices of State; to the end that, in time, Africa be ruled by consent of the Africans. . . .[26]

Two subsequent Pan-African congresses were held in Lisbon in 1923 and in New York City in 1927. Although Africa was virtually unrepresented, other delegates made it clear on both occasions that the demands were made by the "Negro race through their thinking intelligentsia." Du Bois admitted that at the time the Pan-African idea was still "American rather than African." [27] Nigerians did not participate in the congresses, but reports of the proceedings in the local press stimulated among some of them an awareness of belonging to a wider cause.

The second development was the emergence of the militant and race-conscious Garvey movement. Marcus Garvey, a Jamaican Negro, visited London from 1912 to 1914. While there he came into contact with several Africans resident in London who told him of alleged atrocities in Africa. Garvey returned to Jamaica and founded the Universal Negro Improvement Association, and its affiliate the African Communities League, to unite "all Negro peoples of the world into one great body and to establish a country and government absolutely their own." [28] He received little support from his countrymen in Jamaica, and, at the invitation of Booker T. Washington, went to the United States in 1916, presumably for a lecture tour. Within four years he had become the acknowledged leader of the largest Negro mass organization in modern times. He published a newspaper, *Negro World,* which achieved an unprecedented circulation. His name became "a byword among Negroes in the new world and on the Dark Continent," as well as among worried security agents in African territories.[29] Between 1920 and 1925 Negro conventions in New York City, attended by delegates from many parts of Africa, made elaborate plans for the establishment of a Negro state in Africa, adopted declarations of independence, selected a flag and a national anthem, and elected Garvey as the provisional president of Africa.

Garvey sought to gather together into one nationalist ideology the strands of cultural, economic, and political nationalism which had been developing over a period of several decades in American Negro circles. His central argument was that there could be "no other salvation for the Negro but through a free and independent Africa." He stressed the overriding priority of political independence:

Wake up Africa! Let us work towards the one glorious end of a free, redeemed and mighty nation. . . . Nationhood is the

only means by which modern civilization can completely protect itself. . . . Prejudice of the white race against the black
race is not so much because of color as of condition; because as
a race, to them, we have accomplished nothing; we have built
no nation, no government; because we are dependent for our
economic and political existence. . . . every race must find a
home; hence the great cry of Palestine for the Jews—Ireland
for the Irish—India for the Indians and . . . "AFRICA FOR
THE AFRICANS." [30]

Garvey not only demanded a separate state for Negroes in
Africa, but proposed to use force to recapture the African homeland: "If England wants peace, if France wants peace, I suggest
to them to pack up their bag and baggage and clear out of Africa.
. . ." [31] Many themes in latter-day Nigerian nationalism have
been cast in the spirit if not in the exact words of Garvey.

Garvey was deported from the United States in 1927, largely
in response to a petition signed by certain American Negro intellectuals whose leadership he had challenged and whom he had
called "traitors to the race." [32] Although one of his organizations
still exists in New York, the main mass movement he had created
collapsed upon his departure. His appeals for racial solidarity
and the integral and exclusive form of his nationalism did, however, have several significant long-term effects. The widespread
support he received from the masses in America compelled
middle-class mulatto leaders like Du Bois and others to reassess
their stand on the racial issue. Du Bois, who had sought by
persuasion and exhortation to obliterate the American caste
system for the "talented tenth" of his race, ultimately turned to
communism and after 1945 spoke and wrote in words not unlike
those of his famous antagonist of the early 1920's. It is likely
that Garvey's pronounced cultural nationalism helped to stimulate the "Negro Renaissance" in which Negroes turned increasingly to the study and glorification of African history and culture.
Garvey had said that when whites were apes, Africans had a
"wonderful civilisation on the banks of the Nile." [33] Finally, although his movement was centered primarily among the Negro
masses of the eastern seaboard of the United States, and particularly in Harlem, he had made every effort to emphasize Africa as
the fatherland of all Negroes everywhere.

A Lagos branch of the Garveyite movement (Universal Negro Improvement Association) was organized in the fall of 1920. The leaders included Patriarch J. G. Campbell, head of one of the Christian separatist sects, the Reverend W. B. Euba, and the Reverend S. M. Abiodun. The association was strongly supported by John Payne Jackson and the *Lagos Weekly Record.* One young member, Ernest Ikoli, was later one of the founders of the Nigerian Youth Movement. The organization, however, made little headway, and soon became moribund. Yet the ideas propagated by Garvey had made a deep impression on some Nigerians who would not embrace the movement openly. Its indirect effects —on Azikiwe when he was in America, and on the interwar Soviet strategy toward the Negro and the African—were substantial. It is reported that a portrait of Marcus Garvey hangs over the entrance door to the study of Prime Minister Kwame Nkrumah of Ghana.

Influenced partly by these developments among Negro groups elsewhere, inspired by the example of the Indian Congress party, and stimulated by the climate of idealism generated by the war, a few educated Africans in the British West African territories organized the National Congress of British West Africa. The congress was formally established as a result of a conference held in Accra in 1920 at the invitation of Casely Hayford, a distinguished Gold Coast barrister and early nationalist leader. Delegates at the conference included representatives of educated groups in Nigeria, the Gold Coast, Sierra Leone, and Gambia.[34] The conference adopted several resolutions which were subsequently embodied in a memorandum taken to London and presented to the Secretary of State for the Colonies.[35] Among other items, the congress asked for:

1) A legislative council in each territory, half of whose members would be elected Africans.
2) African veto over taxation.
3) Separation of the judiciary from the legislative branch of the government.
4) Appointment and deposition of chiefs by their own people.
5) Abolition of racial discrimination in the civil service.
6) Development of municipal government.
7) Repeal of certain "obnoxious" ordinances.

8) Regulation of immigration of Syrians and other non-Africans.
9) Establishment of a university in West Africa.

The delegation that presented the petition remained in London from October, 1920, until February, 1921. It established contact with the League of Nations Union,[36] the Bureau International pour la Défense des Indigenes, the Welfare Committee for Africans in Europe, the African Progress Union, and West African students resident in London. While in London the delegation endeavored to gain the support of friendly members of Parliament and of prominent Afrophiles such as Sir Sydney Olivier, J. H. Harris, and Sir Harry Johnston. But Lord Milner, Secretary of State for the Colonies, having received unfavorable reports on the delegation from the governors of the British West African territories, rejected its demands. Meanwhile the delegation encountered certain characteristic financial difficulties. These problems, plus tensions within the delegation and the repudiation of certain of its members by prominent Africans at home, brought about its demise.

The activities of the National Congress of British West Africa attracted greater support from educated elements in the Gold Coast and Sierra Leone than from those in Nigeria. Actually, the idea of a West African conference and of a permanent body had first been advanced in 1913 by a Nigerian, Dr. Akinwande Savage, who was then resident in the Gold Coast. He returned to Nigeria in 1915 and tried unsuccessfully to organize a group to sponsor the project. The leadership ultimately passed to educated groups in the Gold Coast, in particular to T. Hutton Mills and Casely Hayford, and there it remained.[37]

There are several reasons for the comparative failure of the congress movement in Nigeria. In the first place, the Lagosians who actively supported the idea fell to fighting among themselves. This internal struggle was aggravated by Dr. Savage, whose personality alienated many actual and potential supporters. Second, the Nigerian government opposed the idea from the very beginning. Indeed, Sir Hugh Clifford, then governor, denounced the congress and its pretensions in strong language. In his memorable address to the Nigerian Council on December 29, 1920, Clifford ridiculed the leaders of the congress as

. . . a self-selected and self-appointed congregation of educated African gentlemen who collectively style themselves the "West African National Conference," . . . whose eyes are fixed, not upon African native history or tradition or policy, nor upon their own tribal obligations and the duties to their Natural Rulers which immemorial custom should impose upon them, but upon political theories evolved by Europeans to fit a wholly different set of circumstances, arising out of a wholly different environment, for the government of peoples who have arrived at a wholly different stage of civilization.[38]

Sir Hugh went on at great length to point out that in his view the Nigerian delegates at the conference were completely unrepresentative of Nigerian peoples and ignorant of Nigerian conditions:

I will leave Honourable Members to imagine what these gentlemen's experiences would be if, instead of travelling peacefully to Liverpool in a British ship [they] could be deposited, unsustained by [British] . . . protection, among . . . the . . . cannibals of the Mama Hills, . . . the determinedly unsocial Mumuyes of the Muri Province, or the equally naked warriors of the inner Ibo country, and there left to explain their claims to be recognized as the accredited representatives of these, their "fellow nationals." [39]

The most illuminating feature of Sir Hugh's speech was his discussion of nationality in its Nigerian context:

. . . the suggestion that there is, or can be in the visible future, such a thing as a "West African Nation" is as manifest an absurdity as that there is, or can be, an "European Nation," at all events until the arrival of the Millennium. . . . The peoples of West Africa do not belong to the same stock and are not of common descent; . . . [they have] no common language . . . [and] no community of religious belief. . . . As a matter of fact, the Hausas of Zaria, the Bantu tribesmen of the valley of the Benue and, say the Fantis of Cape Coast are less nearly allied to one another than are, for example, the Scandinavians of the Baltic, the Slavs of Bulgaria and the Semitic peoples of Egypt and Morocco. . . . Any advancement or recognition of . . . these ridiculous claims and pretensions . . . is mischievous, because they are incompatible with that natural development of real national self-government which all true patriots in Nigeria

. . . should combine to secure and maintain. . . . It is the consistent policy of the Government of Nigeria to maintain and to support the local tribal institutions and the indigenous forms of Government . . . which are to be regarded as the natural expressions of [African] political genius. . . . I am entirely convinced of the right, for example, of the people of Egbaland, . . . of any of the great Emirates of the North, . . . to maintain that each one of them is, in a very real sense, a nation. . . . It is the task of the Government of Nigeria to build up and to fortify these national institutions.[40]

Finally, in one long sentence, Sir Hugh dismissed as dangerous the idea of a "Nigerian" nation:

Assuming . . . that the impossible were feasible—that this collection of self-contained and mutually independent Native States, separated from one another, as many of them are, by great distances, by differences of history and traditions, and by ethnological, racial, tribal, political, social and religious barriers, were indeed capable of being welded into a single homogeneous nation—a deadly blow would thereby be struck at the very root of national self-government in Nigeria, which secures to each separate people the right to maintain its identity, its individuality and its nationality, its own chosen form of government; and the peculiar political and social institutions which have been evolved for it by the wisdom and by the accumulated experience of generations of its forebearers.[41]

This speech has been quoted at length because it not only expressed the hostility of the government to the National Congress, but also revealed its basic attitude toward the concepts of self-government, patriotism, nationality, and nation: (1) the idea of a Nigerian nation was inconceivable, and the government was determined to oppose its development; (2) national self-government was a concept applicable only to "self-contained and mutually independent Native States"; (3) true patriotism and nationalism were sentiments that must be directed to those "natural" units; and (4) the question of ultimate control of the superstructure binding these separate states together in a modern political unit was then outside the realm of permissible discussion.

The Nigerian section of the National Congress was not only torn from within and opposed from without by the full power and influence of the government, but it was also repudiated by several prominent Lagosians who undertook to organize a pro-government Reform Club. The Lagos section of the congress did not, however, admit complete defeat. In 1930 the fourth session of the congress was held in Lagos, and, with the support of the Nigerian Democratic party, its deliberations attracted considerable attention. In 1931, a deputation from the Lagos section visited the governor and requested extension of the franchise, but reaffirmed that the aim of the congress was "to maintain strictly and inviolate the connection of British West African Dependencies with the British Empire." [42] With the departure in 1933 of J. C. Zizer, its indefatigable secretary and also the editor of its weekly organ, *West African Nationhood,* the congress movement in Nigeria became moribund. Weak efforts to revive the organization in 1947 proved abortive.[43]

Another reason for the waning of enthusiasm in the National Congress after World War I was the concern of many politically-minded Lagosians in the *eleko* question. The complex history of the relationship between the government of Nigeria and the House of Docemo has been recounted in detail elsewhere.[44] When Lagos was annexed in 1861 and made a crown colony, the Eleko (King) of Lagos, who was head of the ruling House of Docemo, was given a pension on the condition that he, and presumably his successors, would renounce kingship. Thus the House of Docemo became one of the few traditional authorities in Nigeria which were not brought under the system of indirect rule.

On several occasions between 1916 and 1934 the government punished or treated in cavalier fashion the head of the house because of his alleged participation in or support of political agitation in Lagos. Although denied political power, the eleko was ordered in 1915 to have his bellman go about the town asking the people to pay a new water rate. When he refused, the governor deprived him and his chiefs of their salaries for more than a year. Again, in 1919 recognition of the eleko was withdrawn for a month because he sided with a Muslim faction that had opposed the water rate. Finally, in 1920 the government published a notice "ceasing to recognize" Eshugbayi (the eleko), and subsequently deported him, because he refused to repudiate certain misleading pretensions allegedly made by Herbert Macaulay, who was in London with one Chief Oluwa to appeal to the Privy Council. They were appealing from a decision of the Full Court of Nigeria affirming that the British government possessed rights over the Lagos land that Docemo had ceded by treaty in 1861. The Privy Council upheld the appeal, declaring that the treaty had not changed the "undisputed right of the Community." [45] The deposition and deportation of the eleko unleashed a wave of popular agitation, and for the next decade monopolized attention that might otherwise have been drawn to such broader issues as self-determination. And yet the eleko issue itself embodied important elements of the larger questions. The government's treatment of the House of Docemo, as a crude and irritating manifestation of alien rule, endowed the eleko with a very special symbolism, not unlike that attaching to the Sultan of Morocco and the Kabaka of Buganda in a later period.[46]

POSTWAR LAGOS POLITICS

The new Legislative Council inaugurated for the colony and southern Nigeria in 1923 had four elected African members, three from Lagos and one from Calabar. These members were the first elected Africans in legislative councils in British Africa. The National Congress had stressed the elective principle as one of its main objectives, but the Gold Coast—where the congress was centered and had its greatest strength—did not gain such a concession until 1925. This raises a serious question as to whether the congress' agitation was in any way responsible for adoption of the elective principle in 1922. In 1919, a year before the congress was formed, a motion introduced in the Nigerian Council requested that "the Council be either reconstructed so as to make it a serious factor in the governing of this Colony or Protectorate, or else be abolished." [47] At the same session Sir Hugh Clifford expressed his hope and his belief that within a few years constitutional changes could be introduced. Moreover, leaders of the Reform Club, whom the government usually accepted as spokesmen for their countrymen, had made deferential suggestions for greater participation by educated Africans in the imperial system. Without full access to official papers, it is of course impossible to identify the factors behind the decision to permit the election of Africans to the council. It is not unreasonable to suggest, however, that one of the factors was the ferment of nationalistic thinking among educated Nigerians during the immediate post–World War I period.

The political history of Lagos during the period 1923–1938 centered in the quinquennial elections for the Legislative Council, the triennial elections for the Lagos Town Council (to which the elective principle was partially extended in 1920), and the perennial issue of the status and headship of the House of Docemo. The crucial and dominant personality was Herbert Macaulay, founder of the Nigerian Democratic party.[48] Macaulay was the bête noire of the Nigerian government for nearly forty years, from the water-rate agitation in 1908 to the Nigeria-wide campaign against the so-called "obnoxious ordinances" in 1946. The many and varied antigovernment activities of his long and eventful career won him the popular title of "father of Nigerian nationalism." The chief sources of Macaulay's strength were his newspaper, the *Lagos Daily News;*[49] the Nigerian National Democratic party (NNDP); the highly organized Lagos market-women; the House of Docemo and its supporters; and his unique ability to fire the imagination of the semiliterate and illiterate masses of Lagos. Although trained as a civil engineer, Macaulay made his living mainly by political agitation. At times he demonstrated great loyalty to the British Crown and devotion to the British cause, as when he said, in 1940, "Let us all pray for the success of British arms"; at other times his remarks drove the British administration to near distraction: "I would far sooner place a good reliable native in a position of responsibility than a weak or vicious European." He was twice imprisoned, once for the misapplication of trust funds, and the second time for criminal libel. His prison record, of course, disqualified him for election to office, which no doubt intensified his bitterness. For nearly four decades he did more than any other man to create divisions among the educated elements of Lagos. His ruthless abandon in vilifying his opponents in his paper and on the platform left deep and unhealed scars which decidedly influenced later developments within the nationalist movement. But whether his motivation was personal gain or a genuine desire to achieve justice for his people, he consistently espoused the cause of Africans against the European intruder and master. Most Nigerians regard him as a great nationalist crusader.

When the new constitution went into effect in 1923, the in-

tense competition for the three elective positions allocated to
Lagos stimulated an unprecedented political awakening. Two
new political parties sprang into being, and within a few years
five new newspapers began publication. The NNDP, under the
leadership of Herbert Macaulay, emerged as the most powerful
group; its candidates were victorious in the Legislative Council
elections of 1923, 1928, and 1933. Until 1938 this party was the
major force in Lagos political life. Although its principal function
was to support candidates for the Lagos seats on the Legislative
Council, its stated aims asserted a broader responsibility:

> To secure the safety or welfare of the people of the Colony and
> Protectorate of Nigeria as an integral part of the British Imperial
> Commonwealth and to carry the banner of "Right, Truth, Liberty
> and Justice" to the empyrean heights of Democracy until the
> realization of its ambitious goal of "A Government of the People,
> by the People, for the People," . . . and, at the same time, to
> maintain an attitude of unswerving loyalty to the Throne and
> Person of His Majesty the King Emperor, by being strictly con-
> stitutional in the adoption of its methods and general procedure.[50]

The party included the following specific objectives and demands
in its program:

1) In regard to Lagos:
   a) the nomination and election of the Lagos members of the
   Legislative Council (this was in fact the party's main function);
   b) the achievement of municipal status and complete local
   self-government for Lagos.
2) In regard to Nigeria:
   a) the establishment of branches and auxiliaries of the party
   in all areas of Nigeria;
   b) the development of higher education and the introduction of compulsory education throughout Nigeria;
   c) economic development of the natural resources of Nigeria
   under controlled private enterprise;
   d) free and fair trade in Nigeria and equal treatment for native traders and producers of Nigeria:
   e) the Africanization of the civil service;
   f) the recognition of the National Congress of British West
   Africa and the pledge to work hand-in-hand with that body
   in support of its entire program.[51]

Notwithstanding its claim to be "Nigerian" and "national," the Democratic party remained throughout its long history an exclusively Lagos organization, although abortive efforts were made to establish branches at Abeokuta, Ibadan, and Kano. The failure to nationalize the party was due in part to Herbert Macaulay, who was not only thoroughly preoccupied with the defense of the House of Docemo, but also determined to keep the party under his firm control. The establishment of branches outside Lagos could have challenged his leadership. The constitution of the party clearly stated that branches in the protectorate would be "subject to the direction and control of the Parent Body in Lagos." [52] Secondly, until 1951 Lagos was the only area in Nigeria (except for Calabar which had one representative) where Africans could directly elect a legislative representative. The native administration system, which prevailed throughout the protectorate, did not allow for party activity. In a few native authority areas in the Southern Provinces, as well as in second-class townships (for example, Port Harcourt, Aba, Enugu, and Kaduna), there was a fairly early development of local political organizations, but variations in the systems of government and in the scope allowed local bodies made affiliation with the NNDP pointless, even if there had been a desire for such affiliation. Thus parochialism, the lack of common consciousness, and the desire of Lagos leaders to retain leadership were crucial determinants in confining Western-style political activity to Lagos. But the system of indirect rule and the limitation of the elective principle to Lagos were equally important. In Calabar, where one member was elected to the Legislative Council, the Calabar Improvement League engaged in some political activity.[53] Certainly extension of the principle of direct election to other urban centers in the interior would have greatly accelerated political awakening and party development.[54]

Although the Democratic party confined its activities to Lagos, it frequently took a "national" stand on issues; thus it fostered the consciousness, among Lagosians at least, that Lagos was part of a larger territory called Nigeria. In 1930 the party sent a deputation to the governor to discuss such national matters as the trade depression and the appointment and deposition of chiefs. At a series of mass meetings held periodically throughout the fifteen years of its dominance (1923–1938), the party occasionally raised issues of an all-Nigerian nature and frequently criticized the government. Moreover, Dr. C. C. Adeniyi-Jones, president of the party and one of its representatives in the Legislative Council from 1926 to 1938, was the most militantly critical member of the council; he frequently raised provocative and challenging questions which applied to all Nigeria or, more frequently, to the African race. The debates of the Legislative Council during his tenure in office provide a good index to the growth of racial and national consciousness.[55]

CHAPTER 9

Nationalist Developments in the Interwar Period

Between the collapse of the congress movement in the early 1920's and the arrival of Nnamdi Azikiwe in the late 1930's there was comparatively little nationalist activity in Nigeria. Writing in 1927, Sir William Geary, a long-time British resident of Lagos, observed that there was "no unrest in Nigeria—no political assassination—no non-cooperation, no bombs. The Prince of Wales had a universal welcome of enthusiastic loyalty." [1] Again, in 1936 W. R. Crocker, an Australian who had just resigned from the Nigerian colonial service, stated that Nigeria

> . . . has fewer problems than any other governing unit of the same population in the world. There is no problem of racial antagonism; there are no economic problems, . . . there is no conflict between white capital and coloured labour, . . . and there are no political problems, internal or external, of any kind. Social problems like caste, economic problems like agricultural indebtedness, political problems like nationalism, as in India, are all non-existent. [2]

The following year (1937) Lord Hailey, surveying the whole question of nationalism in Africa, observed that in British West Africa

> . . . one encounters movements of a more definitely political nature . . . [and] a class which more nearly resembles the Indian politician type than can be seen elsewhere in Africa. But prominent as this class is in the local politics, it has not proceeded beyond the ideals of early Victorian radicalism; its ambition is a larger representation in the legislature, and a greater share in Government employ; it seems to make little appeal to the uneducated or rural element. [3]

On the basis of evidence drawn from a study of interwar political activity in Nigeria, these appraisals have a certain validity. The interwar period was largely one of nationalist gestation, when new influences were being felt, new associations were being formed, and a new generation was coming of age.

EXTERNAL INFLUENCES BETWEEN THE WARS

The Nigerians most profoundly affected by the play of external influences were those who resided abroad, mainly as students pursuing higher studies in the United Kingdom and the United States. Physically removed from their traditional environment, and placed in strange and usually hostile surroundings, they formed attitudes and made resolutions that were crucial to the growth of racial consciousness not only in themselves but among other Nigerians with whom they came in contact either through correspondence, or upon their return home. It was Africans who had spent some time abroad who usually founded and assumed the leadership of associations in Africa. Their need for companionship and mutual protection while they were abroad, together with their urge to give expression to their aspirations, led them to establish or join various organizations.

Before 1919 there were two associations formed by Africans and persons of African descent living in the United Kingdom— the African Progress Union and the Society of Peoples of African Origin. The former was founded in 1918 "to promote the social and economic welfare of the Africans of the world," and included among its officers Duse Mohammed Ali, an Egyptian who later moved to Lagos and founded the Lagos *Comet*. In 1919 the two associations amalgamated to form the Union of African Peoples, whose main object was "to teach the people of Britain to understand that all were subjects of the same King, and according to British ideas, were all entitled to the same consideration." [4] In 1931 the Union of African Peoples was succeeded by the League of Coloured Peoples, a larger organization founded by a Jamaican doctor. Membership was open to all non-Europeans, including not only West Indians and Africans, but also Indians, Ceylonese, Burmese, and others. The league was, however, predominantly an association of West Indians, and this partly accounted for its moderation and conservatism. It was pledged to protect and advance the interests of its members and of the whole colored race, as well as to "improve relations between the Races." Nevertheless, as a forum for the discussion of topics, including political topics, which agitated the minds of all colored peoples, it contributed substantially to the growth of racial consciousness. The following is a sample of the proceedings at the league's annual week-end conferences in the period 1933–1938:

1) A West Indian demanded absolute freedom from and abolition of crown colony government, and urged the development of a West Indian consciousness.

2) An Indian encouraged Africans to join Indian student organizations.

3) A strong protest was made in regard to the Scottsboro case and the conquest of Ethiopia, the "rape of a coloured empire."

4) Frequent discussions were held on African art, history, and culture.

5) H. O. Davies from Nigeria affirmed in 1936: "Africans should follow India—the only way out is for Africans to cooperate and to make sacrifices in the struggle for freedom."

6) Paul Robeson and Jesse Owens participated in the conference; the former spoke on "The Negro in the Modern World." [5]

In the main, however, the league was a moderate association; its permanent president was a devout Christian who personally avoided politics. Except for barrister H. O. Davies, none of the league's Nigerian members became prominent nationalists upon their return to Nigeria; indeed, Louis Mbanefo and Stephen Thomas ultimately became puisne judges in the Nigerian judiciary. The league was not a center for either nationalism or inflammatory racial agitation. On the contrary, it sought to ameliorate the lives of colored peoples by persuasion and the display of a coöperative spirit.

It was from the associations organized explicitly by and for students that a more pronounced nationalist spirit gradually emerged. Organizations of Negroes who were more or less permanent residents in England tended to be accommodationist in their outlook, but students who intended to return to their home countries were less conformist. The first formal association of students was the Union for Students of African Descent organized by a few West Indians and West Africans in 1917. The union eschewed politics, since political agitation did not "seem likely to serve the best interests of the average student." [6]

Immediately after the war the number of West African students in London sharply increased. One of the new arrivals was Ladipo Solanke, a Yoruba law student from Abeokuta, who received his degree in 1926. While pursuing his studies he had a dream from which he derived the firm conclusion that "until Africans at home and abroad, including all persons of African descent, recognize and develop the spirit of the principles of self-help, unity and cooperation among themselves . . . they would have to continue to suffer the results of colour prejudice, and remain hewers of wood and drawers of water for the other races of mankind." [7] In 1924, Solanke took the initiative in organizing the Nigerian Progress Union, which in 1925 was replaced by the West African Students' Union (WASU). All the original members of WASU were, like Solanke, barristers or law students. [8] Between 1925 and 1945 the West African Students' Union was the principal social and political center for Nigerian students in the United Kingdom.

The declared objectives of WASU included the following:

1) To provide and maintain a hostel in London for students from West Africa.

2) To act as a center for information and research on African history, culture, and institutions.

3) To promote good will and understanding between Africans and other races.

4) To present to the world a true picture of African life and philosophy.

5) To foster a spirit of self-help, unity, and coöperation.

6) To foster a *spirit of national consciousness and racial pride* among its members.

7) To publish a monthly magazine called *WASU*. [9]

The journal *WASU* provided an early literary outlet for many members of the union who are now West Coast leaders. The issues published during the late 1920's were of unusually high quality. The union's main function has been to provide a hostel for West African students in London, maintained in part by funds collected during Solanke's two extended tours of the West Coast.

During the interwar period the union's leaders, prompted by the "joy of independence, even in poor surroundings," [10] resisted all efforts of the Colonial Office to substitute the more attractive and officially sponsored Aggrey House for the WASU hostel. WASU's greatest contribution by far, however, has been its stimulation of political and racial consciousness among Nigerians who came under its influence. Two of its leading members, Solanke, a Nigerian, and J. W. de Graft-Johnson, a Ghanaian, produced in 1927 and 1928, respectively, the first major literary works of a nationalist character to appear since Blyden's writings in the late nineteenth century. Johnson described the hope of African youth as

> . . . the great yearning for freedom, for emancipation from the yoke of centuries. The youth of Africa everywhere is assailed by the alluring thoughts of a free Africa, of an Africa owing no foreign burden, but stepping into her rightful place as a unit in the powerful army of the human family,

and asserted that the first step toward nationhood was

> . . . to change the attitude of the white man toward the educated African. . . . The white man should not be surprised when he finds the literate African conducting himself in much the same way as his illiterate brother . . . [and should not expect him] to approximate the European in life, conduct, and ideas.[11]

Solanke's unpublished manuscript, completed in 1927 and entitled "United West Africa (or Africa) at the Bar of the Family of Nations," reflected the influence of Garveyism and of the "Negro Renaissance." [12] In it Solanke glorified African history:

> In ancient and medieval negroland . . . West Africa had organized governments of her own creation whose standard was . . . equal to . . . any other of the then known world; . . . in Europe at this period there was as yet neither a nation, . . . nor a constitution, nor a Parliament [sic]. . . .

He ascribed Africa's decline to the slave trade: ". . . for about 500 years she was slowly, systematically and completely ruined. . . . Europe and America robbed her to improve and enrich themselves . . . while Africa had retrogressed almost to the

primitive stage. . . ." In order to restore and regenerate West
Africa, "all foreign names should be discouraged and ultimately
abolished. . . . British Imperialism and African Nationalism are
two conflicting aspirations, theories and practices."

Solanke went on to advocate a "real African National Church,"
and then turned to the most bitter grievance felt by educated
Africans:

> . . . the Political Officer . . . should give up the idea of re-
> garding every educated element as his enemy. . . . If he wants
> to understand the natives properly he can only do so through
> the educated element. . . . Let him embrace the educated as
> his brother, his co-partner in the duty of guardianship of Africa.

Solanke warned the British that sooner or later the educated
elements and their natural rulers would become united and in-
flict retribution upon the white man. Moreover, he endeavored
to refute the oft-repeated plea for gradualism:

> It took the white race a thousand years to arrive at their present
> level of advance: it took the Japanese, a Mongol race, fifty
> years to catch up; . . . there is no reason why we West Africans
> should not catch up with the Aryans and the Mongols in one
> quarter of a century.[13]

These quotations from Johnson and Solanke are fairly characteristic of the thinking of African students in London in the late
1920's.

The role of WASU in the growth of nationalist sentiment was
not limited to the indoctrination of impressionable students in
London. The union also played an important part in the spread of
ideas and in the development of associations in Nigeria. Between
1929 and 1932 Solanke visited all the major centers of Nigeria,
and other parts of British West Africa, to collect funds for the
WASU student hostel in London and to establish branches of
WASU. These subsidiary organizations attracted not only the
intelligentsia but also traditional leaders.[14]

Partly because of his Yoruba background, Solanke endeavored
to bring together the nationalist-minded educated elements and
the natural rulers. Nana Sir Afori Atta of the Gold Coast and
Ademola II, Alake of Abeokuta, were made patrons of WASU in
1930. Even the Emir of Kano was brought into this predominantly

southern movement by being made a patron of the Kano branch. On his tour Solanke invariably approached the natural rulers and elders first, to enlist their sympathy and support on behalf of WASU. This show of deference to indirect rule no doubt made Solanke's activities less suspect and aggravating to the British administration; indeed, it probably made his excursions into the interior possible.[15]

In the late 1930's, certain elements in WASU became increasingly attracted to left-wing ideology; they placed less emphasis upon coöperation; their criticism became more emphatic and uncompromising; and they revealed a growing concern over the political future of their home countries. World War II greatly accelerated this process. These developments will be examined later, but here it need only be noted that Solanke and WASU influenced a critical segment of a whole generation, from which many of Nigeria's most militant post–World War II leaders emerged. From a historical standpoint Solanke was an outstanding figure in the nationalist awakening in Nigeria.

A second external development between the wars was the effort of the Comintern to stimulate and infiltrate a global Negro nationalist movement. Until 1928, Comintern policy toward the American Negro was dominated by Trotsky's admonition that "black chauvinism" should be avoided. In that year, however, the Sixth World Congress in Moscow decided on a new program. Benjamin Gitlow reports that

> It was hoped through a Negro minorities movement in the U.S. to give leadership to a colored nationalist movement of world proportions in the countries of South and Central America, Africa, Asia, and the Antipodes. . . . The American Nationalist Negro Movement, Moscow believed, would provide the leadership for such a world movement.[16]

Although many American Negro Communists were repelled by the idea of creating a "Black Belt Republic" in the United States, Moscow ordered them to infiltrate such Negro organizations as the Universal Negro Improvement Association. This change in strategy suggests that Moscow had been impressed by Marcus Garvey's revolutionary success, and hoped to spread communism through Garveyism—a communized Negro national-

207

ism. In addition to giving orders to the American Communist party, the Comintern in 1932 invited a group of selected Negroes from colonial territories to visit Moscow. Among them were George Padmore, a Jamaican, and I. T. A. Wallace-Johnson, a Sierra Leonian then resident in Lagos; the latter was acting editor of the *Nigerian Daily Telegraph* and general secretary of the African Workers' Union of Nigeria, which he had organized in 1931. Padmore, after his indoctrination in Moscow, went to London and became the leader of the left-wing and Pan-African element of African nationalism in the imperial capital. Although he broke with the Communist party in 1938, he has maintained his leadership ever since. Wallace-Johnson, who became associate editor of the Communist publication *Negro Worker* (Paris), returned to Lagos to organize the Nigerian labor movement. The Nigerian government banned the *Negro Worker,* and soon thereafter Wallace-Johnson moved to the Gold Coast (now Ghana) where he ultimately joined Nnamdi Azikiwe in the publication of a new nationalist newspaper.[17] Subsequently he returned to Sierra Leone where he continued his nationalist career.

In the meantime, literature from Communist and pro-Communist sources, such as the International Trade Union Committee of Negro Workers of the Profitern and the League Against Imperialism (London), had begun to filter through to key individuals in Nigeria. One of the principal points on the program of the former organization was self-determination for Negroes:

> . . . the trade unions of the Negro workers should seek to widen the scope of the economic struggles of the Negro workers, transforming them into political struggles, with the aim of turning it ultimately into a combined economic and political struggle for power and self-determination.[18]

In 1934 Nancy Cunard, a devoted Afrophile, published a monumental anthology of Negro writings, which incorporated literary contributions from prominent Negroes and others in support of the new line: "The Communist world-order is the solution of the race problem for the Negro," "To-day in Russia alone is the Negro a free man," and "The White Man is killing Africa." [19] The section devoted to Africa contained articles written by a few Nigerians, including Adetokunbo Ademola (son of the

Alake of Abeokuta and now a justice on the Supreme Court of Nigeria), Nnamdi Azikiwe, T. K. Utchay, and Ladipo Odunsi. The really significant feature of the anthology was its great emphasis on African history, art, and culture, as a basis for a "national" renaissance. The title of Justice Ademola's article was "The Solidarity of the African Race."

By 1935–1936 it was clear that few American Negroes were attracted to Moscow's plan for a Black Republic in America; besides, at that time the Soviet government had just made one of its sudden policy shifts, and popular fronts and collective security with Britain and France became keynotes of the new line. The Communists therefore temporarily abandoned their open courting of Africans. But informal contact between the British and American Communist parties and some African students was maintained throughout the late 1930's and World War II. In 1946, as will be noted, the direct, open, frontal-assault approach was resumed.

The Italian invasion of Ethiopia gave African racial conscious-ness a far more influential boost. One of the most militant and uncompromising nationalists in Nigeria, now a minister in a regional government, informed me that the Italian conquest of Africa's historic kingdom made him aware for the first time that the struggle of the future was between white and black. Ethiopia had everything that was meaningful to Africans under colonial-ism: an ancient history, independence, equality in diplomatic relations, and black supremacy. To the African it was a symbol of racial achievement which was incomprehensible to most Europeans. The subjugation of Ethiopia by the white man, after 2,000 years of independence, branded as futile all gains the Nigerians had made, or hoped to make toward equality and inde-pendence.

In 1935 a mass meeting convened by the leading Lagosians of all political factions protested the aggression against Ethiopia and passed a resolution urging the British government to take all possible steps to restrain Italy.[20] The Abyssinia Association, formed to support the Ethiopian cause, counted among its mem-bers most of the leading figures in Lagos. In London, WASU formed the Ethiopian Defense Committee and undertook similar protest action. The subsequent failure of the European powers, particularly the United Kingdom, to carry out sanctions against Italy, and the ease with which they accommodated themselves to Italy's conquest, served to strengthen the conviction that white men were by instinct and interest united against black men.[21]

In concluding this brief description of external influences during the interwar period, we should note that they were directed toward the awakening of a racial, not a territorial, consciousness. In no instance were native-born Nigerians encouraged or stimulated to think of Nigeria as an individual national entity or to feel that they were Nigerians. "Race," "African," and "nationality" were interchangeable, almost synonymous, terms. It is true that WASU and the National Congress of British West Africa fostered a nationalism subject to territorial limitations, but even this applied to a fragmented and unconnected portion of the African continent. Solanke, although a Nigerian, tended to think in terms of either "Yorubaland" or "West Africa," and avoided any particularization of thought or organization along territorial lines. In short, color, and therefore race, were the transcendent criteria of nationality.

The tendency to think of nationality in terms of race or tribe, rather than in terms of an artificial territorial unit under British control, was characteristic of the early exponents of nationalism. For this there are several explanations. In the first place, the British themselves did little if anything to encourage the feeling of "Nigerian" nationality; indeed, Sir Hugh Clifford made it emphatically clear that the idea of a Nigerian nation was both inconceivable and dangerous. The system of native administration was designed to foster love for and loyalty to the tribe. Few Nigerians were aware that they belonged to any other community than their lineage, their tribe, or their race; such an identification could be stimulated only by subordination to a race of the opposite color.

Secondly, in the late 1920's, and to an increasing extent throughout the 1930's and 1940's, those Nigerians who would have been most predisposed toward nationalist ideas—the so-called "detribalized," Western-educated, and urbanized elements—were preoccupied in organizing tribal unions for the purpose of establishing or maintaining an identity with their lineage, clan, or tribe of origin. This, of course, is a phenomenon characteristic of individuals only recently removed from their close-knit home communities. It will be treated in more detail at a later point.

Finally, most of the early leaders of thought in Nigeria were non-Nigerian Africans, or Nigerians with very weak roots in the country outside Lagos. For example, Edward Blyden and John Payne Jackson were Liberians; Herbert Macaulay, the grandson of Bishop Crowther, was culturally a Freetown Creole; J. E. Egerton-Shyngle was a Gambian by birth and early education; C. C. Adeniyi-Jones, long-time president of the Democratic party, and J. C. Zizer, editor of *West African Nationhood* (Lagos) and secretary of the Lagos branch of the National Congress of British West Africa, were Sierra Leonians. Many other early leaders had similar backgrounds. Although most of them regarded Lagos and Yorubaland as their home—indeed, they felt they had "returned home" to the land of their ancestors—it was nearly as difficult for them to conceptualize a separate Nigerian nation as it was for Sir Hugh Clifford. It was the task of a new generation of native-born Nigerians to territorialize or Nigerianize the broad racial consciousness that the early leaders at home and the external influences from abroad had begun to arouse.

THE EMERGENCE OF ASSOCIATIONS BETWEEN THE WARS

Another aspect of the interwar period of gestation was the emergence and proliferation of an array of new associations, whose membership, or at least leadership, was drawn largely from Nigerians who came of age in the interwar period. This development resulted from changes, such as increased mobility and social restratification, brought about by the Western impact. The new associations were of crucial significance in the development of the nationalist movement because they enabled nationalist leaders to mobilize and manipulate important segments of the population. Moreover, many of the leaders of these associations, which were primarily nonpolitical in origin, became leaders of formal nationalist organizations. Thus the associations were training grounds for the new nationalist elite.

Special-interest groups appeared on the scene in increasing numbers. As early as 1909 a Niger Traders' Association had been organized at Onitsha to pressure the government into assisting local African traders. In 1919 a group of Nigerian exporters combined to form the West African Federation of Native Shippers and Traders, which sent a delegate to London to request the improvement of shipping facilities.[22] In 1923 the barristers of Nigeria formed the Nigerian Law Association and launched a quarterly journal of high quality. In the late 1930's the Ibibio Farmers' Association, an auxiliary of the powerful Ibibio Welfare Union, agitated for direct representation in the Legislative Council.[23] About the same time African produce buyers, under the leadership of Obafemi Awolowo (now premier of the Western Region), organized the Nigerian Produce Traders' Association. African lorry owners—lorry transport was one of the few enterprises in which European firms did not compete—organized the Nigerian Motor Transport Union. The wave of organizational enthusiasm that hit most urban centers in Nigeria is illustrated by the following list of a few of the many associations organized in Lagos:

> Lagos Fishermen's Association (1937)
> Alakoro Union Women's Trading Company (1939)
> Farina Women Sellers' Union (1940)
> Lagos Wholesale Butchers' Union (1939)
> Taxi Drivers' Association (1938)
> Lagos Canoe Transport Union (1938)
> Lagos Night Soil Removers' Union (1942)
> Lagos Union of Auctioneers (1932)
> Palm Wine Sellers' Association (1942)

Some of these modern organizations, with all the paraphernalia of secretaries and executive committees, were based on traditional guilds and associations. But in the main they reflected the growth of new ties based on the common interests that developed in new urban centers.

In the meantime, the idea of collective action among wage-earning groups had begun to spread. It first took root in 1912 when African clerks in the government service organized the Southern Nigeria Civil Service Union and petitioned Lugard for certain reforms. As the union grew in strength and influence, it changed its name to the Nigerian Civil Servants' Union and again pressed for reforms, with special emphasis upon the elevation of Africans to senior posts in the civil service.[24] In 1921 the artisans employed on the government railroad, who had joined with other technical workers to form the Mechanics' Union, struck against a threatened reduction in wages. They won the strike.[25] In 1931 the mission schoolteachers, recruited from many ethnic groups and scattered throughout the Southern Provinces, organized the Nigerian Union of Teachers (NUT). As the organization grew in strength, branches were established in almost every town in Nigeria. The leadership was not only responsible and active, but genuinely multitribal—the secretary was an Efik, the president a Yoruba, and the vice-president an Ibo. From the beginning the leadership and organization of the NUT had a genuinely "national" orientation.[26]

New economic forces accelerated the tempo of social mobilization throughout the interwar period. As the members of new occupational and professional groups became increasingly aware of the links that bound them together, organizational activity was certain to expand. Most of it was spasmodic and parochial, many organizations collapsed the day they were formed, and others were created by individuals who sought only to exploit their unsuspecting fellow men; but a number of the organizations survived to become the nucleus of regional or national associations. The importance of these organizations lay not in whatever immediate success they might achieve, but in their reflection of new forces groping for expression and of new interests in the process of birth.

From the late 1920's on, kinship and tribal unions sprang up in the main urban centers of Nigeria. These associations were known by various names: for example, Naze Family Meeting, Ngwa Clan Union, Owerri Divisional Union, Calabar Improvement League, Igbirra Progressive Union, and Urhobo Renascent Convention. They gave organizational expression to the persistent feeling of loyalty and obligation to the kinship group and the town or village where the lineage was localized. Although based mainly on kinship groups indigenous to southern Nigeria, branches of such associations were ultimately established in every multitribal urban center, including those in Muslim areas of the Northern Region, and in Fernando Po and the Gold Coast. As the new urban centers either were artificial and lacking in civic consciousness (for example, Minna, Gusau, Kaduna, Nguru, Jos Enugu, Aba, Sapele, and Tiko), or were completely dominated by an inhospitable indigenous group which treated expatriates as unwelcome intruders (for example, Ibadan, Kano, Makurdi, Onitsha, Calabar, and Victoria), these associations represented the human impulse for "brothers abroad" to come together for mutual aid and protection.[27]

At an early date the members of these associations began to export to their rural homelands the enlightenment, modernity, and civilization they encountered in urban centers. This was the result of (*a*) their feeling of obligation toward the homeland, which has been a striking characteristic of African social organizations; (*b*) their acute awareness of the wide gap between the higher standards of living in the urban centers and the poverty of their rural villages; and (*c*) the steady wages that enabled them to undertake programs of community development. The associations played a dynamic role in the material improvement of rural villages, especially in the field of education. Small unions built primary schools and sponsored scholarships to secondary schools, and larger federated unions financed the construction of "national" or "state" secondary schools and sent promising young men abroad for higher studies. A substantial number of the educated members of Nigeria's postwar elite were supported through all or part of their university training by their local unions.

The organizational development of tribal associations took two main forms: diffusion and integration. The association idea spread rapidly from the urban centers in three directions: (*a*) to the rural communities of expatriate groups where "home branches" were formed; (*b*) to previously inarticulate ethnic groups among whom there had been no associational development (for example, Idoma, Tiv, Birom, and Bakweri); and (*c*) to special-interest groups within the kinship system (for example, women's, students', and farmers' associations). While this process of diffusion was going on, a program of conscious integration and federation was being pursued. This integrative effort had three phases: (*a*) the federation of all branches abroad; (*b*) the integration of federated groups abroad with the home branch; and (*c*) the formation of all-tribal federations in a pyramidal structure, beginning with the primary association (the extended family among the Ibo and the large urban towns among the Yoruba) and extending upward through the various social levels of the tribe. The first all-tribal federation was the Ibibio Welfare Union (subsequently the Ibibio State Union), organized in 1928. It was not until the end of World War II that the Edo National Union, the Ibo Federal Union, and the Pan-Yoruba Egbe Omo Oduduwa, among others, were formed.

Although the impetus for the formation of these associations came from educated elements in the urban centers—who usually retained the leadership—the membership normally included all types, from the illiterate peasant or laborer to the wealthy trader, titled native ruler, or Lagos barrister. There have been several exceptions, of course, where the tribal union was the exclusive preserve of young schoolboys. Membership has always been restricted to the kinship group, but within that group it is inclusive; affiliation is considered a duty, the shirking of which often results in social ostracism.

Since the educated elements were excluded from the government, it is not surprising that these associations became the media for their political expression. While the leaders of most of the associations were disclaiming interest in explicitly political affairs, they were in fact engaging in important political activities. They exercised a powerful influence in the democratization of native authority councils. In multitribal urban centers the associations eventually won official recognition and secured representation on township advisory boards or native authority councils. They provided a forum for political expression and a structure within which new groups could assert their leadership. It is significant that the overwhelming majority of the members elected to the Eastern and Western Houses of Assembly in 1951 were prominent leaders of their local tribal associations. Indeed, during the interwar period, the energies of most of the westernized elements outside Lagos were channeled into this type of organizational activity. At the time of its inauguration in 1944, the National Council of Nigeria and the Cameroons (NCNC) was to a large extent a federation of tribal and improvement associations.

In addition to economic and tribal associations, others were organized as media for the new intelligentsia. In the early 1920's literary societies began to emerge; one of the first was the Youngmen's Literary Association organized by Nnamdi Azikiwe and others in 1923, before his departure for America.[28] About the same time the Literary and Debating Society and the Study Circle appeared. The membership of the latter included the prominent young Lagosians H. A. Subair, R. A. Coker, Olatunji Caxton-Martins, Adetokunbo Ademola, and Samuel Akinsanya. The group sponsored essay writing, lectures, debates, and book reviews. In 1935, for example, it arranged a public debate at Glover Memorial Hall on the subject of indirect rule.[29] As time passed the number of literary societies increased, and their discussion of political questions became more frequent. There were public debates on such issues as "Resolved that all sane literate males in the municipality of Lagos . . . should be granted suffrage," and "Resolved that Capitalism is a better institution of National Economics than Socialism." [30] In 1940, eleven such groups organized the Federation of Nigerian Literary Societies for the purpose of improving literary standards and establishing "unity among the literary societies of Nigeria." [31] This type of associational development reflected the intellectual ferment of the times. Many of the participants in literary activity emerged as the leaders of thought and the verbalizers of opinion in the postwar period.

During the interwar period other types of associations also made their appearance. The Lagos Women's League, organized in 1936, petitioned the governor to increase the number of openings for women in the civil service. In later years, women in different parts of Nigeria organized similar associations. In 1924 the Islamic Society of Nigeria was founded in Lagos for the purpose of creating a "non-party and non-sectarian body of Muslims serving the Muslims of Nigeria and watching over the political interest of the Society." A year earlier the Young Unsar-Ud-Deen Society was organized to carry out a scheme for Muslim education, and in succeeding years branches were formed in some of the major centers of Nigeria. These were early manifestations of a new awareness among special-interest groups that they shared common problems, and of a desire to unite to advance their common interests. At most they were only pressure groups, but pressure groups in any society are the raw materials of politics.

In addition to these forms of group activity, there were associations of young men whose orientation was more self-consciously political. They represented the coming of age of a new generation which made its presence known immediately after the 1923 elections to the Legislative Council. Under the leadership of Dr. J. C. Vaughn (Yoruba), Ayo Williams (Yoruba), and Ernest Ikoli (Ijaw), the Union of Young Nigerians was inaugurated for the purpose of interesting "the young men of the country in the doings of their country." [32] They desired to emancipate themselves from the parties dominated by such older figures as Herbert Macaulay and Dr. John Randle. When this proved impossible, the movement became moribund after a short life of five years. Shortly after its demise, however, developments in the field of education occasioned a new burst of consciousness and organizational activity among the literate elements of Lagos and Calabar.

In 1929, when the government was planning educational reforms, the educated elements denounced the plan to substitute a Nigerian certificate for the Oxford and Cambridge certificate in use until that date. A mass meeting was called, the National School Committee formed, and a drive launched to collect £10,000 to build a national school. The Lagos leaders, in order to stimulate popular enthusiasm, extolled the self-help measures taken by American Negroes and by Indians, and sought to shame Nigerians into donating for the national cause. As Dr. C. C. Adeniyi-Jones admonished: "This is an opportunity whereby we might prove to the world that we are indeed enterprising Negroes, not unenterprising niggers as we have quite recently been described." [33]

Despite the support of the press and frequent mass meetings, however, the movement collapsed, although £1,600 had been collected. One reason for its demise was that the government abandoned the project of substituting the Nigerian certificate. Another was the increase in the number of secondary schools in the early 1930's. A third was the failure of the community to contribute adequate funds and the inability of the National School Committee to carry the project through to completion.[34] In any event, during the campaign the ideal of a national institution had received wide publicity.

Five years after the 1929 protest, the educated elements in

Lagos were again agitated over an educational question. The issue this time was higher education in general, and the allegedly inferior status of the Yaba Higher College in particular. The background to the question of higher education and its symbolism for educated Nigerians have already been discussed; here we are concerned only with the stimulus that government policy on this specific issue gave to the nationalist awakening. The leading younger critics—Ernest Ikoli, Samuel Akinsanya, Dr. J. C. Vaughn, and H. O. Davies—formed the Lagos Youth Movement (successor to the Union of Young Nigerians), which became the nucleus of Nigeria's first genuine nationalist organization. Once agitation over the Yaba College issue died out, other issues, such as the appointment of Africans to higher posts in the civil service, and discriminatory legislation against African lorry owners, were taken up by the leaders of the movement. In 1936, at the prodding of the editor of the *Comet*, the name of the organization was changed to the Nigerian Youth Movement; until 1938, however, it remained a predominantly Lagos affair. Apart from occasional outspoken criticisms of government policy by individual members, the policy of the movement was moderate: "Long Live our Prince and Long Live their Majesties. The Nigerian Youth Movement will never fail to cooperate with . . . [the governor]." [35]

Before discussing the nationalist phase of the Nigerian Youth Movement (1938–1941), we must briefly mention other important instances of self-help in the field of education. The central figure in what was later known as the National Education Movement was Professor Eyo Ita, who returned to Nigeria from America in 1934 with a list of academic degrees and a burning passion to organize national schools as instruments in the "war of liberation." In the four years following his return, Ita emerged as Nigeria's foremost pamphleteer on the subject of youth. In 1934 he organized, largely on paper, the Nigeria Youth League Movement. His program for this stillborn organization was built around the imperative, "Youth Must Save Society." He was Nigeria's example par excellence of a sensitive individual who returned from abroad with a strong cultural nationalism. Through pamphlets, newspaper articles, and public lectures Ita sought to awaken in Nigerians a love of their own culture:

This is the day of Nigerian Youth. It must build a new social order. . . . Mother Africa calls us to the battle front. . . . The thrill of the songs which we make and the rhythm of our drums contribute to the building of our souls. . . . Nigeria is our home of beauty. . . . Our God is He Who cares for our homes, our woman-hood, our childhood. . . . He is the God of Nigeria, her abiding genius, her sustaining power. The Youth must realize that it is serving His cause through the activities of its movement.[36]

Eyo Ita consistently stressed the need for unity arising from the evils of tribalism: "We need a magic wand of nature that can create a universal kinship among us that all Nigerians are 'fellow citizens'; . . . the greatest need of Nigerians today is to become a community, . . . to evolve a national selfhood. . . ."[37] Ita admonished Nigerians to "seek coordination among them [tribal unions] in a way that will help to build a strong national consciousness." Just as Mazzini had created a hierarchy of loyalties, so Ita stressed duties and loyalties to a local community, to Nigeria, to Africa, and to humanity:

The love of Calabar must consume us. . . . We are either Calabarians or nothing.[38]

[Youth] must realize that the whole of Nigeria is a supreme value before God, and that its creative work is part of the vast plan of the Divine Conserver of our values.[39]

Our devotion to our mission of service to Mother Africa must become unquenchable.[40]

I believe that nation states are out of date and I believe also that empires are as out of date as the African Camel in agriculture.[41]

It was Ita's firm belief that if Nigeria were free, Africa would be free, as would Europe, Asia, and humanity. Nigerian independence was an essential prerequisite for the higher goal of international and interracial citizenship.

Eyo Ita's national influence in the interwar period was limited by his residence in remote areas; he lived for several years in Ogbomosho, deep in the Yoruba hinterland, and later in Calabar, which was isolated from the rest of Nigeria. He returned to his home in Calabar in 1938 to assume leadership of the National Institute founded by educated elements of that community.

219

Later he established his own institution, the West African People's Institute. Throughout his career he has been associated with other Nigerian educators crusading for educational independence. He demanded a "national education" for a "new Africa." This education, he said, must "make our youth hyper-sensitive to the sacredness of equal social justice. . . . It must fill our youth with sublime moral passion, must teach them to respect themselves, their land and its cause." [42] Ita's ceaseless campaign for self-help in educational development—and he is but the most articulate of many—has been an important element in the nationalist awakening.

THE ARRIVAL OF AZIKIWE

Several developments in the latter part of 1937 and in 1938 produced a radically new twist in nationalist thinking and organizational activity in Nigeria. Two militant nationalists with strong personalities returned from abroad with fresh ideas, and with zeal and determination to arouse a more positive nationalism: Nnamdi Azikiwe (Ibo), an American-trained political scientist and journalist; and H. O. Davies (Yoruba), a former student of Harold Laski. Their arrival, coupled with developments within Nigeria, rejuvenated the Lagos-centered Youth Movement which, in the next three years, became the first Nigeria-wide multitribal nationalist organization in Nigerian history. Events during these three crucial years laid bare certain underlying factors which were destined to shape the subsequent course of the nationalist movement.

During the fifteen-year period 1934–1949, Nnamdi Azikiwe was undoubtedly the most important and celebrated nationalist leader on the West Coast of Africa, if not in all tropical Africa. To the outside world "Zikism" and African nationalism appeared to be synonymous. A brief review of Azikiwe's background and of the influences that shaped his ideas is essential. Azikiwe was born in Zungeru in northern Nigeria in 1904, the son of an Ibo clerk in the Nigerian Regiment. He attended mission schools in Onitsha, Lagos, and Calabar, completing his studies in Lagos in 1921. During the next four years he was employed as a government clerk in the Nigerian Treasury in Lagos. In 1925 he sailed for the United States to undertake higher studies. He was first enrolled in Storer College but later transferred to Lincoln

University, and subsequently to Howard University in Washington, D.C. After securing his degree he was appointed instructor in political science at Lincoln University. While teaching there he obtained postgraduate degrees at Columbia University and the University of Pennsylvania. In 1934 he applied to the Nigerian government for appointment as a teacher at King's College in Lagos, but his application was rejected, presumably on the grounds that his American education did not qualify him for the position. He returned to Nigeria for a brief visit at the end of 1934 but moved shortly thereafter to Accra, Gold Coast (now Ghana). On January 1, 1935, he became editor of the Accra *African Morning Post*. In 1937 he and Isaac Wallace-Johnson were convicted of sedition for an article appearing in the *Post*, although Azikiwe's sentence was ultimately quashed. In the same year he published his book *Renascent Africa*, and returned to Lagos and launched a daily newspaper, the *West African Pilot*.[43]

Even before Azikiwe left for the United States in 1925, many aspects of his early life and experiences predisposed him to nationalism. He was born into a "detribalized" milieu, and, except for occasional trips to Onitsha, his father's home, spent his early life in urban centers and at mission schools. His father's bitterness over his treatment in the Nigerian Regiment, from which he resigned after being insulted by a young British officer, left a deep impression upon young Azikiwe. Nnamdi Azikiwe was a characteristic representative of the generation that came of age in the interwar period.

As a government clerk Azikiwe personally shared the grievances felt by that crisis group. Moreover, his last two years in Lagos (1923–1925) before his sojourn in the United States were years of unprecedented political activity, as has been shown. It was during his nine years in the United States (1925–1934), however, that Azikiwe was exposed to new ideas and patterns of protest behavior which were undoubtedly crucial in forming his attitudes and in conditioning his subsequent activity.

Azikiwe spent his first seven years in America at segregated Negro colleges in the Southern atmosphere of discrimination and caste. Profound changes were occurring in the character of protest activity among American Negroes; the growth of a militant press, the emergence of a "Negro Renaissance" with a new emphasis upon the rediscovery of Africa, the "Black Nationalism" of Garveyism, Communist party activity, race riots, lynchings, and mass demonstrations all reached a high pitch during the four years preceding the depression. As a poor student, Azikiwe was compelled to work as a dishwasher, a steward, a coal miner, and even as a boxer. Thus he felt the full impact of the discrimination and economic insecurity that befell the average American Negro. As a result of his experiences in the United States, and of the influences he encountered during his nine years' residence there, Azikiwe was determined to be a leader, with the West Coast of Africa as his arena, in the world-wide struggle to emancipate the Negro race.

There are two suggestive connections between Azikiwe's American background and his subsequent activity in West Africa. First, from the time of his return in 1934 until the late 1940's, Azikiwe tended to think and act along universalist and racial lines. His motto was that "man's inhumanity to man" must cease. His first two published works, *Liberia in World Politics* and *Renascent Africa,* were written with the basic preconception that the struggle of the future was racial, between black and white. In propagating his ideas, Azikiwe was just as much at home in Accra as in Lagos or Onitsha. Lynchings in America, pass laws in South Africa, or boycotts in the Gold Coast (now Ghana) received just as much emphasis in his newspapers as did the problem of creating an independent Nigerian nation-state. Indeed, Azikiwe at first condemned territorial nationalism as detracting from racial sentiment:

> The West African Colonies have a common foe. . . . So long as we think in terms of Nigeria, Gold Coast, Sierra Leone, Gambia, and not as one United West Africa we must be content with a Colonial Dictatorship instead of a Government of the people by the people for the people—namely, Democracy.[44]

In the early years of his career Azikiwe seldom if ever referred to a person as a "Nigerian"; invariably it was "African" versus "European." The title of his main organ, *West African Pilot,* is suggestive of his expansive, universalist, racialist orientation. Azikiwe arrived in time to carry on the tradition of Jackson and Solanke.

The second element in his American experience which helped to shape Azikiwe's subsequent activities was the sensationalism and pugnacity of American yellow journalism, and particularly the obsessive race-consciousness of American Negro newspapers.[45] The connection becomes strikingly clear in an analysis of the format, style, and content of the newspapers Azikiwe founded and edited on the West Coast. Azikiwe began an entirely new era of journalism in both the Gold Coast and Nigeria. The boldness, daring, and sometimes shocking directness of his editorials and news items radically differentiated them from those of his predecessors. Whereas J. E. K. Aggrey, another American-trained African, had emphasized the need for both black and white piano keys to achieve musical harmony, a European friend of Azikiwe's noted that "most of Zik's music is played on the black keys and it is sweet, exciting, and stirring in African ears; . . . the white keys when used are often employed to stress a contrast or a disharmony." [46] Azikiwe centered his journalism on the theme of racial inequalities and injustices and the need for positive action to right historic wrongs. His combative and provocative journalism was the principal source of his fame and power, and the most crucial single precipitant of the Nigerian awakening. In his *Renascent Africa* Azikiwe advises that "there is no better means to arouse African peoples than that of the power of the pen and of the tongue." [47]

Another factor contributing to the power and influence of Azikiwe's newspapers was his determination to make them commercially successful. Most of the African-owned newspapers previously published in Nigeria had been poor business propositions. Azikiwe's detractors frequently referred to his journalism as "commercial nationalism." In the decade following his return to Lagos, he zealously sought to increase circulation by appointing agents in the provinces, by including provincial news in his columns, and by establishing four provincial dailies (in Ibadan, Onitsha, Port Harcourt, and Kano) in the three regions of the interior. His was the first major effort to Nigerianize journalism. The Nigeria-wide circulation of his *West African Pilot*, supported by the smaller provincial subsidiaries, was crucially significant in the spread of racial consciousness and ideas of nationalism in the interior. Nigerian political activity was still Lagos-centered, but Nigerians throughout the country were for the first time permitted the stimulation of vicarious participation.

Although Azikiwe's power and influence resulted partly from

his fresh and militant approach, they also reflected the fact that he was the first non-Yoruba Nigerian (apart from Ernest Ikoli, an Ijaw) to emerge into prominence. For thirty-five years the Ibo had been on the periphery of Nigerian politics. They were the last of the major groups in southern Nigeria to be pacified. Their passion for education and their desire to catch up with other groups were insatiable. It was commonly remarked by Ibos themselves that "an Ibo would accept education from anyone, even from the Devil." During the 1920's and 1930's educational facilities in Iboland expanded at a far greater rate than in any other area of Nigeria. Until 1935, however, no Ibo had achieved professional status, although tens of thousands of them were clerks in government service and in business firms. Thus, when Azikiwe arrived, he found waiting not only a large number of young Yorubas who were dissatisfied with the conservatism and moderation of their traditional Lagosian leadership, but also all the educated elements of one of the largest tribes of Nigeria which until then had had no spokesman. Azikiwe at once became a symbol of Ibo (indeed, of non-Yoruba) achievement and emancipation, and he was able to mobilize the political support of Ibos, who by then were scattered all over Nigeria; there were more than 10,000 in Lagos alone.

These, then, were the three new elements that Azikiwe brought to Nigeria and to the Nigerian Youth Movement in 1938: militant racial consciousness; an expanding sensationalist press; and a large number of educated Nigerians previously excluded or unmobilized. To his contribution was added the personality of another individual, H. O. Davies, who had just returned from the London School of Economics where he had been a student of Laski and socialism. His roommate in London was Jomo Kenyatta. Between 1938 and 1951, when he resigned to found his own party, Davies was one of the dominant figures in the Nigerian Youth Movement. The characteristic theme in his nationalism has been the unity of Nigeria: "We can never split—no, never. We are not a party, we are a national government whose mission is the regeneration of our fatherland." [48]

THE NIGERIAN YOUTH MOVEMENT

Stimulated by these new, provocative influences, the Nigerian Youth Movement assumed a more active political and national role. It contested and won the Lagos Town Council elections; then it turned to challenge the fifteen-year domination of Macaulay and his National Democratic party over Lagos politics and representation on the Legislative Council. Until 1938, nomination and election to the three Lagos seats in the Legislative Council had usually been settled within the confines of Herbert Macaulay's home. In the October, 1938, elections, however, the Youth Movement, which had in the meantime established its own journal, the *Daily Service,* launched a vigorous campaign and defeated Macaulay's party. This meant a radical change in traditional leadership. One of the main points in the platform of the Youth Movement was that Nigerians should assume the leadership of the country, referring, no doubt, to the fact that many Democratic party leaders had been native foreigners.[49] This was the first major step in the Nigerianization of the nationalist movement.

In 1938 the Youth Movement, confident with success, published the *Nigerian Youth Charter,* which set forth the objectives of the rejuvenated movement. Among them were (1) the unification of the tribes of Nigeria through the encouragement of better understanding and coöperation to the end of creating a common ideal; and (2) the education of public opinion to a higher moral and intellectual level, so that national consciousness could be developed and the common ideal realized.[50] The political section of the charter described the goal of the Youth Movement as

. . . complete autonomy within the British Empire, . . . a position of equal partnership with other member States of the British Commonwealth . . . and complete independence in the local management of our affairs. . . . Our movement accept the principle of trusteeship as the basis of co-operation with the British Government in Nigeria.[51]

As part of its effort to achieve national unity, the Youth Movement organized branches in key centers throughout Nigeria. Actually, many branches had been formed in Yorubaland as early as 1936; in 1938 new branches were opened at Ibadan, Ijebu-Ode, Warri, and Benin City in the west; at Aba, Enugu, Port Harcourt, and Calabar in the east; and among southern expatriate groups in Jos, Kaduna, Zaria, and Kano in the north. In some areas the provincial branches were local tribal unions which affiliated with the Youth Movement, and in others, such as Jos, they were old WASU branches which changed their names. By the end of 1938 the movement claimed a national membership of more than 10,000, and nearly twenty provincial branches in all parts of Nigeria, though predominantly in the south.[52]

An event that helped to center attention on a non-Lagos issue was the protest organized by the Youth Movement over the "Cocoa Pool," a buying agreement signed in 1938 by ten leading European firms exporting about 90 per cent of Nigerian cocoa. The result was that educated politicians in Lagos, for the second time in Nigerian history, took a positive and crusading interest in affairs outside Lagos.[53] A mission appointed by the Youth Movement and composed of some of its prominent members toured the cocoa-growing areas of western Nigeria and gathered data for a report which it subsequently submitted to the government. In the meantime a Lagos mass meeting protested against the measure, and a dramatic and effective boycott against the exporting firms was instituted in the Gold Coast (now Ghana). When the Cocoa Commission appointed by the imperial government arrived in Nigeria, the Youth Movement and its affiliate, the Nigerian Produce Buyers' Union, gave evidence before it and recommended a cocoa exchange system not unlike the marketing boards established after the outbreak of war. In any event, the activities of the Youth Movement during the cocoa agitation contributed significantly to a wider popular awareness of its existence as a national institution.

In 1938 and again in 1940 the leaders of the Youth Movement summoned delegates from all branches to attend a representative conference in Lagos. The following list of a few of the items discussed at the 1940 meeting indicates the tenor of nationalist thinking at the time:

a) Abolition or reform of indirect rule
b) Higher appointments in the civil service
c) Representation of provinces, including the north, in the Legislative Council
d) Representation of Nigerians in London
e) Problems of the farmer and rural communities
f) Aid and support to African business entrepreneurs
g) Conditions of service of African employees in mercantile firms

This array of interests suggests that leaders of the Youth Movement at the outbreak of World War II were thinking more in terms of "national" interests than in terms of particularistic Lagos issues.

In February, 1941, the Nigerian Youth Movement was dealt a devastating blow from which it never really recovered. Actually, dissension had been rife among the principal leaders during the preceding three years. In June, 1938, Ernest Ikoli, a founder and active leader of the movement, had become editor of the *Lagos Daily Service*, which claimed to be the official organ of the movement. From that time on, Azikiwe's enthusiasm for the movement reportedly cooled. His critics allege that he bitterly resented the competition that adversely affected his own journalistic enterprises. In an editorial Ikoli rejected the suggestion and accused Azikiwe of being a megalomaniac. Thus began a breach within the movement which was never successfully closed. Shortly after this incident, Azikiwe resigned from the executive committee, and a year later announced, but later retracted, his withdrawal from the movement itself. His reason was his preoccupation with business affairs. Finally, in February, 1941, the Legislative Council seat held by Dr. K. A. Abayomi, then president of the movement, became vacant as a consequence of his resignation and his ultimate appointment to the governor's Executive Council. Abayomi's resignation precipitated within the movement's leadership—and ultimately within its membership—a struggle over the selection of his successor. The principal contestants were Ernest Ikoli (Ijaw) and Samuel Akinsanya (Ijebu Yoruba), both among the founders of the movement. The selection of Ikoli as the candidate of the movement was interpreted by Akinsanya and Ijebu Yorubas, and by Azikiwe and the Ibos who supported Akinsanya, as a manifestation of tribal prejudice against Ijebus and Ibos. The result was that Azikiwe and most Ibos, as well as Akinsanya and some Ijebus, left the movement. A press war between the *Pilot* and the *Daily Service* ensued. Azikiwe and the Ibos never rejoined the movement, which after 1941 was composed mainly of Yorubas.

The Akinsanya crisis was the first major manifestation of a tribal tension that affected all subsequent efforts to achieve unity. From the beginning the mass membership of the Youth Movement was predominantly Yoruba in origin. Because of certain historical factors many Yorubas were prejudiced against the Ijebu Yoruba. The Ijebu had never come completely under the old Yoruba Kingdom centered at Oyo. During most of the nineteenth century the Ijebu controlled the main trade routes into the interior, and they had acquired the reputation of being the Jews of Yorubaland. Situated as they were on the edge of the Lagos Lagoon, they had supplied most of the middlemen in the slave traffic. Yorubas from Oyo, Ibadan, Lagos, and the Egba Kingdom tended to look down upon or dislike the Ijebu. Akinsanya, an Ijebu, felt that he had been discriminated against on the basis of this prejudice when Ikoli won out over him. It mattered little that Ikoli was an Ijaw. It is not known whether Azikiwe quit the movement because of intertribal antagonisms, or because he was dissatisfied with his role. In any event, the struggle within the nationalist movement after 1941 was conditioned, if not dominated, by the fateful Akinsanya crisis of that year.[54]

Shortly after the incident most of the leaders of the Nigerian Youth Movement turned to other affairs and the organization became virtually moribund. Azikiwe, of course, had resigned; Dr. Abayomi, the president, joined the governor's Executive Council in 1943; H. O. Davies withdrew to accept a government appointment as a marketing officer; Akinsanya retired to his home village as a chief; and others drifted away through indifference or dissatisfaction, or were otherwise distracted by wartime changes. The one exception to the process of disintegration was a development at Ibadan during the period 1941–1944. A new group of traders and intellectuals under the leadership of Chief Obafemi Awolowo, then an Ijebu cocoa trader, made serious efforts to reform the movement and keep it alive in order to lay a foundation for what was later to become the Action Group, one of the best organized and most powerful nationalist organizations in the Western Region, if not in all Nigeria. The description and evaluation of this development belong to a subsequent chapter.

As noted previously, most of the leaders of thought and of organization during the four decades preceding World War II either were native foreigners or descendants of native foreigners, like Macaulay and such Brazilians as the Da Rochas, Alakijas, and

Silveras, or were Egba Yorubas who, because of early contact with Christianity and Western education, had emerged as the dominant group in Lagos society. Secondly, they were older men: Herbert Macaulay was sixty in 1923, when he founded the Democratic party, and H. S. A. Thomas was fifty-seven when elected to the presidency of the Youth Movement in 1939; in fact, the average age of leaders of the Youth Movement was forty. Finally, until 1938, although the stated aims of various organizations frequently referred to "Nigeria," political activity was limited to Lagos and Calabar. During the brief period 1938–1941, when Davies and Azikiwe (both in their early thirties) were active in the Youth Movement, there was a remarkable awakening among three new and potentially powerful groups: educated non-Yorubas, youths of all tribes, and the emergent middle class in the cocoa areas of the Yoruba provinces.[55] After the Akinsanya affair, the first two groups were increasingly attracted to Azikiwe through his newspapers and public lectures, and the leadership of the third group was slowly being consolidated by Awolowo in Ibadan. A fourth group—organized labor—was just beginning to emerge.

The early years of World War II therefore marked the beginning of a new era in which the nationalist movement was destined to be of an entirely different order from that of the preceding two generations. It was a period of transition from a tired and parochial older set, more inclined toward gradualism and accommodation to colonial status, to a younger group of intellectuals whose ambitions and aspirations were far more intense, positive, and urgent. The Youth Movement had tried but failed to embrace both elements: the old who were weary and discredited, and the young who were zealous, impatient, and leaderless. The profound social and economic changes during World War II brought forth new leadership, mobilized new forces, and created a radically different climate of opinion and a setting more congenial to the development of a positive nationalism.

CHAPTER 10

The Impact of World War II

Although the West Coast of Africa was hardly touched by the events of World War I, the high idealism and revolutionary character of the immediate postwar period awakened aspirations and stimulated organizational activity among educated Nigerians on a scale sufficient to provoke the censure of officialdom. Profound changes occurred in Nigeria in the two decades following World War I: the number of educated Nigerians increased from a few thousand to more than a million; the Nigerian economy was drawn deeper into the maelstrom of world economic forces; the national ideal was beginning to excite the minds of an increasing number of Nigerians; and new social groups within Nigeria were groping for expression.

The great events and intellectual ferment of World War II operated to bring about a new attitude both among important elements of the British public and among British officials regarding imperial responsibility and the political and economic development of the colonies. The same events accelerated nationalist developments in Nigeria. In this chapter we shall analyze the more significant external factors and influences that impinged upon imperial policy and the nationalist movement, and in the following chapter we shall examine in detail the wartime developments in Nigeria, and the effect they and the external influences had upon the growth of nationalism.

WARTIME INFLUENCES AFFECTING BRITISH POLICY

One of the first influences to compel a reëxamination of British colonial policy came from the West Indies. By 1938 discontent and unrest in British dependencies in that area resulted in the appointment of a royal commission to conduct an inquiry and make recommendations on future policy. The commission's report indicated that a radically new departure in social and economic policy was urgently required. Its proposals culminated in the Development and Welfare Act for the colonies, approved by Parliament in 1940, which pledged imperial financial support for "schemes for any purpose likely to promote the development of the resources of any colony or the welfare of its people." [1] The new law reflected in part the idea, which had begun to influence local British politics, that government should be a positive agency for the promotion of social welfare and economic well-being. Although most of the funds appropriated during the war were earmarked for the Caribbean area, it was generally agreed by all parties in the United Kingdom that economic development and social welfare were the new imperatives of imperial policy for all the colonies. This idea was restated in the Development and Welfare Act of 1945, upon which postwar development planning and expenditure in Nigeria have been partially based.[2]

A second influence that stimulated a reorientation of traditional policy was the loss of the Far Eastern colonies and the nationalist struggle in India. The fall of Malaya not only struck a severe blow to white prestige throughout the non-European world, but also brought into serious question the oft-repeated argument that colonial systems were ethically justified by the protection great powers could give technologically backward peoples. Moreover, the developments in the Far East directly affected Nigeria in that certain items of Nigerian produce assumed greater, if not vital, importance. The stature of Nigeria, and of other African territories, was further heightened by their contribution of voluntarily recruited military man power to Britain's struggle to maintain or to regain control over her Asian colonies. In short, losses in Asia enhanced the value of tropical Africa, which acted as a subtle prod to the reëxamination of imperial policy.

A third development was the publication of the Atlantic Charter and the subsequent public discussion that centered in its famous third clause: ". . . the right of all peoples to choose the form of government under which they will live. . . ." It is a commonplace that the charter excited the hopes of colonial nationalists everywhere.[3] Prime Minister Churchill's subsequent qualifications—that he and President Roosevelt had only European states in mind, that "the Atlantic Charter is a guide and not a rule," that he would not preside over the liquidation of the British Empire, and that "we mean to hold our own"—did little to dampen the aspirations the charter had aroused. On the contrary, Churchill's rather cavalier rejection of the suggestion that colonial peoples were covered by the charter served only to intensify nationalist sentiment. His remarks were interpreted not only as a betrayal of a promise but also as a reaffirmation of imperialism and of the white-man's-burden concept of empire at a time when the climate of world opinion tended to view colonialism as archaic. This interpretation was fortified by the intensity of the criticism heaped upon Churchill not only by Asians and Africans, but by British critics as well. In commenting on the British self-criticism, Nnamdi Azikiwe said:

> These British criticisms leave me and those of my kind who are living in the outposts of the British Empire to begin to ponder (as we did after his ominous explanation, in 1941, that the Atlantic Charter was not applicable to the colonies) whether we should not prepare our own blueprint ourselves, instead of relying on others who are too busy preparing their own? I can see no hope for a more prosperous and contented Nigeria under the present colonial status.[4]

But it was American criticism that especially provoked Churchill's ire and unleashed a trans-Atlantic debate over the ethics of colonialism and the justification for the British Empire. Shortly after the United States entered the war, the British Empire, and particularly the British presence in India, were vigorously attacked not only by American intellectuals, political leaders, and journals like *Life* and *Fortune* (whose foreign editor was Raymond Leslie Buell, one of America's foremost Africanists), but also by President Roosevelt, Vice President Henry Wallace, Secretary of State Cordell Hull and Under Secretary of State Sumner Welles.[5] The statements of Wendell Willkie were particularly provocative. Following his world tour in 1942 Willkie announced in a national broadcast:

> I found the dread of imperialism everywhere. . . . In Africa, in the Middle East, as well as in China and the whole Far East

freedom means the orderly but scheduled abolition of the colonial system. . . . The rule of people by other people is not
freedom and not what we must fight to preserve. . . .[6]

It is generally believed that Prime Minister Churchill's famous
Mansion House speech, in which he repudiated any suggestion
of imperial liquidation, was a response to such public statements
by American political leaders.

The notion that after the war there should be a new deal in
colonial empires figured prominently in most postwar schemes
advanced by private American individuals and organizations.[7]
It was also advocated by liberal groups in other countries, and
ultimately found expression in Chapter XI of the United Nations
Charter. As an alternative to liberationist and internationalist
proposals, the Churchill government proposed regional coöperation of colonial powers along functional lines. In Africa this regional concept took the form of *ad hoc* interimperial conferences
on specific technical questions; as America possessed no dependent territories in Africa, membership was confined to the imperial
powers.

As the war progressed, a previously inarticulate group of American critics displayed an increasing interest in the aspirations of
Africans and in colonial policy in Africa. These critics were Ameri-
can Negroes. Before the great Negro Renaissance which followed
Garveyism and gained strength during the 1930's, American
Negroes had tended to avoid identification with Africa. A leading
American Africanist observed that "no group in the population
[of the United States] has been more completely convinced of
the inferior nature of the African background than have the
Negroes." [8]

There had been several exceptions to this avoidance by American Negroes of the African connection. The activities of American
Negro religious sects have already been noted. There were also
occasional but abortive Back-to-Africa movements long before
the time of Garvey.[9] In 1912 Booker T. Washington convened
the International Conference on the Negro at Tuskegee Institute
for the purpose of ascertaining to what extent methods used by
Negroes in America might be appropriate for Africa. A year earlier
the Phelps-Stokes Fund had been established; it has sponsored

the publication of a series of studies on race relations and education in Africa, and was responsible for the famous Educational Commission which toured Africa in 1920. After a visit to Africa in the early 1930's, Ralph Bunche emerged as one of America's outstanding Africanists and as a responsible critic of colonialism.[10] In the mid-1930's Eslanda Goode Robeson, wife of Paul Robeson, toured Africa and published her critical observations.[11] The early Pan-African activities of W. E. B. Du Bois and of Marcus Garvey, during his residence in America, have already been discussed.

During the war these pioneering individuals and groups, together with other prominent Negro leaders and scholars, endeavored to awaken a new interest in Africa among the American public, particularly among American Negroes. The Phelps-Stokes Fund sponsored a critical but responsible study prepared by a committee of missionaries and scholars, Negro and white, which advocated positive policies of development.[12] Ralph Bunche, although partially immobilized by his official status, nevertheless contributed both directly and indirectly to the awakening of a new appreciation of Africa as an important but neglected area, especially in his capacity as delegate to international conferences on postwar planning. The foremost spokesman for African interests, however, was Du Bois. Throughout the war he conducted a militant campaign demanding that Africa receive recognition and justice in the postwar world. In surveying the plans for Africa he lamented:

> One can see in . . . postwar plans—the persistence of the old pattern of thought: the white man's need of African labor and raw materials and the assumption that these must be cheap in order to yield maximum profits. . . . the only problem so far as Africa is concerned is that the various dominating nations of the world must henceforth be treated equitably in sharing the material and the labor.[13]

At the San Francisco conference (UNCIO), Du Bois sought an independent hearing for Africa. He then participated in the organization of the Fifth Pan-African Conference in London in 1945, which demanded, among other things, the immediate emancipation of Africa. Finally, in New York, with Paul Robeson and Max Yergan, he organized the Council on African Affairs, which published the journal *New Africa*. The journal became one of the main outlets for African nationalist propaganda in the English-speaking world. By 1948, however, it was obvious that the council had become a Communist front organization. It immediately lost most of the little influence and following it had attained among non-Communist American whites and Negroes. During its short life, however, it exerted no little influence on Nigerian nationalism, either through Nigerian students resident in America, through George Padmore and Ladipo Solanke in London, or through Azikiwe's press in Nigeria. Azikiwe's *Pilot*, which frequently quoted inflammatory articles from *New Africa* on the front page, gave literate Nigerians the impression that 15 million American Negroes were closely following their nationalist movement with sympathy and strong moral support.

The question immediately arises: What influence did all this American criticism have upon British policy? It is impossible, of course, to isolate the American influence from other determinants of policy. Churchill's oft-repeated "no liquidation" remark would suggest that it had no effect. In 1943 Oliver Stanley, Secretary of State for the Colonies, bluntly and publicly stated: "I am more interested in what Britain thinks of the British Empire than what the United States thinks of it." [14] In a more conciliatory vein, Margery Perham, in a series of articles in the London *Times*, sympathetically evaluated the background and importance of American criticism. She concluded that, "taken broadly and at best, the American challenge to us to hasten the work of de-imperializing the Empire can lead only to good." [15] Although history suggests that external criticism usually provokes a defensive reaction in any nation, nevertheless the prodding from American and British critics nudged British officialdom into enunciating a policy that would be less open to criticism. Perhaps the most important effect of American criticism, however, was its influence upon Nigerian nationalists, a point to be examined later.[16]

In addition to the ferment in the West Indies, the debacle in Asia, the Atlantic Charter, and American criticism, other factors brought pressure to bear upon British policy-makers. The most influential of these was undoubtedly the Labour party and its close associate, the Fabian Colonial Bureau. The strong anti-imperialism of the Labour party is common knowledge. In its early history the slogan was doctrinaire: "Socialization and self-determination." [17] During the early years of World War II the party's leaders stated its aims:

> Labour . . . repudiates imperialism. We believe that all peoples of whatever race and colour have an equal right to freedom and to an equitable share in the good things of the world.[18]

> "We in the Labour Party have always been conscious of the wrongs done by the white races to the races with darker skins. We have always demanded that the freedom which we claim for ourselves should be extended to all men. I look for an ever-increasing measure of self-government in Africa." [19]

> "Britain today is in the colonies and she cannot withdraw; nor do I think it desirable that she should. We are pledged, in these Colonial territories, to the pursuit of a policy of constructive trusteeship, a policy which is to lead, we hope, to partnership inside the British Commonwealth." [20]

It soon became clear that in the new Labour approach to empire there was a sharp difference between "constructive trusteeship" and "imperialism." The former implied that the whole process of government was geared "to the supreme purpose of fitting the native races to determine their own destiny," [21] whereas the latter meant capitalist exploitation. Thus, although there was no question of immediate independence, it was imperative that the tempo of imperial liquidation be greatly accelerated. The only other changes advocated by the party were larger imperial subsidies for colonial development and a more thoroughgoing socialization of colonial economies.

Within the confines of these moderate but progressive objectives, Labour party spokesmen agitated inside and outside Parliament for the application of the "spirit" of the Atlantic Charter to the colonies, as well as for the promulgation of a separate colonial charter which would give expression to imperial aims.[22] During the course of the war the party shifted from its original suggestions for international administration of the colonies to the general principle of "international accountability." It is more than likely that the Labour members of the coalition government privately promoted all these objectives inside the government.

The full extent of their influence upon postwar policy cannot be precisely determined, but in all likelihood it was substantial.

As the war progressed it became increasingly evident that leaders of all parties were developing unity of thought on the colonial problem. Colonial affairs rapidly approached the status traditionally held by foreign affairs as a subject upon which national interest dictated unity and a minimum of open criticism. Although this drift may have resulted from the growing dominance of the Labour view on colonial policy, yet the apparent growth of a united imperial front caused some African nationalist leaders, who had traditionally looked upon the Labourites as their metropolitan spokesmen, to suspect an imperial conspiracy. This disaffection, however, did not become significant until the postwar period.

It is important to observe that even before wartime developments began to influence British planning, officials in the Colonial Office were actively considering substantial revisions in policy. Indeed, from about 1936 on, official circles had felt that indirect rule required review. As a result of this kind of thinking, Lord Hailey was appointed by the Secretary of State in 1939 to appraise political forces in African territories, as a preliminary to policy reconsideration and revision. Although Hailey's report was never published, it was generally believed that the Colonial Office was ready to give considerable weight to the new forces in Africa in its plans for the future. During the war, of course, the full impact of the military conflict upon African dependencies could not be evaluated. This indeterminateness partly accounted for the silence and, to some, the inactivity of the Colonial Office regarding postwar political arrangements for the colonies. It is not unreasonable to assume, however, that the various external influences examined herein helped to determine postwar imperial policy.

What was this policy? In the first place, there was no colonial charter to outline a postwar plan, for three very good reasons. First, such a scheme would have been very un-British. It is a commonplace that the British, unlike the French, lean toward a pragmatic, muddling-through approach to problems of state, especially those involving imperial or foreign affairs. Second, the British recognize and encourage diversity in development.

Innovations and reforms—in a word, progress—must come about by varying methods and at varying rates of speed according to the requirements of each individual territory. Third, responsible colonial officials had a profound antipathy to "constitution mongering," and not necessarily for reactionary reasons.

Many responsible and liberal-minded colonial experts, including most notably Lord Hailey himself, were not thoroughly convinced that self-government along Western parliamentary lines was the best form of political development for African territories. Postwar objectives were therefore necessarily cast in very general terms, and such proposals as scheduled independence, universal suffrage, and dyarchy were categorically eschewed.

It was generally agreed by the British government that a major feature of the new policy would be, in Churchill's words, "the fullest possible political, economic and social development within the British Empire." [23] Beyond that broad objective, three other features of the new policy relevant to this study were set forth by the Secretary of State for the Colonies during the period 1943–1945: First, the British presence would be maintained:

> . . . throughout the greater part of the Colonial Empire, it is, for the present, at any rate, the British presence alone which prevents a disastrous disintegration, and British withdrawal today would mean for millions a descent from nascent nationhood into the turmoil of warring sects.[24]

Second, development would be along natural lines:

> . . . our object is to see the various peoples of the various territories develop themselves along the lines of their own national aptitude, their own culture, and their own tradition.[25]

Third, economic and social development would be a necessary precondition for political advance:

> . . . educational advance and economic development . . . [are] the twin pillars upon which any sound scheme of political responsibility must be based.[26]

From the standpoint of Nigerian nationalists, these policy aims were exasperatingly noncommittal, and left two crucial questions unanswered: (1) When was self-government to be achieved? (2) What was the "national" unit to be trained for self-government? Was it the subtribe or emirate referred to by Sir Hugh Clifford in 1920, or a region, or Nigeria as a whole? Since 1942 the struggle between the nationalists and the British and among the nationalists themselves has centered around these two vital issues, the time factor and the space factor.

WARTIME ACTIVITIES OF NIGERIAN STUDENTS ABROAD

Other developments outside Nigeria had important repercussions upon the growth of postwar nationalism. These centered mainly around the activities of Nigerian students abroad. Toward the end of the 1930's an increasing number of private students were going to the United Kingdom for higher studies. By 1945 the number was approximately 150. The majority of these students either were members of or came under the influence of the West African Students' Union in London. During the war years WASU became a beehive of nationalist activity, absorbing influences from sources ranging from idealistic and repentant Christian missionaries to Communist infiltrators. It established close liaison with the Colonial Bureau of the Fabian Society, whose chairman was A. Creech Jones, and with other more left-wing organizations such as the Congress of Peoples Against Imperialism.

In 1940 WASU informed the Secretary of State for the Colonies that "it is the desire of the people of West Africa to become, remain and form a definitely distinct and integral political unit." This subcontinental approach reflected the persistence of Ladipo Solanke's influence. In 1941, shortly after publication of the Atlantic Charter, WASU submitted a memorandum to Clement Attlee which drew attention to the fact that "Great Britain has proclaimed her determination to re-establish and support the national independence of the countries of Europe, of Ethiopia, and of Syria, but what about West Africa?" [27] Shortly thereafter WASU held a conference on West African problems and submitted to the governor of Nigeria a resolution requesting, among other things,

. . . a United Nigeria with a Federal Constitution based on a Swiss or USA model with necessary modifications. . . . Local tribal loyalty [should] be gradually transcended, submerged, and suppressed by the creation and development of Nigerian National Loyalty.[28]

239

It is noteworthy that the conference and the resolution had been sparked by Attlee's remark at the earlier meeting that he hoped for "an ever-increasing measure of self-government and political freedom in Africa." This is only one instance among many of the direct and positive effects that wartime discussion of colonial aims and objectives by Europeans had upon the thoughts and activity of budding Nigerian nationalists. Another example is to be found in a memorandum submitted by WASU to the Under Secretary of State for the Colonies on April 6, 1942:

> In the interest of Freedom, Justice, and true Democracy, *and in view of the lessons of Malaya and Burma,* as well as the obvious need of giving the peoples of the Empire something to fight for, the WASU in Great Britain strongly urges the British Government to grant to the British West African colonies and Protectorates Internal Self-Government Now, with a definite guarantee of complete self-government within five years after the war.[29]

Despite questions put in the House of Commons by one pro-WASU member of Parliament, the British government did not respond to this memorandum.

In 1943, eight journalists from West Africa were invited to London as guests of the British Council. Among these was Nnamdi Azikiwe, who assumed leadership of the group. Close liaison was established with WASU, and just before the delegation returned to the West Coast it submitted to the Secretary of State for the Colonies a memorandum composed principally by Azikiwe and entitled "The Atlantic Charter and British West Africa."[30] The document first quoted several British commentaries on colonial development, including a pro-African Labourite's statement that "it is the duty of the Africans themselves to get together now and hammer out unceasingly what they want for Africa." It then made the following proposals based upon "the declaration of Clause III of the Atlantic Charter": immediate abrogation of the crown colony system of government; immediate Africanization; the award of 400 scholarships annually; and ten years of "representative" government to be followed by five years of full responsible government. Thus the delegation believed that by 1958 West African territories would be "independent and sovereign political entities, aligned or associated with the British Common-wealth of Nations." It is a striking fact that exactly fifteen years later, in 1958, the Western Region and the Eastern Region (under Azikiwe's premiership) of Nigeria became self-governing, with the assurance of complete independence for all Nigeria in 1960.

In 1943, however, the memorandum evoked no response from the Colonial Office, and, embittered, Azikiwe returned to Nigeria and expressed his disappointment at British indifference in a private letter to Dr. Akinola Maja, president of the Nigerian Youth Movement. He concluded:

> Nigeria has very few friends in England . . . so far as our political aspirations are concerned. . . . [We] must close ranks, work co-operatively and carry forward any reconstruction that is practicable, . . . show that we are able to rise beyond our minor internal differences; . . . most of our critics use that argument to prevent the realization of our aspirations.[31]

From this time on Azikiwe became increasingly militant in his demands and activities. The year 1943 marked a turning point in his career.

In the meantime, back in London, a few young and energetic leaders of WASU organized a WASU Parliamentary Committee which twice a month met with members of Parliament who were particularly interested in Africa. With the coöperation of the Colonial Bureau of the Fabian Society, the committee became a channel for bringing African grievances before Parliament during the question hour or in the debate on an adjournment motion. At the same time, new trends began to be discernible in the activities of WASU. As more and more students arrived in England, separatist tendencies became manifest in the form of student unions organized along territorial lines. This threatened the monopoly long held by WASU as the sole organ of West African student expression. As the war came to a close, the process was accelerated by the formation in London of nationality or party organizations such as the Egbe Omo Oduduwa (a Yoruba cultural organization founded by Obafemi Awolowo and others), and a London branch of the National Council for Nigeria and the Cameroons. By the end of the war it was clear that WASU was being eclipsed by the growth of a territorial consciousness, and the initiative was rapidly passing into the hands of nationalists on the coast. In the postwar period WASU came increasingly under left-wing influence, or possibly, because of rebuffs from the Colonial Office, it became more and more attracted to radical solutions.[32]

The wartime activity of Nigerian students across the Atlantic was perhaps of even greater importance in the development of the nationalist movement. Until 1938 only twenty Nigerians, including Eyo Ita and Nnamdi Azikiwe, had gone to the United States to study. Most of these pioneers had been sent by missionary societies for religious studies; none of these religious students, except Ita, had returned as active nationalists. In 1938 twelve Nigerians sailed for America, and not until 1945 did others join them. Of these twelve, three were Ibibios sent for higher studies by the Ibibio State Union, and eight were Ibos who had been under the influence of Azikiwe.[33] Eleven of the twelve went to Lincoln University, Azikiwe's Alma Mater. The Nigerian students were joined at Lincoln by three Gold Coastians, also inspired by Azikiwe, and a few students from Sierra Leone. These Africans, educated in America during the war, have been leading figures in postwar nationalism on the West Coast. A brief description of their activities, and of the influences brought to bear upon them in the United States, is therefore warranted.

In 1941 these students organized the African Students' Association of the United States and Canada, and commenced publication of a monthly organ entitled the *African Interpreter*. Close liaison was established with WASU in London, and each organization followed the activities of the other. The association's charter, adopted at the second conference, said:

> . . . we strongly urge the governing bodies of the British Empire, and their Allies, in the cause of democracy, to grant internal self-government to the colonial peoples of Africa. . . . The fundamental principles of democracy as expressed in the Four Freedoms and the Atlantic Charter . . . must be applied immediately. . . . [We] emphatically demand that those who claim to be fighting for democracy implement their expressed ideals by considering Africa a sovereign land in all of its glorious heritage and history. . . .[34]

Here was a recurrence of the tendency, manifest in the early history of WASU, to think of nationalism in continental terms. In 1943 the association endorsed Azikiwe's memorandum to the Secretary of State for the Colonies demanding constitutional reform. Throughout the war it held conferences and symposiums on Africa, mainly in the New York area, for the purpose of educating American opinion.

What were the influences that impinged upon Nigerians who studied in America? Most of the students left Lincoln University and shifted to other Northern and predominantly white institutions. In the rather liberal and idealistic milieu characteristic of many Northern college campuses, they encountered a strong anti-imperialist sentiment mixed with no little Anglophobia. They were particularly impressed by the wartime statements of Franklin Roosevelt, Henry Wallace, and Wendell Willkie, which found frequent mention in their monthly journal. The constitutional reforms granted to Jamaica in 1943 undoubtedly raised their hopes and increased their demands.[35] They had close contacts with prominent American negroes, and through their journal were informed of the views of leading spokesmen for the principles of racial equality and self-government for all peoples.

Three of the Nigerian students (Mbonu Ojike, Nwafor Orizu, and Ozuomba Mbadiwe—all Ibos) made lecture tours of the United States, and published one or more books each. Their writings were the first contribution to Nigerian nationalist literature since Azikiwe's *Renascent Africa*.[36] Upon their return to Nigeria these three became crusaders for American practical—or what Orizu called "horizontal"—education, as contrasted to the British literary ("vertical") tradition. Their agitation in behalf of American education, coupled with Azikiwe's great success, was one of the principal reasons for the postwar migration of hundreds of Nigerians to America. Their propagation of the American educational ideal and their positive nationalism contributed to the antipathy of both the British and the British-educated Nigerians toward American education and American-educated Nigerians.[37]

The determinative influences of America on the twenty-eight African wartime students can best be shown by a brief description of the subsequent careers of seven of them:

243

Name	Country	Subsequent career
Ako Adjei	Ghana	Barrister; currently Minister of Commerce, Ghana (CPP) government
I. U. Akpabio	Nigeria	College principal; now Minister of Education and Deputy Premier, (NCNC) government of Eastern Region
W. H. Fitzjohn	Sierra Leone	Professor at Fourah Bay College; member of executive of Sierra Leone People's party
H. A. B. Jones-Quartey	Ghana	Deputy Director, Department of Extra-Mural Studies, University College, Ghana
Ozuomba Mbadiwe	Nigeria	Minister of Commerce and Industries, federal government of Nigeria
Kwame Nkrumah	Ghana	Prime Minister of Ghana; founder and lifetime president of Convention People's party
John Karefa-Smart	Sierra Leone	Physician; Minister of Lands, Mines and Labor, government of Sierra Leone

With one or two exceptions the other wartime students became leaders in the nationalist movements of their respective countries. One of the Nigerian students put it this way: "The first skirmishes in the struggle for political freedom of the 21 million people of Nigeria are being fought today in the colleges of the U.S." [38]

There can be no doubt that the American influence was a crucial factor in accelerating the growth of Nigerian nationalism, just as it had been in Jamaican nationalism. Certain features of American culture—the lack of class consciousness; the heterogeneity and mobility of the population; the anti-imperialist tradition; the dynamic and competitive nature of political, social, and economic behavior—were unsettling and highly contagious influences which undoubtedly had a profound impact upon African students. The special situation of the American Negro, into whose company an African student is inevitably thrown, was likewise an important conditioning factor. African students in America were perforce made acutely aware of color discrimination, in itself provocative of racial consciousness. Moreover, Nigerians, like other West Africans, did not meet in their own countries the highly institutionalized and omnipresent discrimination characteristic of Southern states, and to a degree also of Northern states, in America. Racial discrimination in Nigeria (it was formally outlawed in 1948) was irritating and embittering mainly as a symbol of European imperialism; it did not engulf the individual and plague him at every turn. Thus, many Nigerians encountered racial discrimination on a large scale for the first time when they arrived in the United States. The same would have been true, to a lesser extent, in the United Kingdom. Racial discrimination hit Nigerians at an impressionable age, when their personality structures were most vulnerable. Along with the very different and for them difficult climate, financial worries, and academic curricula for which they were not prepared, it was psychologically an overwhelming and traumatic experience.

In addition to racial consciousness, many of the African students in America acquired the aggressiveness, the uncompromising determination to achieve equality, and the crusading zeal of American Negroes. Yet the Nigerians, like most American Negroes, were ambivalent in their attitude toward America. Although they suffered the hardships and adopted the retaliatory techniques of the American Negro, they also shared the latter's loyalty to the American ideal, the confident expectation of improved status, and the admiration for a dynamic society. In any event, it is remarkable how many younger brothers have followed the footsteps of students who returned to Nigeria after studying in America.

Analysis of the ethnic origins of Nigerians who have studied in the United States during the past three decades reveals a striking predominance of Ibos. Although the Ibo peoples constitute no more than 17 per cent of the total population of Nigeria, until the late 1940's more than two-thirds of the Nigerian students in the

United States were Ibos. As the figures in table 19 show, the Ibos were still in the majority as late as 1954.

There are several reasons for the Ibo predominance. One is the strong influence of Azikiwe, Ojike, Mbadiwe, and Orizu, who were among the first university-educated Ibos and who consciously sought to popularize the virtues of American education.

TABLE 19

ETHNIC ORIGIN OF NIGERIAN STUDENTS IN THE UNITED STATES [a]

Period	Ethnic group					Total
	Ibo		Yoruba	Efik-Ibibio	Others and unknown	
	Number	Per cent				
Pre-1938	1 [b]	5	5	2	12	20
1938–1945	8	67	1	3	0	12
1946–1948	114	65	45	11	5	175
1953–1954	165	51	73	38	43	318

[a] Because numbers have been calculated from lists of names, they are only approximations. "Others and unknown" may possibly include several Yorubas who retained their Anglicized names. The Efiks and Ibibios are counted together because it is difficult in most instances for a non-Efik or a non-Ibibio to distinguish between Efik and Ibibio names.
[b] Nnamdi Azikiwe.

Indeed, Mbadiwe and Orizu fostered scholarship schemes designed to send Nigerian students to America, and most of the successful candidates were Ibos. In contrast, most of the older-generation Yorubas had been educated in the United Kingdom, and the later generation tended to adhere to that tradition. In addition, by 1945, the Ibos were the upcoming group, and the number of Ibos in British universities may well have equaled or exceeded the number of Yorubas. For by the late 1940's the number of Ibos with a secondary school education, a prerequisite for university training, actually exceeded the number of Yorubas with a similar qualification. In any event, the preference of Yorubas for British education and of Ibos for American education, coupled with militant Ibo claims of the superiority of American education and of the easier-to-get American degrees, has exacerbated Yoruba-Ibo tension. As table 19 indicates, however, the differential is rapidly changing.

It is difficult, and indeed hazardous, to seek an explanation for the attitudinal and behavioral tendencies of university-educated Nigerians in the differences of their overseas environments. Most of the students who went to Oxford or Cambridge returned to Nigeria with a more conservative nationalism than those who had studied in Ireland or the United States, or at institutions in the London area. Presumably students at Oxford and Cambridge were more thoroughly exposed to English values; they escaped the greater impersonality and color discrimination, and the more intensive left-wing pressures, prevalent in other places. On the other hand, it can be argued that students who attended Oxford and Cambridge would have come from older and more affluent families with stronger pro-British ties and sentiments. Yet any generalization is difficult to support in the face of such imponderables as nationalist predispositions acquired before departure from Nigeria, individual differences in personal stability and integration, and the expectation of entering upon careers at home which might require political moderation.

Although any one of these variables might be decisive in individual cases, it is generally true that students while abroad were emphatic and radical in their nationalism. They held utopian and grandiose visions of the national potentialities of their homeland. Complete physical separation from Nigeria dulled their awareness of homeland realities and aroused a desire, particularly among the more sensitive and impressionable, to glorify their traditional culture, usually by suppressing its unattractive features and exaggerating the qualities that they believed were superior or unique. It is not a coincidence that most of the efforts to awaken respect for and appreciation of African culture started among African students abroad.[39] Also, while abroad students could observe the white man as he actually is—stupid and intelligent, cruel and kind, evil and virtuous, filthy and immaculate, irrational and rational—and thus become aware of the universalities of human nature and behavior. They could see little fundamental difference between the bushman at home and the European peasant, between the Boma Boys of Lagos and the adolescent delinquents of London's East End or New York's tenement areas, between the beggars and petty thieves in the towns of Nigeria and their counterparts on Skid Row; in short, between the average

Nigerian and the average American or Englishman. The doctrine of white superiority, and with it the justification for imperial rule, was crushed by their devastating critique of the white man as he is versus the pretentiousness of his ideals.

Nigerians who studied abroad returned home with greater self-confidence, based on the conviction that technology alone separated them from the rest of mankind. Captivated by the idea of progress, they were convinced that it was their manifest destiny to bring their homeland to the material level of the countries where they had studied. They were profoundly struck by the tremendous differences in material well-being between Nigeria and Europe or America—man-made differences which they, the creative minority, could eliminate if they were given power in their own country. The stigma of backwardness, the real reason for their being under colonial rule, was removable.

THE RUSSIAN MODEL

After the German invasion of Russia and the formation of the wartime alliance of Britain, Soviet Russia, and the United States, a new and sympathetic interest in Soviet Russia and communism developed among Africans. The chief wartime and postwar sources of pro-Communist thought were the Council on African Affairs in New York; the British Communist party; and the left wing of the Labour party. In the pro-Soviet climate of opinion that prevailed during the war, Nigerian students in London and New York, and Nigerian readers of Azikiwe's publications in Nigeria, had Russia presented to them as an ideal, as the unique foreign country whose experience and techniques Nigerians might well emulate. The raw materials with which Russia started were believed to be not unlike those of Nigeria. In 1944 Max Yergan, a prominent American Negro and director of the Council on African Affairs, wrote:

> The Soviet Union has demonstrated to the world how generous planning can in 25 years transform a feudal, illiterate, impoverished and heterogeneous society—such as was Eastern Russia under the Czar, and such as is most of Africa today—into a strong, intelligent, capable and unified people.[40]

In the same year Leonard Barnes, an English Russophile, published a book expounding the same theme; [41] shortly thereafter George Padmore concluded that

> This example of the almost lightning transmutation of disunited backward peoples . . . into a solid unity of intelligent workers . . . is the best repudiation of the oft-repeated falsity that Colonial peoples are inherently incapable of adapting themselves to Western civilization and of taking over their own self-government.[42]

Pro-Communist literature of this nature was widely quoted in Nigerian newspapers throughout the war. Nigerian youths formed the Red Army Club, and in 1943 the Nigerian Youth Movement cabled the leaders of Soviet Russia: "We hope this event [the 25th anniversary of the Red Army] will bring the youths of Nigeria closer to the youths of Soviet Russia." [43]

There are three very special reasons why Nigerian students and leaders have been fascinated with Soviet Russia. The first of these is the alleged absence of color discrimination within Soviet Russia and among Communists. The second is the rapid social, educational, and economic transformation of primitive and backward areas which Communists have claimed was brought about in the Soviet Union. According to one nationalist, the "consuming passion [of Nigerian nationalism] is modernisation, the desire to catch up with the more advanced countries of the world." [44] The third is the political and economic unity imposed upon a large and culturally heterogeneous mass of peoples. These three aspects of Soviet society and development were dominant themes in Communist propaganda, and corresponded to three of the strongest nationalist imperatives: equality, rapid technological progress, and Pan-Nigerian unity. Enchantment with the ends reportedly achieved by the Soviet Union dulled Nigerian sensitivity to the dictatorial means used to achieve those ends. In an effort to dampen enthusiasm for Soviet educational development, the Nigerian director of education pointed out that "the spearhead of the movement was the Red Army, and the methods employed might not commend themselves to the inhabitants of Nigeria." [45] But the fact that most anti-Communist arguments came from spokesmen of the imperial or Nigerian government made them immediately suspect.

Shortly after the end of the war, the Soviet Union renewed its efforts, hastily dropped in 1934, openly to support colonial nationalist movements in their drive for independence. Throughout the postwar period it became clear that colonial students in the United Kingdom, and student groups and labor organizations in the colonies, were primary targets in Soviet propaganda strategy. The main channels of approach appeared to be front organizations, such as the Communist-dominated World Federation of Trade Unions (of which the Nigerian Trades Union Congress was for some time a member), the International Union of Students in Prague (with which WASU was affiliated), and other agencies and individuals previously mentioned.

In the meantime, developments within Nigeria had created an entirely new situation. Within the limits of the broad and, to the nationalists, vague statements of postwar imperial policy, Nigerian officialdom was under pressure to formulate a specific policy of constitutional reform. This pressure was applied with increasing intensity by nationalist leaders as the war progressed, partly as a result of external influences and partly in response to internal forces and events in Nigeria. In the next chapter we shall analyze these wartime developments within Nigeria.

CHAPTER 11

Wartime Developments in the Nationalist Movement

EFFECTS OF WORLD WAR II UPON NIGERIA

In appraising the impact of the war upon West Africa, Meyer Fortes, a wartime resident in the area, remarked:

> Great, perhaps revolutionary, changes have been taking place in certain sectors of West African social and economic structure since the outbreak of the war. . . . It may well be that the war will prove to have been the outstanding instrument of social progress in West Africa for fifty years.[1]

There can be little doubt that the war greatly accelerated the processes of societal disintegration and social mobilization (urbanization, expansion of the wage-labor force, extension of the money economy, and the development of communications) which have been crucial, if not indispensable, to the rise and growth of Nigerian nationalism.

Wartime developments in the economic sphere were perhaps the most important. After the fall of Britain's Far Eastern colonies, the Nigerian government abandoned its historic attitude of comparative neutrality in economic matters. Prompted by a desire to protect the Nigerian primary producer, as well as by a determination to mobilize Nigerian resources for the prosecution of the war, the government asserted control over the entire economic structure, including the regulation of transport, price controls, wage ceilings, and, as discussed in chapter 3, the marketing of export crops. In 1942 the imperial government decided to buy up the entire cocoa crop for the duration of the war. This policy was eventually extended to palm oil, rubber, cotton, and groundnuts, until all strategic sectors of the economy were under the direction of the government.

This wartime change from neutrality and *laissez faire* to statism had significant implications. Before the war it was difficult to focus economic grievances directly upon the government, except for its inaction. Once the government assumed complete control of the economy, it rendered itself vulnerable to blame for all grievances of an economic nature, whether real or imaginary. As marketing boards set the purchase price for primary products, and as these prices were, for sound economic reasons, usually far lower than could be secured in a free market, the thousands of peasant producers became easy targets for antigovernment agitators with a nationalist bent. Government controls also affected unfavorably the activities of middlemen and traders in export products.

Most aggrieved, however, were the emergent Nigerian entrepreneurs who desired to break into the lucrative export-import trade. As noted earlier, the superior competitive position of European and Levantine firms had effectively frozen them out of this field in the prewar period. By the late 1930's, however, many ambitious traders had made good profits in the expansion of the cocoa industry and hoped to use their capital to establish direct relations with foreign manufacturers. It was at this juncture—the outbreak of war—that the government assumed complete control over all exports and imports, and adopted an inflexible policy of issuing licenses only to established "trade channels" (that is, the established non-African firms). In the meantime, the firms themselves concluded an agreement which created a rather effective oligarchy in the import trade. Aspiring African exporters and importers were, or considered themselves to be, victims of a government-firm conspiracy. By the end of the war this small but politically important group was ready to finance and support any movement that would further what they felt to be their legitimate aspirations.

The really significant point here, however, is that all these groups—peasant producers, middlemen, exporters, and importers—as well as wage earners confronted with wage ceilings and market-women affected by price controls, felt the direct impact of government for the first time, and they considered the relationship onerous. Far removed from the war and the great issues at stake, they were understandably insensitive to government appeals for self-sacrifice. Their strong resentment of *étatisme* gave the nationalist cause a tremendous boost. It is an ordinary phenomenon for the people of independent countries to desire a change in government at the expiration of a war, if only in the belief that a new government will remove wartime controls. But in a colonial territory there is no provision for choosing an alternative government; the choice lies between a permanent European bureaucracy and aspiring nationalists. It is easily understandable, therefore, that Herbert Macaulay was able to mobilize the Lagos market-women at a moment's notice, that trade unions could bring about a country-wide general strike, or that a farmers' union, 50,000 strong, could be organized.[2]

Another wartime development added fuel to the nationalist cause. The lack of shipping, plus wartime shortages of imported foods and consumers' goods, resulted in a remarkable growth of local industries (shingles, furniture, butter, potatoes, sugar, and, later, cigarettes, beer, and soap). Moreover, the local products were cheaper than the imported ones. Here was the proof the nationalists had been waiting for; here was conclusive evidence that the only bar to industrialization in Nigeria was the desire of the British administration to protect home manufactures. The nationalists believed that the evidence gave substance to the charge of exploitation. The growth of local industries not only increased the urban labor force, but also created new tastes and new wants.[3]

The spread of the war to North Africa, the Middle East, and India enhanced the strategic value of Nigeria, which became an important station for troops and supplies bound for those theaters of war. The ensuing construction of modern airports, military camps, and new roads increased business activity in key urban centers throughout Nigeria, particularly Lagos, Ibadan, Kaduna, Kano, Maiduguri, Jos, and Enugu. More than 100,000 British troops, and several thousand American troops, passed through West Africa during the war, many remaining as long as eighteen months. Thus the war accelerated urbanization and expanded the wage-earning force in both services and construction.

The presence of large numbers of white troops unconnected

with the colonial government and not always scrupulous in their observance of the established pattern of Eurafrican relationships was of great importance to the growth of nationalism. The color bar and the doctrine of white superiority were dealt fatal blows. For the first time in Nigerian history dance halls, bars, and houses of prostitution became centers of racial commingling. Tens of thousands of Nigerians discovered for themselves what their European-educated brothers had been telling them: that the ordinary white man had all the basic vices.

Although most white troops were egalitarian and uninhibited in their relations with Africans, some of them were arrogant, crude, and provocative. On the other hand, a few left-wing intellectuals who had been conscripted and found themselves stationed in Nigeria entered into covert liaison with nationalist leaders, offering them suggestions regarding future strategy and tactics. In short, few of the many thousands of white troops in Nigeria during the war behaved as custom dictated that white men should behave.

Army life was not confined to white troops; more than 100,000 Nigerians served in the military forces during the war. Two divisions, with more than 30,000 men, had experience in the Middle East, East Africa, Burma, and India.[4] For large numbers the army became a school where they learned new skills and trades, as well as the English language. The necessities of effective command, battle discipline, and communication required a common language; except for the Hausa contingents, this had to be the English language. While in the army, most men enjoyed a standard of living higher than they had ever experienced before— regular money income, clothing, food, and medical care. They also were taught combativeness and violence. It is therefore not surprising to find ex-servicemen among the more militant leaders of the nationalist movement during the postwar period.[5]

Another wartime development that accelerated the growth of nationalism was the government's use of the latest propaganda techniques to promote wartime production of desperately needed raw materials and to foster enthusiasm for the Allied cause. Over the radio, in the press, and through masses of free literature Nigerians were exhorted to join in the crusade for freedom, democracy, and a better postwar world. In Accra educated men from many

254

tribes along the West Coast were employed to broadcast in the vernacular over a rapidly expanding radio diffusion service. Some of the leaders in the nationalist awakening in the north were Hausa-speaking broadcasters who had spent the war in Accra. Government propaganda and extended use of mass communications media served to broaden horizons, to create a new awareness, and to excite hopes and ambitions.

It is difficult to measure the total effect of these internal wartime changes and developments. As previously suggested, in many instances the war merely accelerated existing trends. For example, the total number of wage and salary earners in Nigeria in 1939 was approximately 183,000; in 1946 it was estimated at about 300,000. The trend toward urbanization was most marked in centers of military and industrial activity. The population of Enugu, capital of the Eastern Region, for example, increased 400 per cent during the period 1939–1946. The value of Nigerian exports during the same period rose from £10,300,000 to £24,-600,000; of imports, from £6,800,000 to £19,800,000.[6] These figures are only surface reflections of the deeper and more complex sociopsychological ferment caused by both internal and external wartime developments. It is against this background, however, that we turn to the more specific developments related to this study—the growth of an organized labor movement and wartime organizational developments in the nationalist movement.

ORGANIZED LABOR AND THE GENERAL STRIKE OF 1945

Before World War II the wage and salary earners of Nigeria, with certain exceptions, were either not inclined or not encouraged to participate in organizational activity. The exceptions, the Nigerian Union of Civil Servants and the Nigerian Union of Teachers, have already been noted. Early in the war, however, the number of labor unions rose phenomenally from five to seventy, and the Nigerian Trades Union Congress was organized as a central coordinating body. There were three reasons for this. The first and most important was the decision of the British government to encourage and sponsor labor unionization. Although there had been pressures upon the government as early as 1930 through the activities of the International Labor Organization, the decisive stimulus to a new official attitude toward African labor was the stipulation in the Colonial Development and Welfare Act of 1940 —included at the insistence of the Labour party—that no grants would be made to a territory unless reasonable facilities existed for the establishment of trade unions. In 1941 the government appointed a labor officer for Nigeria, and thereafter steadily expanded its supervisory and counseling services in the field of labor.

Although official toleration, and subsequently encouragement, provided a favorable milieu, the most positive stimulus was the large wartime increase in the cost of living. During the period 1939–1942 the cost of living rose by 50 to 75 per cent in urban centers. In 1940 considerable unrest developed among railway workers, and by 1942 the idea of unionization had spread rapidly to many other occupational groups. This burst of organizational activity, precipitated by the rapid decline in real income, compelled the government to grant a cost-of-living allowance to its employees. The other major employing agencies subsequently took similar action. As the war progressed inflationary tendencies were aggravated, and this in turn led to stronger and more widespread grievances.

The third stimulus to labor organizational activity was a government order of October, 1942, enacted under the Nigerian General Defence Regulations, which made strikes and lockouts illegal for the duration of the war. This measure, of course, merely followed similar legislation in the United Kingdom. Nigerian labor leaders, however, interpreted it as a calculated and arbitrary, even if temporary, curb upon their efforts to organize the workers. They responded by launching a campaign for a trade-union congress through which they could demonstrate the strength of labor. Mass meetings were held, and in November, 1942, a central organization, the Federated Trades Union of Nigeria, was formed. In July, 1943, the organization became the Nigerian Trades Union Congress, which received the full support of all the leading politicians of Nigeria, including Azikiwe, Ikoli, Macaulay, and Awolowo. The congress established a secretariat and began publication of a quarterly bulletin, the *Nigerian Worker*, under the editorship of Obafemi Awolowo. The constitution demanded, among other things, industrialization, nationalization of all natural resources and public utilities, establishment of a labor party, and the unity of all Nigerian trade unions.[7]

During the period 1943–1945 the Trades Union Congress gave promise of becoming a Nigeria-wide organization. In September, 1943, its leaders presented their demands to the Secretary of State for the Colonies. As time passed the government gave increasing recognition to the congress as the accepted representative of Nigerian labor. In 1944 a series of mass meetings and public debates were held, including one on the subject: "That in the hands of workers and not capitalists lies the freedom of the world." [8] Other evidences of left-wing influence were a May Day celebration and the establishment of a "Workers' Week" in the same year. The congress explicitly eschewed politics; the leaders had resolved to work through, but not to become affiliated with, existing political groups until such time as they could organize a labor party.[9]

The international contacts established by the congress reflect the influences that helped to shape its ideology and objectives. The congress corresponded with the Negro Labor Victory Committee and the Council on African Affairs in New York; the Fabian Society in London through its local branch in Nigeria; the British Trades Union Congress; and the World Federation of Trade Unions (WFTU), then in Paris. The president of the Nigerian TUC attended both the London and the Paris meetings of the WFTU. Prior to the general strike of 1945, however, the leadership of the congress was very moderate, a fact which ultimately led to its repudiation by the workers.[10]

By the end of the war certain distinguishing features of the organized sector of the labor force affected its political role. First, despite the rapid increase in unionization during the war, as shown by the figures in table 20, organized labor in 1946 was only 17 per cent of the estimated total wage-labor force. The latter, in turn, represented no more than 4 per cent of the total adult male population (or about 1 per cent of the total population) of Nigeria. Thus, quantitatively at least, organized labor included but a tiny fraction of the population. Second, the vast majority of the unions were small, consisting usually of only one branch. By late 1944, at least sixty-eight of the eighty-five registered unions had a membership of less than 500; only seven unions had a membership exceeding 1,000, and the largest union, the Nigerian Union of Teachers, claimed a membership of only 2,251.[11] Moreover, of the seventeen unions having a membership of more than 500, only five were affiliated with the Nigerian Trades Union

TABLE 20

GROWTH OF LABOR UNIONIZATION IN NIGERIA, 1940–1955

Year	Number of unions	Number of members
1940	12	4,337
1941	36	17,144
1942	77	26,346
1943	83	27,284
1944	85	30,000
1946	100	52,747
1952–1953	131	143,282
1954–1955	177	165,130

Sources: *Annual Report,* Department of Labour, 1951 (Lagos: Government Printer, 1952); *Annual Report,* Department of Labour, 1954–1955 (Lagos: Federal Government Printer, 1956), p. 15; A. A. Adio-Moses, "Notes on the History of Nigerian Trade Unionism" (unpublished manuscript).

Congress.[12] Also, many of the unions either were centered in one town (for example, the Calabar Mercantile Employees' Union and the Ajijaawe Native Herbalist Union) or were "house" unions (for example, the K. Chellaram Tailors' Union and the Ollivant African Staff Union). Finally, the unionized sector of the labor force was composed exclusively of southerners. In 1945 there were no all-northern labor unions in the north.

The cost-of-living allowance granted to most workers in 1942 was not considered adequate, and as the cost of living continued to mount labor unrest kept pace. By 1945 workers claimed that the cost of living had gone up 200 per cent, with no corresponding relief in wages. As a result, the African Civil Service Technical Workers' Union took the lead in demanding an increase of 50 per cent in the cost-of-living allowance together with a minimum daily wage of 2/6 for laborers. This action represented the economic side of the workers' grievance; an equally important source of bitterness was racial discrimination. Labor leaders pointed out that whereas European civil servants in Nigeria had been given allowances which were revised upward according to a sliding scale, the allowances of African workers had not been altered since 1942.[13] As a result seventeen unions consisting of about 30,000 workers went out on strike for thirty-seven days, despite last-minute appeals by the acting governor and revocation of the strike order by labor leaders the day before the walkout was scheduled to occur.

It was not the number of strikers that made the work stoppage significant, but the fact that most of them were performing services indispensable to the economic and administrative life of the country; they were railway workers, postal and telegraph employees, and technical workers in government departments.[14] Moreover, these vital Pan-Nigerian unions were rigidly controlled by union headquarters in Lagos. Although in many places the workers went back to their jobs after a few days, the strike was not terminated until the government had given assurances that there would be no victimization and that an impartial commission of inquiry would look into their grievances.

The general strike of 1945 was an important event in several respects. In the first place, it virtually wrecked the Trades Union Congress. The president of the major striking union, who was defied and repudiated by the members of his union, was also president of the congress. Moreover, since the congress failed to take a positive stand on the strike, it was stigmatized as an ineffectual instrument for ameliorating workers' grievances. Secondly, the strike had the strong support of Azikiwe and his press, which enabled him to emerge from the event with increased stature and a reputation as the champion of labor. It was the first and most successful step in his postwar effort to politicize the labor movement and link it to the nationalist movement. Indeed, the strike served as a dramatic opening of a new nationalist era. Finally, the strike shocked both Europeans and Africans into the realization that Nigerians, when organized, had great power, that they could defy the white bureaucracy, that they could virtually control strategic centers throughout the country, and that through force or the threat of force they could compel the government to grant concessions. One of the present leaders of the Northern Region informed me that the general strike of 1945 marked the beginning of racial and political consciousness in the north, although only a few northerners had participated in it.

259

ORGANIZATIONAL DEVELOPMENTS IN THE NATIONALIST MOVEMENT

The wartime influences from abroad and the great social and economic changes at home had a profound effect upon the growth of nationalist sentiment and upon organizational activity. But these two elements—sentiment and organizational development—must be considered separately. The war produced a new awareness, excited new hopes, and intensified aspirations among all Nigerians who felt its disorganizing impact. Yet the manner of utilizing this sentiment was in large measure determined by the activities of existing organizations. The split that had occurred in the Nigerian Youth Movement as a result of the Akinsanya crisis in February, 1941, was never healed. Many politically conscious Nigerians, whose number had swelled enormously during the war, were therefore adrift, waiting for a force that would channel their energies into purposeful activity in tune with their intensified hopes. During the period 1941–1944, nationalist leaders (Azikiwe, Ikoli, Macaulay, and Awolowo) all shared the determination that Nigeria should have a radical "new deal" at the end of the war, but they were unable to unite in pursuit of this objective.

Azikiwe's defection from the Youth Movement eliminated all possibility that it would become a Nigeria-wide nationalist body. During the war three efforts to rejuvenate the movement failed; but, despite the failure, the efforts in themselves were important indicators of future developments. First, the Lagosian leaders of the Youth Movement appealed to the other so-called nationalist organizations in Lagos (Macaulay's Nigerian National Democratic party and its youth wing, the Nigerian Young Democrats) for a united front in order to meet Nigeria's postwar problems. The response was favorable; the Joint Council was formed, and the parties agreed to share representation on the Legislative Council and on the Lagos Town Council. Apart from this agreement, the Joint Council's only known activity was a protest to the Secretary of State for the Colonies in 1943 against restrictions imposed by the Nigerian government upon students proceeding to the United Kingdom for study. In September of the same year —one month after Azikiwe, dejected and embittered, returned from England—Macaulay resigned from the Joint Council. This ended the first effort to achieve a national front.

The second effort came from the Ibadan branch of the Nigerian Youth Movement. Commencing in June, 1940, a group of young Yoruba intellectuals, cocoa traders, and lorry owners tried to revive the movement. Obafemi Awolowo, an Ijebu cocoa trader and secretary of the Nigerian Motor Transport Union, supplied the initiative and the leadership. During the succeeding four wartime years this group debated, planned, and organized with great enthusiasm and realism. The full importance of Awolowo's guiding genius was revealed by the cessation of activity in 1944 when he left for the United Kingdom to study law. But before his departure the pattern of his thinking and of his plans for the future had become abundantly clear. Four themes dominated his wartime thought. The first was his contempt for all previous political and nationalist activity, especially for Lagos politics. In his efforts to rejuvenate the movement he demanded that supreme authority be taken from the Lagos branch "with its never-ending pettiness, intrigues and crises," and be placed instead in a nationwide representative council.[15] He condemned the Lagosian leadership for its failure to instill discipline, and respect for and obedience to authority, in the rank and file. Second, from 1942 on Awolowo insisted that the movement should be regionalized to fit the major administrative divisions of Nigeria, and he proceeded to put life into the idea by convening two Western Regional conferences (1942 and 1944) at which all western branches of the movement were represented. Third, while advocating constitutional reforms in the central government (such as an African majority and extension of the franchise), he placed primary emphasis upon immediate and wide-scale reform of the native authority system. Actually, Awolowo was one of the few Nigerian nationalists who had ever made a thorough study of that system and had worked out constructive measures for modernization.[16] Reform of indirect rule was a prominent item on the agenda of both regional conferences. Apart from democratization, Awolowo was most emphatic about amalgamating the native authorities:

> What we of the Nigerian Youth Movement are visualising is a Nigeria of tomorrow in which the various linguistic units of

Nigeria will federate to form a single nation. But such is impossible if each little native authority is separate from and totally independent of the rest.[17]

The last Western Regional Conference of the NYM held before Awolowo's departure for London passed a resolution of no confidence in the Lagos executive of the movement, and established a provisional committee to conduct the affairs of the movement during the interim before the All-Nigeria Representative Council was convened in June, 1944. Before the council could meet, however, Awolowo had left for England, and the movement for reform and rejuvenation of the NYM which he commenced was largely abandoned.

Early in 1942 Nnamdi Azikiwe had taken the initiative in organizing the Nigerian Reconstruction Group (NRG), a small private study circle which undertook research into the political, social, economic, and cultural problems that would confront Nigeria at the end of the war. This group of fourteen, mainly non-Yoruba, was composed of two trade unionists (one each from the Nigerian Union of Teachers and the Railway Workers' Union, the largest and most powerful unions), two teachers and four students from Yaba Higher College, a medical practitioner, a few senior government clerks, and occasionally—and surreptitiously—a friendly British noncommissioned army officer stationed in Nigeria.[18] Although the members of the NRG felt that a "national front" should be formed, they did not intend that the NRG should itself become a political organization. Rather, as Dr. Azikiwe reports, they decided "to seek the co-operation of the Nigerian Youth Movement and to request that political body to spearhead this National Front." [19] Private efforts to persuade the NYM leadership to assume this role proved abortive, and after functioning for a little more than a year the NRG became moribund.[20]

In November, 1943, a youth rally was held on the grounds of a private estate in Ojokoro, on the outskirts of Lagos. The speakers and heads of the discussion circles included nationalist leaders from all groups (for example, Nnamdi Azikiwe of the NRG, Rotimi Williams of the NYM, H. O. Davies of the Nigerian Youth

Circle (NYC) and the NYM, and leaders of the Nigerian Union of Students (NUS) who had organized the rally). Many resolutions were passed on subjects relating to the future of Nigeria. One in particular affirmed the need for the national front urged by the NRG and Azikiwe. The rally is generally considered to have been one of the critical events in the political mobilization of youth in World War II. Hundreds of nationalist-minded students from the secondary schools in the Lagos area were in attendance. Many militant nationalists look back upon the Ojokoro youth rally as the occasion on which their enthusiasm for political action was first aroused.[21]

There are two possible explanations why the Lagos leaders of the NYM declined the vanguard role in launching the new national front. The first was the bitter personal hostility that some members of the NYM felt toward Azikiwe. This was the product in part of Azikiwe's journalism, in part of the feeling among some of the leaders that he was solely responsible for the Akinsanya crisis of 1941 and for the ensuing decline in the movement, and that it was impossible, because of his political ambitions and tactics, to work amicably with him on a collegial basis in any political organization. The second reason for the NYM leaders' declination of the invitation was that their ideas about the future of Nigeria and the pace of political development differed substantially from Azikiwe's, at least at that time. Actually the NYM had independently submitted its own demands for postwar reforms to the Secretary of State for the Colonies about the same time that Azikiwe presented his. Azikiwe had spoken of the natural right of self-determination and had demanded self-government within fifteen years from 1943; but the leaders of the NYM were less emphatic: ". . . we are deeply conscious of the fact that self-government does not come by the mere asking for or granting of it. It is the final consummation of the political, economic and cultural state of a people."[22] The NYM memorandum then outlined specific reforms which its leaders believed would advance them on the road to self-government. Between 1943 and Awolowo's return in 1948 this difference in orientation between Azikiwe and the NYM persisted. As a result, the Lagos branch of the NYM was comparatively inactive and the initiative in the nationalist movement passed into the hands of Azikiwe and the newly inaugurated National Council of Nigeria and the Cameroons.

Toward the end of the war, the new generation of educated Nigerians were impatient over the lack of an active organization to spearhead the drive for self-government. Throughout the war Azikiwe's *Pilot* had done a great deal to generate enthusiasm and strengthen nationalist feeling, but there was no organizational structure to give expression to this sentiment. It was from the new generation of secondary school students and young educated Nigerians that the initiative finally came for the inauguration of a militant nationalist organization. The Nigerian Union of Students (NUS) had been founded as early as 1939, and by 1943 there were three branches in urban centers outside Lagos.[23] It had played an important role in organizing the Ojokoro rally in 1943. In August, 1944, a group of students and ex-students of King's College, who were prominent members of the NUS, visited Azikiwe and complained that the youth of the country were ready but there was no leadership. At Azikiwe's suggestion, and with the strong support of his press, the students called a conference in Lagos of all organizations (including the NYM, which declined to send representatives) for the purpose of organizing a national council to "weld the heterogeneous masses of Nigeria into one solid block." On August 26, 1944, the inaugural meeting of the conference was held, like all nationalist gatherings, in Glover Memorial Hall, and resolved:

> Believing our country is rightfully entitled to liberty and prosperous life . . . and determined to work in unity for the realization of our ultimate goal of self-government within the British Empire, we hereby bind ourselves together forming the Nigeria National Council.[24]

Herbert Macaulay was elected president, and Azikiwe general secretary.[25] Membership was organizational and included the following: 2 trade unions, 2 political parties (Democratic party and Young Democrats), 4 literary societies (for example, the Youths' Literary Improvement Circle), 8 professional associations (for example, the National Herbal Institute of Medicine and the Society of Native Therapeutists), 11 social clubs (for example,

Zik's Athletic Club and the Merry Rose Club), and 101 tribal unions (for example, the Ibo Union and the Ijebu National Union).[26] Because Cameroonian associations in Lagos desired to affiliate (that is, the Bamenda Improvement Association, the Bakweri Union, and the Cameroons Youth League), the name of the movement was changed to the National Council of Nigeria and the Cameroons (NCNC).[27]

Between 1944 and 1957 the NCNC was the leading all-Nigerian nationalist organization. Its distinguishing features should therefore be noted. First, until 1952 membership was restricted to organizations. In the early postwar period, all but a few of these were Lagos bodies. Moreover, the majority of the hundred-odd tribal unions were not tribal at all, but were town, clan, or lineage unions; and even in some of the genuine tribal unions the leaders of the Lagos branch were the most active participants. Yet the affiliation of an organization with the NCNC was a subtle but powerful means of awakening political consciousness among individuals in the provinces by the filtration technique.

Second, of equal significance are the organizations that did not affiliate with the NCNC. The Nigerian Youth Movement, of course, held aloof, as did the Nigerian Union of Teachers, the largest trade union. In fact, very few trade unions applied for membership, partly because the government strongly opposed political activity by labor, and partly because the leadership of many trade unions was in the hands of older Yorubas who, for various reasons, were not attracted to the NCNC banner. An important feature of NCNC history has been the abortive efforts of Azikiwe and other leaders to win over the labor movement. Their failure does not indicate a lack of rank-and-file support for the NCNC. On the contrary, many wage earners belonged to the organization, but they came in through the urban branches of tribal unions—usually the Ibo Union—instead of through trade unions.

Third, participation in the NCNC was in the beginning largely confined to southerners and, to a lesser extent, to northerners of the Middle Belt. Although branches were established in more than a dozen urban centers in northern Nigeria, virtually all the active members in those branches were southerners temporarily resident in the north where they were employed by the government or by business firms as clerks or artisans. An appreciation of this fact is of crucial importance. In chapter 17 the rise of northern nationalism will be discussed; until then any mention of nationalism in northern Nigeria refers primarily to southern nationalists living in the north.

Fourth, the Azikiwe-Macaulay rapprochement brought about by the formation of the NCNC was of signal importance in assuring the council of its domination of Lagos politics, at least until the emergence of the Action Group in 1951. Azikiwe's press plus the solid support he obtained from all non-Yoruba Lagosians—whose number was rapidly increasing—was fused with Macaulay's traditional sources of strength, the Lagos market-women and the followers of the House of Docemo. The alliance was a mixed blessing for Azikiwe. On the one hand, Macaulay was more in the tradition of Victorian radicalism and thus was more conservative and "constitutional" than Azikiwe would probably have been. Where Macaulay would demand his rights as a British subject, Azikiwe would talk of natural rights. In a sense, therefore, Macaulay in the early period served as a brake upon Azikiwe's leadership of the NCNC. On the other hand, although a Yoruba, Macaulay was a poor instrument for gaining widespread Yoruba support. Azikiwe, leveler and iconoclast that he was, had already done much to alienate the old conservative Yoruba families through his journalism. By joining with Macaulay, however, Azikiwe and the NCNC inherited all the enmities and personal rivalries accumulated by Macaulay during his forty-year domination of Lagos politics. The alliance gave them both power over the masses in Lagos, but it also exacerbated the tension between them and the educated Yoruba middle class. The latter were effectively if temporarily eclipsed, however, and their hostility was not a matter of concern until Awolowo's dramatic reappearance in 1948.

In January, 1945, the NCNC held its Constitutional Convention. Included among its objectives were:

1) To extend democratic principles and to advance the interests of the people of Nigeria and the Cameroons under British mandate.

2) To impart political education to the people of Nigeria with a view to achieving self-government.

3) To provide NCNC members with a "medium of expression in order to secure political freedom, economic security, social equality, and religious toleration in Nigeria and the Cameroons under British mandate, as a member of the British Commonwealth of Nations." [28]

It is of interest to note that at this point the idea of scheduled self-government (contained in Azikiwe's original proposals for constitutional reform) was absent, and that continued membership in the Commonwealth was planned.

In March, 1945, Governor Sir Arthur Richards (now Lord Milverton) presented to the Legislative Council his proposals for revision of the 1923 Constitution. These official proposals fell far short of the postwar reforms envisaged by most Nigerians. Moreover, the somewhat arbitrary and cavalier manner in which they were introduced provided a timely issue upon which the newborn NCNC could focus nationalist agitation. The postwar activities of the NCNC and the growth of nationalism form the subject of the following chapter.

PART IV

Postwar Developments in the Nationalist Movement

CHAPTER 12

The Richards Constitution and the NCNC

It has been observed that during the war Nigerian students abroad and nationalist leaders at home envisaged a radically new constitutional system for postwar Nigeria. Their plans ranged from WASU's demand for immediate internal self-government to the more moderate proposals of the Nigerian Youth Movement (NYM) that educated Nigerians be given a greater share in the government. It has also been pointed out that wartime influences and events resulted in the adoption of a new approach to the problem of political development in the colonies. As a consequence, officials in the Colonial Office and in the Nigerian government sought to devise a new constitution for postwar Nigeria. On March 6, 1945, Governor Sir Arthur Richards presented their proposals to the Legislative Council of Nigeria.[1] The proposals were approved after slight modification, and the so-called "Richards Constitution" became the law of the land. It remained so until replaced by the Constitution of 1951.

In planning the postwar constitutional structure, Nigerian officialdom struggled with two knotty, interrelated problems. One was peculiar to Nigeria, and to similar African territories where indirect rule had been instituted. The crux of this problem was how to reconcile the native authority system, as the primary unit of African self-government, with a parliamentary system of government at the central territorial level. In 1937 Margery Perham urged that officialdom persevere in the development and modernization of the native authority system, and that the educated elements be integrated into that system, but she cautioned against admitting them to the central superstructure or giving them any further powers in the Legislative Council. In pursuing this "policy of gradual development through local government," she advised that "we must be prepared for unexpected developments, and perhaps for an unexpected rate of development." [2] The exigencies of the war prevented officials from pushing the modernization of local government. Again because of the war and other factors the rate of unexpected developments was staggering, as noted previously. In any event, postwar planners in officialdom were plagued with the same dilemma that had confronted Miss Perham, and before her Sir Hugh Clifford. Indeed, as has been shown, this dilemma derived from a contradiction that had existed in British policy since the beginning of British administration in Nigeria. By 1945, however, the nationalists were in a position to force the issue.

The second and related problem, which has plagued Britain throughout her imperial history, was how to give the centrally-minded nationalists a larger role in the government without relinquishing ultimate imperial authority. It was, in short, a question of how to maintain a balance between authority and responsibility. The late Sir Bernard Bourdillon, Nigeria's wartime governor, described the problem in these terms:

> An official majority in a colonial legislature, bound to vote as they are instructed, and therefore able to carry any measure that the Governor wishes must, even if it is never used, induce a feeling of frustration and impotence in the mind of the unofficials. . . . On the other hand an unofficial majority, when the executive is irremovable, represents that political anathema, power without responsibility.[3]

The fear of creating an "unofficial" majority in Nigeria was heightened by the fact that devolution of power to the majority in order to balance power with responsibility would place centrally-minded nationalists over traditional leaders of the native authority system. Every governor of Nigeria since Lord Lugard had explicitly rejected this possibility.

Nigerian officialdom thus had to find a political formula that would not only meet these problems but would also anticipate the ultimate political destiny of Nigeria. The latter issue could not be dismissed, as it had been in the past, with the vague shibboleth of "ultimate self-government within the Commonwealth," and left for subsequent generations to handle. Specifically, government officials had to decide whether postwar political development in Nigeria should be directed toward the creation of a modern Nigerian state with parliamentary institutions, or toward the continued development of the native authority system with the ultimate coördinating or cementing link left unspecified. Nigerian nationalists and a few colonial officials pressed for the former; British imperial traditions and interests, the inertia of the Nigerian masses, the conservatism of chiefs and traditionalists, and the persuasion of most colonial officials pointed to the latter. The final product was pretty much a compromise which pleased very few, least of all the nationalists.

Broadly speaking, official planners held two views regarding future relations among the native authorities, the artificial administrative regions, and the central superstructure. One school, composed mainly of officials in northern Nigeria who had had experience with large emirates, urged that the native authorities be given progressively wider powers until they became self-governing, presumably with an attenuated British superstructure holding them together in a loose confederation. Some members of this school even advocated complete separation of northern Nigeria from the rest of the territory so as to permit it to pursue its own independent constitutional development. Early in the war, officials in the Colonial Office leaned toward a similar view, advocating radical decentralization of authority to existing regional governments, with the ultimate objective of making each region a virtually self-governing country. Both Governor Bourdillon and Lord Hailey were, however, opposed to this extreme view; Hailey maintained that separatist tendencies should not be encouraged because the future of the country lay in political unity. In the final count the views of the first school, insofar as they related to the development of native authorities as self-governing units, were rejected, but its concept of regionalism was accepted in modified form.

The second school urged that the native authorities be continued only as agencies of local government which would also serve as units of representation to regional or central legislatures in a modern parliamentary state. There were variations on this

273

main theme. Some officials proffered the advanced idea that parliamentary government with electoral constituencies could be the only possible objective; others suggested that, although this might be acceptable as an ultimate goal, native authorities be utilized in the meantime as electoral units. The distinguishing features of this school, however, were the beliefs that the native authorities were not the be-all and end-all of practical political institutions, that the unity of the country must be preserved, and that regional and central parliamentary bodies should be imposed upon the native authority system.

As the discussions progressed, the idea of regionalism gained adherents, as did the idea of utilizing the native authorities as electoral units for representatives to higher councils. In the end, both were adopted. It was believed that the latter scheme would provide the essential link whereby the native authority system and the superstructure would be made complementary elements in a single harmonious system. Moreover, in the eyes of officialdom it solved the problem of the educated elements in an electoral system. British officials had grave apprehensions regarding the institution of direct elections by geographical constituencies. The presumption was that the educated elements, who of course were the centrally-minded nationalists, would through demagoguery or the inertia of the masses capture all elective seats. Although postwar planners realized that the educated elements had to be given a role in the future government, they believed the best way of doing it was to democratize the native authorities and permit educated men to advance indirectly to the higher councils.

The idea of regionalism offered three special attractions to its British votaries. In the first place, it would partially satisfy the agitation for a separate and independent development of the Northern Region. Second, it would prevent the Legislative Council from becoming large and unwieldy, as it was certain to do if all native authorities of Nigeria were to be represented, and would also avoid an unofficial majority without responsibility. This point is of signal importance. Nigerian officialdom was not prepared under any circumstances to grant Nigerians responsible government at the end of the war; neither was it willing to compromise the undeniably sound tradition of avoiding an unofficial majority without responsibility. As there were not enough

European officials to constitute an official majority in the central Legislative Council, regional advisory councils with unofficial majorities would permit representation of native authorities and at the same time solve the dilemma of numbers at the center. The Legislative Council could then be constituted along orthodox lines without the fear of an irresponsible unofficial majority. Third, regionalism was believed to be a defense against a possible seizure of central power by an educated minority in Lagos. Colonial officials were fearful that in a unitary scheme the educated elements in coastal towns would become predominant. Indeed, Governor Richards later remarked that his constitution made a deliberate attempt to break the "absurdly predominant influence" of Lagos.[4] To this last argument for regionalization might be added the nationalist contention that it was a stratagem of divide and rule. This motivation cannot be ruled out, but there is no written evidence that it was operative. One could argue that it was the inarticulate major premise behind the whole regionalizing endeavor; it is believed, however, that the idea evolved in the manner and for the reasons indicated above.

It is unfortunate in many respects that Sir Arthur Richards was governor of Nigeria during the delicate period 1943–1947. He came to Nigeria from Jamaica, where his record reflected unfavorably on his capacity to deal effectively with colonial nationalists.[5] His handling of constitutional reform and nationalism in Nigeria followed a similar pattern. He seemed to have a special knack for antagonizing the educated elements; in Nigeria, at least, his name is at the bottom of their popularity list.[6]

The overwhelming majority of politically conscious, educated Nigerians had two major objections to the Richards Constitution. The first centered around the manner in which it was brought into being; the second concerned its substantive deficiencies. When Sir Bernard Bourdillon relinquished the governorship of Nigeria in 1943, he assured the people that they would have adequate opportunity to discuss the draft of their future constitution at the end of the war. In March, 1945, Governor Richards submitted to the Legislative Council his proposals for constitutional reform. This was the first chance Nigerians had had to learn of their political future; yet the governor urged quick approval in order that the constitution might be considered by

275

Parliament before the general election in June. After a brief debate in the Legislative Council, the constitution was approved by all but one of the African unofficials, and then hastily dispatched to the United Kingdom. Even ex-Governor Bourdillon, who agreed with the substance of the constitutional proposals, expressed regret that the people were given little or no opportunity to shape their own constitution.[7] Nigerian nationalists were embittered by this cavalier treatment, and their grievance was in no way assuaged by the approval given to the constitution by the African unofficials in the Legislative Council; the unofficials had already been repudiated by the majority of the nationalists.

The concept of regionalism was the most distinguishing innovation in the new constitution. As previously noted, the regional plan emerged as a compromise from wartime discussions between regional separatists, who envisaged the creation of three separate states, and strong federalists, who wanted to link the native authority system with a central parliament but were troubled about the problem of an unofficial majority in a large unwieldy council. Under the Richards proposals, three new regional Houses of Assembly would be established at Kaduna, Ibadan, and Enugu; they would merely discuss general legislation but would have the right to pass their own regional budgets. This devolution of budgetary functions was to be matched by a corresponding decentralization of administrative authority to regional governments. The members of the regional houses would be selected from existing native authorities and would in turn select five of their number as representatives to a broadened Nigeria-wide Legislative Council, which would meet successively in Lagos, Ibadan, Kaduna, and Enugu. Sir Arthur Richards argued that this embryonic, quasi-federal structure was a practical means of obtaining two of his major objectives: it would promote Nigerian unity and at the same time would provide within that unity for the country's diverse elements. The suggestion that the regionalism of the Richards Constitution would contribute to separatist tendencies was countered by Sir Bernard Bourdillon, who argued:

. . . in fact this measure represents not the division of one unit into three, but the beginning of the fusion of innumerable small units into three and from these three into one. . . . The [regional] Houses of Assembly will encourage not only a very useful interchange of ideas, but the beginning of that widening of the social, economic and political horizon which is essential if the unity of Nigeria is ever to have any real meaning to its inhabitants.[8]

Moreover, although regionalism later became a bone of contention among various elements in the nationalist movement, not all nationalists were opposed to it. Azikiwe and many others in the NCNC preferred to have a federal commonwealth consisting of not three but eight constituent units which would be given a substantial degree of power. However, one member of the NCNC delegation, which opposed many other features of the constitution, remarked: "One good feature of the Richards Constitution was . . . the regionalization it afforded; this was generally applauded in Nigeria." [9] The federal idea was also strongly endorsed by Awolowo and other prominent members of the Nigerian Youth Movement.[10] Needless to say, to all northerners it was the single most attractive feature of the constitution.

Other features of the constitution, however, evoked bitter indignation from nationalists of all camps. Awolowo remarked that the new constitution "retains some of the objectionable features of the old, contains unsavoury characteristics of its own, and falls short of expectation." [11] Azikiwe and H. O. Davies were even more vehement in their denunciation of the constitution's gross inadequacies and its failure to satisfy any nationalist demands. There were two major points of conflict between the aspirations of most nationalists and the maximum concessions Sir Arthur Richards was willing to make. The first of these was the psychologically crucial question of the powers and functions of Nigerian representatives under the new constitution. Whereas the minimum demand of the nationalists had been the appointment of a few Nigerians as heads of departments, as a step toward responsible government which would give them a share in the *management* of their own affairs, the most that the Richards Constitution envisaged was "greater participation by Africans in the *discussion* of their own affairs." [12] As Davies remarked:

"Discussion" seem the crux of the principle. There is neither intention nor the pretension to secure greater *participation* by the Africans in the direction, management, or control of their affairs. . . . No attempt is made to democratize . . . bureaucrative [*sic*] rule or make it sensitive to public opinion. . . . The head of Department . . . formulates policy, he legislates it, and afterwards administers it; . . . as an executive, he is irresponsibly backed by the law and all its sanctions. . . .[13]

In short, nationalists viewed the new constitution as representing no advance whatsoever in the training of Nigerians for responsible self-government in executive functions. The net result of this agitation was the addition of the word "management" to the constitutional proposals, the chief secretary explaining that it had inadvertently been omitted.[14]

The second point of conflict was the composition and manner of selection of the "unofficial majority" proposed by the governor. Although the proposals provided for such a majority in the regional Houses of Assembly and in the central Legislative Council, the nationalists maintained that from the composition of the so-called "unofficial" element the government would always be assured of a majority. In the regional houses, the ratio of officials to unofficials was to be 19:20 in the north, 14:15 in the west, and 13:14 in the east; at the center it was to be 20:29. Included in the unofficial category for each of the regional houses were five or more Africans or Europeans who would be nominated by the governor; and, at the center, ten of the twenty-nine unofficials were to be either chiefs or Europeans nominated by the governor.[15]

In the eyes of the nationalists the government proposals for an unofficial majority represented a calculated deception, for it was most unlikely that a chief, a European trader, or an African who owed his position to the governor would ever take a really independent position or oppose the government on any crucial issue.[16] Thus nationalist resentment over the denial of a real Nigerian majority was intensified by the government's pretense that it was granting such a majority. Moreover, the nationalists were annoyed by the curious and arbitrary manner of determining the number of African representatives. As Awolowo put it: "The unofficial majority of one in each House of Assembly is governed solely by a consideration of the number of Official members available in each Region, and not by the desire to give wider and adequate representation to the people." [17] This resulted in gross disparities in the ratio of representation to population; in the north it would be 1:575,000; in the east, 1:336,000; and in the west, 1:233,000.

Nationalists also objected strongly to the inclusion of chiefs and emirs in the unofficial category.[18] It was their contention that under indirect rule, as operated in Nigeria, the chiefs and emirs owed their position to the government and they should therefore be categorized as "officials." The nationalists could cite statements, such as the one made by the Oni of Ife that "we [chiefs] are part and parcel of the Government and we must support the Government as well as serve our people." [19] Nationalists also argued that placing chiefs on the same level as commoners, and bringing them into the Western apparatus of government, affronted their dignity and disparaged their symbolic role within the traditional system.[20] The government's response was that chiefs and emirs served in a dual capacity:

> [The chiefs] . . . have been appointed to these traditional posts in accordance with the traditions and customs of the areas over which they exercise jurisdiction. They are also Native Authorities appointed by Government to carry out the duties of Native Authorities under the Native Authorities Ordinance. In the latter capacity they do, as the Oni remarked, form part of the machinery of administration though they are not a part of the central Government. It is, however, in their capacity as traditional leaders of their people that they will attend Legislative Council in order to represent the views of their people in that Council and it is therefore proper that they should sit on the Unofficial side of the House. . . . The chiefs, however, will be under no obligation to support Government measures or to vote in favour of such measures and will enjoy the same freedom of speech and vote as other Unofficial members.[21]

From the nationalist viewpoint there was implicit in this arrangement a conflict in roles, which the chiefs and emirs usually resolved by siding with the government, upon which they were dependent for their positions both as traditional rulers and as members of the Legislative Council. The fact that the overwhelming majority of chiefs and emirs supported the Richards Constitution (for example, the Oba of Benin believed that "the Richards political and constitutional reform for Nigeria is, without mincing words, the best that Nigeria can have at the present moment")[22] further strengthened the nationalist argument.

Nationalists also strongly resented the system of election provided for in the Richards proposals. No change was made in the number of Legislative Council members elected directly by Nigerians. Only the people of Lagos and Calabar were given the opportunity to elect representatives directly to the Legislative Council, a privilege they had exercised since 1923. All other representatives were to be elected indirectly through the native authorities. The nationalists believed that this system, controlled as it would be by traditionalists on the native authority councils, would produce representatives inclined to be progovernment and antinationalist. Moreover, since representation was to be on a provincial basis, the nationalists believed that British administrative officers (residents) would exercise undue influence over the selection of representatives, at least in provinces having several native authorities.[23]

In addition to the foregoing, other aspects of the new constitution were unacceptable to the nationalists. As in other British colonies which have started up the "constitutional ladder" from crown colony status to responsible government, nationalist leaders in Nigeria criticized the governor's veto power ("reserved powers" in official jargon). To British authorities, of course, the veto power was an indispensable corollary to an unofficial majority. Another irritating feature was the continued provision for representation on the Legislative Council of "vested European interests" (that is, banking, shipping, industrial, and mining interests). Again, the property or income qualification for voting in Lagos and Calabar (£100) was viewed as a calculated effort to exclude "all the labour classes who are sufficiently conscious of their rights as to integrate themselves into one Trade Union. . . ."[24] These criticisms reflect the range of objections registered by the nationalists, and show that the Richards Constitution, taken as a whole, overlooked what Azikiwe called the "categorical imperative" of constitutional development in Nigeria, namely, Nigerian management of Nigerian affairs as soon as possible.[25]

Although the overwhelming majority of educated Nigerians

strongly objected to the manner in which the constitution was introduced and to several of its provisions, there were differences among them in regard to its acceptability. One group, represented by such men as H. O. Davies, Obafemi Awolowo, and the members of the Nigerian Youth Movement–*Daily Service* school of thought, although highly critical of the constitution, concluded that "it has got to be accomodated [*sic*] anyhow. . . . That is one rotten fruit of imperialism, and we shall have to adjust ourselves to it as best we can, at least for the time being. . . ."[26] Writing from the United Kingdom, Awolowo took the following position:

> The people of Nigeria have expressed their bitter indignation both at the act of the African unofficial members, and at the conduct of the Government. Only a minute fraction of their counter-proposals has been considered. Nevertheless, when the Constitution is put into operation, they can be relied upon to suppress their feelings, and to co-operate in testing the new machinery. Maybe this new contrivance is, after all, not so defective as the people thought. Its actual working will show.[27]

By 1947, however, elements in this group became less conciliatory and began to speak of boycotting Legislative Council elections as a protest against the constitution.[28]

Another group, represented by Nnamdi Azikiwe and Herbert Macaulay, leaders of the NCNC, decided to launch a continuing protest and demonstration against the constitution. Associated with them was a third and more militant wing whose temper was reflected in the writings of Anthony Enahoro, then editor of the *Daily Comet*. Certain elements in this latter group undertook to form the Zikist Movement, which will be examined at a later point.

Although the nationalists' objections to the Richards Constitution motivated their protest campaign, their appeals to the peasants and chiefs stressed the threats to their land and status allegedly implicit in the four so-called "obnoxious ordinances." These ordinances were enacted in the same session of the Legislative Council (March, 1945) that had approved the Richards proposals for a new constitution. By combining the frustration and bitterness of the educated elements regarding the new constitution with the apprehensions of the peasant masses and traditionalists regarding the allegedly confiscatory and oppressive intent of the obnoxious ordinances, the NCNC leaders were able to generate unprecedented popular support. Indeed, their protest campaign of 1945–1947 showed how, in a colonial milieu, an array of disparate grievances, fears, hopes, and ambitions could be subsumed under the rubric of "nationalism," how a universal belief that both relief and fulfillment were possible through self-government could be created, and how previously unmobilized groups could be drawn into a nationalist movement.

Three of the obnoxious ordinances—the Minerals Ordinance, the Public Lands Acquisition Ordinance, and the Crown Lands (Amendment) Ordinance—gave the impression that the British administration was seeking to arrogate to the Crown (and, by implication, to the British people) the title to Nigerian minerals and lands. The Minerals Ordinance was categorical: "The entire property in and control of all minerals, and mineral oils, in, under, or upon any lands in Nigeria, and of all rivers, streams and water courses throughout Nigeria, is and shall be vested in, the Crown. . . ."[29] The other two ordinances designated as crown lands all lands acquired by the government for public purposes, including those in the protectorate.[30] The purpose of the ordinances was clearly protective, and certainly the Minerals Ordinance was a step toward a more thorough application of the principle of trusteeship. The assertion of the Crown's rights over minerals and land was but one manifestation of the trend toward nationalization of the natural resources of Nigeria preparatory to subsequent state development. Indeed, because of their statist and Socialist orientation, most nationalists would normally have applauded at least the intent of these measures, and later would themselves have enacted them.

The issue in dispute—the meaning of the term "Crown"—was partly semantic and partly psychological. In a strictly legal sense the "Crown" was synonymous with the "Nigerian government," and according to declared British policy, the Nigerian peoples were ultimately destined to control that government. Yet, in drafting the ordinances, the law officers and the Attorney General were obliged to conform to the technical legal jargon customarily employed. But in view of the circumstances in 1945 and the vital interests involved, it is understandable that the nationalists, whether motivated by genuine apprehension or by the simple desire to use the ordinances as instruments to alarm the people, were able to link the term "Crown" with the idea of a rapacious and exploitative imperialism progressively asserting its control over African minerals and lands. As the Richards Constitution offered the nationalists little prospect of controlling either the Crown or the Nigerian government, it was very difficult indeed for them to appreciate the basic intent and the long-term purposes of the ordinances. A large part of the conflict over the term "Crown," therefore, derived from the profound distrust of most nationalists regarding the sincerity of British intentions on the one hand, and, on the other, the insensitivity of the British authorities to nationalist sentiments, particularly as reflected in their tendency to cling to forms and terminology designed for the days of Lugard.

There was one respect, however, in which the issue went deeper. Under international law Nigeria was an amalgam of a colony and two protectorates. Theoretically the Crown had complete sovereignty over the colony, but the power of the Crown over the protectorates was presumed to be limited by treaty. In actuality, while maintaining the theoretical distinction in legal instruments, under the unilateral Foreign Jurisdiction Act of 1890 Britain has usually ignored the distinction and treated her African protectorates as conquered territory. This *de facto* assimilation of protectorates to colonies has been accepted, or at least recognized, in international law.[31] In the eyes of Nigerian nationalists, however, and particularly to Nnamdi Azikiwe, an ardent student of international law, the minerals and lands ordinances represented an illegal extension to the protectorate of the absolute powers possessed only in the colony.[32] Thus nationalists regarded 1945 as a year of further extension and consolidation of British imperial power, rather than as a year marking the commencement of imperial withdrawal. Yet here again there was a paradox. Nigerian unity was one of the objectives most passionately sought by the nationalists. The lands and minerals ordinances ignored the colony-protectorate distinction and imposed a Nigeria-wide uniformity, and in this sense they fostered Nigerian unity. In the psychological climate of 1945, however, the nationalists were more disposed to emphasize the threat of an imperialist consolidation than the residual contribution to Nigerian unity.

The fourth "obnoxious" ordinance—the Appointment and Deposition of Chiefs (Amendment) Ordinance—was not an innovation at all, but rather a consolidation and restatement of existing legislation which empowered the governor to appoint and depose chiefs as he had always done. Because of their deep-seated prejudice against indirect rule, however, this ordinance gave nationalists an opportunity to dramatize what they believed to be the shortcomings of that system. The all-embracing manner in which the ordinance was written conveyed the impression that the governor had the powers of an absolute dictator vis-à-vis the chiefs. The nationalists therefore cited the ordinance as providing visible proof (1) that it was a sham for the chiefs to be categorized as "unofficials" in a legislative body; (2) that as a rule the chiefs were not representatives of the people even at the local level, but were obedient servants of the government; and (3) that the whole native authority structure, and particularly its role in the indirect electoral system, was an instrument for an increasingly oppressive imperial rule.

Armed with these grievances—the shortcomings of the Richards Constitution, the alleged seizure by the imperial government of Nigerian lands and minerals, and the rankling reminder that the chiefs were but puppets of the British administration—the leaders of the NCNC decided to tour the country and arouse the people, and then with the people's mandate to send a delegation to the Secretary of State for the Colonies to demand reforms. One year elapsed between the time this decision was made (April, 1945) and the NCNC tour of Nigeria, and another before the delegation visited the United Kingdom. During these two years the center of nationalist propaganda was the Zik press —Azikiwe's chain of five dailies in Lagos, Ibadan, Onitsha, and Port Harcourt. It was during this period that Azikiwe made his most dramatic and successful bid for national leadership.

AZIKIWE'S EMERGENCE AS A NATIONAL LEADER

Two months after publication of Richards' constitutional proposals and enactment of the four obnoxious ordinances, the general strike of June, 1945, occurred. As has been shown, Azikiwe emerged from that event with enhanced prestige and a reputation as the champion of labor. At the time, however, he took special precautions to disavow any connection with the strike.[33] Yet Anthony Enahoro, one of Azikiwe's former editors, later reported that "the general concensus of opinion in the provinces was, and still is, that Nnamdi Azikiwe engineered and inspired the strike."[34] Moreover, as a result of a series of events during and after the strike, Azikiwe secured international attention, and his name and the NCNC became known in the remotest villages of Nigeria.

On July 8, 1945, Azikiwe's two Lagos dailies, *West African Pilot* and *Daily Comet*, were banned by the government for misrepresenting facts relating to the general strike. This action had little effect on Azikiwe's press agitation, however, because his editorials and news articles on the strike appeared in the Port Harcourt *Guardian*, printed by the press of the *Pilot*. A week later Azikiwe wrote his "last testament" and then fled to Onitsha, where he went into hiding. In the testament he alleged that

> Some unknown persons have planned my assassination. . . . I go away to the Niger whence I came. If it is the will of Providence that I should depart from this world through the bullet of an assassin, then I have no choice. . . . But I go full of supreme confidence and spiritual satisfaction that I have served Mother Africa to the limit of my physical ability—and even gave my most prized possession—my life—for the redemption of Africa.[35]

He then sent an omnibus cablegram to several key individuals and organizations in the United Kingdom (including Reuters, George Padmore, and the National Council of Civil Liberties), which read: ". . . implore you humbly for last time contact highest authorities . . . definite plot to murder me stop please insist that local government be instructed protect my life otherwise this is last cablegram from me alive. . . ."[36]

One of the Nigerian recipients of this cablegram, then resident in London, organized the National Committee of Africans for the purpose of mobilizing world opinion. The committee sent cables to scores of prominent individuals, institutions, and journals throughout the world—including President Truman, Stalin, De Gaulle, *Pravda,* the Indian National Congress, the *Daily Worker,* and many American and West Indian papers—protesting against the suppression of Azikiwe's newspapers and the threat to his life. The organization then wired the governor of Nigeria: ". . . opinion of the world has been mobilised . . . the safety, life, and liberty of Zik is on the conscience of the world." [37] Mass meetings were held in London and the Pan-African Federation issued a broadsheet, "Governor Richards, true to his Fascist Tradition in Jamaica, has decided to prolong the agony of our people." In the meantime Azikiwe had petitioned the Secretary of State for the Colonies for protection, arguing:

> I submit that, if any British Protected Person, like me, cannot feel safe and secure in his person, even under the canopy of the Union Jack, then I fail to appreciate the necessity for the sacrifice in Men, Money, Man Power, and Material Resources which the Colony and Protectorate of Nigeria had contributed, and are contributing, to the war efforts of the British Empire and the United Nations.[38]

The Nigerian government immediately issued a disclaimer maintaining that Azikiwe had declined to meet with the chief secretary to discuss the allegation, that at no time did he ask for police protection nor make available to the police or to the government evidence to support his charge. At the next meeting of the Legislative Council, Governor Richards, referring to the "silly invention that a certain journalist was in danger of his life," claimed that Azikiwe had nothing more "to fear than the dark shadows of his own imagination." [39] In the meantime the government refused to renew Azikiwe's wireless license, since Azikiwe had said that his wireless operator revealed the plot to him, and banned representatives of the *Pilot* from Legislative Council meetings because of allegedly false reports of the council's proceedings.

This "assassination" incident had a significant effect upon Azikiwe's stature and popularity, as well as upon subsequent developments within the nationalist movement. Azikiwe became a national hero in the eyes of the less sophisticated masses of Nigeria, who heard of the alleged plot either as readers of

Azikiwe's newspapers or by word of mouth, which travels very fast in the bush. In his biographical sketch of Azikiwe, Enahoro pointed out:

> But let there be no two opinions about this—the common people believed and were completely satisfied that the white man had planned to assassinate him. Look at the picture of those times from the eye level of the man in the street. The Richards Constitution had appeared four months before. They believed that Nnamdi Azikiwe had told Government not to take our land and gold, and to let our chiefs alone. On top of this, they were convinced that he had organised the General Strike to win better wages for the worker. Naturally the people thought to themselves, the white man would not like him. And to confirm this deduction, his Lagos papers had been banned. . . .[40]

It was widely believed that Azikiwe's life had been threatened because of his efforts to redeem Africa. "Parents named their babes after him. . . . [Azikiwe] became a household word even in remote villages." [41] Furthermore, because of world-wide publicity at a time when anticolonialism was emerging as a dominant theme, Azikiwe's name became the symbol of African nationalism. It was known both at home and abroad to a degree never before achieved by a Nigerian leader.

But the incident also brought Azikiwe strong criticism from Nigerian officialdom and his political opponents. Although the vigor of his journalism had already infuriated and alienated most British officials in Nigeria and London, the assassination incident hardened their feelings of distrust. The incident similarly repelled the leaders of the Youth Movement. Whether motivated by jealousy over his successful bid for leadership over the masses, or by revulsion at his exploitation of their credulity, they launched a full-scale attack upon him for his propagation of a "colossal falsehood." They alleged that he had no reason to be apprehensive about his life, and that he had deliberately invented the story to make himself a martyr and gain cheap popularity.

A violent press war ensued between the Zik group of newspapers and the *Daily Service*. It was the first major flare-up in the ranks of nationalist papers since the Akinsanya crisis of 1941.[42] Actually, between 1941 and 1945, mutual tolerance had prevailed in the Nigerian press. In the two years preceding the introduction of the Richards Constitution, virtually all African newspapers were united in a demand for substantial postwar reforms; and when the constitution and obnoxious ordinances were first made known, the Nigerian press presented a common front in its condemnation of them. Even at the time of the general strike, the Zik group of papers and the *Daily Service* were in general agreement in their support of the workers. When the *Pilot* and the *Comet* were banned during the strike, the *Daily Service* criticized the government for its action.[43] But the assassination episode in July, 1945, terminated the good will. Although a truce was negotiated in April, 1946, mainly as a result of the conciliatory intervention of the Alake of Abeokuta, the press war was renewed with greater violence a year later. In fact, except for short periods of friendliness, the two major sections of the Nigerian press (Azikiwe's group and the *Daily Service*) have been engaged in violent attacks on each other ever since the assassination episode.

The *Daily Service*'s attacks on Azikiwe in connection with the assassination plot provoked a small group of his most enthusiastic followers to organize the Zikist Movement in February, 1946. For several years it was a militant auxiliary of the NCNC. Although full description and analysis of the new organization will be reserved for a subsequent chapter, it is important to note here that the formal battle line between the two wings of the nationalist movement was drawn as early as 1945. At this stage the more moderate nationalists were eclipsed by Azikiwe's phenomenal popularity and charismatic qualities; they either were silent or passive, or pursued a negative policy of disparaging Azikiwe.

Azikiwe's ascendancy during the immediate postwar period was based in part upon support from the following principal groups:

1) *Organized and unorganized labor.* The popular belief that Azikiwe was connected with the general strike, coupled with his consistent championing of workers' grievances, brought him the support of the rank and file. The following is typical of his appeal to labor:

The array of natural rulers of the eastern, western, and northern provinces, ministers of religion, members of the Executive and Legislative Council, the various professional classes, all were alike in their passive and indifferent attitude towards the workers, which attitude indicated that the latter had lost their confidence and sympathy.[44]

2) *Clerks, artisans, and teachers.* Azikiwe was the "great leveler"; the *Pilot* became the champion of clerks, artisans, and teachers. All previous newspapers had limited their coverage to the social and political activities of old Lagos families; Azikiwe increasingly directed his columns and editorials to the social and recreational pursuits of the common clerk or artisan, who, flattered to see his name in print or his picture in the paper, was inspired to support Azikiwe politically and to become a habitual reader of his papers.

3) *Youths.* Azikiwe's display of erudition and academic achievement, his genuine efforts to encourage athletics, his heroic Horatio Alger career, his interest in educational development, his vigorous press attacks upon Europeans and their follies, and his strong support of youth groups won for him a large following in the generation that came of age during the war and in the mid-1940's. The main accent of Azikiwe's *Renascent Africa* was upon youth.[45]

4) *Special-grievance groups.* Realizing that there was little likelihood that he would be called upon to assume responsibility for the policies he advocated, and driven by an intense resentment against alien rule, Azikiwe used his press to exploit all the grievances that came to his attention. He became the watchdog of African rights, and any African from the lowliest messenger to the wealthiest trader, resident anywhere in Nigeria, could secure immediate front-page publicity on any complaint against the government or against Europeans. Administrative officers, even in the remotest districts, were frequently harassed by urgent wires from central, regional, or provincial headquarters, requesting inquiries into allegations of "brutal and inhuman" treatment, discrimination, or denial of rights which appeared daily in the columns of Zik's papers. With few exceptions, Azikiwe's allegations were so worded as to avoid charges of libel or sedition, but

were sufficiently clear in meaning and intent to have the required psychological effect. As one of his older admirers put it:

> . . . now we have the opportunity to "speak out" not like the old days when one had to adopt the Elephant ways of Hear, See, and be Silent. . . . All will be well with Nigeria with that great and good soul Zik the Saviour of Africa and a God sent man, he is a Super Genius more than a superman, God bless him, we absolutely worship that good soul.[46]

5) *Organizational leaders.* Azikiwe's newspapers gave full publicity to the activities of all tribal unions, social clubs, and other organizations throughout the provinces. Azikiwe sent agents for his press to the major urban centers, and for the first time in Nigerian history the thousands of clerks and artisans employed by the government or the firms in the more remote towns of Nigeria (for example, Sokoto, Gusau, Maiduguri, Jos, Lokoja, Minna) felt as though they were part of the great drama unfolding at Lagos. These groups in the provinces were the first to organize branches of the NCNC or, if they were radically inclined, of the Zikist Movement.

6) *Non-Yoruba educated elements.* In Iboland, and among virtually all Ibos spread throughout Nigeria, Azikiwe was deified; his name became a legend; he was the incarnation of all their hopes and aspirations. From personal investigation deep in the bush of Iboland, I am convinced that the impact of Azikiwe on the masses, including the illiterate, was profound and exhilarating. His worst enemies admit this; indeed, in many instances, it is their awareness of his profound influence which intensified their enmity. Although blind devotion to Azikiwe was more pronounced among the Ibo, he was likewise the idol of many previously inarticulate groups such as Cameroonians, Nupe, Tiv, Igbirra, Birom, and Idoma, and indeed of most of the Middle Belt; and a growing number of Hausa, Fulani, and Kanuri youths looked up to him as the national leader.

Azikiwe gained his influence mainly through his press. He also used the technique of frequent mass meetings in Lagos at which his lectures glorifying Africa, vilifying Europeans, and denouncing imperialism evoked great enthusiasm among his eager listeners. An event that brought him even greater prominence as a national figure was the NCNC tour of the provinces in 1946.

The NCNC tour of the provinces was conducted to raise funds to send a delegation to London in order to protest against the constitution and the four obnoxious ordinances. It was an unprecedented venture. Except for infrequent tours previously made by governors, it was the first time in the history of Nigeria that large numbers of people were made conscious of Nigerian unity. The tour commenced at the end of April, 1946, and was led by the "Zimonists" (Nnamdi Azikiwe, Herbert Macaulay, Michael Imoudu—"Nigeria's Labor Leader No. 1"—and two others). From Lagos the touring delegation went first to the Northern Provinces. In Kano, however, the tour was cut short by the death, at eighty-two, of Herbert Macaulay. His funeral, held in Lagos, was the largest in Nigerian history, with more than 100,000 in attendance. Azikiwe delivered the funeral oration:

> Come and mourn with me, heroes and heroines of the New Africa. . . . He had one life: yet this has been sacrificed for the redemption of Africa. . . . [He] has left us an imperishable legacy, the struggle for the attainment of social equality, economic security, religious tolerance and political freedom. . . . Let us perpetuate his ideas of freedom; they can be realised in our lifetime.[47]

Immediately after the funeral, the delegation resumed its tour of the north, with Macaulay's son serving in his stead. It visited the principal urban centers, including the remote Maiduguri, and although mass meetings and public appeals had to be limited to the sabon garis (isolated quarters in urban centers in the Moslem North inhabited by southern clerks and artisans), all the southerners, and many younger northerners, were excited by this dramatic and visible intrusion of nationalism.

It was in the Eastern Provinces, however, that the delegation made its greatest impact and achieved its greatest financial success.

> By car, lorry, horseback, accompanied by brass bands, flute bands, cowhorn bands, dancers and soldiers, in schoolrooms,

halls, compounds, cinemas, and churches, they touched the lives of hundreds of isolated communities in a way never known before.[48]

In one month the delegation had visited more than forty-five towns and had collected more than £2,500. Its members preached the ideal of self-government, and ceaselessly blasted the constitution and the ordinances. They argued that repeal of the constitution and the ordinances and achievement of self-government would usher in an era of equality and prosperity which would make everybody happy and free. Like the touring governors, they willingly accepted petitions covering all local grievances, including demands for wells, roads, and maternity homes.

In the Western Provinces the delegation was less successful, but its accomplishments were by no means unimpressive. Although chiefs in the west were often hostile or indifferent, Yoruba youths were very much attracted by the new nationalist spirit. The delegation finally terminated its tour at Lagos in late December, 1946, after eight months on the road. It was given a reception by an enthusiastic crowd of 30,000. It had collected £13,000 and had stimulated hundreds of thousands of Nigerians in the interior to an awareness of the nationalist ideal. Azikiwe and the NCNC were at the peak of their power and prestige, atop the crest of the highest wave of postwar nationalism. This was confirmed a few months later by the overwhelming victory of the three NCNC candidates, led by Azikiwe, in the Lagos elections.

Armed with new self-confidence, the nationalists of the NCNC were in the mood to force the government's hand on racial discrimination, one of the most embittering of all grievances. At this point a dramatic incident unified all nationalists and brought this issue to a head. An official in the Colonial Office, who was of African descent, visited Lagos in mid-April, 1947. He was denied accommodation at the Bristol Hotel, even though the Nigerian government had reserved a room for him. When this news reached the Lagos press, there was an instantaneous reaction. The leaders of the NCNC and of the NYM abandoned their differences and immediately formed the United Front Committee (UFC) to demand total elimination of all discrimination. Mass meetings were convened and a deputation visited the governor. In response to an overwhelming demonstration of unity and determination, the governor issued a circular condemning all forms of discrimination in public facilities. This decisive victory for the nationalists marked the beginning of a long series of government concessions.[49]

Although the nationalists tried to make the United Front Committee a permanent organization, the endeavor collapsed over the eternal question of which organization—the NCNC or the UFC—would absorb the other. The NCNC emerged with popularity and prestige unimpaired, although a few critics were beginning to ask questions about the disposition of the £13,000 raised on the tour of Nigeria.

In June, 1947, the long-awaited NCNC delegation to London left Lagos to lodge a formal protest with the Secretary of State for the Colonies, having, as they claimed, a mandate from the people. The delegation was reputedly "national," for it was composed of the following persons: Nnamdi Azikiwe (Ibo), Adeleke Adedoyin (Ijebu Yoruba), Dr. Abu Bakr Olorun-Nimbe (Ilorin Yoruba), Mallam Bukar Dipcharima (Hausa), Chief Nyong Essien (Ibibio), P. M. Kale (Bakweri Cameroonian), and Mrs. Funmilayo Ransome-Kuti (Yoruba). Before visiting the Secretary of State, members of the delegation met with leaders of the Fabian Colonial Bureau, the Labour Party Imperial Committee, WASU, and other organizations, and took a short trip to Eire where the Lord Mayor of Dublin assured them that the "Irish people were always on the side of all peoples struggling for national independence regardless of race, color, or creed." [50]

On August 13, 1947, the delegation held its fateful meeting with A. Creech Jones, Secretary of State for the Colonies. In addition to demanding radical revision of the Richards Constitution, the delegation submitted a memorandum setting forth thirty-three other grievances, ranging from the employment of European wives and the refusal to grant freehold tenure in Lagos to the appointment of "sole native authorities." In accepting the memorandum, to which he later replied in writing, the Secretary of State assured the delegation that it was the desire of the British government to press for self-government and that the Richards Constitution was not static but would be subject to later revision based on experience; but he emphatically insisted that the constitution would not be amended or replaced without a period of trial. He urged the delegates to return home and participate in this trial.[51]

Nearly two months later the delegation returned to Lagos and was met by a "mammoth crowd of 100,000" shouting "NCNC: Freedom or Death!" "We want self-government!" and "Nigeria first, Nigeria last, Nigeria all the time!"[52] "State" services were held at the Lagos Cathedral. The elected Lagos members of the Legislative Council (Azikiwe, Olorun-Nimbe, and Adedoyin) resolved to boycott the council. Subsequently, however, the delegation was requested to report on its achievements and account for the £13,000. As to the former, the *Pilot* argued that no one expected the Colonial Office to say, "Well done, go home and take over the Government of Nigeria."[53] As to the latter, it was pointed out that tours of Nigeria and trips to England were more expensive than might be expected. Members of the delegation began to squabble among themselves, and soon the pages of the local press were filled with mutual recriminations. Those who criticized the delegation for its failure to account for the £13,000 became increasingly vocal. The *Daily Times* editorialized:

> We would like to remind the delegation that what has been achieved could have been obtained in Nigeria by airmail at the very modest cost of one shilling, whereas the delegation has been ever so expensive. If therefore this is the sort of unthinking and wasteful leadership being thrust on us, we will have none of it.[54]

Although the delegation did not exact concessions or achieve immediate self-government,[55] and although its failure to account for funds made it vulnerable to relentless criticism, nevertheless its visit to the United Kingdom undoubtedly dramatized the existence of a nationalist movement in Nigeria and the discontent of certain politically important elements of the population. During its stay the delegation received considerable publicity, both critical and reflective, in the British press. For example, shortly after its arrival the *Daily Mirror,* referring to Azikiwe, commented:

> "Six feet of charm, of eloquence, of dignity, of ability. Six feet of stupidity, of folly, of hate-blended prejudice. . . . A man who could have done much for his country, who could have been a real leader, he has degenerated into a will-o'-the-wisp, a figure

of straw blown all ways by his own passions. . . . Zik could have helped in the wonderful future of his country." [56]

On the other hand, the influential *Economist* endeavored to draw a lesson from the delegation's visit:

> "But could not more be done in associating the Colonial peoples more directly with the responsibilities of government? . . . If intelligent Africans could be given more responsibility than they are at present, some counter-weight of Zikism might be provided. . . . Could not there be less of the . . . outward symbols of the British raj that irritate the sensitive, educated African as much as they impress the illiterate?" [57]

The latter observation no doubt reflected the growing apprehension in responsible British circles that the postwar policy in Nigeria was inadequate. In this sense, it is reasonable to conclude that the visit of the delegation had some influence upon the significant policy changes of 1948.

In an effort to recover from what was interpreted at the time as a failure, the leaders of the NCNC convened a national assembly in Kaduna in April, 1948. In his presidential address Azikiwe maintained that the NCNC had fulfilled the dreams of its founders by unifying the various elements of Nigeria, by crystallizing and articulating their aspirations, and by preparing the nation for the struggle for emancipation. After adopting a Freedom Charter the assembly adjourned, and for the next three years the NCNC, as an organization, was virtually moribund. During that period its name and its objectives were kept alive only in the person and activities of Nnamdi Azikiwe and in the pages of his newspapers. When the NCNC was reactivated in 1951, it was in response to a completely new situation.

CHAPTER 13

The Rise and Fall of Militant Nationalism

Militant nationalism in the postwar period was a child of Azikiwe's journalism and charismatic qualities. The militant nationalists included genuine idealists, Communist sympathizers, and political opportunists who were the shock troops of the NCNC during the height of its activity, and who were not impressed by nor content with the reforms of 1948 (see chapter 14). The enthusiasm and ambitions that Azikiwe had aroused in them were too strong, and their impatience was too great, for them to wait until the reforms matured. During the two-year period 1948–1950, they plotted to capture power through "positive action" and through the assertion of political control over the Nigerian labor movement. Their principal organizations were the Zikist Movement (later known as the Freedom Movement), the National Church of Nigeria, and the Nigerian National Federation of Labour (later known as the Nigerian Labour Congress), all of which were moribund by the end of 1951.

THE ZIKIST MOVEMENT (1946–1950)

Late in 1945, when Azikiwe was under heavy attack by his critics because of the assassination plot, three of his young admirers inaugurated the Zikist Movement. Its immediate objective was to defend Azikiwe. The tribal origin of the founders—Kolawole Balogun (Yoruba; now a chief and federal Minister of Information), M. C. K. Ajuluchuku (Ibo), and Abiodun Aloba (Edo)—reflected the multitribal character of Azikiwe's youthful following at that time. The organization came into being early in 1946 with the pledge: "Nevermore shall we allow this evangelist [Azikiwe] to cry his voice hoarse when millions of youths of Nigeria can take up his whisper and echo it all over the world. . . . He has lived a life that must live as long as Nigeria lives." [1] During the rest of 1946 and the early part of 1947 the organization expanded, claiming twenty-nine branches in the provinces and including most politically conscious young nationalists in Nigeria. On November 16, 1946, Azikiwe's birthday, all branches held special mass meetings at which the Zikist flag was unfurled and the Zikist song ("My Life Has Been a Joy to Me") was sung to celebrate "Zik Day." [2]

The objectives of the movement were wrapped up in a vague "Zikist philosophy" which had been advanced by A. A. Nwafor Orizu, an Ibo follower of Azikiwe's, in his book *Without Bitterness*, written in America during World War II. Orizu defined his philosophy as follows:

> I have coined the philosophy of "Zikism" to express the unconscious yearnings of my soul. . . . Zikism is irredentism. It is a God-sanctioned plan. It is a rejuvenated universal philosophy; it is not jingoism; it is not racialism; it is not anarchism; it is not monistic; it is not sarcastic; it is not apologetic; it is faith in life, a creative impulse. . . . Zikism must grow and spread on one social myth; namely, African irredentism, which must mean "the redemption of Africa from social wreckage, political servitude and economic impotency." . . . Africa is then to be saved from ideological confusion, psychological immaturity, spiritual complacency, and mental stagnation. [3]

Armed with this new philosophy, the Zikists sought not only to defend Azikiwe against his critics but to deify him as a leader and immortalize him for posterity. Azikiwe's *West African Pilot* was the principal organ of publicity for the movement.

Until the latter part of 1948 the Zikist Movement was, in effect, the youth branch of the NCNC. This is reflected in the following demiofficial status report of 1948:

> Whenever a few admirers of Zik are gathered together they usually form a branch of the movement and there is a central branch in Lagos, though the latter exercises little, if any control. Although the movement occasionally makes representations to Government it seldom takes any very active part in politics. Its principal function appears to be to arrange public lectures by supporters of Azikiwe.

297

The secretariat of the NCNC defined the relationship as follows: "The NCNC is the whole and the Zikist Movement is only a part of that whole." [4]

As the influence and *élan* of the NCNC began to wane toward the end of 1948, a few of the most zealous Zikists decided to take a more positive line. In October a leading Zikist, Osita C. Agwuna (Ibo), in a public lecture entitled "A Call for Revolution," demanded a new philosophy besides Zikism: "Those who shall be its adherents will see nothing good in co-operating with the British Government as long as we remain enslaved. . . ." [5] He then enumerated thirteen measures requiring positive action, including a country-wide general strike, a refusal to pay taxes, a boycott on all things foreign, and a demand that all students going overseas take a course in military science. [6] He was supported by another Zikist, Ogedengbe Macaulay (son of Herbert Macaulay), who argued: "If we tell the Governor to come down, he will not; we must drag him down and take over." [7] Shortly thereafter Mallam H. R. Abdallah (Igbirra), president of the movement, gave a public address entitled "The Age of Positive Action," in which he declared:

> I hate the Union Jack with all my heart because it divides the people wherever it goes. . . . It is a symbol of persecution, of domination, a symbol of exploitation, . . . [of] brutality.
>
> We have passed the age of petition, . . . the age of resolution, . . . the age of diplomacy. . . . This is the age of action— plain blunt and positive action. [8]

In the meantime leaders of the Zikist Movement launched a campaign against all those opposed to its aims. In the words of Agwuna:

> Our campaign will not be limited to imperialism, but it will be carried out against African nationals and semi-nationals, institutions, organisations, and establishments that are opposed in any way to our march towards immediate irredentism, for the enemy is no less a danger than his ally. [9]

The government acted quickly in response to these statements, arresting ten of the leaders and charging them with sedition. They were tried in February, 1949. In his trial Mallam Abdallah addressed the court for more than ninety minutes, charging: "My country has for over half a century been panting under the oppressing heels of British imperialism." During the trials the Lagos members of the movement conducted services in Lagos at which patriotic songs were sung ("Our Desire Is for Freedom," "Alien Rule Must Go") and lessons were read from Azikiwe's *Renascent Africa*. The services closed with a prayer to the "God of Africa." Most of the Zikists under trial were convicted and given heavy fines and sentences. The government's decisive action, which immobilized several of the most militant leaders, temporarily arrested the drift toward overt manifestations of extremism.

That the lull was only temporary was well demonstrated by the activities of certain Zikists during the disorders in the Eastern Provinces which followed the fatal shooting of twenty-one miners at the Enugu colliery on November 18, 1949. The shooting was the climax of a protracted period of unrest among the Enugu coal miners who had become embittered over their belief, encouraged by the local nationalist press, that large sums of arrears in pay were due them and were being withheld by the colliery management. That in fact was untrue.[10] As a consequence of their economic grievance, however, the miners staged a "go-slow" strike; the government, fearful that the miners or the Zikists would seize the stocks of explosives in the mines, ordered a contingent of armed police to guard the explosives while they were being removed. The miners in turn feared that once the explosives were removed nothing would prevent the management from closing the mines and thereby effecting a lockout. A large mob of aroused women and miners carrying sticks and machetes thereupon proceeded to the place where the explosives were stored in order to prevent their removal. When a jittery European police officer directed the police to fire upon the mob, twenty-one miners were killed and fifty-one were wounded. This was the signal for the Zikists to move into action. It appeared for a time as though the political moderation and quiescence produced by the reforms of 1948 would end. The government immediately appointed a commission, which included two prominent African judges, to inquire into and report upon the incident and the events that followed.

The immediate reaction of all nationalists to the shooting incident was profound shock and resentment. They quickly closed ranks and formed a coalition called the National Emergency Committee (NEC). The president of the NYM, Dr. Akinola Maja, and the vice president of the NCNC, Mbonu Ojike, became respectively the president and vice president of the new organization. Its cabinet included all leading nationalists in Nigeria, drawn from all factions of the nationalist movement. From November, 1949, until September, 1950, the NEC showed promise of becoming a permanent coalition of nationalist forces. But shortly after representatives of the NCNC and the NYM had signed an "Instrument of Coalition" on September 30, 1950, the NEC collapsed. In a large measure the failure to merge resulted from competition for positions within the hierarchy of the new organization, as well as from the revival of the ever-present sentiment of tribalism. During the period of its existence, the only tangible "nationalist" achievement of the NEC was the abolition of discrimination on the teaching staff at University College.[11] In historical perspective, the NEC, like its predecessor, the United Front Committee of 1947, was an exception to the chronic disunity that characterized the nationalist movement. Its failure suggested that only an acute crisis, when the issue was barefaced discrimination or ill-treatment of black by white, could unite all nationalists in a common endeavor.

Actually, the NEC, insofar as it was a coalition of nationalist leaders in Lagos, was not a militant organization. It was the Zikist Movement operating under its own name or that of the NEC, or even of the NCNC, which was responsible for a revival of militancy immediately after the tragic shooting at Enugu. Riots and looting by frenzied mobs and additional shootings by the police occurred in four eastern towns: Port Harcourt, Onitsha, Calabar, and Aba.[12] All these disturbances conformed to a common pattern: local Zikists, with a few highly mobile leaders who sped from one town to another immediately after a shooting, convened mass meetings and organized demonstrations; once a mob was mobilized it would proceed to assault Europeans, damage or destroy government property, and loot the stores of European firms; in order to disperse the mobs, the police were ordered to fire upon their leaders. The Zikists who instigated the riots in Aba explained their motivation as follows: ". . . all the people in the country regard one another as comrades in arms against the rule of the present Government, if for no other reason than that it is a foreign Government voted to power not by the people but imposed upon them by the might of British arms. . . ." [13] The Zikists had tried, unsuccessfully, to seize upon the tension created by the shootings to further the ends of militant nationalism.

During the proceedings of the Commission of Enquiry, a government security officer reported that since early in 1948 it had been known that the Zikists were encouraging the formation of terrorist parties, that they had tried to acquire arms and explosives, and that actually thirty cases had been stolen from the colliery magazine.[14] Moreover, immediately after the Enugu incident, Zikists in Enugu and Onitsha were prevented by the police, only at the last minute, from delivering lectures having such titles as "The Hour Has Struck." [15] Finally, on February 18, 1950, a Zikist attempted to assassinate the chief secretary to the government. Because of this growing evidence of a conspiratorial network, the government police carried out a surprise search of the houses of Zikists all over Nigeria and uncovered large quantities of seditious literature. Later, during his trial, the secretary of the movement, a twenty-four-year-old ex-serviceman, defied the judge in these terms:

> . . . with the immense resources and the coercive state machinery behind you and the Government you represent, I do not as a Zikist recognize the right of this court to try this case. . . . You are a symbol of that imperialist machine which I and my colleagues abhor; therefore I am not pleading before this court. . . .[16]

This quotation reveals the uncompromising militancy characteristic of many Zikists.

In April, 1950, the governor declared the Zikist Movement unlawful: "Although the movement is small and unrepresentative its purposes and methods are dangerous to the good government of Nigeria and it is essential to make it quite clear that such purposes and methods will not be tolerated." [17] The following month in Port Harcourt the Zikists reorganized as the Freedom Movement, which aimed at the destruction of "all forms of imperialism and the establishment of a free Socialist Republic of Nigeria fighting in and out of Parliament employing nonviolent revolutionary tactics." [18] Except for Zikists who were in jail, the membership of the new organization was the same as that of its predecessor. Branches were organized throughout the Eastern Provinces, and a few were formed in the north and the west; in fact, the Freedom Movement even claimed to have a branch in New York City. Its total strength, concentrated mainly in Lagos and in cities of the east and the north, was not much more than 1,500. For several reasons the new movement was short-lived: enthusiasm among its members rapidly dwindled, and factional feuds developed, mainly between the Lagos and Port Harcourt leadership. After a few months it became moribund. Its demise was hastened by the reorganization of the NCNC on the basis of individual rather than organizational membership in 1951 and the formation of the NCNC Youth's Association in 1952.

THE NATIONAL CHURCH OF NIGERIA

In the latter part of 1948 the National Church of Nigeria was founded at Aba, and became the religious wing of the Zikist Movement. According to Mbonu Ojike, one of its strongest supporters, "all churches exist to serve a given people and not purposelessly. Our National Church must therefore serve us." [19] The superintendent of the Church, though denying that he was antichrist, argued:

> God sends His prophets to various nations from age to age to lead, teach, succour, defend and reform His human creations in travail, despair and decay. Thus the Arabs had Mohammed. . . . [The] Russians had Lenin. . . . [The] Indians had Ghandhi. . . . And Africa has Dr Nnamdi Azikiwe.[20]

At special services in November, 1950, when Azikiwe worshiped in the National Church, the superintendent who blessed him compared him to Christ. Azikiwe himself had written in an earlier period:

> I will publicly admit that I have never claimed to be a New Messiah, although for reasons best known to a section of the West African Press I have been elevated to that creditable and immortal position. It is possible that I may be one of the apostles of the new Africa. . . .[21]

A characteristic church service included the following: lessons from the NCNC Manifesto, the American Declaration of Independence, Zik's *Renascent Africa,* and the Bible; a sermon in the form of a political campaign speech extolling nationalists and condemning their opponents; and selections from a book of National Hymns and Prayers, including the following National Prayer:

O Almighty and everlasting God of the universe, God of Africa. . . . Give ear to the prayers of Thy children who assemble here . . . to implore Thee to give us . . . freedom from foreign domination, and freedom to own and enjoy this portion of Thy earth which Thou hast, without a mistake allocated to us. . . .[22]

The National Church occasionally held memorial services for Herbert Macaulay; it gave Paul Robeson the title of "Champion of African Freedom"; and, whenever a "national" tragedy like the Enugu shooting occurred, it conducted mourning services.[23]

The National Church was virtually coextensive in its membership and branch organization with the Zikist (and subsequently with the Freedom) Movement. In fact, in some towns the leaders of the two organizations were identical. Whereas the Zikist Movement expressed protest against the political aspects of imperial rule, the National Church represented revolt against white European churches. The title of one sermon delivered by a spiritual leader was "Nigeria in the Tentacles of Religious Imperialism." In fact, from 1949 on, radical, militant nationalists became increasingly critical of Christian missions. Statements such as the following frequently appeared in the nationalist press:

None [of the alien missionary societies] has helped Nigerians in their struggle for freedom. . . . They are enemies of our Freedom; . . . in the guise of Christianity they use our churches and schools to suppress and ridicule our political consciousness.[24]

The [European Church] will wax or wane according as it identifies itself with, or keeps aloof from, the interests of the African body politic.[25]

The basis for revolt against European churches has been treated at length in chapter 4. The main objectives of the National Church apparently were the glorification and awakening of racial and national consciousness. As such the Church was not so much a religious enterprise as a strand in the nationalist movement.

THE NIGERIAN LABOUR CONGRESS

This brief survey of the more militant manifestations of nationalism would be incomplete did it not mention the meteoric rise of
a young Ibo Zikist to a position of power and influence within the
labor movement. Nduka Eze personified militant nationalism in
the economic sphere just as the Zikist Movement and the National Church (he was a member of both) represented it in the
political and religious spheres, respectively. After being educated
in mission schools Eze worked as a clerk in the United Africa
Company (UAC). He was one of the first to join the Zikist Movement in 1946; he became successively a member of the executive
committee, acting secretary, and finally acting president during
1949–1950, the period of its most militant activity. Although he
was one of the movement's powerful forces pushing for "positive
action," his greatest influence was exerted in the Nigerian labor
movement. He concentrated on organizing the workers in European firms and politicizing the Nigerian Trades Union Congress (TUC).

Prior to 1946 employees of large European firms had been
unable to organize, due mainly, they allege, to the resistance of
management and its victimization of workers. The general strike
of 1945 was overwhelmingly an affair of government employees.
By the end of 1946, however, Nduka Eze had founded the UAC
Workers' Union, of which he became the first secretary. In 1947
he commenced to organize UAC workers in earnest, and by 1950
he had made the Workers' Union the second largest labor organization in Nigeria (18,000 members), with branches in most
of the towns. Eze's personal control over both branch leaders and
membership was decisive. His personal hatred of the UAC and
of the type of economic enterprise it represented was intense
and uncompromising, and had a heavy Leninist flavor:

> . . . not very many people in this country are aware that the
> introduction of imperialism in this country has as its essential
> motive the sapping of the vitality of the worker and the ap-
> propriation of the surpluses of whatever the worker has, leaving
> him with a bare minimum to subsist in order to adorn the im-
> perialist design.[26]

In August, 1950, Eze brought all unionized mercantile workers out on strike and won for them a 12½ per cent cost-of-living allowance. At that point his power in the UAC union was at its zenith. Four months later he was repudiated and disowned, principally as a consequence of his more ambitious activities in politics and the central labor movement.

As the first field secretary of the Zikist Movement, Eze had laid much of the groundwork for the enthusiastic reception accorded the NCNC delegation on its 1946 tour. In the next year he brought about the affiliation of the Trades Union Congress with the NCNC, an accomplishment that ultimately won for him a position in the NCNC cabinet. When the majority of the TUC voted in 1948 to disaffiliate, Eze and others split the labor movement by organizing a new central body, the Nigerian National Federation of Labour, which became the labor wing of the NCNC. At the time of the Enugu shooting (November, 1949), when Eze was acting president of the Zikist Movement, he organized the National Labour Committee. This act, together with a speech he made in Enugu, suggested that he was prepared to launch the long-awaited "positive action" with the labor movement as his weapon. But Eze's subsequent prosecution for sedition, and the collapse of the Zikist disturbances in the east, lost him whatever opportunity the Enugu shooting might have presented.

Undaunted, however, Eze proceeded to unite all labor in a new central organization, the Nigerian Labour Congress, embracing his federation, the TUC, and the Government Workers' Union. This amalgamation was brought about at the end of May, 1950. Three months later Eze had established himself firmly in power as general secretary, and his associates held the key centers of authority throughout the new structure. In the meantime he had used funds belonging to his UAC union, plus others received from Communist front organizations abroad, to establish a daily paper in Lagos, the *Labour Champion*.[27] By early 1951 Eze was unemployed and had lost all his positions and most of his influence.

There are several reasons for Eze's fall from power just at the moment when he seemed to have achieved a position and an organizational apparatus enabling him to challenge directly the government of Nigeria. The first was his difficulty with funds, both those of the union and those received from abroad. This was the principal reasons for the collapse of his newspaper, an indispensable instrument for establishing an independent political base. Second, the Nigerian Labour Congress which Eze indisputably controlled pushed its members' loyalty beyond the breaking point by calling an ill-planned and ill-timed strike in December, 1950, in which the workers lost heavily in wages, jobs, and prestige. The entire central labor organization, as well as the UAC union, virtually disintegrated. Third, Eze had been openly critical of the existing so-called "bourgeois" leadership, and had made it emphatically clear that he had strong political ambitions of his own. In January, 1951, he tried unsuccessfully to organize a labor party; two months later at a Freedom Movement meeting he said:

> Nigeria is pregnant with political confusion; . . . there are so many parties . . . and yet the yearnings and aspirations of the people remained unfulfilled. . . . The masses and workers are the backbone of the country. Experience in Russia and China proved that conclusively. The masses must recognise and accept their position as the vanguard of the liberation movement.[28]

In the same month Azikiwe expelled Eze from the NCNC cabinet on grounds of disloyalty and breach of trust, alleging that Eze had carried out a "denigration" campaign against him both in Nigeria and abroad. Moreover, Azikiwe regarded the "egocentric activities of Mr. Eze" as the principal cause of the lamented suppression of the Zikist Movement.[29] By 1954, however, Eze was back in the NCNC fold as an unofficial member of its national executive committee.

Azikiwe's critics have alleged that he was inconsistent in his attitude toward militant nationalists. At times he would caution them against extremism: "But we must warn the youngsters, as ever we have done, that hard work and diligent studies will fetch far richer dividends than high-sounding slogans and plans that fizzle out into a nine days' wonder." [30] Azikiwe tried to avoid open identification with the leadership of the Zikist Movement at the height of its militant activity. At other times he would encourage radicals, even creating the Order of African Freedom to be awarded to all those imprisoned for sedition. They were to be the African heroes who would receive preference and veneration in public places.[31] Some nationalists believed that this off-and-on attitude of Azikiwe's was one of the reasons for the disaffection of Eze and others of a militant persuasion, particularly those who had served prison sentences in pursuit of the Zikist ideal.

After Eze's break with Azikiwe, this small group of unreconciled Zikists continued to organize for positive action. Impressed by the astounding successes of the militant Convention People's party (CPP) in the Gold Coast (now Ghana), they organized a Nigerian CPP which openly opposed Azikiwe and the NCNC in the Eastern Region. Partly in response to this challenge the NCNC Youth's Association was organized in 1952 for the purpose of attracting the more militant youths, both of the upcoming generation and from the membership of the former Zikist and Freedom movements and of the CPP. Azikiwe's disinclination to give radicals his continuous support—possibly a reflection of his own hesitation about the feasibility or desirability of revolutionary measures—was a crucial element in their inability to exert much influence during the period 1948–1951. Perhaps another reason for the failure of militant nationalism was the untimeliness of its appearance. In short, it failed for the same reasons that brought about the decline of the NCNC. During the years 1948–1951 most educated Nigerians were not in the mood for positive action, either because they were busy consolidating gains already achieved, or because they were not in agreement on the ends toward which such action was to be directed. Their disagreement on objectives was a factor in the emergence of regional nationalist organizations in 1951, a development to be covered in succeeding chapters.

CHAPTER 14

The Beginning of a New Era

The year 1948 was a turning point in Nigerian nationalism. The three-year period from April, 1945, to April, 1948, had opened with the general strike and the provocative constitutional proposals of Governor Sir Arthur Richards, and had closed with the National Assembly of the National Council of Nigeria and the Cameroons and the publication of its Freedom Charter. During that period the NCNC had made an effort to Nigerianize and territorialize the nationalist movement, and as an organization it had attained unprecedented recognition and influence among important segments of the population. In the succeeding three-year period, from April, 1948, to April, 1951, the NCNC became relatively inactive and its more militant offshoots or affiliates failed to gain widespread support for positive action. To some extent the decline in overt and organized nationalist activity was the result of new developments in British policy and of the situation that began to take shape in 1948. In this chapter we will analyze these new factors and appraise their impact upon the development of nationalism.

The year 1948 was one of great change and reform. It was ushered in by two crucial events. The first was the decision of Nnamdi Azikiwe and the other two elected NCNC members to abandon their boycott of the Legislative Council. Azikiwe affirmed: "We will go to Kaduna . . . [and] nothing which will be inimical to your interests will be left unchallenged." [1] He was determined to use the council as a platform for the continuing assertion of nationalist demands and aspirations. In this sense he was carrying on the tradition of harassing officialdom, a tradition set by the Honorable C. C. Adeniyi-Jones in the prewar period, but by 1948 nationalist criticism of officials was more pointed and nationalist demands were far more emphatic.

The second significant development was the retirement of the unpopular Governor Richards and the arrival of Sir John Macpherson, a tactful and conciliatory official. Governor Richards had acquired the stigma of being antinationalist. Both within and outside the Legislative Council he had directly and indirectly criticized Azikiwe and the NCNC. For example, in an address at Onitsha, Azikiwe's home town, in October, 1946, he had said of the NCNC: "This, to begin with, is a curious name, because it is neither 'national' nor a 'council.' It consists of a group of individuals who have claimed to be, and consider themselves, leaders. . . . I am well aware that this National Council has attempted by abuse, untruths and exaggeration to deceive the people of this country." [2] There can be little question that Governor Richards found his tenure in office very trying and irritating. Nevertheless, his personal and official relations with the nationalists had deteriorated to a point where it was difficult for both sides to move away from the dead center of hostility.

The change in governorship, therefore, was of crucial significance. For the British it meant that concessions could be granted with a minimum loss of face and a minimum inflation of nationalist prestige. As long as Governor Richards remained it was psychologically impossible to create the impression that the government was giving in to nationalist demands. The change also meant that A. Creech Jones, the new Labourite Secretary of State for the Colonies and a sincere Afrophile of long standing, was in a stronger position to institute positive reforms which the Fabian Colonial Bureau, whose founder and president he was, had espoused. In short, these changes in the position of the principal antagonists in the struggle—the foremost nationalist and the leading imperial representative—cleared the air for a new era in Anglo-Nigerian relationships.

By the end of 1948 great strides had been taken toward eliminating several of the nationalists' grievances, either by outright concession or by the declaration of revised objectives and timetables and the establishment of machinery for their achievement. Several of the reforms had been in the process of maturation since the beginning of the war; others were clearly the product of a new awareness among colonial officials that the nationalists' demands could no longer be ignored, either because they were patently reasonable or because political stability and peaceful evolution required a radical change in approach. Although some of the reforms would have been introduced irrespective of nationalist demonstrations, the nationalists can point out that the more important reforms were granted at the height of their agitation, or soon thereafter.

The arguments of both groups are partially correct. There can be no question that the United Kingdom, particularly after the advent of the Labour government in 1945, was dedicated to a radically new policy of positive development. Yet there is no doubt that Azikiwe and the NCNC during the period 1945–1948 compelled both the imperial and the colonial governments to accelerate sharply the tempo of that development.

What, then, were the changes of 1948? The four most important were (1) the new governor's announcement that the Richards Constitution would be revised earlier than had been planned and that such revision would be based on the wishes of the people; (2) an explicit statement that it was the policy of the government to accelerate the Africanization of the senior service and of advisory boards and committees; (3) the rapid and substantial democratization of the native authority system; and (4) the extension of facilities for higher education. It is important to note that these changes occurred in the aftermath of the great nationalist victory on the issue of racial discrimination at the time of the Bristol Hotel incident and the United Front Committee one year earlier. The decisive removal of this psychological hurdle provided a climate in which subsequent reforms could be instituted by the government and accepted by many nationalists with fewer inhibitions and less suspicion.

This crucial change in the psychological realm was accelerated by the spirit that lay behind the reforms of 1948. Whether they liked it or not—and many emphatically did not—British officials in Nigeria were under pressure to adopt an entirely new attitude toward educated Africans. Whereas previously it was the chiefs and elders who had received or, according to policy, should have received official recognition, deference, and courtesy, the new emphasis was upon winning the good will of all educated Africans. District officers began to invite more and more educated Nigerians to tea or cocktails; mixed clubs, like the Island Club in

Lagos and the Niger International Club in Aba, became increasingly popular; sports events became multiracial endeavors (for example, the Nigerian Boxing Board of Control); and all along the line cracks began to appear in the great barriers that had separated the European from the African.

In a special address before the Legislative Council in August, 1948, Governor Macpherson made the following rather startling announcement:

> The progress already made [under the Richards Constitution] . . . has been, in my considered view, so rapid, and so sound that I suggest that we might be justified in *reviewing our timetable*, and that *we might consider together* what changes should be made, and whether they should be made earlier than originally intended.[3]

At the next session of the Legislative Council a select committee proposed

> . . . that a series of conferences be held, first at village and divisional level, and then at provincial level, when the various Provincial Conferences would make recommendations to be considered by Regional Conferences. . . . The views of the four Regional Conferences were then to be considered by a Drafting Committee, . . . then a General Conference, and the resolutions of this Conference would then be debated in the Regional Houses and by the Legislative Council *before being submitted to the Governor* and the Secretary of State for the Colonies.[4]

This unprecedented proposal for constitutional revision, in which theoretically every Nigerian from the most illiterate peasant to the Emir of Kano and Nnamdi Azikiwe was to be consulted on what form of government he desired, was in part an effort to make amends for the cavalier manner in which Governor Richards had instituted his constitution three years earlier.

In practical effect, the proposed method of popular consultation not only absorbed the time and attention of large numbers of people for more than two years, but it also provided a structure through which nationalists could advance their own proposals. The formula for revision, and particularly the protracted manner in which it was to be carried out, significantly weakened the

NCNC, whose *raison d'être* had been agitation for constitutional revision. Because the new constitution would establish the power structure of the Nigeria of the future, internal tensions between leaders of different ethnic or cultural groups were exacerbated in the open competitive struggle over such issues as representation, regional powers, and revenue allocation. During the ensuing two years less was heard about "British autocracy" and "rapacious colonial exploitation," and more about Fulani threats either to continue their interrupted march to the sea or to withdraw to the western Sudan, about Yoruba allegations of threatened Ibo domination, and about the NCNC and unitarian nationalists accusing the British of "divide and rule."

The nationalists of NCNC persuasion were not pleased with the proposed method of consultation. They would have preferred a national constituent assembly. The official method of country-wide grass-roots participation appeared to them to give too much weight to traditional authorities, who, they feared, could be manipulated or influenced by British officials. Their reasons for objecting were not unlike their reasons for opposing the system of indirect elections under the Richards Constitution. In any event, whatever the nationalist motivation may have been, there can be little doubt that the method of constitutional revision did in fact give heavy weight to rural and traditionalist elements and minimized the influence of urban, educated, and nationalist elements.

It has previously been pointed out that the failure of the British to Africanize the senior service was of great importance in propelling educated elements into nationalist activity. In May, 1948, the new governor appointed the Nigerianization Commission to make recommendations about the recruitment and training of Nigerians for the senior service. Two of the governor's appointees on the commission were Nnamdi Azikiwe and another officer of the NCNC. In its report, which was approved unconditionally by the government and the Legislative Council, the commission affirmed a nationalist demand of long standing:

> The training and recruitment of Nigerians for senior posts in the Government Service is not only necessary to enable Nigerians to take an *increasing share in the management of their own affairs*

and to allow the Service to keep in step with the pace of constitutional advance: it is also essential for the development and progress of the country.[5]

The commission recommended as a fundamental guiding principal that "no non-Nigerian should be recruited for any Government post except where no suitable and qualified Nigerian is available." [6] Other important recommendations, all of which were approved, were that public service boards with Nigerian majorities should be appointed to select all candidates for the senior service, and that during the following three years (1948–1951) 385 scholarships should be awarded by the government for the education and training of Nigerians for that service. These were reforms for which nationalists had been agitating ever since Azikiwe published his plans for postwar Nigeria in 1943.

It is likely that one of the factors prompting the Nigerian government to make this remarkable concession was the growing inability to obtain European recruits for service in Nigeria. Actually, by 1948 some progress had been made in Africanization, and after that year the number of Africans inducted into the senior service increased rapidly. In 1939 there were only 23 Africans in the senior service; in 1947 the number stood at 182; by 1951 it had reached 628; and in 1953 it was 786. The significant fact, however, is not the number involved, but rather that many of the appointees were nationalists—which, of course, quickly immobilized them politically—and certainly the vast majority of them were potential nationalists. Azikiwe lost several of his most able editors to the expanding and heavily Africanized Public Relations Department. Moreover, the opening of careers to the talented meant higher pay, perquisites, and status, and greater economic security for thousands of educated Nigerians who had aspired to such appointments. In short, except among educated Nigerians who either were not attracted to the senior service or felt that they had no chance of securing positions in it, the change in policy had a substantial impact on the nationalist movement.

The accelerated program of Africanization was not confined to the senior service. By 1948 the Ten-Year Plan of Development and Welfare was getting under way. In order to carry out the plan, the government created a hierarchy of executive and advisory institutions, including central, regional, provincial, and local development committees and boards to which educated Africans were appointed, frequently in the majority. In many other spheres, such as transport, health, communications, and education, the government established advisory institutions and manned them mainly with educated Nigerians. Although this reform did not provide remunerative careers, nominal honorariums were attached to such appointments. The real significance was psychological and not economic, for educated Africans began to feel that they were being given a share, albeit limited, in the management of their own affairs at the executive level.

It was at the native authority or local government level, however, that reform was most pronounced. It had, of course, been under way for some time but the shortage of staff during the war and the immediate postwar period had retarded its full implementation. Upon his arrival in Nigeria on April 14, 1948, Sir John Macpherson declared: "I shall devote my special interest to the problems of local government." [7] Democratization of the native authority system, and diversion of the energies of educated Nigerians into it, were a favorite theme not only of Obafemi Awolowo, but also of A. Creech Jones.[8] No doubt the new governor had been well briefed by the latter before leaving London. In addition to this external stimulus, early in 1948 senior administrative officers in the Eastern Provinces had arrived at a similar conclusion. They recognized that "native administration" was suspect to the educated class; yet it was from that class alone that the political leadership of the future must come. They were convinced that if the educated nationalists were to remain outside the machinery of government they would become increasingly critical, suspicious, and hostile. As a result of the ferment in policy circles in the Eastern Provinces, it was decided to scrap the entire native authority system in the east and to substitute a completely modern form of democratic local government. The new system, to be modeled after that of the United Kingdom, would be a hierarchy of elected councils (local, district, and county). All councils would be self-governing within the limits of their allocated powers, and district officers would act only as advisers. Although officialdom in the north and the west was disinclined to introduce such radical innovations, the authorities in those two regions undertook to accelerate their programs of democratization already under way.[9]

The significant feature of the 1948 reforms in the east, however, was the scrupulous manner in which the government avoided giving the impression that the new system was being imposed upon the people. An all-African select committee of the Eastern House of Assembly toured the entire Eastern Region and conferred with native authority councils and tribal unions, as well as with prominent nationalists. After protracted consultation, the new scheme was adopted almost unanimously by Nigerian representatives. In the meantime, of course, the existing native authorities were rapidly being democratized. By the end of 1949, the people of the Eastern Region (and to a lesser extent elsewhere) were so thoroughly involved in discussions about their political and economic future—local government reform, constitutional revision, and development planning—that even the most militant nationalist had difficulty in finding an issue or an audience.

Finally, the year 1948 marked the turning point in education. In August of that year the Education Ordinance, the first major educational plan applying to the whole of Nigeria, was approved by the Legislative Council. It proposed the establishment of a wide network of boards and commissions, which would be heavily Nigerianized; a new system of grants-in-aid; and an appropriation for education which was double that of 1945, and five times that of 1940.[10] In addition, the ordinance gave native authority councils the power, previously denied in the south, to levy local rates. For the first time in history the people of southern Nigeria were forced to realize that alleviation of their insatiable hunger for education was limited only by what they were willing to pay in taxes.

The developments in primary and secondary education were matched by two innovations in higher education, which were perhaps of far greater political importance. In January, 1948, the University College of Nigeria was opened in Ibadan with a highly qualified staff and the power to confer degrees from the University of London. Ultimately it was to accommodate 500 students. This development was supplemented by the government's award of scholarships for higher education over the following three years (1948–1951). Thus ambitious and zealous students in the sec-

315

ondary schools of Nigeria could look forward to and work for a better future than an £8-a-month junior clerkship in Lagos.

These major changes in policy came at a time when Nigeria was entering upon the period of its greatest prosperity. The post-war demand for vegetable oils, rubber, timber, cocoa, and other Nigerian exports rose to heights never before known. The expansion in export-import trade is indicated by the following schedule of values: [11]

Year	Exports	Imports
1939	£ 10,469,000	£ 6,757,000
1948	62,472,000	41,947,000
1951	130,358,000	84,401,000

Even more remarkable was the tremendous increase in the importation of certain high-valued items: [12]

Item	1939	1948	1951
Manufactured apparel	£155,000	£ 765,000	£1,093,000
Boots and shoes	33,000	417,000	1,064,000
Cars and trucks	177,000	1,945,000	3,998,000
Bicycles	46,000	983,000	1,581,000

These figures are indicators of the rapid rise in the standard of living of wage earners, primary producers, and other groups involved in the commercialized sector of the economy.

At this point one might ask: What was left of nationalist grievances? Discrimination had been declared illegal; the Richards Constitution was being revised, presumably by Nigerians themselves; the senior service was being Nigerianized as fast as qualified recruits could be found; indirect rule was rapidly being replaced by elected councils upon which educated elements would ultimately displace traditional elements; and education was being expanded along lines proposed by the nationalists. To the casual observer, the answer would be nothing.

But this conclusion is superficial and inadequate, because it reduces nationalist motivation to a level of rationalism and hedonism which the facts do not support. As previously remarked, suspicion and distrust, and the conviction that educated Nigerians had a natural right to rule their country, were critical features of the nationalist mentality. Moreover, the legal prohibition of discrimination—as any American well knows—does not extinguish all its subtle social manifestations. Most of the 1948 reforms were mere declarations of future policy; European officials remained as deeply entrenched in the key centers of power as they had always been. Finally, despite an awareness of his limitations, and his apparent readiness to accept temporarily a "partnership" arrangement in an imperial system in the process of liquidation, the educated Nigerian retained deep in his soul the conviction that he would never feel free until he was his own master and could, for good or for ill, shape his own destiny.

There remained the intangible and insatiable yearning for equality; and to the educated Nigerian equality was not simply a matter of sitting at a desk opposite a European and earning the same salary, or of drinking at the same bar; it would never be complete until he and his fellow Africans were no longer dependent upon Europeans for advice, skill, technology, or power, but were their own masters. All the reforms described above looked toward this final objective; but the point is that the Nigerian nationalist saw little likelihood that the objective would be reached in his lifetime.

Furthermore, the suggestion that colonial nationalism can be arrested by the removal of material grievances, by prosperity, and by the mere prospect of rapid political advance, overlooks crucial elements in the psychology of nationalism. A sense of oppression and deprivation is only one of many sources of nationalism. Of equal importance are hope and expectancy. Indeed, one of the reasons colonial governments have endeavored to ignore nationalist movements, or at least look upon them with indifference, has been the very sound assumption that recognition and concessions would inflate their importance and create new aspirations which would in turn stimulate fresh activity. As nationalists become more hopeful of victory, their grievances multiply and become more intolerable. Eric Hoffer makes this particular point very well:

Discontent is likely to be highest when misery is bearable; when conditions have so improved that an ideal state seems almost

within reach. A grievance is most poignant when almost re-
dressed. . . . The intensity of discontent seems to be in inverse
proportion to the distance from the object fervently desired.[13]

Thus organized nationalism, though less in evidence during the
period 1948–1951 than before, had not been "bought off." But the
prospects of substantial political reform, together with prosperity
and the elimination of discrimination, produced a temporary lull
in the overt manifestations of nationalist activity. In part this was
because many people were deeply involved in a variety of new
arrangements and institutions. Moreover, a large number of those
predisposed to nationalism had left to study abroad. Azikiwe's decision to work within the Legislative Council and not to give indiscriminate support to his more militant followers was another
factor. It was, in short, a period of consolidation. It was also a
period during which new political alignments were being formed
with a somewhat different orientation from that of the Pan-
Nigerian NCNC. These developments will be discussed in succeeding chapters.

CHAPTER 15

The Regionalization of Nationalism

The year 1948 was significant not only because political reforms for which nationalists had agitated since 1945 were introduced, but also because important segments of the population, previously inactive or opposed to the NCNC, became increasingly articulate and commenced to organize along different lines. These elements had been temporarily eclipsed by the dramatic activities of Nnamdi Azikiwe and the NCNC during the period 1945–1947. Their appearance in 1948 was in part a reaction to those activities. Whereas the NCNC had emphasized Pan-Nigerian nationalism, the new elements, including Yoruba leaders in the west and Fulani-Hausa leaders in the north, placed greater stress upon regionalism as the primary focus of Nigerian nationalist development. Before analyzing these developments, however, we will review certain background factors.

UNIFYING AND DIVISIVE ASPECTS OF BRITISH POLICY

One of the most common themes in colonial nationalist literature is the allegation that imperial powers inevitably pursue a policy of "divide and rule" in order to thwart nationalist unity and maintain the imperial presence. This view is based not only upon substantial historical evidence of the effectiveness of such a policy, but also upon political realism. And most nationalists are realistic about human motivation. Political realists, including Nigerian nationalists, would therefore be ready to believe that Britain, in her own interests, would pursue a Machiavellian policy of "divide and rule." But no definitive conclusion can be reached until, through the publication of memoirs and the declassification of relevant documents, the actual facts are available. In the meantime we can only make a reasonable interpretation, realizing that the attribution of motive is a hazardous undertaking.

At the outset, at least four special observations are in point. One is that except for Nigerian nationalists, who are of course themselves a product of the British presence, the British are the sole creators of the political entity known as Nigeria. This elementary truth has been put most forcefully by two of Nigeria's leading statesmen. In 1947 Premier Obafemi Awolowo, founder and leader of the Egbe Omo Oduduwa and the Action Group, wrote as follows:

> Nigeria is not a nation. It is a mere geographical expression. There are no "Nigerians" in the same sense as there are "English", "Welsh", or "French". The word "Nigerian" is merely a distinctive appellation to distinguish those who live within the boundaries of Nigeria from those who do not.[1]

In 1948 Prime Minister Abubakar Tafawa Balewa, a leader of the Northern Peoples' Congress, affirmed in the Legislative Council that

> Since 1914 the British Government has been trying to make Nigeria into one country, but the Nigerian people themselves are historically different in their backgrounds, in their religious beliefs and customs and do not show themselves any sign of willingness to unite. . . . Nigerian unity is only a British intention for the country.[2]

Of course, Britain did not consciously plan to create an independent Nigerian nation when it established Nigeria's boundaries; developed a common administrative system; constructed a common transportation grid and a communications network; introduced a common currency, a lingua franca, and an educational system; and recruited a corps of Nigerian clerks and artisans who developed Pan-Nigerian perspectives and aspirations—all were simply requisite to the administration of an arbitrary chunk of Africa as an overseas dependency.

Second, the idea of a united and self-governing Nigeria was not absent from British declarations of policy. Mention has already been made of Sir Hugh Clifford's statement in 1921 that in the course of time the Legislative Council would become the Supreme Parliament of Nigeria. In 1937 Margery Perham wrote: "Among many doubts and uncertainties, however, one thing is certain, that it is both our duty and our interest to assist the Africans of Nigeria to build a sound united state." [3] Sir Bernard Bourdillon, governor of Nigeria during the early war years, argued that the Richards Constitution represented "not the division of one unit into three, but the beginning of a fusion of innumerable small units into three and from these three into one." [4] From 1948 on Governor Macpherson spoke repeatedly and emphatically in favor of a united Nigeria, on many occasions publicly deprecating manifestations of disunity and tribalism among Nigerian political groups.[5]

Third, it is also clear that before 1948 the British government did not anticipate that a united and independent Nigeria would emerge for a very, very long time. Even such a strong Afrophile as Raymond Leslie Buell had placed it a century away.[6] In her foreword to Premier Awolowo's book, written in December, 1946, Miss Perham concluded that "the day when Nigeria from being a name written on a map by Sir George Goldie and an administrative framework put together by Lord Lugard, becomes a true federation, still more a nation, is still far away." [7]

Finally, it is likely that the British policy, regarded by nationalists as a calculated policy of fostering tribalism and preventing the development of a Nigerian national consciousness, was rooted in the ordinary Englishman's Burkean concept of nationalism. Carlton Hayes's commentary on Burke's traditional nationalism illuminates this point:

> Nationality, according to Burke, does not signify a mere geographical entity or just an aggregate of individuals who happen at a given moment to live under a common government. . . . Not all human loyalties were to be absorbed into a supreme loyalty to the democratic national state. On the contrary, Burke advanced and pressed the idea of a hierarchy of loyalties, each supreme in its own sphere and all perfectly "natural," because all are "traditional." . . . man is and should be loyal to his family . . . [and] to his locality or "region;" "regionalism" is traditional and hence natural, and the nation should respect and foster it as a necessary preliminary to love of an extensive country or nationality.[8]

Thus, whereas most Englishmen—and some Nigerians—would be instinctively attracted to a Burkean concept of nationalism, Nigerian nationalists seeking the rapid transformation of Nigeria into a modern and united state would incline more to a Jacobin nationalism, which would extinguish all obstructive intermediate groups. Recognition of this difference places a somewhat different light on Sir Hugh Clifford's assertion in 1921 that "real national self-government" must be obtained through "local tribal institutions and the indigenous forms of government, . . . the natural expressions of their [Nigerians'] innate political genius." [9] Once this is noted, it is understandable that, given the highly conservative system of indirect rule and the policy of excluding the educated elements from the government, the Englishman's concept of nationalism was interpreted as a rationalization of protracted imperial rule.

Perhaps the most telling indictment of British policy, in terms of its declared aims, is Awolowo's observation that, though Nigeria was admittedly the artificial creation of the British and was "made up of a large number of small, unintegrated tribal and clannish units . . . ," British policy nevertheless helped to maintain the *status quo*.[10] In this respect, by far the most important single feature of British policy was the effort made to preserve the Muslim North in its pristine Islamic purity by excluding Christian missionaries and limiting Western education, by denying northern leaders representation in the central Nigerian Legislative Council during the period 1923–1947, and by minimizing the contact between the northern peoples and the more sophisticated and nationally-minded southerners temporarily resident in the north. All these aspects of British policy, and others, tended to perpetuate the individuality and separateness of the north.

It has already been pointed out that in 1939 the Southern Provinces were divided into two groups which ultimately became known as the Western and Eastern regions. During World War II, shortages of administrative personnel, and other factors, necessitated a substantial devolution of administrative power to the three regional governments. The Richards Constitution of 1946 brought about not only further administrative devolution but a political and budgetary regionalization as well. The declared purpose of this new quasi-federal system was to "promote the unity of Nigeria," on the assumption that regional political integration was a necessary first step to national political integration. After 1948 every effort was made to encourage "regional thinking." In the balance, it is clear that British policy has been directed toward the development of a federal system based upon regions as the constituent units.[11]

During the interwar period official efforts were made, first in the north and later in the west, to bring the principal traditional leaders together in periodic meetings. When the British conquered the north in 1901, the emirs of the large Hausa states had little contact with each other. As one writer put it, "So widely separated were they by distance and by point of view that they would not unite to face what was then a common danger in their minds— the approach of British sovereignty." [12] In 1930 the first full conference of northern rulers was convened by the lieutenant governor of the Northern Provinces. This ultimately became the Advisory Council, in some respects the precursor of the present Northern House of Chiefs. During the 1930's a similar effort was made to bring the Yoruba chiefs together, and this was ultimately extended to include non-Yoruba rulers such as the Oba of Benin. These efforts suggest that indirect rule did not necessarily mean the preservation of scattered political units having no linkages and developing no common institutions. But, since these chiefs' conferences excluded the educated elements, it is understandable that the nationalists were not attracted to them.

The attitudes of nationalists toward these various issues, particularly toward regionalism and a federal system, reveal interesting similarities. With the exception of the NCNC during the period 1951–1954, all nationalists agreed that some form of territorial grouping was necessary at a level intermediate between the native authorities and the central government. The regionalization features of the Richards Constitution were not opposed, and it will be recalled that during the period 1940–1944 the Ibadan branch of the NYM advocated the regionalization of the NYM and, indeed, organized conferences of the branches representing the Western Provinces. It was Awolowo's intent that the same organizational development take place in the other two regions. In this respect he no doubt felt that political organization had to fit the structure of government. In 1947 Awolowo strongly rejected the idea of a unitary system: "Since the amalgamation all the efforts of the British Government have been devoted to developing the country into a unitary State. . . . This is patently impossible. . . ." [13] He argued that the existing three regions had been established merely to suit administrative convenience, and that a true federal system would require the readjustment of the boundaries so that "each group, however small, is entitled to the same treatment as any other group, however large. . . . Opportunity must be afforded to each to evolve its own peculiar political institution." [14] Provisionally, however, he accepted the regions.

Similarly, Azikiwe and the NCNC were guided by Azikiwe's *Political Blueprint of Nigeria* (1943) in which he envisaged a federal commonwealth of Nigeria made up of eight "protectorates," whose boundaries roughly followed ethnic lines. During the period 1948–1950 leaders of the NCNC in the Legislative Council and in the conferences held in connection with the revision of the Richards Constitution repeatedly demanded a federal system based on ethnic units. In March, 1948, one of the three NCNC members of the Legislative Council introduced a resolution stating that the "House approves of the unity of Nigeria by federation of the various regions which should become autonomous in due course, and that the whole country be developed towards self-government on this federal basis." [15]

At its third annual convention at Kano in August, 1951, however, the NCNC reversed its position on the federal issue, for the following stated reason:

> That in view of recent divisionist tendencies in the country and to accelerate the attainment of our goal for a united Nigeria, a unitary form of government with the acceptance of the principle of constituencies will be better for Nigeria and the Cameroons.[16]

One interpretation of this shift in position is that after 1948 it became increasingly clear (1) that the NCNC would not be able to gain the support of the bulk of the Yoruba or of the Hausa, the tribes that dominated respectively the Western and Northern regions; but (2) that it was likely to secure the support of groups in the Middle Belt of the Northern Region, in the non-Yoruba areas of the Western Region, and in virtually all the Eastern

Region as well as the southern Cameroons. Either a unitary system or a federal system based upon ethnic or linguistic groups promised the NCNC a chance of winning a national majority, whereas regionalism based upon artificial administrative units might well mean anti-NCNC Yoruba control of the Western Region and anti-NCNC (and pro-British) Fulani-Hausa control of the Northern Region. In certain respects this is in fact what happened as a result of the 1951 elections. At the London Constitutional Conference in 1954, however, the NCNC agreed to a federal system based on the existing three regions.[17]

As noted in chapter 2, British policy was directed toward the inculcation of loyalty to and participation in the traditional political systems. Limited efforts were made to integrate traditional groups which either had no recent history of tribal unity or had lost it during intratribal wars immediately before the imposition of British authority (for example, the Conference of Yoruba Chiefs, the Tiv Central Council, the Idoma Central Council, and the Ekiti Confederation). On the other hand, during the 1930's there was a countermovement toward increasing fragmentation.[18] The policy of preserving traditional institutions appeared also in the economic sphere in connection with the system of land tenure. This not only prevented an influx of European settlers, for which Nigerians are most grateful, but also precluded the free movement of Nigerians from an area where there was a land shortage, such as Iboland, to other less populated areas, particularly in the west and the north. Except in urban centers, this meant that existing ethnic groups were virtually frozen in the areas they occupied when the British arrived. In the balance, such a policy tended to perpetuate localism and foster tribalism.

There remains, however, the question of what other policy would not have brought problems of even greater magnitude. The survival of the House of Docemo provided strong evidence of the persistence of people's loyalties to traditional political institutions. If the British had forcibly abolished the traditional form of landownership in order to facilitate the redistribution of peoples, there is no doubt that while social mobility would have been increased, tribal animosities would probably have been greatly exacerbated. It is therefore difficult to evaluate the British record without reference to ultimate objectives. If, on the one hand, a socially and politically integrated Nigerian nation had been the overriding imperative, which it was not, then old forms, customs, and loyalties would have been discouraged, and new symbols and wider political groupings fostered. On the other hand, if the slow transformation of societies and the minimization of social disintegration had been the aims of policy, which they were, then not only should a policy of indirect rule have been followed, but all the other forces and processes at work in the urban centers should have been rigidly circumscribed and controlled.

Before 1945 official circles were clearly disinclined to accelerate the emergence of wider loyalties, to inculcate the idea of a Nigerian "nation," or to fashion Nigerian symbols upon which loyalties and sentiments could be focused. The one significant exception was the Nigerian Legislative Council. Indeed, to a limited extent it has played the same role in Nigerian history that the parliaments of early modern Europe played in the development of national viewpoints. But even here, representation in the Legislative Council was restricted to the southern provinces, and even then the Western Region had a disproportionate share. The upper ranks of the administrative superstructure were largely closed to Nigerians; hence there did not emerge a multitribal corps of qualified Nigerian administrators, skilled in the management of large-scale affairs, who would have had both the urge and the capacity to govern a Nigerian nation. The closest approximation to such a corps was the centrally- and nationally-minded group of clerks and artisans employed by the government, who, as has been shown, were in fact in the vanguard of the Nigeria-wide nationalist movement.

Apart from the governor and the King of England, there was no "national" symbol in the form of a head of state. Needless to say, the national flag was the Union Jack; the national anthem was "God Save the King"; the national army was a British-officered corps of Africans having the unnational title of "West African Frontier Force"; and the national holiday was Empire Day, when British officials throughout Nigeria, in full ceremonial regalia, read a message from their great white father, the King of England, to the schoolchildren, who were dutifully marched to the local parade grounds. Although such symbols were accepted in the early days of British rule, the degree of acceptance diminished in direct ratio to the rise of nationalism.

In the latter part of the nineteenth century pamphlets and booklets written by Nigerians began to appear. Samuel Johnson's monumental *History of the Yorubas* (1897) was perhaps the best known of these early works. Also, most students who had studied abroad began to take an interest in and to appreciate African culture. By the early 1950's the number of tribal histories and works on African culture, both serious and polemical, had vastly increased. It has been a crucial, but frequently neglected, aspect of African nationalist development.

As there is not a Nigerian nation, so there is not a distinctive Nigerian culture. The literary works devoted to cultural subjects, therefore, relate either to Africa or to a tribe, a subtribe, or a town. Among the more important works on African culture are W. E. B. Du Bois, *The World and Africa* (1947); Raymond Michelet, *African Empires and Civilisation* (1945); R. E. G. Armattoe, *The Golden Age of West African Civilization* (1946); J. C. de Graft-Johnson, *African Glory: The Story of Vanished Negro Civilisations* (1954); and certain sections of Nnamdi Azikiwe, *Renascent Africa* (1937). These writings served two purposes: (1) to correct prejudiced European interpretations of Africa's past; and (2) to inculcate racial pride and self-respect, or what Nnamdi Azikiwe has called "mental emancipation" from a servile colonial mentality.[19] Literature of this type is addressed to the educated African and is most directly related to political nationalism.

At another level are tribal and national histories of major ethnic groups. Among such works written in English are the following: [20]

Ajayi Kolawole Ajisafe, *The Laws and Customs of the Yoruba People* (1946)
G. I. Amangala, *Short History of Ijaw* (1939)
Jacob U. Egharevba, *A Short History of Benin* (1953)
Dixon Ogaranya Ewo, *History and Customs of Egbaland* (1952)
Adebesin Folarin, *The Laws and Customs of Egbaland* (1939)
Sa'id Hajji, *History of Sokoto* (1949)

Sarkin Ruwa Hassan, *A Chronicle of Abuja* (1952)
Akwaelumo Ike, *Great Men of Ibo Land* (1952)
Jonathan Olumide Lucas, *The Religion of the Yorubas* (1948)
Frederick Yamu Numa, *Pride of Urhobo Nation* (1950)
G. A. Obano, *Path to National Unity in Benin* (1950)
Peter I. Omo-Ananigie, *Brief History of Etsakor* (1946)
C. O. Omoneukanrin, *Itsekiri Law and Custom* (1942)

In addition, there are many pamphlets and books on similar subjects in the vernacular languages.

This ever-growing body of literature dealing with local history, famous African leaders, proverbs and traditional institutions, and a variety of other topics, clearly reflects a strong respect for and interest in the African past and in the distinctive institutions, forms of aesthetic expression, and customs of the diverse peoples who make up modern Nigeria. It is this cultural strand in African literature which brings into serious question the usual clichés about the "detribalized" and "westernized" African.

It is difficult to establish the political significance of these forms of expression. One reasonable hypothesis might be that such works, particularly the historical ones, tend to revive or exacerbate old tensions between groups, or create new ones—in short, that they foster tribalism or subgroup nationalism which militates against the development of a wider Nigerian nationalism. A case in point is a history written by an Efik historian who sought to prove, among other things, that the Ibibio were once the slaves of the Efik. Obviously such literary activity would not facilitate Efik-Ibibio coöperation in the larger political nationality of Nigeria. On the other hand, most nationalists recognize and appreciate the diversity of Nigerian cultures and, except for the centralizing Kemalistic Jacobins, share Nnamdi Azikiwe's view that the "various communities or nationalities inhabiting this country have great traditions, and a rich heritage of cultures which, if pooled together, can make Nigeria great and enable her to take her rightful place among the family of nations." [21] Probably in itself such literature has not had a divisive political influence, but it might well be used by tribally-oriented political movements which have other bases for their separatist urges.

In their admirable study of the geography of Nigeria, K. M. Buchanan and J. C. Pugh have emphasized the dual make-up of the three regions of Nigeria (see map 12): "Not one of the existing Regions approaches the ideal of an ethnic unit; rather does each present a dual personality, consisting in each case of a 're-gional nucleus' occupied more or less compactly by a dominant group—Yoruba in the West, Ibo in the East, Hausa-Fulani in the North—with a peripheral zone occupied by minority groups." [22]

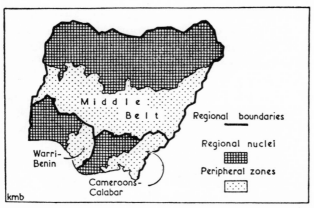

Map 12. The dual make-up of the three regions (from K. M. Buchanan and J. C. Pugh, *Land and People in Nigeria*)

Moreover, in each region the dominant group is characterized by a more advanced degree of economic development. The unique clustering of cultural groups on a dominant-minority basis within the regions, and the uneven character of the economic development of those groups, as well as the regions themselves, are significant elements in the background of intergroup and interregional political tensions in modern Nigeria.

In the historical introduction it has been shown that Nigeria was not created as a complete whole, but was rather a composite political unit which emerged in 1914 as a result of the final political merger of areas acquired from three main centers of British expansion—the Colony of Lagos, the Oil Rivers Protectorate at Calabar, and the Royal Niger Company at Lokoja. As a result

329

of this composite political origin, westernizing influences (missionaries, traders, and schools) impinged unevenly upon the peoples of Nigeria, as to both time and space. Lagos was the funnel through which such influences spread into western Nigeria, beginning in 1860; the trading depots at the mouths and along the banks of the Niger and Cross rivers were the focal points for the penetration of eastern Nigeria several decades later. As a result of the protective policies of Sir George Goldie, Lord Lugard, and their successors, such influences had very little impact upon the Muslim North.

Partly as a result of these temporal and spatial differences in Western penetration, the areas concerned have developed unevenly in education, communications, sanitation facilities, hospitals, public works, housing, and other aspects of modern civilization. This unevenness has been compounded by differences in the capacity and desire for, or the resistance to, the forces making for change. For example, the Hausa and the Birom, for very different reasons, have been slow in accepting Western forms, whereas the Ibo have been extremely adaptable to new ideas, and have demonstrated a remarkable capacity for self-transformation. The net result is that, as Nigeria entered upon its national era, politically conscious leaders became acutely aware of the relative position of their groups and regions on the scale of modernity.

This awareness unleashed competitive drives on the part of the groups and regions that were low on the scale to overtake those above them; the latter, challenged by the threatened loss of their early advantage, have responded with renewed efforts to retain their lead. The same passionate quest for modernity and equality which formed so crucial an ingredient in the motivation of Nigerian nationalists was also operative among the leaders of newly awakened groups inside Nigeria. Thus, unevenness in development sharpened the awareness of group and regional differentiation which in turn intensified intergroup and interregional competition and tensions. The decisively important feature of this phenomenon, however, was that in most instances the appeal for united action for self-improvement was made to the kinship, tribal group, or nationality, and, to a limited extent, the region.

From a political standpoint the three most important manifestations of tribal or regional tension arising from uneven development were (1) the struggle between Yorubas and non-Yorubas (mainly Ibos) in the southern provinces; (2) the rivalry between the peoples of the southern provinces and the Muslim peoples of the north, isolated as they were in their northern fortress by an official policy of controlled acculturation; and (3) the tensions between the dominant group within each region (Fulani-Hausa, Yoruba, and Ibo) and the regional minorities. The early advantages of the Yoruba peoples in regard to educational and professional attainments have been noted. Until the mid-1930's the overwhelming majority of higher positions in the African civil service and in business firms were held by Yorubas. Until the NCNC emerged, Yorubas had had a near monopoly over modern political activity, centered as it was in Lagos, a predominantly Yoruba city. As a result of these initial differences and of other factors to be analyzed later, the Ibo and Ibibio strove to assert themselves. This was the setting for Yoruba-Ibo competition and disharmony.

The tensions between north and south, however, were far deeper and less easily dissipated. In the period 1920–1950, the Ibo, by great individual and group effort, had been able to eliminate the gap between themselves and the Yoruba—at least insofar as education was concerned—but it was not until 1948 and after that the northern peoples were shocked into a terrifying awareness of the great divide that separated them from the south; indeed, so wide was the gap that it was patently impossible for them to catch up. Needless to say, when northern leaders contemplated the rapidity of political advance and saw that the trend of events was leading inexorably to a self-governing Nigeria at a much earlier date than any of them had previously contemplated, north-south tensions were greatly exacerbated. It is against this background that the post-1948 drift to regional separatism must be examined. These developments will be discussed in the two succeeding chapters. The issue of regional minorities, which arose later, will be discussed in chapter 18.

CHAPTER 16

The Ibo and Yoruba Strands in Nigerian Nationalism

THE IBO AWAKENING

Iboland is one of the most densely populated rural areas in the world. In some places the density is more than 1,000 persons to the square mile. Moreover, the soil is comparatively poor. As a result, in the past the Ibo expanded territorially and exported to other areas large numbers of seasonal laborers and even semi-permanent residents. In fact, the Ibo were expanding territorially in many directions at the time of the British intrusion. Since then this outward thrust has continued and has been the source of anti-Ibo feeling among the tribes bordering Iboland (for example, the Igala, the Idoma, the Tiv, and even the Ibibio). The Nigerian historian Dike argues that "perhaps the most important factor conditioning Ibo history in the nineteenth century and in our own time is land hunger. . . . The Ibos pressing against limited land resources had, of necessity, to seek other avenues of livelihood outside the tribal boundaries." [1] British policy has been, in effect, one of containment, mainly by supporting the peripheral tribes through land regulations designed to halt Ibo expansion. But this policy did not prevent Ibos from migrating to other areas, particularly Yorubaland, to work as farm laborers or as servants and unskilled workers.

After British pacification, individual Ibo colonizers steadily drifted to other areas. During the forty-year period 1911–1951, the number of Ibos in Lagos increased from 264 to 26,000. [2] In the Northern Provinces there were less than 3,000 Ibos in 1921, and nearly 12,000 by 1931; by 1951 the number had increased to more than 120,000, excluding settled Ibo minorities along the boundary

332

between the Eastern and Western regions. These figures become more meaningful when it is realized that most of the Ibo immigrants gravitated to the urban centers where wage employment could be obtained. By the end of World War II Ibo clerks, artisans, traders, and laborers constituted a sizable minority group in every urban center of Nigeria and the Cameroons, as indicated in table 21.

As a consequence of the comparative lack of opportunity in their homeland, and other factors to be noted subsequently, the Ibo embraced Western education with great enthusiasm and determination. Christian missions were welcomed, and were encouraged to set up schools in Iboland. Village improvement unions sponsored scholarships, and Ibo students flocked to secondary schools in what is now the Western Region. By the late 1930's the Ibo were more heavily represented than any other tribe or nationality in Yaba Higher College and in most Nigerian secondary schools. Thenceforward the number of Ibos appointed to the African civil service and as clerks in business firms increased at a faster rate than that of any other group. By 1945 the gap between Yorubas and Ibos was virtually closed. Increasing numbers of Ibo barristers and doctors began to arrive from England. By 1952 the number of Ibos (115) enrolled at University College, Ibadan, was nearly equal to the number of Yorubas (118). The influx of Ibos into the towns of the west and the north and their rapid educational development, which made them competitors for jobs and professional positions, were two indicators of their emergence as an active group in Nigerian affairs.

Another factor of indeterminate significance in the Ibo awakening was certain characteristic personality and behavioral traits attributed to the group. Some observers have sought to relate such traits to distinctive patterns of Ibo culture. M. M. Green points out that it is the "go-getter" who is admired, "the man who has wives and children and bestirs himself and makes money. . . . A man who just sits quiet is not respected." [3] Life in some traditional Ibo societies tends to be highly competitive, and great stress is placed upon achieved status. Some of these traits are particularly characteristic of the Aro, a subgroup within Ibo society. Fanning out from Arochuku, their homeland, the Aro, by shrewdness, strong familial bonds, and hard work, acquired substantial in-

333

TABLE 21

ETHNIC COMPOSITION OF POPULATIONS OF SELECTED URBAN CENTERS IN NIGERIA

Region and center	Indigenous group	Northern groups		Western groups		Eastern groups		Total other	Non-Africans Nigerian	Total lation popu-	Per cent digenous noninn-
		Hausa	Nupe	Yoruba	Edo	Ibo	Ibibio-Efik				
Western Region											
Ibadan	Yoruba	5,538	2,177	434,732	3,500	7,335	943	4,541	430	459,196	5.4
Lagos	Yoruba	4,132	444	195,974	5,708	31,887	1,921	18,518	8,823	267,407	26.7
Abeokuta	Yoruba	1,499	75	80,648	300	1,119	83	572	155	84,451	4.0
Ilesha	Yoruba	850	132	69,833	183	398	10	603	20	72,029	2.0
Benin City	Edo	306	19	2,124	43,676	5,411	66	2,024	127	53,753	18.7
Sapele	Mixed	635	78	2,428	3,335	11,974	333	14,681	174	33,638	77.2
Eastern Region											
Onitsha	Ibo	3,339	1,813	2,693	799	66,119	314	1,688	156	76,921	14.0
Enugu	Ibo	1,557	71	1,574	862	54,465	1,331	2,427	477	62,764	13.3
Port Harcourt	Ibo	624	64	1,935	889	45,503	2,022	6,733	1,076	58,846	22.6
Aba	Ibo	259	14	590	162	52,888	1,947	1,695	232	57,787	8.4
Calabar	Efik	384	a	665	219	15,613	15,952	13,386	486	46,705	65.8
Northern Region											
Kano	Hausa	100,834	1,103	5,783	839	11,135	564	8,437	1,478	130,173	22.5
Zaria	Hausa	73,435	1,169	4,346	529	7,385	a	4,885	459	92,208	23.5
Sokoto	Hausa	42,863	1,202	476	a	1,151	a	6,226	68	51,986	17.5
Ilorin	Yoruba	4,561	1,147	34,573	a	342	a	360	11	40,994	15.6
Kaduna	Mixed	24,482	1,707	4,888	571	10,645	a	7,799	543	50,635	51.6
Jos	Birom	14,097	259	5,061	243	8,889	a	2,472	561	31,582	99.1
Minna	Gwari	3,056	1,659	2,182	a	2,988	a	2,819	106	12,810	98.1

a Exact number not known.

Sources: *Population Census of the Western Region of Nigeria, 1952* (Lagos: Government Statistician, 1953–1954); *Population Census of the Northern Region of Nigeria, 1952* (Lagos: Government Statistician, 1952), pp. 26–28; *Population Census of the Eastern Region of Nigeria, 1953* (Lagos: Government Statistician, 1953–1954).

fluence in many Ibo towns where Aro colonies were formed.[4] These facts are, of course, very suggestive, but generalizations about "national character" and culturally determined behavioral traits must be treated with great caution. Competitiveness, materialism, and emphasis upon achieved status are not unique with the Ibo, nor necessarily common to all Ibo. At the very highest level of generalization and comparison, however, they are traits that gave birth to certain national stereotypes and provided a basis for distinguishing the attitudes and behavior of the typical Ibo from those of the typical Yoruba or Hausa. But even here a distinction would have to be made between generations, as second- and third-generation Yoruba and Hausa youths have been less affected by traditional cultural determinants.

One of the most provocative features of the emergence of the Ibo has been their role in political activity and in the nationalist movement. At the outset it should be noted that Ibos overwhelmingly predominated in both the leadership and the mass membership of the NCNC, the Zikist Movement, and the National Church.[5] Postwar radical and militant nationalism, which emphasized the national unity of Nigeria as a transcendent imperative, was largely, but not exclusively, an Ibo endeavor. The important and relevant questions here are: (1) Why did politically conscious Ibos tend to gravitate toward radical and militant nationalism? (2) Why did they incline toward a Pan-Nigerian ideal as the nationalist objective? (3) What was the effect of these orientations upon the development of nationalism among other nationalities?

There are several possible answers to the first question. In the first place, certain aspects of traditional Ibo culture might predispose an Ibo toward nationalist activity. Three such aspects—expansiveness, competitiveness, and emphasis upon acquired status —have been discussed in preceding paragraphs. In addition to these, the traditional pattern of Ibo political organization is of decided significance. As one observer has written:

The fact . . . that they possessed traditionally a form of political organization within which power was widely distributed, and were not encumbered with chiefs or held back by excessive respect for authority, made them naturally inclined, once they

335

turned their attention to national politics, to question the principles on which colonial rule was based.[6]

The Ibo attitude toward authority and Ibo individualism in political affairs were partly the outgrowth of the conciliar and "democratic" character of Ibo political processes. Moreover, the Ibo political system gave great latitude to youth. An enterprising, talented young man who acquired wealth could attain political power, even over his elders.[7] Ibo youths were organized into age-grade associations which not only had disciplinary power over their members but also played important political and judicial roles within the community.[8] In these features, Ibo culture differed rather markedly from both Yoruba and Hausa cultures, which placed a great value on age and ascribed status.

Nnamdi Azikiwe's leadership provides another explanation for the inclination of many Ibos toward a more emphatic nationalism. His special role in the awakening of the Ibo peoples, and the charisma with which he was endowed in their eyes, have already been mentioned. Azikiwe's own nationalist orientation helped to shape the attitudes of his large Ibo following. As we have seen, however, Azikiwe's attitude cannot be dissociated from his American experience; nor can one ignore the fact that a substantial number of postwar Ibo political leaders had had a similar experience. This suggests that politically conscious Ibos were unusually assertive in their nationalism because their leaders, more than the leaders of any other nationality in Nigeria, were strongly influenced by America and, more particularly, by the American color problem.

Finally, of the three major groups in Nigeria, the Ibo had historical and environmental justification for a militant protest against the existing order. In a sense their anti-British nationalism was but an extension of their competitive struggle within Nigeria to overcome their technological underdevelopment. The powerful urge for progress and self-transformation which drove them to assert themselves in the affairs of Nigeria was in effect the same that drove them on to take the lead in early postwar nationalism.

The special predisposition of the Ibo for assertive nationalism is thus partly explainable in terms of certain unique traits of their traditional culture, the influence of Azikiwe and the American

Negro, and their reaction against their status in Nigeria. But what about the second question we have asked? In contrast to most educated Hausas and Yorubas, why, in the immediate postwar period, was the educated Ibo nationalist more attracted to Pan-Nigerian objectives? This question is not meant to suggest that non-Ibo nationalists had a lesser objective, but rather that those from other dominant groups (Hausa and Yoruba) placed greater emphasis upon their own cultural heritage, even though they too believed a Nigerian federation was desirable. The difference is one of emphasis and degree, but it is an important difference. A partial answer to the question is provided by the same factors that inclined the Ibo to a more emphatic nationalism. Azikiwe's own tendency to define nationalism in Pan-Nigerian or Pan-African terms was undoubtedly communicated to his large Ibo following. Azikiwe's mission was to free Africa, to free the African wherever he lived. He affirmed that "an African is an African no matter where he was born, whether at Kibi or at Zungeru . . . Bathurst or Accra, Patagonia . . . or Tuscaloosa . . . Nairobi or Amedica [*sic*]. . . ." [9] It was the force of circumstances and the obvious need to work within a particular political framework which forced Azikiwe to localize his nationalism in the core area of Nigeria and the Cameroons.

A student of Ibo culture has suggested that the scale and form of their traditional political organization made it easier for the Ibo, as distinguished from the Hausa or the Yoruba, to be attracted to Pan-Nigerian or Pan-African ideals. The argument runs as follows:

One of the most striking features of present nationalist agitation is the conspicuous role of leaders and spokesmen originating in the region of Nigeria which was completely uninvolved in any of the former large-scale states. . . . There actually seems to be an inverse relation between the passion for modern [territorial] nationhood and the long-standing indigenous experience of large-scale organization. Thus the Ibos have carried a minimum of excess baggage so to speak, in the way of tribal or quasi-national organization crystallized around symbols which inhibit broader, trans-tribal identification of indefinitely broader scope. [10]

This is certainly a suggestive hypothesis, yet, as Professor Dike has pointed out, "beneath the apparent fragmentation of authority [in Iboland] lay deep fundamental unities not only in the religious and cultural sphere, but also . . . in matters of politics and economics." [11] The crux of the distinction, which would lend some validity to the hypothesis, is not that strong unifying forces were absent in Iboland (Dike has shown that there were many), but that for environmental and historical reasons the Ibo did not develop a highly centralized, monolithic Pan-Ibo state structure, whereas the Hausa, for the same reasons, did develop such a structure. Once this is noted, it is not unreasonable to suggest that differences in the scale and form of traditional political organization might well have contributed toward different perspectives regarding larger-scale modern political systems.

Educated Ibo leaders have been particularly resentful over the cliché that Africans have no culture and no history. It is axiomatic that all societies have a culture (that is, a way of life) as well as a history (even though it be oral history, as in large areas of Africa). What uninformed and ethnocentric critics probably had in mind, however, was a culture and a history which they themselves found attractive either because of its quaintness or because of its functional virtues, or which the advanced and educated members of the group concerned found meaningful and worthy of development. In this sense, many early European observers glorified the cultures, traditions, and histories of the Hausa states, and, to a lesser extent, of the Yoruba kingdoms, to which the Ibo, and other groups similarly placed, were invidiously contrasted.[12]

Another possible explanation for the Ibo gravitation toward a Pan-Nigerian objective lies in cruel economic realities. As described above, a mixture of poor soil and extreme overpopulation made Iboland in particular, and the Eastern Provinces in general, the "depressed areas" of Nigeria. Moreover, the poverty, lack of opportunity, and overcrowding would, in the absence of rapid industrialization or drastic and compulsory resettlement, continue indefinitely. The wide dispersion of educated Ibo clerks, artisans, and traders throughout Nigeria and the Cameroons has resulted not only in increased tension between Ibo colonizers and the non-Ibo populations among whom they live, but it has fostered among the Ibos abroad a consciousness of the potentialities of Nigerian unity and a more universalist frame of mind. The Ibo, as well as the Ibibio, had strong personal economic reasons for wanting Nigeria to be a nation with freedom of movement and enterprise. The existence of this sentiment was well demonstrated by a minority report submitted by representatives from the Eastern Region (six Ibos, four Ibibio-Efiks, one Cameroonian, and one Ijaw) as part of the recommendations of the General Conference on the review of the Nigerian constitution in January, 1950. They protested against the majority recommendation whereby southerners resident in the north would be rendered ineligible for election to the Northern House of Assembly:

It is in our view invidious that any Nigerian could under a Nigerian constitution be deprived of the right of election to the House of Assembly in any region in which he for the time being —or permanently—has his abode merely by reason of the accident of birth or ancestry. . . . In the last analysis the unity of Nigeria is the unity of the individuals in it. The individuals are bound together by political ties of nationality. Identical nationality of any country must surely carry with it identical political rights. . . .[13]

It is significant to note that of the twelve eastern signatories to this report, only three were supporters of Azikiwe and members of the NCNC; indeed, the remaining nine opposed Azikiwe in varying degrees, and some were definitely pro-British. It is equally important to emphasize that the discriminatory provision opposed by the easterners was supported by all representatives from the Northern and Western regions. In short, the Pan-Nigerian ideal was a more emphatic objective of the Ibo and of others from the Eastern Region because the growth and the institutionalization of regional separatism might well have affected the careers and future opportunities of large numbers of easterners resident abroad.

These, then, are some of the historical, cultural, and economic factors that help to explain why the Ibo were predisposed toward an emphatic assertion of nationalism, as well as toward a Pan-Nigerian focus of that nationalism. This predisposition was only part of what can be termed the "Ibo challenge"; other aspects of the challenge were (1) the growth of a Pan-Ibo movement, and (2) the political and journalistic activities of Nnamdi Azikiwe.

The Ibo drive for rapid educational advance began in the early 1930's. Educated Ibos, domiciled in Lagos and other urban centers throughout Nigeria, organized village, town, and clan "improvement" and "progress" unions. The admirable activities of these unions in furthering the progress of rural areas have been discussed elsewhere. In 1935, when Sir Francis Ibiam, the first Ibo doctor, returned from Europe, a few energetic Ibos in Lagos urged the formation of a federation of all the small Ibo village and clan unions organized during the previous decade, to be called the Ibo Union (Lagos). This was the beginning of a Pan-Ibo movement, the main purpose of which was to advance the Ibo peoples, principally in the field of education. As one of the leaders argued in 1933:

> . . . education is the only real agent that will give rebirth to the dying embers of the Ibo national zeal. . . . It will be the means to free the Ibos from the throes of both mental and moral thraldom and I see no better place to start the work of reunion than Lagos.[14]

At the inaugural meeting of the Ibo Union (Lagos), held in June, 1936, the leader of the movement stated:

> Brethren, this is the day and the hour when the Ibos of Nigeria should rally together . . . [and] sink all differences—geographical, lingual, intellectual, moral and religious, and unite under the banner of our great objective—the tribal unity, co-operation and progress of all the Ibos.[15]

Since most non-Yorubas resident in Lagos suffered varying forms of discrimination, particularly in regard to housing, it is not unlikely that this Ibo drive to unity stemmed in part from a real common grievance. In 1943 the general secretary of the Ibo Union (Lagos) launched a campaign to federate all Ibo unions throughout Nigeria. The following year the Ibo Federal Union, a Pan-Ibo organization, was inaugurated with headquarters in Lagos. Its specific objective was to raise money to build and maintain five secondary schools in Iboland. One of the leaders affirmed: "Give a boy a good secondary education and he can rise to any height in the world without being dragged down by the dead weight of inferiority complex." Since that time Ibo leaders have insisted that "there is nothing tribal in the affair," pointing out that the fund would be open to all subscribers and the schools to all tribes. The sincerity of this pledge cannot be questioned, particularly in view of the nondiscriminatory policy of the Ibo secondary school in Kano, an institution which became a center of enlightenment for the children of all Nigerian groups in that education-starved northern city.

During the period 1944–1947 the Ibo Federal Union, under the leadership of the Lagos branch, made great strides toward the realization of an Ibo educational plan. At one Lagos mass meeting Azikiwe donated £100 to the scheme. The meeting ended with the singing of the Ibo "national anthem." [16] A decision was made later to found a national bank of Iboland. [17] During this same period the Ibo Union (Lagos) was one of the most active member organizations supporting the NCNC; and the provincial branches of the Ibo Federal Union often took the initiative in organizing the reception of the NCNC delegation during its famous tour of the country in 1946. It was this apparently close alliance between the Pan-Ibo movement and the NCNC Pan-Nigeria movement which alarmed the leaders of other nationalities, who saw what they suspected to be a growing threat of Ibo domination. In actual fact, the Ibo Federal Union devoted its attention solely to the problems of education and of the material improvement of Iboland. It was not until 1948, after the outbreak of Yoruba-Ibo conflict in Lagos, that Ibo leaders converted the Pan-Ibo federation into a quasi-political organization.

Perhaps the most provocative features of the Ibo entrance into Nigerian politics were the political activities and journalistic enterprise of Nnamdi Azikiwe. Some Yoruba and Hausa leaders resented Azikiwe and his associates because they felt he threatened their positions and challenged their own aspirations for leadership. The Ibo as a group tended to be the victims of this resentment either because Azikiwe was an Ibo or because they were among his principal supporters. A not uncommon sentiment expressed by non-Ibo leaders was that, if Azikiwe had never intruded himself upon the Nigerian political scene, tribal tension and separatism would not have developed in the nationalist movement.

The animosity toward Azikiwe might have been linked to two characteristic themes in Azikiwe's political thought. Azikiwe firmly believed that there could be no compromise on the question of imperialism. In his view imperialism was based upon the ethics of force and could be liquidated only by a radical alteration of the power structure. His belief on the priority of power was cast in these terms:

> After having studied the history of man through the ages, I have come to the conclusion that control of political power is the only key which can open the door of happiness and contentment to man as a political animal. Without political power no country can live a full life.[18]

Azikiwe's critics accused him of being power-mad, of being intolerant of any political competition, of shunning any political movement unless he could dominate it, and of having a consuming passion to be Nigeria's first president. Besides the emphasis upon power, Azikiwe believed that in a renascent Africa the young must displace the old:

> If the New Africa must be realized, then the Old Africa must be destroyed because it is at death-grips with the New Africa. . . . Renascent Africans must be equal to the task and must salvage the débris of Old Africa through the supreme efforts of Youth.[19]

Statements of this sort, and frequent press criticisms of traditional rulers, tended to antagonize some of the Yorubas and chiefs of the west, and some of the emirs in the north.

Guided by these imperatives—the priority of power and the reformation of African society by youth—Azikiwe carried out a frontal attack upon what he called "Uncle Tom Mis-leadership": ". . . these mis-leaders developed a psychosis which had emasculated them so that they had to cringe and to curry for favours, making dolts of themselves and their posterity." [20] As the chiefs, emirs, and educated Yorubas were the Nigerian leaders at the time Azikiwe wrote these lines, it is understandable that they interpreted his remarks as a direct attack upon themselves.

Azikiwe's critics further allege that through his *West African Pilot* he exercised a tyranny based on fear—fear that anyone who dared to oppose or criticize Azikiwe would have his career or reputation shattered by being branded as an "Uncle Tom" or an "imperialist stooge." They also point out that from the beginning Azikiwe's newspapers glorified the achievements of individual

Ibos at home and abroad, but seldom gave publicity to the activities of prominent Yorubas; they claim, on the contrary, that Azikiwe carried on a sustained program of character assassination against them.[21]

In his public statements and in many of his activities, Azikiwe consistently opposed tribalism. As he points out in *Renascent Africa,* his newspaper office in Accra was a "miniature West Africa, . . . a laboratory of intertribal fellowship" in which most of the major West Coast tribes and nationalities were represented.[22] There is, in fact, little evidence to support the charge that Azikiwe deliberately favored Ibos in the employment policy of his newspaper enterprises. He made an effort to present a multitribal front in the NCNC. In his newspapers, and later in the Legislative Council, he consistently denounced tribalism and separatism. Yet, even though he was not a conscious tribalist, his objectives, his methods, and his ambitions, and the predominance of Ibos among his political supporters, provoked strong opposition among the leaders of other groups, particularly the Yoruba.

THE GROWTH OF YORUBA NATIONALISM

Modern associational activity among the Yoruba has a rich history. In 1918 the Egba Society was founded in Lagos to promote the interests of Egbaland. Throughout the interwar period similar associations were formed, first in Lagos, and subsequently in the urban centers of Yorubaland and elsewhere (for example, the Union of Ijebu Youngmen in 1923, the Yoruba Union in 1924, the Egbado Union, the Ekiti National Union, the Ife Union, the Ijaiye National Society, the Offa Descendants' Union, the Ogbomoso Progressive Union, the Owo Progressive Union, and the Oyo Progressive Union). In the late 1930's these associations formed a federation. In 1942 the Yoruba Language Society was organized (*a*) to awaken and foster among the Yoruba people a pride in their mother tongue, (*b*) to encourage the study of Yoruba, (*c*) to raise funds to train eligible Yorubas in scientific studies, (*d*) to encourage the formation of societies and groups of students, and (*e*) to give financial and moral support to the publication of works written in Yoruba.[23] Thus, by the end of World War II there existed a wide network of Yoruba associations which undertook to act collectively for certain purposes. There were also Pan-Yoruba

343

associations devoted to the study and development of Yoruba culture. This associational development paralleled, but was independent of and in no respect competitive with, the similar development among the Ibo people.

In London, in 1945, a small group of Yoruba students founded a Pan-Yoruba cultural organization called the Egbe Omo Oduduwa, which translated means the Society of the Descendants of Oduduwa, who was the mythical founder of the Yoruba peoples.[24] One of the founders of this organization was Obafemi Awolowo, who had endeavored to reorganize and rejuvenate the Nigerian Youth Movement during the period 1941–1944. Until 1948 the Egbe functioned only in London. Meanwhile, certain Yoruba circles in Nigeria had become agitated about the activities of the NCNC and the more general problems of Nigerian political development. Several of the leading Yoruba chiefs, in particular, were apprehensive over the political orientation of Yoruba youth. Prominent Yorubas in Lagos were also concerned over Azikiwe's assumption of a commanding position in the nationalist movement. Upon Awolowo's return to Nigeria in 1948 these elements joined together to found the Egbe Omo Oduduwa as a Yoruba cultural organization in Nigeria. At the time of its founding in 1948 it had the following objectives, among others: [25]

1) *Cultural development:* ". . . to foster the study of the Yoruba language, culture and history."

2) *Educational advancement:* ". . . to plan for the improvement of educational facilities . . . especially by means of Scholarship awards by the Society . . . [for] the pursuit of Secondary and university education by Yoruba boys and girls."

3) *Yoruba nationalism:* ". . . to accelerate the emergence of a virile modernised and efficient Yoruba state with its own individuality within the Federal State of Nigeria . . . [and] to unite the various clans and tribes in Yorubaland and generally create and actively foster the idea of a single nationalism throughout Yorubaland."

4) *Protection of chiefs:* ". . . to recognise and maintain the monarchical and other similar institutions of Yorubaland, to plan for their complete enlightenment and democratisation, to acknowledge the leadership of Yoruba Obas."

5) *Nigerian federation:* ". . . to strive earnestly to co-operate

with existing ethnical and regional associations and such as may exist hereafter, in matters of common interest to all Nigerians, so as thereby to attain to unity in federation."

That one of the Egbe's objectives was inculcation of the "idea of a single nationalism throughout Yorubaland" did not necessarily mean that Yoruba leaders wished to minimize or detract from any movement for Nigerian independence. Yet it might well have had that effect. But the concept of Yoruba nationalism was nothing new; indeed, as has been shown, there were early efforts in that direction. As early as 1908, a member of the Legislative Council spoke in favor of reconstructing the boundaries of Yorubaland so as to have all Yorubas together. During 1911–1912 E. D. Morel, a strong Afrophile, argued repeatedly for an official policy of creating a united Yoruba state: "It is from Oyo that Yoruba nationalism could be revived if the Yorubas could be brought to appreciate all that they have lost from its decay, all that they might gain from its re-birth." [26] The Conference of Yoruba Chiefs, the United Kingdom visit of the Alake of Abeokuta as a representative of the Yoruba obas, the founding of the Yoruba Literary Society in 1942—all these were developments logically preceding the formation of a Pan-Yoruba cultural organization. Moreover, most Yoruba leaders thought in terms of a federal Nigeria in which cultural diversities would be explicitly recognized. The previous quotations from Awolowo's *Path to Nigerian Freedom* make this abundantly clear.

The original founders of the Egbe realized that the inauguration of the organization might be misinterpreted. As one of them subsequently remarked:

When at the end of 1945 a handful of us in London came together to form the Egbe . . . we foresaw that the allegation would be made that the aim of the Egbe was anti-Ibo . . . and decided that not only must we not be anti-Ibo but we must not make it appear that we were anti-Ibo.[27]

Apprehension on this point was the primary motivation for including among the Egbe's objectives the encouragement of similar organizations among other ethnic groups in Nigeria. When advocating such an organization in 1944, the editor of the *Daily Service* remarked: ". . . we anticipate . . . an era of wholesome rivalry among the principal tribes of Nigeria . . . [and] while they must guard against chauvinism and rabid tribalism the great Yoruba people must strive to preserve their individuality." [28]

Despite such efforts to avoid provocation, leading Yorubas did make statements both before and after the organization of the Egbe which were interpreted as tribalistic. Thus, when the Egbe held its inaugural conference at Ile Ife in the early part of June, 1948, Sir Adeyemo Alakija, the president, stated: "This Big To-morrow . . . [for the Yoruba] is the future of our children. . . . How they will hold their own among other tribes of Nigeria. . . . How the Yorubas will not be relegated to the background in the future." [29] As Ibo-Yoruba tension mounted during the summer of 1948, remarks like the following, made by a member of the Egbe, became more common:

> We were bunched together by the British who named us Nigeria. We never knew the Ibos, but since we came to know them we have tried to be friendly and neighbourly. Then came the Arch Devil to sow the seeds of distrust and hatred. . . . We have tolerated enough from a class of Ibos and addle-brained Yorubas who have mortgaged their thinking caps to Azikiwe and his hirelings.[30]

Statements of this type, and intemperate retaliatory remarks made by prominent Ibos, resulted in a press war of unprecedented violence, in which the *West African Pilot* and the *Daily Service* were the principal contestants.

From July to September, 1948, Yoruba-Ibo animosity boarded on the verge of violence. At the height of the tension, radicals on both sides descended upon the local markets and bought up all available machetes. At a mass meeting the Ibos of Lagos decided that all personal attacks on Azikiwe would be considered attacks upon the "Ibo nation," because "if a hen were killed, the chickens would be exposed to danger." [31] Azikiwe's *Pilot* declared:

> Henceforth, the cry must be one of battle against Egbe Omo Oduduwa, its leaders at home and abroad, up hill and down dale in the streets of Nigeria and in the residences of its ad-vocates. . . . It is the enemy of Nigeria; it must be crushed to the earth. . . . There is no going back, until the Fascist Organization of Sir Adeyemo has been dismembered.[32]

346

The most significant outcome of the "cold war" of 1948 was the politicization of the Pan-Ibo (Ibo Federal Union) and Pan-Yoruba (Egbe Omo Oduduwa) nationality federations. In December, 1948, at a Pan-Ibo conference at Aba, the Ibo Federal Union was converted into the Ibo State Union, ostensibly to organize the "Ibo linguistic group into a political unit in accordance with the NCNC Freedom Charter." [33] Nnamdi Azikiwe was elected Ibo state president, and other prominent Ibos—both NCNC and anti-NCNC—joined to form the Provisional Committee. At the first Ibo State Conference in 1949, Azikiwe, doubtless hoping to foster self-respect among the Ibo, made certain statements in his presidential address which his critics ultimately turned against him:

> . . . it would appear that the God of Africa has specially created the Ibo nation to lead the children of Africa from the bondage of the ages. . . . The martial prowess of the Ibo nation at all stages of human history has enabled them not only to conquer others but also to adapt themselves to the role of preserver. . . . The Ibo nation cannot shirk its responsibility. . . .[34]

Such statements, coupled with Azikiwe's position as president of both the Ibo State Union and the Pan-Nigerian NCNC, were interpreted to mean that the NCNC was determined to impose Ibo dominion over Nigeria. These fears were not assuaged by such statements as the following, which appeared in the *West African Pilot:*

> Nigerian nationalists, in this year of destiny, are not only struggling for freedom. They are seeking to impose freedom upon all worshippers of servitude and "pakistan." And relying on the NCNC we shall build the nucleus of a Socialist Commonwealth of Africa.[35]

As previously noted, between 1943 and 1948 Azikiwe had advocated a federal system for Nigeria, with eight protectorates, some of which would roughly coincide with tribal boundaries. At the Kaduna National Assembly of the NCNC, held in 1948 after the inauguration of the Egbe Omo Oduduwa, the NCNC further defined its stand in its Freedom Charter, advocating a federal system based strictly upon tribal units. Thus, its federalistic aims were quite similar to those which the Egbe supported. Indeed, it would seem that the NCNC was nudged into such a position by the action of the Egbe. In any event, as noted above, the Ibo organized the Ibo State Union and other groups followed suit; for example, the Edo National Union, the Ibibio State Union (a new name for the oldest all-tribal federation in Nigeria), and the Warri National Union were organized. Finally, at the NCNC convention held at Kano in September, 1951, the NCNC leaders suddenly decided to abandon federalism and switch to a unitarian position, because of their belief that the government and anti-NCNC Nigerians were using federalism as a cloak for dismembering Nigeria.[36]

In addition to the reasons previously given for this dramatic about-face on the part of the NCNC, two others should be noted: (1) the emergence of a strong and well-organized political party in the Western Region; and (2) the structure and organization of power under the new Macpherson Constitution of 1951. The first point cannot be fully understood without a brief description of the new constitution and the manner in which it evolved. It will be recalled that in 1948 the new governor, Sir John Macpherson, proposed that the hated Richards Constitution be revised as soon as possible and that such revision be carried out in full consultation with the peoples of Nigeria. Throughout 1949, village, provincial, and regional conferences were held, and in January, 1950, a general conference of representatives from all sections of Nigeria assembled to reconcile the regional recommendations. At that conference the majority voted to retain the existing regions as the political units into which Nigeria was to be divided, although the question of the status of Lagos was held over for consideration by a select committee of the Legislative Council. This committee, composed of all unofficials of the old council (including Azikiwe), recommended that Lagos be abolished as a colony and be incorporated into the Western Region. In a well-documented minority report, Azikiwe recorded his dissent (and that of the NCNC) from both regionalization and the inclusion of Lagos in the Western Region. He objected to the tripartite division of the country on the grounds that "it is an artificial creation and must inevitably tend towards Balkanization"; he recommended instead "the division of the country along the main ethnic and/or linguistic groups [i.e., ten] in order to enable each group to exercise local and cultural autonomy." In the course of his argument he stressed the desire of the non-Yoruba peoples of the Western Region to "re-main masters of [their] own destiny in a separate region." His critics allege that the position assumed by Azikiwe and the NCNC during the period 1948–1951 is proof positive that in his quest for power Azikiwe was the foremost tribalist, playing upon tribal sentiment, especially among the non-Yoruba tribes in the Western Region and the Middle Belt tribes in the Northern Region, in order to dissociate them from the Yoruba and the Hausa in a regionalized Nigeria.

On the incorporation of Lagos into the Western Region, which the select committee approved, Azikiwe and three other dissent-ing members argued that "Lagos representation in the Central Legislature should be direct and unfettered—and not through the Western House of Assembly which must, in turn, select the same Lagos Representatives in that House to the Central Legislature." Azikiwe's Yoruba critics argue that he opposed the merger of Lagos with the Western Region because he feared that an anti-Azikiwe, Yoruba-dominated, Western House of Assembly would not only freeze him out of the central House of Representatives (for which it was the electoral college), but would also legislate for Lagos, the main center of his political power and his business enterprises. Actually, in 1952 Azikiwe was excluded from the cen-tral House in this manner.

These constitutional provisions regarding regionalization and the status of Lagos would not have been consequential had it not been for the emergence of a new Western Regional political party, the Action Group. By the beginning of 1950 it had become evident that the new constitution would not only preserve the regions, but would also greatly increase their powers. At that time Awo-lowo called a secret meeting of several of his Yoruba followers, as well as of selected individuals from other groups in the west, such as the Edo, the Ishan, and the Jekri. In March, 1951, this small group, after some months of planning, publicly inaugurated the Action Group.

The new organization received its strongest support from the old Yoruba families and the Yoruba professional class of Lagos, from the growing Yoruba middle class based upon the cocoa trade, from Yoruba chiefs (who were patrons of the Egbe Omo Odu-duwa, of which Awolowo was general secretary), from Yoruba

349

intellectuals opposed to the NCNC on grounds of principle, and from selected leaders of minority groups (the Jekri and the Edo) in the Western Region. Awolowo and the other leaders made special efforts to prevent the organization from being stigmatized as Yoruba-dominated. This was difficult because Yorubas constituted the majority of the population of the Western Region.

The Action Group aimed at one specific objective: the capture of power in the Western Region under the electoral system of the new constitution. It differed from all previous Nigerian political organizations in several respects: (1) its leadership was collegial —and this at Awolowo's insistence; (2) it developed a definite program in a series of policy papers dealing with all aspects of governmental activity (for example, education, agriculture, health, and local government), and pledged reforms if elected; (3) it developed a permanent organizational structure and utilized modern techniques of mass persuasion and electoral campaigning; and (4) it shunned Lagos, partly because of Awolowo's emphatic belief that the capital city was a cesspool of intrigue, petty bickering, and confusion.

The aims of the Action Group included the following: (1) "to encourage and strengthen most sedulously all the ethnical organizations in the Western Region"; and (2) "to explore all possibilities for and to co-operate wholeheartedly with other nationalists in the formation of a Nigeria-wide organization which shall work as a united team towards the realization of immediate self-government for Nigeria." Awolowo consciously sought and largely succeeded in obtaining the coöperation of prominent leaders of some of the non-Yoruba tribes in the Western Region.

The dominant theory of the Action Group leaders was that under the circumstances then prevailing in Nigeria the only certain avenue to power was a regional political party.[37] Accordingly, one of the main themes in the group's electoral campaign was common opposition to Azikiwe and to the threat of Ibo domination under a unitary scheme. In response, the NCNC felt compelled to use tribalism among the non-Yoruba and quasi-Yoruba tribes of the west as an instrument to undermine the Yoruba-dominated Action Group. Thus, during the three-year period 1948–1951, tribalism and regional nationalism became not only the most legitimate but the most effective means for educated nationalists to secure power.

The victory of the Action Group over the NCNC by a sizable margin in the 1951 elections in the Western Region was the triumph of regional nationalism.

These, then, were the steps in the evolution of subgroup nationalisms from a vague awareness of differentiation to a sentiment employed as a conscious instrument in politics. Certain basic underlying differences in history, culture, temperament, and levels of development and acculturation provided the classical setting for intergroup friction. The net effect of British policy was to aggravate these differences. The decisive determinants, however, were educated Nigerian nationalists, and among this group Azikiwe and Awolowo were the most influential. Azikiwe had a burning passion to liberate Africa, but circumstances limited his field of operation to Nigeria and the British Cameroons. An important ingredient in his zeal was his great desire to elevate his own people—the Ibo—who were behind other major groups in the race toward modernity. Although he publicly eschewed tribalism, most Ibos looked upon him as the leader not only of the Ibo nationality but also of the Nigerian nation of their dreams, and Ibos were in the front ranks in his Pan-Nigerian crusade. These circumstances aroused apprehensions that Azikiwe's crusade was in reality a Pan-Ibo affair. On the other hand, more in the tradition of Burke, Awolowo had always been a Yoruba nationalist first and a Pan-Nigeria nationalist second. From the beginning, therefore, there was a fundamental difference in attitude regarding the ends toward which the nationalist movement should be directed.

The cleavage and tensions produced by this difference were further aggravated by an equally basic difference in attitude regarding the tempo at which nationalists should pursue their common objective of a self-governing Nigeria. The crucial point is that all these differences fell roughly along nationality or regional lines. From our discussion it is clear that in the early postwar period Azikiwe and his Ibo followers tended to be more militant in their nationalist demands and more emphatic in their desire for and expectation of early self-government than were Awolowo and most educated Yorubas, as well as most northerners. Yet there can be no doubt that this very difference compelled the Yorubas to assume a more radical position. In order to compete for leadership with Azikiwe and the NCNC in the 1951 electoral campaign in the

Western Region, the Action Group took an uncompromising stand on the question of self-government. This change in tempo is brought out most vividly by a comparison of the political thought of Awolowo as set forth in his book in 1947, with the views he propagated in his Ibadan daily, the *Nigerian Tribune*, during the period 1950–1952.

There can be little doubt that the implementation of the Constitution of 1951 accelerated the drift toward subgroup nationalism and tribalism. Educated Nigerians who aspired to fill the new positions of power and status opened up to Nigerians by that constitution realized that their most secure base of support would be the people of their own groups. The indirect electoral system strengthened this realization. They also recognized that the disagreement among themselves regarding nationalist objectives, and the tempo with which those objectives were to be pursued, would be fairly well settled by the outcome of the constitutional elections. In the struggle that ensued, tribalism was the dominant note; but when appealing to the people for support, the competing parties strove to outdo each other in the use of nationalist slogans.

In our discussion thus far, the Northern Region, which includes more than half of both the land area and the population of Nigeria, has been largely ignored. In the main, before 1951 nationalism was a phenomenon of the two southern regions. Either through ignorance, or on the bland assumption that the so-called backward north could be manipulated at will, many southern nationalists felt that once they achieved self-government and freed their brothers in the north from the autocratic emirs, all Nigerians would unite spontaneously in a natural brotherhood. Very few southerners seriously considered the possibility that the Northern Region, once awakened, would seek its own separate destiny, or even impose its own conception of political development on the rest of the country. Thus, in pushing toward their own nationalist objectives in the postwar period, most southerners tended to take the north for granted. The northern awakening is the subject of the next chapter in this study.

CHAPTER 17
The Northern Awakening

Throughout this study the separate development of the Northern Region has been repeatedly emphasized. With certain exceptions previously noted the peoples of the north missed the unsettling influences of relatively uncontrolled missionary activity, and of Western education divorced from the values and sanctions of traditional society. Moreover, the shift to the production of cash crops for export occurred much later in the north than in the southern areas.[1] The highly stratified authoritarian political structure of the Hausa states was buttressed by their rulers' use of certain interpretations of Islam designed to inculcate habits and attitudes of subordination. These authoritarian systems were further strengthened by the thoroughgoing application of indirect rule.[2] Largely because of the success of this policy, there were few overt manifestations of modern nationalist activity or sentiment among the peoples of the Northern Region before the late 1940's.[3] Until then such overt activity as did take place was the exclusive preoccupation of southerners temporarily domiciled in the sabon garis of northern urban centers.

Both the Nigerian Youth Movement (1938–1941) and the National Council of Nigeria and the Cameroons (1945———) established branches in the urban centers of the north, but, with certain exceptions to be noted subsequently, membership was confined to southerners.[4] In this chapter we are not concerned with the nationalism of southerners in the north, although they were influential in sparking northern nationalism, but rather with the development of nationalist sentiment and activity among the northern peoples themselves. The distinction between sentiment and

353

activity is crucial, and we shall note their relationship when relevant.

A second initial point requiring emphasis is that the Northern Region is not a cultural or a historical unit. Indeed, from a tribal standpoint, the north is far more heterogeneous than the south. The integrative bonds of Islam and the Fulani Empire, however, have given a large part of the north a certain feeling of identity. For purposes of analysis, the Northern Region can be divided into three areas: (1) the predominantly Muslim areas (hereafter referred to as the "Muslim North"), inhabited mainly by the Kanuri, Fulani, and Hausa peoples; (2) those areas of the Middle Belt inhabited by peoples who were subjects in the Fulani Empire and who have been, or are being, assimilated to the culture of the Muslim North; and (3) those areas of the non-Muslim Middle Belt which escaped the Fulani conquest, have been to some extent influenced by Christian missionaries and Western education, and are only partially integrated into the dominant northern culture.

For the purposes of this study there are four important classes in the Muslim North:

1) The traditional ruling class (*Filanin gida*—"House Fulani") which constitutes the political elite in all but two or three of the northern emirates and includes all officials in the traditional political structures, ranging from emir to district head, and, in some instances, even to village head. Entrance into this class is mainly hereditary within titled families, but commoners, including slaves, can also achieve titles.

2) The Western-educated class (*ma'aikata*) of clerks, teachers of secular subjects, and skilled artisans, which constitutes the "crisis stratum" of the Muslim North.

3) The merchant class.

4) The peasant masses (*talakawa*), who constitute the overwhelming bulk of the population and were, until the early 1950's, politically inert and fully accommodated to the overlordship of the Fulanini gida.

SPECIAL FACTORS IN THE NORTHERN SITUATION

Against this background, the first and most pressing question that emerges is: What are the reasons for the delayed nationalist awakening in the north? Islam, linked with an authoritarian political structure, is the first and most obvious answer. The Filanin gida, supported as they were by British power, were avowedly anti-nationalist and opposed to social and political reform. Moreover, as Smith has observed, the "Hausa regard obedience to their superiors and loyalty to their chief as one of the doctrines of Islam—*'addinimmu addinin biyayya ne'* ('our religion is a religion of obedience')." Thus, he adds, "in the attitudes it inculcates towards both external groups and internal stratification, Islam acts as another force giving definition and stability to the [northern] social system." [5]

Perhaps the most striking feature of the northern situation is that certain groups that elsewhere have taken the lead in nationalist activity have either been absent or silent in the north, at least before the early 1950's. Two groups in particular—the Western-educated class and the merchant class—faced a situation very different from that faced by their counterparts in the south. In regard to the Western-educated class (ma'aikata), several points should be noted. The first is that the carefully planned educational system in the north was closely geared to the requirements of the native administrations. With few exceptions, most youths who received even the rudiments of Western education were absorbed by those administrations. The demand for Western-educated northerners in the native administration system alone, not to mention the government and the firms, has always been far greater than the supply. Thus there has been no large class of unemployed "Standard VI Boys," who played such an important role in the nationalist movement in the south. Moreover, as few educated northerners sought employment in the African civil service (British superstructure) or in commercial firms, most educated northerners did not suffer personally from the abusive behavior and prejudiced attitudes characteristic of some European officials and firm employees. Few educated northerners were taught, or felt inclined, to ape the white man; hence the psychology of revolt stemming from frustration over the denial of equal social status, which was such a significant factor among educated southerners, did not develop in the north.

Another factor relates to the composition of the Western-educated class. A substantial number of those northerners who were so educated in the interwar period were sons of titled families or of high-ranking officials in the native administrations. This was particularly true at the secondary level of education. Their future careers and status were assured. For the rest there was no dearth of career openings in the native administrations, and strong social and political forces compelled them to accommodate themselves to the *status quo*. Smith has argued that the ma'aikata present a picture of "social insecurity and psychological confusion" and seek "reintegration with the traditional social and political system by exchanging their clerical jobs for some form of political office where possible."[6] The fact that the traditional northern political system provided for a certain measure of vertical mobility, even for commoners, further strengthened the spirit of accommodation and the drive for reintegration.

Another important factor is that, with one exception, no northerners went abroad for higher studies until 1945. Beginning in that year the Nigerian government annually sent four northern teachers to the United Kingdom for study. Early nationalist leadership in the north came principally from this small group of London-educated northerners. The present prime minister of the Federation of Nigeria, Sir Abubakar Tafawa Balewa, was a member of this group. Mallam Aminu Kano, president of the Northern Elements' Progressive Union (NEPU), was another member. In fact, in 1947 he organized in London what later came to be known as the Northern Teachers' Association, the first northern labor union. Most nationalist organizations founded in the north since 1947 trace a lineal descent from this association.

Another factor, frequently overlooked, is that reforms in the northern system of native administration were inaugurated by British officials before northerners became openly critical of the system. In their admirable report on local government in the north, Maddocks and Pott point out that the Residents' Conference of 1945 decided that immediate steps should be taken to bring the native authorities into closer contact with public opinion, and that the best means would be to promote the growth of "vigorous District and Village Councils." They note that whereas "in the past the natural leaders of public opinion were the powerful feudal fief-holders, the military commanders and influential religious teachers," the changes introduced by the Western impact made it necessary that the older councilors have a "leavening of younger and more progressive blood."[7] There is no lack of evidence that behind the scenes the British authorities exerted pressure upon the emirs to delegate some of their powers and to admit the educated elements to their councils. It was a course of action which was at least extremely delicate and at most could have provoked strong reaction. In any event, insofar as it was successful—and by 1950 a great deal had been accomplished—it created openings, at first on a very modest scale, for younger Western-educated Nigerians in the formal structure of government.

Thus the north did not have an uprooted and acutely aggrieved Western-educated class; it also lacked a claimant and nationalist-minded commercial class, partly owing to certain aspects of its traditional social system. Actually, very few of the modern successful merchants are Fulanis. Although wealth carried prestige, it did not confer political status. The net effect of this and other factors was that wealthy merchants gained status and acceptance by presenting large gifts to high political figures. They became accommodationist rather than revolutionary.

Another reason for the delayed northern awakening, which also explains the unusual development of northern nationalism, was the comparative lack of freedom of speech, of association, and of the press in the north. Emirs and chiefs limited the expression of dissent mainly by the threat of victimization. Unlike the loosely organized chiefdoms of the south, the northern emirates were monolithic and totalitarian. A clerk in a native administration in the south could, in off-duty hours, serve as secretary of the local Zikist Movement, but in the north any suggestion of political activity while on or off duty might well have led to dismissal. With the exception of mission schools in the Middle Belt, most northern schools were controlled by the native administrations; hence teachers, who elsewhere became nationalist leaders, were limited in the extent to which they could participate in politics.

THE DEVELOPMENT OF NATIONALISM IN THE NORTH

In 1943 two young northerners living in Bauchi organized the Bauchi General Improvement Union. One of the founders, Mallam Sa'ad Zungur, had been in continuous firsthand contact with nationalist activity in the south as the first northern student to attend Yaba Higher College. During the early postwar period Mallam

357

Sa'ad became Azikiwe's strong man in the north, and was finally elevated to the position of general secretary of the NCNC. The second founder was Mallam Aminu Kano, a Fulani schoolteacher who, as already mentioned, emerged as the leader of the NEPU, the radical nationalist movement. A third member of the Bauchi Union, Mallam Abubakar Tafawa Balewa, onetime headmaster of the Bauchi Middle School, has become one of the leaders of the Northern Peoples' Congress (NPC), the more conservative wing of the northern nationalist movement, and is now the federal prime minister of Nigeria. The Bauchi Union soon became moribund, however, largely because of the opposition of the Emir of Bauchi. Two years later (1945) the Northern Elements' Progressive Association (NEPA) was founded in Kano under the leadership of Mallam H. R. Abdallah, an Igbirra from the Middle Belt. A year later Abdallah also organized the Kano branch of the Zikist Movement, of which organization he later became national president. The NEPA was the northern extension of Azikiwe's nationalist crusade, but it had a short life, owing mainly to the strong opposition of the Kano Native Authority. Like its successor, the NEPU, it suffered from identification with Azikiwe and the NCNC.

When Mallam Aminu Kano returned to Nigeria in 1947, he and a few others from the small European-educated group (Dr. A. E. B. Dikko, Mallam Balewa, and Mallam Yahaya Gusau), began to plan a pannorthern cultural organization. As a result of subsequent discussions, which included some leaders of the Northern Teachers' Association, the Northern Peoples' Congress (Hausa: Jam'iyyar Mutanen Arewa) was formally inaugurated at a conference in Kano in December, 1949. The leaders of the congress, Dikko and Gusau, declared at the conference that the north must and could only be saved by northerners; that the peoples of the north felt "cautious friendship" for the other peoples of Nigeria; and that the organization was not subversive:

> Jam'iyyar does not intend to usurp the authority of our Natural rulers; on the contrary, it is our ardent desire to enhance such authority whenever and wherever possible. We want to help our Natural rulers in the proper discharge of their duties. . . . We want to help them in enlightening the *Talakawa*.[8]

The claims and pretensions of the NPC were exceedingly modest; in fact the congress appeared so harmless and deferential that the

Sultan of Sokoto and the Emirs of Kano and Zaria sent telegrams of congratulation.

Several young northerners, including Aminu Kano, were dissatisfied with the congress, believing that it was overly deferential toward the emirs and the British authorities. They were not convinced that the emirs could be reformed by persuasion. They felt that, to be effective, such an organization must take a positive stand on political reform. Their nationalist activities increased after Azikiwe began to publish his *Daily Comet* with one page written in Hausa. Finally, in August, 1950, a small group of dissidents in Kano broke with the congress and inaugurated the Northern Elements' Progressive Union (Jamiyar Naman Sawaba), which flatly demanded radical political reforms. Because of this secession of its more militant elements, and of other developments to be mentioned later, the congress became moribund. In the middle of the general elections of 1951, however, it was revived and declared a political party by an alliance hastily formed by conservative nationalists and the Filanin gida in order to meet the threat posed by the remarkable victories of the radical NEPU in the Kano elections. The unifying element in the alliance was common opposition to the NEPU, mainly because of its working alliance with the NCNC, the symbol of potential southern domination.

It is clear from this necessarily brief summary of organizational development that nationalism in the Muslim North is a recent phenomenon, and that in its early stages it took two forms: (1) a coalition of Western-educated conservatives with the Filanin gida as a reaction against the threat of southern domination; and (2) a small, highly articulate, radical group of northerners who felt that the real enemy was not future southern domination but the existing autocracy of the northern system. The nationalism of the first group was essentially a defensive reaction to southern Pan-Nigerian nationalism, and took refuge in regional separatism, whereas the nationalism of the second group was a demand for radical reform in the north and for northern participation in a united Nigerian nationalist movement as the best way to achieve such reform. With this background we may analyze the political thought and activities of these groups and then relate to them a third strand, the growth of nationalism in the Middle Belt and other areas.

359

The Northern Peoples' Congress

Southern nationalists have stirred the north out of its lethargy. The awakening has been largely a reaction to southern prodding, and not the result of a spontaneous self-generated northern consciousness. Certainly it did not come from a feeling of common identity with the south. Mutual opposition to the British produced southern unity which, as we have seen, has never been very strong, but common opposition to the advanced and claimant southerners created northern unity, a unity not only among northern ethnic groups but among classes within those groups.

What are the bases for this antisouthern feeling? It is not necessary, nor is there space, to catalogue all the elements that have contributed to such a sentiment. Differences in religion, culture, and temperament, as well as disparities in the level of material development, are the obvious underlying reasons for intergroup tension. The strength of northern hostility, however, points to something beyond these. Perhaps the most serious cause of provocation has been the attitude of the educated southerner vis-à-vis the north. Northern opinion on this score was emphatically expressed as early as 1943 by Mallam Abubakar Imam, long-time editor of *Gaskiya Ta Fi Kwabo* (a Hausa weekly), and onetime general secretary of the Northern Peoples' Congress. He was the only member of the West African press delegation to London in 1943 who refused to associate himself with the memorandum on postwar reforms which Azikiwe submitted to the Secretary of State for the Colonies. At a meeting at WASU House in London he bluntly told the southerners what the average educated northerner thought: "We despise each other; . . . we call each other ignorant; the South is proud of Western knowledge and culture; we are proud of Eastern [culture]. . . . To tell you the plain truth, the common people of the North put more confidence in the white man than in either their black Southern brothers or the educated Northerners. . . ." [9] With great candor Imam listed northern grievances against southerners, pointing out that the southern press ridiculed the Hausa and made disrespectful attacks on the emirs; and that southern clerks in the north discriminated against northerners in government offices, in railroad ticket offices, and in commercial firms.[10] He then attacked the southerners at their most vulnerable point: their tendency to take the north-erners for granted and assume that in a self-governing Nigeria the north would in effect be a backward protectorate governed by southerners. These frank statements followed an even more out-spoken rebuff given WASU by the Sultan of Sokoto a year earlier, when his views on the WASU memorandum on constitutional re-form were solicited: "People who do not habitually reside in a country are in no position to know the customs and outlook of its people—much less make proposals for its government." [11] The sul-tan added that those southerners who desired a united Nigeria should embrace the religion of the Prophet.

During the period 1945–1950 the attitude of most educated northerners toward southern nationalists was perhaps most force-fully expressed by Mallam Abubakar Tafawa Balewa. At the budget session of the Nigerian Legislative Council in March, 1948, Azikiwe introduced a motion condemning the creation of ill will among the peoples of Nigeria and urging a united Nigerian out-look. In the debate on that motion Balewa reaffirmed the northern position:

Many [Nigerians] deceive themselves by thinking that Nigeria is one, . . . particularly some of the press people. . . . This is wrong. I am sorry to say that this presence of unity is artificial and it ends outside this Chamber. . . . The Southern tribes who are now pouring into the North in ever increasing numbers, and are more or less domiciled here do not mix with the Northern people . . . and we in the North look upon them as invaders.[12]

He added that the north was not ready for self-government, but this should be no obstacle to the other regions: ". . . no Region should be denied self-government because the others are not ready for it; . . . as each Region develops to the stage of free self-government . . . by all means let them have it." [13] At the same time he reiterated the fear that under self-government in a united Nigeria the north would furnish only the labor. These sentiments were echoed by other educated northerners and emirs, both inside and outside the Legislative Council, throughout the postwar period, and were also frequently expressed in editorials in *Gaskiya Ta Fi Kwabo*. For example, the editor of that paper

361

stated that if Nigeria were granted self-government, he believed that

> . . . Southerners will take the places of the Europeans in the North. What is there to stop them? They look and see it is thus at the present time. There are Europeans but, undoubtedly, it is the Southerner who has the power in the North. They have control of the railway stations; of the Post Offices; of Government Hospitals; of the canteens; the majority employed in the Kaduna Secretariat and in the Public Works Department are all Southerners; in all the different departments of Government it is the Southerner who has the power. . . .[14]

Another source of antisouthern sentiment has been the British administration in the north. Governor Bourdillon alluded to this in his analysis of the Richards Constitution. He suggested that one of the main reasons for the exclusion of northern representatives from the old Legislative Council (1923–1947) was that northern administrative officers had tended to exaggerate the isolationism of the northern peoples. In order to overcome this sentiment Bourdillon in 1942 personally visited all the important emirs and suggested that they take a different attitude: "We will not have the Southerners interfering in our affairs . . . [but] we ought to have at least an equal say with the Southerners in advising the Governor as to the affairs of the whole country." [15]

Accordingly, during the period of constitutional review (1949–1950), the north emphatically asserted its intention to play a full and equal role in the future government of Nigeria. Northern representatives (emirs and educated northerners) made the following demands, hinting that if they were not granted the north would, in effect, secede from Nigeria: (1) that there be no alteration of the north-south boundary in favor of the south; (2) that regional representation in the central House of Representatives be on a democratic (per capita) basis, and that the north therefore be given a minimum of 50 per cent of the representation in that house; and (3) that central revenue be allocated to the regions on a democratic (per capita) basis. Thus the northerners employed against southern nationalists the democratic ideals the latter had been propagating. After protracted debate it was agreed to leave the determination of the first and third points to the governor and to a special commission, respectively; but in regard to the 50 per cent representation, the north remained adamant and forced the other regions to capitulate. In the meantime, the north demonstrated its determination to enforce its ultimatum by launching a campaign to raise the Northern Self-Development Fund, financially the most successful public collection in Nigerian history.

There can be little doubt that the threat of southern domination, fancied or real, was the major stimulant in the northern awakening. But just as Yoruba nationalism was accompanied by an intensified anti-British nationalism in order to meet the threat of Azikiwe and the NCNC, so the awakening in the north was marked not only by a negative antisouthern sentiment but also by a positive urge to bring about reform. As Mallam Balewa asserted: "We have come to a point when we realize that we must move fast and faster than any Region in the country." [16] It was at this point that the antisouthern coalition began to reveal inner stresses. Moderates would readily join conservatives and traditionalists to protect the north from southern domination, but at the same time they realized that the only way to remove that threat permanently was to institute radical reforms in the north, including a rapid democratization of the native authority system. Balewa revealed this element in the thinking of educated northern nationalists when, in a speech in the Northern House of Assembly in 1950, he strongly criticized the undemocratic political institutions that kept the north backward.

Immediately before the first elections to the new Northern House of Assembly, held in the latter part of 1951, the Northern Peoples' Congress was revived and declared to be a "Progressive Political Party as from October 1st, 1951." Partly because its membership was drawn largely from the ranks of higher officials in the native administrations (emirates), and partly because the indirect system of election permitted the emirs to exercise substantial influence over the electoral colleges, the NPC won a safe majority in the first Northern House of Assembly, and, except for a few emirs and chiefs, all northern representatives in the first Nigerian House of Representatives were members of the NPC.

Again, in the federal elections of December, 1954, the NPC won eighty of the ninety-two northern seats in the reconstituted Nigerian Federal House of Representatives.

As an organization the NPC represents an effort to transfer power progressively into the hands of a conservative coalition of younger educated elements identified with the Filanin gida (for example, the *Sardauna* of Sokoto) and the moderate elements among the ma'aikata. The NPC's declared aims reflect this effort to combine traditionalism with moderate but progressive reform: (1) regional autonomy within a united Nigeria; (2) local government reform within a progressive emirate system; (3) the voice of the people to be heard in all the councils of the north; (4) retention of the traditional system of appointing emirs with a wider representation on the Electoral Committee; (5) drive throughout the north for education while retaining and increasing cultural influences; (6) eventual self-government for Nigeria with dominion status within the British Commonwealth; and (8) one north, one people, irrespective of religion, tribe, or rank.[17] In pursuit of these objectives, the leadership of the NPC was burdened with the task, on the one hand, of resisting the reactionary drag from the emirs who feared the loss of their powers and prestige, and, on the other, of restraining the more radical elements of the ma'aikata from gravitating toward the camp of the Northern Elements' Progressive Union. With the strong support of the British administration, the NPC leadership was able to go a long way toward democratizing the native authority system, although by no means far enough to satisfy radical reformists. In any event, the NPC, as the government of the day, inevitably became the target of opposition movements, primarily of the radical NEPU.

Northern Elements' Progressive Union

As previously noted, in 1950 a small group of northern youths who were dissatisfied with the conservatism of the NPC organized the NEPU. In its Declaration of Principles, issued before the elections of October, 1952, at which time it declared itself to be a political party, the NEPU made a frontal assault upon the emirs and the native authority system, alleging that "the shocking state of social order as at present existing in Northern Nigeria is due to nothing but the Family Compact rule of the so-called Native

Administrations in their present autocratic form." Arguing that "all political parties are but the expression of class interests," and that there was a class struggle between the members of the "vicious circle of Native Administrations" on the one hand, and the ordinary talakawa on the other, the NEPU leaders declared that the talakawa must "organize consciously and politically for the conquest of the powers of Government." [18] By placing itself in militant opposition to the Filanin gida and the accommodationist ma'aikata, and by calling upon the talakawa to emancipate themselves, the NEPU revealed that its objectives were indeed extremely radical, at least for the north.

It is striking that nothing in the NEPU's Declaration of Principles referred to the British presence. This shows that, whereas the conservative wing of the political activists (NPC) was initially stimulated by the fear of southern domination and of domestic levelers, the radical wing (NEPU) was primarily concerned with the reform of northern institutions. Except as they were held responsible by the NEPU for maintaining the Filanin gida in power, the British, instead of being the target of nationalist activity, were in a sense obliged to play the role of neutral referee.

Apart from the talakawa, the primary targets of propaganda and agitation, NEPU leaders have appealed to all dissident groups in the Northern Region. Indeed, Aminu Kano, president-general of the NEPU, declared that his party did not intend to impose its ideas on the people, but "to take each district as it is, find out what grievances the people have, and assist them to remedy them." [19] In particular, the NEPU appealed to the mallamai, and efforts were made under its auspices to organize a network of Koranic schools, as well as a Nigerian Muslim congress, to spearhead a drive for the reform and modernization of Islam in the north. The NEPU also made special efforts to win over the leaders of tribal unions in the Middle Belt (for example, the Birom Progressive Union, the Idoma Union, the Ilorin Youth League, the Tiv Progressive Union), principally by supporting their demands for greater tribal autonomy or for their own region. The main support of the NEPU came from (1) Muslim northerners of the ma'aikata class, such as ex-servicemen, teachers, and native administration workers, particularly those in the last category who had been dismissed for "inefficiency or insubordination" (an omnibus charge allegedly used by the emirs to get rid of any obstreperous individual, whether a genuine rogue or a militant nationalist);[20] (2) northerners from Middle Belt groups, such as the Nupe, the Igbirra, the Birom, the Ilorin Yoruba, and the Yagba Yoruba (the primary organizer and onetime general secretary of the NEPU was a mission-educated Yoruba from Kabba Province who for several years was a clerk for the United Africa Company); (3) northerners resident in urban centers abroad, primarily in the southern regions; and (4) the postwar Hausa youths.

A dominant theme in the NEPU program has been the idea of a united Nigeria, as distinguished from the strong regional separatism of the NPC. From the very beginning the NEPU was an autonomous northern organization, but it was also in active liaison with, and received some assistance from, the NCNC. This alliance proved to be one of the NEPU's greatest handicaps, for it made the organization extremely vulnerable to the charge of being an agent of southern domination. Despite the manifest disadvantages of such an alliance, the NEPU leadership maintained its links with the NCNC. Its main propaganda outlet was Azikiwe's *Comet* in Kano, and his chain of southern newspapers. Again, some of the NEPU's strength came from the Middle Belt, and the ideal of a united Nigeria or of a separate Middle Belt region was strongly supported in that area. Also, it is not unlikely that the leaders of the NEPU firmly believed that only an alliance would enable them to be victorious over the northern emirate system.

NATIONALISM IN THE MIDDLE BELT

In the early part of 1950 the Birom Progressive Union initiated a new organization known as the Middle Zone League (MZL) with the object of achieving a federation of all peoples living in the Middle Belt (Birom, Tiv, Gwari, Ilorin Yoruba, Nupe, Idoma, etc.) of the Northern Region. In July, 1953, a second organization, the Middle Belt Peoples' Party (MBPP), was founded in Jos, largely, it is reported, at the initiative of the national executive of the NCNC. The declared aims of the MBPP, which were almost identical with those of the NEPU and of the NCNC, were to fight for the unity and progress of the people in the Middle Belt, to demand a separate region with a house of assembly and a house of chiefs, to agitate for self-government in or before 1956, and to support Nigerian federation "with a strong Central Government to control all the Regions." In 1955, these two parties merged to form the United Middle Belt Congress (UMBC), but it immediately broke into two factions, one headed by David Lot (founder of the MZL), which allied itself to the NPC, and the other headed by Moses Rwang (one of the founders of the MBPP), which remained allied with the NEPU and the NCNC.

These organizational developments reflected the two initial strands in the political orientation of the Middle Belt—one leaning toward accommodation to and integration with the Muslim North and the other toward the creation of a separate Middle Belt region as a means of undermining the traditional domination of the Filanin gida and the potential domination of the numerically superior Fulani-Hausa. The NPC sought to encourage and establish an alliance with the integrationist wing (that is, the David Lot faction of the UMBC), whereas the NEPU, supported by the NCNC, endeavored to work with the separatist wing. Thus, as the peoples of the Middle Belt entered into their nationalist era and into ever-increasing political involvement, they became the center of a tug of war beween the major Nigerian parties.

Nationalism in the north is clearly a very recent phenomenon.[21] Three main influences have operated to bring it into existence. The first and most obvious is strong support from southern nationalists. The postwar nationalist activities of the southerners domiciled in the north were bound to have a stimulating effect upon potentially nationalistic northerners. Many of the latter were also profoundly influenced by temporary residence in the south, either as students or as traders. A second stimulus has come from the handful of northerners who visited the United Kingdom during the period 1945–1950. Several of these returned with definitely nationalist ideas and intentions. A third stimulus, and perhaps the most powerful of all, has been the rapid postwar constitutional developments within Nigeria. When they were drawn into the mainstream of Nigerian political life, thoughtful northerners of all classes were shocked into an acute awareness of their educational and material backwardness in contrast with other areas, an awareness that was sharpened by their realization that, if the postwar pace of constitutional advance continued, they would, in a self-governing Nigeria, be subordinate to the more sophisticated southerners. This produced a strong drive for unity and reform among northerners who wanted the north to hold its own in a future self-governing Nigeria.

This chapter has covered only the background of the northern awakening and the distinctive features of the birth and early stages of regionalism and nationalism in the north. Subsequent developments in the northern political scene will be surveyed in chapter 18.

CHAPTER 18

The Final Phase and Self-Government

As noted in the Introduction, the beginning of the year 1952 was selected as the terminal point for this study on the background to Nigerian nationalism. That date marked the inauguration of the 1951 Constitution, which Nigerians had helped to write; and the nationalist movement became formally structured in political parties, functioning within an electoral system. The purpose of this final chapter is to provide a brief survey of political developments during the period 1952–1957, as well as an analysis of three special aspects of those developments: the character of the new political elite which emerge from the several elections held in that period; the formal appearance of state and minority movements as Nigeria approached her independence; and the drive to set a date for self-government.

SURVEY OF DEVELOPMENTS, 1952–1957

It was intended that the Richards Constitution of 1946 would last for nine years. Largely because of strong nationalist agitation, however, it was decided to initiate a general review just three years later, in March, 1949. As previously noted, during 1949 conferences were held throughout the country at divisional, provincial, and regional levels, culminating in the Ibadan General Conference of January, 1950. Although that conference recommended that the "constitution should be reviewed as seems necessary from time to time within a period of five years," [1] the Secretary of State for the Colonies decided not to set any time limit for its operation:

I do not myself think it wise to fix definite timetables for constitutional advance, whether these take the form of laying down that a particular change will be made after a given period of years or of stating that no review will take place until a given period has elapsed. Constitutional advance must in my opinion depend on the political development of the country concerned. . . . I would nevertheless urge that, when the new constitutional arrangements have been introduced, they should be allowed to operate for a reasonable period before further changes are considered.[2]

Thus, when the so-called "Macpherson Constitution" was inaugurated under the Nigeria (Constitution) Order in Council of June 29, 1951, its life was not absolutely certain. Just two years later, however, on July 30, 1953, Nigerian political leaders met with representatives of the British government in London to discuss "the defects in the present constitution," "the changes required to remedy these defects," "what steps should be taken to put these changes into effect," and "the question of self-government in 1956." [3]

After hardly more than one brief year of operation (1952), the Macpherson Constitution proved unworkable, not only because of its manifest deficiencies and structural anomalies, but also because important political elements became increasingly determined that it should be immediately and drastically revised. Between June, 1951, when the constitution came into operation, and the end of the year, the British administration and the Nigerian peoples were preoccupied with the elections for representatives to the three regional houses of assembly. The year 1952 was one of comparative amity and calm, during most of which leaders endeavored to adjust to their new roles, to avoid open interparty strife, and to give, or to create the impression they were giving, the constitution a "fair trial." Toward the end of that year, however, there was increasing evidence of stress and dissatisfaction. Leaders became more and more involved in political maneuvering in an effort to retain or acquire a monopoly over nationalist symbols. As the year 1953 opened, the tempo and intensity of political agitation sharply increased, leading to a succession of dramatic events which culminated in a constitutional stalemate in the Eastern Region and at the center, and finally in the tragic Kano riots in May. These crucial developments in the first half of 1953 will be examined in more detail at a subsequent point.

Suffice it to note here that they were of such gravity that the British government was finally compelled to convene the famous London Conference of July–August, 1953.

The London Conference of 1953 (including the resumed conference held in Lagos early in 1954) was the most fateful constitutional deliberation in modern Nigerian history. It is noteworthy in terms both of the character of the participants and of the substantive decisions reached. As for the participants, one of them (Dr. K. O. Mbadiwe) subsequently observed—correctly, I believe—that the 1953 conference "marked the first time in our history when Nigerian political parties, acting through their various leaders, decided on the type of constitution under which Nigeria should be ruled." [4] As for the substantive decisions, the following are among the more important: (1) Nigeria would be a truly federal state with limited and specific powers allocated to the federal government and residual powers inhering in the regional governments, rather than, as under the 1951 Constitution, an essentially unitary state with specific powers devolving from the center to the regions; (2) within a greatly increased sphere of power and responsibility each of the regional governments would be controlled by Nigerian ministers having effective authority over the personnel and affairs of their departments, with a Nigerian "premier" as their head; (3) full internal self-government would be granted to those regions desiring it in 1956; and (4) within three years (that is, no later than August 31, 1956) another conference would be held for the purposes of reviewing the 1953–1954 agreements and examining further the question of self-government.[5] A summary of the changes that were made in the 1951 Constitution as a result of the 1953 conference, together with subsequent revisions agreed upon at a 1957 conference, is set forth in table 22.

The 1953–1954 constitutional decisions came into force on October 1, 1954, and for the balance of that year interests and energies were absorbed by the first federal elections to the reconstituted federal House of Representatives. Throughout 1955 Nigeria's leaders were deeply involved in the exercise of the new powers and responsibilities granted to them by the 1954 Constitution. With agreement reached on two fundamental issues—the federal character of the Nigerian political system and the goal of

TABLE 22

PRINCIPAL CHANGES IN THE CONSTITUTION OF NIGERIA, 1951–1958

Subject	Constitution of 1951	Constitution of 1954	Constitutional agreements of 1957
Territorial distribution of powers	Devolution to regional governments of legislative and financial powers on specified range of subjects	Allocation of specified subjects to federal government; specified list of concurrent subjects; residual powers to regional governments	Essentially same as 1954
Central legislature	Unicameral; 148 members (north and south each 50 per cent) elected by and responsible to regional legislatures	Unicameral; 184 members (north and south each 50 per cent) elected separately from and not responsible to regional houses	Bicameral in 1959; House of Representatives of 320 elected directly; Senate of 52 members representing regions and Lagos, plus special and ex officio members
Central executive	18 members (6 ex officio; 4 nominated by each regional house); all ministers equal; initially no direct individual ministerial responsibility	13 members (3 ex officio; 3 from each region and 1 from Cameroons recommended by majority party leaders); individual ministerial responsibility	11 members: prime minister plus any 10 other members drawn from either House or Senate, recommended by him and serving at his discretion
Nigerian heads of government	All ministers equal; no premiers or prime minister	Three regional premiers	Federal prime minister; three regional premiers; premier, Southern Cameroons
British heads of government	Governor of Nigeria; regional lieutenant-governors	Governor-General of Federation; governors of regions	Same as 1954
Public service; judiciary; marketing boards	Unitary public service under control of governor; centrally controlled judiciary and marketing boards	Regional public services; regional judiciaries and marketing boards established alongside similar federal bodies	Same as 1954
Status of Cameroons	Northern Cameroons integral part of Northern Region; Southern Cameroons part of Eastern Region	Northern Cameroons same; Southern Cameroons a quasi-federal territory	Same as 1954, but greater regional autonomy for Southern Cameroons; Cameroonians to decide own status upon Nigerian independence
Status of Lagos	Integral part of Western Region	Excised from Western Region; created federal capital under federal government	Same as 1954
Self-government	Ultimate self-government implied only; timetable unspecified	Full internal self-government in 1956 for regions so requesting; independence for all Nigeria undecided	Eastern and Western regions ask for and secure internal self-government in 1957; Northern Region defers to 1959; leaders propose Nigerian independence April, 1960
Future constitutional review	Unspecified	Review conference to be held before August, 1956	Resumed conference to be held to consider reports of special commissions on minorities and other matters

self-government in 1956, even though the latter applied only to the regions—attention became increasingly diverted to the knotty problems of internal development, to the challenging task of fulfilling nationalist promises and campaign slogans, and to party maneuvering at the local level, as well as to planning for the constitutional conference scheduled for 1956. As Premier Awolowo is reported to have remarked in a speech in early February, 1955: "Less is heard of attacks on 'British Imperialism' in Nigeria today than of intelligent discussion on economic problems . . . now of practical and urgent importance." [6]

In mid-1955 Sir John Macpherson, whose name had become popularly linked with the much-lamented 1951 Constitution, as well as with British intransigence on the issue of scheduled self-government, was succeeded by Sir James Robertson, whose recent service in the Sudan qualified him, in the eyes of many, as an administrator of terminal arrangements (one paper likened him to Lord Mountbatten of India). Indeed, Sir James's arrival in 1955—not unlike Sir John's arrival in 1948—marked the beginning of a new era in Anglo-Nigerian relations. The changed character of those relations was emphasized by the fact that Sir James was sworn in as governor-general by a Nigerian (Acting Chief Justice Olumuyiwa Jibowu), and by his public declaration that "it will be my duty not so much to decide policy directly myself, or through my officials, as to look to my [Nigerian] Ministers, themselves responsible to a freely elected legislature, to formulate and decide major policies." [7]

The most spectacular dramatization of the new era of amity in Anglo-Nigerian political relations, as well as of the widespread existence of pro-British sentiment among Nigerians, was the highly publicized royal tour of Nigeria in early 1956. This event introduced Nigeria to the British people and to the world as a result of its extensive press, newsreel, radio, and television coverage. It also helped in many ways to introduce the peoples of Nigeria to each other, contributing, in the view of some, to a Nigerian sense of unity. Moreover, it provided an occasion on which Nigerian leaders could comment on the noncontentious aspects of the Anglo-Nigerian relationship. Mbadiwe, long a strong NCNC critic of the British presence, remarked that the "bonds between Britain and Nigeria grew stronger each year";

Chief S. L. Akintola, one of the most outspoken nationalists among the leaders of the Action Group, affirmed that Nigeria was "undivided and indivisible" in its welcome and that the Queen's visit signified the "unity of the Commonwealth to which Nigeria hoped to belong"; and Alhaji Abubakar Tafawa Balewa extolled the value of the British connection and felt that the Commonwealth was the "only effective League of Nations." [8] Indeed, by merely substituting the word "Queen" for "Prince of Wales" one could, with few reservations, repeat the observation made by Sir William Geary thirty years before: "There is no unrest in Nigeria—no political assassination—no non-cooperation, no bombs. The . . . [Queen] had a universal welcome of enthusiastic loyalty." [9]

Toward the end of 1955 and during the first half of 1956 party leaders gave increased attention to the positions they would take on outstanding issues at the constitutional review conference finally scheduled for September 19, 1956. At a preparatory meeting convened by the governor-general of the Federation in Lagos in early January, 1956, the leaders agreed that the conference should be held in London, rather than in Nigeria, as originally intended. In the meantime, the Action Group government of the Western Region had taken the initiative in working out detailed proposals for the structure of government and the distribution of powers under regional self-government. These proposals, which assumed that the Western Region would request and receive self-government in 1956, were embodied in a white paper approved by the Western House of Assembly in December, 1955. In subsequent months the positions of the leaders of the other parties on these issues were progressively disclosed in reports of party meetings, public statements, and press comments. By June the major questions requiring negotiation and agreement, and the party positions thereon, were fairly clear. The following month, however, the long-awaited conference was postponed to allow for an official inquiry into allegations of improper conduct on the part of Dr. Nnamdi Azikiwe in connection with the affairs of the African Continental Bank. [10]

The report of the (Foster-Sutton) Commission of Enquiry into those allegations was not published until January 16, 1957. It concluded that Azikiwe's conduct in connection with the affairs of the bank fell short "of the expectations of honest, reasonable,

374

people . . . [unbiased by their political opinions]." [11] In commenting on the report the NCNC government of the Eastern Region stated that the report of the commission fell short "of the expectations of honest, reasonable people uninfluenced by the very nature of their appointment." [12] Popular reaction to the report differed considerably. Azikiwe's supporters felt that his actions were directed solely at breaking Nigeria's foreign banking monopoly, and quoted that portion of the report which stated that his "primary motive was to make available an indigenous bank with the object of liberalising credit for the people of this country." [13] His critics, on the other hand, emphasized the derogatory passages in the report, stating that Azikiwe was "attracted by the financial power his interest in the Bank gave him," and that "the control of the newspapers included in the Zik Group of Companies gave Dr. Azikiwe a degree of political power which we think he was anxious to retain." [14] In any event, the publication of the report meant the end of that particular crisis in Nigeria's affairs, thus making it possible to resume planning for the long-delayed constitutional conference.

Any doubts that the commission's report may have raised regarding Azikiwe's claim to participate in the conference were largely resolved by two actions taken a few days after its publication. The first was the announcement by the NCNC national executive that it had "advised the Premier—and he has accepted—to transfer all his rights and interests in the bank to the Eastern Nigeria Government." [15] The second was Azikiwe's decision to dissolve the Eastern Region House of Assembly and to schedule new elections for March 15, 1957. [16] These elections returned Azikiwe and the NCNC to power with a large majority, thereby renewing, in the eyes of his supporters, his mandate to speak for the Eastern Regional Government and the NCNC in the constitutional discussions held in London between May 23 and June 26, 1957. [17]

One observer at the 1957 conference aptly remarked that "this is a far less exciting Conference than the one in 1953. Not only was the agenda fairly obvious in advance, but the Premiers' spadework limited the area of possible disagreement." [18] There are other reasons for the relative absence of drama and crisis. One is the remarkable spirit of unity and good will which pervaded the conference deliberations. Another is that much of the conference time was devoted to the detailed discussion of constitutional arrangements relating to self-government for the Eastern and Western regions in 1957, and for the Northern Region in 1959, as well as to specific provisions concerning the structure of the federal government and the division of functions between the federal and regional governments.[19] Finally, decisions on several critical issues were avoided or postponed. Although Nigerian leaders had agreed upon a date for independence of the Federation (April 2, 1960), the Secretary of State for the Colonies argued that he could not at that time commit the British government. Again, no decision was taken on such troublesome issues as minorities, the demands for new states, the allocation of revenue, and fundamental rights. These problems were referred to special commissions and similar bodies, whose reports were to be considered by a resumed conference. Thus, the 1957 conference was one of solid achievement as regards the details of the evolving political structure, but also one of postponement of some of the more provocative political issues.[20]

The 1957 conference made possible two momentous developments which occurred in rapid succession after its adjournment. The first was the formal attainment of self-government by the Eastern and Western regions on August 8; the second was the creation, a few weeks later, of a "national government" under federal Prime Minister Alhaji Abubakar Tafawa Balewa. These developments were a substantial advance toward the two goals most desired by Nigerian nationalists—self-government and national unity. To one unfamiliar with Nigerian constitutional history, the achievement of "regional self-government" in these days of "national independence" is not a particularly impressive event —indeed, it suggests little more than the progress connoted by "provincial autonomy" or "municipal self-government" in other political systems. In view, however, of the important and extensive powers held by Nigeria's regional governments under the federal constitution, as well as of the size and population of the regions, it was a historic occasion. Even Premier Azikiwe, who lamented the failure to achieve self-government for all Nigeria, called it a "major achievement" marking "the end of the beginning of the struggle for freedom from political tutelage. . . ."[21] Premier Awolowo observed that the "burden of administering this Region and providing for the general well-being of its people now devolves entirely on the shoulders of the leaders of our Party. We are now free, within our clearly prescribed jurisdiction, to do just what we like, without let or hindrance from any quarter." But, he cautioned, "whilst we rejoice . . . we must realize that this event carries with it very grave responsibilities."[22] This awareness of the magnitude and reality of their new responsibilities, and the completeness of their freedom to handle them as they saw fit, permitted Nigerian leaders—if, indeed, it did not compel them—at last to shift from the role of political agitators to that of responsible statesmen. There remained, of course, the final hurdle—Nigerian independence in 1960.

Between 1952 and 1957 one of the major shortcomings of the Nigerian constitution, both in theory and in actual operation, was the weakness of the central Council of Ministers. This failure at the center unquestionably facilitated the drift to regionalism. Had there been a truly national party, commanding majority support in all three regions, the story would have been quite different. But parties, as well as membership in the central House of Representatives and Council of Ministers, had a regional basis. It was impossible under these circumstances to secure a politically homogeneous council. Even had that been possible, however, there was no provision for a Nigerian head of the council. Thus, when it was agreed at the 1957 conference that the office of federal prime minister would be created, and that the holder of that office could nominate his own cabinet, and subsequently that Alhaji Abubakar Tafawa Balewa would fill that office, fresh hope was aroused regarding the possibility of establishing a genuinely national government for all Nigeria.

In assuming office as Nigeria's first prime minister, Alhaji Balewa immediately undertook to form a "national" government representative of all major parties. This involved persuading the Action Group leaders, excluded from the previous council, to join the new government, as well as obtaining the consent of NCNC leaders, then in a majority on the council, to accept them.[23] In a letter to Chief Rotimi Williams, Prime Minister Balewa invited the

377

Action Group to "come into the Council and share with us in carrying the burden of piloting Nigeria to independence." He continued:

> I have given this matter of a National Government very careful thought and I now feel confident that if Nigeria is to achieve independence on April 2, 1960, it is essential that the three major political parties should work together in close co-operation on all matters of policy and planning.[24]

The Action Group accepted the invitation, and an all-party government was formed which reflects fairly accurately the existing party strengths in the House of Representatives. If this national government at the center can endure until the next federal elections in late 1959, the British government would undoubtedly be more disposed to consider favorably the demand for Nigerian independence on April 2, 1960.

THE CHARACTER OF THE NEW ELITE

During the period 1951–1957 the Nigerian electorate participated in seven elections to the three regional houses of assembly and two elections to the central House of Representatives. Although the elections in 1951 were largely indirect, and a variety of charges have been made about the representativeness of victorious candidates, the results provide insight into the character of the new political elite in Nigeria. The data in table 23 show the age, occupation, and education of members of the first two regional houses elected in each region since the inauguration of the 1951 Constitution, and of members of the House of Representatives elected in 1951 and 1954. In table 24 these same data are shown for the second regional houses by party affiliation.

One of the most striking facts revealed by these data is the youthfulness of the members. There are very few over sixty. The median age of the members of the several bodies varies between the high thirties and low forties. Among the regions, the Eastern Region has elected the most youthful legislators, with the median age between thirty-five and thirty-nine. In terms of education, northern representatives, as would be expected, are not so well educated as those from the south, especially at the university level. It is also noteworthy that northern members of the House of Representatives have a higher educational level than members of the Northern House of Assembly. As to occupations, educators and barristers are heavily represented in the southern membership; educators constitute 30 per cent of the eastern and barristers 25 per cent of the western membership in the 1952 House of Representatives. There are no northern members who are barristers. Rather, there is an extremely heavy representation from the native authorities, ranging from 75 to 95 per cent of the total northern membership. The majority of these members are either central officials or district heads, which emphasizes the extent to which the Filanin gida have been institutionalized in the new western councils.

As to the attributes of members by party affiliation, the NCNC members in the Eastern House are the most youthful. Older members of both parties tend to predominate in the Western House of Assembly. On the score of education, members of the United National Independence party (merger of the UNP and NIP) rank highest and NPC members lowest at the university level. Northern parties have the highest percentage of their members in the primary education category. As to occupation, the NCNC in the Western Region ranks highest in the number of members drawn from the professions (40 per cent), the NPC highest in members from native administration (81 per cent), the Action Group highest in members engaged in private enterprise (32 per cent).

In addition to data shown in the tables, there are other points of interest in the social background and career history of these legislators. More than two-thirds of the southern members started their careers either as employees of Christian missionary societies, usually as teachers in mission schools, or as members of the junior civil service in the government of Nigeria. In sharp contrast, the overwhelming majority of the northern members started their careers in the native administration system, where most of them remain. Between 42 and 50 per cent of the members of the 1952 House of Representatives had either visited or resided in the United Kingdom; and 30 per cent of the northern members had been to Mecca, but none to the United States. Eleven per cent from the Eastern Region had been to the United States, but only 3 per cent from the Western Region.

TABLE 23

SELECTED ATTRIBUTES OF ELECTED NIGERIAN REPRESENTATIVES, 1952–1957

(All figures in percentages [a])

Attribute	Northern Region				Western Region				Eastern Region			
	Regional House of Assembly		House of Representatives		Regional House of Assembly		House of Representatives		Regional House of Assembly		House of Representatives	
	1952	1956	1952	1957	1952	1956	1952	1957	1952	1953	1952	1957
Age:												
20–29	9	12	7	11	8	4	3	3	17	14	22	5
30–39	32	39	35	44	26	39	22	28	47	53	59	46
40–49	46	34	51	40	42	39	53	40	30	26	19	33
50–59	12	15	7	5	21	16	19	20	6	6	0	8
60 and over	1	0	0	0	1	0	3	6	0	1	0	3
Unknown	0	0	0	0	1	2	1	3	1	0	0	5
Occupation:												
Educational	5	7	2	10	29	33	25	20	39	28	45	28
Headmaster or principal	(3)	(5)	(2)	(5)	(24)	(27)	(25)	(17)	(24)	(24)	(30)	(20)
Teacher	(2)	(2)	(0)	(5)	(5)	(6)	(0)	(3)	(15)	(4)	(15)	(8)
Professional	2	1	2	0	21	19	38	23	21	20	22	20
Barrister	(0)	(0)	(0)	(0)	(14)	(11)	(25)	(20)	(9)	(5)	(11)	(15)
Other professional [b]	(2)	(1)	(2)	(0)	(7)	(8)	(13)	(3)	(12)	(15)	(11)	(5)
Private enterprise	3	16	0	5	30	35	22	43	22	30	18	26
Trader or businessman	(2)	(14)	(0)	(5)	(27)	(27)	(19)	(37)	(13)	(26)	(11)	(23)
Farmer	(1)	(2)	(0)	(0)	(3)	(8)	(3)	(6)	(9)	(4)	(7)	(3)
Firm manager [c]	0	0	0	0	9	3	3	6	0	0	0	3
Native authority and local government	89	75	95	63	7	2	9	0	17	18	15	15
Central official	(66)	(43)	(77)	(52)								

District head	(15)	(20)	(12)	(20)[d]								
Clerk or technician	(2)	(6)	(2)	(5)								
Headmaster or prin-cipal or teacher	(3)[d]	(5)[d]	(2)[d]	(3)[d]								
All other	(3)	(1)	(2)	(3)								
Education:												
Koranic	6	10	2	0	0	0	0	0	0	0	0	0
Primary	19	25	7	14	21	8	19	6	9	11	0	5
Post-primary[e]	57	46	63	37	10	20	3	20	31	26	22	31
Secondary	11	15	18	41	38	40	34	37	24	35	30	28
University[f]	4	2	7	8	30	31	44	34	36	28	48	36
Unknown	3	2	3	0	1	1	0	3	0	0	0	0

[a] The data for all the 1952 houses of assembly, the 1952 House of Representatives, and the 1956 Northern House of Assembly are complete; those for the remaining houses ranges from 68 to 96 per cent of the total membership.

[b] Includes medical doctor, pharmacist, journalist, and minister of religion.

[c] Member of managerial staff of a European expatriate firm.

[d] Duplicate entry; included also under educational occupations.

[e] Includes teacher training colleges and middle schools.

[f] Attendance at a university-level institution, including Yaba Higher College and Fourah Bay College.

Sources: Amicus, Who's Who in Nigeria (Lagos: Advent Press, 1949); Who's Who in the Eastern House of Assembly (Lagos: Public Relations Dept., 1952); Who's Who in the Western House of Assembly (Lagos: Public Relations Dept., 1952); Who's Who, Northern Regional Who's Who (Kaduna: Public Relations Dept., 1952); Who's Who, Northern Regional Legislature, 1957 (Kaduna: Government Press, 1957); Who's Who in Nigeria (Lagos: Nigerian Printing and Publishing Co., Ltd., 1957); and personal interviews.

TABLE 24

Selected Attributes of Elected Nigerian Representatives, Regional Houses of Assembly, by Party Affiliation

(All figures in percentages)

Attribute	Northern Region, 1956				Western Region, 1956		Eastern Region, 1953	
	NPC	NEPU and BYM	UMBC	Action Group and allies	Action Group	NCNC	NCNC	NIP and UNP
Age:								
20–29	11	0	34	0	2	10	16	0
30–39	35	56	50	75	41	35	52	55
40–49	37	44	8	0	41	35	26	27
50–59	17	0	8	25	14	20	4	18
60 and over	0	0	0	0	0	0	0	0
Unknown	0	0	0	0	2	0	2	0
Education:								
Koranic	11	11	0	25	0	0	0	0
Primary	27	33	8	0	7	10	13	0
Post-primary [a]	46	45	67	25	21	20	30	0
Secondary	15	0	17	50	45	25	35	36
University [b]	1	0	8	0	27	40	22	64
Unknown	0	11	0	0	0	5	0	0
Occupation:								
Educational								
Headmaster or principal	3	0	34	0	32	15	25	37
Teacher	1	0	17	0	9	0	1	9
Professional								
Barrister	0	0	0	0	5	25	3	18
Other professional [c]	0	0	8	0	4	15	17	0
Private enterprise								
Trader or businessman	11	56	0	50	32	20	31	0
Farmer	0	11	8	0	9	5	1	18
Firm manager [d]	0	0	0	0	0	10	0	0

Native authority and local government

Central official	49	11	25	0	2	0	19	18
District head	24	0	0	0				
Clerk or technician	7	0	8	0				
Headmaster or principal or teacher	(3)[e]	(0)[e]	(25)[e]	(0)[e]				
Other	1	0	0	0				
All other	1	22	0	50	5	10	3	0
Unknown	3	0	0	0	2	0	0	0

[a] Includes teacher training colleges and middle schools.
[b] Attendance at a university-level institution, including Yaba Higher College and Fourah Bay College.
[c] Includes medical doctor, pharmacist, journalist, and minister of religion.
[d] Member of managerial staff of a European expatriate firm.
[e] Duplicate entry; included also under educational occupations.

383

An analysis of the leadership roles played by the members of this new elite in extraparliamentary activities reveals that about 12 per cent of the members from the Eastern and Western regions in the 1957 House of Representatives, and none from the Northern Region, have been officials of trade unions; 55 per cent of the easterners and 32 per cent of the westerners, but only 8 per cent of the northerners, have been officials of or active in tribal and nationality associations. Only a few activists of the Zikist Movement gained entry into the 1957 House of Representatives (3 per cent from the west, but none from either the north or the east). Among the members of that same house, 43 per cent from the east, 23 per cent from the west, and 13 percent from the north were political activists who had held office in nationalist organizations, or were known by their other activities to have been active nationalists. About 40 per cent of the members from the two southern regions were elected as councilors or had otherwise participated in local government bodies.

By contrast with the substantial overlap of membership between the present regional and central houses on the one hand, and present local government bodies on the other, there has been very little carry-over from the pre-1951 regional and central representative institutions. Only two persons from the two southern regions and two from the north were members of the pre-1948 Legislative Council; four from the east, one from the west, and five from the north had been members of the 1948–1951 Legislative Council; and from all regions only ten members had also been members of regional houses of assembly during the period 1948–1951. This illuminates with striking clarity the extent to which those who had played political roles during the period of the Richards Constitution were repudiated or otherwise passed from the political scene. The year 1952 clearly ushered in a new elite.

MINORITIES, SEPARATE STATES, AND NIGERIAN UNITY

In an address in London in July, 1956, Dr. K. O. Mbadiwe stated succinctly the twin goals of Nigerian nationalism: "First, to attain full self-government and independence; secondly to see that all the component parts of Nigeria remain united." [25] The questions of how and with what success Nigerians have pursued these two objectives have been the central focus of this study. In the remaining sections of this chapter we will briefly analyze, first, the emergence of minority and separatist (state) movements, and, second, the development of the idea of setting a firm date for self-government and independence.

Given Nigeria's cultural heterogeneity it can be stated at the outset that no matter how rationally internal political boundaries are drawn, there would still be cultural minorities. This is, of course, a problem common to all multinational or multitribal political systems, on which there is an extensive literature. In earlier chapters we stressed the accidental and arbitrary manner in which many of Nigeria's internal boundaries were established, particularly those of the present three regions. During the early period of British rule, however, there was no minority problem. For this there are two explanations. First, the native authority system was specifically directed toward the development of each tribal or nationality group according to the peculiar institutions and requirements of that group. Thus, in general, one cultural group was not coercively made subordinate to another cultural group, except, of course, in the pagan Middle Belt where British policy legitimized an indigenous imperial system.

Second, there was no minority problem in the early period simply because minority grievances and the recent drive to create new states are the result of, or a reaction to, modern political development. Three aspects of that development are particularly in point: (1) the growth of nationalism among the principal nationalities, as reflected in the Pan-Yoruba Egbe Omo Oduduwa and the Ibo State Union; (2) the approach of self-government; and (3) interparty rivalry. As for the first, the formation of tribal and "state" unions in the postwar period has been discussed in detail in chapter 15. Although the original objective may have been self-improvement or the fostering of respect for traditional culture, tribal and nationality associations in time acquired political importance. Through their leaders they became identified with factions within the nationalist movement, and later with political parties. Thus, the Action Group was considered by some to be the political wing of the Egbe Omo Oduduwa (Chief Awolowo was a founder and leader of both), and the NCNC to be the political arm of the Ibo State Union (Dr. Azikiwe was president of both). When the political parties acquired power in the regions, opposi-

385

tion groups stressed or exaggerated these links, stigmatizing, for example, the Action Group government of the Western Region as Yoruba domination and the NCNC government in the Eastern Region as Ibo domination.

The promotion of cultural nationalism among tribal and nationality groups also led to political minority movements. Ibibio cultural consciousness, strengthened by the activities of the Ibibio State Union, is one of the major factors in the anti-Ibo and anti-NCNC movement to form a separate C-O-R state. A long-time president of the union is now secretary-general of the C-O-R State Movement and a national officer of the anti-NCNC United National Independence party. Yoruba cultural consciousness, fostered by the Egbe Omo Oduduwa, is the main ingredient in the Action Group's demand for the transfer of the Yoruba areas in the Northern Region (Ilorin and Kabba divisions) to the Western Region and in the minority consciousness of that area. And Ibo cultural consciousness, espoused by the Ibo State Union, is one among several factors in the movement for a Mid-West state (see map 13) in the non-Yoruba areas of the Western Region. It is not without significance that the chairman of that movement, who is also a national officer of the NCNC, pioneered the formation of the Ibo State Union.[26] In sum, the interlocking leadership of the principal cultural and political associations has furthered the tribalization of political groups—whether in fact or in the popular image—as well as the politicization of cultural groups, even though the leaders themselves may not have desired this result.

As Nigeria approached self-government leaders of minority groups became more articulate and insistent in their demands either for constitutional safeguards or for separate states of their own. The reason is apparent. Self-government meant that power would pass from British to Nigerian hands, that is, to the hands of those Nigerians able to command a majority in the existing political subdivisions, the regions. As the major regional parties were believed to be effectively controlled by leaders of the numerically dominant cultural groups (that is, the NPC by the Hausa-Fulani, the Action Group by the Yoruba, and the NCNC by the Ibo), it followed—not necessarily, of course, but at least in the eyes of many minority leaders—that self-government would

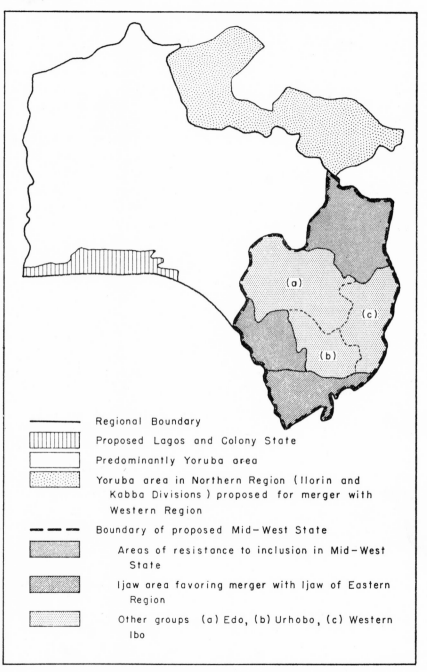

Map 13. Proposed Mid-West State in the Western Region

Legend:

— Regional Boundary

Proposed Lagos and Colony State

Predominantly Yoruba area

Yoruba area in Northern Region (Ilorin and Kabba Divisions) proposed for merger with Western Region

– – – Boundary of proposed Mid–West State

Areas of resistance to inclusion in Mid–West State

Ijaw area favoring merger with Ijaw of Eastern Region

Other groups (a) Edo, (b) Urhobo, (c) Western Ibo

mean permanent Hausa, Yoruba, or Ibo domination. Clearly, therefore, the most effective safeguard for a minority group would be a redrawing of the map and the creation of additional political subdivisions in which their minority status was either extinguished or minimized. Moreover, this would have to be done before self-government and the removal of the British presence.

In examining the third factor, interparty rivalry, we must take into consideration not only the preceding argument, but also the development of political associations discussed in earlier chapters. It should also be noted that in contemplating the ideal constitution for Nigeria both Awolowo and Azikiwe have repeatedly and consistently argued that the cultural factor should be the ultimate and overriding criterion in the territorial organization of Nigeria. In 1947 Awolowo wrote that "our ultimate goal" is "a true federal constitution" whereby "each group, however small, is entitled to the same treatment as any other group, however large. . . . Each group must be autonomous in regard to its internal affairs. Each must have its own Regional House of Assembly." [27] Again, in 1953 he suggested a redivision of the country into nine states (Northern Region—4, Western Region—2, and Eastern Region—3),[28] and on many occasions since he has reaffirmed the desirability of recognizing the ethnic factor. Similarly, in 1943 Azikiwe proposed the regrouping of Nigeria's twenty-five provinces into eight new political units.

The principal difference between Awolowo and Azikiwe on the issue of territorial subdivisions was the former's willingness to accept and work within the existing regions until such time as Nigeria had sufficient revenue and administrators of its own to support and justify a larger number of states (or regions, as the words are used interchangeably). By 1956, however, Awolowo and his party were prepared to recommend

> That in order to promote the success of a federal constitution for Nigeria it is desirable to have more states provided that no Region is split into states unless there is a majority of the people wanting the separate state in the area concerned, that there are sufficient resources in the area to support such a state and that there shall be no fragmentation of existing ethnic units.[29]

Azikiwe, on the other hand, was more outspoken in his condemnation of the regional framework until, in his 1957 Aba speech, he opposed the fragmentation of the Eastern Region. In any event, the important point is that the two southern leaders have been much closer in their ideas on the ultimate territorial framework than has usually been acknowledged. This should be kept in mind in any evaluation of the activities of their respective parties in each other's regional minority areas.

Both the Action Group and the NCNC seek to be genuinely national parties. The NCNC is the older of the two and, until the 1957 elections in the Eastern Region, it was more determined and energetic in its efforts to achieve that goal. In seeking to organize on a national basis, both parties have, for reasons discussed, operated from a political core area (that is, an area in which they are consistently predominant). For the Action Group this has been Yorubaland in the Western Region; for the NCNC it has been Iboland in the Eastern Region. As would be expected, the Action Group has received its greatest support in the non-Ibo areas of the Eastern Region, the NCNC in the non-Yoruba areas of the Western Region.[30] In the 1956 elections to the Northern House of Assembly the Action Group was the only southern party to win any seats, but these were confined, significantly, to the Yoruba area of the Middle Belt. The territorial distribution of party strength in the three regions is shown by the data in tables 25, 26, and 27, which are keyed to maps 13, 14, and 15.

TABLE 25

PARTY STRENGTH IN MINORITY AREAS OF THE WESTERN REGION, 1956

Area	Number of seats in Western House of Assembly		
	Action Group	NCNC	Total
Proposed Mid-West State			
Edo, Urhobo, and Western Ibo areas	0	11	11
Areas of resistance to inclusion in Mid-West State	4	3	7
Western Ijaw area	0	2	2
Total	4	16	20
Remainder of region	44	16	60
Regional total	48	32	80

The NCNC Freedom Charter of 1948 prescribed that the "Commonwealth of Nigeria and the Cameroons . . . shall be organized into States on [a] National and linguistic basis." [31] In the several southern centers where the NCNC had a strong and active branch, "state" unions were formed; or existing tribal or nationality unions, like the Ibo and Ibibio unions, inserted the word "state" in their titles. The movement to establish a Benin-Delta State had its origin in this period. In 1951 Chief Anthony Enahoro, a leader of the Action Group, called a conference in Sapele which again demanded a Benin-Delta State. In 1952 and 1953 this demand was reaffirmed, and finally, in 1955, the Western House of Assembly unanimously passed a resolution supporting the creation of the Benin-Delta State, whose name was later changed to "Mid-West State." In the meantime similar demands for a separate state were made by minority groups in the Middle Belt in the Northern Region, by the Ijaw peoples of the Delta area, and elsewhere.

The decision of the 1953 London Conference to separate the Southern Cameroons from the Eastern Region was undoubtedly taken as a precedent and served to stimulate additional demands. In elections held in 1954, 1956, and 1957 in the southern regions the NCNC and the Action Group competed for votes by promising to support the several state movements at the 1957 conference. In a nationwide broadcast during the election campaign of 1957, Azikiwe stated: "My last argument for persuading the electorate to return the N.C.N.C. candidates to the Eastern House of Assembly is based on our claim that we have re-affirmed our faith in the right of any community to self-determination. . . . The right of the people of former Calabar, Ogoja and Rivers Province to determine their political future is conceded." [32] Thus when the 1957 London Conference met, the delegations from both southern parties were committed to supporting the creation of additional states.

The 1957 conference devoted considerable time to discussion of the problems of regional minorities, specific proposals for the creation of new states, and the desirability of breaking up existing regions. It was finally agreed that the problem was of such complexity that a commission of inquiry should be appointed "to ascertain the facts about the fears of minorities in any part of

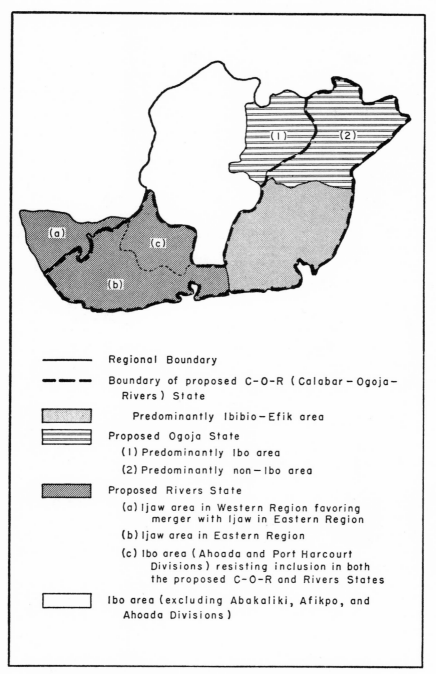

Map 14. Proposed new states in the Eastern Region

TABLE 26

PARTY STRENGTH IN MINORITY AREAS OF EASTERN REGION, 1957

Area	Number of seats in Eastern Regional House of Assembly		
	NCNC	Action Group and UNIP	Total
Proposed C-O-R State			
Ibibio-Efik area (Calabar Province)	7	11	18
Non-Ibo area of Ogoja Province	2	4	6
Rivers Province: { Ijaw area	3	3	6
{ Ibo area	5	0	5
Total	17	18	35
Proposed Ogoja State (Ogoja Province)			
Non-Ibo area	2	4	6
Ibo area	7	0	8 [a]
Total	9	4	14
Proposed Rivers State			
Rivers Province: { Ijaw area	3	3	6
{ Ibo area	5	0	5
Total	8	3	11
Remainder of region (Ibo area)	40	0	41 [a]
Regional total	64	18	84 [a]
Recapitulation			
All Ibo areas	52	0	54 [a]
All non-Ibo areas	12	18	30
Regional total	64	18	84 [a]

[a] Figures include two independents: one from Ibo area, Ogoja Province; one from Ibo area in remainder of region.

Nigeria and to propose means of allaying those fears whether well or ill founded." [33] To emphasize its strong opposition to fragmentation, the British government stated that it would not consider the creation of more than one new state in each region, and that even then it would

> . . . have to take into account the effect of the establishment of any such new States on the existing Regions in the Federation and on the Federation as a whole . . . [and] would also have to be satisfied by the Commission that any such new State would be viable from both the economic and administrative points of view, since it was the view of the United Kingdom Government

that administrative and other practical reasons would inevitably limit most severely the possibility of the further sub-division of Nigeria into States modelled on the present Regional system.[34]

The commission of inquiry into the problem of minorities held hearings throughout Nigeria during the latter part of 1957 and the first part of 1958. It received lengthy memoranda from minority groups, state movements, antistate movements, and individuals having their own schemes for redrawing the political map of Nigeria. The principal proposals for changes are illustrated in maps 13, 14, and 15.

The positions of the major political parties will clearly affect final decisions on the several proposals that have been made. The leaders of the NPC have repeatedly and emphatically rejected any suggestion either to alter the present northern boundaries in order to assuage aggrieved minorities, or to create new states in the north. Their program remains as announced in 1952: "One North, one people, irrespective of religion, rank or tribe." Firm in their resolve to preserve the integrity of the north, the leaders have taken several steps to meet the challenge. First, they have increased the powers of provincial governments in the Northern Region under a policy known as "provincialisation." Second, they have sent two delegations abroad, one to Libya and Pakistan and the other to the Sudan, "to ascertain at first hand how these predominantly Moslem states have adapted their systems of administration . . . to meet the problems raised by the diversity of racial origins and religious beliefs in their territories." [35] Third, and perhaps most important, they have adopted a positive policy of winning Middle Belt leaders to their side. In this respect it is significant that Middle Belt forces are divided on the issue of a separate state, and that some of the more important and capable young leaders from that area hold high posts in the NPC government. The effectiveness of this policy is further illustrated by the fact that the NPC won twenty-eight of the forty-three Middle Belt seats in the 1956 regional elections in the north (see table 27). Finally, the northern leaders have suggested that the Eastern and Western regions be merged in order to end the southern complaint that an undivided north would dominate the south in an independent Nigeria.

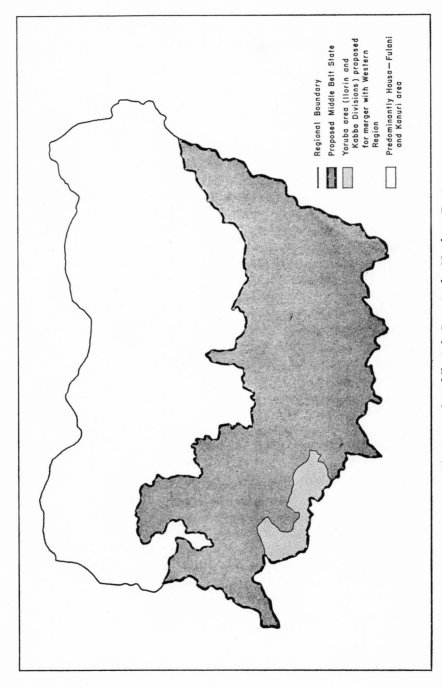

Map 15. Proposed Middle Belt State in the Northern Region

TABLE 27

PARTY STRENGTH IN MINORITY AREAS OF NORTHERN REGION, 1956

Area	Number of seats in Northern House of Assembly				
	NPC	NEPU and BYM	UMBC	Action Group and allies	Total
Proposed Middle Belt State					
Non-Yoruba areas	27	1	10	0	38
Yoruba areas					
Ilorin Division	0	0	0	4	4
Kabba Division	1	0	0	0	1
Total	28	1	10	4	43
Remainder of region	78	8	2	0	88
Regional total	106	9	12	4	131

Although leaders of the NCNC and the Action Group have long been committed to the principle of ethnic self-determination (as well as to specific proposals for new states in the Middle Belt, the Benin-Delta area, and the Calabar-Ogoja-Rivers provinces), nevertheless they have sought to limit the full application of self-determination in the regions they control. Thus the Action Group has consistently supported a Mid-West state, but it would not agree to the inclusion therein of peoples who currently oppose such inclusion (see map 13). Again, Azikiwe has been the foremost proponent of the principle of new states, but he qualified his position in various speeches made in 1957, arguing that the "situation in the Eastern Region is exceptional" and that the "East can no longer stand dismemberment as a sacrifice either for administrative convenience or for national unity." [36] Azikiwe objects particularly to the present leaders of the C-O-R State Movement, his main political opponents in the Eastern Region, because he feels that they base their claim for a separate state primarily on anti-Ibo sentiment.

The appearance of a plethora of minority, separatist, and tribal movements in new states on the threshold of independence has frequently evoked suggestions that self-government would lead to anarchy or civil war, that Africans are incorrigible tribalists incapable of organizing national parties, or that dominant cultural groups are exploiting or oppressing minority groups. Although in concrete instances there may be some basis for certain of these apprehensions, it would seem that such movements are perfectly natural phenomena of terminal colonialism, particularly in British dependencies like Nigeria where freedom for individual and group self-expression is greatest. The minority problem in Nigeria was bound to arise before the departure of the British. The fact that it is being objectively examined by an independent commission of inquiry warrants modest hope that equitable, but rational, decisions will be made on the issue before independence is achieved.

TOWARD A DATE FOR SELF-GOVERNMENT

It is a commonplace that one of the cardinal principles of British colonial policy has been the ultimate attainment of self-government for its overseas dependencies. When burgeoning forces in Africa began to demand application of the principle in the late 1930's, four questions arose. First, was it indeed applicable to Africa? The answer was clearly in the affirmative for so-called "white" Africa (that is, those African territories inhabited by a substantial number of resident Europeans). There was some doubt about its full applicability to so-called "black" Africa (in which category, of course, Nigeria belongs), although ultimate self-government was implicit in the Anglo-Saxon concept of "trusteeship." Second, to whom was self-government to be granted? In white Africa it was, of course, the "kith and kin" overseas, the resident Europeans; in black Africa, if the question was answered at all, it was the "natural rulers." Lord Lugard and Sir Hugh Clifford were quite clear on this point. Third, was the ultimate self-governing unit in black Africa to be the "native authority" or the artificial territory as a new potential national entity? Again, it was to be the "native authority." Finally, when would self-government be granted? Here, for reasons of both common sense and imperial interest, the British government was disinclined to commit itself beyond the promise that self-government would be granted when the peoples concerned were ready for it. But, when is a country ready? The argument, of course, could be terminated only when nationalists were able to mobilize and display sufficient power and national unity to compel a commitment.

396

Unlike white colonial subjects, who had only to force the issue of timing, Nigerian nationalists—and their counterparts in Ghana —were obliged to seek and obtain a commitment on all four of the above questions. Aided by a major transformation in attitudes toward colonialism, and the growth in and display of their own strength, Nigerian nationalists progressively won answers to all but the last of these questions. The principle of self-government was most emphatically applicable to black Africa; the heirs to British power were not the natural rulers, but the educated nationalists; the highest unit of self-government was not the tribe or native authority, but the territory, that artificial creation known as Nigeria. With the attainment of regional self-government in 1957, the final date of complete Nigerian independence remained the only unanswered question.

As noted in chapter 10, the first occasion on which Nigerian nationalists demanded that a definite date be fixed for self-government was the memorandum submitted by the West African Students' Union (London) to the Secretary of State for the Colonies on April 6, 1942. This proposal was also supported at the time by the African Students' Association of the United States and Canada (New York). WASU requested "Internal Self-Government Now [1942], with a definite guarantee of complete self-government within five years after the war [1950]." [37] In 1943 Dr. Nnamdi Azikiwe proposed a period of fifteen years' tutelage, at the end of which time Nigeria would become independent. He envisaged a preparatory stage of ten years, and a final stage during which Nigerianization would be completed, and then full self-government.[38] As Azikiwe's proposal was advanced at the very end of 1943, it meant that the preliminary stage would have been completed by the beginning of 1954, and the second stage by 1959. Although Azikiwe's 1943 proposals were completely ignored at the time, his prophecy of what "progressive dreamers and schemers should bear in mind" has been largely fulfilled.

Between 1943 and 1951 the idea of setting a specific date for Nigerian self-government was not seriously and consistently espoused by any of Nigeria's nationalist leaders or groups. Throughout this period many individual Nigerians, particularly students and intellectuals, advocated immediate or early British withdrawal in principle, but no precise year or target date became a politically relevant symbol. The NCNC Constitution of 1945 stated as one of its objectives the achievement of "internal self-government for Nigeria whereby . . . [Nigerians] . . . shall exercise executive, legislative and judicial powers," [39] but no date was set. The NCNC Freedom Charter of 1948 was a proposal for a constitution for the "Commonwealth of Nigeria and the Cameroons." Adopted by the so-called "Peoples National Assembly" at Kaduna, its preamble cited Article III of the Atlantic Charter and proclaimed that the "Tribes, Nations and Peoples of Nigeria and the Cameroons . . . Now undertake, as of right, to arrogate to themselves the status of an independent self-governing political community." [40] This was not seriously intended to be an immediately operative declaration of independence; rather it was an expression of aspiration, a model for the future.

The first explicit target date advocated by an organized nationalist body was the year 1956. There was no special significance attaching to that year; it simply marked the end of the normal five-year term of the regional houses of assembly whose members were elected in 1951 and took office in 1952. The date was first declared a nationalist goal by the National Rebirth Assembly which met in Lagos on March 27, 1951, for the purpose of recommending changes in the organizational structure and constitution of the NCNC in preparation for the electoral campaign later that summer.[41] At its Owo conference the following month, the Action Group decided that Nigeria must be free "within five years." [42] In the subsequent electoral contest between the NCNC and the Action Group in the Western Region (including Lagos), politicians and their followers became irrevocably committed to, if not prisoners of, the mutual target date their electoral competition had established. Thereafter it would have been political suicide for either party to slacken its drive toward that "year of destiny." Thus interparty rivalry to maintain mastery over nationalist symbols was a major factor in date-fixing and in accelerating the drive for self-government. Such mastery could be achieved only by stressing ever more emphatically and categorically the irrevocability of 1956 as the fateful year of independence. As Chief Anthony Enahoro stated, "1956 is a position from which it is impossible to retreat." [43]

On March 31, 1953, Enahoro moved in the House of Representatives "that this House accepts as a primary political objective the attainment of self-government for Nigeria in 1956." In arguing the desirability of having Nigeria's central parliament set a firm date simply as an objective toward which to work, he stated that

. . . the bare idea of self-government is no longer attractive, is no longer enough. Whether it is expressed as 'self-government in our life-time' or 'self-government in the shortest possible time' or 'self-government as soon as practicable', it has ceased to be a progressive view, because Nigerian nationalism has moved forward from that position. The question in the public mind since the end of the war has been, 'self-government, when? What time, what date?' [44]

To this motion Alhaji Ahmadu, Sardauna of Sokoto and leader of the Northern Peoples' Congress, moved the adoption of an amendment changing the words "in 1956" to "as soon as practicable." The debate on the amendment was bitter and tempestuous, and ended only when the NCNC and Action Group members walked out of the House. Subsequently they formed an alliance to force the issue of self-government in 1956.

After the adjournment of the House of Representatives the northern members were subjected to insults and abuse by Lagos crowds, and during the ensuing weeks they were ridiculed and strongly criticized by the southern press. Upon their return to the north they determined never to be subjected to such indignities again; within a few weeks they announced an eight-point program which, if implemented, would have meant virtual secession of the Northern Region from Nigeria. This action provoked even harsher criticism from the southern press and from Action Group and NCNC leaders. The northern leaders were repeatedly charged with being unrepresentative of their people; they were called "imperialist stooges"; and they were criticized as having "no minds of their own." Leaders of the NCNC and the Action Group then undertook to send delegations to northern cities to campaign for self-government in 1956. One such delegation, led by Chief S. L. Akintola of the Action Group, scheduled a meeting in Kano at the very height of the north-south tension. This led to a chain of events culminating in four days of rioting in the Kano sabon gari which resulted in 277 casualties, including 36 deaths (15 northerners and 21 southerners).[45] Two days later, on May 21, 1953, the Secretary of State for the Colonies announced the convening of the London Conference to revise the Nigerian constitution.

The crisis provoked by the debate in early 1953 on Enahoro's self-government motion and culminating in the Kano riots was but the surface manifestation of deep and unresolved tension in two interrelated areas—northern fear of southern domination in a self-governing Nigeria, and southern dissatisfaction with the 1951 Constitution in particular and frustration over the slow rate of advance toward self-government in general. In previous chapters we have examined in detail the bases for the northern fear: the gross disparities in the level of development in all fields; the heavy concentration of educated southerners at strategic points of control in the administrative, commercial, and transportation sectors of northern society; the condescending and exploitative attitudes and behavior attributed to southerners living and working in the north; and the leveling and disorganizing impact of southern ideologies and patterns of politics on the highly stratified and aristocratic northern social system. Moreover, despite the devolution of certain functions to regional governments, the 1951 Constitution was essentially unitary in character, and there was little evidence in 1953 that a constitution written for a self-governing Nigeria would be any different in this respect. Thus, northern leaders believed that unless there was a drastic alteration of the structure of government and of the division of powers between the regions and the center, creating a truly federal system, self-government in 1956 would mean unquestioned southern predominance in the higher ranks of the central civil service and police. It could, and probably would, also mean eventual southern predominance in the central legislature as a result of the ceaseless efforts of southern parties to detach or to penetrate the Middle Belt and construct alliances with dissident groups there and in the Muslim North.

Southern leaders also had their case against the north. They had most reluctantly accepted the allocation of 50 per cent of the seats in the House of Representatives to the north under the 1951 Constitution. They believed—and subsequent events proved them substantially correct—that because of the northern social system and indirect electoral arrangements, the north would vote as a monolithic bloc and thereby control not only the deliberations of the House of Representatives, but also, because of the presence of six ex officio members, those of the Council of Ministers.[46] They also believed that the northern leaders were the primary obstacle to the early attainment of self-government. As one commentator put it: "To such a man [as Awolowo] it must be infinitely frustrating that Nigerian self-government has to wait on the leaden feet of the North—the North whose rulers he sincerely condemns as despots, whose leading politicians he believes to be British stooges."[47] Moreover, southern leaders were growing weary of recurrent threats of northern secession and withdrawal to the western Sudan.

Southern leaders were also dissatisfied with the actual working of the 1951 Constitution. On several occasions the Action Group leaders felt they were obstructed in carrying out their program. They were particularly annoyed by the decision of the Council of Ministers that ministers should not speak or vote on the Enahoro self-government motion. The effective exclusion of Azikiwe and several other powerful NCNC leaders from any meaningful role in the formal structure of government not only intensified their opposition to the constitution, but caused a complete split in the ranks and leadership of the NCNC, which led in turn to a protracted crisis in the government of the Eastern Region.[48] In May, 1953, the crisis was resolved by the dissolution of the Eastern House and the holding of a new election in which Azikiwe and other leaders previously excluded from office were returned with an overwhelming majority. From the very beginning of the operation of the 1951 Constitution, however, Azikiwe strongly criticized it not only because of what he regarded as its shortcomings, but also because of his disagreement with those elements in the NCNC who were trying to make it work, namely, Eyo Ita and other ministers in the Eastern Region and the three NCNC ministers in the central Council of Ministers.[49]

On the eve of the 1953 conference southern leaders were determined to take an uncompromising stand on the issue of self-government in 1956. Action Group leaders had been fortified in their position by a resolution passed unanimously by the Western House of Chiefs accepting and approving the Enahoro motion on self-government debated earlier in the House of Representatives. The southern position was further strengthened by the united front formed by Awolowo and Azikiwe, who closely collaborated in all negotiations with the governor and the Secretary of State for the Colonies on the terms of reference for the conference. Their letter to the governor finally accepting the invitation to the conference reflected their determination and self-confidence:

> This . . . is the last constitution conferring dependent status which we are willing to operate. The Constitution will come to an end . . . in 1956 or by earlier breakdown or abrogation. If any of these . . . events occur we demand that Britain, in all friendly spirit, should accord us Dominion status within the British Commonwealth of Nations. If she refuses to do so we would unhesitatingly declare our independence and proceed to assert it whatever the consequences might be.[50]

The north, of course, was equally determined not to accept self-government in 1956 without basic structural changes in the political system. The outlook for the conference was not considered encouraging.

The essential features of the 1953 constitutional agreements have been described. They reflected an ingenious compromise of what had been regarded as intractable positions. The acceptance of federalism and the allocation of residual powers to regions reassured the north, as it also pleased the west. The British government firmly refused to fix a definite date for self-government for Nigeria as a whole, "the more so as the Northern delegation, representing over half the population of Nigeria, was unable to depart from its policy of self-government as soon as practicable."[51] But it accepted the principle of scheduled self-government for 1956 at the regional level. In retrospect it could be argued that it was the north that won the day. The northern leaders obtained much greater autonomy for the regions, and they really conceded nothing on the issue of scheduled self-government. In the debate on the self-government motion Alhaji Ahmadu, Sardauna of Sokoto, had stated categorically that "we from the Northern Region never intended, nor do we intend to retard the progress of any Region."[52] In the balance, however, the idea of a united Nigeria was the real victor. The conference produced a profound transformation in attitudes, not only between British and Nigerians, but also among Nigerian leaders themselves. Yet it did not weaken the determination of southern leaders to pursue the objective of self-government for all Nigeria in 1956.

This determination was repeatedly affirmed by southern leaders during the three years following the 1953 conference, as was the equally emphatic northern determination not to accept a firm date for independence.[53] As the conference scheduled for 1956 approached, however, a marked change occurred in party attitudes on the issue. This change resulted from the unexpected announcement on May 30, 1956, that northern leaders would demand regional self-government in 1959. At last the north had abandoned the vague and frustrating phrase "as soon as practicable," and had accepted the principle of scheduled self-government. Southern leaders promptly qualified their positions. Awolowo reaffirmed that the Action Group desired self-government for the Federation in 1956, but would not "seek to coerce the North" on the issue.[54] A month later Azikiwe proposed a new timetable specifying self-government for the southern regions in 1956 and, after a three-year transitional period, independence for the Federation of Nigeria in 1959. He added that 1959 was selected because it was more suitable for the Northern Region.[55] The factors making for compromise are clear—southern determination to set a firm date provoked the northern leaders to take a more advanced position much earlier than they had planned, and northern resistance forced the southerners to be less doctrinaire on the issue. Each had come to realize that it could neither dominate nor do without the other, a situation usually conducive to temperance and mutual respect.

As previously noted, the enquiry into Azikiwe's connections with the African Continental Bank resulted in the postponement of the 1956 conference until May, 1957. On March 26, two months before the rescheduled conference met, Chief Akintola of the Action Group introduced a motion in the federal House of Representatives that "this House instructs the delegates . . . to the forthcoming Constitutional Conference to express the views of this House to do all in their power to secure the grant of self-government to the Federation of Nigeria in 1957." [56] To this motion J. A. Wachuku of the NCNC moved an amendment changing the year from 1957 to 1959. Akintola promptly accepted the amendment because he considered the subject of "great national importance" and the "best way to give it the importance that is due to it is that it be faced with the utmost spirit of unanimity." [57] Immediately thereafter Alhaji Balewa said, on behalf of the members of the Northern Peoples' Congress in the House, that his party, although it had never reached a firm decision on a definite date for the attainment of Nigerian independence, saw "no reason why we of the Congress should refuse to allow the House of Representatives the opportunity to instruct their political delegates to press for the fixing of a date for Nigerian independence in 1959. (*Loud applause.*)" [58] The amended motion setting 1959 as the "year of destiny" was then passed unanimously. Nigerian leaders were at last united on an issue which for six years had not only plagued all internal relationships but had also threatened the very existence of Nigeria as an emergent national entity. An editorial in *West Africa* called the event the most important in "Nigeria's history since 1900, and, for Africa, scarcely less important than Ghana's independence. . . ." [59]

Fortified by this new spirit of unity and common purpose the three regional premiers and the Leaders of Government Business in the Southern Cameroons agreed upon a joint memorandum requesting the British government to grant independence to the Federation of Nigeria in 1959. This memorandum was submitted at the beginning of the 1957 conference in London. In response to it, the Secretary of State reaffirmed his government's opposition in principle to date-fixing, pointing out that the memorandum was only a request for the British government to draw a "blank cheque" in favor of independence for Nigeria in 1959 and that he could not reasonably go to his colleagues in the cabinet without knowing "how the cheque will be filled in," or "what the face of Nigeria in 1959 would be likely to be." [60] He emphasized, however, that his government stood as firmly behind the objective of full self-government within the Commonwealth as any one in Nigeria. He proposed that when the federal elections of 1959 were over government leaders in Nigeria and the United Kingdom "might confer together to determine the processes by which Nigeria might attain that common objective." [61]

This response did not satisfy the Nigerian leaders. After con-

sidering the several complex issues left unresolved by the conference, they decided to shift the final target date for self-
government from 1959 to 1960. They then informed the Secretary
of State that early in 1960 the new Nigerian parliament would
adopt a resolution setting a precise date for independence, and
asked him for a more specific commitment on behalf of the British
government. Although suggesting that an informal consultation
between Nigerian and British leaders precede such action, the
Secretary of State did promise that upon receipt of the proposed
resolution his government would

> . . . consider it with sympathy and will then be prepared to fix a
> date when they would accede to the request. We would not at
> this stage give any undertaking that the date would be the same
> date as asked for in the resolution, though we would do our
> utmost to meet the resolution in a reasonable and practicable
> manner.[62]

The next day the Sardauna of Sokoto, speaking for the still dissatisfied Nigerian leaders, made the following statement:

> We have given further consideration to the Secretary of State's
> statement on the independence of the Federation of Nigeria. We
> feel bound to express our disappointment that it has not been
> possible for Her Majesty's Government to give an undertaking to
> grant independence to Nigeria on a date to be named in 1960 by
> the new Nigerian Parliament.
> The year 1959 has been unanimously proposed by the people
> of Nigeria, and we have given consideration to a date in 1960
> only because we appreciate that the solution to the various
> problems that must be disposed of before independence will take
> longer time than we had thought.
> Having gone thus far on the path of reason and realism, we
> had thought that the Secretary of State would accede to our
> united wishes. In the circumstances we can do no more than to
> take note of the Secretary of State's statement, while reserving
> to ourselves the right to pursue the issue further with a view to
> impressing upon Her Majesty's Government the necessity for
> granting independence to the Federation of Nigeria not later than
> 2nd April, 1960.[63]

Although disappointed, the Nigerian leaders were not inclined
to force the issue. The Secretary of State had not refused self-

government in 1960; nor had he refused to consider a formal request for it at that time. Indeed, he had stated that he would do his utmost to meet it. Nigerian students in the United Kingdom engaged in demonstrations of protest, but the nationalist press at home was remarkably restrained in its comment. The pro–Action Group *Nigerian Tribune* editorialized:

> . . . our freedom ambassadors are expected back today . . . the talks have been an unqalified success. This is not because we are necessarily unaware of the disappointment of all Nigerians at the attitude of the British Government to the question of fixing a target date for the independence of the Nigerian Federation. But whatever the view of the individual on this issue, the fact still remains that Nigeria has moved closer to its objective than one could have imagined six months ago.[64]

Azikiwe's *West African Pilot* argued that

> . . . we do not see how any sensible man should blame our leaders. . . . To have pressed the British Government into committing itself to any definite date for Nigerian independence, in the face of its obvious reluctance to do so, would have involved the conference into a stalemate or even a crisis. . . . And instead of whimpering, let all Nigerians gird their loins and face our last and final task—which is to do everything constitutionally possible to force Britain to bow to the inevitable on or before 1960. This is the only way to over-come her artful dodging.[65]

This moderation, and the comparative absence of invective, are explainable simply by the fact that Nigerian leaders knew their battle was won, and that if they really wanted to force the issue they could do so at any time. They were returning home from the London Conference laden with unprecedented powers and responsibilities, the exercise and discharge of which would not be furthered by campaigns of positive action, by nationalist riots, or by the immediate expulsion of the remaining British civil servants. Since they had just inherited the bulk of British power in a wide range of fields, it was important that they not encourage defiance of authority or other forms of unconstitutional action.

The prevailing assumption following the 1957 conference was that Nigerians could and would obtain their independence in 1960 if it was seriously desired. There were, of course, the congenital cynics, as well as those who found emotional relief or political advantage in arguing the near-dead issue of subservience to British imperialism. Most reflective nationalists, however, felt a new sense of urgency in tackling the staggering problems that had to be solved in order to make their long-sought independence a reality. In their view, accelerated Nigerianization in all fields had the highest priority, for these reasons: only 24 per cent of the higher positions in the federal civil service were held by Nigerians; only a tiny cadre of foreign service officers were in training; British officers filled the upper ranks of the army and police; and a growing number of expatriates were departing under the lump-sum compensation scheme approved by the 1957 conference. Speakers in debates at the 1958 budget session of the House of Representatives revealed not only this sense of urgency, but also an infectious spirit of hopeful expectancy regarding the approach of independence. Indeed, a motion was approved setting up a national committee to prepare proposals for independence celebrations in 1960 and to consider such obvious requisites of an independent state as a national anthem and flag.[66]

Even though Nigerians now have ultimate effective control over the timetable, it is not at all certain that April 2, 1960, will usher in their independence. Dates have been set before and allowed to pass. In 1953, for example, Enahoro proclaimed that it was impossible to retreat from the year 1956, and Awolowo and Azikiwe stated that they would "unhesitatingly declare" Nigeria's independence if they encountered resistance. Again, at the 1957 conference, the leaders easily persuaded themselves—and subsequently their followers—that the "year of destiny" should be changed from 1959 to 1960. The same pattern of categorical demand and subsequent adjustment characterized the terminal stages of colonialism in the Gold Coast. In 1952 Dr. Kwame Nkrumah came to power under the slogan, "Self-government Now," yet it was five years before that cherished status was finally achieved. On the other hand, the Sudan unilaterally declared its independence in advance of the timetable under which it was operating.

There are at least three considerations that will dictate the actual date of Nigerian independence, apart from whatever position the British government might take when, and if, it receives a resolution from the Nigerian House of Representatives requesting self-government: (1) the degree of national unity prevailing in Nigeria at the time—and here the decisions on boundaries, minorities, and new states, the tensions between traditionalists and modernists in the Northern Region, and the durability of Alhaji Balewa's national coalition, as well as of the Awolowo-Azikiwe-Sardauna alliance, are all in point; (2) the time required for legal experts to complete the necessary constitutional instruments, which could, from a purely technical standpoint, easily exceed the period from January to April 2, 1960; and (3) the status of political forces at the time, including particularly the significance of the interparty struggle for mastery over nationalist symbols. As new elections to the federal House of Representatives will probably be held in late 1959, it is not unlikely that "self-government in 1960" will emerge as the central campaign slogan of all parties. And in that event the victorious party will feel a compelling obligation to win independence for Nigeria and to make it a full-fledged member of the Commonwealth.

Critique and Conclusions

A student of African nationalism finds it difficult to contribute original conclusions regarding the nature of colonial nationalism, especially in the light of the growing mass of literature on nationalism in the Middle East and Asia. The most he can do is to show that the African response to alien rule and to the stimulus of westernization follows a historic pattern; that the idea of national self-determination has been given a new lease on life in an area into which many believed it would not penetrate, at least for a very long time; and that the knotty problem of how to create nations out of heterogeneous cultural materials is not peculiar to non-African areas. The same old ingredients that elsewhere combined to produce a nationalist reaction to colonial rule have also been present in Nigeria. Once this confession is made, however, one hastens to add that it is this very sameness that is important to the social scientist. It is believed that this case study of Nigerian nationalism supports Deutsch's proposition that the process of nation-building shows "a number of patterns which seem to recur," as well as Cobban's statement that "the problems created by the attempt to put the theory of national self-determination into practice reappear in the most diverse environments." Studies that reveal the normality of African political phenomena are important in breaking down the great wall of prejudice and misconception that has surrounded Africa and its peoples.

Nationalism in Nigeria is the product of certain unplanned developments that have occurred since that territory came under British administration a little more than fifty years ago. Until the Nigerian nationalists forced a change, the general assumption underlying British policy was that British control would endure for a long time. Northern Nigeria had become the show place for the policy of indirect rule, which envisaged a gradual adaptation of traditional African communities to the requirements of a modern state. Nationalism emerged to challenge this assumption, and proceeded at once to undermine the structure of indirect rule and to attack the British presence itself.

Our discussion of the Western impact upon Nigeria has suggested that nationalism was the end product of three major developments or conditions. The first was the "social mobilization," to use Karl Deutsch's phrase, of substantial numbers of Nigerians as a result of a policy of determined Europeanization by Christian missionaries, a literary educational curriculum, and the growth of an urbanized wage-labor force whose members were haunted by a sense of economic and psychological insecurity. The second was the accumulation of conscious economic grievances among the mobilized groups, derived from the presence and the practices of large-scale European enterprise and what was believed to be government indifference regarding economic development. The third, and decisive, development was the emergence of a Western-educated minority whose members were employed as clerks, artisans, and subalterns in the government and in the firms, and who suffered most acutely from the inequalities and the frustrations of colonial rule. At the top of the new social structure was an exceedingly small group of European- or American-educated professional men (lawyers, doctors, journalists, teachers) who had become saturated with Western ideas, particularly the ideas of democracy, large-scale political organization, national self-determination, and rapid economic development. Under the system of indirect rule these Western-educated elements were largely excluded from any meaningful role in the government of the country. As a consequence many were attracted to nationalism in a mood having certain striking characteristics: a profound distrust and suspicion of the European; a deep bitterness regarding racial discrimination; a passionate belief in the idea of progress and the power of technology which convinced them that they, the enlightened few, were not only destined by right to rule, but also that by an act of will they could create an independent Nigerian nation which would allow them, in the words of their prophet Nnamdi Azikiwe, to walk "majestically with the other races of mankind."

410

The external influences that helped to shape the ideas and awaken the aspirations of what was at first a very small claimant minority came from India, the United Kingdom, America, and Soviet Russia. Nigerian students in America were compelled to partake of the color consciousness, as well as the hopeful expectancy, of the American Negro. Soviet Russia offered an example of the capacity of man to transform his environment and liquidate the stigma of backwardness within a single generation. Most of the nationalist leaders came from the small group of Nigerians who had studied in American and British universities. While abroad their sense of distinctness was sharpened by the cruder forms of color discrimination they were compelled to suffer. Their detachment from their traditional culture, their bitterness over their exclusion from white culture, their resentment of the inferiority implications in the European allegation that they had no history and no culture, and their critical observation of the shortcomings of Western culture, all combined to stimulate among these students a deeper appreciation of their own culture and history, or a determination to create a neo-African culture.

Most Nigerian nationalists are not cultural nativists; they are eclectics, desiring to keep what is useful and attractive in the old and fuse it with the new. From the West they have absorbed the scientific attitude and the idea of progress. These distinctly exotic notions have inspired their conviction that man can manipulate nature and creatively shape his own destiny. A factor of even greater importance has been the nationalists' desire to liquidate the stigma of inferiority and backwardness; and they are convinced that the only way to accomplish this is to utilize modern forms and techniques. However, it is their belief that modernity and progress are the standards by which they have been judged and will continue to be judged. Indeed, they are the standards by which they tend to judge themselves. Nigeria has not had a Gandhi.

Most nationalist leaders, as well as their active supporters, are members of the second or third generation since culture contact. This is borne out by the initiative taken by educated "native foreigners" in early nationalist activity. The changing perspectives of each succeeding generation have been succinctly described by

411

Premier Awolowo: "Our grandfathers, with unbounded gratitude adored the British. . . . Our immediate fathers simply toed the line. We of to-day are critical, unappreciative, and do not feel that we owe any debt of gratitude to the British. The younger elements in our group are extremely cynical, and cannot understand why Britain is in Nigeria."

A colonial nationalist movement normally has two main objectives. The first is to terminate imperial rule; the second is to create a modern nation-state. During the period covered by this study Nigerian nationalists pursued these two objectives with increasing vigor. At times it seemed as though the impatient southern drive to achieve self-government might destroy the possibility of attaining national unity. On the other hand, many southern nationalists desiring self-government in their own day found intolerable the delay expected and demanded by the north in exchange for her consenting to be part of "one Nigeria," and they were not at all sure they would pay the price. But the vision of the prestige and power that a united Nigeria would bring was highly seductive, and therefore sobering. As a result, self-government was postponed for a few years, the north drastically revised its timetable, and a new unity was achieved.

Nigerian nationalists encountered several special difficulties. One of these was the lack of external support, both moral and physical. On the moral side Awolowo pointed out that "reasonable men" unanimously supported India, Burma, and Ceylon, but were hesitant regarding Nigeria. Three old and trusted friends of colonial nationalism cooled noticeably after 1945. The Fabian Society and the Labour party placed more and more emphasis upon economic and social development as a precondition for political freedom, and the people and government of the United States increasingly recognized that expanding Soviet imperialism, which thrived on instability in newly independent colonial areas, was a far greater threat to civilization than British colonialism seemingly in the process of orderly liquidation. From the standpoint of physical support, the isolation of Africa from potential allies, the control over the importation of arms and ammunition, and the totality of European control over the African continent left Nigerian nationalists of militant bent with little more than machetes and stones to carry out their threats of "positive action."

Another handicap suffered by the nationalists was the difficulty of Nigerians in conceptualizing a Nigerian nation. Since they lacked cultural unity, their moving sentiment was racial consciousness. The common subjection of most of Africa to white rule, and the relatively short period of imperial rule, are two obvious explanations for this. Another reason is the great freedom of movement across frontiers. As Lord Hailey put it: "There must often be an inclination for natives to look on themselves rather as members of a common African stock than as subjects of a particular colonial power."

A final disability suffered by the Nigerian nationalists was the absence of a strong transtribal and transregional class, which could have been a cementing link and a sustaining force in the nationalist drive. Commencing in the late 1930's, however, a sizable middle class began to emerge in the rubber and cocoa areas of the Western Region. But the power, the influence, and the nationalism of this emergent group were diverted to the support of a Yoruba nationalism midway in the nationalist build-up. The absence of a transtribal class, or of an economic-interest group, means that the Nigerian nationalist movement has been supported principally by a mélange of individuals whose only basis for unity was the desire for self-government, the symbol for all things desirable.

In glancing over the map of Africa one is prompted to ask why the Gold Coast (Ghana) and Nigeria should have spearheaded Africa's entry into a national era. A few tentative explanations may be offered. What is said here regarding Nigeria is equally applicable to the Gold Coast. In the first place, in contrast to most of the rest of Africa, the peoples of Nigeria have enjoyed greater freedoms—freedom of speech, of press, of assembly, and of movement, including the freedom to study abroad. The exercise of these freedoms has not been curtailed by the presence of a large number of white settlers. Moreover, the British policy of encouraging territorial self-sufficiency, coupled with the fact that Nigeria is completely surrounded by French territory with a different form of administration and a different official language, has sharpened Nigeria's territorial individuality. Third, the declared

413

political objective of British colonial policy has been self-government. As noted in this study, British officials and Nigerian nationalists disagreed on the meaning of this objective; but its declaration as a final goal of policy served to awaken aspirations as well as to provide a standard by which British policy could be criticized. By contrast, the policy of the French and Portuguese governments has been one of assimilation to the metropolitan country; the Belgian and Spanish governments have been noncommittal, at least until recently. In British Central and East Africa the objective of self-government has been blurred and complicated by the presence of white settlers and other aliens.

Again, the British, in contrast to the officials of other colonial powers in Africa, have been freer in their open self-criticism. Any serious disturbance in the colonies has usually resulted in the appointment of a commission, whose reports are invariably made public. The British Left has carried on a ceaseless crusade on behalf of Africans through pamphlets and questions in Parliament, and their pronationalist literature has been available to Africans in Nigeria and in London. British self-criticism (Burke, Mill, Macaulay, Hobson, and Laski) has bulked large in nationalist literature. Moreover, British colonial critics have been active on the organizational side. In 1911 the British leaders of the Anti-Slavery and Aborigines Protection Society of London took the initiative in organizing an African branch in Nigeria. This was the first Western-style organization in Nigeria, and the postwar nationalist movement traces a fairly direct lineal descent from it. In short, nationalism in Nigeria is as much the product of British liberalism as it is of British colonialism.

Nationalism in Nigeria, as in the Gold Coast, is a manifestation of long-dormant peoples groping their way to nationhood in order that they may enter the life of the world community as equal participants. Just as Japan and India spearheaded the Asian revolt, so the Gold Coast and Nigeria have been the vanguard in the African awakening. The lift-pump effect of developments in these two territories upon other areas of Africa has been, and will be profound. Nationalism in both Togoland and the Cameroons under British and French trusteeship is in a large measure the direct by-product of developments in the Gold Coast and Nigeria. The national idea is rapidly spreading to the neighboring territories of French West Africa. For good or ill, Africa has crossed the threshold and is beginning its own national era. Azikiwe's dream of a "New Africa" is slowly becoming a reality. How new, or how much better it will be, cannot yet be discerned.

Appendix

A Note on Concepts and Terms

In constructing a conceptual framework for the presentation and analysis of data on the subject of nationalism in Nigeria one is at once struck by the imprecision and general inadequacy of many of the key concepts of the social sciences. In numerous instances the indiscriminate and uncritical use of traditional concepts in political science would create a distorted picture of African realities. Moreover, the concepts developed by anthropologists—until recently the only scholars who have systematically studied African political phenomena—would lead to additional ambiguities. In short, recent and contemporary political developments in Africa have created a new frontier for the social sciences in which concept formation and clarification must be accorded first priority.

There are several explanations for this conceptual poverty. The vocabulary of political science has been elaborated with specific reference to Western political systems. In general, the modern states system and the explicit institutions of government (legislatures, executive and judicial institutions, and political parties) have constituted the limited universe of the political scientist. In part his neglect of or indifference to non-Western political systems has been the consequence of the widely accepted assumption, based upon such theses as Maine's status-to-contract evolutionism, that those systems were irrelevant or destined for extinction. Another explanation is that political science as a discipline is a product of Western scholarship, and until recently neither the imperatives of public or foreign policy nor the availability of foundation grants have stimulated or encouraged an interest in non-Western systems. Political science is also a young discipline, which emerged after Western colonial rule had been established over most of the non-West and legitimized by traditional international law. The institutions of colonial government, endowed as they were with both legitimacy and political relevance, have engaged the attention of those few political scientists who were attracted to the study of non-Western situations. These are a few of the more obvious explanations for the conceptual ethnocentrism characteristic of contemporary political science.

Despite their admirable effort to develop universal categories for the study of man, wherever he is, anthropologists have been preoccupied with preliterate societies. Their use of certain concepts central to this study (for example, "nation," "state," and "nationalism") lacks rigor and tends to have specific relevance only to such societies.[1] Thus, whereas the political scientist has limited his focus to the institutions of colonial government, the anthropologist has restricted his interest to the political institutions of traditional African societies. These different orientations mean that neither discipline has been conceptually prepared to cope with the new institutional patterns and social relationships— partly modernist and partly traditionalist—which characterize much of emergent Africa.

The purpose of this note is neither to bring about a *rapprochement* between the political scientist and the anthropologist, nor to introduce new concepts. Rather it is to set forth certain working definitions in order that the data and analysis presented in this study will be both intelligible and consistently treated. At the present developmental stage of the social sciences the most one can require and expect of any analyst is that he be *explicit* in his conceptualization and *consistent* in the use of his concepts.

People. A human group without emphatic reference to any particular criterion for grouping, such as consanguinity, cultural or linguistic affinity, or political unity. Thus, the "Islamic peoples of Northern Nigeria," or "the peoples of Nigeria." [2]

Society. A human aggregation whose members have become interdependent through the exchange of goods and services, a division of labor, and a network of relationships and interactions which distinguishes them as a group from other groups.[3] A society is normally, but not necessarily, a community. The objective factors that create a society tend also to create a sense of community. A society is a "system of action in operation," with emphasis upon a mechanistic interrelatedness.[4] A community is a "sentiment area," with emphasis upon affective interrelatedness. Thus it is possible to speak of a Nigerian society (as a human aggregation distinct from, say Dahomey), but this does not necessarily mean that Nigeria constitutes a community.

Culture. The distinctive patterns of behavior, symbols, artifacts, ideas, and values of a human group.[5] All human groups have a culture.[6] Culture in general refers collectively to the objective constellation of traits and patterns which differentiate one human group from another. Particular groups (that is, lineage, tribe, nationality, nation, or civilization) are bearers of particular cultures; hence the use of the concept "culture" in a concrete situation depends upon the analyst's frame of reference and level of abstraction (for example, Western culture, Islamic culture, African culture, Yoruba culture, Onitsha culture).

Community. A human group of any size whose members have a consciousness of living a common life and sharing a common destiny. Communities are culture-bearing social units. There is a hierarchy of communities ranging from the family or village to the region or nation. The strength of community feeling varies according to the size of the group, the intensity of social communication among its members, and the sense of in-group identification. In the modern world, the nation is usually regarded as the terminal community.[7]

Race. Broadly, a division of mankind distinguished by color of skin, stature, head shape (prognathism), and general physiognomy. Although the term "race" is generally avoided because of its imprecision and the qualitative implications it has acquired, it is used herein merely to distinguish between two distinct physical types: those predominantly white and those predominantly black in color. Hence the descriptive expressions "white race" and "black race."

State. A territorial political system having the following attributes: (1) a single and self-sufficient legal order, (2) a concentration of power sufficient to maintain that system, (3) centralized and explicit forms of government, and (4) criteria of membership participation which are not based solely upon kinship. It is necessary in this study, however, to distinguish between two general types of states on the one hand, and so-called "stateless societies" on the other:

1. *Modern state.* A state which is a participating unit in the international states system as evidenced by recognition by some or all other states, by the maintenance of diplomatic relations with other states, and, in general, by accepted participation in international affairs on the basis of sovereign equality. In these terms, the Federation of Nigeria is an emergent state, but not a *de facto* state.

2. *Traditional state.* A state which is not—though it may have been or it may become—a participating unit in the international states system. This type of state has been referred to frequently by anthropologists as a "primitive" or "archaic" state.[8] It is essentially a historical category, referring to precolonial African political systems having all the attributes of statehood, except recognized and accepted participation in international affairs. Such early African states as existed in Kebbi, Dahomey, Yorubaland, Benin, Hausaland, and Bornu are examples of this category.

3. *Stateless society.* A society whose political system lacks one or more attributes of statehood as defined above. The category includes those traditional African societies that have no centralized and explicit forms of government.

Nation. A large group of people who feel that they form a single and exclusive community destined to be an independent state. The three key criteria of nationhood are (1) largeness in scale, which, although imprecise, at least excludes city-states, principalities, and small tribal societies; (2) the existence of an in-group sentiment and belief that the nation constitutes the terminal community; and (3) the assumption of a national destiny of independent statehood in the modern world. Apart from largeness in scale, there are several objective criteria by which a nation is normally, but not necessarily, defined. A common culture and historical tradition, and a common language, are usually attributes of a concrete nation. But in the last analysis, a nation is defined by subjective criteria; objective factors tend to create a subjective feeling of nationhood, but the causal link is not necessary. Moreover, the nation is essentially a modern phenomenon, not because modernity has any special legitimizing quality, but because modern technology makes largeness in scale and closeness of contact physically possible, and modern ideology postulates the necessary coincidence of nation and state. In any event, by these criteria Nigeria has never been and is not yet a nation; nor is any one of the three regions of Nigeria a nation. This study is primarily concerned with the processes of nation-building and national awakening in Nigeria.

Nationality. A people distinguished from other peoples by one or more common cultural traits (a common language, a shared historical tradition, a common mythology as to origin, or similar customs). A nationality is the largest traditional African group above a tribe which can be distinguished from other groups by one or more objective criteria (normally language). Present or recent political unity is not necessarily a characteristic of a nationality, although such unity no doubt prevailed in the original core group (tribe) from which many of the Nigerian nationalities have developed historically.

The concept of "nationality," or an equivalent, is considered essential for any working classificatory scheme for Nigerian social and political groupings. As yet none of the Nigerian "peoples" are "nations," at least as defined herein; neither are they all "tribes," which they have often been called.[9] In some respects nationalities may be considered as "extended tribes," in other respects as "incipient nations." Yet the former conveys the notion of greater cohesion than really exists, and the latter has a teleological implication that is unwarranted. Moreover, whereas several nationalities are both potential and incipient nations (for example, the Hausa, the Yoruba, and the Ibo), others are too small or awkwardly situated to become nations. In sum, the concept of nationality is simply a convenient intermediate category introduced to refer to a people larger in population than a tribe, which is not yet and may never be a nation, but which offers the strongest cultural basis for nationhood at the highest level and on the largest scale of all traditional African groupings. The major so-called "language groups" of Nigeria are regarded as nationalities within the framework of this study.

Tribe. A relatively small group of people who share a common culture and who are descended from a common ancestor. The tribe is the largest social group defined primarily in terms of kinship, and is normally an aggregation of clans. Within the present conceptual scheme it is a group intermediate between the lineage or clan and the nationality.[10]

Clan. A group consisting of one or more extended families descended from one historical ancestor, speaking the same language and dialect, and observing one common shrine.

Lineage. A group that is a portion of a clan living together in a given locality. "The loyalties which bind an individual to his clan members, and particularly to the members of his lineage, are the strongest bonds in African society." [11] The lineage is the basic socioeconomic unit in most traditional African societies.

Association. A group of people united and organized for the purpose of pursuing a common interest. The four principal types of associations referred to in this study are: [12]

1. *Nationalist movement.* An association organized to achieve self-government for the people whom its members claim to represent. Its aim is to obtain a fundamental change in the colonial relationship which terminates with complete African control of the government.

2. *Political party.* An association that competes with other similar associations in periodic elections in order to participate in formal government institutions and thereby influence and control the personnel and policy of government.

3. *Pressure group.* An association that endeavors to influence, but not necessarily to control, the government on behalf of the special interests of its members. It presses for favors, or for the redress of grievances within a *status quo* which it does not challenge.

4. *Tribal union.* Loosely, any association organized for the purpose of promoting a loyalty toward, and advancing the progress and prosperity of, any one of several communities to which the members belong. "Tribal union" is the popular Nigerian name for associational activity on at least two levels:

a) Kinship and village associations, whose interests are centered upon, and whose bonds of unity are derived from, the kinship group (family, lineage, or clan) or the village or town

424

where the lineage is localized. Herein associations of this type will be referred to as *kinship associations*.

b) Pantribal and nationality associations, whose interests are centered upon the progress and integration of the widest traditional community (tribe or nationality) to which the members belong. Herein associations of this type will be referred to as *tribal unions*.

Nationalism.[13] Broadly, a consciousness of belonging to a nation (existent or in the realm of aspiration) or a nationality, and a desire, as manifest in sentiment and activity, to secure or maintain its welfare, prosperity, and integrity, and to maximize its political autonomy. The reference group for "nationalism" can be a *de facto* nation or nationality, or a territorially defined group in which certain members believe and advocate that it ought, or is destined, to become a nation. If the reference group is an existent *nation* (as in much of Europe), nationalism is directed toward the attainment, maintenance, or restoration of its political independence as a nation-state in the international states system. If the reference group is an existent *nationality*, nationalism refers to sentiment and activity directed toward maximizing its political autonomy either as a separate state, or as a constituent member of a multinational state in the international states system. If the reference group is a territorially defined group which is neither a nation nor a nationality, nationalism refers to sentiment and activity directed toward the creation of a nation and the attainment of independent statehood. For the purposes of this study at least four reference-group foci of nationalism can be distinguished.

1. *Pan-African nationalism.* A belief on the part of certain Africans or individuals of African descent that the continent of Africa is a national homeland, a desire that it be united and independent under African leadership, and activity directed toward spreading that belief and desire. Herein this phenomenon is referred to as "Pan-Africanism," and an advocate as a "Pan-Africanist."

2. *Nigerian nationalism.* Sentiment and activity on the part of Africans who claim some part of Nigeria as their home, aimed at the establishment of an independent Nigerian state and the creation of a Nigerian nation coextensive with that state. Herein

this phenomenon is referred to simply as "nationalism," and an adherent as a "nationalist."

3. *Regional nationalism.* Activity on the part of Africans who claim some part of Nigeria as their home, directed toward the maximization of the political autonomy of a region and the creation of a regional sentiment. Herein this is referred to as "regionalism," and an adherent as a "regionalist." Derivative terms are "Western regionalism (-ist)," "Eastern regionalism (-ist)," and "Northern regionalism (-ist)." The COR, Mid-West, and other "state movements" which emerged in the mid-1950's would also be considered manifestations of regional nationalism.

4. *Group nationalism.* A consciousness, on the part of members of a traditional Nigerian community, of membership in that community, and the manifestations of sentiment and activity aimed at maximizing the political autonomy of that group. For the major Nigerian cultural groups (nationalities), this phenomenon is herein referred to as "group nationalism," and, for specific nationalities, as "Yoruba nationalism," "Ibo nationalism," and so on. For the minor Nigerian cultural groups (tribes), this phenomenon is referred to as "tribalism."

Cultural nationalism. A consciousness, on the part of Africans, of the distinctive culture of their own group, or of Africa in general, and activity directed toward developing, glorifying, and generalizing an appreciation of that culture. Conceptually this phenomenon should be distinguished from the predominantly political nationalism referred to above, although concretely cultural nationalism and political nationalism are but two aspects of a single phenomenon.

Race consciousness. The awareness of membership in a distinctive race, and the desire to maintain the integrity and to assert the equality of that race. In regard to Africans and members of the Negro race in general, this sentiment has no specific territorial connotation, unless it be "wherever black men dwell." A related concept, *racialism,* refers to a race consciousness characterized by animosity toward other races. "African racialism" would be indiscriminate and pronounced antiwhite sentiment.

Acculturation (also westernization, Europeanization). Refers to changes that have occurred, or are in process, in the original cultural patterns of either or both of two groups of individuals having different cultures and coming into continuous firsthand contact. In Nigeria, although there is a fair amount of internal acculturation among different nationalities and tribes, the term refers specifically to the changes in African culture which have come about, or are in process, as a result of contact with European culture; hence the terms "westernization" and "Europeanization." The latter terms refer to the adoption or adaptation of forms of behavior and production, and values and ideas, characteristic of "Western" or "European" culture.

Detribalization. A loose and inaccurate concept which denotes the weakening of loyalties and attachments of Africans to their traditional social group of origin as a result of acculturation. Despite its many ambiguities, the term is employed herein with the appropriate qualifications. In general, a Nigerian who has been "westernized" or "Europeanized" is presumed to be "detribalized."

Africanization. Refers to the process whereby Africans replace non-Africans in positions of administrative or executive authority in the government of Nigeria or in positions in any other enterprise or endeavor normally occupied by non-Africans (that is, commercial firms, the upper levels in the social and technical services, and the educational system).

European. A common term used by Africans and non-Africans to refer to any white person irrespective of nationality.

African. A loose term employed mainly by Europeans in referring to members of the Negro race, except those from the United States, who are called "American Negroes," or those from the West Indies, who are called "West Indians."

Nigerian. An African, irrespective of tribe or nationality, who is an indigenous inhabitant of some part of Nigeria. The related terms *westerner, easterner,* and *northerner* refer to Africans who inhabit the Western, Eastern, and Northern regions of Nigeria, respectively.

Expatriate. A non-African, normally a European, who is employed by some branch of the government of Nigeria or by foreign commercial firms.

Notes

Notes

[1] The recency and significance of the "colonial revolution" are revealed in Hans Morgenthau's substantial revision of this subject in *Politics among Nations* (2d ed.; New York: Knopf, 1954). The subject is further illuminated by the disproportionate amount of attention devoted to colonial and self-determination questions in most of the organs of the United Nations over the past ten years.

[2] *The World and the West* (New York: Oxford, 1953), pp. 70–71. For a similar view see Alfred Cobban, *National Self-Determination* (Chicago: University of Chicago Press, 1944), pp. 123–138. Also see Joseph Stalin, *Marxism and the National Question* (New York: International Publishers, 1942), especially pages 54–55, where the application of the principle to the Caucasus was declared "meaningless and nonsensical in relation to Caucasian conditions." Also, Lord Hailey prefers to use the term "Africanism" rather than "nationalism" when he refers to African sentiment and activity directed toward the creation of new nations. His reasons are similar to those of Toynbee quoted in the text. See *An African Survey Revised 1956* (London: 1957), pp. 251–260.

[3] E. H. Carr, *Nationalism and After* (London: Macmillan, 1945), pp. 34–71.

[4] The most recent affirmation of this argument is set forth in Boyd C. Shafer, *Nationalism: Myth and Reality* (New York: Harcourt, 1955); for example, on page 235 the author speaks of "the arbitrary divisions into which petty patriots, narrow scholars, sadistic dictators, cheap journalists, and popular novelists have divided mankind." For earlier arguments on the essentially destructive, tyrannical, and aberrant character of nations and nationalism see Carlton J. H. Hayes, *The Historical Evolution of Modern Nationalism* (New York: Macmillan, 1931), and W. Friedmann, *The Crisis of the National State* (London: 1943). A related argument which equates nationalism and nations with the bourgeois class and the capitalist state is contained in the writings of Joseph Stalin, especially *op. cit.*, pages 98–100, and also in those of the Chinese Communist theoretician, Liu Shao-Chi, in his *Internationalism and Nationalism* (Peking: 1952).

[5] *Op. cit.*, p. 134.

[6] "The British Problem in Africa," *Foreign Affairs,* 29 (July, 1951), 638. For a penetrating critique of Miss Perham's statement see K. Onwuka Dike, "African History and Self-Government," *West Africa,* Feb. 28, 1953, p. 177.

[7] Arthur N. Cook, *British Enterprise in Nigeria* (Philadelphia: 1943), p. 272.

[8] *Empire and After* (London: 1949), p. 5.

[9] *Path to Nigerian Freedom* (London: 1947); *Renascent Africa* (Accra: 1937).

[10] "The Growth of Nations," *World Politics,* V (Jan., 1953). See also his *Nationalism and Social Communication* (New York: 1953).

CHAPTER 1: *The Geography and Peoples of Nigeria*
(Pages 11–35)

¹ *Report of the Commission on Higher Education in West Africa*, Cmd. 6655 (London: H.M.S.O., 1945), p. 4.

² *Ibid.*

³ *Ibid.*, p. 5.

⁴ For a survey of Nigerian ethnic groups see Margery Perham, ed., *The Native Economies of Nigeria* (London: 1946), pp. 26–28; C. K. Meek, *The Northern Tribes of Nigeria* (London: 1925), I, 23–50; P. Amaury Talbot, *The Peoples of Southern Nigeria* (London: 1926), IV, 16–72; and K. M. Buchanan and J. C. Pugh, *Land and People in Nigeria* (London: University of London Press, 1955).

⁵ The classificatory scheme employed here is that proposed by Joseph H. Greenberg, *Studies in African Linguistic Classification* (New Haven: 1955), pp. 1–61. Cf. Diedrich Westermann, "African Linguistic Classification," *Africa*, XXII (July, 1952), 250–256; and Buchanan and Pugh, *op. cit.*, pp. 82–87. Greenberg's complete genetic reclassification of the languages of Africa has stimulated a revision of many current assumptions about the relationship among language, culture, and behavior, including particularly the long-standing implication that peoples speaking languages of a "Hamitic" character were *ipso facto* superior. Greenberg, *op. cit.*, pp. 52–54.

⁶ As used here, language "groups" include both "tribes" and "nationalities" as defined in the Appendix. Two of the four major language families represented in Nigeria include, according to Greenberg's classification, the following Nigerian language groups: Niger-Congo family: Kwa Branch (Yoruba, Nupe, Edo, and Ibo), Ijo Branch (Ijaw), Central Branch (Efik, Ibibio, and twelve other Cross-River languages), Adamawa Branch (Mumuye, Vere, and several smaller groups); and the Afroasiatic family: Berber Branch and Chad Branch (Hausa and several small groups). Greenberg, *op. cit.*, pp. 10–12, 48–49.

⁷ *Ibid.*, pp. 24–32; F. W. de St. Croix, *The Fulani of Northern Nigeria* (Lagos: 1944); C. L. Temple, ed., *Notes on the Tribes, Provinces, Emirates and States of the Northern Provinces of Nigeria* (Lagos: 1922); Mohammed Bello, *The Rise of the Sokoto Fulani*, trans. E. C. Arnett (Kano: 1929).

⁸ For the Hausa see S. J. Hogben, *The Muhammedan Emirates of Northern Nigeria* (London: 1930); M. G. Smith, *The Economy of Hausa Communities of Zaria* (London: 1955); Diedrich Westermann, "The Development of the Hausa People," *African Abstracts*, 3 (April, 1952), 69–70; Mallam Abubakar Imam, "Daura Sword is the Symbol of the Seven States of Hausaland," *West African Annual* (1950), 114–115; D. P. L. Dry, "The Social Structure of a Hausa Town" (unpublished paper read before the Royal Anthropological Institute, Nov. 4, 1950); Temple, *op. cit.*, pp. 405–408.

⁹ A. Schultze, *The Sultanate of Bornu*, trans. P. A. Benton (London: 1913); E. W. Bovill, *Caravans of the Old Sahara* (London: 1933); Hogben, *op. cit.*; Lady Lugard, *A Tropical Dependency* (London: Nisbet, 1905).

¹⁰ S. F. Nadel, *A Black Byzantium* (London: 1942); Daryll Forde and others, *Peoples of the Niger-Benue Confluence* (London: 1955).

¹¹ Laura and Paul Bohannan, *The Tiv of Central Nigeria* (London: 1953); Paul Bohannan, "Migration and Expansion of the Tiv," *Africa*, XXIV (Jan., 1954), 2–16; R. East, ed., *Akiga's Story* (London: 1939).

¹² For the Yoruba see Daryll Forde, *The Yoruba-Speaking Peoples of South-Western Nigeria* (London: 1951); S. O. Biobaku, "An Historical Sketch of Egba Traditional Authorities," *Africa*, XXII (Jan., 1952), 35–49; P. C. Lloyd, "The Traditional Political System of the Yoruba," *Southwestern Journal of Anthropology*, 10 (Winter, 1954), 366–384; P. C. Lloyd, "The Yoruba Lineage," *Africa*, XXV (July, 1955), 235–251; William B. Schwab, "Kinship and Lineage among the

Yoruba," *Africa*, XXV (Oct., 1955), 352–374; S. O. Biobaku, "The Kingly Titles of Western Nigeria," *West Africa*, May 3, 1952, pp. 391–392; Chief Samuel Ojo, *The Origin of the Yorubas* (Ibadan: 1952); E. A. Kenyo, *Origin of the Progenitor of the Yoruba Race* (Lagos: n.d.); Ajayi K. Ajisafe, *The Laws and Customs of the Yoruba People* (Lagos: 1946).

[13] W. Northcote, *Anthropological Report on the Edo-Speaking Peoples of Nigeria* (London: 1910); M. R. Bradbury, *The Benin Kingdom and the Edo-Speaking Peoples of South-Western Nigeria* (London: 1957); Jacob U. Egharevba, *Benin Laws and Customs* (Lagos: 1947), and *A Short History of Benin* (1st ed.; Lagos: 1936); Samuel O. Omoregie, *Binis Own Lagos* (Benin City: 1954); M. D. W. Jeffreys, "The Origins of the Benin Bronzes," *African Studies*, 10 (June, 1951), 87–91; S. W. Nee-Ankrah, *Whither Benin?* (Benin City: 1951); Uviri Okegberu, *A Short History of Isoko People* (Kano: n.d.); Peter I. Omo-Ananigie, *A Brief History of Etsakor* (Lagos: 1946).

[14] See Daryll Forde and G. I. Jones, *The Ibo and Ibibio-Speaking Peoples of South-Eastern Nigeria* (London: 1950), pp. 45–50; S. M. Juwe, *The Western Ibo People and the Coming Days* (Port Harcourt: 1953).

[15] As table 1 shows, more than 70 per cent of the Ijaw inhabit the Eastern Region. On simple arithmetic grounds they are, therefore, a people of the Eastern Region, and the 79,079 (1952 census) Ijaw inhabitants of the Western Region constitute a minority of that region. Culturally and linguistically the Ijaw are no more related to the Ibo or Ibibio than they are to the Edo or the Yoruba. There is no comprehensive ethnographic study of the Ijaw. See P. Amaury Talbot, *Tribes of the Niger Delta* (London: 1932); S. K. Owonaro, *The History of Ijo (Ijaw) and Her Neighbouring Tribes in Nigeria* (Lagos: 1949); Isaac Warrior-Osika, *Rivers Man! Separate State!* (Port Harcourt: 1955); and K. Onwuka Dike, *Trade and Politics in the Niger Delta, 1830–1885* (Oxford: 1956), pp. 24–46.

[16] Forde and Jones, *op. cit.*, pp. 9–27; M. M. Green, *Ibo Village Affairs* (London: 1947); C. K. Meek, *Law and Authority in a Nigerian Tribe* (London: 1937); Dike, *op. cit.*, pp. 20–46; Ben N. Azikiwe, "Nigerian Political Institutions," *Journal of Negro History*, XIV (July, 1929), 328–340.

[17] R. Kanu Umo, *History of Aro Settlements* (Yaba: n.d.); Dike, *op. cit.*, pp. 37–41.

[18] *Op. cit.*, p. 44.

[19] Under previous classificatory systems Ibo was a "Sudanic" language and Ibibio "semi-Bantu." According to Greenberg's revised system, both belong to the larger Niger-Congo family, but Ibo (together with Yoruba and others) belongs to the Kwa subfamily and Ibibio to the large Central Branch subfamily. *Op. cit.*, pp. 6–23, 33–42. For ethnographic data on the Ibibio, see Forde and Jones, *op. cit.*, pp. 67–92; P. Amaury Talbot, *Life in Southern Nigeria* (London: 1923) and *The Peoples of Southern Nigeria*; E. U. Udoma, "Law and British Administration in South-Eastern Nigeria" (unpublished Ph.D. dissertation, University of Dublin).

[20] Dike, *op. cit.*, pp. 24–26; Bassey P. Ituen, *The Ibibios and the Efiks* (Kano: n.d.).

[21] Ituen, *op. cit.* Forde and Jones classify the Efik as one of the main groups of the Ibibio-speaking people, and, *op. cit.*, page 69, state that "Efik is generally accepted among the Ibibio as the literary language."

[22] Schwab, *op. cit.*; Lloyd, "The Yoruba Lineage"; Dry, *op. cit.*; William R. Bascom, "West and Central Africa," in Ralph Linton, ed., *Most of the World* (New York: 1949), pp. 352 ff.

[23] *Census of Nigeria, 1931* (Lagos: 1932), II, 1.

CHAPTER 2: *The Historical Background*
(Pages 36–60)

[1] Thomas Hodgkin stated that "for the Hausa States and for Bornu it was above all the links with Tunisia and Tripolitania that mattered. For almost the last thousand years the Fezzan has been their window on the wider world." *West Africa*, Aug. 24, 1957, p. 799. See also E. W. Bovill, *Caravans of the Old Sahara* (London: 1933), pp. 25 ff.; J. D. Fage, *An Introduction to the History of West Africa* (Cambridge: 1955), pp. 9–39; C. K. Meek and others, *Europe and West Africa* (London: 1940), pp. 7–14.

[2] For a discussion of contacts between northern Nigeria and the Maghreb and the Middle East see Thomas Hodgkin, "Islam and Politics in West Africa," *West Africa*, Sept. 15, 1956, p. 703; L. A. Fabunmi, "Egypt and Africa," *West Africa*, Dec. 28, 1957, p. 123; C. R. Niven, "Nigerian Pilgrimage to Mecca," *Corona*, 2 (Nov., 1950), 408–410.

[3] C. K. Meek and others, *op. cit.*, pp. 7–8; C. K. Meek, *The Northern Tribes of Nigeria* (London: 1925), II, 1–131. The existence of historical links with Egypt is still very much in dispute.

[4] P. C. Lloyd, "Dom Domingos, Prince of Warri" (unpublished MS).

[5] Alan Burns, *History of Nigeria* (4th ed.; London: 1948), pp. 62–85, 97–108.

[6] For a discussion of the abolition of the slave trade and its effect upon Nigerian slave dealers, see K. Onwuka Dike, *Trade and Politics in the Niger Delta, 1830–1885* (Oxford: 1956), pp. 11 ff.

[7] See Melville Herskovits, *The Myth of the Negro Past* (New York: 1941), pp. 143–261; Pierre Verger, "Yoruba Influences in Brazil," *Odú*, 1 (Jan., 1955), 3–11.

[8] The history of this period is covered by Dike, *op. cit.*, pp. 208–214. See also D. Wellesley, *Sir George Goldie* (London: 1934).

[9] Margery Perham, *Native Administration in Nigeria* (London: 1937), p. 3. See also S. E. Crowe, *The Berlin West African Conference, 1884–1885* (London: 1942).

[10] A. H. M. Kirk-Greene, "Who Coined the Name 'Nigeria'?" *West Africa*, Dec. 22, 1956, p. 1035. Cf. rejoinder of S. I. Edokpayi in *West Africa*, March 16, 1957, p. 252.

[11] Margery Perham's Introduction to Joan Wheare, *The Nigerian Legislative Council* (London: 1950), p. x.

[12] This was especially true in the Eastern Region and the Middle Belt of the Northern Region, where the absence of sociological data made administrative convenience the guiding principle.

[13] See Lord Hailey, *Native Administration in the British African Territories* (London: 1951), III, 108–113; L. Gray Cowan, *West African Local Government* (New York: 1958); T. Olawale Elias, "Makers of Nigerian Law," *West Africa*, Dec. 31, 1955, p. 1233. In reflecting on Lugard's early policies, Dr. Elias concludes that "in excluding Northern Nigeria from the Legislative Council Lugard missed a great opportunity of carrying his epoch-making task to its logical conclusion. He centralised the administration; he universalised the principles of Indirect Rule; he unified the judiciary; he even created a new country as one political unit; but he hesitated to build a Nigerian nation. Had North and South been brought into a common forum . . . and encouraged with the authority and prestige of this man of destiny to look upon themselves as fellow-countrymen they probably would have started earlier to learn to co-operate in a common political endeavour. . . ." *Op. cit., West Africa*, Jan. 7, 1956, p. 7.

[14] *Memorandum on Local Government Policy in the Eastern Provinces* (Lagos: 1949); Cowan, *op. cit.*; R. A. Stevens, "Progress in Local Government in the Eastern Region of Nigeria," *Journal of African Administration*, 5 (Jan., 1953), 15–21.

[15] *Annual Reports,* Plateau and Benue provinces, 1945–1950; Laura and Paul Bohannan, *The Tiv of Central Nigeria* (London: 1953), pp. 31–41; Hailey, *op. cit.,* III, 53–61.

[16] *Minutes of the Proceedings of the Conference of Chiefs, Northern Provinces,* 1931–1938; *Proceedings of the Conference of Yoruba Chiefs, Western Provinces,* 1938–1942.

[17] Quoted in Allan McPhee, *The Economic Revolution in British West Africa* (London: 1926), p. 106.

[18] Quoted in *ibid.*

[19] Quoted in *ibid.,* p. 117.

[20] *Annual Report,* Nigeria, 1950 (London: H.M.S.O., 1951).

[21] McPhee, *op. cit.,* p. 120.

[22] *Nigeria Handbook, 1926* (Lagos: Government Printer, 1926), pp. 161 ff.

[23] McPhee, *op. cit.,* pp. 107–125.

[24] Margery Perham, ed., *The Native Economies of Nigeria* (London: 1946), p. 9.

[25] Quoted in McPhee, *op. cit.,* p. 233.

[26] *Annual Report,* Nigeria, 1950 (London: H.M.S.O., 1951), p. 28.

[27] Quoted in McPhee, *op. cit.,* p. 217.

[28] See Hailey, *op. cit.,* III, 179 ff.; T. Olawale Elias, *Nigerian Land Law and Custom* (2d ed.; London: 1953), pp. 88–172.

[29] See McPhee, *op. cit.,* p. 7; S. H. Frankel, *Capital Investment in Africa* (London: Oxford, 1938), pp. 156–162.

[30] The discrimination about which southerners complained is that northerners in the south could obtain freehold or long-term leases, whereas southerners in the north could acquire only a "certificate of occupancy." See Elias, *Nigerian Land Law and Custom,* pp. 298–299.

[31] *The Native Economies of Nigeria,* p. 16.

CHAPTER 3: *Western Economic Forces*
(Pages 63–90)

[1] Allan McPhee, *The Economic Revolution in British West Africa* (London: 1926), pp. 39–40; C. K. Meek and others, *Europe and West Africa* (London: 1940), pp. 80–93.

[2] One of the most perceptive and penetrating analyses of the distortion in classical concepts of the economics of traditional societies is Lucy P. Mair, "The Growth of Economic Individualism in African Society," *Journal of the Royal African Society,* 33 (July, 1934), 261–273. At page 200 she notes that "we still find it assumed as axiomatic that there is some fundamental difference between the African attitude to property and our own. Even if the word 'communist' is no longer used, the attempt persists to describe this supposed difference by some such term as 'communalist' or 'collectivist.'"

[3] See especially M. G. Smith, *The Economy of Hausa Communities of Zaria* (London: 1955), p. 100. The behavioral and attitudinal differences among representatives of different Nigerian groups, and their cultural correlates, are phenomena requiring much more intensive and systematic study. I believe, however, that the nonhierarchical and segmentary character of Ibo society, in contrast to the extreme stratification in both Yoruba and Hausa societies, helps to explain the differences noted.

[4] K. Onwuka Dike, *Trade and Politics in the Niger Delta, 1830–1885* (Oxford: 1956).

[5] On the growth of an internal exchange economy see Margery Perham, ed., *The Native Economies of Nigeria* (London: 1946), pp. 32–35; K. M. Buchanan and J. C. Pugh, *Land and People in Nigeria* (London: 1955), pp. 100 ff.; and E. A. Keukjian, "Commercializing Influences of the Development of Exports of

Indigenous Agricultural Economies in Tropical Africa" (unpublished Ph.D. dissertation, Harvard University, June, 1953).

[6] Perham, *op. cit.*, p. 33.

[7] The Eastern Region, however, is dangerously dependent upon one major item (palm products), which constitutes nearly 80 per cent of its exports. There is a similar but less acute danger in the cocoa-growing areas of western Nigeria.

[8] T. Olawale Elias, *Nigerian Land Law and Custom* (2d ed.; London: 1953), pp. 173 ff.

[9] Quoted in *ibid.*, p. 296.

[10] Buchanan and Pugh point out that the background to the agricultural economy of Nigeria is found in the "fundamental doctrine" announced by Governor Sir Hugh Clifford in the early 1920's: "Land policy should aim primarily, mainly and eventually at the development of the agricultural resources of these countries through the agency of their indigenous inhabitants." (*Op. cit.*, p. 100.) It was in this same period that Sir Hugh categorically rejected Lord Leverhulme's proposal for Nigerian plantations.

[11] Calculated from figures in Margery Perham, ed., *Mining, Commerce, and Finance in Nigeria* (London: 1948), pp. 18, 97; *Nigeria Handbook, 1936* (Lagos: 1937); *Annual Report*, Department of Education, 1938 (Lagos: Government Printer, 1939). These figures are estimates only, having been collected from several sources of unknown reliability.

[12] See Geoffrey Tooth, *Studies in Mental Illness in the Gold Coast* (London: H.M.S.O., 1950).

[13] See *Enquiry into the Cost of Living and the Control of the Cost of Living in the Colony and Protectorate of Nigeria, 1946,* Colonial no. 204 (London: H.M.S.O., 1946), pp. 53–66.

[14] Mair, *op. cit.*, p. 270, argues that "the separation of economic privilege from social obligation . . . seems to be almost universal among primitive peoples when they are brought into contact with European trade and initiated into the use of money."

[15] The acculturative role of the city in Nigeria has been not unlike that of the city in Yucatan, where urban influences extended into the hinterland to the town, the peasant village, and the tribal village. See Robert Redfield, "The Second Epilogue to Maya History," in *Supplementary Publications*, no. 28 (Washington: Carnegie Institution, 1937), pp. 12–22.

[16] The consequences of urbanization in Nigeria were but approximations of the general characteristics of "urbanism" as described by Louis Wirth in "The Urban Society and Civilization," *American Journal of Sociology*, XLV (March, 1940), 752, and "Urbanism as a Way of Life," *American Journal of Sociology*, XLIV (1938), 1–8.

[17] See William R. Bascom, "Urbanization among the Yoruba," *American Journal of Sociology*, LX (March, 1955), 446–453. Bascom notes that the estimated index of urbanization of Yoruba cities falls between the indexes of the United States and of Canada, and the urban pattern among the Yoruba is not unlike that of modern France.

There is continuing debate among anthropologists and sociologists regarding the criteria for the definition of a city. It could be argued that the concentrated aggregations in Yorubaland are not properly cities because they lack the heterogeneity and impersonality characteristic of the modern city. William Schwab, for example, has suggested that such aggregations are urban in form but "folk" in terms of social organization and process. Although acknowledging the importance of the distinction between the industrial and the nonindustrial city, Bascom contends that the Yoruba cities satisfy the principal criteria of a city (*ibid.*, p. 446). For the purposes of this study, the concentrated aggregations of Yorubas will be referred to as cities.

As Ralph Beals has argued, technological specialization and industrialization, as well as secularization, the cash nexus, and a high degree of individuation, "may be characteristics primarily associated with urbanized societies, yet not be necessary attributes of the city itself." See his "Urbanism, Urbanization, Acculturation," *American Anthropologist,* 53 (Jan.–March, 1951), 9.

An offsetting factor that could not be evaluated because of the absence of census data is the countertendency in Yorubaland, during the past fifty years, for farmers to live more and more on their farms, rather than to cluster together in the cities. Several Yoruba cities emerged as war camps during the intertribal wars of the nineteenth century, and this return-to-the-farm movement is explained in terms of the British pax. I do not believe, however, that this factor would significantly alter the general observations stated in the text.

[18] This has been confirmed in a letter from Peter Lloyd, former Research Fellow in the West African Institute of Economic and Social Research, who writes: "It is true the Yoruba are highly urbanized and acculturated, but Yoruba towns are tribal towns. Wealth weakens but does not break; the richest Ijebus still live in the ancestral compound and belong to their proper age sets. Most traders and craftsmen live at home—only the literates move." Again, as Bascom points out, "the *anomie* stressed by Durkheim and later sociologists does not seem to be apparent, unless it is to be found among the rural Yoruba who find themselves in the city. Since the lineage is the residential unit and involves reciprocal social and economic obligations, the city dweller need not feel lonely or insecure. Competitiveness is strong, and economic failure can lead to frustration or suicide but not to starvation." *Op. cit.,* p. 451.

It should be stressed that the differences in acculturation between the members of a continuing social group in a traditional city and the uprooted migrants inhabiting a heterogeneous new city are essentially quantitative and not qualitative. Cf. the hypotheses advanced by Beals, *op. cit.,* p. 7.

[19] See Gideon Sjoberg, "The Preindustrial City," *American Journal of Sociology,* LX (March, 1955), 438–445.

[20] The variation in the degree to which traditional cities have been caught up in modern urban activities has frequently been the result of chance or caprice. Ogbomosho, in 1911 the second largest city in Nigeria, stagnated for more than three decades because the rail line was routed via Oshogbo; Abeokuta, a famous Yoruba city, was eclipsed by Lagos and Ibadan as a result, in part, of its location midway between these two larger centers; and Kaduna, rather than Zaria or Kano, became the center of government and administration in northern Nigeria largely as a result of the personal wish of Lord Lugard. Kaduna is, of course, more in the center of the region than other cities. The famous centers of Sokoto, Katsina, and Yerwa have been retarded in their urban development because of location and poor communications, among other reasons.

[21] An interesting parallel is the personal status and political orientation of the first-generation native-born American of foreign parentage. See Gabriel Almond, *The Appeals of Communism* (Princeton: Princeton University Press, 1954), pp. 203–210. Almond challenges Philip Selznick's hypothesis that the processes of industrialization, urbanization, and democratization operate to create "an unstructured collectivity withdrawn from the normal, spontaneous commitments of social life, . . . a glob of humanity," affirming that it ignores the human capacity "to create new and comparatively satisfying primary and community ties to take the place of older ones which have been eroded by social mobility." One might add that the hypothesis also overlooks the demonstrated capacity of Africans to preserve and adapt original primary group ties in the new urban situation. These observations do not refute the substance of the Selznick thesis; rather they qualify its rather rigid sociological determinism.

[22] In the Northern Region both the ruling emirs and the British authorities had good political reasons for maintaining the separation between the traditional sector and the stranger sector. It was a logical corollary of indirect rule, but it has also

served to shield the peoples of the indigenous sector from unsettling political ideas and from active contact with the more nationalist-minded southerners living in the sabon garis. In the Yoruba cities of the west, the separation was partly economic in character.

²³ *Legislative Council Debates,* Nigeria, March 5, 1945, p. 38.

²⁴ The United Africa Company, a subsidiary of Unilever, is the lineal descendant of the National African Company (formed in 1879 by Sir George Goldie as a result of the merger of all British companies trading on the Niger), the Royal Niger Company (which operated under a royal charter giving it the powers of government from 1886 to 1900, when the charter was revoked), and the Niger Company (1900–1930), acquired by Unilever and Lever Brothers in 1930. See Perham, *Mining, Commerce, and Finance in Nigeria,* pp. 60 ff.; Dike, *op. cit.,* pp. 203 ff.; P. T. Bauer, *West African Trade* (Cambridge: 1954), pp. 107–108.

²⁵ P. T. Bauer, "Concentration in Tropical Trade," *Economica,* XX (Nov., 1953), 302–321.

²⁶ P. T. Bauer, a Cambridge economist and author of an exhaustive and widely debated study of oligopoly and monopoly in Nigerian trade, states that although the firms in the AWAM have at various times acted in concert in the import trade, the association does not permanently commit them to such a policy. The five firms associated with the UAC in the AWAM are two British firms, John Holt and Co. Ltd. (Liverpool) and Paterson, Zochonis and Co. Ltd.; two French firms, Compagnie Française de L'Afrique Occidentale, and the Société Commerciale de L'Ouest Africain; and a Swiss firm, the Union Trading Company Ltd. See Bauer, *West African Trade,* pp. 66–67.

²⁷ *Ibid.,* pp. 180–191.

²⁸ *Ibid.,* pp. 145–155.

²⁹ *Ibid.,* pp. 246–259. Bauer points out (p. 250) that in actual practice the AWAM worked out the quotas for its various members and informed the Colonial Office, which in turn simply issued instructions to the Produce Control Board conforming to the AWAM formula. See also Perham, *Mining, Commerce, and Finance in Nigeria,* pp. 102 ff.

³⁰ J. Mars, "Extra-Territorial Enterprises," in Perham, *Mining, Commerce, and Finance in Nigeria,* pp. 95–96, 113–122; William N. M. Geary, *Nigeria under British Rule* (London: 1927), pp. 191 ff.

³¹ *West African Trade,* pp. 22–34, 104–111. See also Bauer, "Concentration in Tropical Trade," pp. 305 ff.

³² See McPhee, *op. cit.,* pp. 85 ff., and Dike, *op. cit.,* pp. 97–218. The elimination of African middlemen in the Delta area during the last two decades of the nineteenth century was one side of the establishment of a practical trade monopoly by the Royal Niger Company; the other side was the elimination or amalgamation of the 200-odd European traders and firms that existed at mid-century. The elimination of the African middlemen has been defended on economic and welfare grounds. Thus McPhee argues that it was necessary in order to break the ruthless monopoly held by the coastal chiefs and to establish direct contact with the native producers in the hinterland. (*Op. cit.,* p. 85.) Also, Macgregor Laird, the pioneer European trader in the lower Niger Basin, strongly believed that Africans should be partners in development, but he had in mind the "tribal inhabitants" and not the "degraded" Delta middlemen. (Dike, *op. cit.,* pp. 115–116.)

³³ See J. Mars, *op. cit.,* p. 120; Bauer, *West African Trade,* pp. 118–119. Bauer draws attention to another factor, that in the aggregate the activities of these pre–World War I traders were on a very small scale compared with subsequent trading operations, and that the "African share in direct foreign trade declined primarily as a combined result of the increased capital requirements of a rapidly growing trade and of a money economy, and of the losses sustained in trade fluctuations." (P. 118.) One African trader in 1910 pointed out that the "extension of the railroad to the hinterland has not been an unmixed blessing—at least not

to the native. Cotton and other imported European goods can now be carried to the interior so conveniently that the big mercantile firms are always able to keep a large and varied stock on hand at all their branch factories which they could not do some time back, owing to the difficulty and expense of transport. The result is that the trade for the native in the interior is just as unprofitable as it is in Lagos, the middleman system having been abolished, the big firms selling direct to the consumers, carrying the goods to their very doors, so to speak. In this line of business the native trader is absolutely nowhere." *African Mail,* Sept. 23, 1910. Cf. McPhee, *op. cit.,* p. 85: "European houses are gradually eliminating the middlemen from the south and establishing direct relations with the native producers, to the mutual profit of [these houses and the producers]."

[34] Gilbert Burck, "The World of Unilever," *Fortune* (Jan.–Feb., 1948), 136.

[35] For a fairly comprehensive summary of the role and function of the middlemen in the cocoa trade of western Nigeria, see K. D. S. Baldwin, *The Marketing of Cocoa in Western Nigeria* (London: 1954), especially pp. 7–10, 34 ff. Although the elimination of the prewar type of middleman was more or less a by-product of wartime marketing controls, the Nowell Commission in 1938 explicitly recommended a reorganization of cocoa marketing for the specific purpose of extinguishing the middleman. See *Report of the Commission on the Marketing of West African Cocoa,* Cmd. 5845 (London: H.M.S.O., 1938).

[36] The following list of percentages of cocoa purchased in different periods by different types of firms shows the changing character of racial participation in one aspect of the Nigerian export trade (figures for 1940–1941 are estimates):

Period	European firms	Levantine firms	African firms	Association of Nigerian Co-operative Exporters
1940–1941	92	7	1	—
1948–1949	78	9	2	11
1949–1950	76	12	3	9
1950–1951	72	14	4	10
1951–1952	70	15	7	8

See Baldwin, *op. cit.,* p. 21.

[37] As one leading nationalist paper editorialized, "The system . . . assures the capitalist middlemen huge and stable profits and virtually destroys African middlemen who might otherwise have been shippers themselves." *Daily Service,* Oct. 30, 1944.

[38] Bauer lists several "local conditions" and various recent factors that have made the capital requirements for successful business operation exceptionally high in Nigeria, thereby favoring expatriate firms with large capital resources. These include physical conditions that require a large inventory, the absence of a local capitalist class (though this argument can be circular), and especially high costs incident to initial entry into the field. See *West African Trade,* pp. 106–107.

[39] See Mars, *op. cit.,* p. 101. The factors influencing the conservatism of European banks, and their allegedly prejudiced practices, are critically analyzed in Bauer, *West African Trade,* pp. 180–188.

[40] A brief history of the indigenous banking movement in Nigeria appears in W. T. Newlyn and D. C. Rowan, *Money and Banking in British Colonial Africa* (Oxford: 1954), pp. 97–122. Between January, 1945, and March, 1952, 11 African companies using the name "bank" were formed (p. 107). On the 49 African bank offices established by 1952 more than half (26) were in the Western Region, 8 were in the Northern Region, 6 were in the Eastern Region, and 9 were in the colony (p. 109).

[41] *Annual Report,* Nigerian Farmers and Commercial Bank Ltd., 1951 (Lagos: 1951).

[42] Several prominent figures in the National Bank of Nigeria were also active in the Action Group (the majority party in the Western Region after 1952); and

leaders in the National Council of Nigeria and the Cameroons (including particularly Nnamdi Azikiwe) were prominent in the original management of the African Continental Bank. See Newlyn and Rowan, *op. cit.*, pp. 96 ff.; *Proceedings of the Tribunal Appointed to Inquire into Allegations of Improper Conduct by the Premier of the Eastern Region of Nigeria in Connection with the Affairs of the African Continental Bank Limited and Other Relevant Matters* . . . (2 vols.; Lagos: Federal Government Printer, 1957).

[43] *Report of the Commission of Enquiry into Conditional Sales* (Lagos: Government Printer, 1948). See also Suzanne Comhaire-Sylvain, "Le Travail des Femmes à Lagos, Nigérie," *Zäire*, 5 (May, 1951), 475–502.

[44] See *Report of the Commission of Enquiry into Disturbances in the Gold Coast, 1948*, Colonial no. 231 (London: H.M.S.O., 1948), pp. 34–47; *Report of an Enquiry into the Cost of Living . . . in . . . Nigeria, 1946*, Colonial no. 204 (London: H.M.S.O., 1946).

[45] P. Bower, "The Mining Industry," in Perham, *Mining, Commerce, and Finance in Nigeria*, p. 5. During the period 1937–1947, however, the Secretary of State for the Colonies, A. Creech Jones, announced that the UAC had agreed to let its share of mineral royalties revert to the government fifty-two years earlier than the 1900 agreement had provided. For nationalist criticism of the 1900 agreement see Nnamdi Azikiwe, *Land Tenure in Northern Nigeria* (Lagos: 1942).

[46] In 1946 the chairman of Lever Brothers declared that "the pattern of the businesses of the United Africa Company is . . . gradually changing from general wholesaling and retailing to one of specialized wholesaling, with retailing passing more and more into the hands of the Africans." London *Times*, Nov. 30, 1946.

[47] The number of Nigerian managers employed by the UAC nearly doubled (43 to 79) during the period 1946–1952. An interesting feature of the UAC Africanization program at the management level is that African politicians frequently cite the example of the UAC when exhorting others firms, and even governments, to proceed with greater speed. For details on Africanization in the UAC see *Statistical and Economic Review*, no. 5 (March, 1950), 42; no. 12 (Sept., 1953), 40–41.

[48] W. K. Hancock, *Survey of British Commonwealth Affairs* (London: 1952), Vol. II, Part 2.

[49] *West African Trade*, pp. 31–32.

CHAPTER 4: *Christianity and European Missionaries*
(Pages 91–112)

[1] In discussing the factors that impelled Western missionaries to undertake evangelical work in Africa, we will note only selected aspects of the African situation. A complete explanation of missionary motivation would necessarily include many elements in nineteenth-century Europe which stimulated and fostered extra-European expansion. Africa was just beginning to be opened up by traders and adventurers during the latter part of the great evangelical revival that commenced toward the end of the eighteenth century and had its roots in European social history. Carlton J. H. Hayes has suggested that the very materialism that weakened Christianity in Europe tended to foster a spiritual crusade abroad. See his *A Generation of Materialism* (New York: Harper, 1941), pp. 148–151, 223–224. In a not unrelated vein, K. Onwuka Dike, a Nigerian historian, has argued that whereas diverse noneconomic forces affected the "movement for the penetration of the West African interior, . . . the economic change taking place in Europe at the time . . . canalized these discordant elements [adventurers, scientific explorers, missionaries, humanitarians, and European nationalists] into one channel and provided a common ground for unity. . . ." *Trade and Politics in the Niger Delta, 1830–1885* (Oxford: 1956), p. 14.

[2] Eugene Stock, ed., *The History of the Church Missionary Society* (London: Church Missionary Society, 1899), I, 45.

³ Quoted in Edward W. Blyden, *Christianity, Islam and the Negro Race* (London: 1887), p. 65.

⁴ The number of European missionaries (including ordained priests as well as lay helpers) per million of population was as follows: Asia, 29; India, 24; tropical Africa, 183; and southern Nigeria, 81. Computed from statistics in Joseph I. Parker, ed., *Interpretative Statistical Survey of the World Mission of the Christian Church* (London: International Missionary Council, 1938), pp. 18–22, 33–35.

⁵ *Church Missionary Atlas* (London: Church Missionary Society, 1896), p. 11.

⁶ William J. W. Roome, "Strategic Lines of Christian Missions in Africa," *International Review of Missions*, V (July, 1916), 353–354.

⁷ Quoted in *ibid.*, p. 354.

⁸ *Ibid.*, p. 354.

⁹ P. Amaury Talbot, *The Peoples of Southern Nigeria* (London: 1926), IV, 115.

¹⁰ *Ibid.*, pp. 103 ff.; J. Lowry Maxwell, *Nigeria, the Land, the People and Christian Progress* (London: 1931), pp. 105 ff.

¹¹ By 1931 there were only 20,000 Christian converts in the Northern Region, and of this number more than half belonged to the Yoruba elements in Ilorin Province. The rest came from the Nupe and other Middle Belt groups. See *Census of Nigeria for 1931* (Lagos: 1932), II, 63–64.

¹² See James S. Coleman, "Nationalism in Tropical Africa," *American Political Science Review*, XLVIII (June, 1954), 416–417.

¹³ The Ibo have been in the forefront of southern and Pan-Nigerian nationalism, and educated Kanuri have been prominent in the more radical movements in northern Nigeria. Despite great contrasts in culture and history, there is evidence that the two groups had one cultural trait in common, an emphasis upon achieved status.

¹⁴ H. Kraemer, *The Christian Message in a Non-Christian World* (London: 1938), p. 342.

¹⁵ *Ibid.*, p. 230.

¹⁶ David Livingstone, *Missionary Travels and Research in South Africa* (London: 1857), p. 5.

¹⁷ Roome, *op. cit.*, p. 353.

¹⁸ In a message to the Yoruba chiefs, Queen Victoria remarked: "Commerce alone cannot make a nation great: England has become great through the knowledge of God in Jesus Christ." Quoted in J. Du Plessis, *The Evangelization of Pagan Africa* (Capetown: J. C. Juta, 1930), p. 137.

¹⁹ Cf. K. M. Panikkar, *Asia and Western Dominance* (London: Allen and Unwin, 1953), pp. 455–456.

²⁰ Kraemer, *op. cit.*, p. 55.

²¹ Edwin W. Smith, *The Christian Mission in Africa* (London: 1926), p. 49.

²² Quoted in *ibid.*, p. 48.

²³ *Ibid.*, p. 132. See also p. 19.

²⁴ Quoted in Salo Wittmayer Baron, *Modern Nationalism and Religion* (New York: Harper, 1947), p. 157.

²⁵ "Many missionaries are not good revolutionaries, but blind ones, because their minds are closed to the inestimable advantage they can derive from the labours of the anthropologists." Kraemer, *op. cit.*, p. 343.

²⁶ *Ibid.*, p. 347.

²⁷ The literature of Protestant missionary societies has given marked attention to traditional African culture, reflected in the recasting of educational objectives, in new attitudes toward the marriage payment and dancing, and in a new appreciation of African religious and cosmological concepts. In particular, see J. H. Oldham and M. Gibson, *The Remaking of Man in Africa* (London: Oxford, 1931); Edwin W. Smith, ed., *African Ideas of God* (London: 1950); and Geoffrey Parrinder, *West African Religion* (London: 1949). The relatively large number of articles on African cultural subjects in the *International Review of Missions*

(quarterly journal of the International Missionary Council) provide further evidence of the new orientation of missionaries.

[28] Propositions regarding the atomizing tendencies of Protestant evangelization are advanced by Kraemer, *op. cit.*, p. 350. Busia cites an official report of 1905 describing the conflict induced by Christian conversion: "The tendency of Christian converts to alienate themselves from the communities to which they belong is very marked, and is naturally resented by the chiefs who claim their hereditary right, in which they are supported by Government, to make the converts in common with their fellow tribesmen obey such laws and orders as are in accordance with native custom, not being repugnant to natural justice, equity and good conscience." See K. A. Busia in Daryll Forde, ed., *African Worlds* (London: International African Institute, 1954), p. 207.

[29] Du Plessis, *op. cit.*, p. 141.

[30] *Op. cit.*, pp. 12–13.

[31] Stock, *op. cit.*, I, 114–115, 118; II, 453, 455, 535, 646. Bishop Crowther published a Yoruba vocabulary in 1843.

[32] *Ibid.*, II, 459.

[33] Maxwell, *op. cit.*, pp. 154–155.

[34] See M. A. Rawling, *Bibliography of African Christian Literature* (London: 1923), pp. 108–127.

[35] Smith, *op. cit.*, p. 47.

[36] Stock, *op. cit.*, II, 101, 426, 454; III, 4811; Talbot, *op. cit.*, IV, 112, 123. It has been reported that in 1851 Henry Venn, early leader of the Church Missionary Society, thought "the ultimate object of a mission, viewed under its ecclesiastical result, to be the settlement of a Native church, under Native pastors, upon a self-supporting system." *East Africa and Rhodesia*, Sept. 8, 1949, p. 9.

[37] Maxwell, *op. cit.*, pp. 112–113.

[38] Stock, *op. cit.*, II, 414. See also Du Plessis, *op. cit.*, p. 140; Blyden, *op. cit.*, p. 48.

[39] Stock, *op. cit.*, III, 737 ff.; Du Plessis, *op. cit.*, pp. 144–145. Although the CMS criticized aspects of Bishop Crowther's administration, they subsequently paid glowing tribute to his achievements.

[40] Diedrich Westermann, *The African To-day* (London: 1934), p. 236.

[41] Cf. Gunnar Myrdal, *An American Dilemma* (New York: 1944), p. 858, for comparison with American Negro churches.

[42] Cf. *ibid.*, p. 863.

[43] *African Mail*, Nov. 12, 1909.

[44] Blyden, *op. cit.*, p. 66.

[45] *Ibid.*, pp. 78–79.

[46] *Daily Service*, July 2, 1945.

[47] During a tour of Nigeria in 1911, the Reverend J. H. Harris warned that "the greatest problem which faces the missionary societies in West Africa is that of polygamy, for the whole social fabric of the race rests upon a polygamous basis." *African Mail*, Aug. 11, 1911.

[48] Isaac Delano, *One Church for Nigeria* (London: 1945), p. 12.

[49] *Ibid.*, p. 15.

[50] Quoted from the Treaty with the King and Chiefs of Opobo, 1884, in Alan Burns, *History of Nigeria* (4th ed.; London: 1948), p. 338.

[51] The concept of close missionary-government collaboration in Central Africa was in fact espoused by one prominent Christian spokesman. Although this recommendation was made with specific reference to Northern Rhodesia, it was made in terms of general application. See J. Merle Davis, *Modern Industry and the African* (London: Macmillan, 1933), pp. 346–357.

[52] *Ibid.*, pp. 356–357.

[53] The Society of Friends in both the United Kingdom and the United States has been particularly active in its support of African students and nationalists. Several

of the most active members in pronationalist groups such as the Africa Bureau, the Fabian Society, and the Movement for Colonial Freedom have been prominent Christian leaders. Some unusually outspoken Christian agencies have directly challenged alien rule. For example, in 1947 the Catholic Association for International Peace declared: "Imperialists like Lord Hailey keep repeating that the ultimate aim of British colonial policy in Africa and elsewhere is self-government for all dependencies. However, they all seem rather vague about the length of the period of tutelage necessary before subject peoples can assume political responsibility. . . . The Church teaches that one of the just causes of war is the securing of the independence of a nation or the recovering of territory taken unjustly from a people. . . . Our sympathies should be and are with [the Africans]." *Symposium on Africa,* Catholic Association for International Peace (New York: 1947). Again, at the annual London meeting of the Universities Mission to Central Africa, the Reverend R. W. Stopford stressed the fact that nationalism was the result of Christian influence and ought not to cause surprise; indeed, it would be surprising if there had been no growth of nationalism. *East Africa and Rhodesia,* Sept. 8, 1949, pp. 9 ff.

[54] *East Africa and Rhodesia,* March 22, 1945, p. 664.

[55] "Easter Reflection, the Missionary in West Africa," *West Africa,* April 5, 1947, p. 280.

CHAPTER 5: *Western Education*
(Pages 113–140)

[1] The concept "Western education" (as distinguished from traditional African education) is employed herein to refer to formal and systematic instruction in subjects characteristic of the curricula used in Western countries (reading, writing, and arithmetic as core subjects, to which are added courses in the humanities, arts, and sciences). This system of instruction was designed to standardize the training of young people not only in the values of a modern industrialized and commercialized society, but also in the necessary skills for meaningful participation in that society.

[2] A. Victor Murray, *The School in the Bush* (London: 1929), p. 65.

[3] See *Ten-Year Educational Plan,* Nigerian Sessional Paper no. 6/1944, p. 13.

[4] See H. S. Scott, "The Development of the Education of the African in Relation to Western Contact," *The Year Book of Education, 1938* (London: 1938), pp. 693–739; Murray, *op. cit.,* p. 218.

[5] It is noteworthy that some early government officials criticized missionaries for their tendency "to discourage the teaching of English by the teaching of the native languages and dialects and to seek to perpetuate them as written languages." *Annual Report,* Department of Education, Southern Provinces, 1926 (Lagos: 1927), p. 7. On the role of missionaries in the development of the vernacular see Diedrich Westermann, *The African To-day and To-morrow* (3d ed.; London: 1949), pp. 117–128.

[6] For nationalist criticisms on education see Kingsley Ozuomba Mbadiwe, *British and Axis Aims in Africa* (New York: 1942), pp. 173–203; A. A. Nwafor Orizu, *Without Bitterness* (New York: 1944), pp. 140–143; Mbonu Ojike, *My Africa* (New York: 1946), pp. 54–55; and Nnamdi Azikiwe, *Renascent Africa* (Accra: 1937). Azikiwe said: *"Africans have been mis-educated. They need mental emancipation so as to be re-educated to the real needs of Renascent Africa"* (p. 135). "Why should African youth depend upon Oxford, Cambridge, Harvard, Yale, Sorbonne, Berlin, Heidelberg, for intellectual growth? These universities are mirrors which reflect their particular societal idiosyncrasies" (p. 140).

[7] *Op. cit.,* pp. 101–102.

[8] *Report of the Commission on Higher Education in West Africa,* Cmd. 6655 (London: H.M.S.O., 1945), pp. 51–61.

⁹ G. A. Fabure, "Anomalies in Nigeria's Education System," *African World* (Feb., 1950), 16.

¹⁰ F. D. Lugard, *The Dual Mandate in British Tropical Africa* (4th ed.; London: 1929), p. 428; Arthur Mayhew, "A Comparative Survey of Educational Aims and Methods in British India and British Tropical Africa," *Africa*, VI (April, 1933), 172 ff.

¹¹ See especially Westermann, *op. cit.*, pp. 98–128; and Murray, *op. cit.*, pp. 337–370.

¹² Scott, *op. cit.*, p. 711.

¹³ *Education Policy in British Tropical Africa*, Cmd. 2374 (London: H.M.S.O., 1936), p. 4. Although not published until 1936, the policy statement was presented to Parliament in March, 1925.

¹⁴ *Memorandum on the Education of African Communities*, Colonial no. 103 (London: H.M.S.O., 1935), par. 29.

¹⁵ *Education Policy in British Tropical Africa*, p. 4.

¹⁶ *Education in Africa*, Phelps-Stokes Fund (New York: 1932), pp. 145 ff.

¹⁷ Edwin W. Smith, *The Christian Mission in Africa* (London: 1926), pp. 62–63.

¹⁸ Quoted in *Annual Report*, Department of Education, 1926 (Lagos: Government Printer, 1926), p. 2. See also p. 6.

¹⁹ Address to the Nigerian Council, Dec. 29, 1920 (typed copy), Macaulay Papers.

²⁰ *Annual Report*, Department of Education, 1926, p. 16.

²¹ *Ten-Year Educational Plan*, p. 4.

²² Certain interwar developments should be noted. In the field of agriculture, some of the missions on their own initiative established school farms and taught gardening. Training colleges for government teachers were opened on sites adjoining experimental farms of the Agriculture Department, and courses in rural science were taught by agricultural officers. After 1930 agricultural instruction and workshop practice were taught in schools that were preparing for the new school-leaving examination. In several areas the Agriculture Department worked closely with mission schools to train students in the proper cultivation of the oil palm and cocoa plant, as well as in the growing of food crops. In 1937 the government seriously undertook to give all elementary school teachers a satisfactory course of training in school agriculture, to be supplemented by follow-up work by agricultural officers. By the outbreak of World War II, however, the government and the missions were still experimenting with new schemes, and very little real progress had been made.

In the field of vocational and technical training, the prewar story was much the same. The Hope-Waddell Training Institution, established in 1895, was for three decades the only secondary school that offered meaningful vocational training, but its students were few, and the skills acquired were limited to carpentry, printing, and tailoring. Even when workshop practice was included in the required curriculum in accordance with the post-1930 policy, the instruction was not designed to equip the student for specific occupations. The great majority of Nigerian artisans secured their training the hard way—as low-paid laborers and long-term apprentices in the garages and workshops of commercial firms and of government departments. The technical departments of government (Public Works, Railways, Marine, Posts and Telegraph, and Lands and Survey) conducted small-scale technical training programs for future recruits. Although the quality of this instruction was excellent—especially because it provided a sandwich course of practice and theory—it was usually limited quantitatively to the number of vacant posts in the respective departments. During the first thirteen years of its course, the Public Works Department trained only 107; and as late as 1944 the average annual entry was only 10. Annual entry figures for the other departments were: Marine Department, 12; Railways, 6–8; and Posts and Telegraph, 4–6.

Before 1940 only about 300 Nigerians had had an opportunity to receive formal instruction and training for technical occupations. (*Report of the Commission on Higher Education in West Africa*, pp. 115–118, 188–189.)

A familiar theme in most of the prewar annual reports of the Department of Education was: ". . . the Department makes no attempt to train artisans, or to give technical instruction." In planning for postwar educational expansion the Nigerian government did not intend to alter their historic attitude toward technical education, as it was "doubtful whether a big trade school or a technical college is necessary at the present stage. Such a school would be extremely expensive to build and equip, require a large European and African staff and there would be no great demand for its products when trained." (*Ten-Year Educational Plan*, p. 18.)

The economic depression of the early 1930's and the coming of the war in the late 1930's serve in part to explain government inactivity regarding educational change.

[23] W. E. B. Du Bois, *The Souls of Black Folk* (Chicago: McClurg, 1903), p. 105. See also his attack upon the theories of Booker T. Washington, pages 41–59.

[24] See editorials in *Nigerian Advocate*, Aug. 29, 1923, and *Lagos Daily News*, Nov. 19, 1928; also Du Bois, *op. cit.*, p. 105, and Mbonu Ojike, *I Have Two Countries* (New York: 1947), pp. 20–45.

[25] *Education Policy in British Tropical Africa*, p. 4.

[26] Quoted in H. S. Scott, "Educational Policy in the British Colonial Empire," *The Year Book of Education, 1937* (London: 1937), p. 435. The recommendations made in the 1930's by the Advisory Committee on Native Education on the subject of higher education were not published; but they are briefly summarized in *ibid.*, pages 434–435, and in Lord Hailey, *An African Survey* (London: 1938), pp. 1231–1233. At page 1288 Lord Hailey stated that "the considerations which decide the character of higher education are largely political, for the type of instruction given depends on the view held of the place in the society which the educated African may be expected to fill." He concluded (p. 1289) that as British administrations in Africa were disinclined to commit themselves to a definite view of the political future of the educated African they were, as a consequence, unable to give any "decisive direction to the educational system."

[27] Correspondence between Dr. Edward W. Blyden and Sir Gilbert T. Carter, May–June, 1896, Lagos.

[28] Correspondence between the Union of Students of African Descent and the Secretary of State for the Colonies, March, 1926–Nov., 1927, Lagos.

[29] *Report of the Commission on Higher Education in West Africa*, p. 38.

[30] *Ibid.*, p. 36. Above all, however, was the embittering fact that Yaba graduates were officially rated as inferior to graduates of British universities. For example, a Yaba graduate in medicine was called a "medical assistant," while a graduate of a European university was designated "medical officer."

[31] *Ibid.*, pp. 185–188; *Legislative Council Debates*, Nigeria, Dec. 10, 1945, pp. 23–24.

[32] *Nigerian Advocate*, Aug. 29, 1923.

[33] The remarks of Chief Essien in the Legislative Council illustrate the high priority accorded to education by Nigerian political leaders: "Our Nigeria is a horde of depression, a land of ignorance and illiteracy, therefore a land of poverty and death. . . . Without education it will be impossible for us to get to our destination which is, Nigeria's economic independence and Nigeria's political independence. . . ." *Legislative Council Debates*, March 8, 1939, pp. 167–169. See also B. N. Azikiwe, "How Shall We Educate the African?" *Journal of the African Society*, 33 (April, 1934), pp. 143–151.

[34] *Annual Report*, Department of Education, 1938 (Lagos: Government Printer, 1939), p. 8. As late as the early 1950's Nigeria still had a lower percentage of

children of school age actually in school than many other African territories (e.g., Northern Rhodesia, 46 per cent; Gold Coast, 45 per cent; Belgian Congo, 42 per cent; Kenya, 32 per cent; Uganda, 28 per cent; and Nigeria, 19 per cent).

[35] *Ibid.*

[36] *Ten-Year Educational Plan*, pp. 28–31.

[37] *Ibid.*, p. 11.

[38] *Ibid.*, p. 29.

[39] Mbadiwe, *op. cit.*, p. 191; *Legislative Council Debates*, March 5, 1945, p. 22.

[40] *Ten-Year Educational Plan*, p. 13; *Report of the Commission on Higher Education in West Africa*, pp. 19–22, 181–185.

[41] *Annual Report*, Department of Education, 1938, pp. 11–16.

[42] Scott, "The Development of the Education of the African in Relation to Western Contact," p. 737.

[43] *Education Policy in British Tropical Africa*, pp. 4–5; *Memorandum on the Education of African Communities*, pp. 6–7.

[44] In 1926 the governor said that the main cause of his negative attitude toward a proposal for government scholarships to King's College was the "absence of demand from the people of the Protectorate."

[45] See "Africans Want To Be Clerks," *Round Table* (Dec., 1949).

[46] Murray, *op. cit.*, pp. 328–329.

[47] Although literacy in Arabic script, as distinguished from roman script, is significant in a cultural and religious sense, as well as in a political sense, it had little relevance during the early period of political development. English, and Hausa in roman script, were the media for political debates and discussion, and of the political press and pamphlets.

[48] See C. W. J. Orr, *The Making of Northern Nigeria* (London: 1911), p. 289.

[49] F. D. Lugard, *Annual Reports*, Northern Nigeria, 1900–1911, p. 135.

[50] *Ibid.*, pp. 518 ff.

[51] The most noted leader was Dr. A. E. B. Dikko, a founder and the first president of the Northern Peoples' Congress (the majority party in the Northern Region). He was converted to Christianity by Dr. Miller.

[52] Lugard, *Annual Reports*, p. 125.

[53] Quoted in Orr, *op. cit.*, p. 263.

[54] Lugard, *Annual Reports*, p. 646.

[55] *Ibid.*

[56] *Ibid.*, p. 469.

[57] *Ibid.*, p. 761.

[58] Suggested Policy in Primary and Elementary Education in Kano Province, Jan. 14, 1928.

[59] Address to the Nigerian Council.

CHAPTER 6: *The Westernized Elite*

(Pages 141–166)

[1] Obafemi Awolowo, *Path to Nigerian Freedom* (London: 1947), p. 31.

[2] These tribal figures have been calculated from P. Amaury Talbot's analysis of the 1921 census in *The Peoples of Southern Nigeria* (London: 1926), IV, 166–168. *Nigeria Handbook, 1926* (Lagos: 1926), pp. 386–387, lists 56 African barristers and solicitors and 23 medical practitioners, of whom at least 12 were Africans. In 1936 the number of African barristers, including "native foreigners," was 62. Of these 13 were in the Eastern Provinces, and only 1 was in the Northern Provinces. None were from the Ibo tribe. *Nigeria Handbook, 1936* (Lagos: 1936).

[3] Percentages were computed from the population censuses cited as sources for table 16.

[4] *African Mail*, July 9, 1909.

[5] *Ibid.*, Dec. 13, 1912.

[6] "Achimota," *Round Table,* no. 61 (Dec., 1925), 85.

[7] Charles Roden Buxton, "Some African Friends," *Spectator,* Dec. 28, 1934, p. 986.

[8] Gunnar Myrdal, *An American Dilemma* (New York: 1944), p. 963.

[9] Americans returning from the West Coast of Africa have frequently been heard to exclaim: "They always dress for dinner!"

[10] A. Victor Murray, *The School in the Bush* (London: 1929), p. 384.

[11] As Nnamdi Azikiwe put it in his *Renascent Africa* (Accra: 1937), p. 9, ". . . the Renascent African must be rid of the inferiority complex and all the trappings of hat-in-hand Uncle Tom-ism." See also his *Political Blueprint of Nigeria* (Lagos: 1943), pp. 7–8.

[12] *Renascent Africa,* pp. 9, 29 ff. "Mental emancipation . . . includes education of the sort which should teach [an] African youth to have faith in his ability: to believe that he is the equal of the people of other races of mankind—mentally and physically . . ." (p. 9).

[13] *Op. cit.,* p. 655.

[14] J. Mars in Margery Perham, ed., *Mining, Commerce, and Finance in Nigeria* (London: 1948), pp. 96, 98. Buxton, *op. cit.,* p. 986, offered another explanation: "Less than half a century ago practically no African had ever had the experience of holding trust moneys, or of being an official with the power of a European government behind him. In our country we have become accustomed to these situations by centuries of tradition, and we have gradually learned the terrible consequences of dishonesty. . . ."

[15] A. J. N. Tremearne, *Niger and the West Sudan* (London: 1900), p. 75.

[16] *Op. cit.,* p. 975.

[17] Letter to the editor, *African Mail,* Dec. 13, 1912.

[18] W. R. Crocker, *Nigeria: A Critique of British Colonial Administration* (London: 1936), p. 211. Crocker wrote this after he had resigned from the Nigerian administrative service, and the degree to which he correctly represented the views of others still in the service is problematical. But it is noteworthy that in 1956, exactly two decades after Crocker issued his warning, a London conference agreed to transfer power from the British government to the Nigerian educated elite. In 1949 Crocker published *Self-Government for the Colonies,* in which he stated (p. v): "It is not so long ago . . . since I did not fully appreciate the urgency [of colonial dissident movements]. . . . It took India to bring home to me the meaning and the explosiveness of nationalism amongst dependent peoples. And after seeing India I saw at first-hand something of the psychology of the movement amongst individuals drawn from the intelligentsia of Negro America, the West Indies, and Africa." He argued (p. vi) that "the essence of the colonial grievance is not economic. It is political. . . . The biggest fact of all in the colonial world today is not poverty, but passion. . . . The root of the matter is that the colonial peoples are ruled by a handful of aliens and that enough of the colonial peoples resent the rule. A disconcerting truth is that a very small minority can constitute 'enough of the colonial peoples' in the sense of being enough to disrupt government."

[19] Address to the Nigerian Council, Dec. 29, 1920 (typed copy), Macaulay Papers.

[20] *West African Review,* XIV (Jan., 1943), 21.

[21] D. W. Brogan has pointed out that throughout the colonial world the educated group is a "class that the imperial powers cannot help creating. . . . The imperial powers *must* create this class, since they need cheap clerical aid and they cannot make this class literate only in book-keeping and copying. The man who can keep accounts or a register can also read John Stuart Mill, Macaulay and Marx." *The Price of Revolution* (London: Hamish Hamilton, 1951), p. 139.

[22] The discussion in this section refers exclusively to pre–World War II British policy. The revolutionary postwar reforms will be discussed in detail in Part IV.

[23] Between 1862 and 1922 there was a Legislative Council for the Colony of

447

Lagos, and during the period 1900–1914 this council also legislated for the Protectorate of Southern Nigeria. The council had two nominated African members. See Raymond Leslie Buell, *The Native Problem in Africa* (New York: 1928), I, 738 ff.

[24] During the period 1913–1921 a few chiefs from the Northern Region (then the Northern Provinces) were members of the Nigerian Council. Also, during the life of the first Legislative Council (1923–1946), the lieutenant governor and the secretary of the Northern Provinces were members representing northern interests. But there was no African representative from the north. See Joan Wheare, *The Nigerian Legislative Council* (London: 1950), pp. 29–30, 198–203; Buell, *op. cit.*, I, 739 ff.

[25] Awolowo, *op. cit.*, p. 42.

[26] *Nigeria Handbook, 1936*, pp. 225, 357–359.

[27] *Report on the Amalgamation of Southern and Northern Nigeria, and Administration, 1912–1919*, Cmd. 468 (London: H.M.S.O., 1920), p. 19.

[28] Quoted in Wheare, *op. cit.*, pp. 31–32.

[29] For statistics see Talbot, *op. cit.*, IV, 16 ff., 124 ff., 160 ff., 175 ff.; C. K. Meek, *The Northern Tribes of Nigeria* (London: 1925), II, 175 ff., 215 ff., 254 ff.

[30] William N. M. Geary, *Nigeria under British Rule* (London: 1927), p. 268: "The usual legal term for a European is 'non-Native'; and this sometimes includes a 'Native foreigner', which refers to an educated Native."

[31] Perham, *op. cit.*, pp. 324–325.

[32] It is noteworthy that in 1925 only twelve of the fifty-six African barristers in Nigeria had purely African names (e.g., Akinsemoyin, Inyang, etc.). The rest were either members of old Lagos families of Yoruba extraction, or Gold Coastians, Brazilians, Sierra Leonians, and West Indians.

K. Onwuka Dike points out that Macgregor Laird, one of Nigeria's early European pioneers, felt that there were two types of Africans with whom the European must coöperate: "The tribal inhabitants, men who though ignorant were not 'degraded' like the Delta middlemen, formed the first group. The other, and from Laird's point of view the more important, were Negroes from the West Indies and from Sierra Leone, men who would act as intermediaries between their 'benighted brethren' and the new Europeans (as opposed to the 'degraded' white men of the coast) in their attempt to develop and civilize Africa." Dike adds that the second group (native foreigners), through their "belief in the superiority of their acquired culture and religion," were divorced from the indigenous peoples, and "although they became the pioneers of education and other beneficent movements of the nineteenth century, few were leaders of tribal thought, which they despised and misunderstood." *Trade and Politics in the Niger Delta, 1830–1885* (Oxford: 1956), p. 116.

[33] James S. Coleman, "Current Political Movements in Africa," *The Annals* (March, 1955), 100–101.

[34] F. D. Lugard, *The Dual Mandate in British Tropical Africa* (4th ed.; London: 1929), p. 84.

[35] For example, in 1946 the attorney general of Nigeria said: "There is nothing more detrimental to a young nation than to put incompetent people into responsible positions. . . ." *Legislative Council Debates*, Nigeria, March 22, 1946, p. 324.

[36] It could be argued, of course, that in any imperial system there is a danger point beyond which, in terms of imperial interests, entry must be denied to indigenous inhabitants. Any political system, and particularly a colonial political system, must have its arcana, and one of the great problems of British colonial administration was the protection of secrets of state. Many educated Nigerians were nationalists, and so by definition were subversive of the existing political order. Leakages through clerks were known to be common. The problem would have been of far wider, if not unmanageable, scope if Africans had had access to higher

offices where knowledge of such secrets was indispensable for the proper functioning of the administration.

[37] Lugard, *op. cit.*, p. 225. Italics added.

[38] Margery Perham, *Native Administration in Nigeria* (London: 1937), p. 361.

[39] *Ibid.*, p. 362. In discussing the character of higher education and the role of the educated African in the African territories in 1938, Lord Hailey noted that "British policy as yet exhibits no clear view of the future of the educated African. . . . Accepting the general value of an education based on the European model, British governments have been content to wait until the product of that type of education has asserted his claim to a position in the political or administrative life of the country. . . . It may be justifiable to conclude that for some time at least it is unlikely that British administrations in Africa will commit themselves to a definite view of the future of the educated African. . . ." *An African Survey* (London: 1938), p. 1289.

[40] *Nigerian Pioneer*, Feb. 4, 1921. Italics added.

[41] *Native Administration in Nigeria*, p. 360.

[42] *Nigerian Pioneer*, Feb. 4, 1921.

[43] *Op. cit.*, p. 86. See also pp. 193–229.

[44] Speech of the governor to students at Igbobi College, April 1, 1933, quoted in *Nigerian Daily Times*, April 4, 1933.

[45] Quoted in *African Mail*, May 31, 1912.

[46] *Op. cit.*, p. 986.

[47] *Native Policies in Africa* (London: 1936), pp. 283–286.

[48] *Native Administration in Nigeria*, p. 361.

[49] *Ibid.*

[50] See Wheare, *op. cit.*, pp. 151–157.

[51] Margery Perham in *ibid.*, p. 151 n. 1.

[52] Quoted in Awolowo, *op. cit.*, p. 57.

CHAPTER 7: *Early Resistance and Protest Movements*
(Pages 169–182)

[1] Dike's study is one of the most detailed accounts of early resistance in the Niger Delta area. See K. Onwuka Dike, *Trade and Politics in the Niger Delta, 1830–1885* (Oxford: 1956), especially chap. 1.

[2] *Ibid.*, p. 10.

[3] Alan Burns, *History of Nigeria* (4th ed.; London: 1948), pp. 108–130; A. McL. Davidson, "The Origin and Early History of Lagos," *Nigerian Field*, 19 (Apr., 1954), 52–69.

[4] See William N. M. Geary, *Nigeria under British Rule* (London: 1927), pp. 153–244; C. W. J. Orr, *The Making of Northern Nigeria* (London: 1911); Burns, *op. cit.*, pp. 169–194.

[5] *Op. cit.*, p. 185.

[6] In an early essay, Nnamdi Azikiwe affirmed that "the history of Nigeria cannot be complete without reference to the various uprisings of the native chiefs against foreign imperialism." See "Nigerian Political Institutions," *Journal of Negro History* XIV (July, 1929), 330.

[7] Burns, *op. cit.*, p. 154. See also Geary, *op. cit.*, pp. 191–197; Dike, *op. cit.*, p. 212.

[8] Raymond Leslie Buell, *The Native Problem in Africa* (New York: 1928), I, 710 ff.; Ajayi K. Ajisafe, *History of Abeokuta* (Suffolk: 1924), pp. 198–204.

[9] Lord Hailey, *Native Administration in the British African Territories* (London: 1951), III, 159. See also Margery Perham, *Native Administration in Nigeria* (London: 1937), pp. 206–220; C. K. Meek, *Law and Authority in a Nigerian Tribe* (London: 1937), pp. ix–xvi, 325–356.

[10] Ralph Linton, "Nativistic Movements," *American Anthropologist,* 45 (April–June, 1943), 230–240.

[11] Meek, *op. cit.,* pp. 201 ff.

[12] Quoted in Perham, *op. cit.,* p. 219.

[13] For an analysis of such phenomena see A. Irving Hallowell, "Sociopsychological Aspects of Acculturation," in Ralph Linton, ed., *The Science of Man in the World Crisis* (New York: Columbia, 1945), pp. 171–200.

[14] Burns, *op. cit.,* pp. 189–193. See A. Le Grip, "Aspects actuels de l'Islam en A.O.F.," *L'Afrique et L'Asie,* no. 24 (Fourth Quarter, 1953), 6–20; Alphonse Gouilly, *L'Islam dans l'Afrique Occidentale Française* (Paris: Larousse, 1952); Thomas Hodgkin, "Arab Africa and West Africa," *West Africa,* Aug. 24, 1957, pp. 799–800; Thomas Hodgkin, "Islam and Politics in West Africa," *West Africa,* Sept. 15, 1956, p. 703; Sept. 22, 1956, p. 727.

[15] The issue of polygyny has usually been regarded as the dominant motive in the religious secessionist movements. Certainly all the separatist churches permitted it, except for their ministers. Geoffrey Parrinder argues, I believe correctly, that it was primarily the desire for independence which motivated the secessionist leaders. See his *Religion in an African City* (London: 1953), pp. 107 ff.

[16] G. A. Oke, *A Short History of the United Native African Church* (Lagos: 1936), p. vi.

[17] *Lagos Weekly Record,* Dec. 23, 1890. "By this we mean a Native Christian Church to be composed of Natives, supported by Natives, and governed by Natives." *Ibid.,* Jan. 14, 1891.

[18] Parrinder, *op. cit.,* pp. 111 ff.

[19] Isaac O. Delano, *Notes and Comments from Nigeria* (London: 1944), pp. 36 ff.

[20] *Lagos Times,* March 7, 1891.

[21] Parrinder, *op. cit.,* pp. 126–127.

[22] There were many manifestations of protest and resistance from the very beginning of the expansion of British influence. Some of these are briefly described in Volume I of P. Amaury Talbot, *The Peoples of Southern Nigeria* (Oxford: 1926). At the time of the economic unification of the Lagos Settlements with the Gold Coast in 1883, the African traders and merchants of Lagos and along the Niger and Benue strongly protested. After the Berlin Conference of 1885, these groups intensified their agitation, demanding the formal separation of Lagos from the Gold Coast. Partly in response to this pressure, a new charter was granted by the imperial government in January, 1886, making Lagos a separate colony. See T. Olawale Elias, "Makers of Nigerian Law," *West Africa,* Dec. 3, 1955, p. 1135.

[23] Buell, *op. cit.,* I, 662.

[24] *African Mail,* Jan. 31, 1908. The government expropriated a Baptist chapel and dispossessed sixty-five African residents. All unofficial members (both European and African) of the Legislative Council protested the appropriation of £5,000 for the purpose of carrying out the expropriation. (*Ibid.,* Dec. 6, 1907.)

The Secretary of State for the Colonies supported the governor's position on the Land Acquisition Ordinance and rejected the petition sent to him. (*Ibid.,* Feb. 14, 1908.)

A prominent English resident of Lagos, who frequently identified himself with the African cause, stated: "It means that an unofficial European or native is to be driven out of a sanitary house into an unsanitary house for the benefit of an official, which is so odious in principle that it has only to be stated so as to appear inherently indefensible. . . . There are inevitable causes of friction when a black race has to be ruled by Europeans; and it is most impolitic to add to these unnecessarily. To expropriation for works of public utility—railways, roads, fortifications—the leaders of the public raise no objection; but they protest strongly against their houses being pulled down to make sites for official residences." (*Ibid.,* March 13, 1908.) Another measure that increased native discontent at the time was the erection of a church at public expense for the use of Europeans only.

The opposition on this occasion was not unlike that which occurred more than forty years later, when Nigerian leaders themselves tried to carry out a slum clearance program in Lagos.

[25] In addition to strong running criticism in the local press and the convening of several mass meetings, there was one occasion in November, 1908, when some 400 youths marched around Lagos demonstrating against the water supply and smashing the windows of expatriate firms. In December, Lagos chiefs and landowners presented a long petition to Governor Egerton opposing the new rate.

[26] *African Mail*, Dec. 24, 1915.

[27] "Plenty of pure water is already available. . . . People have got it . . . from time immemorial, and paid nothing for it. Also many had tanks for collecting rain water. There was never a water famine, and Lagosians themselves feel no need for the water supply." *Ibid.*, Feb. 26, 1909.

[28] Report of the Proceedings at an Interview on the Water Rate Question, May 6, 1916 (typed copy), Macaulay Papers.

[29] *African Mail*, Dec. 24, 1915.

[30] Actually, it was not simply the absence of representation, but the idea of taxation per se that caused resentment. At one of the mass meetings a Lagos chief affirmed: "Since the assessment Committee distributed the Blue Notices, we have all become dead men. When His Excellency, Sir Walter Egerton, started the work, the people including the chiefs went to him and said they did not want water. We are saying the same thing today and that is we do not want your water. We would rather die than admit taxation among us. Taxation is against our national tradition." Quoted in Buell, *op. cit.*, I, 662.

The government position included the following arguments: (1) for health reasons the people needed pure water; (2) a good water supply, like electric lights, was not meant exclusively for the Europeans; (3) the landowners of Lagos, and not the general public, were behind the protest movement; (4) all previous Lagos improvements had been paid for by revenues from the country (i.e., including the interior) and not by Lagosians only; (5) the native community was not too poor to afford the water supply, since many natives were very well off; and (6) the measure had received the unanimous assent of the Legislative Council in which there was African representation.

[31] *African Mail*, Feb. 26, 1909. That the water rate agitation exacerbated Nigerian sentiment toward the British administration was confirmed in an interview with S. H. Pearse, a Lagosian who was politically active during this early period. He said: "The feeling that Government was trying to oppress the people began with the introduction of water rates."

[32] Beginning in 1910 the British Anti-Slavery and Aborigines Protection Society undertook to stimulate organizational activity among Africans. It invited "enlightened and humane British subjects on the African continent to organize themselves into responsible Committees with the object of watching over the liberties of local British subjects, assisting the Society with their work of maintaining such rights and securing freedom for the unfortunate natives whose liberties are at present taken from them and their persons subjected to barbarous and inhuman treatment in the economic interest of groups of organised speculators." *Lagos Weekly Record*, Aug. 13, 1910.

There was, of course, no suggestion that this development was intended to lead to anti-British political activity or to any questioning of the imperial connection. In the Gold Coast, an early organization known as the Aborigines Rights Protection Society actually became a prominent nationalist association; it was, as Apter states, "hailed by the chiefs and more vociferous public opinion as a body representative of Gold Coast Colony public demands." David E. Apter, *The Gold Coast in Transition* (Princeton: 1955), p. 36.

[33] Buell, *op. cit.*, I, 770–771. Nigerian allegations in this particular instance had

no foundation in fact. The idea of extending the northern Nigeria system to the south was actually proposed by a few leading English Afrophiles (e.g., E. D. Morel, Noel Buxton, J. Ramsay MacDonald, and Joseph Wedgwood). Nevertheless, although the northern Nigeria system of land tenure was clearly intended to protect the native inhabitants, it did deprive them of their freedom to exercise one of the fundamental rights of ownership, namely, the right of disposition. This special system of land tenure in the north ultimately caused serious resentment among southerners desiring to acquire land in the north. See also *The Land Tenure Question in West Africa*, People's Union (Lagos: 1913); and Elias, *op. cit., West Africa*, Jan. 28, 1956, p. 81.

During June and July, 1913, a press battle raged over the composition and conduct of the deputation to London, not unlike the press war that followed the dispatch of a delegation to London by the National Council of Nigeria and the Cameroons in 1947 (see chap. 12). For the 1913 polemic see issues of the *African Mail* for September, 1913.

It should also be noted that the so-called threat posed by the 1912 West African Lands Commission followed only three years after the Foreshore case in 1909, in which the courts held that the land of Lagos had been the property of King Docemo in 1861 when it was ceded to the British government. The Lagos auxiliary of the Anti-Slavery and Aborigines Protection Society strongly objected to this decision, maintaining that Lagos land belonged to the White Cap chiefs and therefore had not been legally ceded by Docemo. See Buell, *op. cit.*, I, 755. This issue ultimately became linked with the famous *eleko* case, to be discussed later. See Elias, *op. cit., West Africa*, June 9, 1956, pp. 367–368.

[34] *Lagos Weekly Record*, May 7, 1910.

[35] *Ibid.*, Jan. 8, 1910. The same editor added that a "just and generous mind would only see in the Native Press a needed though feeble instrument for voicing the Native side of matters under the aegis of an absolute system of government which is altogether a law unto itself, and the only appeal against which for the people is the authorities in Downing Street, and who more often than not, take their facts and findings from the absolute authority appealed against." *Ibid.*, March 19, 1910.

[36] Interview with H. S. A. Thomas, Lagos, Nigeria. Clifford's complaint led ultimately to the formation of the Reform Club, "composed of a few gentlemen of high standing in the Community . . . [who] are regarded by the Government as holding the sanest views on matters affecting the public welfare. High officials used to accept invitations from them and attend their meetings." *Nigerian Advocate*, Aug. 15, 1923.

[37] *Ibid.*

CHAPTER 8: *The Beginnings of Nationalist Thought and Activity*

(Pages 183–200)

[1] Correspondence with Edith Holden, Blyden's biographer. Blyden's obituary appeared in the *Sierra Leone Weekly News*, February 10, 1912. Blyden first sought to gain entrance to an institution of learning in the United States, but this was denied him on grounds of color. He then became the principal of Liberia College, and later served as the Liberian minister to the Court of St. James. Extracts from his lectures and speeches were frequently printed in the *Lagos Times*, commencing in 1880, and after 1891 by John Payne Jackson in the *Lagos Weekly Record*. In 1890–1891 Blyden visited Lagos for the purpose of encouraging the formation of an African church, and his visit was not unrelated to the subsequent separatist religious movements discussed in chapter 7. In 1896 he was in active correspondence with

Governor Gilbert T. Carter in connection with his long-time aspiration to establish a West African university.

[2] It is not unreasonable to assume that Blyden was influenced by the back-to-Africa movement among American Negro intellectuals in the pre–Civil War period, particularly the Liberia Emigration Society and the National Emigration Convention. Similarly, the ideas he developed during the last four decades of the nineteenth century were rather closely related to the cultural nationalism of contemporary Negro intellectuals in America. See Wilson Record, "The Negro Intellectual and Negro Nationalism," *Social Forces*, 33 (Oct., 1954), 11–12.

[3] Blyden's writings include *From West Africa to Palestine* (Freetown: 1873); *Christianity, Islam, and the Negro Race* (London: 1887); *The African Problem, and the Method of Its Solution* (Washington: 1890); and *West Africa before Europe* (London: 1905).

[4] "The Nigerian Press," *West African Review* (June, 1950), 625.

[5] *Lagos Weekly Record*, Feb. 26, 1910.

[6] *Ibid.*, June 12, 1919.

[7] *Ibid.*, June 14, 1919.

[8] *Ibid.*, Jan. 31, 1920.

[9] *Ibid.*, April 10, 1920.

[10] *Ibid.*, Feb. 19, 1921.

[11] A. B. Laotan, "Notes on the History of the Nigerian Press" (typed copy). Laotan was editor of the *Catholic Press*, Lagos, Nigeria.

[12] Ajasa spent more than twelve years of his life in England, beginning in his early teens. The *Nigerian Pioneer* gave unqualified support to the British connection, but from time to time it made suggestions for reform and improvement. Concerning the government Ajasa wrote: "We in West Africa have been for generations under British rule and with that rule we are satisfied." (*Nigerian Pioneer*, Sept. 7, 1917.) "Nigeria's lot is cast, and God grant it will, nay, and must be cast for years to come in and within the Empire. . . ." (*Ibid.*, Oct. 17, 1930.) But, although acknowledging that "it might be suicidal for any Empire to let the subject races into its secrets by having them employed in positions of trust," he asked that the government "look upon the educated natives as an asset of the Empire to be utilised in Imperial interests. . . ." (*Ibid.*, Sept. 7, 1917.) And he warned: "An educated class is fast growing among natives throughout . . . the African continent. The more highly educated the African is the more intense is his love for his country, the more he presses for a greater and more effective voice in the shaping of the destiny of his people. . . . But the educated native still cries in the wilderness; . . . his cry must be heeded some day. . . ." (*Ibid.*, Sept. 14, 1917.) On his alleged collusion with the government, Ajasa stated that the *Pioneer* "existed in order to interpret thoroughly and accurately the Government to the people and the people to the Government." (*Ibid.*, March 16, 1923.) Sir Kitoye, like Dr. Henry Carr, belonged to the first generation of "black Englishmen." Relations between most Europeans and members of this first generation were in general very free, friendly, and characterized by mutual respect. One likely reason is that Africans of this type offered no serious threat to the British presence. Another, suggested by the biographer of Mrs. Jessica Otonba-Payne (widow of the late John Adepeyin Otonba-Payne), is that "because there were so few Africans in the United Kingdom, or because manners were more polished in those days, 'colour bar' appears to have been unknown. [Mrs. Otonba-Payne] certainly never experienced any racial discrimination, and to this day, she is wholly without racial consciousness." ("Victorian Lagos Lady," *West Africa*, Jan. 14, 1956, p. 29.) Most members of this set were frequent guests at Government House.

[13] Increase Coker has pointed out that record-keeping was poor or nonexistent in the early days; hence "the question of what newspaper is the earliest on the scene in Nigeria is a matter for speculation." *Seventy Years of the Nigerian Press* (Lagos: 1952), p. 2.

[14] Between 1890 and 1950, more than 100 newspapers and periodicals were registered in Nigeria; although many were short-lived and fatality rates were high, there was no cessation of agitation for reforms, increased self-government, and removal of grievances. At least three editors were jailed for seditious or libelous publications against the government before the arrival of Nnamdi Azikiwe in 1937. Of the fifty publications registered before 1937, nearly half contained the word "Nigerian" as part of the title. The first was the *Nigerian Chronicle,* which began publication in 1908.

[15] James Africanus Beale Horton, *Political Economy of British Western Africa; with the Requirements of the Several Colonies and Settlements. (The African View of the Negro's Place in Nature)* (London: 1868). A select committee of Parliament in 1865 also recommended Britain's withdrawal from her settlements in West Africa; but, as Dike has pointed out, the policy of retrenchment was not applicable to the Niger territories: "Here the British Government and her traders launched a vigorous policy of expansion during the sixties." K. Onwuka Dike, *Trade and Politics in the Niger Delta, 1830–1885* (Oxford: 1956), p. 166.

Horton used the Parliamentary Report of 1865 as the basis for another book, *West African Countries and Peoples, British and Native, with Requirements necessary for establishing that self-government recommended by the House of Commons, 1865; and a Vindication of the African race* (London: 1868).

[16] *Lagos Times,* March 9, 1881.

[17] *A Preliminary Bibliography of the Literature of Nationalism in Nigeria* (London: [1955]), pp. 4–5. An example of the early literature is Adeoye Deniga, *African Leaders Past and Present* (2 vols.; Lagos: 1915).

[18] Samuel Johnson, *The History of the Yorubas,* ed. O. Johnson (London: 1921).

[19] J. W. E. Bowen, ed., *Addresses and Proceedings of the Congress on Africa* (Atlanta: Gammon Theological Seminary, 1896), pp. 37–46. Edward Blyden, then the Liberian minister to the Court of St. James, also contributed to the congress proceedings.

[20] G. Spiller, ed., *Papers on Inter-racial Problems Communicated to the First Universal Races Congress* (London: 1911).

[21] *African Mail,* Sept. 1, 1911.

[22] "The Africa of the Immediate Future," *Journal of the African Society,* 18 (April, 1919), 161.

[23] H. L. Ward-Price, *Dark Subjects* (London: 1939), p. 48.

[24] W. E. B. Du Bois, *The World and Africa* (New York: 1947), p. 8.

[25] *Ibid.,* p. 9. Blaise Diagne at the time was *commissaire-général* in charge of recruiting African troops for the French army. He emphatically rejected self-determination for Africa in a letter to Marcus Garvey on July 3, 1922: "We French natives wish to remain French, since France has given us every liberty and since she has unreservedly accepted us upon the same basis as her own European children. None of us aspires to see French Africa delivered exclusively to the Africans as is demanded, though without any authority, by the American negroes, at the head of whom you have placed yourself." Quoted in Buell, *op. cit.,* II, 81.

[26] Du Bois, *op. cit.,* pp. 11–12.

[27] *Ibid.,* p. 242. Du Bois argued that the "idea of one Africa to unite the thought and ideals of all native peoples of the dark continent belongs to the twentieth century and stems naturally from the West Indies and the United States. Here various groups of Africans, quite separate in origin, became so united in experience and so exposed to the impact of new cultures that they began to think of Africa as one idea and one land." (*Ibid.,* p. 7.)

The 1923 and 1927 congresses urged a more comprehensive system of trusteeship over colonial territories, and demanded that Africans have a greater voice in their own government, free elementary education, and socialistic economic development. Inflammatory racialism was conspicuously absent.

[28] Robert H. Brisbane, "His Excellency: The Provincial President of Africa,"

Phylon, X (Third Quarter, 1949), p. 259. The literature on Garvey is now extensive. The only study of book length is Edmund D. Cronon, *Black Moses* (Madison: 1955). There is a selected list of secondary literature in Wilson Record, *op. cit.*, pp. 15–17.

[29] Buell mentions the gratitude expressed by the governor of Sierra Leone to President King of Liberia for having had "nothing to do with any movement having as its avowed object the fomenting of racial feeling of hatred and ill-will. Your Excellency, by slamming the door on spurious patriots from across the Atlantic, . . . deservedly earned the gratitude not only of every West African Government but of all who have the true welfare of the African at heart." (*Op. cit.*, II, 733.) The biographer of the late J. E. K. Aggrey repeats a story that the Gold Coast CID "were very worried about Aggrey—for these, of course, were the stormy days after the First World War. . . . [A letter, presumably in the CID files] suggested that Aggrey had sympathy with the Marcus Garvey extremist faction." William M. Macartney, *Dr. Aggrey* (London: 1949), p. 57.

[30] Amy Jacques Garvey, ed., *Philosophy and Opinions of Marcus Garvey* (New York: 1923), pp. 5–6, 18, 34.

[31] *Ibid.*, p. 40.

[32] At the time Du Bois was Garvey's chief antagonist. He had signed the petition, which asked the United States Department of Justice to prosecute Garvey and have him deported.

Wilson Record has analyzed the hostility between Marcus Garvey and American middle-class Negro intellectuals. The intellectuals wanted to identify themselves with American culture and to make their way within, while trying to ameliorate, the American racial situation. The Garvey movement was a racial class movement, whose adherents were drawn almost exclusively from lower-strata and darker-skinned American Negroes. Most of the intellectuals were from the upper strata and were lighter in color. Garvey stressed the superiority of the Negro, which meant that a dark skin brought higher status. Moreover, Garvey's appeal tended to deprive the intellectuals of whatever leadership they had acquired over the American Negro mass, and his organization competed with the established Negro organizations under their control. See Record, *op. cit.*, pp. 16–17.

[33] Brisbane, *op. cit.*, p. 259. Garvey stated: "I am only the forerunner of an awakened Africa that shall never go back to sleep." Quoted in Cronon, *op. cit.*, p. 39. "Garvey proudly recalled for his followers, though not always with complete accuracy, the stirring heroism of such leaders of American slave rebellions as Denmark Vesey, Gabriel Prosser, and Nat Turner. The struggles of Zulu and Hottentot warriors against European rule, the histories of Moorish and Ethiopian empires, and the intrepid exploits of Toussaint L'Ouverture against the French in Haiti were not neglected in the effort to make Negroes conscious and proud of their racial heritage." *Ibid.*, p. 47.

[34] Among the Nigerian delegates were Patriarch J. G. Campbell and Adeoye Deniga, founder of the weekly Yoruba newspaper *Akede Eko* (1927), as well as other Lagosians, and a few representatives from Calabar.

[35] *Petition to King George V for the reconstitution of the several Legislative Councils and the constitution of Houses of Assembly and other reforms*, National Congress of British West Africa (London: 1920); *Resolutions of the Conference of Africans of British West Africa held at Accra, Gold Coast, from 11th to 29th March, 1920*, National Congress of British West Africa (London: 1920); *Memorandum of the case of the National Congress of British West Africa for a memorial based upon the resolutions to be presented to His Majesty the King Emperor in Council through the Right Honourable the Secretary of State for the Colonies*, National Congress of British West Africa (London: 1920).

[36] *Report of the Proceedings of a meeting held in London between the League of Nations Union and the delegates of the National Congress of British West Africa*, National Congress of British West Africa (London: 1920).

[37] George Padmore, *Africa, Britain's Third Empire* (London: 1949), pp. 201–205.
[38] Address to the Nigerian Council, Dec. 29, 1920 (typed copy), Macaulay Papers.
[39] *Ibid.*
[40] *Ibid.*
[41] *Ibid.*
[42] *West African Nationhood*, July 7, 1931.
[43] Notes on the National Congress of British West Africa, Macaulay Papers.
[44] Buell, *op. cit.*, I, 662–667; Margery Perham, *Native Administration in Nigeria* (London: 1937), pp. 264–271; *Gazette Extraordinary*, Aug. 29, 1933, Commission of Enquiry regarding the House of Docemo; Herbert Macaulay, *Justitia Fiat: the Moral Obligation of the British Government to the House of King Docemo of Lagos* (London: 1921); T. Olawale Elias, "Makers of Nigerian Law," *West Africa*, June 9, 1956, p. 367; E. A. Akintan, *The Closing Scene of the Eleko Case and the Return of Prince Eshugbayi Eleko* (Lagos: 1931). Both Buell and Perham criticized the government's policy regarding the House of Docemo and its role in the political life of Lagos. The gist of their criticism was that the government should have recognized the respect of the people for the traditional authorities, and that some formula could have been devised to integrate the eleko into the Lagos system of local government. It is not without significance that, when the Action Group party came to power in 1951, the Oba of Lagos was made chairman of the Lagos Town Council.
[45] Buell, *op. cit.*, I, 755–756, and Elias, *op. cit.*
[46] The history of the changing fate of the House of Docemo provides startling proof not only of the tenacity of ancient loyalties but also of the virtue in the system of indirect rule. Although Lagos was atypical as an urban metropolis, it is quite clear that had the British attempted to institute direct administration throughout the protectorate they would have required, as Margery Perham suggests, "an army of Government agents." *Op. cit.*, p. 269.
[47] Buell, *op. cit.*, I, 740.
[48] Herbert Samuel Heelas Macaulay was born in Lagos on November 14, 1864. He was the grandson of the Reverend Samuel Ajayi Crowther, first African bishop of the Niger territory. He received his secondary school education in Lagos, spent several years in England where he qualified as a licensed surveyor, and returned to Lagos in 1893. For his biography see Isaac B. Thomas, *Life History of Herbert Macaulay* (3d ed.; Lagos: 1948), and Obadia Adegboyega Sobande, *Notes and Comments on the Life of Mr. H. Macaulay* (Lagos: n.d.). In addition to *Justitia Fiat*, previously cited, Macaulay's published pamphlets include *An Antithesis . . . on the Public Lands Acquisition (amendment) Ordinance, 1945* (Lagos: 1946), and *An open comment upon the views on Nigerian public affairs expressed in London by Dr. John Randle* (Lagos: 1922).
A full account of Macaulay's life and his contribution to the development of early nationalism in Nigeria has yet to be written. Within the limits of this brief survey of early nationalism, less than justice can be given to his role. He is recognized by the present generation of Nigerians as the father of Nigerian nationalism. His championing of the famous Appapa land case, *Amodu Tijani v. Secretary, Southern Nigeria* (1921), his prominent role behind the scenes in the National Congress of British West Africa, and his leading part in the *Eshugbayi Eleko v. Government of Nigeria* case (1928), are but the highlights of his leadership in the early nationalist awakening.
[49] The *Lagos Daily News* succeeded Jackson's paper, the *Lagos Weekly Record*, as the principal Nigerian nationalist organ in the interwar period. Publication of the *News* commenced in 1925 and was continued irregularly until the late 1930's. Although Macaulay was equally as trying to the government as Jackson—the two were cofounders of the Democratic party—he was so saturated in the British tradition that his articles and editorials lacked the sharpness and outspoken boldness of Jackson's. Macaulay would normally conclude a caustic attack upon the govern-

ment with the phrase, "God Save the King"; and his appeals for the redress of grievances were usually made on the grounds of the "inviolate rights" of "British subjects," or of the "manifold blessings of Pax Brittanica."

[50] *Constitution of the Nigerian National Democratic Party* (Lagos: n.d.), p. 1.

[51] Macaulay Papers.

[52] *Constitution of the Nigerian National Democratic Party*, p. 4.

[53] Historical Records of the Calabar Improvement League, Calabar, Nigeria.

[54] There were other reasons for the confinement of early Nigerian politics to Lagos: the city's unique legal status as a crown colony; its longer and more intensive contact with Western forces stimulating change; its status as the political and commercial capital of the country; the paucity of opportunities outside Lagos for meaningful careers for educated and professional classes; the lack of means outside Lagos; the resistance of officials and traditionalists; and the deep involvement of Lagosians in local issues and political intrigues. Moreover, many of the principal participants in pre-1938 political agitation were repatriated Brazilians or native foreigners from Liberia, the Gold Coast, and Sierra Leone—all of whom had limited familial ties with the peoples of the interior.

[55] In 1934 Sir Donald Cameron referred to the "tornado of questions" submitted to the Legislative Council by Adeniyi-Jones. The questions covered a wide range of issues and grievances, including, for example, a request for the names, designations, and departments of Africans who had been appointed or promoted to European posts during the period 1927–1934. (*Legislative Council Debates*, Nigeria, June 12, 1934, pp. 42–43.) At the same session Adeniyi-Jones attacked proposed restrictions on Japanese imports: "I have not been able to discover a single clause which I can consider as designed to offer any kind of protection to native interests. . . . The measures now introduced are of an Imperial nature designed to protect what an Englishman will call home markets." (*Ibid.*, p. 50.) Throughout the period 1926–1938 Adeniyi-Jones maintained a relentless campaign of questioning, not unlike that conducted by Nnamdi Azikiwe during the period 1948–1951. See *Address given by Hon. Dr. C. C. Adeniyi-Jones, President of the Nigerian National Democratic Party, at a Mass-Meeting held at Glover Memorial Hall, Lagos, on 1st October 1938* (Lagos: 1938). His criticism of the 1923 constitution is contained in his *Political and Administrative Problems of Nigeria; an Address Delivered to the West African Students Union in London* (London: 1929).

CHAPTER 9: *Nationalist Developments in the Interwar Period*
(Pages 201–229)

[1] William N. M. Geary, *Nigeria under British Rule* (London: 1927), p. 14.

[2] W. R. Crocker, *Nigeria: A Critique of British Colonial Administration* (London: 1936), p. 235.

[3] Lord Hailey, "Nationalism in Africa," *Journal of the African Society*, 36 (April, 1937), pp. 140–141.

[4] Macaulay Papers.

[5] *The Keys*, official organ of the League of Coloured Peoples, 1933–1938.

[6] *West Africa*, Oct. 25, 1924. By 1921 the union had 25 members, and 120 by 1924. As early as 1913 a conference had been held in London to consider the position of African students in London. Sponsored by the African Society and the Anti-Slavery and Aborigines Protection Society, it was attended by many distinguished Englishmen, Duse Mohammed Ali, and about 40 African students. "Conference with Africans," *Journal of the African Society*, 12 (July, 1913), 425–431.

[7] Quoted in Philip Garigue, "The West African Students' Union," *Africa*, XXIII (Jan., 1953), 56.

[8] The original members included, besides Solanke (who remained in London), Kusimo Soluade (a Jos barrister), Olatunde Vincent (a Lagos barrister), three Nigerian barristers now deceased (Ekunday Williams, M. A. Sarinola Siffre, and B. J.

Forreira), and about six others from the Gold Coast, Sierra Leone, and Gambia. *Ibid.,* p. 57.

⁹ Ladipo Solanke, *United West Africa (or Africa) at the Bar of the Family of Nations* (London: 1927).

¹⁰ Robert Gardiner, "WASU," *African Interpreter,* I (April, 1943), 7.

¹¹ J. W. de Graft-Johnson, *Towards Nationhood in West Africa* (London: 1928).

¹² The first WASU hostel, acquired in 1928, was given to the association by Marcus Garvey. Garigue, *op. cit.,* p. 58.

¹³ These quotations are all from Solanke, *op. cit.*

¹⁴ In Nigeria, branches were established at Lagos, Ebute-Metta, Abeokuta, Ijebu-Ode, Jos, Zaria, Kano, Ibadan, Ago-Iwaye, Ile Ife, Enugu, and other centers. See Garigue, *op. cit.,* p. 58.

¹⁵ Solanke's visits occasionally provided an opportunity for others to make off-the-cuff nationalistic speeches. Thus, when Solanke visited Kano, the Reverend S. O. Odutola preached a sermon beginning with the salutation, "My dear fellow nationalists," and affirming that "no right thinking African will acquiesce in white domination and exploitation." *Ibid.,* p. 59.

¹⁶ Benjamin Gitlow, *I Confess* (New York: 1940), p. 482. For a more detailed discussion of the development of this particular Communist line, see Wilson Record, *The Negro and the Communist Party* (Chapel Hill: 1949), chap. 3.

¹⁷ Isaac T. A. Wallace-Johnson, *Trade Unionism in Colonial Dependent Territories* (London: 1946), pp. 17 ff. At one of its meetings, the African Workers' Union of Nigeria resolved that a management committee be empowered to form a syndicate for the purpose of taking a directorship share in the Nigerian Mercantile Bank, that the union establish a monthly journal "to be devoted entirely to the subject of the improvement of the condition of the working class and of native industries," and that an agricultural school be established for the education of the "working class." *West African Nationhood,* Oct. 13, 1931.

¹⁸ Macaulay Papers.

¹⁹ Nancy Cunard, ed., *Negro Anthology* (London: 1934), pp. iii–iv.

²⁰ *Nigerian Daily Telegraph,* Sept. 21, 1935.

²¹ In commenting on the Italian conquest, Lord Hailey observed: ". . . it may well be that to thinking Africans the fact that its three most prominent colonising nations were not competent to check the militaristic aggressiveness of a new arrival was more striking than the evidence that Europeans could still desire to possess themselves of African lands. But I feel that the Abyssinian campaign may yet be destined to have its effect on African thought, for it breaks harshly into the era of the altered attitude towards the African Native which the Mandate policy had seemed to signalise." *Op. cit.,* p. 143.

²² The federation was organized to overcome shipping difficulties arising from the war. Among the original members were J. H. Doherty; Fred E. Williams, a wealthy cocoa trader; Salami Agbaje, a wealthy Ibadan merchant; and J. K. Coker. The representative sent to London in 1919 was Sam H. Duncan, author of a pamphlet entitled *Reconstruction: Self-Determination* (London: 1919). *Nigerian Advocate,* Dec. 5, 1923.

²³ *Nigerian Eastern Mail,* Nov. 29, 1941.

²⁴ The Southern Nigeria Civil Service Union, in its petition of 1912, demanded higher salaries and positions better than clerkships for members of the native staff. (*Lagos Weekly Record,* June 14, 1919.) In 1919 Sir Kitoyi Ajasa's paper strongly supported similar demands, pointing out that Nigerians who are denied senior posts "are then left with the other alternative that it is a policy of the Government to repress the Natives to a position of inferiority in every department of service." (*Nigerian Pioneer,* Feb. 14, 1919.)

²⁵ A. A. Adio-Moses, "Notes on the History of Nigerian Trade Unionism" (unpublished MS).

²⁶ *Nigerian Teacher,* official organ of the Nigerian Union of Teachers, 1935–1950.

[27] The discussion of lineage and tribal unions is drawn from my unpublished paper entitled "The Role of Tribal Associations in Nigeria," read at the Annual Conference of the West African Institute of Social and Economic Research, Ibadan, Nigeria, April 15–19, 1952. See also Thomas Hodgkin, "Towards Self-Government in British West Africa," in Basil Davidson and Adenekan Ademola, eds., *The New West Africa* (London: 1953); Thomas Hodgkin, *Nationalism in Colonial Africa* (London: 1956), chap. 2; Lord Hailey, *Native Administration in the British African Territories* (London: 1951), III, 18–20; and Simon Ottenberg, "Improvement Associations among the Afikpo Ibo," *Africa*, XXV (Jan., 1955), pp. 1–28. Cf. K. A. Busia, *Social Survey of Sekondi-Takoradi* (Accra: 1951), pp. 77–83, 111–112.

[28] *Nigerian Advocate*, Nov. 14, 1923.

[29] *Nigerian Daily Telegraph*, March 20, 1935.

[30] *West African Pilot*, June 14, 1940.

[31] *Ibid.*, Jan. 23, 1940.

[32] *African Messenger*, July 5, 1923. Nnamdi Azikiwe notes that Chief Ayo Williams became the leader of the Union of Young Nigerians, and also was responsible for organizing the Nigeria Union of Young Democrats in 1938. *The Development of Political Parties in Nigeria* (London: 1957), p. 6.

[33] *Lagos Weekly Record*, June 8, 1929.

[34] The failure of the national school campaign provoked endless self-criticism among Nigerians throughout the following two decades. In 1929 the editor of the *Lagos Weekly News* charged that "the project of a national school has been laid before us at least six times, but what have we done in the shape of practical action save to talk it out in nothingness?" (*Lagos Weekly News*, May 11, 1929.) In 1930 Herbert Macaulay editorialized in his *Lagos Daily News*: "What has become of the National School?" In 1938, in a biting editorial, Azikiwe wrote: "We submit that the failure of the project reflects discreditably on the capacity of Africans to manage their own affairs in this particular aspect of their community life. . . . When Africans whine that they have no opportunities they are simply exhibiting their childish nature, because opportunities abound in Africa. It would seem as if our real need today is leadership . . . with character." (*West African Pilot*, Aug. 9, 1938.) In 1947 the effort to carry out the project was renewed, but nothing significant came of it.

[35] *Service*, official organ of the Nigerian Youth Movement, May 16, 1935.

[36] Eyo Ita, *Nigeria Youth League Movement* (Calabar: n.d.). Quotation includes excerpts from pp. 1–7.

[37] *West African Pilot*, June 2, 1945.

[38] Ita, *op. cit.*, p. 6.

[39] *Ibid.*, p. 7.

[40] *Ibid.*, p. 6.

[41] *West African Pilot*, Jan. 23, 1951.

[42] Ita, *op. cit.*, p. 6. Ita's other publications include the following, all published in Calabar by his West African People's Institute Press: *The Assurance of Freedom* (1949), *Crusade for Freedom* (1949), *The Revolt of the Liberal Spirit in Nigeria* (1949), *Sterile Truths and Fertile Lies* (1949), *Two Vital Fronts in Nigeria's Advancement* (1949), *A Decade of National Education Movement* (1949), *National Youth Renaissance* (n.d.), and *Reconstructing towards Wider Integration; a Theory of Social Symbiosis* (1951). Nnamdi Azikiwe, first a collaborator and later a political opponent of Ita's, has appraised Ita's contribution in *op. cit.*, pp. 6–7.

[43] Azikiwe's writings extend over a period of a quarter of a century. While in America he contributed articles to three learned journals, under his baptismal name, Ben (Benjamin) N. Azikiwe: "Nigerian Political Institutions," *Journal of Negro History*, XIV (July, 1929), 328–341; "Fragments of Onitsha History," *Journal of Negro History*, XV (Oct., 1930), 474–497; and "How Shall We Educate the African?" *Journal of the African Society*, 33 (April, 1934), 143–151. He published all subsequent works under his African name, Nnamdi Azikiwe. His two major

works are *Liberia in World Politics* (London: 1934), and *Renascent Africa* (Accra: 1937). Subsequent publications include *Land Tenure in Northern Nigeria* (Lagos: 1942); *Political Blueprint of Nigeria* (Lagos: 1943); *Economic Reconstruction of Nigeria* (Lagos: 1943); *Taxation in Nigeria* (Lagos: 1943); *Suppression of the Press in British West Africa* (Onitsha: 1946); *"Before Us Lies the Open Grave"* (London: 1947); and *The Development of Political Parties in Nigeria* (London: 1957).

⁴⁴ *West Africa Pilot,* July 21, 1938.

⁴⁵ Professor Frazier has painstakingly analyzed the content of the American Negro press over the years. He points out that in the early 1920's 21 per cent of the news items and 40 per cent of the editorials were on the subject of racial wrongs or clashes. As late as 1949 two-thirds of the front-page stories in Negro newspapers dealt with Negro-white relations, and only one-third with strictly Negro news. E. Franklin Frazier, *The Negro in the United States* (New York: 1949), pp. 411–415.

⁴⁶ W. T. Fox quoted in *West African Pilot,* March 22, 1947.

⁴⁷ P. 17. "The Press is an avenue. Schools are important, but the Press is a much wider and more potent avenue for this particular mission. And the pen is said to be mightier than the sword." *Ibid.*

⁴⁸ *Daily Service,* Oct. 5, 1938.

⁴⁹ *Ibid.,* Oct. 17, 1938.

⁵⁰ *Youth Charter and Constitution and Rules,* Nigerian Youth Movement (Lagos: n.d.), pp. 15 ff.

⁵¹ *Ibid.,* p. 1.

⁵² Historical Records, Ibadan Branch of the Nigerian Youth Movement.

⁵³ The first occasion was in 1912, when educated Lagosians aroused chiefs in the Yoruba hinterland over an alleged threat to their land. See chap. 8.

⁵⁴ For Azikiwe's appraisal of the Akinsanya crisis see *The Development of Political Parties in Nigeria,* p. 8.

⁵⁵ In the late 1930's H. O. Davies led in the organization of Youth Study Circles, which flourished in Lagos and other parts of southern Nigeria. The circles were conducted as seminars at which papers were read on the problems of Nigeria. The circles at Yaba Higher College and King's College were particularly active.

CHAPTER 10: *The Impact of World War II*
(Pages 230–250)

¹ *Public General Acts* (1940), 3 & 4 George VI, chap. 40.

² *Preliminary Statement on Development Planning in Nigeria,* Sessional Paper no. 6 (Lagos: 1945).

³ In regard to Nigerian nationalists, see A. A. Nwafor Orizu, *Without Bitterness* (New York: 1944), pp. 271 ff.; Nnamdi Azikiwe, *Political Blueprint of Nigeria* (Lagos: 1943), pp. 71 ff.

⁴ Azikiwe, *op. cit.,* p. 72.

⁵ Raymond Leslie Buell, *Isolated America* (New York: 1944), pp. 409–414; President Roosevelt's remarks celebrating the seventh anniversary of the Philippine Commonwealth, *Fortune* (March, 1943), 86 ff.; Elliot Roosevelt, *As He Saw It* (New York: 1946), pp. 35–36, 77; Cordell Hull, *The Memoirs of Cordell Hull* (New York: 1948), pp. 1235 ff.; Sumner Welles, *The World of the Four Freedoms* (New York: 1943), p. 75; Henry Wallace, *Democracy Reborn* (New York: 1944).

⁶ *New York Times,* Oct. 27, 1942.

⁷ See M. J. Bonn, "The Future of Imperialism," *The Annals* (July, 1943), 71–77; George Soule, *America's Stake in Britain's Future* (New York: 1946); Louise Ragatz, *Africa in the Post-War World* (New York: 1944); Paul Redwood, "The New Colonialism and American Opinion," *Journal of Legal and Political Sociology,* III (Summer, 1945), 29–40; and the reports of the Commission to Study the Organ-

ization of the Peace, in *International Conciliation,* no. 405 (Nov., 1944), 696–710.

[8] Melville Herskovits, *The Myth of the Negro Past* (New York: 1941), p. 31. Carter G. Woodson, one of the American leaders in the "Negro Renaissance" during the 1930's, said: "Negroes themselves accept as a compliment the theory of a complete break with Africa, for above all things they do not care to be known as resembling in any way these 'terrible Africans.' " Quoted in *ibid.*

[9] For early American Negro interests in Africa, see Wilson Record, "The Negro Intellectual and Negro Nationalism," *Social Forces,* 33 (Oct., 1954), 10–15. On back-to-Africa movements, Ralph Bunche observed that "the glamour of a black state, either as a 49th state or in Africa, as an independent nation, has not caught the imagination of the Negro—either of the Negro intellectual or the Negro in the mass. The Negro in his thinking, and in his aspirations is an American, and he regards America as his home." Quoted in *ibid.,* pp. 10–11.

[10] Ralph J. Bunche, "French and British Imperialism in West Africa," *Journal of Negro History,* 21 (Jan., 1936), 31 ff.; "Africa and the Current World Conflict," *Negro History Bulletin* (Oct., 1940), 11–15.

[11] *African Journey* (New York: John Day, 1945).

[12] *The Atlantic Charter and Africa from an American Standpoint* (New York: 1942).

[13] "The Realities in Africa," *Foreign Affairs,* 21 (July, 1943), 729.

[14] London *Times,* March 6, 1943.

[15] *Ibid.,* Nov. 21, 1942, p. 5.

[16] See Azikiwe, *op. cit.,* pp. 74 ff. Obafemi Awolowo, *Path to Nigerian Freedom* (London: 1947), p. 23, asks: "What is going to be Nigeria's ultimate goal—Independence or Self-government? This question . . . had never received the attention it deserved until the people of the United States of America forced it into prominence."

[17] *The Colonial Empire,* Labour Party (London: 1933).

[18] C. R. Attlee, *Labour's Peace Aims* (London: 1939), p. 4.

[19] C. R. Attlee quoted in the London *Daily Herald,* Aug. 16, 1941.

[20] A. Creech Jones in *Debates,* House of Commons, June 6, 1944, col. 1250.

[21] "The Old World and the New Society," in *A Report on the Problems of War and Peace Construction,* prepared by the National Executive Committee of the Labour party for the annual party conference, May, 1942, p. 21.

[22] London *Times,* June 19, 1943; *Debates,* House of Commons, June 6, 1944, cols. 1224 ff.

[23] *Debates,* House of Commons, March 17, 1943.

[24] Remarks of Oliver Stanley before the Foreign Policy Association in New York City on Jan. 19, 1945, reported in *New York Times,* Jan. 20, 1945, p. 5.

[25] Remarks of Oliver Stanley in *Britain Looks Ahead,* III (1943), 72–73.

[26] Oliver Stanley in *Debates,* House of Commons, July 13, 1943, col. 142.

[27] *West African Pilot,* Oct. 8, 1941.

[28] *Ibid.,* Oct. 5, 1941. See also Resolutions of a Conference on West African Problems, London, Aug. 29, 30, 1941.

[29] Memorandum from WASU to the Under Secretary of State for the Colonies, April 6, 1942. Italics added.

[30] The memorandum, dealing with postwar reconstruction of the colonies and protectorates of British West Africa, was submitted on August 1, 1943.

[31] Macaulay Papers. In a letter to me dated March 12, 1958, Premier Azikiwe authorized the quotation from his letter to Dr. Maja.

[32] See Philip Garigue, "The West African Students' Union," *Africa,* XXIII (Jan., 1953), 65–70. On October 10, 1944, Dr. Akinola Maja, Chief Ladipo Solanke, and H. O. Davies cabled Dr. Azikiwe supporting the demand for immediate self-government, and suggesting that leaders in Nigeria should tour the country to gain the support of the people for this demand. See Nnamdi Azikiwe, *The Development of Political Parties in Nigeria* (London: 1957), pp. 12–13.

[33] The twelfth student was a Yoruba employee of Azikiwe's press.

[34] *African Interpreter,* I (March, 1943), 4.

[35] *Ibid.,* pp. 8, 13.

[36] See Orizu, *op. cit.;* Kingsley Ozuomba Mbadiwe, *British and Axis Aims in Africa* (New York: 1942); Mbonu Ojike, *My Africa* (New York: 1946), and *I Have Two Countries* (New York: 1947). It is significant that all major nationalist works, except for Azikiwe's *Renascent Africa,* have been written and published by Africans while abroad (e.g., Blyden, de Graft-Johnson, Solanke, Awolowo, Orizu, Mbadiwe, and Ojike).

[37] Many American-educated Nigerians complained of the discrimination they received at the hands of the Nigerian government when they sought employment upon their return to Nigeria. See *A Survey of African Students Studying in the United States,* Phelps-Stokes Fund (New York: 1949), pp. 33 ff.

[38] Prince Okechukwu Ikejiani, "Nigeria's Made-in-America Revolution," *Magazine Digest* (Jan., 1946), p. 57.

[39] In 1931 the African Academy was founded in London by students who felt that African art, science, and philosophy must be preserved. (*Nigerian Daily Times,* April 4, 1933.) In 1949 the West African Society was formed in London by a group of students who affirmed: "No people can achieve greatness without a literature of their own. Their thoughts, their aspirations and achievements, their history, their art and culture patterns, in fact, their whole story, must be recorded in a way that they feel to be their own and that the world may recognize as distinctive." See also Udemezue Onyido, "The Nigerian Institute of Music," *The Rhodes-Livingstone Journal,* no. 19 (1955), 46–47.

[40] *New Africa* (Feb., 1944). Yergan broke with Paul Robeson and W. E. B. Du Bois in the late 1940's, and since then has become an outspoken anti-Communist. See his "The Communist Threat to Africa," in C. Grove Haines, ed., *Africa Today* (Baltimore: 1955), pp. 262–280.

[41] *Soviet Light on the Colonies* (New York: Penguin, 1944).

[42] George Padmore and Dorothy Pizer, *How Russia Transformed Her Colonial Empire* (London: Dobson, 1946), p. 117.

[43] *Daily Service,* March 1, 1943.

[44] Ayo Ogunsheye, "Nigerian Nationalism, 1919–1952," *Nigerian Year Book, 1953* (Lagos: 1953), p. 117.

[45] *Legislative Council Debates,* Nigeria, March 12, 1948, p. 599.

CHAPTER 11: *Wartime Developments in the Nationalist Movement*

(Pages 251–267)

[1] Meyer Fortes, "The Impact of the War on British West Africa," *International Affairs,* XXI (April, 1945), 206.

[2] The market-women were particularly aggrieved by a practice known as "conditional sales"; that is, the firms would sell them popular items for resale in the local markets only if they would also accept slow-moving items. See *Report of the Commission of Enquiry into Conditional Sales* (Lagos: 1948).

[3] Fortes, *op. cit.,* pp. 206–219.

[4] See E. E. Sabben-Clare, "African Troops in Asia," *African Affairs,* 44 (Jan., 1945), 151–156.

[5] The administration had its greatest difficulty with the resettlement of ex-servicemen in the Eastern Region. This was partly because a substantial number of Ibos had been recruited for the army, and partly because there were fewer career openings in the Eastern Region. In 1951 an organization known as the Unemployed Ex-Servicemen's Union literally captured the large eastern town of Umahia and kept the European community and officers of the provincial administration incommunicado for several days.

[6] *The Economic Development of Nigeria,* International Bank for Reconstruction and Development (Baltimore: 1955), p. 666.

[7] Notes on the History of the Trades Union Congress, supplied by T. A. Bankole, first president of the congress.

[8] *Ibid.*

[9] *Ibid.*

[10] One reason for the moderation was that several of the leaders were older men and held fairly high positions in the government service.

[11] *Department of Labour Quarterly Review,* II (Sept., 1944), 7. Between 1944 and 1953 the number of larger unions, but not of all unions, increased substantially:

	No. of unions (500–1,000)	No. of unions (1,000–5,000)	No. of unions (more than 5,000)
1944	9	7	0
1953	16	14	6

Five of the largest unions in 1953 were the Railway Workers' Union (10,296), the Public Utility Technical and General Workers' Union of Nigeria and the Cameroons (26,542), the Nigerian Union of Teachers (5,880), the Cameroons Development Corporation Workers' Union (19,700), and the Nigeria African Mine Workers' Union (12,377). See *Annual Report,* Department of Labour, 1952–1953 (Lagos: 1954), pp. 98–100.

[12] The larger unions affiliated with the NTUC were the Railway Station Staff Union (729), the PWD (Public Works Department) Workers' Union (950), the Nigerian Mercantile Workers' Union (1,500), the UAC (United Africa Company) African Workers' Union (530), and the large Federal Union of Native Administration Staffs (2,029). See *Nigerian Worker,* I (July, 1943), 4.

[13] *Enquiry into the Cost of Living and the Control of the Cost of Living in the Colony and Protectorate of Nigeria,* Colonial no. 204 (London: H.M.S.O., 1946), pp. 9–10. Although there was some substance to the charge of discrimination, European civil servants in Nigeria were also painfully hit by wartime inflation. See *Report of the Commission on the Civil Services of British West Africa, 1945–46,* Colonial no. 209 (London: H.M.S.O., 1947).

[14] The most powerful, highly organized, and politically conscious unions were those of government workers. About one-third of unionized labor in Nigeria belonged to this category in 1945.

[15] Historical Records, Ibadan Branch of the Nigerian Youth Movement.

[16] Awolowo's recommendations for reform of the native authority system appeared first in the local press, then in the journal *West Africa,* and were finally embodied in synthesized form in his admirable *Path to Nigerian Freedom* (London: 1947), pp. 56–134.

[17] Historical Records, Ibadan Branch of the Nigerian Youth Movement.

[18] The origin and activities of this group are discussed in detail by Nnamdi Azikiwe in *The Development of Political Parties in Nigeria* (London: 1957), pp. 8–9. The members included B. O. S. Adophy, Azikiwe, Moses O. Balonwu, S. I. Bosah, C. Enitan Brown, T. E. E. Brown, Dr. E. C. Erokwu, E. E. Esua, Dr. Okoronkwo Ogan, M. E. R. Okorodudu, L. A. Onojobi, Dr. T. O. na Oruwariye, and Albert I. Osakwe. The European member was Henry Collins, author of "Economic Problems in British West Africa," in Basil Davidson and Adenekan Ademola, eds., *The New West Africa* (London: 1953), pp. 102–140.

[19] Azikiwe, *op. cit.,* p. 9.

[20] Negotiations were carried on for six months between the Nigerian Reconstruction Group (NRG) and the Nigerian Youth Movement (NYM), through the good offices of the Nigerian Youth Circle (NYC), an organization closely linked to the NYM. (*Ibid.,* p. 9.) In a personal interview Dr. Azikiwe told me that upon his return from the United Kingdom in August, 1943, after his memorandum on postwar reforms had been ignored by the Colonial Office, he offered the Lagos

leaders of the NYM the results of the studies made by the NRG and requested them to assume leadership to pursue the political objectives of his memorandum. This they declined to do for reasons explained in the text. Despite these failures on the organization side, the discussions of the NRG led to two publications, both authored by Azikiwe: *Political Blueprint of Nigeria* (Lagos: 1943), and *Economic Reconstruction of Nigeria* (Lagos: 1943).

[21] See issues of the *West African Pilot* and *Daily Service* for November, 1943. See also Azikiwe, *The Development of Political Parties in Nigeria*, p. 9.

[22] *Memorandum Submitted by the Nigerian Youth Movement to the Rt. Honourable Colonel Stanley, M.P.* (Lagos: 1943), p. 1.

[23] "The N.U.S. [Nigerian Union of Students] had its origin at the Abeokuta Grammar School, where it was founded in October, 1939. Among its leaders were Adewale Fashanu, I. O. Dafe, Olubumi Thomas, B. B. Bamgbose and P. N. Malafa. Among its patrons were the following personalities: Rev. I. O. Ransome-Kuti, Herbert Macaulay, Dr. Akinola Maja, Ernest S. Ikoli, Mrs. Stella Marke, and Nnamdi Azikiwe." Azikiwe, *The Development of Political Parties in Nigeria*, p. 9.

[24] Macaulay Papers.

[25] Leaders of the Nigerian Youth Movement and all other existing associations were invited to the inaugural session of the National Council of Nigeria and the Cameroons. At its third meeting provisional officers for the NCNC were elected. Some of those elected declined to serve. The final roster of officers included Herbert Macaulay, president; Nnamdi Azikiwe, general secretary; Oyeshile Omage, financial secretary; Dr. Abu Bakr Olorun-Nimbe, treasurer; L. A. Onojobi and A. Ogedegbe, auditors; and E. A. Akerele and Ladipo Odunsi, legal advisers. See Azikiwe, *The Development of Political Parties in Nigeria*, p. 10.

[26] *African Affairs*, 44 (Oct., 1945), 165. This listing differs from others, but only in unimportant details.

[27] The exclusion of the Cameroons from this study is mentioned in the Introduction. It should be noted at this point, however, that Cameroonian nationalism was greatly stimulated by the birth of the NCNC.

[28] *The Constitution of the National Council of Nigeria and the Cameroons* (Lagos: 1945), p. 1.

CHAPTER 12: *The Richards Constitution and the NCNC*
(Pages 271–295)

[1] *Proposals for the Revision of the Constitution of Nigeria*, Cmd. 6599 (London: H.M.S.O., 1945).

[2] Margery Perham, *Native Administration in Nigeria* (London: 1937), p. 362.

[3] Bernard Bourdillon, "Nigeria's New Constitution," *United Empire*, XXXVII (March–April, 1946), p. 78.

[4] Quoted in *West Africa*, Aug., 7, 1948, p. 792.

[5] See Alex Zeidenfelt, "Political and Constitutional Development in Jamaica," *Journal of Politics*, 14 (Aug., 1952), 512–540.

[6] Yet even Nnamdi Azikiwe remarked on one occasion that Governor Richards had arrived at a very difficult time.

[7] *Op. cit.*, p. 76.

[8] *Ibid.*, p. 78.

[9] Notes of a Meeting with the National Council for Nigeria and the Cameroons held on 13th August, 1947 at the Colonial Office (mimeographed copy), p. 6. The delegate who made the remark was Adeleke Adedoyin. The evolution of the NCNC position on regionalism and federalism is discussed in detail in chapter 15. In the early postwar years nationalists did not fully appreciate the separatist tendencies inherent in regionalism.

[10] Obafemi Awolowo, *Path to Nigerian Freedom* (London: 1947), p. 53. As

noted elsewhere, throughout the period 1941–1944 Awolowo and the Ibadan branch of the Nigerian Youth Movement strongly favored the regionalization of Nigeria.

[11] *Ibid.*, p. 125.

[12] On March 27, 1945, the NCNC submitted a memorandum to the governor for transmission to the Secretary of State for the Colonies stating that the new constitution should not only seek to secure greater participation by Africans in the discussion of their own affairs, which was its declared intention, but it should enable them to secure *"greater* participation in the *management* of their own affairs." Nnamdi Azikiwe, *The Development of Political Parties in Nigeria* (London: 1957), p. 13.

[13] H. O. Davies, "Nigeria's New Constitution," *West African Review*, XVI (May, 1945), 15.

[14] In the Legislative Council debates on the Richards proposals, the chief secretary to the government said: "I can assure [the member criticizing the omission of the word "management"] on Your Excellency's authority that the word 'management' was so firmly fixed in your mind at the time that you omitted to set it down in the passage, which should of course read 'discussion *and management* of their own affairs.'" *Legislative Council Debates*, Nigeria, March 22, 1945, p. 543. Italics added.

[15] See Joan Wheare, *The Nigerian Legislative Council* (London: 1950), pp. 135 ff.

[16] British and Nigerian officials have consistently held that *nominated* unofficials were not necessarily progovernment members of legislative councils. Although it is true that in many instances, in Nigeria and elsewhere, unofficials have sharply criticized the government and have occasionally voted against it on grounds of "personal conviction," nevertheless it is equally true that such members have been less critical and less inclined to vote negatively than *elected* unofficials. This is largely explained by the fact that nominees, in order to secure a government appointment in the first place, must have met certain criteria of "moderation" and "responsibility," and that, since they lacked permanent tenure, their renomination depended upon the degree to which they had met those criteria while in office.

[17] *Op. cit.*, p. 126.

[18] The third Lagos member of the Legislative Council, E. A. Akerele, affirmed: "I cannot see any argument . . . that can convince me that the four Emirs and two Chiefs are not Official Members." *Legislative Council Debates*, March 22, 1945, p. 531.

[19] Quoted in *Daily Service*, Nov. 4, 1946.

[20] Charles Bishop, in an article entitled "Let's Call a Western Boycott," protested against a unicameral assembly: "The people inhabiting the Western Provinces have been known for their traditional political organization culminating in the evolution of a monarchical form of Government. . . . For reasons best known to Sir Arthur Richards . . . he has chosen deliberately to insult the highly organised family of Yoruba Kingdoms . . . by setting up a single House of Assembly for Kings and Commoners at Ibadan." *Daily Service*, Feb. 12, 1947.

[21] Remarks of acting chief secretary to the government, when queried about the statement of the Oni of Ife quoted in the text.

[22] Quoted in *West African Pilot*, March 22, 1945.

[23] It did not, in fact, turn out this way. Provincial conferences established in most of the provinces subsequently extended their purview to cover the discussion of provincial development.

[24] Davies, *op. cit.*, p. 18.

[25] *West African Pilot*, March 22, 1945.

[26] *Daily Service*, July 23, 1946.

[27] *Op. cit.*, p. 119.

[28] "Let us call a Western Boycott of the Richards Constitution as the only

effective means of vindicating the Honour and Traditions of the great and loyal Yoruba Commonwealth of Nations." *Daily Service,* Feb. 12, 1947.

[29] Quoted in T. Olawale Elias, *Nigerian Land Law and Custom* (2d ed.; London: 1953), p. 57.

[30] See Herbert Macaulay, *An Antithesis . . . on the Public Lands Acquisition (amendment) Ordinance, 1945* (Lagos: 1946).

[31] See M. F. Lindley, *The Acquisition and Government of Backward Territory in International Law* (London: 1926), pp. 204 ff. "Great Britain, for some purposes, treats her protectorates of the African type as if they were Crown Colonies, . . . as if they were ceded or conquered territory" (p. 204). See also Martin Wight, *British Colonial Constitutions* (London: 1950), pp. 3–4.

[32] See especially Nnamdi Azikiwe, *Land Tenure in Northern Nigeria* (Lagos: 1942). During the post-1945 period Azikiwe occasionally made his appeals as a "British protected person" to the Secretary of State for the Colonies.

[33] See his *Suppression of the Press in British West Africa* (Onitsha: 1946); *Assassination Story: True or False* (Onitsha: 1946); and his series of articles entitled "History of General Strike" in *West African Pilot,* Nov. 1–Dec. 17, 1945.

[34] Anthony Enahoro, *Nnamdi Azikiwe, Saint or Sinner?* (Lagos: n.d.), p. 16. Enahoro analyzes (pp. 8–19) the main factors and historical events contributing to Azikiwe's emergence as a national hero in the early postwar period.

[35] Nnamdi Azikiwe, *Assassination Story,* p. 9.

[36] *Ibid.,* p. 8.

[37] Macaulay Papers.

[38] Azikiwe, *Assassination Story,* p. 12.

[39] *Legislative Council Debates,* Dec. 10, 1945, p. 9.

[40] *Op. cit.,* p. 16. Enahoro observed that whether Azikiwe deliberately "bamboozled this country is a question time will answer. . . . We interpret Nnamdi Azikiwe's prompt retirement to Onitsha as a huge joke, a cowardly act or a wise and judicious step, according to our several opinions of the man." *Ibid.*

[41] *Ibid.,* p. 17.

[42] See daily issues of the *Daily Service* and the *West African Pilot,* Aug., 1945–April, 1946.

[43] *Daily Service,* July 10, 1945.

[44] Macaulay Papers.

[45] P. 21.

[46] Macaulay Papers.

[47] Quoted in Obadia Adegboyega Sobande, *Notes and Comments on the Life of Mr. H. Macaulay* (Lagos: n.d.), pp. 16–17, 21–22.

[48] *African Affairs,* 45 (Oct., 1946), 168.

[49] At the meeting between the governor and the deputation from the "Island Club United Front Committee," which included among others Dr. Akinola Maja, Dr. Nnamdi Azikiwe, and Chief H. O. Davies, the governor stated that he would request the licensing boards "to make it a condition in future hotel and bar licenses that there shall be no racial discrimination, . . . [that future hospitals] would not be either European or African but general hospitals catering for patients of all kinds, . . . [that the time for European reservations] was passing away, . . . [and that] as African officers increasingly filled the higher posts [in the civil service] they would live in what were formerly European reservations. . . ." "Racial Discrimination," *Circular* no. 25 of 21.3.47 (Lagos: Government Printer, 1947), pp. 5–7. The notes of this meeting were published by the government, with the following preface (p. 1): "As a result of the recent incident at the Bristol Hotel, Lagos, His Excellency has given very careful consideration to various aspects of inter-racial contact in Nigeria with a view to eliminating all possible grounds for suspicion that it is the policy of Government in any way to countenance, let alone to encourage, colour discrimination in any shape or form."

[50] *West African Pilot,* Sept. 23, 1947.

[51] Notes of a Meeting with the National Council for Nigeria and the Cameroons held on 13th August, 1947 at the Colonial Office, pp. 11–12. The history of the delegation has been written by Udemezue Onyido, *The N.C.N.C. Delegation to London of 1947* (Aba: 1949). A brief account by Nnamdi Azikiwe, head of the delegation, is set forth in *The Development of Political Parties in Nigeria*, pp. 12–15.

[52] *West African Pilot*, Aug. 3–8, 1947.

[53] *Ibid.*, Oct. 15, 1947.

[54] Aug. 15, 1947.

[55] The delegation did not in fact request immediate self-government. It demanded that steps be taken *toward* self-government for Nigeria and the Cameroons. It further requested that Nigeria and the Cameroons be granted political autonomy in two stages, "the first stage to last for ten years: during which period the country could be governed conjointly with the citizens, and the second stage to last for five years: during which period the Anglo-Nigerian Government would be liquidated and an Interim Nigerian Government substituted." Onyido, *op. cit.*, p. 13.

[56] Quoted in *ibid.*, p. 22.

[57] Quoted in *ibid.*, p. 23.

CHAPTER 13: *The Rise and Fall of Militant Nationalism*
(Pages 296–307)

[1] *West African Pilot*, March 2, 1946.

[2] *Ibid.*, Nov. 3, 1948.

[3] *Ibid.*, June 17, 1946. In his book Orizu states that the word "Zik" is derived from the "African name Azikiwe: Azi-eweka-iwe, or Azi-akalilika-n'iwe, or Azi-erika-n'iwe, any of which can be translated: 'The Youth is overwhelmingly indignant,' or 'The New Age is full of revenge.'" A. A. Nwafor Orizu, *Without Bitterness* (New York: 1944), p. 293.

[4] *West African Pilot*, Oct. 29, 1948.

[5] *Ibid.*, Oct. 27, 1948.

[6] *Ibid.*, Feb. 10, 1949.

[7] *Ibid.*

[8] *Ibid.*

[9] *Ibid.*, Dec. 31, 1947. In an address given at the time of his election as president of the NCNC (May 7, 1947), Azikiwe expressed his own views: "Let it be firmly impressed upon the minds of any person in this country that I regard all people who uphold the *status quo* and regard the present political servitude of Nigeria as the best of all possible worlds as enemies of progress. Just as worshippers of imperialism must be viewed as international criminals, like their Nazi counterparts, so must their adherents and stooges, who are in reality, accomplices. . . . But I warn [the stooges] that, when Nigeria shall come into her own, and we are in power . . . every one of them, indigenous or alien, shall be held to strict accountability and shall be impeached for high treason against the safety of the State of Nigeria." *"Before Us Lies the Open Grave"* (London: 1947), p. 2.

[10] See *Report of the Commission of Enquiry into the Disorders in the Eastern Provinces of Nigeria, November, 1949* (Lagos: 1950), p. 35.

[11] See *West African Pilot*, July 28, 1950.

[12] See *Report of the Commission of Enquiry into the Disorders. . . ,* pp. 41 ff.

[13] *Ibid.*

[14] *Ibid.*, pp. 34 ff.

[15] See *West African Pilot*, March 24, 1950.

[16] *Ibid.*, March 8, 1950.

[17] *Ibid.*, April 14, 1950.

[18] *Eastern States Express*, Feb. 26, 1951.

[19] *West African Pilot*, Aug. 5, 1950.

[20] K. O. K. Onyioha, *The National Church of Nigeria: its Catechism and Credo* (Yaba: 1950), p. 36.

[21] *Renascent Africa* (Accra: 1937), p. 17.

[22] *National Hymns and Prayers,* National Church of Nigeria and the Cameroons (Aba: n.d.), p. 45.

[23] E.g., see *West African Pilot,* April 12, 1951.

[24] *Ibid.,* Oct. 24, 1949.

[25] *Ibid.,* July 7, 1950.

[26] *The People,* May 21, 1951.

[27] The *Labour Champion* was published from September, 1949, to June 30, 1950. Eze's financial transactions were reported in the *Nigerian Tribune,* Jan. 26, 1952, and in the *Daily Times,* Dec. 22, 1951.

[28] *West African Pilot,* March 21, 1951.

[29] *Northern Advocate,* March 1, 1951.

[30] *West African Pilot,* Oct. 14, 1947.

[31] *Ibid.,* July 7, 1950.

CHAPTER 14: *The Beginning of a New Era*
(Pages 308–318)

[1] *West African Review* (March, 1948).

[2] *Nigerian Review,* Oct. 16, 1946. Salt was rubbed into the wound when the government-sponsored newspaper, the *Nigerian Review,* reproduced the governor's critical speech verbatim in a special edition.

[3] Speech of the Governor to the Legislative Council, 17 August 1948, pp. 8–9. Italics added.

[4] *Annual Report,* Nigeria, 1950, p. 124. Italics added.

[5] *Report of the Commission . . . to make recommendations about the recruitment and training of Nigerians for Senior Posts in the Government Service of Nigeria* (Lagos: 1948), p. 4. Italics added.

[6] *Ibid.,* p. 17.

[7] *West African Review* (June, 1948), 695.

[8] A. Creech Jones, "Labour's Colonial Policy," *United Empire,* XXXVI (July–August, 1945), 127–131; see also "African Local Government," *Colonial Office Summer School on African Administration,* African no. 1173 (London: H.M.S.O., 1947).

[9] See Lord Hailey, *Native Administration in the British African Territories* (London: 1951), III, 38–182; *Memorandum on Local Government Policy in the Eastern Provinces* (Lagos: 1949); *Local Government in the Western Provinces of Nigeria, 1951* (Ibadan: 1951); K. P. Maddocks and D. A. Pott, *Report on Local Government in the Northern Provinces of Nigeria* (Kaduna: 1951).

[10] *Memorandum on Educational Policy in Nigeria,* Sessional Paper no. 20, 1947; *Grants in Aid of Education—A Review with Recommendations* (Lagos: Government Printer, 1948).

[11] *Nigeria Year Book, 1953* (Lagos: 1953), pp. 133–135. Cf. *The Economic Development of Nigeria,* International Bank for Reconstruction and Development (Baltimore: 1955), pp. 18–19.

[12] *Nigeria Year Book, 1953,* p. 135.

[13] *The True Believer* (New York: Harper, 1951), pp. 27–28. At page 11 Hoffer states: "For men to plunge headlong into an undertaking of vast change, they must [among other things] be intensely discontented yet not destitute, . . . have an extravagant conception of the prospects and potentialities of the future . . . [and] be wholly ignorant of the difficulties involved in their vast undertaking. Experience is a handicap." And at page 48 he says: "Unlimited opportunities can be as potent a cause of frustration as a paucity or lack of opportunities. . . . Patriotism, racial solidarity, and even the preaching of revolution find a more

ready response among people who see limitless opportunities spread out before them than among those who move within the fixed limits of a familiar, orderly and predictable pattern of existence." Cf. Joyce Cary, *The Case for African Freedom* (London: 1941), especially pp. 16–25.

CHAPTER 15: *The Regionalization of Nationalism*
(Pages 319–331)

[1] Obafemi Awolowo, *Path to Nigerian Freedom* (London: 1947), pp. 47–48.
[2] *Legislative Council Debates,* Nigeria, March 4, 1948, p. 227.
[3] *Native Administration in Nigeria* (London: 1937), p. 363.
[4] "Nigeria's New Constitution," *United Empire,* XXXVII (March–April, 1946), 78.
[5] In his letter to Macpherson approving the proposals of the Nigerian General Conference on the Constitution of 1950, the Secretary of State for the Colonies, James Griffiths, said that "any tendency to break up Nigeria into separate parts would in the view of His Majesty's Government be contrary to the interests of the peoples of all three Regions and of Nigeria as a whole. I therefore warmly welcome the recommendations for a strong Central Legislature and Executive for Nigeria."
[6] "The Struggle in Africa," *Foreign Affairs,* 6 (Oct., 1927), 1–21.
[7] Awolowo, *op. cit.,* p. 16.
[8] *The Historical Evolution of Modern Nationalism* (New York: Macmillan, 1931), p. 93. Of course the "regionalism" to which Burke was referring was not exactly the same as the "regionalism" in Nigeria, although the analogy would obtain if Yorubaland, Hausaland, and Iboland were thought of as regions.
[9] Quoted in Joan Wheare, *The Nigerian Legislative Council* (London: 1950), p. 32.
[10] Awolowo, *op. cit.,* p. 32.
[11] In his letter to Sir John Macpherson approving the proposals of the Nigerian General Conference on the Constitution of 1950, the Secretary of State for the Colonies stressed "how much importance I attach to the principle of greater regional autonomy. One of the great advantages of encouraging the Regions to develop each along its own characteristic lines will be that by that very process the unity of Nigeria will be strengthened." Cf. n. 5, above.
[12] *West Africa,* Aug. 22, 1931, p. 1017; *Journal of the African Society,* 30 (July, 1931), 424. In addition to the conferences of chiefs, there were also annual regional conferences of residents, first in the north (1926) and later in the east and the west.
[13] *Op. cit.,* p. 47. Cf. n. 11, above.
[14] *Ibid.,* p. 54. In a brief survey in *The Development of Political Parties in Nigeria* (London: 1957), Dr. Nnamdi Azikiwe states that the late Chief Bode Thomas, a leading figure in the Action Group, was the first principal Nigerian exponent of what Azikiwe terms "regionalisation," that is, that Nigeria should be permanently divided into three regions (p. 15). Actually, it appears that Chief Thomas was primarily interested at that time (1947) in the organization of political parties on a regional basis, rather than the permanent delineation of regional political entities, although such a pattern of political organization could result in the latter. Azikiwe argued at the time that the regionalization of political parties "would encourage separatist movements in Nigeria and the Cameroons, and destroy our corporate existence as a Commonwealth of Nations." *Ibid.,* p. 17.
[15] *Legislative Council Debates,* March 24, 1948, p. 719. Azikiwe notes, however, that the late Mbonu Ojike and Eyo Ita, both NCNC delegates at the Ibadan General Conference (1950) "strongly opposed the division of the country into Regions. . . ." (*Op. cit.,* p. 17.) But Ojike and Ita were not opposed to federalism; they simply did not want the existing three regions to be the constituent units

in a federal system, which virtually all nationalists supported at that time. Their minority report read, in part, as follows: "Regionalisation is opposed because it divides the country. . . . What we want is a strong federated Nigeria with local government based on natural and not artificial geographical boundaries. Grouping of Nigeria along ethnic and linguistic units would serve to remove the problems of Boundaries, minority and Pakistanistic dangers now threatening the unity of Nigeria." *Proceedings of the General Conference on Review of the Constitution, January, 1950* (Lagos: 1950), p. 244.

¹⁶ *Forward to Freedom and Progress*, National Council of Nigeria and the Cameroons (Yaba: 1951), p. 26.

¹⁷ *Report by the Conference on the Nigerian Constitution*, Cmd. 8934 (London: 1953), pp. 4–5.

¹⁸ Awolowo, *op. cit.*, pp. 112 ff.

¹⁹ *Renascent Africa* (Accra: 1937), p. 25; see also p. 135.

²⁰ Ruth Perry, *A Preliminary Bibliography of the Literature of Nationalism in Nigeria* (London: [1955]).

²¹ *Legislative Council Debates*, March 4, 1948, p. 219.

²² K. M. Buchanan and J. C. Pugh, *Land and People in Nigeria* (London: 1955), p. 94.

CHAPTER 16: *The Ibo and Yoruba Strands in Nigerian Nationalism*

(Pages 332–352)

¹ K. Onwuka Dike, *Trade and Politics in the Niger Delta, 1830–1885* (Oxford: 1956), p. 28.

² P. Amaury Talbot, *The Peoples of Southern Nigeria* (Oxford: 1926), Vol. IV; *Population Census of the Western Region of Nigeria, 1952*, Bulletin no. 5 (Lagos: 1953).

³ *Ibo Village Affairs* (London: 1947), p. 255.

⁴ On the role of the Aro in the history of Iboland see Dike, *op. cit.*, pp. 39 ff.

⁵ With few exceptions, the Freedom Movement which succeeded the Zikist Movement was an Ibo group. The National Church membership was almost wholly Ibo.

⁶ Linville Watson, "Some Cultural Aspects of Nigerian Nationalism" (unpublished manuscript), p. 17. See also Thomas Hodgkin, "Background to Nigerian Nationalism," *West Africa*, Sept. 1, 1951.

⁷ C. K. Meek, *Law and Authority in a Nigerian Tribe* (London: 1937), pp. 197 ff.

⁸ Talbot, *op. cit.*, IV, 191.

⁹ Nnamdi Azikiwe, *Renascent Africa* (Accra: 1937), p. 24.

¹⁰ Watson, *op. cit.*, p. 12.

¹¹ *Op. cit.*, p. 44.

¹² See, for example, F. D. Lugard, *The Dual Mandate in British Tropical Africa* (4th ed.; London: 1929), pp. 64 ff.

¹³ *Proceedings of the General Conference on Review of the Constitution, January, 1950* (Lagos: 1950), p. 246.

¹⁴ *Nigerian Daily Telegraph*, Feb. 3, 1933.

¹⁵ *Comet*, June 27, 1936.

¹⁶ *Daily Times*, Sept. 24, 1944.

¹⁷ *West African Pilot*, March 7, 1946.

¹⁸ Nnamdi Azikiwe, *Political Blueprint of Nigeria* (Lagos: 1943), p. 54.

¹⁹ *Renascent Africa*, pp. 18, 21.

²⁰ *Political Blueprint of Nigeria*, p. 7.

[21] The main criticisms of Azikiwe and the NCNC have been published in a pamphlet entitled *NCNC: Their Black Record* (London: n.d.).

[22] P. 29.

[23] *Daily Times*, Oct. 7, 1942.

[24] See J. O. Lucas, *Oduduwa* (Lagos: 1949).

[25] *Constitution of the Egbe Omo Oduduwa* (Ijebu-Ode: 1948), pp. 5–6.

[26] *African Mail*, Aug. 29, 1912.

[27] Ayotunde Rosiji, "The Egbe and Nigerian Unity," *Egbe Omo Oduduwa Monthly Bulletin*, I (Dec., 1948), 7.

[28] *Daily Service*, Oct. 17, 1944.

[29] Minutes of the First Inaugural Conference of the Egbe Omo Oduduwa, June, 1948 (typed copy).

[30] Oluwole Alakija in *Egbe Omo Oduduwa Monthly Bulletin*, I (Dec., 1948), 4.

[31] *West African Pilot*, Aug. 30, 1948.

[32] *Ibid.*, Sept. 9, 1948.

[33] Minutes of First Pan-Ibo Conference, Aba, 1948 (typed copy).

[34] *West African Pilot*, July 6, 1949.

[35] *Ibid.*, May 25, 1951.

[36] *Daily Times*, Sept. 8, 1951.

[37] For Chief Bode Thomas' suggestion that regional political parties be formed, see Nnamdi Azikiwe, *The Development of Political Parties in Nigeria* (London: 1957), p. 16. In a speech made at the time of the laying of the foundation stone of the Action Group headquarters building, on September 14, 1954, Premier Obafemi Awolowo recounted the early history of the Action Group. The first meeting, called by Awolowo, was held in his Ibadan home on March 26, 1950. Although fifty persons had been invited, only eight attended. The purpose of the meeting, as explained by Awolowo, was "to try and devise some means whereby it would be possible to have an organised body of people in the New House of Assembly who would be capable of representing the Western Region." It was decided to organize a new association for this purpose because the existing associations were considered to be poorly organized, lacking in popular support, or otherwise unsuitable for the new situation.

CHAPTER 17: *The Northern Awakening*

(Pages 353–368)

[1] William N. M. Geary, *Nigeria under British Rule* (London: 1927), pp. 237 ff., points out that by 1910 the estimated value of imports into northern Nigeria was only £ 331,000 and the value of exports was not much more than £ 400,000. The lack of transport was a critical obstacle to development, as was the official discouragement of immigrant traders from southern Nigeria. The traditional legal system of the north, whose penalties were very severe, also acted as a deterrent. The different land policy in the north was another. See T. Olawale Elias, *Nigerian Land Law and Custom* (2d ed.; London: 1953), pp. 298 ff.

[2] See M. G. Smith, *The Economy of Hausa Communities of Zaria* (London: 1955), p. 93.

[3] During the period British authority was being established in northern Nigeria there were several Mahdist uprisings; but once full control was established, there were few overt manifestations of Mahdism, although the British authorities were sensitive to the possibilities of their recurrence. See Alan Burns, *History of Nigeria* (4th ed.; London: 1948), pp. 182 ff. Thomas Hodgkin notes that northern Nigeria was, until recently, more or less isolated from the political reforming movements found elsewhere in the Muslim world. "Tradition and Reform in Muslim Africa," *West Africa*, Sept. 22, 1956, p. 727. On Mahdism in the French Sudan and northern Nigeria see A. Le Grip, "Aspects actuels de l'Islam en A.O.F.," *L'Afrique et L'Asie*, no. 24 (Fourth Quarter, 1953), 6–20.

[4] ". . . [the National Council of Nigeria and the Cameroons and the Action Group] are Southern movements and membership is virtually confined to Ibo and Yoruba immigrants and kindred Southern communities residing in the Sabon Garis or in the Business Layouts in the Districts." *Report on the Kano Disturbances, 16th, 17th, 18th and 19th May, 1953*, Northern Regional Government (Kaduna: 1953), p. 2.

[5] *Op. cit.*, p. 93.

[6] *Ibid.*, p. 100.

[7] K. P. Maddocks and D. A. Pott, *Report on Local Government in the Northern Provinces of Nigeria* (Kaduna: 1951), p. 1. See also *Recent Trends and Possible Future Developments in the Field of Local Government in the Northern Region* (Kaduna: 1952); and D. A. Pott, *Progress Report on Local Government in the Northern Region of Nigeria* (Kaduna: 1953).

[8] *Daily Comet*, Dec. 29, 1949.

[9] Quoted in *Nigerian Citizen*, July 1, 1949.

[10] See editorials from *Gaskiya Ta Fi Kwabo* quoted in *Report on the Kano Disturbances* . . . , pp. 42 ff.

[11] Macaulay Papers.

[12] *Legislative Council Debates*, Nigeria, March 4, 1948, p. 227.

[13] *Ibid.*

[14] An editorial published in *Gaskiya Ta Fi Kwabo* of Feb. 18, 1950, quoted in translation in *Report on the Kano Disturbances* . . . , p. 43.

[15] Bernard Bourdillon, "Nigeria's New Constitution," *United Empire*, XXXVII (March–April, 1946), 77.

[16] *Proceedings of the General Conference on Review of the Constitution, January, 1950* (Lagos: 1950), p. 65.

[17] Manifesto of the Northern Peoples' Congress, October 1, 1951, quoted in *Report on the Kano Disturbances* . . . , p. 45.

[18] Declaration of Principles of the Northern Elements' Progressive Union, quoted in *ibid.*

[19] *West Africa*, July 19, 1952, p. 650.

[20] The *Report on the Kano Disturbances* . . . (p. 3) describes the membership of the NEPU as follows: "In the main provincial centres and other large towns there is usually a hard core of ten to thirty members, mostly young, discontented and often insecurely employed, either owing to temperament or past history." It should be noted that the report was issued by the Northern Regional government, which at the time was controlled, theoretically at least, by the Northern Peoples' Congress, NEPU's main political opponent. Cf. the evaluation in the report of the NPC: ". . . the programme it outlines expresses the general trend of public opinion in the Region, and its leaders have had almost unanimous support from all public meetings and all conferences. . . ." *Ibid.*, p. 3.

[21] "As far as the Northern political parties are concerned, the party system and organisation in this Region are, as yet, in an embryonic stage." *Ibid.*

CHAPTER 18: *The Final Phase and Self-Government*

(Pages 369–408)

[1] *Proceedings of the General Conference on Review of the Constitution, January, 1950* (Lagos: Government Printer, 1950), p. 241.

[2] *Review of the Constitution of Nigeria: Despatch dated the 15th July, 1950 from the Secretary of State for the Colonies*, Sessional Paper no. 20, 1950 (Lagos: Government Printer, 1950), p. 8.

[3] *Report by the Conference on the Nigerian Constitution held in London in July and August, 1953*, Cmd. 8934 (London: H.M.S.O., 1953), p. 3.

[4] *West Africa*, July 7, 1956, p. 477. The members of the 1950 General Conference, which helped fashion the 1951 Constitution, were Nigerian, but they

were not representatives of political parties. At that time parties were not regarded as legitimate or even as suitable instruments for elevating leaders to roles within the formal structure of government. Moreover, the majority of the members of the 1950 conference were at that time either antinationalists or conservative nationalists. Of its 50 members, 18 were emirs or conservatives from the north (Alhaji Abubakar Tafawa Balewa possibly excepted), and 20 were antinationalists or moderates from the south (e.g., such members of the old Legislative Council as the Reverend T. A. J. Ogunbiyi and Dr. F. A. Ibiam), leaving only 12 (24 per cent) who at that time could have been called nationalists in terms of their political activity and public statements. Of those 12, by coincidence, 6 identified themselves, then or subsequently, with the NCNC and 6 with the Action Group. Of the 19 delegates to the 1953 conference, 15 (79 per cent) were nationalists in varying degrees (including Mallam Ibrahim Imam of the NPC), although they belonged to different parties. Most significant of all, perhaps, is that neither Awolowo, Aminu Kano, nor Azikiwe (although formally a member) participated in the 1950 General Conference. Finally, the conference atmosphere and the concept of the role of Nigerians in the two conferences differed. Legally the role of Nigerians was the same, but actually a profound change had occurred in power relationships. In 1950 Nigerian conferees were, in effect, colonial subjects submitting their humble proposals to the Secretary of State for the Colonies for his consideration and unilateral decision; in 1953 they were coparticipants negotiating a definitive multilateral agreement.

[5] For a full account of the decisions see *ibid.* and *Report by the Resumed Conference on the Nigerian Constitution held in Lagos in January and February, 1954,* Cmd. 9059 (London: H.M.S.O., 1954).

[6] *West Africa,* Feb. 12, 1955, p. 124.

[7] *Ibid.,* June 25, 1955, p. 591.

[8] *Ibid.,* Feb. 5, 1956, p. 100.

[9] *Nigeria under British Rule* (London: 1927), p. 14. Cf. par. 1, chap. 9, above.

[10] The allegations of improper conduct were made in a letter to Azikiwe from E. O. Eyo, at the time chief whip (NCNC) in the Eastern House of Assembly and chairman of the Eastern Region Development Corporation, and formerly deputy speaker of the Eastern House of Assembly. Eyo alleged that Azikiwe had permitted public funds of the Eastern Region to be invested in the African Continental Bank in which he continued to have an interest. Eyo resigned as government chief whip and from the NCNC and subsequently requested that an independent commission of inquiry be appointed. On July 24, 1956, the Secretary of State for the Colonies (Lennox-Boyd) announced in the House of Commons that he had decided to appoint such a commission, which necessarily meant a postponement of the scheduled constitutional conference. Azikiwe at first opposed the proposal for a commission, alleging that the Secretary of State had acted in a "dictatorial way" and favored United Kingdom banking interests, but after the formal announcement he expressed willingness to appear before the commission as he had "nothing to hide." In August, 1956, the Eastern House of Assembly approved a motion welcoming the decision to appoint a commission of inquiry, but criticized the "high-handed" manner in which the whole affair had been handled. *West Africa,* Aug. 18, 1956, p. 615.

[11] *Daily Times,* Jan. 17, 1957. For the full report see *Proceedings of the Tribunal appointed to Enquire into Allegations of Improper Conduct by the Premier of the Eastern Region of Nigeria in connection with the affairs of the African Continental Bank Limited and other relevant matters, August–November, 1956* (Lagos: Government Printer, 1957).

[12] *West Africa,* Jan. 26, 1957, p. 79.

[13] *Daily Times,* Jan. 17, 1957.

[14] *Ibid.* For an analysis of reaction to the report see the following issues of *West Africa:* Jan. 19, 1957, pp. 49–50; Jan. 26, 1957, p. 79.

[15] *Daily Times,* Jan. 19, 1957.

[16] The pro–Action Group *Daily Service* editorialized that the dissolution of the Eastern House was justifiable only if the fiscal policy of the whole Eastern Regional government, rather than merely the conduct of one minister, had been in question. It further argued that a general election could not exonerate Azikiwe. *West Africa,* Jan. 26, 1957, p. 79.

[17] The NCNC's manifesto for the March, 1957, elections in the Eastern Region embodied its proposals for changes in the constitution and its position on the various issues involved in regional self-government. In effect, therefore, the electorate of the Eastern Region was asked to support or reject the NCNC position at the constitutional conference.

[18] *West Africa,* June 1, 1957, p. 507.

[19] The 1957 constitutional agreements relating to regional self-government went a long way toward granting maximum autonomy in a wide sphere of governmental activity, while at the same time providing safeguards not only against a misuse of power by regional governments, but also against any threat to the functioning of the federal government and the continuance of federation. Under self-government regional governors would cease to preside in the respective regional executive councils, and would lose virtually all their reserved powers. Provisions were included to guarantee the independence of the judiciary, the civil service, the Audit Department, and the director of public prosecution. And the governor-general of the Federation was empowered, in his discretion and with the approval of the Secretary of State for the Colonies, "to issue such directions to a Region as might appear to him to be necessary for the purpose of ensuring that the executive authority of the Region was not exercised in such a way as to impede or prejudice the performance by the Federal Government of any of its functions or to endanger the continuance of federal government in Nigeria." *Report by the Nigeria Constitutional Conference Held in London in May and June, 1957,* Cmd. 207 (London: H.M.S.O., 1957), p. 8. See also "Regional Self-Government," *West Africa,* July 13, 1957, p. 655.

[20] Agreement was reached, however, on two rather important political issues. One of these concerned control over the police. It was decided to give both federal and regional governments concurrent responsibility for law and order prior to independence; thereafter, ultimate responsibility would be inherited by the federal government. It was also agreed that the Cameroons under United Kingdom trusteeship (both the northern portions forming part of the Northern Region of Nigeria, and the Southern Cameroons) had the right to decide whether it desired to remain a part of Nigeria after independence was achieved.

[21] *Daily Times,* Aug. 9, 1957.

[22] *Ibid.,* Oct. 14, 1957.

[23] Under the 1954 Constitution the governor-general was obliged to appoint the three ministers from each region on the recommendation of the leader of the party holding a federal majority in the region. It was tacitly assumed at the time the constitution was drawn that this party would be the same as the one commanding a majority in the regional House of Assembly. This assumption was invalidated when the NCNC obtained a majority in both Eastern and Western regions in the federal elections of 1954, although the Action Group was the majority party in the Western House of Assembly. This meant that the NCNC was entitled to, and was given, positions on the Council of Ministers while the Action Group received none. Thus, from January, 1955, until September, 1957, the Council of Ministers was composed of one minister representing the Southern Cameroons (Kamerun National Congress), three ministers from the Northern Region (NPC), and six ministers from the Eastern and Western regions (NCNC). When Alhaji Balewa formed his "national" government in September, 1957, the party strengths in the council were NCNC—6; NPC—4; Action Group—2; and KNC—1.

[24] *West Africa,* Sept. 7, 1957, p. 855.

474

[25] *Ibid.*, July 7, 1956, p. 477.

[26] This is not meant to imply that the Mid-West State Movement is primarily an Ibo affair, but certainly modern Ibo political consciousness, like Edo consciousness aroused by the Otu Edo, is an important factor in it.

[27] *Path to Nigerian Freedom* (London: 1947), p. 54. Awolowo estimated that this might necessitate more than ten houses of assembly, but added that, in view of Canada's nine provinces and Switzerland's twenty-two cantons, "even as many as thirty to forty Regional Houses of Assembly would not be too many in the future United States of Nigeria."

[28] *West Africa*, Dec. 26, 1953, p. 1215. It is interesting that on this occasion Awolowo argued his case in terms of his fear of "Northern domination" under the new 1954 Constitution.

[29] *Daily Times*, June 28, 1956.

[30] As shown in table 25, the NCNC won as many seats in Yoruba areas as it did in the non-Yoruba parts of the Western Region in the 1956 elections. On a proportionate basis, however, the Action Group clearly predominates in the Yoruba areas.

[31] *Freedom Charter* (Lagos: 1948), p. 2.

[32] *Daily Times*, March 13, 1957.

[33] *Report by the Nigeria Constitutional Conference . . .* , p. 13.

[34] *Ibid.*, p. 14.

[35] *West Africa*, March 8, 1958, p. 231.

[36] *Daily Times*, Oct. 29, 1957.

[37] Memorandum from WASU to the Under Secretary of State for the Colonies, April 6, 1942.

[38] *Political Blueprint of Nigeria* (Lagos: 1943), pp. 9–10. Azikiwe submitted these proposals as the "foundation for the erection of a political structure, which progressive dreamers and schemers should bear in mind in planning a free Nigeria" (p. 9).

[39] *The Constitution of the National Council of Nigeria and the Cameroons* (Lagos: 1945), p. 1.

[40] *Freedom Charter*, pp. 1–2.

[41] National Council of Nigeria and the Cameroons, *Forward to Freedom and Progress* (Yaba: 1951). The recommendation that the NCNC "should declare its intention to win Independence for Nigeria by 1956" (p. 12) was one of five proposals submitted by the National Rebirth Assembly to the NCNC. These were later debated and accepted by the third annual convention of the NCNC held at Kano on August 30 and 31, 1951. In its manifesto issued in connection with the federal elections in 1954, the Action Group claimed that it first declared 1956 to be the year of self-government. Referring to the Action Group's Benin conference of December, 1952, at which December 1, 1956, was fixed as the date for independence, the manifesto states that "it was the first time in Nigeria, or indeed in the history of colonialism, that a political party in a dependent country had fixed a target date for the liberation of its country from foreign yoke. The idea and the date caught like wildfire, and after some doubt and hesitation, both the British Government and major political parties in Nigeria have come to adopt 1956 as Nigeria's year of destiny." Action Group, *Forward to Freedom* (Lagos: n.d.), p. 4. Only subsequent research can prove the accuracy of this claim. The setting of the precise date of December 1, 1956, may support it. But the chronology given in the text is, I believe, essentially correct. The mere fact that there was and is competition in claiming priority serves only to enrich my main argument advanced in the text.

[42] *Forward to Freedom*, p. 4.

[43] *House of Representatives Debates*, 2d sess., Vol. II (March 19–April 1, 1953), p. 989. Chief Enahoro's speech elucidated in great detail the many reasons for the selection of 1956.

[44] *Ibid.*, p. 987.

[45] *Report on the Kano Disturbances, 16th, 17th, 18th and 19th May, 1953* (Kaduna: 1953), p. 21.

[46] The concluding remarks of Premier Awolowo in the debate on the Enahoro self-government motion, made just before the Action Group–NCNC walkout, points up southern resentment at what was felt to be northern domination of the proceedings: "There is no doubt in anybody's mind that when the division comes, the North will win the day, and this momentous motion would have been postponed indefinitely. . . . With a situation like that . . . we are not prepared to accommodate ourselves. . . . We will not stay here to continue this debate. We will allow the North alone to run the show by themselves." *House of Representatives Debates*, p. 1000.

[47] *West Africa*, April 11, 1953, p. 319.

[48] For the background to and running commentary on the split that occurred within the NCNC during 1952–1953, as well as the crisis in the Eastern House of Assembly, see the excellent series of articles by Abiodun Aloba in the following issues of *West Africa*: Nov. 1, 1952, p. 1019; Dec. 13, 1952, p. 1162; Dec. 27, 1952, p. 1202; Jan. 17, 1953, p. 35; and March 21, 1953, p. 247.

[49] Even before the 1951 Constitution came into operation, Azikiwe sent an open letter to Awolowo urging an Action Group–NCNC alliance in the Western Region: "We of the N.C.N.C. can count on a surprisingly commanding number of members to support us in the Western House of Assembly; with your equally large number of members the two parties can present a united front and create such a deadlock in the Western Provinces as to force the hands of Government to concede us a better constitution whose provisions would make party politics more effective." *West Africa*, Dec. 29, 1951.

[50] *Ibid.*, June 20, 1953, p. 554.

[51] *Report by the Conference on the Nigerian Constitution . . . .* , pp. 10–11.

[52] *House of Representatives Debates*, p. 991. In the same debate Mallam Mohammed, Waziri of Bornu, stated (p. 993): ". . . we are not asking any Region to wait for the Northern Region. They can do what they like in their Region. . . ."

[53] See, for example, *Forward to Freedom*, p. 4; *West African Pilot*, Sept., 1953–June, 1956; and the summary of the proceedings of the 1955 convention of the Northern Peoples' Congress in *West Africa*, July 9, 1955, p. 627.

[54] *West Africa*, June 16, 1956, p. 385.

[55] *Ibid.*, July 14, 1956, p. 495. A further explanation and rationalization of Azikiwe's changed position on the self-government issue appeared in the *West African Pilot*, his leading paper, on July 10, 1956: "[Dr. Azikiwe's revised proposal for self-government] . . . is another sacrifice which is bound to be made if the unity of Nigeria is to be preserved. Except those who want to live in a world of make-believe, there is no lover of Nigeria who will not acclaim Dr. Zik's suggestion as a piece of masterstroke. With the North fixing 1959 as the dateline for her self-government, and the other two regions clamouring for it this year, practical politics dictate that a compromise must be sought lest the whole edifice breaks down. Nigeria, as a strong united country, stands the chance of leading the whole of Africa and that is why all those who have the interest of the country at heart should strive to do everything possible to keep it as an entirety. Dr. Zik's suggestion is neither humiliating to the South nor revolutionary for the North."

[56] *House of Representatives Debates*, Official Report, Session 1957–58, Vol. II, p. 1407.

[57] *Ibid.*, p. 1423.

[58] *Ibid.*, p. 1426.

[59] *West Africa*, April 6, 1957, p. 313. Some planning had apparently gone into the 1957 debate on self-government, for several days before the debate the names of two prominent members of the Northern Peoples' Congress and of two prominent members of the NCNC had appeared together on the amendment setting 1959

as independence year; and Mallam Maitama Sule of the NPC promptly seconded the amending motion introduced by Wachuku of the NCNC. It was also believed that the date had been discussed by Chief Awolowo and the Sardauna of Sokoto.

[60] *Report by the Nigeria Constitutional Conference Held in London in May and June, 1957*, p. 24.

[61] *Ibid.*, p. 26.

[62] *Ibid.*

[63] *Ibid.*, p. 27.

[64] June 28, 1957.

[65] June 28, 1957.

[66] *West Africa*, April 5, 1958.

APPENDIX

(Pages 419–427)

[1] M. Fortes and E. E. Evans-Pritchard, eds., *African Political Systems* (London: 1940), pp. xiii, 4–5.

[2] Cf. Karl W. Deutsch, *Nationalism and Social Communication* (New York: 1953), p. 70, where a "people" is defined specifically in terms of a wide complementariness of social communication among its members.

[3] *Ibid.*, pp. 61–65; Ralph Linton, ed., *The Science of Man in the World Crisis* (New York: Columbia University Press, 1945), p. 79. Cf. R. M. MacIver, *Society* (New York: Farrar and Rinehart, 1937), pp. 4–8; John W. Bennett and Melvin M. Tumin, *Social Life* (New York: Knopf, 1948), pp. 197–222.

[4] Marion Levy, *The Structure of Society* (Princeton: Princeton University Press, 1952), p. 113. Cf. Louis Wirth, "World Community, World Society, and World Government: An Attempt at a Clarification of Terms," in Quincy Wright, ed., *The World Community* (Chicago: University of Chicago Press, 1954), pp. 9–20. "When we are dealing with human beings as aggregates of population distributed in space and in relationship to resources, it is useful to employ the concept 'community.' When, on the other hand, human groups are thought of as held together by communication, by the bonds of interest, and when they move toward common collective goals for which they require a common understanding of symbols and a sharing of common norms, we are dealing with a society" (p. 12).

[5] See A. L. Kroeber and Clyde Kluckhon, *Culture* (Cambridge: Peabody Museum Press, 1952), pp. 180 ff. See also George P. Murdock, "The Processing of Anthropological Materials," in A. L. Kroeber, *Anthropology Today* (Chicago: University of Chicago Press, 1953), for a listing of "culture-bearing units" and corresponding "culture units," a conceptual scheme that differs from the one employed here.

[6] Culture is used here in its anthropological sense, not in the popular literary sense of cultivation or in the sense of a higher stage of perfection.

[7] Cf. Deutsch, *op. cit.*, pp. 62–64; MacIver, *op. cit.*, pp. 8–11; S. F. Nadel, *A Black Byzantium* (London: 1942), p. 17.

[8] See Fortes and Evans-Pritchard, *op. cit.*, pp. 5–7; Daryll Forde, "The Conditions of Social Development in West Africa," *Civilisations*, III (1953), 471–488; Paula Brown, "Patterns of Authority in West Africa," *Africa*, XXI (Oct., 1951), 261–278; and Daryll Forde, "The Cultural Map of West Africa," *Transactions of the New York Academy of Sciences*, 15 (April, 1953), 206–218.

[9] E.g., *Nigeria Handbook, 1953* (Lagos: 1953), p. 20, refers to even the Hausa people as a "tribe." Cf. the definition of "tribe" given by Okoi Arikpo, Nigeria's leading anthropologist, in *West Africa*, June 23, 1956, p. 420.

Many educated Nigerian nationalists resent the indiscriminate application of the term "tribe" to all Nigerian communities, not only because of its manifest inapplicability but also because of the backward, inferior, or primitive connotation they believe it has acquired. As one nationalist put it, "the word 'tribe' though it may have been respectable in the Roman days, has fallen into disrepute in the modern world." *West Africa*, June 23, 1956, p. 420. Another inquired why "the word 'Tribe' is used to describe only ethnic groups in Africa." *West Africa*, April 14, 1956, p. 180.

[10] The term "tribe" has been used extensively by anthropologists, but few of them have given it a precise definition. As previously noted, Meek was indiscriminate in his use of the concept. The British administration in Nigeria has used the following definition: ". . . one or more clans descended from one legendary ancestor, though the legend may have been lost; originally observing one common shrine though the memory may have been lost; speaking one language, though perhaps not the same dialect, and enlarged by assimilated peoples." Cf. Daryll Forde, *The Yoruba-Speaking Peoples of South-Western Nigeria* (London: 1951), and Daryll Forde and G. I. Jones, *The Ibo and Ibibio-Speaking Peoples of South-Eastern Nigeria* (London: 1950), both of which use the categories of tribe, subtribe, group, and village group with some precision and consistency.

[11] William R. Bascom, "West and Central Africa," in Ralph Linton, ed., *Most of the World* (New York: 1949), p. 352.

[12] See James S. Coleman, "The Emergence of African Political Parties," in C. Grove Haines, ed., *Africa Today* (Baltimore: 1955), pp. 226–227.

[13] Cf. Lord Hailey, *An African Survey Revised 1956* (London: 1957), pp. 251–260. At page 251 Lord Hailey states that "it seems advisable . . . to give prominence to the use of the term 'Africanism' rather than 'nationalism'. In Europe nationalism is a readily recognizable force, even though it may not be easily definable, but as a concept it has associations which make it difficult of application in the conditions of Africa. . . . the population of most of the countries of Africa south of the Sahara consists of peoples who have been brought together under one form of government by the accidents of history; they have for the most part no tradition of a common origin nor common outlook on their political future." Although the concept "Africanism" has a certain usefulness, its substitution for the concept "nationalism" would seem most unfortunate. It not only tends to perpetuate the erroneous notion that Africans are essentially different from the rest of mankind, but it also exaggerates the differences in the operation of the historical process of nation-building in Europe and in Africa. If one goes far enough back into European history, one can find some very interesting parallels; and recurrent patterns are the lifeblood of the social scientist.

Bibliography

Bibliography

BOOKS

Abraham, R. C. *The Tiv People*. Lagos: Government Printer, 1933.
Anderson, J. N. D. *Islamic Law in Africa*. London: H.M.S.O., 1955.
Apter, David E. *The Gold Coast in Transition*. Princeton: Princeton University Press, 1955.
Austin, Dennis. *West Africa and the Commonwealth*. London: Penguin, 1957.
Baldwin, K. D. S. *The Marketing of Cocoa in Western Nigeria*. London: Oxford University Press, 1954.
Bauer, P. T. *West African Trade*. Cambridge: Cambridge University Press, 1954.
Bohannan, Laura and Paul. *The Tiv of Central Nigeria*. London: International African Institute, 1953.
Bovill, E. W. *Caravans of the Old Sahara*. London: Oxford University Press, 1933.
Bowen, G. Elenore Smith. *Return to Laughter*. London: Gollancz, 1954.
Bradbury, M. R. *The Benin Kingdom and the Edo-Speaking Peoples of South-Western Nigeria*. London: International African Institute, 1957.
Buchanan, K. M., and J. C. Pugh. *Land and People in Nigeria*. London: University of London Press, 1955.
Buell, Raymond Leslie. *The Native Problem in Africa*. New York: Macmillan, 1928. 2 vols.
Burns, Alan. *History of Nigeria*. 4th ed. London: George Allen & Unwin, Ltd., 1948.
————. *In Defence of Colonies*. London: George Allen & Unwin, 1957.
Cameron, Donald. *Principles of Native Administration and Their Application*. Lagos: Government Printer, 1934.
Cary, Joyce. *The Case for African Freedom*. London: Secker and Warburg, 1941.
Communist Party of Great Britain. *Allies for Freedom*. London: 1954.
————. *The Crisis of Britain and the British Empire*. London: Lawrence and Wishart, 1953.
Cook, Arthur N. *British Enterprise in Nigeria*. Philadelphia: University of Pennsylvania Press, 1943.
Cooksey, J. J., and A. McLeish. *Religion and Civilisation in West Africa*. London: World Dominion Press, 1931.
Cowan, L. Gray. *West African Local Government*. New York: Columbia University Press, 1958.
Crocker, W. R. *Nigeria: A Critique of British Colonial Administration*. London: George Allen and Unwin, 1936.
————. *Self-Government for the Colonies*. London: Allen and Unwin, 1949.
Cronon, Edmund D. *Black Moses*. Madison: University of Wisconsin Press, 1955.
Crowe, S. E. *The Berlin West African Conference, 1884–1885*. London: Longmans, 1942.

Bibliography

Cunard, Nancy, ed. *Negro Anthology*. London: Wishart & Co., 1934.

Davidson, Basil, and Adenekan Ademola, eds. *The New West Africa*. London: Allen and Unwin, 1953.

Deutsch, Karl W. *Nationalism and Social Communication*. New York: John Wiley, 1953.

Du Bois, W. E. Burghardt. *The World and Africa*. New York: Viking, 1947.

East, R., ed. *Akiga's Story*. London: International African Institute, 1939.

Fage, J. D. *An Introduction to the History of West Africa*. Cambridge: Cambridge University Press, 1955.

Forde, Daryll. *The Yoruba-Speaking Peoples of South-Western Nigeria*. London: International African Institute, 1951.

————, ed. *Efik Traders of Old Calabar*. London: Oxford University Press, 1956.

Forde, Daryll, and G. I. Jones. *The Ibo and Ibibio-Speaking Peoples of South-Eastern Nigeria*. London: International African Institute, 1950.

Forde, Daryll, and others. *Peoples of the Niger-Benue Confluence*. London: International African Institute, 1955.

Fortes, M., and E. E. Evans-Pritchard. *African Political Systems*. London: Oxford University Press, 1940.

Frobenius, Leo. *The Voice of Africa*. London: Hutchinson, 1913. 2 vols.

Galletti, R., K. D. S. Baldwin, and I. O. Dina. *Nigerian Cocoa Farmers*. London: Oxford University Press, 1956.

Garvey, Amy Jacques, ed. *Philosophy and Opinions of Marcus Garvey*. New York: Universal Publishing House, 1923.

Geary, William N. M. *Nigeria under British Rule*. London: Methuen, 1927.

Gitlow, Benjamin. *I Confess*. New York: Dutton, 1940.

Green, M. M. *Ibo Village Affairs*. London: Sidgwick and Jackson, 1947.

Greenberg, Joseph H. *Studies in African Linguistic Classification*. New Haven: Compass Publishing Company, 1955.

Groves, C. P. *The Planting of Christianity in Africa*. London: Lutterworth Press, 1955. 3 vols.

Gunn, Harold D. *Peoples of the Plateau Area of Northern Nigeria*. London: International African Institute, 1953.

Hailey, Lord. *An African Survey*. London: Oxford University Press, 1938.

————. *An African Survey Revised 1956*. London: Oxford University Press, 1957.

————. *Native Administration in the British African Territories*. London: H.M.S.O., 1951. 5 vols.

Haines, C. Grove, ed. *Africa Today*. Baltimore: Johns Hopkins Press, 1955.

Hancock, W. K. *Survey of British Commonwealth Affairs*. London: Oxford University Press, 1952. 2 vols.

Harris, Philip. *Local Government in Southern Nigeria*. Cambridge: Cambridge University Press, 1957.

Hazlewood, Arthur. *The Finances of Nigerian Federation*. London: Oxford University Press, 1956.

Herskovits, Melville. *The Myth of the Negro Past*. New York: Harper, 1941.

Hinden, Rita. *Empire and After*. London: Essential Books, 1949.

Hodgkin, Thomas. *Nationalism in Colonial Africa*. London: Muller, 1956.

Hogben, S. J. *The Muhammedan Emirates of Northern Nigeria*. London: Oxford University Press, 1930.

Hubbard, John W. *The Sobo of the Niger Delta*. Zaria: Gaskiya Corporation, n.d.

International Bank for Reconstruction and Development. *The Economic Development of Nigeria*. Baltimore: Johns Hopkins University Press, 1955.

Jennings, W. Ivor. *The Approach to Self-Government*. Cambridge: Cambridge University Press, 1956.

Johnson, Samuel. *The History of the Yorubas*. Lagos: C.M.S. Bookshop, 1937.

Kingsley, Mary H. *Travels in West Africa*. London: Macmillan, 1900.

————. *West African Studies*. London: Macmillan, 1899.

Kraemer, H. *The Christian Message in a Non-Christian World.* London: Edinburgh House Press, 1938.

Lindley, M. F. *The Acquisition and Government of Backward Territory in International Law.* London: 1926.

Lugard, F. D. *The Dual Mandate in British Tropical Africa.* 4th ed. London: William Blackwood, 1929.

————. *Report on the Amalgamation of Southern and Northern Nigeria and Administration, 1912–1919.* London: H.M.S.O., 1920.

Macartney, William M. *Dr. Aggrey.* London: S.C.M. Press, 1949.

Macmillan, W. M. *Africa Emergent.* London: Penguin, 1949.

McPhee, Allan. *The Economic Revolution in British West Africa.* London: Routledge, 1926.

Mair, Lucy P. *Native Policies in Africa.* London: George Routledge, 1936.

Malinowski, Bronislaw. *The Dynamics of Culture Change.* New Haven: Yale University Press, 1945.

Maxwell, J. Lowry. *Nigeria, the Land, the People and Christian Progress.* London: World Dominion Press, 1931.

Meek, C. K. *Law and Authority in a Nigerian Tribe.* London: Oxford University Press, 1937.

————. *The Northern Tribes of Nigeria.* London: Oxford University Press, 1925. 2 vols.

————. *A Sudanese Kingdom.* New York: Humanities Press, 1950.

Meek, C. K., and others. *Europe and West Africa.* London: Oxford University Press, 1940.

Miller, Walter R. *Have We Failed in Nigeria?* London: Lutterworth Press, 1947.

————. *Success in Nigeria?* London: Lutterworth Press, 1948.

Morel, E. D. *Nigeria, Its Peoples and Its Problems.* London: Macmillan, 1912.

————. *Trading Monopolies in West Africa.* Liverpool: Richardson and Sons, 1901.

Murray, A. Victor. *The School in the Bush.* London: Longmans, 1929.

Myrdal, Gunnar. *An American Dilemma.* New York: Harper, 1944.

Nadel, S. F. *A Black Byzantium.* London: Oxford University Press, 1942.

Newlyn, W. T., and D. C. Rowan. *Money and Banking in British Colonial Africa.* Oxford: Clarendon Press, 1954.

Nicholson, Marjorie. *West African Ferment.* London: Fabian Publications, 1950.

Niven, C. R. *How Nigeria is Governed.* London: Longmans, 1950.

————. *Nigeria, Outline of a Colony.* 2d ed. London: Nelson, 1955.

————. *A Short History of Nigeria.* London: Longmans, 1937.

Nuffield Foundation and Colonial Office. *African Education: A Study of Educational Policy and Practice in British Tropical Africa.* Oxford: 1953.

Oldham, J. H., and M. Gibson. *The Remaking of Man in Africa.* London: Oxford University Press, 1931.

Orr, C. W. J. *The Making of Northern Nigeria.* London: Macmillan, 1911.

Padmore, George. *Africa, Britain's Third Empire.* London: Dobson, 1949.

————. *How Britain Rules Africa.* London: Dobson, 1936.

————. *How Russia Transformed Her Colonial Empire.* London: Dobson, 1946.

————. *Pan-Africanism or Communism.* London: Dobson, 1956.

Parrinder, Geoffrey. *West African Religion.* London: Epworth Press, 1949.

————. *Religion in an African City.* London: Oxford University Press, 1953.

Pedler, F. J. *West Africa.* London: Methuen, 1951.

Perham, Margery. *Native Administration in Nigeria.* London: Oxford University Press, 1937.

Perham, Margery, ed. *Mining, Commerce, and Finance in Nigeria.* London: Faber, 1948.

————. *The Native Economies of Nigeria.* London: Faber, 1946.

Perry, Ruth. *A Preliminary Bibliography of the Literature of Nationalism in Nigeria.* London: International African Institute, [1955].

Bibliography

Phelps-Stokes Fund. *The Atlantic Charter and Africa from an American Standpoint.* New York: 1942.
———. *Education in Africa.* New York: 1932.
———. *A Survey of African Students Studying in the United States.* New York: 1949.
Political and Economic Planning. *Colonial Students in Britain.* London: P.E.P., 1955.
Quinn-Young, C. T., and T. Herdman. *Geography of Nigeria.* London: Longmans, 1954.
Rawling, M. A. *Bibliography of African Christian Literature.* London: 1923.
Read, Margaret. *Education and Social Change in Tropical Areas.* London: Nelson, 1955.
Record, Wilson. *The Negro and the Communist Party.* Chapel Hill: University of North Carolina Press, 1949.
St. Croix, F. W. de. *The Fulani of Northern Nigeria.* Lagos: Government Printer, 1944.
Schultze, A. *The Sultanate of Bornu.* Trans. by P. A. Benton. London: Oxford University Press, 1913.
Smith, Edwin W. *The Christian Mission in Africa.* London: International Missionary Council, 1926.
Smith, M. G. *The Economy of Hausa Communities of Zaria.* Colonial Research Studies no. 16. London: H.M.S.O., 1955.
Stock, Eugene, ed. *The History of the Church Missionary Society.* London: Church Missionary Society, 1899. 4 vols.
Talbot, P. Amaury. *The Peoples of Southern Nigeria.* London: Oxford University Press, 1926. 4 vols.
———. *Tribes of the Niger Delta.* London: Sheldon Press, 1932.
Taylor, J. V. *Christianity and Politics in Africa.* London: Penguin African Series, 1957.
Temple, C. L., ed. *Notes on the Tribes, Provinces, Emirates and States of the Northern Provinces of Nigeria.* Lagos: C.M.S. Bookshop, 1922.
Thorp, Ellen. *Ladder of Bones.* London: Jonathan Cape, 1956.
Tremearne, A. J. N. *The Niger and the West Sudan.* London: Stoughton, 1900.
Trimingham, J. P. *The Christian Church and Islam in West Africa.* London: S.C.M. Press, 1955.
Ward-Price, H. L. *Dark Subjects.* London: Jarrolds, 1939.
Wellesley, Dorothy. *Sir George Goldie.* London: Macmillan, 1934.
Westermann, Diedrich. *The African To-Day.* London: Oxford University Press, 1934.
———. *The African To-day and To-morrow.* 3d ed. London: Oxford University Press, 1949.
Westermann, Diedrich, and M. A. Bryan. *Languages of West Africa.* London: Oxford University Press, 1952.
Wheare, Joan. *The Nigerian Legislative Council.* London: Faber and Faber, 1950.

ARTICLES

Alderton, E. C. "Developments in Local Government in the Eastern Region of Nigeria," *Journal of African Administration,* VIII (Oct., 1956), 169–174.
Allott, A. N. "Legal Problems in Northern Nigeria," *West Africa,* Mar. 9, 1957, p. 223.
Apter, David E. "British West Africa: Patterns of Self-Government," *The Annals,* 298 (March, 1955), 117–129.
Bascom, William R. "African Culture and the Missionary," *Civilisations,* III (no. 4, 1953), 451–501.

————. "The Principle of Seniority in the Social Structure of the Yoruba," *American Anthropologist*, 44 (Jan.–March, 1942), 37–46.

————. "Social Status, Wealth and Individual Status among the Yoruba," *American Anthropologist*, 53 (1951), 490–505.

————. "Urbanization among the Yoruba," *American Journal of Sociology*, LX (March, 1955), 446–453.

————. "West and Central Africa," in Ralph Linton, ed., *Most of the World*. New York: Columbia, 1949. Pp. 331–405.

Bauer, P. T., "Concentration in Tropical Trade," *Economica*, XX (Nov., 1953), 302–321.

Bennett, George. "Local Government in Practice," *West Africa*, Oct. 16, 1954.

————. "Unrule and Divide," *West Africa*, Sept. 4, 1954.

Bourdillon, Bernard. "Nigeria's New Constitution," *United Empire*, XXXVII (March–April, 1946), 76–80.

Brisbane, Robert H. "His Excellency: The Provincial President of Africa," *Phylon*, X (Third Quarter, 1949), 257–264.

Brown, R. E. "Local Government in the West Region of Nigeria, 1950–1955," *Journal of African Administration*, VII (Oct., 1955), 180–187.

Bunche, Ralph J. "Africa and the Current World Conflict," *Negro History Bulletin* (Oct., 1940), 11–15.

Burck, Gilbert, "The World of Unilever," *Fortune* (Jan.–Feb., 1948).

Buxton, Charles Roden, "Some African Friends," *Spectator*, Dec. 28, 1934, pp. 986–987.

Carr, Bernard. "Fifty Years of the Eastern Provinces," *West Africa*, Sept.–Oct., 1950.

Coleman, James S. "Current Political Movements in Africa," *The Annals*, 298 (March, 1955), 95–108.

————. "The Emergence of African Political Parties," in C. Grove Haines, ed., *Africa Today*. Baltimore: Johns Hopkins Press, 1955. Pp. 225–255.

————. "Nationalism in Tropical Africa," *American Political Science Review*, XLVIII (June, 1954), 404–426.

————. "The Problem of Political Integration in Emergent Africa," *Western Political Quarterly*, VIII (March, 1955), 44–57.

————. "A Survey of Selected Literature on the Government and Politics of British West Africa," *American Political Science Review*, XLIX (Dec., 1955), 1130–1150.

Comhaire-Sylvain, Suzanne. "Le Travail des Femmes à Lagos, Nigérie," *Zäire*, 5 (May, 1951), 475–502.

Davidson, A. McL. "The Origin and Early History of Lagos," *Nigerian Field*, 19 (April, 1954), 52–69.

Deutsch, Karl. "The Growth of Nations," *World Politics*, V (Jan., 1953), 168–196.

Dry, D. P. L. "The Social Structure of a Hausa Town" (unpublished paper read before the Royal Anthropological Institute, Nov. 4, 1950).

Du Bois, W. E. Burghardt. "The Realities in Africa," *Foreign Affairs*, 21 (July, 1943), 721–732.

Fortes, M. "The Impact of the War on British West Africa," *International Affairs*, XXI (April, 1945), 206–219.

Garigue, Philip. "Changing Political Leadership in West Africa," *Africa*, XXIV (July, 1954), 220–232.

————. "The West African Students' Union," *Africa*, XXIII (Jan., 1953), 55–69.

Goodland, Tim. "Local Government in Aba," *West Africa*, Dec. 8, 1956, p. 991.

Hailey, Lord. "Nationalism in Africa," *Journal of the African Society*, 36 (April, 1937), 134–147.

————. "A Turning Point in Colonial Rule," *International Affairs*, XXVIII (April, 1952), 177–183.

Hargreaves, J. D. "Radicalism and West Africa," *West Africa*, Aug. 24, 1957.

485

Bibliography

Hazlewood, Arthur. "The Finances of Federation," *West Africa*, Aug. 27–Sept. 24, 1955.

Hodgkin, Thomas. "Arab Africa and West Africa," *West Africa*, Aug. 24–Oct. 19, 1957.

———. "Background to Nigerian Nationalism," *West Africa*, Aug. 4–Oct. 20, 1951.

———. "Disraeli on Northern Nigeria," *West Africa*, May 9, 1953.

———. "Islam and Politics in West Africa," *West Africa*, Sept. 15–Nov. 10, 1956.

———. "The Study of African History," *West Africa*, July 25, 1953.

Kirk-Greene, A. H. M. "Who Coined the Name 'Nigeria'?" *West Africa*, Dec. 22, 1956.

Kolarz, Walter. "Moscow in West Africa," *West Africa*, Apr. 4–11, 1953.

Linton, Ralph. "Nativistic Movements," *American Anthropologist*, 45 (April–June, 1943), 230–240.

Little, Kenneth. "The Study of 'Social Change' in British West Africa," *Africa*, XXIII (Oct., 1953), 274–284.

Lloyd, P. C. "Action Group and Local Government," *West Africa*, Nov. 7–14, 1953.

———. "Cocoa, Politics, and the Yoruba Middle Class," *West Africa*, Jan. 17, 1953.

———. "Craft Organization in Yoruba Towns," *Africa*, XXIII (Jan., 1953), 30–44.

———. "Kings, Chiefs and Local Government," *West Africa*, Jan. 31–Feb. 7, 1953.

———. "New Economic Classes in Western Nigeria," *African Affairs*, 52 (Oct., 1953), 327–334.

———. "The Traditional Political System of the Yoruba," *Southwestern Journal of Anthropology*, 10 (Winter, 1954), 366–384.

———. "The Yoruba Lineage," *Africa*, XXV (July, 1955), 235–251.

Mair, Lucy P. "The Growth of Economic Individualism in African Society," *Journal of the Royal African Society*, 33 (July, 1934), 261–273.

———. "Local Government in Nigeria," *West Africa*, Dec. 20, 1952–Jan. 10, 1953.

———. "Nigeria under the Macpherson Constitution," *World Today*, 9 (Jan., 1953), 12–21.

———. "Traditional Authorities in Eastern Nigeria," *West Africa*, Nov. 9–16, 1957.

Morton-Williams, P. "Some Yoruba Kingdoms under Modern Conditions," *Journal of African Administration*, VII (Oct., 1955), 174–179.

Nicholson, Marjorie. "Return to Nigeria," *African Affairs*, 54 (Oct., 1955), 293–299.

Ogmore, Lord. "The Centre and the Regions," *West Africa*, Nov. 12, 1955.

Ottenberg, Simon. "Improvement Associations among the Afikpo Ibo," *Africa*, XXV (Jan., 1955), 1–28.

Perham, Margery. "The British Problem in Africa," *Foreign Affairs*, 29 (July, 1951), 637–650.

Perry, Ruth. "New Sources for Research in Nigerian History," *Africa* (Oct., 1955), 430–431.

Record, Wilson. "The Negro Intellectual and Negro Nationalism," *Social Forces*, 33 (Oct., 1954), 10–15.

"Review of the State of Development of the Native Authority System in the Northern Region of Nigeria on the 1st of January, 1955," *Journal of African Administration*, VII (Jan., 1955), 77–86.

Sabben-Clare, E. E. "African Troops in Asia," *African Affairs*, 44 (Jan., 1945), 151–156.

Schwab, William B. "Kinship and Lineage among the Yoruba," *Africa*, XXV (Oct., 1955), 352–374.

Scott, H. S. "The Development of the Education of the African in Relation to Western Contact," *The Year Book of Education, 1938*. London: Evans Brothers, 1938. Pp. 693–739.

———. "Educational Policy in the British Colonial Empire," in *The Year Book of Education, 1937*. London: Evans Brothers, 1937. Pp. 411–438.

Stevens, R. A. "Progress in Local Government in the Eastern Region of Nigeria," *Journal of African Administration*, 5 (Jan., 1953), 15–21.

486

Verger, Pierre. "Yoruba Influences in Brazil," *Odú*, I (Jan., 1955), 3–11.
Williams, D. M. "West African Marketing Boards," *African Affairs*, 52 (Jan., 1953), 45–54.

OFFICIAL PUBLICATIONS

Publications of the Colonial Office, United Kingdom

Report by the Hon. W. G. A. Ormsby-Gore, M.P. (Parliamentary Under-Secretary of State for the Colonies), on his Visit to West Africa during the Year 1926. Cmd. 2744. London: 1926.
Despatch from the Secretary of State to the Officer administering the Government of Nigeria regarding the Report of the Commission of Inquiry into the Disturbances at Aba and other places in South Eastern Nigeria in November and December, 1929. Cmd. 3784. London: 1931.
Memorandum on the Education of African Communities. Colonial no. 103. London: 1935.
Education Policy in British Tropical Africa. Cmd. 2374. London: 1936.
Report of the Commission on the Marketing of West African Cocoa. Cmd. 5845. London: 1938.
Statement of Policy on Colonial Development and Welfare. Cmd. 6175. London: 1940.
Labour Conditions in West Africa. Cmd. 6277. London: 1941.
Mass Education in African Society. Colonial no. 186. London: 1944.
Report on Cocoa Control in West Africa, 1939–1943. Cmd. 6554. London: 1944.
Proposals for the Revision of the Constitution of Nigeria. Cmd. 6599. London: 1945.
Report of the Commission on Higher Education in the Colonies. Cmd. 6647. London: 1945.
Report of the Commission on Higher Education in West Africa. Cmd. 6655. London: 1945.
Enquiry into the Cost of Living and the Control of the Cost of Living in the Colony and Protectorate of Nigeria. Colonial no. 204. London: 1946.
Statement on the Future Marketing of West African Cocoa. Cmd. 6950. London: 1946.
Memorandum on Colonial Mining Policy. Colonial no. 206. London: 1946.
Report of the Commission on the Civil Services of British West Africa, 1945–46. Colonial no. 209. London: 1947.
Education for Citizenship in Africa. Colonial no. 216. London: 1948.
Report of the Commission of Enquiry into the Disorders in the Eastern Provinces of Nigeria, November, 1949. Colonial no. 256. London: 1950.
Prest, A. R., and I. G. Stewart. *The National Income of Nigeria, 1950–51.* Colonial Research Studies no. 11. London: 1953.
Report by the Conference on the Nigerian Constitution held in London in July and August, 1953. Cmd. 8934. London: 1953.
Report by the Resumed Conference on the Nigerian Constitution held in Lagos in January and February, 1954. Cmd. 9059. London: 1954.
Report by the Nigeria Constitutional Conference Held in London in May and June, 1957. Cmd. 207. London: 1957.

Publications of the Government of Nigeria to 1954

Preliminary Statement on Development Planning in Nigeria. Sessional Paper no. 6, 1945. Lagos: 1945.
A Ten Year Plan of Development and Welfare for Nigeria. Lagos: 1946.
Memorandum on Educational Policy in Nigeria. Sessional Paper no. 20, 1947. Lagos: 1947.
Administrative and Financial Procedure under the New Constitution: Financial

Bibliography

Relations between the Government of Nigeria and the Native Administrations. Lagos: 1947.

Report of the Commission appointed by His Excellency the Governor to make recommendations about the recruitment and training of Nigerians for Senior Posts in the Government Service of Nigeria. Lagos: 1948.

Report of a Select Committee of the Eastern Region House of Assembly set up to review the existing system of Local Government in the Eastern Provinces. Lagos: 1948.

Report of the Commission of Enquiry into Conditional Sales. Lagos: 1948.

Memorandum on Local Government Policy in the Eastern Provinces. Lagos: 1949.

Review of the Constitution—Regional Recommendations. Lagos: 1949.

Proceedings of the General Conference on Review of the Constitution, January, 1950. Lagos: 1950.

Report of the Drafting Committee of the Constitution. Lagos: 1950.

Review of the Constitution of Nigeria: Despatch dated the 15th July, 1950 from the Secretary of State for the Colonies. Sessional Paper no. 20, 1950. Lagos: 1950.

Report of the Commission on Revenue Allocation. Lagos: 1951.

Local Government in the Western Provinces of Nigeria, 1951. Ibadan: 1951.

Maddocks, K. P., and D. A. Pott. *Report on Local Government in the Northern Provinces of Nigeria.* Kaduna: 1951.

A Revised Plan of Development and Welfare for Nigeria, 1951–56. Sessional Paper no. 6, 1951. Lagos: 1951.

Handbook of Constitutional Instruments. Lagos: 1952.

Population Census of the Northern Region of Nigeria, 1952. Bulletin nos. 1–13. Lagos: 1952.

Population Census of the Eastern Region of Nigeria, 1953. Bulletin nos. 1–7. Lagos: 1953.

Population Census of the Western Region of Nigeria, 1952. Bulletin nos. 1–9. Lagos: 1953.

Report of Fiscal Commissioner on Financial Effects of Proposed New Constitutional Arrangements. Lagos: 1953.

Report of the Commission of Inquiry into the Administration of the Lagos Town Council. Lagos: 1953.

The Nigerianization of the Civil Service—A Review of Policy and Machinery. Lagos: 1954.

Legislative Council Debates, 1924–1951.

House of Representatives Debates, 1952–1957.

Northern Region House of Assembly Debates, 1952–1957.

Eastern Region House of Assembly Debates, 1952–1957.

Western Region House of Assembly Debates, 1952–1957.

Nigeria Handbook, 1926, 1930, 1936, 1953.

Publications of the Government of the Federation of Nigeria

Handbook of Constitutional Instruments, 1954. Lagos: 1954.

Conclusions of the Government of the Federation on the Report of the Commission on the Public Services of the Governments in the Federation of Nigeria, 1954–1955. Lagos: 1955.

The Training of Nigerians for the Representation of Their Country Overseas: A Statement of Policy by the Government of the Federation of Nigeria. Sessional Paper no. 11, 1956. Lagos: 1956.

Staff List Revised to 1 April 1957. Lagos: 1957.

Handbook of Commerce and Industry in Nigeria. 3d ed. Lagos: 1957.

Proceedings of the Tribunal appointed to Inquire into Allegations of Improper Conduct by the Premier of the Eastern Region of Nigeria in connection with the

Affairs of the African Continental Bank Limited and Other Relevant Matters, August–November, 1956. Lagos: 1957. 2 vols.

Publications of the Regional Governments

Western Region. *Report of the Commission of Inquiry into the Administration of the Ibadan District Council.* Ibadan: 1955.

————. *Development of the Western Region, 1955–1960.* Sessional Paper no. 4, 1955. Ibadan: 1955.

————. *Report on the Holding of the 1956 Parliamentary Election to the Western House of Assembly.* Ibadan: 1956.

Eastern Region. *Eastern Nigeria.* Enugu: 1956.

————. *Policy for Local Government.* Sessional Paper no. 2, 1956. Enugu: 1956.

————. *Report on Banking and Finance in Eastern Nigeria.* Sessional Paper no. 4, 1956. Enugu: 1956.

————. *Banking Monopoly in Nigeria. Statement made by the Hon. Premier in the Eastern House of Assembly on 8 August 1956.* Enugu: 1956.

————. *Staff List No. 2 revised to 1 June, 1956.* Enugu: 1956.

Northern Region. *Social and Economic Progress in the Northern Region of Nigeria.* Kaduna: 1955.

————. *Preliminary Statement of the Government on the Report of the Commissioner appointed to advise the Government on Devolution of Powers to Provinces.* Kaduna: 1955.

————. *Provincial Authorities.* Kaduna: 1956.

————. *Staff List No. 4 Revised to 1 January 1957.* Kaduna: 1957.

AFRICAN LITERATURE [*]

Aba Community League. *Local Government Reform.* Aba: n.d.

Abuja Native Authority. *A Chronicle of Abuja.* Ibadan: Ibadan University Press, 1953.

Action Group. *Constitution.* Ibadan: 1950.

————. *Lagos Belongs to the West.* London: 1953.

————. *Nigeria Constitution Conference, London, August, 1953.* Minority Report published by the Action Group Delegation. Ibadan: 1953.

————. *Forward to Freedom: Action Group Manifesto for the First Federal Elections under the Amended Constitution.* London: 1954.

————. *The NCNC Regime of Austerity for Workers.* Ibadan: 1955.

Adelabu, Adegoke. *Africa in Ebullition.* Ibadan: 1952.

Adeniyi-Jones, Curtis Crispin. *Political and Administrative Problems of Nigeria: an Address Delivered to the West African Students Union in London.* London: Bonner, 1929.

————. *Address given by Hon. Dr. C. C. Adeniyi-Jones, President of the Nigerian National Democratic Party, at a Mass-Meeting held at Glover Memorial Hall, Lagos, on 1st October 1938.* Lagos: 1938.

Agebebi, Mojola. "The West African Problem," in G. Spiller, ed., *Papers on Interracial Problems Communicated to the First Universal Races Congress.* London: 1911.

Agunbiade-Bamishe, O. *The Case for the Action Group—Party of the Masses.* Ibadan: 1954.

Agwuna, Osita C. *Inside Africa.* Yaba: 1947.

————. *Go With the Masses: Studies in Essential Tactics in National and Colonial Struggles.* Onitsha: 1953.

---

[*] African literature is listed separately only for the purpose of illustrating its quantity and varied character. This selected listing, therefore, includes scholarly works, such as those of Saburi Biobaku, K. Onwuka Dike, and T. Olawale Elias, as well as tribal histories and polemical pamphlets. Articles and books written by the same author have been listed chronologically.

Bibliography

Ajibola, J. O. *Economic Development of West Africa*. London: West African Society, 1948.

Ajisafe, Ajayi K. *History of Abeokuta*. Bungay, Suffolk: Richard Clay, 1924.

———. *The Laws and Customs of the Yoruba People*. Lagos: 1946.

Ajuluchuku, M. C. K. *Workers Versus Whitelegs*. Port Harcourt: 1951.

Akak, Eyo O. *Bribery and Corruption in Nigeria*. Ibadan: Kajola Press, 1953.

Akinfosile, Olu. "Federalism and the Future," *West Africa*, April 2, 1955, p. 299.

Akinsuroju, Olorundayomi. *Nigerian Political Theatre (1923–1953)*. Lagos: n.d.

———. *Zik in Nigeria's Ship of Destiny*. Lagos: 1951.

Akintan, E. A. *Prince Eleko and the Government*. Lagos: 1928.

———. *The Closing Scene of the Eleko Case and the Return of Prince Eshugbayi Eleko*. Lagos: 1931.

———. *English Translation of Yoruba Phrases and Proverbs*. Lagos: 1947.

Akinyele, Chief I. B. *The Outlines of Ibadan History*. Lagos: 1946.

Akpan, Ntieyong U. "Chieftaincy in Eastern Nigeria," *Journal of African Administration*, IX (July, 1957), 120–123.

———. *Epitaph to Indirect Rule*. London: Cassell, 1956.

Akunneto, I. O. *Tribalism in Nigeria*. Lagos: n.d.

Aloba, Abiodun. "Lagos—Nigerian or Yoruba," *West Africa*, Aug. 16, 1952, p. 751.

———. "Tribal Unions in Party Politics," *West Africa*, July 10, 1954.

Aluko, S. A. *The Problems of Self-Government for Nigeria*. Ilfracombe: Stockwell, 1955.

Amanagala, G. I. *Short History of Ijaw*. Port Harcourt: 1939.

Animashaun, Adam I. *The History of the Muslims Community of Lagos*. Lagos: n.d.

Arikpo, Okoi. "Nigeria's Villagers Vote in Their Own Way," *West Africa*, Oct. 6, 1951.

———. "Self-Government and the Tribal Outlook," *West Africa*, June 23–30, 1951.

———. "On Being a Minister," *West Africa*, July 31–Aug. 21, 1954.

———. "Nigeria Overseas," *West Africa*, Oct. 23, 1954.

———. "Zik's First Year in Office," *West Africa*, Feb. 12–19, 1955.

———. "The Future of Nigerian Federalism," *West Africa*, May 28–June 25, 1955.

Atolagbe, D. *Is Nigeria Ready for Self-Government?* Ibadan: 1947.

Awolowo, Obafemi. *Path to Nigerian Freedom*. London: Faber, 1947.

Azikiwe, Nnamdi. "Nigerian Political Institutions," *Journal of Negro History*, XIV (July, 1929), 328–341.

———. "Murdering Women in Nigeria," *Crisis*, 37 (May, 1930), 164–178.

———. "Fragments of Onitsha History," *Journal of Negro History*, XV (Oct., 1930), 474–497.

———. "Our Struggles for Freedom in Africa," *Crescent*, 34 (Spring, 1930), 6–9.

———. "Ethics of Colonial Imperialism," *Journal of Negro History*, XVI (July, 1931), 287–309.

———. "In Defence of Liberia," *Journal of Negro History*, XVII (Jan., 1932), 30–51.

———. "The Negro in Greek Mythology," *Crisis*, 41 (March, 1934), 65–66.

———. "How Shall We Educate the African?" *Journal of the African Society*, 33 (April, 1934), 143–151.

———. "Liberia: Slave or Free?" in Nancy Cunard, ed. *Negro Anthology*. London: Wishart, 1934. Pp. 780–783.

———. *Liberia in World Politics*. London: 1934. 2 vols.

———. *Renascent Africa*. Accra: 1937.

———. *Land Tenure in Northern Nigeria*. Lagos: 1942.

———. *The Atlantic Charter and British West Africa*. Lagos: n.d.

———. *Economic Reconstruction of Nigeria*. Lagos: 1943.

———. *Taxation in Nigeria*. Lagos: 1943.

———. *Political Blueprint of Nigeria*. Lagos: 1943.

———. *Suppression of the Press in British West Africa*. Onitsha: 1946.

490

————. *Assassination Story: True or False*. Onitsha: 1946.

————. *"Before Us Lies the Open Grave."* London: 1947.

————. *The Development of Political Parties in Nigeria*. London: 1957.

Balogun, Kolawole. *As Youth Sees It*. Lagos: 1947.

————. *What Nigeria Wants*. Yaba: 1949.

————. *Home Rule Now*. Lagos: 1952.

————. *Century of the Common Man*. Oshogbo: 1954.

————. *Tax More Abundant or Life More Abundant?* Oshogbo: 1954.

Bassey, Bassey Efiom. *Calabar Youths Can Plan a Future*. Calabar: 1950.

Biobaku, Saburi. "An Historical Sketch of Egba Traditional Authorities," *Africa*, XXII (Jan., 1952), 35–49.

————."The Kingly Titles of Western Nigeria," *West Africa*, May 3, 1952, pp. 391–392.

————. "Lishabi, Father of the Egba," *West Africa*, April 4, 1953.

————. *The Lugard Lectures 1955*. Lagos: Government Printer, 1955.

Blyden, Edward W. "Africa for the Africans," *African Repository*, 48 (Jan., 1872), 14–20.

————. "African Tribes Not All Savages," *African Repository*, 48 (July, 1872), 208–210.

————. *From West Africa to Palestine*. Freetown: 1873.

————. *Christianity, Islam and the Negro Race*. London: Whittingham, 1887.

————. *The African Problem, and the Method of Its Solution*. Washington: 1890.

————. *West Africa before Europe*. London: C. M. Phillips, 1905.

Busia, K. A. *Social Survey of Sekondi-Takoradi*. Accra: Government Printer, 1951.

Campbell, J. G. *Observations on Some Topics, 1913–1917, during the Administration of Sir Frederick Lugard*. Lagos: 1918.

Chukwuemeka, Nwankwo. *African Dependencies: A Challenge to Western Democracy*. New York: William Frederick Press, 1950.

————. *Industrialization of Nigeria*. New York: William Frederick Press, 1952.

————. *The Unity of Nigeria*. Yaba: 1952.

Chukwura, Christopher Okabi. *Short History of Eastern Motor Transport Workers Union, Nigeria*. Aba: 1951.

Coker, Increase. *Seventy Years of the Nigerian Press*. Lagos: 1952.

————. *Grammar of African Names*. Lagos: 1954.

Coker, S. A. *The Rights of Africans To Organize and Establish Indigenous Churches Unattached to and Uncontrolled by Foreign Church Organizations*. Lagos: 1917.

Davies, H. O. "Nigeria's New Constitution," *West African Review*, XVI (May, 1945), 15–18.

Delano, Isaac O. *The Singing Minister of Nigeria*. London: n.d.

————. *The Soul of Nigeria*. London: 1937.

————. *An African Looks at Marriage*. London: 1944.

————. *Notes and Comments from Nigeria*. London: 1944.

————. *One Church for Nigeria*. London: 1945.

Deniga, Adeoye. *African Leaders Past and Present*. Lagos: 1915. 2 vols.

————. *Nigerian Who's Who*. Lagos: n.d.

————. *Yoruba Titles and Their Meanings*. Lagos: 1921.

Dike, K. Onwuka. "African History and Self-Government," *West Africa*, Feb. 28, Mar. 14, 1953.

————. *Trade and Politics in the Niger Delta, 1830–1885*. Oxford: Clarendon Press, 1956.

Dosumu, Gbadebo. *Oduduwa*. Ibadan: 1951.

Dynamic Party. *The Dynamic Party: Our 23 Protocols*. Ibadan: 1954.

Edo National Union. *Constitution and Rules*. Benin City: 1943.

Egharevba, Jacob U. *A Short History of Benin*. 1st ed. Lagos: 1936.

————. *Some Stories of Ancient Benin*. 2d ed. Lagos: 1951.

————. *The Origin of Benin*. Benin: 1953.

Bibliography

Eguoritseyemi, O. *False Accusations on Protected Persons*. Warri: 1950.

Ekwensi, C. *People of the City*. (Novel.) London: Dakers, 1954.

Elias, T. Olawale. *Nigerian Land Law and Custom*. 2d ed. London: Routledge and Kegan Paul, 1953.

——. *Groundwork of Nigerian Law*. London: Routledge and Kegan Paul, 1954.

——. *The Nature of African Customary Law*. Manchester: Manchester University Press, 1956.

——. "Makers of Nigerian Law," *West Africa*, Nov. 26, 1955–Jan. 28, 1956; June 9–July 7, 1956. Republished as *Makers of Nigerian Law*. London: Sweet and Maxwell, 1957.

Emejulu, L. M. E. *A Brief History of the Railway Workers Union*. Lagos: n.d.

Enahoro, Anthony. *Nnamdi Azikiwe: Saint or Sinner?* Lagos: n.d.

Enekwa, E. I. *Guide to Tribal and Trade Unions*. Lagos: 1950.

Fabunmi, L. A. "Nigerians on the Nile," *West Africa*, Aug. 4, 18, 1956.

——. "Egypt and Africa," *West Africa*, Dec. 28, 1957.

Fabure, G. A. "Anomalies in Nigeria's Education System," *African World* (Feb., 1950).

Faduma, Orishetukeh. "Religious Beliefs of the Yoruba People in West Africa," in J. W. E. Bowen, ed., *Addresses and Proceedings of the Congress on Africa*. Atlanta: Gammon Theological Seminary, 1896.

Folarin, Adebesin. *The Demise of the Independence of Egbaland*. Lagos: 1916.

——. *Egba History*. Abeokuta: E.N.A. Press, 1931.

——. *The Laws and Customs of Egba-Land*. Abeokuta: E.N.A. Press, 1939.

Gana, M. Abba. *Our Land and People—The North*. Lagos: P.R.D., n.d.

Graft-Johnson, J. W. de. *Towards Nationhood in West Africa*. London: Headley, 1928.

Hajji, Sa'id. *History of Sokoto*. Trans. by C. E. J. Whiting. Kano: 1949.

Horton, James A. B. *Political Economy of British Western Africa; with the Requirements of the Several Colonies and Settlements*. (*The African View of the Negro's Place in Nature*). London: W. J. Johnson, 1868.

——. *West African Countries and Peoples*. London: W. J. Johnson, 1868.

Idowu, Ishola O. *Pan-African State Organization*. Lagos: 1952.

Ifenkwe, A. N. *The Nigerian Youths and Destiny*. Ibadan: 1951.

Igbirra Progressive Union. *Call for Unity*. Ibadan: 1950.

Ike, Akwaelumo. *The Origin of the Ibos*. Aba: 1950.

——. *Great Men of Ibo Land*. Aba: 1952.

Ikoli, Ernest. *Our Northern Warriors*. Zaria: P.R.D., n.d.

——. "The Nigerian Press," *West African Review* (June, 1950), 625.

Imam, Abubakar. "Nigerian Constitutional Proposals," *African Affairs*, 45 (Jan., 1946), 22–27.

——. "Daura Sword is the Symbol of the Seven States of Hausaland," *West African Annual* (1950), 114–115.

Ita, Eyo. *The Assurance of Freedom*. Calabar: 1949.

——. *Crusade for Freedom*. Calabar: 1949.

——. *A Decade of National Education Movement*. Calabar: 1949.

——. *National Youth Renaissance*. Calabar: n.d.

——. *Nigeria Youth League Movement*. Calabar: n.d.

——. *Revolt of the Liberal Spirit in Nigeria*. Calabar: 1949.

——. *Sterile Truths and Fertile Lies*. Calabar: 1949.

——. *Two Vital Fronts in Nigeria's Advancement*. Calabar: 1949.

——. *Reconstructing Towards Wider Integration; a Theory of Social Symbiosis*. Calabar: 1951.

Ituen, Bassey P. *The Ibibios and the Efiks*. Kano: n.d.

Johnson, Samuel. *The History of the Yorubas*. Ed. by O. Johnson. 1st ed. London: Routledge, 1921.

Jokparoba, R. E. *The Urhobo People in Nigerian Politics*. Lagos: n.d.

Juwe, S. M. *The Dawn of a New Day for Western Ibos*. Kafanchan: 1949.

———. *The Western Ibo People and the Coming Days*. Port Harcourt: 1953.

———. *Zik and the Freedom of Nigeria*. Port Harcourt: 1953.

Kenyo, E. Alademomi. *Origin of the Progenitor of the Yoruba Race*. Lagos: n.d.

Lasekan, Akinola. *Whither Nigeria*. Lagos: 1947.

Losi, John B. O. *History of Lagos*. Lagos: 1914.

———. *History of Abeokuta*. Lagos: 1924. 176 pp.

Lucas, J. O. *The Religion of the Yorubas*. Lagos: 1948.

———. *Oduduwa*. Lagos: 1949.

Macaulay, Herbert S. H. *Justitia Fiat: the Moral Obligation of the British Government to the House of King Docemo of Lagos*. London: St. Clement's Press, 1921.

———. *An open comment upon the views on Nigerian public affairs expressed in London by Dr. John Randle*. Lagos: 1922.

———. *An Antithesis . . . on the Public Lands Acquisition (amendment) Ordinance, 1945*. Lagos: 1946.

Macaulay Papers. Papers of the late Herbert Macaulay on deposit in the library, University College, Ibadan.

Mbadiwe, George Igbodebe. *Golden Dawn*. Lagos: 1947.

Mbadiwe, Kingsley Ozuomba. *British and Axis Aims in Africa*. New York: Malliet, 1942.

Meniru, G. Udegbunem. *African-American Cooperation*. Glen Gardner, N.J.: Libertarian Press, 1954.

National Church of Nigeria and the Cameroons. *Hymns and Prayers*. Aba: n.d.

National Congress of British West Africa. *Memorandum of the case of the National Congress of British West Africa for a memorial based upon the resolutions to be presented to His Majesty the King Emperor in Council through the Right Honourable the Secretary of State for the Colonies*. London: 1920.

———. *Petition to King George V for the reconstitution of the several Legislative Councils and the constitution of Houses of Assembly and other reforms*. London: 1920.

———. *Report of the Proceedings of a meeting held in London between the League of Nations Union and the delegates of the National Congress of British West Africa*. London: 1920.

———. *Resolutions of the Conference of Africans of British West Africa held at Accra, Gold Coast, from 11th to 29th March, 1920*. London: 1920.

National Council of Nigeria and the Cameroons. *The Constitution of the National Council of Nigeria and the Cameroons*. Lagos: 1945.

———. *Freedom Charter*. Lagos: 1948.

———. *Forward to Freedom and Progress*. Yaba: 1951.

———. *The Constitution, Rules & Regulations of the National Council of Nigeria and the Cameroons*. Lagos: 1953.

———. *Lagos is Free. Gedegbe Leko wa. Memorandum of the National Council of Nigeria and the Cameroons on the Lagos separation issue*. Lagos: 1953.

———. *Battle for Unity and Freedom*. Lagos: 1954.

Nee-Ankrah, S. W. *Whither Benin?* Benin City: 1951.

Nigerian Reform Association. *Petition against the Provincial and Native Courts Ordinances*. Lagos: 1917.

Nigerian Young Democrats. *The Constitution of the Nigerian Young Democrats*. Lagos: n.d.

Nigerian Youth Movement. *Youth Charter and Constitution and Rules*. Lagos: n.d.

———. *Memorandum Submitted by the Nigerian Youth Movement to the Rt. Honourable Colonel Stanley, M.P.* Lagos: 1943.

Nigeria Society. *Occasional Paper on Nigerian Affairs, No. 1*. London: 1955.

Northern Peoples' Congress. *Constitution and Rules*. Zaria: 1955.

493

Bibliography

Numa, Frederick Yamu. *Pride of Urhobo Nation.* Lagos: 1950.
Obahiagbon, E. E. "The New Party in Western Nigeria," *West Africa,* May 19, 1951.
Obano, G. A. *Path to National Unity in Benin.* Lagos: 1950.
Obi, Chike. *Our Struggle: A Political Analysis of the Problems of the Negro Peoples in Their Struggle for True Freedom.* Ibadan: 1954.
Oduntan, O. *Just before the 1950 Reforms.* Ibadan: 1949.
Offonry, H. Kanu. "The Strength of Ibo Clan Feeling," *West Africa,* May 26–June 2, 1951.
Ogunsheye, Ayo. "Nigerian Nationalism, 1919–1952," *Nigerian Year Book, 1953.* Lagos: Nigerian Printing and Publishing Company, 1953. Pp. 117–123.
Ojike, Mbonu. *My Africa.* New York: John Day, 1946.
———. *I Have Two Countries.* New York: John Day, 1947.
———. *Functions of a Bank.* Lagos: n.d.
———. *The Road to Freedom.* Calabar: n.d.
Ojo, Chief Samuel. *The Origin of the Yorubas.* Ibadan: 1952.
Okafor, Amanke. *Nigeria, Why We Fight for Freedom.* London: 1949.
Okah, Mallam Jibril. *NCNC or the Action Group; Which for Nigerian Freedom.* Ibadan: n.d.
———. *Native Authorities versus Native Settlers.* Ibadan: 1951.
———. *The Ibo, the Hausa, the Yoruba.* Yaba: n.d.
Oke, G. A. *A Short History of the United Native African Church.* Lagos: 1936.
Okegberu, Uviri. *A Short History of Isoko People.* Kano: n.d.
Oloko, Tunde. "Religion and Politics in Nigeria," *West Africa,* Feb. 2–9, 1957.
Olowu, Olajide A. "Suggestive Principles of National Planning for Nigeria." Lagos: 1944.
Omo-Ananigie, Peter I. *A Brief History of Etsakor.* Lagos: 1946.
Omoniyi, Bandele. *A Defence of the Ethiopian Movement.* Edinburgh: St. James Press, 1908.
Omoregie, Samuel O. *A Glance at Benin Politics.* Sapele: 1952.
Onukaogu, Gabriel Uwakwe. "Conditions Affecting the Administration of Technical Assistance Programs in Nigeria." Unpublished Ph.D. dissertation, Indiana University, 1955.
Onwenu, D. K. *Epic Drama. A Political Crisis in Fiction.* Port Harcourt: n.d.
Onyia, J. I. G. *Review of the Constitution of Nigeria for 1950.* Aba: 1949.
Onyido, Udemezue. *The N.C.N.C. Delegation to London of 1947.* Aba: 1949.
Onyioha, K. O. K. *The National Church of Nigeria: its Catechism and Credo.* Yaba: 1950.
Orizu, A. A. Nwafor. *Without Bitterness.* New York: Creative Age Press, 1944.
Osadebay, Dennis. "Easter Reflection, the Missionary in West Africa," *West Africa,* Apr. 5, 1947, p. 280.
———. *Africa Sings.* Ilfracombe: Stockwell, 1952.
Owonaro, S. K. *The History of Ijo (Ijaw) and Her Neighbouring Tribes in Nigeria.* Lagos: 1949.
Payne, John Augustus. *Lagos and West African Almanack.* Lagos: 1874.
People's Union, Lagos. *The Land Tenure Question in West Africa.* Lagos: 1913.
Ransome-Kuti, Funmilayo. "Women Should Play a Bigger Part in the Elections," *West Africa,* Nov. 3, 1951, p. 1015.
Sobande, Obadia Adegboyega. *Notes and Comments on the Life of Mr. H. Macaulay.* Lagos: n.d.
Solanke, Ladipo. *United West Africa (or Africa) at the Bar of the Family of Nations.* London: 1927.
Sowole, Michael S. *The Federal Union of Native Administration Staffs of Nigeria.* Abeokuta: 1945.
Sowunmi, Akintunde. *Our Land and People—The West.* Lagos: P.R.D., n.d.

494

Talakawa Party. *The way forward for Nigeria; the programme of the Talakawa Party.* Lagos: 1954.

Tepowa, Adebiyi. "A Short History of Brass and Its People," *Journal of the African Society* (March, 1907), 33–88.

Thomas, Isaac B., ed. *The House of Docemo: Full Proceedings of An Inquiry Into the Method of Selection of A Head of the House of Docemo.* Lagos: 1933.

——. *Life History of Herbert Macaulay.* 3d ed. Lagos: 1948.

Tokunboh, M. A. *A Simple Guide for African Trade Unions.* Lagos: 1952.

Tutuola, A. *My Life in the Bush of Ghosts.* (Novel.) London: Faber, 1954.

——. *The Palm Wine Drinkard.* (Novel.) London: Faber, 1952.

Udoma, E. U. "Law and British Administration in South-Eastern Nigeria." Unpublished Ph.D. dissertation, University of Dublin.

Umo, R. Kanu. *History of Aro Settlements.* Yaba: n.d.

Uwanaka, Charles U. *New Nigeria.* Lagos: 1953.

——. *Zik and Awolowo in Political Storm.* Lagos: 1953.

Uzo, Timothy M. *The Nigerian Political Evolution.* Lagos: 1950.

——. *The Pathfinder: A Test of Political Ideals and An Interaction of Facts, Politics and Common-Sense in Nigeria.* Port Harcourt: 1953.

Wachuku, Jaja A. *The Aim and Objectives of the New Africa Party.* Aba: 1950.

Wallace-Johnson, Isaac T. A. *Trade Unionism in Colonial Dependent Territories.* London: 1946.

Warrior-Osika, Isaac. *Rivers man! Separate state!* Port Harcourt: 1955.

JOURNALS

Africa. International African Institute, London.

Africana. West African Society, London.

African Affairs. Royal African Society, London.

African Interpreter. African Students' Association of North America and Canada, New York.

African World. African Publications, Ltd., London.

Anti-Slavery Reporter and Aborigines' Friend. Anti-Slavery Society, London.

Colonial Review. Institute of Education, University of London, London.

Corona. H.M.S.O., London.

Crown Colonist. St. Margaret's Technical Press, London.

Egba Omo Oduduwa Monthly Bulletin. Ibadan.

Journal of African Administration. H.M.S.O., London.

Journal of Negro History. Association for the Study of Negro Life and History, Washington, D.C.

Negro History Bulletin. Association for the Study of Negro Life and History, Washington, D.C.

New Africa. Council on African Affairs, New York.

Nigeria. Nigerian Government, Lagos.

Nigerian Worker. Nigerian Trades Union Congress, Lagos.

Odú. Ibadan.

Oduduwa. Egbe Omo Oduduwa, Ibadan.

Service. Nigerian Youth Movement, Lagos.

Statistical and Economic Review. United Africa Company, London.

The Keys. League of Coloured Peoples, London.

United Empire. Royal Empire Society, London.

Venture. Fabian Colonial Bureau, London.

WASU. West African Students' Union, London.

West Africa. West Africa Publishing Company, London.

West African Review. West Africa Publishing Company, London.

495

Bibliography

NIGERIAN NEWSPAPERS *

African Mail, 1908–1915.
African Messenger, 1926–1930.
Catholic Herald, 1949–1952.
Comet, 1935–1946.
Daily Comet, 1947–1952.
Daily Service, 1938–1958.
Daily Times, 1926–1958.
Eastern Nigerian Guardian, 1949–1952.
Eastern States Express, 1950–1952.
Gaskiya Ta Fi Kwabo (English summaries), 1950–1952.
Lagos Daily News, 1925–1938.
Lagos Weekly Record, 1891–1930.
New Africa, 1950–1952.
Nigerian Advocate, 1923–1930.
Nigerian Chronicle, 1908–1920.
Nigerian Citizen, 1950–1958.
Nigerian Daily Telegraph, 1927–1935.
Nigerian Eastern Mail, 1935–1950.
Nigerian Pioneer, 1914–1925.
Nigerian Tribune, 1949–1952.
Nigeria Review, 1949–1952.
Northern Advocate, 1949–1952.
Southern Nigeria Defender, 1949–1952.
West African Nationhood, 1932–1935.
West African Pilot, 1938–1958.

* This is a selected listing. Inclusive dates are those covered by this study.

Index

Index

Index

American Negro (*continued*)
Africa, 233–235; press of, 460 n. 45;
attitude toward Africa, 461 nn. 8, 9
Anti-Slavery and Aborigines Protection
Society, 181, 451 n. 32, 452 n. 33
Appointment and Deposition of Chiefs
(Amendment) Ordinance, 284
Arab-Asian-African bloc, 1
Arikpo, Okoi, 477 n. 9
Aro, 30, 333
Arochuku, 333
Askia, Mohammed, 36
Assassination incident, 285–288
Association of West African Merchants,
80
Atlantic Charter, 231, 235, 239
Attlee, Clement, 239
Awolowo, Obafemi, 6, 241, 260, 314,
320, 345, 373, 377, 412, 461 n. 16,
463 n. 16; and Nigerian Produce
Traders' Association, 212; and Ni-
gerian Trades Union Congress, 256;
and NYM, 261–262; on Constitution of 1946, 277–278, 281; on regionalism, 323–325; and Egbe Omo
Oduduwa, 344–345; and Action
Group, 349–350, 471 n. 37; on ethnic
grouping, 388–389, 475 n. 27; on
date for Nigerian independence,
402–403, 476 n. 46
Azikiwe, Nnamdi, 6, 159, 208, 216,
235, 242, 246, 248, 260, 264, 277,
280–281, 283, 308, 311–312, 327,
328, 344, 410, 415, 443 n. 6, 447
nn. 11, 12, 449 n. 6, 467 n. 9, 475
n. 38, 476 n. 49; biographical sketch
of, 220–223; experiences in America,
221–223; publications of, 222, 240,
459 n. 43; journalism of, 222–223;
and leadership of Ibo, 224, 336–337,
341–342, 347–348, 385; and Akinsanya crisis, 227–229; and 1943
memorandum to Colonial Office,
240–241, 397; and wartime NRC,
262–264, 463 n. 20; and NCNC,
262–267; on Constitution of 1946,
277; emergence of, as national
leader, 284–291; alleged plot to assassinate, 285–288; sources of political support, 288–291; and 1946 tour
of Nigeria, 291–293; as leader of
NCNC London delegation, 293–295;
British press on, 294–295; and militant nationalism and Zikist Movement, 306–307; on regionalism and
ethnic grouping, 324–325, 347–349,

388–389, 395; Pan-African orientation of, 336–337; political thought
of, 341–343; critics of, 342, 349; on
Constitution of 1951, 348–349, 401;
and bank crisis of 1956, 374–375;
and Constitutional Conference of
1957, 376; on date for Nigerian independence, 397, 403, 476 n. 55

Baldwin, K. D. S., 439 n. 35
Balewa, Alhaji Abubakar Tafawa, 320,
356, 358, 361, 374; and formation
of national government, 376–378;
as Nigeria's first federal prime min-
ister, 377; and self-government mo-
tion of 1957, 404
Balogun, Kolawole, 296
Bank crisis of 1956, 403; background
to, 374, 473 n. 10; report of Foster-
Sutton Commission of Enquiry into,
374–375
Banks, African, 86, 439 n. 42
Banks, European, 85–86
Barnes, Leonard, 249
Bascom, William R., 436 n. 17
Bauchi General Improvement Union,
357
Bauer, P. T., 85, 90, 438 n. 26
Benin, Kingdom of, 27, 75
Benin-Delta state. *See* Mid-West state,
movement for
Berlin Conference of 1885, 41, 450 n.
22
Birom Progressive Union, 365–367
Blyden, Edward Wilmot, 106–107, 123,
187, 211, 452 n. 1, 453 nn. 2, 3;
and United Native African Church,
175–176; biographical sketch of,
183–184
Boma Boys, 78
Bornu, Kingdom of, 23
Bornu, Shehu of, 20
Bornu Youth Movement, 395
Bourdillon, Bernard, 272–273, 275,
276, 321, 362
Brazilians, 154
Bristol Hotel incident, 292–293, 310
British acquisition of Nigeria: Royal
Niger Company and, 41; Niger Coast
Protectorate and Lagos, 42; map, 43;
resistance to, 170–171
British policy in Nigeria: nationalists'
perspectives of, 6; on administrative
divisions, 45–49; on all-Nigerian civil
service, 48, 50; on Legislative Coun-
cil, 50; on native administration and

indirect rule, 50–54, 385; on transportation and communications systems, 54–56; on exports and marketing boards, 54–58, 81–82, 84; on common currency, 56–57; on taxation, 57–58; on indigenous landownership, 58–60; on *laissez faire*, 60, 80; on missionary activity in north, 95–96, 133, 136–137; on Western education, 117–132, 444 n. 22; on education in north, 133–140; on educated class, 150–151, 153–166; ultimate political objectives of, 159–161; early protests in Lagos against, 178–182; on National Congress of British West Africa, 192–195; impact of World War II upon, 230–237; official statement of, 237–239; on 1946 Constitution, 271–275; and reforms of 1948, 308–316; unifying and divisive aspects of, 319–327; on native administration in Northern Region, 356–357; on north-south tension, 362; on separate states, 392–393; on scheduled self-government, 396–397, 399–400, 402, 404

British Trades Union Congress, 257
Brogan, D. W., 447 n. 21
Buell, Raymond Leslie, 232, 321
Bunche, Ralph, 234
Bureau International pour la Défense des Indigenes, 192
Busia, K. A., 442 n. 28
BYM. *See* Bornu Youth Movement

Calabar Improvement League, 199
Cameroons under United Kingdom trusteeship, 5
Campbell, J. G., 191, 455 n. 34
Carr, Henry, 453 n. 12
Caxton-Martins, Olatunji, 216
Chiefs: in Legislative Council, 279–280, 465 nn. 18–20; and NCNC 1946 tour, 292; British efforts to develop unity among, 323
Christian missionaries: Tropical Africa of special interest to, 91–93, 440 n. 1; early perspectives of, 91–94; struggle against spread of Islam, 92–93; early Roman Catholic activity, 93; excluded from Muslim areas of north, 94, 133–137; response to, 94–96; on African customs, 97–98; humanitarianism of, 98; changes in policy of, 98–100; and African so-

cieties, 100–101; and reintegration, 101–104; and nationalist grievances, 105–112; and African nationalism, 108–109, 110–112, 443 n. 53; alleged conspiracy of, with government, 108–111; and Western education, 113–114; sentiment against, 302–303
Christianity: impact of, 94–95; and nationalist grievances, 96–97, 105–112; as integrative force, 104–105
Church Missionary Society, 103
Churchill, Winston, 233, 238
Clerks, 289
Clifford, Hugh, 118, 140, 150, 156, 182, 192, 196, 210, 211, 272, 320, 436 n. 10
Cobban, Alfred, 2, 409
Coker, Increase, 453 n. 13
Colonial Development and Welfare Act of 1940, 256
Colony and Protectorate of Southern Nigeria, 42
Comintern. *See* Communism
Commercialization of land and labor. *See* Money economy
Communism: interwar activities of Comintern, 207; American Negroes and, 207–208; I. T. A. Wallace-Johnson and, 208; and change of strategy in 1936, 209; Council on African Affairs and, 234–235; as model for rapid transformation of society, 248–250; and Nduka Eze, 305
Conference of Missionary Societies in Great Britain and Ireland, 111
Constitution of 1923, 182, 196–198
Constitution of 1946, 47, 322–323, 362; preparation of, 271–275; nationalists' objections to, 275–281; opposition to, linked with obnoxious ordinances, 281–284; NCNC and revision of, 293–295
Constitution of 1951: origin of, 310–312, 348–349; effect of, upon tribalism and regionalism, 352; breakdown of, 369–371, 400–402; Secretary of State on, 469 nn. 5, 11
Constitution of 1954, 48, 324
Constitution of 1957, 474 n. 19
Convention People's Party (Nigeria), 307
C-O-R State Movement: and anti-Ibo sentiment, 386; Azikiwe on, 390, 395
Council of Ministers, 377, 474 n. 23

Index

Macpherson, John, 309, 314, 348, 373
Macpherson Constitution. *See* Constitution of 1951
Maghreb, 22, 36
Mahdism, 175, 471 n. 3
Maja, Akinola, 241, 300, 461 n. 32
Mallamai, 137
Mbadiwe, K. Ozuomba, 243, 244, 246, 371, 373, 384, 443 n. 6
Mbanefo, Louis, 203
MBPP. *See* Middle Belt Peoples' party
Melle, 36
Methodist Church, 176
Middle Belt, 24, 171, 324–325; nationalism in, 366–368; Action Group strength in, 389; and policy of NPC, 393
Middle Belt Peoples' party, 366–367
Middle Belt state, proposal for, 390, 393, 394
Middle Zone League, 366
Mid-West state, movement for, 386–387, 390, 475 n. 26
Militant nationalism, 296–307, 335
Miller, Walter, 136, 139
Mills, T. Hutton, 192
Milverton, Lord. *See* Richards, Arthur
Minerals Ordinance, 282
Minorities, ethnic: created by regional and international boundaries, 16–18; background to problem and politicization of, 384–390; and London Conference of 1957, 390–393; commission of inquiry into, 390–396
Missionaries. *See* Christian missionaries
Money economy: development of, and British policy, 54–58; growth of, 66–72; disintegrative effects of, 67–72; and wage employment, 68–70; and extraterritorial enterprise, 90; expansion of, in postwar period, 316
Morel, E. D., 105
Morocco, Sultan of, 196
Movement for Colonial Freedom, 443 n. 53
Muslim North, 322
MZL. *See* Middle Zone League

National Bank of Nigeria, 86
National Church of Nigeria: as religious wing of Zikist Movement, 302; nature and membership of, 302–303; predominance of Ibo in, 335
National Committee of Africans, 285
National Congress of British West Africa, 210; opposition of Sir Hugh Clifford to, 156, 192–195; origin and program of, 191–192; Nigerian support of, 192; failure of, in Nigeria, 192–195
National Council of Civil Liberties, 285
National Council of Nigeria and the Cameroons, 184, 215, 241, 318–319, 347; origin of, 264–265, 464 n. 25; early character of, 265–267; initial objectives of, 266–267; and 1946 Constitution and obnoxious ordinances, 281–284; 1946 tour of, 291–293; 1947 London delegation of, 293–295, 464 n. 9; 1948 national assembly and Freedom Charter of, 295, 390; and Zikist Movement, 297–298; inactivity during 1948–1951, 308, 311–312; on regionalism, unitary government, and federalism, 324–325, 347–359, 469 n. 15; role of Ibos in, 335–336; and NEPU, 366; and MBPP, 366–367; on bank crisis of 1956, 375; character of elected members of, 379–384; and Ibo State Union, 385; strength of, in non-Yoruba areas, Western Region, 389; on minorities and separate states, 395; and date for Nigerian independence, 398
National Education Movement, 218
National Emergency Committee, 300
National government of 1957, 376
National Labour Committee, 305
National Prayer, 303
National Rebirth Assembly, 398
National School Committee, 217, 459 n. 34
National self-determination, 1; universalization of, 1–3; applicability to Africa, 2–3
Nationalism: and primary resistance, 4; and grievances, 5; and commercialization of labor, 68–72; and urbanization, 79; and economic grievances, 79–89; and economic opportunity, 89–90; and missionary activity, 96–97, 105–112; and grievances regarding Western education, 119–132; and tribal responses to education, 132–140; and European attitudes and official policy toward Westernized elite, 145–166; traditional, distinguished from modern, 169–170; and early resistance move-

and Akinsanya crisis of 1941, 227–228; decline of, 228–229; rejuvenation of, 260–263; Ibadan branch of, 261–262; postwar constitutional reforms, of, 263; and national front, 263–264

Nigerianization. *See* Africanization

Nkrumah, Kwame, 244

NNDP. *See* Nigerian National Democratic party

Non-Onitsha Ibo, 31

North-south tension, 352–364

Northern Elements' Progressive Association, 358

Northern Elements' Progressive Union: origin of, 356–359; and NCNC, 359, 366; objectives and activities of, 364–365; support of, 365–366, 472 n. 20

Northern Nigeria. *See* Northern Region

Northern Peoples' Congress: origin of, 357–359; antisouthern attitude of, 360–364; as political party, 363–364; objectives of, 364; elected members of, 379–384; and separate state movements, 393; and scheduled self-government, 399–404

Northern Provinces. *See* Northern Region

Northern Region: peoples of, 18–24; ethnic map of, 19; early contacts of, 36–39; and trans-Saharan trade, 38–39; and Islam, 39; and British policy, 46–47, 322–323; and Christian missionaries, 133–137; Western education in, 133–140; and relations with south, 329–331; growth of nationalism in, 352–368

Northern Self-Development Fund, 363

Northern Teachers' Association, 356, 358

NPC. *See* Northern Peoples' Congress

NRG. *See* Nigerian Reconstruction Group

Nupe, 23

NUS. *See* Nigerian Union of Students

NYM. *See* Nigerian Youth Movement

Oba of Benin, 28, 280

Obnoxious ordinances and opposition to 1946 Constitution, 281–284

Odunsi, Ladipo, 209

Odutola, S. O., 458 n. 15

Offa Descendants' Union, 343

Ogbomosho Progressive Union, 343

Ogoja state, proposal for, 392

Ogunbiyi, T. A. J., 473 n. 4

Oil Rivers Protectorate, 42, 329

Ojike, Mbonu, 243, 246, 300, 302, 443 n. 6

Ojokoro youth rally, 262–263

Old Calabar, 42, 96

Old Oyo, 25

Olivier, Sydney, 192

Olorun-Nimbe, Abu Bakr, 293

Oni of Ife, 279

Onitsha Ibo, 31

Onyido, Udemezue, 467 n. 51

Oranyan, 25

Order of the Seraphim and Cherubim, 176

Orizu, A. A. Nwafor, 243, 246, 297, 443 n. 6, 467 n. 3

Orunlaism, 177

Osadebay, Dennis, 112

Oshun Federation, 25

Otonba-Payne, John Adepeyin. *See* Payne, John Augustus

Owo Progressive Union, 343

Oyo Progressive Union, 343

Padmore, George, 208, 235, 249, 285

Pan-Africanism: early congresses, 188–189; and Marcus Garvey, 189–191; after World War II, 234–235; Azikiwe and, 336–337; concept of, 425

Pan-Ibo movement. *See* Ibo State Union

Pan-Yoruba movement. *See* Egbe Omo Oduduwa

Payne, John Augustus, 186

Pearse, S. H., 451 n. 31

Perham, Margery, 3, 45, 159, 235, 271, 321, 456 n. 46

Perry, Ruth, 186

Phelps-Stokes Fund, 118, 233, 234

Political party, concept of, 424

Portuguese, early influences of, 39–40

Postpacification revolts: and primary resistance, 172; Akassa Massacre of 1895, 172–173; Egba Uprising of 1918, 173; Aba Riots of 1929, 174–175; Mahdism, 175

Press war: after Akinsanya crisis, 227–228; after assassination incident, 287–288; after Egbe Omo Oduduwa's inaugural conference, 346–347

Protectorate of Northern Nigeria, 41

Protectorate of Southern Nigeria, 42

507

351; cultural associations and, 384–388; approach of self-government and, 386, 388, 396; interparty rivalry and, 388–390; concept of, 426

Tribe, concept of, 423–424; and nationalist attitudes, 477 n. 9, 478 n. 10

Tripolitania, 22, 36

UAC. *See* United Africa Company
UAC Workers' Union, 304
UMBC. *See* United Middle Belt Congress
Union of African Peoples, 202
Union of Ijebu Youngmen, 343
Union of Students of African Descent, 123, 203
Union of Young Nigerians, 217
UNIP. *See* United National Independence party
United Africa Company, 80, 90, 438 n. 24, 440 nn. 46, 47
United Front Committee, 292–293, 300, 310, 466 n. 49
United Middle Belt Congress, 367
United National Independence party, 386
United Nations Charter, 233
United Native African Church, 175–177
United States of America: Azikiwe's experience in, 221–223; wartime criticism in, 232–235; Nigerian students in, 242–246; and nationalism, 244–246; Ibo students in, 245–246, 336. *See also* American Negro
Universal Negro Improvement Association, 189, 207
Urbanization: consequences of, 72–73; degree of, 74; in Yorubaland, 75; in Iboland, 75; among Ibos outside Iboland, 76–77; in "traditional" and "new" cities, 77–79; and nationalism, 79
Utchay, T. K., 209

Vaughn, J. C., 217, 218

Wachuku, J. A., 403
Wahabi movement, 175
Wallace-Johnson, Isaac T. A., 208, 221, 458 n. 17
Warri National Union, 348
Washington, Booker T., 187, 189, 233
WASU. *See* West African Students' Union

WASU Parliamentary Committee, 241
Water rate agitation in Lagos, 451 nn. 25–32; background to, 179–180; British policy toward, 180; People's Union and, 180
Welfare Committee for Africans in Europe, 192
West African Federation of Native Shippers and Traders, 212
West African Lands Commission, 180
West African People's Institute, 220
West African Produce Control Board, 81
West African Settlements, 42
West African Society, 462 n. 39
West African Students' Union, 111, 210, 226, 239, 250, 271; founding and objectives of, 204; role of, 205–207; and Italian invasion of Ethiopia, 209; during World War II, 239–243; northern attitude toward, 360–361; and scheduled self-government, 397
Western education: role of Christian missions in, 113–114; social consequences of, 113–116; and nationalist grievances, 116, 119–132; official views on, 117–119; higher education, 121–124, 449 n. 39; expenditures on, 126; impact of, 132–140; 1948 reforms in, 315–316; concept of, 443 n. 1
Western Region: peoples of, 25–28; ethnic map of, 26; acquisition of, 170–171; self-government in, 374
Westernized elite: and native administration, 53–54; and extraterritorial enterprise, 90; and Western education, 115–116; size and character of, 141–145, 378–384; urban concentration of, 143–145; European attitudes toward, 145–152; official policy toward, 152–166; criticisms of, 156–159; and indirect rule, 165–166; and central government, 166; and tribal unions, 214–215; in the north, 355–356
Williams, Ayo, 217
Williams, F. R. A., 262, 377
Williams, Sapara, 181
Willkie, Wendell, 232
World Federation of Trade Unions, 250, 257
World War I, impact of, 187–188
World War II: impact of, 230–255; Nigerian troops abroad during, 254

Index

Yaba Higher College, 123, 218, 262, 333, 357
Yergan, Max, 234, 248
Yoruba: origin and character of, 25–27; and Edo, 27; political system of, 33; urbanization of, 75; and Ibo, 331, 345–348; nationalism among, 343–352
Yoruba Language Society, 343
Yoruba Literary Society, 345
Yoruba nationalism, 343–352. *See also* Egbe Omo Oduduwa
Yoruba Union, 343
Young Unsar-Ud-Deen Society, 216

Youth study circles, 460 n. 55

Zikism, 220, 297, 467 n. 3. *See also* Zikist Movement
Zikist Movement, 288, 290, 303; **origin** of, 288, 296–297; objectives of, 297; and NCNC, 297–298; activities of, 298–302; and Enugu shooting incident, 299–301; banning of, 301; and Freedom Movement, 301–302; Ibo in, 335
Zimonists, 291
Zizer, J. C., 195, 211
Zungur, Sa'ad, 357

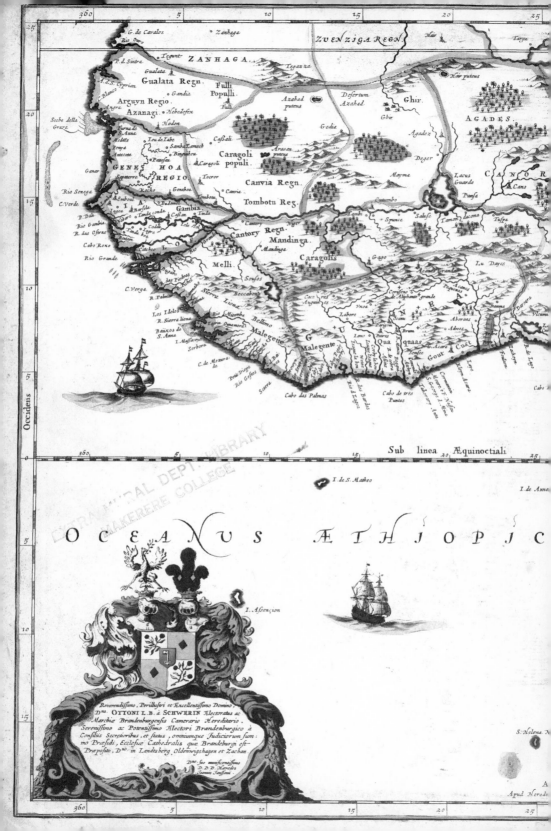